MW01128759

NINETY-EIGHT DAYS

NINETY-EIGHT DAYS

A Geographer's View
of the Vicksburg Campaign

WARREN E. GRABAU

The University of Tennessee Press / Knoxville

Published in cooperation with the United States Civil War Center.

The paper used in this book meets the minimum requirements of ANSI/NISO
Z39.48-1992 (R 1997) (Permanence of Paper). The binding materials have been
chosen for strength and durability. Printed on recycled paper.

Library of Congress Cataloging-in-Publication Data

Grabau, Warren.
Ninety-eight days : a geographer's view of the Vicksburg Campaign /
Warren E. Grabau.—1st ed.
      p. cm.
"Published in cooperation with the United States Civil War Center."
Includes bibliographical references and index.
ISBN 1-57233-068-6 (cl.: alk. paper)
1. Vicksburg (Miss.)—History—Siege, 1863. 2. Vicksburg (Miss.)—History—
Siege, 1863—Maps. I. United States Civil War Center. II. Title.
E475.27 .G79 2000
973.7'344—dc21   99-050509

Contents

Part II: Maps

Maps

(The maps are contained in Part II: Maps, following page 534. This list of maps is repeated in Part II, beginning on page 531, for the convenience of the reader.)

BASE MAPS

DISPOSITION OF FORCES MAPS

Tables

Preface

Geography is a dimension in nearly all human activities, because the characteristics of a place influence the nature of the action that occurs there. Even the pattern of our thoughts is constrained by our physical surroundings. The inhabitant of the plains and the cliff-dweller do not think alike. The conduct of war is the classic example of the impact of geography on human conduct. It is a truism that the commander who wins is the one who takes best advantage of the terrain. Still, there are no absolutes, because other factors enter into the equation. Nevertheless, given approximately equal numbers, technology, training, and morale, the army which exploits the landscape most cleverly is most likely to win.

All considerations of winning or losing aside, battles tend to be fought in particular ways because of the nature of the landscape in which the contest occurs, just as the convolutions of maneuver during a campaign are constrained by the patterns of the countryside. It is probably safe to assume that no military decision is taken without prior contemplation of the terrain. To be sure, a wise general also takes into account the capabilities of his opponent. Indeed, that dichotomy—knowledge of the landscape and of the enemy—is enshrined in military parlance as *terrain intelligence* and *military intelligence,* and every modern army has specialized information-gathering agencies devoted to each. While the concept was firmly entrenched during the Civil War, the specialized agencies existed only in rudimentary form.

Terrain is too restrictive a concept, because it encompasses only the physical landscape. Campaigns are influenced by far less tangible things, such as the political allegiance and economic status of the inhabitants of the region in which the campaign is fought. Such things often have deep roots in the physical landscape. The civilian populace need not pick up arms and join in the fighting to make its influence felt; it need only provide one side with reliable, and the other with unreliable, information!

Two examples will suffice. The prosperity of the towns along the Mississippi River at the time of the Civil War depended upon the trade that flowed between the industrial North and the agrarian South. Thus it was perhaps inevitable that many inhabitants of the river towns deeply deplored the formation of the Confederacy, because they feared that the new nation would erect barriers which would profoundly influence, if not completely ruin, the trade on which they depended. Large numbers of them demonstrated their disapproval of the course of events by remaining steadfastly pro-Union.

The floodplain of the Mississippi was ideal for the production of cotton, a labor-intensive and bulky "industrial" commodity that flourished where transportation was cheap and land easy to cultivate. Before the days of agricultural machines, the preferred means of insuring requisite labor was slavery, so one of the driving forces behind the secession movement was the issue of preserving the "peculiar institution." It was widely and passionately believed that the abandonment of slavery automatically meant the destruction of the economy. Therefore the people of the floodplain were strongly pro-Confederacy, because a plantation economy and pro-secession political persuasion went hand in hand.

Well away from the river, however, the soil was thinner and less fertile, and transportation so costly that such bulk commodities as cotton were less attractive. In such areas, the farm families grew much of their own food and raised cotton only to provide the relatively small amount of cash required to purchase necessities that could not be produced on their own land. The consequence was that the rolling countryside east of the floodplain developed an economy centered not on planters but on yeomen farmers. These latter had little interest in the preservation of slavery, and many of them held their loyalty to "the Old Flag" right through the war years. Of course, there were large areas where combinations of fertile soil, flat lands, and ready transport made plantation agriculture profitable, and this is one of the reasons why the interior of Mississippi became a crazy-quilt of pro- and anti-Union sentiment.

While it is tempting to conclude that geography dictates the outcome of a conflict, the doctrine of geographic determinism should, like Satan, be put firmly behind one. Geography does not define who wins or loses; it only influences the ways in which the campaigns and battles are waged. The Vicksburg Campaign is a notable example. The city was eminently defensible, sitting on its hilltops, with its front guarded by the mighty River and its rear by a terrain that made attacking forces operate at almost insuperable disadvantages. Nevertheless, it fell. Its geography did not dictate the outcome; it only influenced the way in which the campaign was fought. Influenced, not dictated, because tactics other than those actually used by the Federal forces might well have been equally successful.

One of the tasks of history is to illuminate the factors which participants weighed in making their decisions. With such information in hand, it should be possible to deduce the decision-making process itself. My approach to this task was first to provide a detailed summary of the situation as it was known to the commanders at the time, and then to describe how those data could have been used to arrive at the decisions that we know, on the basis of historical evidence, were made.

One of the critical concerns is the matter of supply. There is a military aphorism asserting that "amateurs study tactics; professionals study logistics." The odd thing is that most Civil War histories describe the battles in minute and romantic detail but largely ignore how the men and animals were fed and how ammunition reached the guns, even though it is obvious that the commanders' decisions were profoundly conditioned by considerations of supply and communications.

Another factor was the navy. The navy assured a secure supply line down the Mississippi, but it did far more. It is possible that Alfred Thayer Mahan's concept of a "fleet in being" was inspired by David Porter and his Mississippi River Squadron. The presence of the fleet changed the balance of power.

I have chosen to begin the narrative of the Vicksburg Campaign on 29 March 1863, when Union MG Ulysses S. Grant made his fateful decision to find an undefended landing spot on the Mississippi shore somewhere to the south of the city. It may be argued, of course, that the campaign for Vicksburg began much earlier, because, from the very first, opening the Mississippi River was the principal objective of the Union's war in the West. However, Vicksburg was not identified specifically as the objective early in the war. As it turned out, Vicksburg simply happened to be the place selected by fate—and geography—for the role of final stronghold on the Mississippi. Only a brief prologue, provided to set the stage, covers events prior to March 1863.

The geographic region directly involved in the movements of the principal armies during the final 98 days of the Vicksburg Campaign is quite small. It extends east-west only from the modern city of Tallulah, LA, to Jackson, MS, and north-south from Yazoo City, MS, to Rodney, MS. The respective distances are only 65 and 75 miles, so the entire drama played itself out on a stage with an area of less than 5,000 square miles. If Vicksburg is used as a base of operations, a visit to even the remotest site involves a distance by road of no more than 50 miles.

On the other hand, major movements indirectly (and sometimes not so indirectly) connected with the campaign involved an immense area, extending from Tennessee to the Gulf of Mexico, and from Louisiana to Georgia. Indeed, events in places as far away as the East Coast played a part. Even excluding the East Coast, the theater of operations is an area 400 miles north to south and 500 miles east to west—200,000 square miles. The narrative deals only briefly with those supporting movements of both Federal and Confederate forces that took place outside the "core" area. For example, even though Grierson's Raid had a profound and direct effect on the campaign, only those aspects of the raid that bore directly on the movements of the contending armies in the vicinity of Port Gibson at the time of the Federal landing at Bruinsburg are related in detail. Similarly, Nathan Bedford Forrest's cavalry was billeted at Spring Hill, TN, before being sent south to deal with COL Abel Streight's Union raiders, who managed to march all the way across north Alabama and almost reached Rome, GA, before being brought to a halt. In this instance, the effect on the campaign was indirect; Forrest's cavalry were so exhausted that they could not be sent to Mississippi to help Pemberton in his defense of Vicksburg. MG Nathaniel Banks's offensive into southern Louisiana moved from New Orleans to Alexandria, LA, and in so doing kept Confederate GEN Kirby Smith's army tied up in southern Louisiana while Grant's Army of the Tennessee moved from Milliken's Bend to Bruinsburg. "Pap" Price marshaled Rebel troops from Little Rock and Shreveport to strike at Helena, AR, in a final desperate attempt to assist the trapped garrison in Vicksburg by severing the Union supply route down the Mississippi. Neither of these subcampaigns is described in detail, but general descriptions are given, in order to provide a rounded strategic view of the situation.

Notes conventionally serve two purposes: they identify sources, and they provide supplemental information. I have chosen to identify sources in the conventional manner. It will do no harm simply to ignore the little numbers scattered through the text, because, for all practical purposes, every modern Civil War historian uses exactly the same sources, and I am no different. For an exhaustive list of sources on the Vicksburg Campaign, I can do no better than refer the reader to Edwin C. Bearss's monumental three-volume work, *The Campaign for Vicksburg* (1985–86). Supplemental information is a different matter. For all practical purposes, everything important enough to be included is given in the text, eliminating the need to place such information in the notes.

All the maps and diagrams which accompany the narrative have been drawn especially for this history. The procedure used to construct them is described in a brief section ("About the Maps") at the beginning of the map set at the end of the volume.

The cast of characters for the Vicksburg drama is quite large. The traditional way of keeping track of them is to provide an "Order of Battle," which is no more than a list of the units and their commanders. Unfortunately, such lists often are difficult to interpret, especially when the forces taking part in any one event, such as the Battle of Port Gibson, were only detachments from the much larger totality of forces involved in the campaign. Accordingly, I have provided a special section entitled "Command Structures of the Federal and Confederate Forces," which outlines in diagrammatic form the composition of both Union and Confederate forces as they existed on 29 March 1863. If the reader is curious as to the precise regimental composition of a particular brigade, it usually can be established by referring to the "Command Structures" diagrams.

I have attempted to deal with military nomenclature by adopting a consistent set of abbreviations and conventions, described below. However, problems of terminology persist. There is a naval tradition that salt-water vessels are *ships* and brown-water vessels, such as those that plied the Mississippi, are *boats.* It is a convention often abandoned, and the confusion extends to Civil War scholarship. Paul H. Silverstone's *Warships of the Civil War Navies* (1989) uses the term *ship* for the vessels of both river and saltwater fleets. I have opted to follow Silverstone's example, on the grounds that any one of RADM David Porter's brown-water ironclads handily could have beaten RADM David Farragut's saltwater *Richmond* and thus deserves the dignity of being called a ship.

To the dwellers along the Mississippi, there is only the River; all other flows are trivial. So overwhelming is the sense that the stream is the creator of their lands and the mediator of their lives that their name for it is, simply, the River. I have tried to preserve this sense of the transcendent by using "river" as a proper name whenever the Mississippi is the referent.

Acknowledgments

In 1956, when I first arrived in Vicksburg to live, I very soon visited the Vicksburg National Military Park and in due course made the acquaintance of Edwin C. Bearss, who at that time was the park historian. We were both veterans of World War II and both military historians. To be sure, he was a professional and I was only an amateur, but our common interests created a bond. Both of us felt that, in one way or another, the existing accounts of the Vicksburg campaign were inadequate. It was not long before we decided to write a definitive history of the campaign, and by 1978 we had generated an enormous body of more than a thousand single-spaced, typewritten pages, gleaned from both classical and local sources. This work was great fun.

At that point, my professional life became extraordinarily busy, and I was forced to put the work aside. Ed Bearss, however, carried on, and in due course he published his various works on the Vicksburg campaign. They are, I believe, the most detailed and carefully researched works extant on that remarkable series of events.

The original draft copies of the manuscript still reside in my filing cabinet. That manuscript is the primary (but not the only!) source for the materials included in the present campaign study. It is therefore only fair to say that, without Ed Bearss, this book could not have been written.

I almost certainly would not have carried the work any farther, however, had it not been for Newell Murphy of the U.S. Army Engineers Waterways Experiment Station. In 1989, he asked me to assist in the preparation of materials for a Staff Ride for the U.S. Second Army covering the final phases of the Vicksburg campaign. A primary function of staff rides is to enable military officers to examine the processes by which the contending commanders who were involved in historical military events made their decisions. Because that always had been my primary interest in the study of military history, I felt right at home. After preparing the campaign study for Murphy, I persuaded myself that a similar, albeit somewhat modified and expanded, account would be of interest to civilian historians as well. Thus, I owe Newell Murphy and the U.S. Second Army a profound debt for providing the incentive to carry on. Further, without the patience and support of my wife, Jean Grabau, whose forbearance knows few limits, I never would have finished.

Two local Civil War buffs, Charles "Sonny" Rule and Milton Meyers, both of whom are extraordinarily knowledgeable about the campaign, provided invaluable criticisms. I think they truly enjoyed finding mistakes and challenging me to interpret ambiguities! Let it be understood, however, that the mistakes that remain are mine alone.

I also am deeply indebted to Dr. Glenn Robertson of the Combat Studies Institute, U.S. Army Command and General Staff College, for his encouragement; and to Terrence Winschel, the present historian of Vicksburg National Military Park, and Edwin C. Bearss, who needs no further identification, for many helpful criticisms and suggestions.

It is also important to note that David Madden, of Louisiana State University, founding Director of the United States Civil War Center, played a unique role in the development of this study. Almost alone, he recognized the importance of interpreting historical events on the basis of the environmental context. I think he coined a telling phrase: "Historians must let the terrain testify!" It is a thesis to which I thoroughly subscribe, and I accordingly made many, and critical, changes.

Finally, Richard Cowart of Vicksburg, MS, helped immeasurably by loaning me critical items of equipment, without which the creation of this work would have been very much more difficult.

Calendar: Early Summer, 1863

March

Su	Mo	Tu	We	Th	Fr	Sa
1	2	3	4	5	6	7
8	9	10	11	12	13	14
15	16	17	18	19	20	21
22	23	24	25	26	27	28
29	30	31				

April

Su	Mo	Tu	We	Th	Fr	Sa
			1	2	3	4
5	6	7	8	9	10	11
12	13	14	15	16	17	18
19	20	21	22	23	24	25
26	27	28	29	39		

May

Su	Mo	Tu	We	Th	Fr	Sa
					1	2
3	4	5	6	7	8	9
10	11	12	13	14	15	16
17	18	19	20	21	22	23
24	25	26	27	28	29	30
31						

June

Su	Mo	Tu	We	Th	Fr	Sa
	1	2	3	4	5	6
7	8	9	10	11	12	13
14	15	16	17	18	19	29
21	22	23	24	25	26	27
28	29	30				

July

Su	Mo	Tu	We	Th	Fr	Sa
			1	2	3	4
5	6	7	8	9	10	11
12	13	14	15	16	17	18
19	20	21	22	23	24	25
26	27	28	29	30	31	

Abbreviations, Conventions, and Definitions

Note: Modern abbreviations and conventions are used because they are far more compact, as well as less likely to be ambiguous or misleading, than Civil War–era usage.

ABBREVIATIONS

MILITARY ARMS

ARTY	Artillery
CAV	Cavalry
DSMTD	Dismounted
ENG	Engineers
HVY	Heavy
INF	Infantry
LGT	Light
MTD	Mounted

MILITARY UNITS

(AD)	African Descent; i.e., black troops
BDE	Brigade
BTRY	Battery
CO	Company
CONS	Consolidated Units
DET	Detachment
DIV	Division
IND	Independent Unit
PROV	Provisional Unit

RGT	Regiment
SEC	Section (of artillery)
SQDN	Squadron (of cavalry)
ST TRP	State Troops
UN	Union

Examples

1 OH	1st Ohio Infantry Regiment
7 LA (AD)	7th Louisiana Infantry Regiment (African Descent)
3 MO CAV	3d Missouri Cavalry Regiment
2 BTRY KY LGT ARTY	2d Battery, Kentucky Light Artillery
4 IN DSMTD CAV (DET)	Detachment of the 4th Indiana, Dismounted Cavalry (Detachment)
Bissell's IND CO KY ENG	Bissell's Independent Company of Kentucky Engineers
Jackson's CAV DIV	Jackson's Cavalry Division
17 BN MS ST TRPS (2 COs)	2 Companies of the 17th Battalion of Mississippi State Troops

Notes

1. A unit designation without specification of unit size implies a regiment: 7 IN CAV = 7th Indiana Cavalry Regiment.
2. A unit designation without specification of arm of service implies an infantry unit: 112 IL = 112th Illinois Infantry Regiment.
3. A personal name associated with a unit indicates the commanding officer.
4. ?? indicates that the name of the commanding officer is unknown.

MILITARY RANKS

Navy

ACMR	Acting Master
AEN	Acting Ensign
ALT	Acting Lieutenant
CDR	Commander
COM	Commodore
CPT	Captain
EN	Ensign
FO	Flag Officer
GNR	Gunner

LCDR	Lieutenant Commander
LT	Lieutenant
MR	Master
RADM	Rear Admiral

Army

BG	Brigadier General
COL	Colonel
CPL	Corporal
CPT	Captain
GEN	General
LT	Lieutenant
LTC	Lieutenant Colonel
LTG	Lieutenant General
MAJ	Major
MG	Major General
PVT	Private
SGT	Sergeant

ARTILLERY

in   inch (refers to bore diameter; i.e., a 3-in rifle is a rifled field artillery piece that fires a shell approximately 3 inches in diameter)

pdr   pounder (refers to size of artillery piece; i.e., 10-pdr gun indicates an artillery piece that fires a projectile weighing approximately 10 pounds)

CONVENTIONS

Watercraft names are italicized; e.g., *Lafayette.*
Dates: The military system is used (day number, month, year); e.g., 2 June 1863 = June 2, 1863.
Time: The 24-hour clock is used:
   0030 = 12:30 A.M.
   0415 = 4:15 A.M.
   1600 = 4:00 P.M.
   2345 = 11:45 P.M.
U.S. Postal Code is used to identify states of the United States.
mwl = Mean water level.

DEFINITIONS

The following definitions are primarily terms used in a technical sense in military narratives. Most, but not all, are found in any good dictionary. They are included here for the use of the general reader.

Abatis. An obstacle of sharpened stakes or trees, with sharpened branches directed toward the enemy and often interlaced with wire.

Aspect ratio. Length (l) of an artillery projectile, divided by the diameter (d) of a projectile. A smoothbore cannon fires a spherical projectile, so the l/d ratio is 1.0. However, a rifled cannon fires a projectile that is a pointed cylinder, so the length of the projectile is longer than the diameter. For example, a 30-pdr Parrott rifle shell had a length of 8 inches, and a diameter of 2.9 inches, so the aspect (l/d) ratio was about 2.6. The practical effect is that the rifle projectile applies far more energy at the point of impact than the smoothbore round; therefore its penetration power is greater.

Fort. A completely enclosed earthwork.

Invest. To surround a place with military forces.

Lunette. An earthwork consisting of a salient angle with two flanks and open at the rear.

Redan. A V-shaped earthwork, usually projecting from a fortified line.

Redoubt. An independent earthwork of any shape, usually enclosed or semi-enclosed, and built in advance of a fortified line.

Sap-roller. A movable barrier placed at the head of a sap to protect the sappers from enemy fire. At Vicksburg it was often composed of a large bundle of bamboo stems bound tightly together.

Sap. A trench formed so as to approach an enemy's position. It is usually wide enough to permit the passage of a field artillery piece, and the excavated earth is used to form ramparts on either side to shield the trench from enemy fire.

State Troops. Capitalized words identifies officially designated troops of the state armies. Each of the Confederate states maintained an army of its own, but the troops of such armies were much less effective than those of the Confederate regular army, chiefly because of inadequate training, equipment, and morale.

Tête-de-pont. A fortified bridgehead.

PART I

ORDER OF EVENTS

1

Prologue
6 February 1862–29 March 1863

Maps: 1. The Theater of Operations
      2. Northern Sector
      9. Northeastern Louisiana

Military campaigns, like all other historical events, occur as sequences embedded in complex contexts. Without a reasonable understanding of those contexts, the events themselves often seem to make no sense. So it is with the Vicksburg Campaign, which grew out of a maze of interacting political, social, economic, geographic, and military considerations. Let it not be forgotten that some of those forces were purely emotional, reflecting the personality traits of leaders on both sides.

FEDERAL PERSPECTIVE

If the Federal government were to win its war, it had to occupy the territories of the recalcitrant southern states. The North, then, had to take the offensive, so its armies pressed ever southward. It became clear, almost from the beginning of the war, that offensives deep into the Confederacy would require such mountains of supplies that they could be carried over long distances only by water or by railroad. Thus the Federal lines of advance were restricted to those which could be supported by water-borne or rail-borne transport, or some combination of the two. The geography of the South was such that there were not many routes of these types leading into the Confederate heartland. One, of course, was the East Coast, where advances to the south could be supported by both railroads and ships. The second involved the Cumberland River as far as Nashville, after which a complex of railroads headed south to converge on Chattanooga, TN. The third was the Tennessee River, which could be navigated as far as Eastport, MS, just below the Mussel Shoals. From near Eastport, railroads again led south into the Confederate heartland. And finally, there was the Mississippi River.

The Great River had psychological as well as economic and military significance. To the people living in the Old Northwest (what we now call the Lake States), the river was their lifeline to the outside world, as well as the avenue for much of their internal commerce. It had assumed an almost mystical importance. Listen to John Logan, congressman from Illinois, speaking to Congress assembled in January 1861: ". . . the men of the Northwest would cleave their way down the Mississippi Valley to the Gulf of Mexico with their swords!"[1] He was telling the southern faction, in the plainest words he knew, that his constituents would see red war sweep the land rather than see the Mississippi in the hands of a foreign power. Three months later, with the sound of Fort Sumter's guns scarcely stilled, John Logan was on his way to Illinois to help the men of the Old Northwest take up their swords. We will meet him again on the slopes of Champion Hill, where the life-blood of the Confederacy drained away.

It is hardly surprising that Union grand strategy west of the Appalachian Mountains focused on opening the Mississippi River to Union shipping. At the same time, the Gulf Coast was blockaded to prevent European war materials from reaching the Confederacy. Moves directed to that end began at the very start of the war. On 25 April 1862, New Orleans fell to a Union naval expedition commanded by FO David D. Farragut. Once solidly in possession of New Orleans, Farragut immediately launched a thrust up the river. It reached as far as Vicksburg, but his deep-draft saltwater ships dared not remain in the river during low-water stages, and he had no troops to hold places along the stream, so he was forced to retreat to the mouth of the river and content himself with the occupation of New Orleans.

At the northern end of the Mississippi Valley (that portion extending from the confluence of the Ohio to the Gulf of Mexico), Union forces under MG Ulysses S. Grant won victories at Fort Henry (6 Feb. 1862) on the Tennessee River and Fort Donelson (12–16 Feb. 1862) on the Cumberland River, and then moved southward to Pittsburg Landing on the Tennessee. Here, on 6 and 7 April 1862, Grant was attacked and nearly defeated by a Confederate army under GEN Albert Sidney Johnston. Those victories bear close examination, because, while the army gets all the credit, they would have been impossible without the navy. In fact, Fort Henry fell to COM Andrew H. Foote's gunboats before the army even appeared on the scene! At Fort Donelson, the Rebel defenders beat off a determined attack by Foote's ironclads, but the ever-present naval threat contributed heavily to the Confederate decision to surrender the place. Then, on that terrible Sunday afternoon at Shiloh, Grant's vulnerable left flank, close to the river, was saved by the supporting fire of two of Foote's gunboats, *Lexington* and *Tyler*. Grant never forgot either the debt or the lesson; from that time forward, the war in the West became a truly amphibious war, with army and navy working in such close coordination as to seem a single force.

The Confederacy tried to hang onto Memphis, despite the fact that the city was effectively outflanked after the defeat at Shiloh. One reason for Confederate optimism was that the position was sustained by a powerful Confederate naval squadron, so it could be supplied by water, if not by land. Meanwhile, Foote had been succeeded by COM Charles Davis, under whose command the fleet promptly ended all Confederate hope of holding the town. The Confederate squadron was virtually destroyed during the Battle of Memphis, on 6 June 1862.[2] With the loss of their naval force, the Confederates were forced to evacuate Memphis, and it seemed that this action would open the Mississippi to the Federal fleet all the way to the Gulf.

A squadron promptly sailed downstream, but at Vicksburg it was brought up short by the discovery that the place was heavily fortified. The river front was lined with batteries containing many heavy anti-ship guns, so strong that even the ironclads would be unable to silence them. There was no help for it; the army was going to have to open the way, and at that point Vicksburg became the principal objective of the effort to open the Mississippi. But a land campaign against Vicksburg posed problems. While Shiloh had not been a Union defeat, neither had it been a resounding victory. The Confederate armies were far from destroyed; indeed, they had been damaged no more seriously than the Union Army of the Tennessee. It was clear to everyone who gave the matter thought that getting from Pittsburg Landing on the Tennessee to Vicksburg on the Mississippi was going to be somewhat difficult.

The first move in the Union plan was to secure the Memphis & Charleston Railroad (M&CRR) from the Alabama border to the Mississippi River. This was achieved by Union victories at Iuka, MS, on 19 September 1862, and at Corinth, MS, on 3 and 4 October 1862. This gave the Federals supply depots on both the Tennessee and Mississippi rivers, and these depots were connected by a secure lateral railroad. From this point, the idea was to move south along the Mississippi Central Railroad from Grand Junction, on the M&CRR, toward Grenada and Jackson, MS, with the army supplied from a huge depot at Holly Springs, MS. The Confederates countered by falling back and organizing a defensive line along the Tallahatchie River in northern Mississippi.

The Army of the Tennessee was moving steadily, albeit slowly, southward and had reached the line of the Yocona River, when suddenly three Confederate cavalry brigades came out of nowhere and, on 20 December 1862, turned Holly Springs into an inferno.[3] Grant had no choice but to retreat to Grand Junction, where his troops at least could be fed.

With his drive down the railroad stalled, he thought he might try an end run using the navy as the primary tool. Thus he sent MG William Tecumseh Sherman aboard a transport fleet down the Mississippi and a short distance up the Yazoo River. By this time, RADM David Dixon Porter had replaced Davis in command of the Union fleet on western waters, and he took a squadron of his ironclads along to provide gunnery support. Sherman put his troops ashore and assaulted the northern anchor of Fortress Vicksburg, the Snyder's Bluff–Drumgould's Bluff complex. He had hoped to take the Confederates by surprise, but they were forewarned, and the effort ended on 29 December 1862 in the bloody defeat known as the Battle of Chickasaw Bayou.[4]

It was the Union army which had been defeated; the navy never really had had a chance to get into the fight, so the next effort was built almost entirely around the navy. In effect, during the initial phases, the army troops were to act as scarcely more than a security force for the fleet. The idea was to go through the Yazoo Pass, a gap in the east bank of the Mississippi a few miles downstream from Helena, AR. A navigable channel connected the pass with the Coldwater River, which in turn connected to the Tallahatchie, which then connected with the Yazoo River, thus providing a navigable waterway all the way to Vicksburg's back door. The navy and its big guns would overawe Yazoo City, the army would put troops ashore, and Vicksburg would be taken in flank. Furthermore, a Union army at Yazoo City could be supported entirely by water transport, so there was no possibility of a replay of the Holly Springs disaster.

Initially everything went as planned, but just above Greenwood, on 10 March 1863, the ironclads were fired on by big guns mounted in a strong earthwork called Fort Pemberton. The stream was so narrow that only two gunboats at a time could bring their guns to bear, so, for the first time, the navy was outgunned. Furthermore, pretty much the whole countryside was under water due to spring floods, so it was impossible for the army to get into the act. The expedition started back out on 20 March 1863; the men thought they were lucky to make it with their skins intact.[5]

The defeat at Fort Pemberton rankled Porter. While he was at Chickasaw Bayou with Sherman, his intelligence service informed him that there was yet another water route to Yazoo City. It led from the Yazoo River below the Confederate forts at Snyder's Bluff, up Steele Bayou to Black Bayou, which connected to Deer Creek. From there the route led up Deer Creek to the Rolling Fork, which connected to the Big Sunflower River. That river joined the Yazoo River thirteen airline miles northeast of Haynes Bluff. Once on the Yazoo, it was less than nine river miles to Satartia, from which good roads led into the rear of the Rebel fortifications at Snyder's and Haynes bluffs, as well as into Vicksburg itself. Porter entered Steele Bayou with five of his City Series ironclads and a number of supporting vessels on 14 March 1863. By this time, Porter and Sherman were bosom buddies, and Sherman supported the naval expedition with a division of his XV Corps. It was well that he did. By 22 March, Porter's ironclads had been brought to a stop by trees felled across the Rolling Fork, and Rebel infantry were beginning to drop still others behind the ironclads. At this juncture, Sherman and his infantry arrived, and together Porter and Sherman were able to extricate the precious ships from their deadly trap.[6]

Just prior to this time, Grant had moved most of the Army of the Tennessee down the Mississippi and put them ashore on the Louisiana side of the river a few miles above Vicksburg, at a trio of camps called Lake Providence, Milliken's Bend, and Young's Point. All three places had rather large areas on high segments of the natural levees that border the river, and all were protected by good artificial levees as well, so the camps were well protected from the spring floods which inundated most of the countryside. By 29 March, the Union had a major part of its entire fighting force in the Lower Mississippi Valley concentrated opposite Vicksburg. Present were MG John McClernand's XIII Corps, MG William T. Sherman's XV Corps, MG James McPherson's XVII Corps, and RADM David D. Porter's fleet of ironclad warships. Only MG Stephen Hurlbut's XVI Corps had been left behind, and it guarded western Tennessee and the railroad connecting the bend of the Tennessee with Memphis on the Mississippi. Control of the river all the way back to the immense depots at Cairo, IL, gave Grant a secure and efficient supply route. The Union command had discovered that railroads had their problems; they tied up troops in large numbers, because they were so vulnerable to interruption by cavalry or partisan raids. Every bridge, culvert, and water tank had to be provided with a guard detachment, and each such detachment drained manpower away from the fighting force. The security of the river, on the other hand, could be turned over to the navy, which automatically meant more men in the fighting regiments.

The problem now, therefore, was to find a way to get the army safely onto the Mississippi shore, so that it could come to grips with the Confederate defenders of Vicksburg.

CONFEDERATE PERSPECTIVE

Shiloh had been a close call, and the consensus in the Confederacy was that only bad luck had been responsible for the defeat. As a result, the Confederacy tried to hold the Memphis & Charleston Railroad, which connected Memphis with Chattanooga, TN, primarily because it afforded a very useful and convenient lateral communication line behind what was, after Shiloh, the northern edge of Confederate-controlled territory. A major contributing factor in the decision was the presence of a powerful naval squadron based at Memphis and Fort Pillow. There seemed no reason to doubt that the combination of the naval forces and the barely-defeated army would be able to hold the Federals in check indefinitely. If that could be done, then the River and the enormously rich agricultural resources of northern Mississippi and the Mississippi Delta would be secure.

Their hopes were dashed on 6 June 1862, when the Confederate naval forces were destroyed by a Union squadron of ironclads and rams. Memphis was the last defensible position on the River north of Vicksburg, and in a matter of days the Federal ironclads had appeared just upstream from the town. Fortunately, Vicksburg had been heavily fortified as a precaution, and the Federal thrust to the south came to an abrupt halt just out of range of the big guns of the River Defense batteries. It was clear to everyone that Vicksburg had become the next objective of the Federals.

In the meantime, Union forces in overwhelming strength moved slowly and cautiously southward from Shiloh and, on 30 May 1862, occupied Corinth. Control of the railroad between the bend of the Tennessee River and Memphis, too, fell irrevocably into Union hands. The Confederates had little choice but to fall back. They established a defensive line based on the swampy Tallahatchie River, hoping thus not only to bar the way to Vicksburg, but also to prevent Union cavalry forays into the enormously rich agricultural area of the Mississippi Delta.

It was absolutely essential that Vicksburg be held. By the autumn of 1862, the blockade of southern seaports was beginning to pinch. The Confederacy needed European war materiel and was becoming increasingly dependent upon a supply line that ran from Matamoros, Mexico, up the bays and sounds of the Texas coast to southern Louisiana, then up the rivers and bayous to Monroe, LA. Here the items were put on the railroad to DeSoto, shipped across the Mississippi on ferries to Vicksburg, and then back on the railroad that eventually led to the East Coast. To be sure, there were also railroads leading inland from Port Hudson, Grand Gulf, and Bayou Sara, but they were largely irrelevant because they were only short dead-end spurs. Thus the Monroe–Vicksburg–Meridian railroad was becoming increasingly vital to the Confederacy. If supplies of European war materiel were cut off, the South would be faced with yet another serious difficulty.

Some few southerners appreciated the fact that the fall of Vicksburg also meant that the military resources of the entire Trans-Mississippi would be lost to the Richmond government. No more troops or supplies from Louisiana, Texas, Arkansas, and Missouri—the patrolling warships of the Union navy would see to that. In addition, if the Confederacy could prevent Union commerce from using the River, this would add sensibly to Union discontent and war-weariness, especially in the states of the Old Northwest.

The vulnerability of the supply lines to the Trans-Mississippi was amply demonstrated when FO Farragut's squadron came up the River after the fall of New Orleans in April 1862. Shortly thereafter, on 12 May 1862,[7] BG Martin Luther Smith arrived in Vicksburg to take command of the garrison, and he immediately began fortifying the place. MAJ S. H. Lockett, who eventually became chief engineer of the Department of Mississippi and East Louisiana, arrived on 20 June 1862, and with his arrival the thrust to fortify Vicksburg took on new life. It was he who finally placed the defensive perimeter and designed the various strongpoints and riflepits.

After a long rest, the Yankee armies moved southward and, on 19 September 1862, defeated the Rebel forces attempting to hold Iuka, MS. Then, on 3 and 4 October 1862, the Confederates tried to retake Corinth and failed. These twin defeats convinced the Richmond authorities that the threat to Vicksburg was very real, and they sent the man many believed to be the best general in the Confederacy, GEN Joseph E. Johnston, to take command of the Department of the West, which included Vicksburg and Mississippi. Johnston, however, believed that the principal threat to the Confederacy was Union MG William S. Rosecrans's Army of the Cumberland, which had occupied Nashville and was threatening Chattanooga. Thus, on 4 December 1862, he established his headquarters at Chattanooga, TN, about eighty-five miles southeast of Murfreesboro, TN, which had been occupied by GEN Braxton Bragg's Army of Tennessee on 26 November 1862. The previous month (on 14 Oct. 1862), newly promoted LTG John C. Pemberton had been placed in command of the Department of Mississippi and East Louisiana, with specific orders to defend Vicksburg at all costs.[8] He established his headquarters at Jackson, MS, since it was at the nexus of communications lines leading to his armies in Vicksburg, Port Hudson, and North Mississippi. His department technically was subordinate to Johnston's, but in practice it was virtually autonomous. After the twin victories of Iuka and Corinth, the Federal army established a base at Grand Junction and moved ponderously and cautiously southward along the railroad toward Grenada, MS. The Northerners established a huge supply depot at Holly Springs and, by the middle of December 1862, had reached the Yocona River. There seemed no way to stop them.

Confederate MG Earl Van Dorn, normally not a particularly brilliant soldier, thought the Federal supply system looked vulnerable. In late December 1862, he led three brigades of cavalry on a raid behind the Union lines, and, on 20 December 1862, they penetrated and burned the depot at Holly Springs. With the smoke of the conflagration still rising into the sky, the Federals began a retreat that carried them all the way back to Grand Junction. Clearly, the Confederate defenses of Vicksburg were holding.

The Confederate high command scarcely had time to congratulate itself when suddenly a powerful Union ironclad squadron, escorting a fleet of troop transports, appeared off the mouth of the Yazoo River, only a few miles above Vicksburg. The fleet sailed up the Yazoo and put an army ashore below the Confederate defenses at Snyder's and Drumgould's bluffs. It was no surprise to the Confederates to discover that the Union forces were commanded by William Tecumseh Sherman. To reach the bluffs, the Yankees had to build roads across the water-logged river floodplain and attack across swampy Chickasaw Bayou. That took time, and when the attack finally came, on 29 December 1862, the Southerners were more than ready for them. The assault failed utterly. However, Sherman did not retreat upriver, as everyone expected; instead, he put his men ashore on the Louisiana side of the River. By mid-January 1863, it was clear that his camps at Young's Point, Milliken's Bend, and Lake Providence were going to be permanent fixtures.

The Yankees were not content to stay in their riverside camps; instead, almost immediately they sent patrols to the south to break the railroad from DeSoto to Monroe. That was an irritant, because it prevented the railroad from being repaired (it had been out of service since the summer of 1862) and still further hampered the flow of European war materials coming up from Matamoros. That could be tolerated for a time, because the flow could be diverted to the route following the Red River to Bayou Sara, on the Mississippi. Meanwhile, the Yankee army posed no real threat to the security of Vicksburg, and would not pose such a threat unless somehow it could be put ashore in Mississippi in the vicinity of Vicksburg.

Before long, more blue-clad soldiery began to arrive in those Louisiana camps; by the end of January, it was clear that much of the Army of the Tennessee was in residence. Then, on 2 February 1863, Union engineers appeared on the Mississippi shore at the Yazoo Pass, a few miles below Helena, AR. They proceeded to cut a hole in the levee, and soon gunboats and transports began to pass through the opening. Pemberton realized immediately that such an expedition could follow navigable waterways almost all the way to Vicksburg. He moved quickly to strengthen the earthworks of Fort Pemberton, on the Tallahatchie River above Greenwood, and reinforced its garrison. When the Union warships finally appeared, on 10 March 1863, the Confederate garrison under MG William Wing Loring easily beat them off. There was a good deal of sparring between Federal batteries and the guns of Fort Pemberton after the repulse of the ironclads, but at last, on 4 April, the Yankees gave up and pulled out.

Meanwhile, on about 15 March, word had arrived at Pemberton's headquarters in Jackson that five of the big Union ironclads, apparently unsupported by ground forces, had entered Steele Bayou. Their intention was obvious: they planned to use the interconnecting waterways of the Mississippi Delta to reach the Yazoo River above Haynes Bluff, thus avoiding the guns of both Fort Pemberton and the batteries at Snyder's and Haynes bluffs. It looked like a golden opportunity to create a Confederate ironclad fleet without having to build it, because those waterways were so narrow and tree-lined that a Confederate force could obstruct the channel ahead of and behind the squadron and trap it! Orders went out instantly, and for a while it looked as if the plan might work, but Sherman's infantry marched overland to the rescue, and the damned Yankees were able to back their ships out of the ambush.

Despite their disappointment at the failed effort to capture the ironclads, Pemberton and the rest of the Confederate high command breathed a sigh of relief. Vicksburg again had been held against all threats by both land and water. To be sure, the Army of the Tennessee still remained in those camps on the Louisiana shore, and that was worrisome, but it posed no real threat to the security of Vicksburg. Only if the Union army could be put ashore in Mississippi in the vicinity of Vicksburg would it pose a problem.

It did not escape Pemberton's attention, however, that Federal strategy had changed after Holly Springs; instead of using the railroads as their major supply lines, as everyone expected, they now were using the river. That was a problem, because it was much harder to interfere with fleets of transport steamboats on the river than trains of cars on a railroad. Furthermore, a secure supply system, coupled with lots of troop transports supported by the heavy artillery of the ironclads, meant that Vicksburg was threatened with a direct amphibious assault. Steps were taken immediately to counter this menace, and in the months following the arrival of Lockett, Vicksburg became very strong indeed. By the spring of 1863, it had become a system of four mutually supporting strongpoints. Ten miles north of the city, where the Yazoo River brings navigable water close to the base of the hills, thus affording access to high ground leading to the rear of Vicksburg, the powerful defensive complex of Haynes, Snyder's, and Drumgould's bluffs was constructed. Another major strongpoint was created at Grand Gulf, thirty airline miles south of Vicksburg, where the Mississippi again flows against the valley wall, just as it does at Vicksburg. And finally, about seven miles south of Vicksburg, a strong battery was built at Warrenton, at a place where a tongue of low but flood-free land reached from the bluffs to the river. It was comforting to know that every potential crossing place had been heavily fortified. All indications were that Vicksburg could be held indefinitely.

COMMENTARY

The Confederates thought of Vicksburg as a purely defensive position, never as a base for their own operations. Somehow this doctrine of holding places was built into the southern psyche. Perhaps it stemmed from the doctrine of states' rights, upon which the Confederacy was founded. If one believed that every political entity, such as a state, was sovereign, then one's loyalty was owed to the state and not to the nation of which the state was a part. That being so, the compulsion to defend every place equally, without regard to its actual strategic value to the Confederacy as a whole, was well nigh irresistible. Places, then, became the coin of Confederate strategic thought. The objective always was to hold a place, and the Confederate strategic doctrine was tied tightly into defense.

It may be argued, of course, that this is too simplistic a view. The pervasive influence of the states' rights concept may well have been reinforced by a subconscious realization that the Confederacy did not have to win the war; it had only to hold out until the Union grew tired of fighting. The South did not have to invade and conquer the North; all it had to do was exist until the North was exhausted. Thus defense—making the Yankees pay for every square foot of ground—became basic to the Confederacy's psychological orientation, composed in equal parts of grand strategy and political doctrine.

The South organized its military structure around a set of departments, and surely it is no coincidence that those departments almost always consisted of groups of states. Thus, in the spring of 1863, GEN Joseph Johnston commanded the Department of the West, the western boundary of which was the Mississippi River; and GEN Edmund Kirby Smith commanded the Department of the Trans-Mississippi, the eastern boundary of which was the same river. The River also was the boundary between states, except for that portion of Louisiana below 31°N. That portion of Louisiana east of the river obviously was not in the Trans-Mississippi, so consistency won out, and it was included in Johnston's Department of the West. The result was that the Confederacy created two equal departments to defend the river whose defense was absolutely crucial to the existence of the new nation, and made the river the boundary between the two departments!

The boundary between adjacent units is always a weak spot in any defense line, chiefly because it is so difficult to coordinate actions across it. As a twentieth-century military man would say, it is a command and control problem. All other things being equal, a good strategist or tactician will always attack at a place where two units adjoin. The Confederate high command knew full well that the central Union strategy in the West was to gain control of the River from end to end. That is, the leaders knew that the Federals, sooner or later, would thrust down the river. Despite this, they used the river as the seam between the two military agencies responsible for its defense. One can only conclude that they were defending the states, not the river. They adopted a basic pattern of organization which almost inevitably would grant the Union an important, perhaps a fundamental, advantage. The temptation to assign that oversight to the doctrine of states' rights is compelling. As we shall see, the Confederacy's inability to coordinate the operations of the departments of the West and the Trans-Mississippi runs through the campaign almost like the theme of a Greek tragedy.

2

The Geographic Setting

The northern end of the Confederate defense perimeter at Vicksburg terminates in a little square fort on the summit of Fort Hill, an eminence that looms 255 feet above the plain to the west. The view from the parapet to the western horizon is unbroken. To the north is the deep ravine of Mint Spring Bayou, and beyond it an Indian mound perches near the end of Indian Mound Ridge. It is now surrounded by the Vicksburg National Cemetery, which was established shortly after the end of the Civil War. Below the western parapet of the square fort, the western face of Fort Hill drops steeply to what once was the River. To the east is the sinuous crest of Fort Hill Ridge, along which the Confederate defense line ran away into the distance. The escarpment on which the little fort is perched is characteristic of almost the entire length of the Lower Mississippi Valley. The line of bluffs begins just below the confluence of the Ohio and Mississippi rivers and extends to Baton Rouge, LA. It is not everywhere as high as at Vicksburg, but it is imposing throughout its entire length.

The Mississippi is a classic meandering river, with a highly unstable channel. Left to its own devices, the channel would shift position almost continuously. In the course of millennia, it has wandered widely over its floodplain, and at the time of this writing, as in 1863, much of its course is far out in the middle of the plain, many miles from the line of bluffs that marks the floodplain's eastern limit. In 1863, the river in the lower valley touched the eastern valley wall in only a very few places. From north to south, they were: Columbus, KY; Memphis, TN; Vicksburg, MS; Grand Gulf, MS; Rodney, MS; Natchez, MS; Port Hudson, LA; and Baton Rouge, LA.

In the early days of settlement, these were prime locations for the founding of towns, because they were the only places where one could establish a settlement on the river and still keep one's feet dry during the annual spring flood. Today Grand Gulf, Rodney, and Port Hudson are gone, chiefly because the river changed course and now flows well out in the floodplain. Memphis, Vicksburg, Natchez, and Baton Rouge remain flourishing communities, primarily for two reasons. First, of course, is that the river still impinges on the valley wall at those locations, so they provide essential stopping and trans-shipping sites for river traffic. Second, because the river towns already were bustling ports when the west-seeking railroads were being built, it was perfectly natural—indeed, inevitable—that the railroads should end at the river ports, the only locations where one could be assured that there always would be dry ground on which to make the transfer from ship to rail or vice versa.

One of the Confederate objectives was to close the river to Union traffic. Without an effective navy, the southerners had to rely on batteries of heavy artillery. It was hopeless to mount such batteries where the first flood would inundate them, so they had to be at places like Vicksburg, where flood-free ground came almost to the water's edge. The combination of river, bluff, and railroad strongly influenced the choice of places for the Confederate batteries. The gun-tube of a 10-in columbiad weighs 15,400 pounds. It was possible, of course, to move them with animal power, but it was a lot easier to move them by rail. The choice of Columbus, KY; Memphis, TN; and Vicksburg as positions for big-gun batteries was inevitable; all three had direct rail links to the East Coast. Port Hudson and Grand Gulf did not. To be sure, both towns were served by railroads, but they were only short stubs which did not connect to the primary network. Hauling a big anti-ship gun by wagon over Mississippi's dirt roads was a major problem.

Columbus and Memphis fell very early in the war and do not really figure in the operations relating to the Vicksburg campaign. Grand Gulf was established much later, at the beginning of the last phases of the Vicksburg campaign. The river flows in from the west, strikes the valley wall, and then turns sharply south at Vicksburg, Grand Gulf, and Port Hudson. In 1863, those sharp turns restricted the channel and created very turbulent flows.

This was an important factor in the locations of the anti-ship batteries, because the eddies tended to throw ships out of control as they rounded the bend. At Vicksburg, the Confederates placed the Water Battery, one of the most effective of the River Defenses, almost at the water's edge, right at the base of Fort Hill and opposite the most turbulent stretch of the channel.

The general level of the floodplain at Vicksburg is about 90 feet above mean sea level, and the crest of Fort Hill is 345 feet above mean sea level, a difference of 255 feet. The horizontal distance from the crest of the hill to the water's edge is 1,200 feet, which yields an average slope of a bit over 21 percent, or about 12 degrees. It looks a lot steeper to one standing on the parapet of the fort, or at the bottom of the hill at the water's edge! An escarpment of roughly this order is normal for the entire eastern valley wall for a distance of at least 50 miles in both directions.

Young's Point, one of the two big Union bases on the Mississippi River above Vicksburg, was eight airline miles to the west. It could not be seen from the Confederate observation post on Fort Hill, not because of any intervening hills, but because of the curvature of the earth combined with huge forest trees growing on the intervening floodplain. The second of the big Union bases, Milliken's Bend, was fifteen airline miles away to the west-northwest and was similarly invisible from the Confederate positions on Fort Hill.

The escarpment, and the river at its foot, were the topographic barriers which faced Grant from his position on the western side of the river. If ever one side held the high ground, it was the Confederates at Vicksburg.

MISSISSIPPI RIVER FLOODPLAIN

In 1863, the Mississippi River in the vicinity of Vicksburg differed greatly from its character today. One thing about Old Man River: he doesn't like to stay in the same place for very long. In 1863, the river came down from the southwest until it reached Paw Paw Bend, where it turned and continued south. Within a few miles, it turned again, to the southeast. This reach was so broad and placid that the Union Navy used a large patch of open water off the mouth of the Yazoo River as an anchorage. At this time, the Yazoo joined the Mississippi well out in the valley, almost opposite Young's Point and about nine river miles above Vicksburg.

Below the mouth of the Yazoo, as the river began to approach the wall of the valley, it began a gradual turn to the north. And here the placid stream suddenly began to change in temperament; the current began to move more rapidly until, at a point just above the city of Vicksburg, the channel made a complete 180-degree turn around the tip of DeSoto Point and flowed in a torrent right down the city waterfront. This reach in front of the city had a current velocity of some six knots even during normal water stages, and it was faster when the water was high. Furthermore, as the water made that incredible course reversal around DeSoto Point, enormous and unpredictable eddies formed, which then drifted downstream through the channel in front of the city. The turbulence of this stretch was notorious, and river pilots dreaded the area because the currents made steamboats so hard to control. Despite this difficulty, however, the Vicksburg steamboat landings all were located in a two-mile stretch along the city's waterfront. The singular advantage was that there was always deep water off the bank, regardless of water stage, because the bluffs came down virtually to the water's edge. Under ordinary circumstances, such a bank would have been actively eroding and thus very dangerous; but at Vicksburg, the bluffs at water level are cored in solid limestone and shale, which not even the Mississippi could readily eat away.

DeSoto Point, the long, low-lying peninsula which jutted up between the north- and south-flowing reaches of the river, had a man-made levee surrounding portions of it, which kept the interior more or less dry except during periods of excessively high water. In March 1863, the water was high, but not quite high enough to overflow the DeSoto Point levees, so the little community which clustered around the railroad ferry landing remained dry. The strategic railroad ran southward safely behind the DeSoto Point levees for a mile or so and then turned westward on a combination of trestles and fills across the swamps to Monroe.

The 1863 course of the river persisted with but minor changes all through the Civil War; but finally, during the spring flood of 1876, the river finally cut through the base of DeSoto Point and took a new course to the south. As is usual in such instances, the river quickly built sandbars across the mouths of the abandoned channel and converted DeSoto Bend and the reaches above and below it into an ox-bow lake, which quickly became known as Centennial Lake. Such lakes are common in the Mississippi floodplain. For example, Eagle Lake, a popular resort area eleven airline miles northwest of Vicksburg, is such a lake. Another is Lake Providence, a few miles upstream on the Louisiana side.

The effect of the 1876 DeSoto Cutoff on Vicksburg was devastating. Much of the city's economy depended upon river traffic, and now the town was effectively cut off from the navigation channel. Unless something was done, its days as a river port were over. Early in this century, the problem was solved by damming the natural outlet of the Yazoo River and then cutting a channel connecting it to the north end of Centennial Lake. The flow of the Yazoo keeps the old channel in front of Vicksburg scoured out and navigable, thus preserving the city as a river port. In some ways the present landing is better than the old one. In the "good old days," the rapid and turbulent currents made the steamboat landing a relatively treacherous place, whereas the flow of the Yazoo is much more sedate and thus much easier for pilots to negotiate. So it is that modern Vicksburg, arguably the epitome of river towns, no longer is truly on the river. Few of its citizens call attention to that curious irony.

To the untrained eye, the floodplain west of Vicksburg is scarcely more than an endless, monotonously level surface.[1] In reality, it is a surface of quite astonishing complexity, albeit one of very low relief. It is also entirely a creation of the river. In the untamed days before Europeans appeared on the scene, the river was free to wander where it would. Meander loops formed, were cut off, and new ones formed in an endless cycle. When the river overflowed its banks, as it did virtually every year between February and June, the silt and sand carried by the turgid waters were deposited in successive layers on the banks along the channel., creating an asymmetric ridge along either bank, with a steep bank facing the water and a very gentle slope trending away from the channel. These ridges are called *natural levees,* and they have formed wherever the river has flowed. Most of them are not very high; normally they are 10 to 15 feet above the general level of the landscape, and they may be as narrow as 100 yards or as wide as several miles. The slopes leading away from the river are very real but usually so gentle as to be imperceptible to the naked eye.

In the course of ages, the river has cut off innumerable meander loops, and each such abandoned loop remains as an oxbow lake, a form of lake characteristic of the floodplains of meandering streams. Each such lake is surrounded by a natural levee, formed while the river flowed in the loop. Furthermore, the river sometimes made major changes in its course, abandoning long sections of channels. Such abandoned channels now are occupied by bayous, which are simply modern streams faithfully following the ancient river course. Examples are Walnut and Roundaway bayous, across the river west of Vicksburg, and the Yazoo River north of Vicksburg. Because they follow the ancient courses, the bayous almost always are bordered by natural levees.

In ages past, rivers such as the Arkansas flowed in different courses, and today their abandoned channels also are occupied by rivers and bayous. The Tensas River and Bayou Macon, both flowing southward near the western edge of the floodplain opposite Vicksburg, are examples. They, too, are bordered by natural levees, although theirs are somewhat less extensive than those formed by the Mississippi.

The result of all these course changes and abandonments is an astonishingly complex network of intersecting waterways, many of which were navigable by small steamboats in 1863, especially during periods of high water. Because the ancient courses crossed and recrossed each other, the regions between the modern rivers and bayous eventually formed closed basins called *backswamps*, each walled in by natural levees on all sides. Some of the backswamps drained each year during the low-water periods of late summer and winter, but many of them did not. Those that did not were filled with dense stands of huge bald cypress and tupelo trees, and they became haunts of alligators, water snakes, countless aquatic birds, and innumerable fish. Those that drained each year were covered with tall forests of willow, tupelo, and oak, and were inhabited by white-tailed deer, black bear, cougar, opossum, raccoon, and many other birds and animals. Whether permanently flooded or not, the backswamps were, for all practical purposes, untamed wildernesses, utterly impassable by a man on horseback or by any form of wheeled vehicle, and very difficult even for a man on foot.

Of course, the natural levees were not absolutely continuous; floodwaters could pour through the gaps, so that nearly every year, during the spring flood, the backswamps were deeply inundated. In most years, however, the water did not rise high enough to submerge the natural levees completely. Thus, in a normal year, the major parts of the natural levees remained above flood level. During such times, the floodplain was a vast shallow lake crossed here and there by low, sinuous, narrow ridges of high ground, barely above water level and usually paralleling a river or bayou.

For all practical purposes, the only lands suitable for farming with the technology available in the mid-nineteenth century were the natural levees, and by 1863 most of them had been cleared. While the major crop, by far, was cotton, the exigencies of war forced nearly all the plantations to grow food crops (especially corn, fruit, and vegetables) as well. Each natural levee was occupied by a line of plantation homes built on the highest part of the ridge and always facing the bayou. The bayous were the highways of this strange, watery world. The few extant roads tended to follow the natural levees and were both discontinuous and primitive. The plantations tended to have large acreages, so the houses were almost always a half-mile or more apart. Where the plantation owner was prosperous enough to own slaves, the main house was surrounded by the cabins of Africans who worked the fields and the barns and other buildings required to operate a plantation. A few plantations were so large that the cluster of buildings assumed the proportions of a small town, and indeed functioned as such, for many of them, like the manors of medieval England, were largely self-sustaining communities. Examples are Bruinsburg and Hard Times. By far the majority of plantations, however, were smaller, resembling the Dalkeith plantation, on Walnut Bayou near Vicksburg, which had a modest house with four rooms. Small establishments like Dalkeith normally held only two or three or four slaves, and many had none at all. Nevertheless, slaveholders, whether they held few or many slaves, nearly all conformed to the tenets of the "plantation culture," one of which was the conviction that the "peculiar institution" was not only necessary but proper.

A Mississippi River flood must be seen to be believed. The change in water level between extreme low water, which normally occurs in November and December, and spring high water, which normally occurs sometime between early March and late May, normally is on the order of sixty feet. At low water, the pilot of a steamboat in the channel could not see over the top of the bank even if he climbed to the top of the stacks; during high water, the vessel floated on a water surface higher than the surrounding countryside.

By 1863, the river and many of the bayous were lined with artificial levees, privately constructed by local plantation owners to keep their lands as free of floodwaters as possible. There were no official standards, so the structures were of all heights and shapes. Of course they often failed, and then the waters would roar through the "crevasse" to inundate the landscape beyond. These "fast floods" were greatly feared, for it was all too easy for people and animals to be trapped by the rapidly rising waters. In those days, Old Man River was feared as well as respected.

THE TERRAIN OF THE EAST BANK

LOESS HILLS

At the bottom of the line of bluffs that defines the eastern margin of the floodplain, at approximately river level, there is relatively hard limestone and shale, above which lies a thin and discontinuous layer of soft red

sandy clays and gravels. Above those red clays is a thick layer of a very
special kind of brown silt called *loess*, and it is this material which is responsible for the region's peculiar characteristics. The loess layer is up
to two hundred feet thick close to the river, but to the east it thins rapidly, so that it forms a narrow belt rarely more than fifteen miles wide
paralleling the eastern margin of the floodplain. In many places, the belt
is only five or six miles wide. At Vicksburg, and for many miles north and
south, the belt of Loess Hills is from ten to fifteen miles wide.

Loess is very strange stuff. It is composed of very tiny plate-like particles
which are locked together by calcium carbonate—that is, lime—cement.
The tiny plates are at all angles; geologists call it a "fairy castle" structure.
As a result, undisturbed loess has a high porosity (i.e., there is a lot of empty
space in it); because of that, the soil is very light. However, despite the high
porosity, in its undisturbed state loess is almost completely impermeable.
Because water cannot percolate through it, rainwater cannot penetrate into
it, so water is not stored in the mass of the soil, and accordingly there are
very few springs. Such few springs as exist—and they are very rare—nearly
all go dry in July, August, and September. Streams are even more ephemeral, and the smaller ones may flow only during winter and early spring
months, when episodes of rain are very frequent. The inevitable corollary
of the lack of soil storage of water is that runoff is very rapid, and streams in
the Loess Hills are extraordinarily subject to flash flooding.

Loess is quite soft and easy to work, yet it will stand in a vertical bank
indefinitely, and in its undisturbed state it will support even relatively
large tunnels without revetting or timbering. These seemingly contradic-
tory properties were exploited by both military and civilian populations
of Vicksburg during the siege. The city is built almost entirely on loess,
and the citizenry dug caves in it and lived in them during the fighting.
That sounds damp and uncomfortable, but in fact, because the material
is so impermeable, the caves were dry, cool, and relatively pleasant.

Along with its admirable and useful properties, however, loess has
others which are more troublesome. For one thing, while water will not percolate through the undisturbed material, running water flowing across an unprotected surface will quickly erode it. It is said that, if one scratches the
surface, the first good rain will turn the scratch into a gully ten feet deep.
While perhaps apocryphal, there is enough truth to make it necessary to
protect bare loess surfaces to prevent very rapid erosion. It is this property
that is responsible for the terrain so characteristic of the Loess Hills. Apparently the upper surface of the loess belt originally undulated gently, but over

the millennia, runoff water eroded it into an astonishing complex of deep ravines that seem to run in all directions. The ridges between the ravines generally are flat-topped, but those flat tops may range in width from a few feet to several hundred yards. The slopes that drop into the ravines often are almost unbelievably steep, being in some places vertical. The landscape, then, is a maze of narrow, serpentine plateaus separated by mini-gorges. Before the days of European settlement, the whole complex was covered by tall hardwood forest, dominated in places by black walnut.

The first thing the Europeans did was to cut down the forest so that crops could be planted. In general, the only flat ground was on the tops of the ridges, so that is where the farm buildings and fields were located. Because of the almost total lack of groundwater (an artifact of the lack of permeability of the loess), there were no wells; the farm water supply was provided by rainfall stored in large cisterns dug into the loess. Many still remain, even though all traces of the farm buildings may be gone. The capacity of these cisterns was very limited, and toward the end of the "dry season," which normally falls between late July and mid-October, water often was in short supply.

As soon as the protecting trees were removed by the early settlers, those ridgetop fields began to wash away. While some of the materials were deposited in the ravine bottoms, most were carried to the Mississippi, which eventually dumped them into the Gulf of Mexico. By 1863, after the process had been under way for some seventy-five years, a substantial proportion of the hilltop farmland had been lost, the sides of the ridges were scarred with a multitude of fresh gullies, and the major ravines had been partially filled with silt that stayed wet and boggy the whole year long. The abundant moisture in the boggy ravine bottoms was quickly exploited by the native bamboo (or cane), and by 1863 many of the ravine bottoms had grown into immense canebrakes. The native bamboo grows about fifteen feet tall and, when undisturbed, will grow into almost impenetrable thickets, especially when locked into a tangle with cat's-claw vines (the name is apt!), greenbrier, poison ivy, grape, and honeysuckle.

The slopes between the boggy bottoms and open fields at the top were mostly covered with tangled scrub; the big trees had been cut down for timber and fuel, and the second growth was quite small, scraggly, and tangled with the usual array of vines. The ridgetops tended to be bare of trees and under cultivation, as were the side slopes in those few places where the slopes were gentle enough to permit a man with a mule and a plow to walk without falling into the ravine. Houses always were located on the ridgetops, and roads followed the ridgetops wherever possible; only as a last resort did a road descend from a dry ridgetop to cross one of the boggy stream bottoms. As a result, the roads of 1863 were very tortuous. It is difficult for a modern observer to appreciate those roads. Typically one wagon wide, they often were bordered on either side by ravines 150 feet deep, with appallingly steep sides. When they were forced to drop off a ridge crest in order to cross from one ridge to another, the grade quickly became depressed into the hillside, because every fall of rain eroded ruts into the road surface, and the next time the road was graded, the surface was lowered another inch or so. Before long, the roadbed in many places was at the bottom of a small canyon ten to fifteen feet deep, with vertical sides. Very few of these roads are still in use, although in some places they can be followed—on foot!—for considerable distances. Modern roads cut indiscriminately across the countryside on elaborate cuts and fills, so it is almost impossible to obtain an impression of the region as it was in 1863 without leaving the modern road and walking into the woods.

Most farms in the Loess Hills were abandoned between 1900 and 1920, and the land quickly reverted to hardwood forest, although of course the present-day trees are very much smaller than the forest giants of pre-European days. It may come as a shock to realize that, in most cases, the seemingly primeval forests lining the roads between Vicksburg and Bovina and covering the battlefield of Port Gibson are less than seventy-five years old. Trees grow quickly in Mississippi.

The peculiar topography and soils of the Loess Hills had a profound effect on the nature of human occupancy there. Probably because the Mississippi was so conveniently near, making it relatively easy to get cotton to market, some of the agricultural establishments on the Loess Hills became cotton plantations. However, a substantial number of subsistence farms also existed, as well as a number of establishments which specialized in providing farm produce to Vicksburg, the surrounding towns, and the plantations across the river. Relatively few of the farms and plantations in the Loess Hills around Vicksburg held slaves, and one consequence of that was that Vicksburg and Warren County voted against secession.

The modern Vicksburg–Port Gibson highway follows the base of the bluffs for about fifteen miles south of Vicksburg and only then climbs into the Loess Hills. Even so, today's road is located far from the alignment of the main road in 1863, so the terrain visible from the modern highway, for the most part, is not representative of what one would have seen at the time of the Civil War. In 1863, the main road to Port Gibson first followed the Halls Ferry Road to a point ten miles south of the city, then veered off to the southwest, following one of those sharp ridges which forms the watershed between the Mississippi and the Big Black rivers to a point two miles east of Yokena. There it again turned south, to cross the Big Black on a ferry at Hankinson's Ferry, and Bayou Pierre on the Grindstone Ford suspension bridge. Almost the entire route passed across the tangled terrain of the Loess Hills, and it is a remarkable fact that it followed ridgetops so assiduously that it crossed only four watercourses in the entire distance: Hatcher Bayou (four miles south of Vicksburg), Big Black River, and Big and Little Bayou Pierre. It no longer is possible to follow the entire length of that road even on foot, because the ferry and the bridge have been gone for many years.

Except for very short and discontinuous stretches, all roads were *unmetaled*—that is, no gravel or other material had been applied to stabilize the surface. When the weather was dry, traffic quickly converted the surface into ankle-deep dust; and when the rains came, the surface rapidly degenerated into seemingly bottomless mud. Only rarely were moisture conditions so ideal that neither dust nor mud was a plague. Even so, the roads were mostly graded, so it still was easier to move along the roads than to go across country. Civil War–era armies were far more road-bound than a modern army. All wheeled vehicles—the wagons of the supply train as well as the caissons and limbers of the artillery—ran on rigid wheels surfaced with an iron tire. Under the rare ideal conditions, such a wheel sank slightly into the unmetaled road surfaces just enough to give a contact area of about 16 square inches, so the four wheels of a supply wagon provided about 64 square inches of supporting surface. A wagon plus cargo weighed (very roughly) about 4,000 pounds, so the "contact pressure" of such a vehicle was about 62 pounds per square inch (psi). If the surface is dry and firm, it will support such a load, but if it is wet, the wheel simply sinks into the surface to a depth such that the load can be sustained. The horses and mules do the same, of course. A few vehicles moving along a rain-softened road quickly churned the surface into a morass into which each successive vehicle simply sank deeper. Consider the case of an artillery gun carriage carrying a 12-pdr Napoleon gun (the field artillery piece of choice for both armies). The gun-tube weighed 1,227 pounds, and the carriage another 800 pounds, for a total weight of 2,027 pounds, and it was supported on only two wheels, so the contact pressure rose to about 63 psi. (In comparison, a modern Abrams heavy tank has a contact pressure of about 3.5 psi!) And that is one of the principal reasons why rain tended to bring Civil War armies to a stop.

THE INTERIOR PLAINS

East of the belt of Loess Hills, the land is gently rolling and open. The loess is gone, and the soils are derived from clays and red sandy gravels. This landscape was largely under cultivation in 1863. The only extensive patches of woodland were on the few and scattered hill masses and in the floodplains of the larger creeks, where the soils were too heavy to work and where summer flash floods made cultivation too chancy an affair.

Except in a few limited localities, the soils of this region are not especially fertile, and this factor, plus the relatively long wagon hauls to market, made cotton a less attractive crop than in the Mississippi floodplain or even in the Loess Hills. As a result, most of the agricultural establishments of the Interior Plains were either subsistence farms or farms growing mixed crops. That is, the plantation economy of the floodplain was not so intensively or extensively practiced. This is not to say that cotton was not grown—far from it. But it was grown as a cash-crop component of a relatively diverse agricultural production. Very, very few of these yeomen farmers held slaves, and many of them (perhaps by far the majority) considered the Confederacy to be a creature of the slave owners, for whom they had little liking. There were cotton plantations, of course, but they were very much in the minority, and the "plantation culture" did not dominate the political, economic, and social scene quite so thoroughly as it did in the floodplain of the Mississippi.

Secession sentiment was far from pervasive among the subsistence farmers and small agricultural towns. Jones County, in southeastern Mississippi, actually seceded from the Confederacy! The Confederate government sent in troops, hanged a few of the ringleaders, and effectively suppressed the movement. There is no doubt that the actions of the country people became more circumspect, but is very unlikely that any minds were changed. Today it is widely believed that the modern anti-North sentiment in the region is mostly an artifact of the postwar Reconstruction period, rather than the Secession period.

The clay-rich soils of the Interior Plains are relatively impermeable, so there is very little groundwater. One consequence is that the smaller creeks normally flow only during winter and spring; most are dry by late June. Indeed, any prolonged rainless spell dries them up completely, regardless of the season. Only the largest creeks flow all year round, and even they are reduced to scarcely more than a trickle in late summer and autumn. Indeed, some are little more than discontinuous chains of pools in the sandy and gravelly beds. Nevertheless, these streams have created small floodplains in which the soils are very soft and boggy during the winter and spring. During the summer, and especially during the autumn "dry season," the floodplains dry out, but the streams nevertheless remain as major military obstacles, because their channels are "entrenched" in the floodplain sediments; that is, the water flows in a narrow bed with banks often vertical and ranging from three to ten feet high. The water may be only ankle-deep, but before a horse or a wagon could cross, a ramp had to be cut through the banks.

Mississippi is subject to usually brief but often very intense rainstorms at any season of the year. It is not at all unusual for four inches of rain to fall in two or three hours or less. The soils are unable to absorb such a deluge, so it is quite possible for the runoff waters to convert an almost dry creek, trickling placidly in the bottom of its entrenched channel, into a raging torrent ten feet deep within minutes. Normally such flash floods persist for only a few hours, but while they last they are awesome. Such rapid and extreme changes in water levels and current velocities tended to wash out conventional wooden crib-and-girder bridges every time a major storm crossed the region, so the crossings of choice for the larger streams (such as Big Black River and Bayou Pierre) tended to be floating bridges or ferries, while the smaller streams were crossed by fords. It was easier and more reliable to wait a few hours than to rebuild all the bridges every time it rained. There were a few permanent bridges, such as those across Little Bayou Pierre at Port Gibson and Big Bayou Pierre at Grindstone Ford; rather surprisingly, they were suspension bridges, a technique that made it slightly easier to raise the roadway high enough to clear the inevitable flash floods. The intermediate streams, like Bakers Creek and Fourteen Mile Creek, were a constant problem, because they were too small to justify a floating bridge but too large to make a ford entirely practical. As we shall see, this tendency of Mississippi streams to wash out bridges set the stage for the climactic battle at Champion Hill and thus—if one wishes to indulge in a bit of hyperbole—for the ultimate collapse of the Confederacy.

Most farms depended upon cisterns for the domestic water supply and small stock ponds for the farm animals. The stock ponds were created by constructing small dams across swales. The capacities usually were not large; toward the end of any prolonged dry spell, the few gallons of water remaining became heavily polluted with animal droppings and slime-green with algae.[2]

INTERIOR RIVERS

Two streams large enough to deserve being called rivers flow through the Interior Plains and the Loess Hills: the Big Black River and Bayou Pierre. When one looks at the narrow, snag-choked channel of the modern Big Black River, it is difficult to remember that, in 1863, it was navigable as far upstream as Amsterdam, a hamlet roughly midway between Jackson and Vicksburg. To be sure, the steamboats that plied its waters were not large; RADM Porter on one occasion refused to let one of his ironclads venture up the Big Black. Still, some of the little tinclads, like *Cricket*, could have moved up and down it relatively freely. The result was that the Confederates had a problem, because there was always the danger, however remote, that the Yankees somehow might sneak a tinclad into the Mississippi below Vicksburg and that she might then come nosing up the Big Black. Worse, the ironclad *Essex* had been in the Mississippi below Vicksburg since July 1862; during very high water, even she might have been able to manage the stream. So worrisome was the prospect that the Confederates built a barrier raft below Big Black Bridge, where the Southern Railroad of Mississippi crossed the Big Black between Edwards and Vicksburg, to prevent a gunboat attack on that crucial railroad crossing.

The Bayou Pierre is smaller, but even it was navigable as far upstream as Port Gibson; after all, that is how the town got its name. There was always the possibility that a Yankee tinclad could ride high water as far as the railroad bridge across the bayou two miles northwest of Port Gibson and destroy the bridge. Such an eventuality would not have been a disaster, but it certainly would have been an inconvenience to the garrison at Grand Gulf.

Both streams flow through swampy alluvial valleys which are nothing less than scaled-down versions of the Mississippi floodplain. In 1863, they, like the Mississippi floodplain, were the domains of bald cypress and tupelo, as well as alligators and other unsavory creatures. The valleys were effectively impassable during the spring flood season and difficult in the best of times. People tended to stay out of the floodplains because of the fear of flash flooding, which could be caused at any season by a heavy, widespread, and long-lasting rain. One still can gain some appreciation of this by looking at the floodplain of the Big Black River from the long embankment leading to the modern highway bridge eighteen miles south of Vicksburg. Imagine yourself in a horse-drawn wagon attempting to cross that plain after a period of heavy rain.

While the Big Black was regarded as a navigable stream, it normally could not support steamboat traffic during the late summer and autumn, because the water fell to such low levels. However, it must be recalled that, in 1863, few if any of the very numerous and extensive headwater swamps had been ditched and drained, and as a result the flow regime was considerably more stable than it is today. High waters were not quite so high, and low waters not quite so low.

3

Logistics and Communications

Maps: 1. The Theater of Operations
2. Northern Sector
4. Southern Sector

As a strategic whole, the Vicksburg Campaign can be viewed as a contest between defenders exploiting interior lines of communication and an invader forced to use exterior lines. The Federal armies of the Cumberland and the Ohio, starting in Kentucky and Tennessee, were attempting to move southward toward Chattanooga and Atlanta, the heart of the Confederacy, while the Army of the Tennessee, lodged in Louisiana opposite Vicksburg, was attempting to open the Mississippi to Union traffic and operations. Note that, until 1863, the river was the strategic objective, not Vicksburg. In contrast, the Confederates were trying to hold central and eastern Tennessee and the states of Georgia, Alabama, and Mississippi, as well as to maintain control of the river itself between Vicksburg and Port Hudson.

In addition to being a contest between interior and exterior communications, the campaign was a contest between land and water transportation.

FEDERAL PERSPECTIVE

Rivers were the highways of Federal military power. Troops and supplies flowed freely up and down them, carried by an immense fleet of steamboats. The Union troops at Corinth were fed by ships sailing up the Tennessee River from the Ohio, and the Army of the Tennessee opposite Vicksburg was supplied by others sailing down the Mississippi from St. Louis and Cairo, IL. Cairo, situated at the confluence of the Ohio and Mississippi rivers, was scarcely more than a gigantic military depot and naval station. Memphis, almost midway between Cairo and Vicksburg, was primarily a forward depot, heavily defended to avoid a repeat of Holly Springs.

Getting the mountains of supplies down the Mississippi River from Cairo to the huge encampments at Lake Providence, Young's Point, and Milliken's Bend was not entirely simple and straightforward. Food, ammunition, forage, and all the multitudinous items of materiel that were required to keep an army in the field had to be carried on fragile river steamboats. Natural hazards were bad enough; the channel of the Mississippi was notoriously treacherous, and ships were forever going aground on newly formed sandbars or impaling themselves on "snags." These giant trees, partially embedded in the riverbed, ripped the bottoms out of more boats than ever were lost to enemy action. Nor were the vessels themselves all that reliable; boiler explosions and fires were all too common.

At first the Union transports ran up and down the rivers individually, but soon it became apparent that single steamboats were terribly vulnerable. Many were wood-burners, and they had to put in to shore fairly frequently to replenish. There were favored spots for this—locations where the fuels of choice (oak and pine) were readily available and where there was enough high ground to make stockpiling practical. Soon it was noted that the Confederates had a nasty habit of emplacing a battery of light field artillery at the refueling sites and ambushing ships which stopped. It was not long before the Union naval commanders—most notably, RADM Porter—grasped the pattern and began casting about for a countermeasure. As it happened, there was one ready at hand, in the form of a growing fleet of tinclads.

The Mississippi River campaigns were conceived and managed by westerners, many of whom had grown up along the river and its tributaries, and who therefore were familiar with the fact that the farms and plantations of the Lower Mississippi Valley—the floodplain from Cairo, IL, to the Gulf of Mexico—virtually all were located on natural levees and thus were within rifle-shot of navigable water. Furthermore, the roads of the region, too, were located on those same natural levees. A fleet of shallow-draft gunboats carrying big guns, the leaders reasoned, could perform valuable interdiction service. Thus, late in the summer of 1862, the Union began to purchase a number of river steamboats and convert them into gunboats. The boats came in every conceivable size and configuration, ranging from Porter's giant flagship *Black Hawk* to tiny *Cricket,* which weighed in at a mere 176 tons.

All the vessels had two things in common. First, their lower decks

were converted into casemates armored with about a half-inch of iron—
just thick enough to turn small-arms fire (which is why they were called
"tinclads"). Second, they tended to carry guns far larger than field artillery pieces. Most of them were armed with 12- or 24-pdr howitzers, but
some carried guns as large as 100-pdr Parrott rifles. Little *Cricket* carried six 24-pdr howitzers, astonishing when one considers her draft of
eighteen inches. President Lincoln was enchanted. "We must not forget,"
he said, "our web-footed Navy, which can go wherever the ground is a
little damp." Lincoln was not easily impressed; he knew the river, having twice, in his youth, served as a crew member on flatboats descending from the Ohio River to New Orleans.

Porter's solution to the Confederate artillery ambushes was to station
tinclads at the critical places. A battery of light field guns stood little
chance against a gunboat mounting 12- or 24-pdr howitzers. That improved the situation, but only briefly. Very soon the transport captains
began to report that they were coming under fire wherever the navigation channel came close to the bank. Such places are nearly always at the
outside of meander loops, and, because the Mississippi is an almost pro-
totypical meandering stream, there were a lot of bends. So many, in fact,
that the Union operations officers soon ran out of tinclads, even though
there were about thirty-five of them in operation by the summer of 1863.

The answer to this was the convoy. Going downstream, the fleet of
transports comprising a convoy (it might be anything from two or three
vessels to as many as twenty) would sail in single file, with the tinclad
bringing up the rear. This disposition was almost forced on them, because
any transport in a convoy sailing downstream was always downcurrent
from its escort, which made it easy for the tinclad to get to the scene of
action quickly. Going upstream, the tinclad usually led the procession; she
could get to the scene of action more rapidly by sailing with the current.

The convoy system was not organized in exactly the way one might expect, with a single tinclad assigned to each convoy for the whole trip. Instead,
it was a sort of zone defense. The river was divided up into *reaches*, with a
tinclad assigned to each reach. Thus, a convoy moving either up or down
the stream would, in the course of its journey, be handed off from tinclad to
tinclad. There were some advantages. First, each tinclad captain got to be
very familiar with his stretch of the river and knew all the likely places for
an ambush. A little judicious scouting with landing parties further narrowed
the possibilities, so the tinclad commander almost always knew exactly where
to expect trouble. This was especially useful on those occasions when an

urgent cargo forced a transport to travel alone. The sound of a distant gun reaching a tinclad lying on station between convoys told her captain where the action was likely to be.

Finally, this system saved fuel. A tinclad could lie at anchor between convoys, with steam up but engines idle. An emergency would send her churning into action with a minimum of delay, but also with a minimum of fuel expenditure. Most naval vessels were coal-burners, and coal had to be brought from Kentucky or Pennsylvania, so fuel was always a problem.

By the spring of 1863, the convoy protection techniques had been honed near to perfection.[1] Of course, despite all effort, the Rebels would pick off a transport now and again, but the losses were very few, considering the number of vessels involved. Normal shipwrecks, caused by fires, boiler explosions, or hitting sandbars or snags became a more serious problem than the Confederates. The system worked so well that the Army of the Tennessee, in its camps at Milliken's Bend, Young's Point, and Lake Providence, never suffered from want of supplies.

Once away from the railroads or navigable waters, all supplies were carried on wagons. A regular military wagon theoretically could carry six thousand pounds of cargo, but in practice they rarely carried more than three thousand. Each was drawn by four or six horses or mules, depending upon local conditions. Of course, animals get sick or have accidents, so it was customary, whenever possible, to take along a spare animal per wagon, so the normal complement, under good conditions, was five horses or mules per wagon. It was possible to make twenty-five miles if the roads were dry and in nearly perfect condition, but more commonly the rate was about fifteen miles per day. After a day or two of rain on the unsurfaced roads of the day, any movement at all became excruciatingly difficult. During the march southward through Louisiana at the beginning of the Vicksburg campaign, a Union infantry division, accompanied by its normal wagon train, made exactly four miles, and that left both animals and men totally exhausted.

Consider a fully loaded four-horse wagon, with its spare horse, supplying a place far away from a depot. A horse eats about 20 pounds of fodder and grain per day, a mule rather less. The teamster has to be fed, and he uses about 3 pounds per day. The result is that, for each day of operation, each wagon must devote 103 pounds of its cargo to fuel—i.e., food for animals and men. This results in some interesting arithmetic. The first day out is "free," as the horses presumably have been fed from stores at the depot, but food for the return journey must be carried with them.

So more than 3 percent of the cargo capacity must be devoted to fuel. If the delivery point is two days away, the fuel requirement goes up to more than 10 percent of the total carrying capacity. Assuming near-perfect conditions, a wagon could get about 225 miles away from its base, but in so doing it would need to devote its entire carrying capacity to fuel. Horses are not called "hay-burners" for nothing.

Of course, the calculations above do not tell the whole story. In practice, each wagon train had to carry along a blacksmith, a forge, fuel for the forge, a supply of spare parts, and so on. It also had to take along an ambulance or two, because men, like horses, get sick. Some wagons had to carry camping gear for the teamsters. While in enemy territory, no wagon train dared operate without guards, and those men and animals had to be fed. If the weather was dry, water had to be carried. Food had to be carried in boxes, and the boxes weighed as much as, or more than, the contents. When all these things are added, it becomes clear that a Civil War army found it very difficult indeed to operate at a distance of more than about sixty miles from its base of operations. Moreover, that base had to be supplied from the factories and farms by either steamboats or a railroad.

Consider the problem of supplying a battery of field artillery consisting of six 10-pdr Parrott rifles. The normal animal complement of such an organization was 180 horses. That equates to 3,600 pounds of fodder and grain per day. Of course, foragers could pick up some of their requirements from the countryside, but, in general, the first battery down the road swept up all the readily available forage, and the batteries which followed behind found slim pickings. An army might operate for two or three days without a supply train, but after that, it was necessary to have, in the words of MG W. T. Sherman, "a well-regulated supply system."[2]

It is also worth remembering that the human complement of a Union infantry division of 6,000 men required a minimum of 18,000 pounds of food per day. Double that weight to include the containers, and it follows that twelve wagons per day, with cargoes devoted entirely to food, were required just to feed the troops a minimum ration. And this is just to feed the men; horses and mules are extra. So are ammunition and all the other impedimenta of an army on the march. A Civil War army on the march required a lot of wagons, horses, and mules. An army did not blithely march off into the sunset; that march was supported every inch of the way by an enormous logistical effort.

Message traffic among the far-flung units of the Federal army was a continuing problem. The Federal troops which occupied the Memphis &

Charleston Railroad (M&CRR) between Memphis and Corinth were fortunate in being able to use the telegraph line that followed the railroad. However, getting a message from MG Stephen Hurlbut's headquarters in Memphis to MG Ulysses S. Grant's headquarters at Young's Point was another matter entirely. The only practical method was steamboat. Going downstream and taking full advantage of the current, a fast boat could cover the approximately 325 river miles in about twenty hours. Going upstream, a fast boat and a clever pilot could manage the trip in about forty-four hours. Thus, if Grant sent a message to Hurlbut, he could not expect to receive a reply for at least three days. Given such a situation, micromanaging outlying commands was manifestly impossible. Grant had to trust his subordinate commanders to do the right thing on a day-by-day basis.

This was equally true on a national level. Memphis, the immense and absolutely critical logistical base for all the operations along the Mississippi, had no direct telegraphic communication with the North. There was a line between Memphis and Columbus, KY, but then a twenty-mile boat trip on the Mississippi was required to get the message to Cairo, IL, which had direct telegraphic connections with Washington. When the Memphis-to-Columbus line failed, as it frequently did due to either weather or Confederate guerrilla actions, getting a message from Memphis to Cairo required a long steamboat trip of 240 river miles, which translates into about fifteen hours going downstream or thirty-four hours upstream. If President Lincoln sent a dispatch to Grant on Monday morning, Grant could not hope to receive it until Tuesday afternoon at the very earliest! Thus, message communications between the central government of the Union and the Army of the Tennessee across the river from Vicksburg was neither fast nor particularly secure. Lincoln and General-in-Chief Halleck had no choice but to trust Grant to "do the right thing."

CONFEDERATE PERSPECTIVE

Defending against the Union thrusts were Confederate armies based in Tullahoma, TN, and Jackson, MS. The two field armies were connected only by light, mobile forces guarding a line that ran from Tullahoma to Florence, AL, then westward across northern Alabama and Mississippi to Panola, MS, and thence south to Vicksburg. There were no fortifications except small earthworks at a few key positions.

Supporting these Confederate defensive positions was a rather skeletal network of railroad lines, plus a few critical links of navigable rivers.

Oddly enough, by the summer of 1862, there was no longer a direct rail connection between the capitol of the Confederacy at Richmond, VA, and Vicksburg. There was a railroad from the East Coast, but it terminated at Montgomery, AL, on the Alabama River. At that point, matters grew complicated. Goods and passengers destined for Vicksburg moved from Montgomery to Selma, AL, by steamboat on the Alabama River; then by rail to Demopolis, AL, on the Tombigbee River; then by steamboat once again on the Little Tombigbee River to McDowell's Bluff, AL; and finally by rail via the Southern Railroad of Mississippi to Meridian, MS, and Jackson, MS. The Alabama and Tennessee Railroad ran on from Selma toward the Northeast, but it terminated at Talladega, AL.

It was also possible to use an enormous detour via Mobile Bay. The Alabama & Florida Railroad connected Montgomery, AL, with Tensas Station, thirteen miles northeast across Mobile Bay from Mobile, AL. Tensas Station was connected to Mobile only by steam ferries across Mobile Bay. From Mobile, the Mobile & Ohio Railroad (M&ORR) ran northwest to Meridian, MS, and then on northward to Corinth, MS, where it crossed the Memphis & Charleston Railroad.

The Western & Atlantic Railroad ran from the East Coast to Atlanta and on to the northwest to Chattanooga, at which point it continued on to Stevenson, AL; Tullahoma; and Nashville, as the Nashville & Chattanooga Railroad (N&CRR). At Stevenson, about thirty-five miles west of Chattanooga, the N&CRR connected with the Memphis & Charleston Railroad (M&CRR), which ran via Tuscumbia on the Tennessee River to Memphis. However, the section of the M&CRR between Corinth and Memphis was under Union occupation. Since the only connection between the M&CRR and the M&ORR was at Corinth, the M&CRR was useless to the Confederate armies in Mississippi.

Finally, the New Orleans, Jackson & Great Northern Railroad (NOJ&GNRR) connected New Orleans with Jackson, MS, and continued northward as the Mississippi Central Railroad (MCENRR) through Grenada, MS, to Grand Junction on the M&CRR. The short Mississippi & Tennessee Railroad connected Grenada with Panola, MS, and Memphis, TN.

The carrying capacities of those railroads and their associated water links in the summer of 1863 should not be overestimated. After more than two years of war, both rolling stock and rails were beginning to show serious signs of wear, and the supply of replacement parts was very limited, because most of the shops, factories, and foundries were in the North.

There were good shops in Richmond, VA; somewhat less good ones in Atlanta; and shops capable of minor repairs scattered broadly about the country, including one at Vicksburg, but these could not possibly meet the demand generated by the Confederacy's far-flung rail system. As a result, the railroads were increasingly rickety. Furthermore, the South was chronically short of labor, and the roadbeds soon were in deplorable condition because they could not be maintained. As early as 1863, an average railway speed of fifteen miles per hour was considered remarkable.

Without adequate replacement parts and repair services, and with no possibility whatever of obtaining additional rolling stock, it often was a major achievement to assemble the engines and cars required to transport a brigade of troops. The flow of food and war materials to the fighting fronts could not be interrupted, so it was not uncommon for troops to travel by shank's mare while their gear traveled by rail. When one reads that a large body of troops traveled from Point A to Point B by rail, one must reflect that it wasn't necessarily so.

Of course, the Union high command looked at those long and vulnerable railroad lines and dreamed of destroying or obstructing them. The weapon of choice was the cavalry raid, and the history of the Vicksburg Campaign is replete with examples of such raids. Sometimes they were affective; more often they were not.

Unlike the Union armies, which had to be supplied with virtually everything from farms and factories north of the Ohio River, the Confederate armies tended to live off the country. In general, commissary supplies came from neighboring farms, and only military materiel had to come long distances via the railroads or wagon roads. Of course, a large concentration of manpower in one location for any significant length of time quickly exhausted the local supplies, and in such cases sources had to be found farther afield. The armies concentrated at Vicksburg, for example, drew heavily on the Mississippi Delta, which was the richest agricultural region in the Mississippi Valley east of the river. It had no railroads, and its wagon roads were primitive and discontinuous, but a maze of navigable waterways existed. As a result, fodder and commissary supplies flowed out of the region aboard small steamboats, barges, and even *bateaus* (small oar- or pole-propelled boats designed for use in shallow and restricted waters). The Union Navy, lying off the mouth of the Yazoo River, prevented the cargoes from being brought all the way to Vicksburg by water, so they were landed instead at Snyder's Bluff and sent forward into Vicksburg by wagon along the Valley Road, which followed the base of the bluffs between Vicksburg and Yazoo City. Much of the produce of the rich farms and plantations along the Big Sunflower River, Steele Bayou, and Deer Creek reached Vicksburg by this route.

In contrast, the produce of the northern portion of the Mississippi Delta flowed down the Yazoo River as far as Yazoo City, about forty-five miles northeast of Vicksburg. Yazoo City was connected to Vicksburg with a good wagon road, the Valley Road, but the distance made it almost impracticable. Instead, it was sent over an equally good wagon road which ran from Yazoo City to Benton, and then on to Vaughan, on the MCENRR. This was only twenty-three miles, and in good weather a wagon could make a one-way trip in a single day. From Vaughan, the cargo was carried by rail to Jackson and Vicksburg. The only vulnerable link in this chain was where the MCENRR crossed the Big Black River at Ways Bluff on a long wooden trestle. The Confederates in Jackson were understandably sensitive to any threat to that bridge.

The Confederate high command made elaborate use of electronic communications, which was a major advantage; by 1863, telegraph lines had reached nearly every major town in the South. However, the interconnectivity remained relatively poor. The major lines tended to follow the railroads; towns off the railroads normally were reached only by a branch or stub line. For example, Yazoo City was not on a railroad, but it was reached on a stub line that ran from the railroad at Vaughan. Grand Gulf and Port Gibson were connected by a telegraph line that ran along the little railroad line connecting the two towns, and Grand Gulf was connected to Vicksburg by a stub line, but there was no direct connection between Grand Gulf and Jackson. The result was that a telegraph message from Grand Gulf to Yazoo City had to go to Vicksburg, where it was transcribed by an operator, who sent it to an operator in Jackson, who transmitted it to one in Vaughan, who transmitted it to Yazoo City. Of course, each operator was subject to error, and it was fairly common for a message to be somewhat garbled before it got to its final destination. Nevertheless, the telegraph system gave the Confederate high command the ability to reach very nearly all its major outlying commands within minutes.

Furthermore, President Jefferson Davis, in Richmond, could get a message to LTG John Pemberton in Jackson, MS, in an hour or so, as could GEN Joseph E. Johnston, whose headquarters were with GEN Braxton Bragg's Army of the Tennessee in Tullahoma, TN. Thus, the message communication system among major commands and the central government of the Confederacy was excellent, being both fast and relatively secure.

Mounted couriers "carried the mail" if there were no telegraph. If the weather was good, a mounted courier on a good fresh horse could manage about forty miles in a day; but he wasn't good for much the next day, unless he could get a fresh horse. Good horseflesh was always at a premium; the military demand for anything with a leg on each corner was insatiable. Farmers and planters developed remarkably innovative ways of hiding their horses and mules from the military, and it didn't matter much whether they wore blue or gray uniforms.

4

Defenses of Vicksburg

The defenses of the city of Vicksburg in 1863 were truly formidable and at that time probably were exceeded only by those around Washington, DC, and perhaps by the works protecting the capital of the Confederacy at Richmond, VA. The Confederate troops defending Vicksburg were nominally all under the command of MG Carter Stevenson, who commanded the Army of Vicksburg, which included the Vicksburg garrison. In practice, however, he was responsible only for defending the city from attack by land forces, while the River Defenses, under the command of COL Edward Higgins, were relatively autonomous.

RIVER DEFENSES

The River Defenses of Vicksburg had two missions, a fact that often is overlooked. The first—and the one that has captured the imagination and therefore the attention of historians—was to close the river to the passage of Union shipping. To this end, the defenses included a large array of heavy guns protected by strong earthworks. The second, and far more obscure, mission was to prevent a direct amphibious assault on the city by the Federal army. To achieve this goal, the heavy guns of the anti-ship batteries were backed up by several batteries of field artillery and a small infantry force. Of course, all Carter Stevenson's forces also would be available in an emergency, such as an amphibious landing in force on the waterfront.

In March 1863, the Vicksburg River Defense batteries projected an aura of terrible power. Indeed, the Confederate authorities seem to have been mesmerized by the array of artillery marshaled on Vicksburg's river face. To be sure, the Union commanders seem to have been only slightly less impressed, although, as we shall see, there were important doubters. It has been said that the only truly adequate defensive system is one that so overawes the enemy that it is never challenged. By this criterion, the river-closure mission failed, since the batteries were challenged—successfully—by Porter's Union ironclad squadron. However, by that same criterion, the anti-landing mission succeeded, because the Union high command never seriously contemplated a direct amphibious attack. In that sense, the River Defenses played a vital role in the campaign for Vicksburg, and therefore are worth looking at in some detail.

The men who designed the River Defenses were quite aware of the difficulties posed for steamboats by the notorious turbulence of the water in DeSoto Bend, and their artillery positions were designed to exploit that turbulence. The Water Battery,[1] which was the northern anchor of the Confederate River Defenses and one of the most powerful in the system, was built on a narrow terrace just above flood level, and its guns were designed to command the waters of DeSoto Bend, where the river made its 180-degree turn around the tip of DeSoto Point. The Confederates counted on the fact that the extreme turbulence was likely to make vessels spin out of control while making the turn.

This does not seem so important to us today, when power-driven turrets automatically track targets regardless of the positions of the hulls, but it was extremely important in 1863. All the Union gunboats were casemated craft—i.e., their guns were mounted in a fixed shelter, and they fired through relatively small gunports. In order to train the guns, the entire gun carriage had to be pointed in the proper direction, and this was a very slow and painstaking job. The small gunports made it even more difficult, because, with the ship turning quickly, a target tended to move very quickly across the restricted field of view, before the gun could be readied for firing.

In the context of water conditions in DeSoto Bend, the result of these constraints is easy to imagine. As the ships came into the turn and encountered the enormously powerful eddies, the pilots fought, often unsuccessfully, to keep them turning smoothly so that the gunners would have time to aim their pieces. When they were unable to do so (and that was much of the time), the Confederate gunners in the Water Battery had the game all to themselves; with no counterbattery fire, they could take their time. In effect, a gunboat in the channel could be hit again and again without the ability to hit back. The Confederates hoped that this advantage would enable them so to maul the Union ironclads while they were making the turn at DeSoto Bend that their artillery would be put out of action, giving the gunners in the downstream batteries the same advantage. Things didn't work quite that way most of the time—a testimony to the skill of the pilots in keeping their vessels stable, the excellence of the armor on the casemates, and the skill, courage, and determination of the Union gunners, who somehow were able to fight back effectively even when their ships were yawing wildly.

In the spring of 1863, the River Defense batteries probably contained thirty-seven pieces of ordnance emplaced specifically for an anti-ship mission, and thirteen guns intended primarily for an antipersonnel mission, to be used in the event that the Yankees were so misguided as to make a direct amphibious assault. The anti-ship guns consisted of twenty smoothbores ranging in size from 10-in columbiads to 32-pdr siege guns, and seventeen rifles that varied in caliber from a 7.44-in Blakely to a 2.71-in Whitworth. Many of the guns were scarcely new; some had been used in the War with Mexico sixteen years before. Others, such as the Blakely and Whitworth rifles, were state-of-the-art guns newly purchased from Great Britain.

It should be noted that four of the thirty-seven guns classed as anti-ship artillery in the Vicksburg batteries were not, properly speaking, heavy guns at all; the 2.71-in Whitworth rifle, the 3-in Armstrong rifle, the 18-pdr rifle "Whistling Dick," and the 20-pdr Parrott rifles were only of field-gun caliber. They were emplaced in the River Defenses because it was hoped that their accuracy and high muzzle velocities (and therefore penetrating power) would be useful against armored ships. Thus, at least five of the guns were of very doubtful effectiveness, except perhaps against tinclads and unarmored transports.

Higgins had organized his command into three subcommands. The upper batteries, which defended the waterfront from Mint Spring Bayou on the north to Glass Bayou on the south, were manned by the 1 TN Heavy Artillery and commanded by COL Andrew Jackson, Jr. The center batteries ranged along the city waterfront from Glass Bayou on the north to the old railroad depot on the south. They were commanded by MAJ Fred N. Ogden. The lower batteries extended from the old railroad depot to South Fort, were served by the 1 LA Artillery, and were under the command of LTC Daniel Beltzhoover.[2]

COL Jackson divided the big guns manned by his regiment into six batteries, the northernmost of which was the Water Battery, located on a terrace 30 feet above mean water level (mwl) of the river, and just south of the mouth of Mint Spring Bayou. It mounted three 32-pdr rifles, one 32-pdr smoothbore, and one 10-in columbiad. Battery No. 7, situated 110 feet above the river, mounted two 10-in columbiads. Battery No. 6, constructed on the "Devil's Backbone" 160 feet above the river, emplaced a single 42-pdr smoothbore. Battery No. 5, 90 feet above the water, contained a most effective weapon, a 7-in Brooke rifle. Battery No. 4, situated west of the Harwood house and some 60 feet above the river, emplaced a single 9-in Dahlgren smoothbore. The southernmost of COL Jackson's positions was the powerful Wyman's Hill Battery. It was located about 40 feet above the river, near the mouth of Glass Bayou, and mounted three 10-in columbiads, one 8-in columbiad, one 32-pdr rifle, one 2.71-in Whitworth rifle, and one 3-in Armstrong rifle.[3]

MAJ Ogden's command served only two batteries along the city waterfront. The Whig Office Battery was located near the old steamboat landing, just down the hill from the Court House, and was armed with a 10-in columbiad and a 32-pdr smoothbore. A little to the south and adjacent to the depot was the "Depot Battery," which contained a single 10-in columbiad.

LTC Beltzhoover's regiment manned an array of batteries extending from just below the depot to South Fort, with a detachment serving the guns at Warrenton, five miles south of the city. An 18-pdr rifle ("Whistling Dick") and a 20-pdr Parrott rifle were emplaced in the "Railroad Battery," located 100 feet above the river and just south of the railroad cut.[4] The Marine Hospital Battery, one of the most powerful in the Vicksburg defenses, was located west of the Marine Hospital on a slight elevation 40 feet above the water, and mounted three 42-pdr smoothbores, two 32-pdr smoothbores, and two 32-pdr rifles. Unlike many of the others, the guns of the Marine Hospital Battery were mounted *en barbette,* which means that they fired over the top of a smooth parapet, rather than through embrasures.[5] This method had the advantage of providing a wide and unimpeded field of fire but the disadvantage of leaving the gun crews much more exposed to counterbattery fire from warships in the river.

The Brooke Battery, just north of the Marine Hospital Battery, emplaced a single 6.4-in Brooke rifle. About a quarter of a mile southeast of the Marine Hospital was the Widow Blakely Battery. At 130 feet above the river, it mounted three 32-pdr rifles and one 7.44-in Blakely rifle. The Blakely was called "The Widow" because it had no companion in the city.

South of the Widow Blakely Battery, geography conspired to create a problem, because the river begins to trend away from the bluff line, leaving a wedge of often-flooded plain at the base of the bluff. Thus, a mile below the Widow Blakely Battery, the only battery site safely above flood level was 1,200 yards from the river bank, a distance so great that the effectiveness of even a big gun would be questionable. The engineers who designed the River Defenses would have preferred to terminate the array of anti-ship batteries with the Widow Blakely position, but the configuration of land defenses made it necessary to defend the bluff line for a distance of 1,800 yards to the south. The reason was that MAJ Samuel A. Lockett, the engineer who selected the alignment of the land defenses, had chosen a prominent ridge that circled the southeastern half of the city for his main defensive line, and that ridge terminated just across the deep ravine of Stouts Bayou at a point 1,800 yards south of the Widow Blakely position. The fortress engineers had little choice but to construct a strongpoint on the bluff at that point, 170 feet above the level of the floodplain, to provide a secure anchor for the land defenses. The result was South Fort, in which were emplaced three long-range guns: one 10-in columbiad, a 30-pdr Parrott rifle, and a 10-in mortar.[6] No one had any illusions about the effectiveness of the South Fort guns in an anti-ship role, so South Fort was a part of the River Defenses only by courtesy.

About five miles below the city, at Warrenton, there was a strong casemated water battery, built of cotton bales covered with logs and sheathed with railroad iron, which in turn was covered with earth. Its armament is uncertain, but it appears to have mounted two 20-pdr and two 30-pdr Parrott rifles.[7]

The thirteen pieces of light artillery (that is, field artillery) were emplaced at strategic points along the riverfront, to be used as anti-personnel weapons in case the Federals should launch an amphibious assault directly upon the city.

Contrary to the general impression, only eleven of the anti-ship guns of Vicksburg were emplaced on or near the top of the bluffs. In the case of the 42-pdr smoothbore in Battery No. 7, on the "Devil's Backbone," the Confederates themselves complained that its great elevation made it ineffective. The three most powerful batteries in the defenses were the Water, Wyman's Hill, and Marine Hospital, and these were situated at elevations ranging from thirty to forty feet above the river, just high enough to be out of danger from floodwaters.

Three major factors made guns placed high on the bluffs relatively ineffective. First, very thick parapets were necessary in order to prevent penetration by the heavy shells of the Union naval artillery, but those thick parapets also made it impossible to depress the guns far enough to bear on the river close into shore. The unfortunate consequences of this had been revealed some months earlier, when the Union ironclad *Essex* and the ram *Queen of the West* had rammed the Rebel ironclad *Arkansas* while she was moored under the guns of the River Defenses. They had remained next to the bank for ten minutes or more without sustaining any damage except to their upper works.[8]

Second, placing the guns on the ridgetops meant increasing the range. The riverfront of Vicksburg is very steep, but a gun atop the ridge still was at least 400 yards from the river bank, and this meant approximately doubling the distance to targets in the river. The greater range reduced the penetrating power of the projectiles, and the increased distance to the river made it much more difficult to see and hit objects in the stream, especially amid the smoke of battle.

Third, in order to bear on the river at all, the muzzles of guns on the ridgetop had to be deeply depressed. This is a serious handicap in muzzle-loading artillery, because great care must be taken in bringing the gun into battery (i.e., running it forward into firing position after loading). With the muzzle below the horizontal, a sudden stop will "start" the projectile in the bore (i.e., the shot will slide forward in the bore away from contact with the powder charge). This markedly reduces both accuracy and power. The extreme care required to prevent this from happening automatically reduces the rate of fire, further curtailing the overall effectiveness of such guns. If the bore is raised each time the gun is loaded and run forward into battery, a good deal of time must be taken to set the muzzle angle properly, and that reduces the rate of fire unacceptably.

Union naval gunners fired shell and grape almost exclusively. In general, they did not even bother to aim for the embrasures, because, in the darkness and smoke of battle and firing from a moving gun-platform, a direct hit on a target as small as an embrasure would be nothing more than a stroke of blind luck. They used grape because the shotgun effect gave them at least a finite probability of getting a ball through an embrasure or of taking the head off anyone who was misguided enough to look out over the top of the parapet. The shells were not expected to penetrate the enormously thick parapets. Instead, they were intended to bury themselves in the earth and explode, throwing huge masses of earth into the air. Some of it would rain backward into the works, covering everything with loose dirt. Enough of that, and the guns would be impossible to train or even fire. If the dirt got deep enough, the fortress guns would be put out of action, albeit only temporarily. But, in the view of the attackers, any reduction in the rate or accuracy of fire was a major benefit.

LAND DEFENSES

North of the city, the line was anchored on the very steep Fort Hill, which rose abruptly from the river terrace directly behind the Water Battery. The works on Fort Hill were not elaborate, consisting of only a signal station and emplacements for two 24-pdr siege guns, several small field pieces, and a little brass signal gun. This hill already had earned a measure of fame, for the Spanish explorers had built Fort Nogales at its foot as early as 1791. From the crest of Fort Hill, a continuous line of riflepits (we would call them trenches) crowned the top of precipitous Fort Hill Ridge. Every 250 yards or so, wherever the configuration of the terrain was suitable, a field artillery position was constructed. About a mile and a half west of the river, Fort Hill Ridge branched, with a spur running off to the south while a continuation of the ridge trended off to the northeast. The Graveyard Road approached the city along this ridge, entering the perimeter at the salient angle formed by the south-trending spur.

Salient angles in fortified lines are notoriously weak, so Lockett went to extraordinary lengths to protect this place. The complex incorporated three strongpoints. The powerful Stockade Redan, the major component, had been built at the angle[9] and just south of and commanding the Graveyard Road. North of the road and 75 yards to the west was the 27 LA Lunette, precisely sited so that fire from its parapet would enfilade any force assaulting the north face of the redan. Finally, 75 yards to the south, yet another redan (later called Green's Redan) projected from the line of riflepits, this one sited so that fire from its parapets would sweep the approaches to the east face of the Stockade Redan. The Graveyard Road entered the perimeter between the 27 LA Lunette and the Stockade Redan; to close that gap, a palisade of poplar logs had been constructed, each nine to twelve inches in diameter, with pointed tops, like a frontier fort in the days of Daniel Boone. In the three-inch gaps between the larger palisades were fitted smaller logs with square tops, about four or five inches lower than the pointed ones, so that a rather effective row of loopholes was formed, a refinement unknown to the Indian fighters of yore. It was this palisade that gave the complex its name. In front of the stockade, a ditch was dug, with the earth thrown up against the palisades. In the bank thus formed was planted a formidable row of pointed stakes. Both the lunette and the redan had embrasures for artillery.

From the Stockade Redan, the line of riflepits followed the spur to the south for about 900 yards, where Glass Bayou flowed through a deep but narrow gap in the guardian ridge. Guarding this cut against penetration were trenches in the bottom of the ravine and battery positions sited to sweep all approaches. About 200 yards south of Glass Bayou, the Jackson Road came into the perimeter on the top of the ridge forming the watershed between Glass Bayou and Durden Creek. On the north side of the road was the 3 Louisiana Redan; on the south was the formidable Great Redoubt.[10] The redan had emplacements for two guns but lacked a ditch in front, while the redoubt was pierced for five guns.

About a mile to the south of the Great Redoubt, the Baldwin's Ferry Road came in from the southeast. Just south of the road, on a commanding nose of ridge, was the 2 Texas Lunette; but there was a gap in the line of riflepits about 100 yards wide, between the left flank of the lunette and the beginning of the fortified line north of the road. The lunette had embrasures for two guns. Five hundred yards farther south, the railroad penetrated the guardian ridge through a cut some twenty feet deep. This vulnerable point was guarded by the Railroad Redoubt, which jutted so far beyond the general line that the Confederates often called it the Horn Work.[11] The interior was divided into three approximately equal segments by traverses at right angles to the face of the main parapet. Each segment contained a gun, and the open gorge to the rear was guarded by a second line of riflepits.

Another half-mile to the southwest, on a commanding elevation, stood Square Fort, the only completely enclosed work on the Vicksburg perimeter. It was entered by a drawbridge and mounted three guns. Later, during the siege, it was renamed Fort Garrott.[12] A mile further to the southwest, the Hall's Ferry Road crossed the defense perimeter after reaching the works on a high ridge separating Stouts Bayou from Durden Creek. On the east side of the road and well in advance of the general line was a redan emplacing two guns. This earthwork, called the Salient Work because of its advanced position, was connected to the general line by a line of riflepits east of the road, and was supported by a detached artillery position west of the road. Between the Hall's Ferry Road and the deep ravine occupied by Stouts Bayou was an almost continuous line of trenches but no major works, although the creek bottom was commanded by a strong battery emplacement on the hill to the east. West of the bayou, the riflepits continued until they tied into the flank of South Fort, located on the edge of the bluff overlooking the Mississippi River.[13] Since South Fort ostensibly was a part of the River Defenses, its big guns were mounted so that they could register only on the river, but provision was made so that they could be shifted quickly to bear on the Warrenton Road, in the event that the city should be attacked from the land side. As events were to prove, this was a wise provision; after

22 May, they became the most powerful weapons emplaced in the land defenses of the city.

To command the narrow triangle of land between the base of the bluffs and the river, the line of riflepits had been extended almost a mile along the top of the bluffs north of South Fort.

The nine major works had similar profiles. Each initially had a parapet about fourteen feet thick, and all except the 3 Louisiana Redan were fronted by a ditch six to ten feet deep and ten to eighteen feet wide. The line of riflepits that connected the nine strongpoints had a parapet about six feet thick, but no fronting ditch. This line was studded, however, with artillery positions, each carefully sited on commanding ground or arranged to provide a deadly crossfire against the most likely avenues of approach. There were ten such positions between Fort Hill and the Stockade Redan, five between that strongpoint and the 3 Louisiana Redan, six between Great Redoubt and the 2 Texas Lunette, one between the lunette and the railroad, five between the Railroad Redoubt and Square Fort, seven between Fort Garrott and the Salient Work, and twelve between the Hall's Ferry Road and South Fort.

As an added protective measure and to provide uninterrupted fields of fire, all the trees in the ravine bottoms in front of the works had been cut down and laced together with telegraph wire to form a broad band of abatis. There was an abatis 200 yards deep in front of the Stockade Redan, and another of formidable proportions between the Hall's Ferry Road and Stouts Bayou. Other lesser fields of abatis were formed wherever a grove of trees provided the raw materials.

In addition to the main perimeter, the ridge north of Mint Spring Bayou, called the Indian Mound Ridge by virtue of the small but distinctive Indian mound perched upon its western extremity, also was partially fortified. A discontinuous line of riflepits ran along the crest of the ridge from the river bank past the Indian mound to a point about a mile and a half to the northeast, where a large transverse spur jutted southward toward the Fort Hill ridge. The riflepits extended to the southeast to the end of this spur. At this point, the advanced line was separated from the principal line on Fort Hill ridge by a deep ravine about 400 yards wide, through which flowed Mint Spring Bayou. There were no major works and apparently only one battery position, which was occupied by a 24-pdr gun. MAJ S. A. Lockett, who designed the works, seems to have regarded it as scarcely more than a somewhat strengthened picket line, to be used only to delay the occupation of Indian Mound Ridge by a besieging enemy.

One interesting property of the region occupied by the fortifications is that the ridgetops were under cultivation for miles in every direction, so that visibility from ridgetop to ridgetop was unimpeded. Only in the valley bottoms had there been significant stands of trees. Much of the Vicksburg National Military Park, which occupies much of the area involved in the siege, is heavily wooded with second-growth forest; thus it provides a wholly false perception of the situation in 1863.

As mentioned earlier, the parapets of the strongpoints, such as the Stockade Redan and the Railroad Redoubt, initially were about fourteen feet thick. This was the standard dimension called for by military manuals of the day, based on experience which had shown that fourteen feet of earth was sufficient to stop any field artillery projectile. However, as experience was to demonstrate, there was a flaw in the body of experience. Most of it had been accumulated along the southeastern coast of the United States, where soils are sandy. In Vicksburg, the soil is loess. It is difficult to compact except at exactly the correct moisture content, and Lockett and his fellow officers knew nothing of that. Furthermore, it is by no means as resistant to penetration as sand, but again Lockett knew nothing of that.

VICKSBURG RIVER DEFENSE BATTERIES

JACKSON'S COMMAND (NORTHERN SECTOR)

Water Battery:
Location: 100 yards south of the mouth of Mint Spring Bayou
Elevation above mean water level (mwl): 30 feet
Guns: 3 32-pdr rifles
    1 32-pdr smoothbore
    1 10-in columbiad

Battery 7:
Location: 500 yards south of Mint Spring Bayou
Elevation above mwl: 110 feet
Guns: 2 10-in columbiads

Battery 6:
Location: On "Devil's Backbone," 750 yards south of Mint Spring
    Bayou
Elevation above mwl: 160 feet
Guns: 1 42-pdr smoothbore

Battery 5:
Location: 750 yards north-northeast of the mouth of Glass Bayou
Elevation above mwl: 90 feet
Guns: 1 7-in Brooke rifle

Battery 4:
Location: 400 yards northwest of the mouth of Glass Bayou
Elevation above mwl: 60 feet
Guns: 1 9-in Dahlgren smoothbore

Wyman's Hill Battery:
Location: 200 yards northeast of the mouth of Glass Bayou
Elevation above mwl: 40 feet
Guns: 3 10-in columbiads
    1 8-in columbiad
    1 32-pdr rifle
    1 2.71-in Whitworth rifle
    1 3-in Armstrong rifle

OGDEN'S COMMAND (CENTRAL SECTOR)

Whig Office Battery:
Location: 450 yards south of the mouth of Glass Bayou
Elevation above mwl: approximately 60 feet
Guns: 1 10-in columbiad
    1 32-pdr smoothbore

Depot Battery:
Location: 125 yards south of the mouth of Glass Bayou, 200 yards
    west-southwest of the railroad depot
Elevation above mwl: approx. 100 feet
Guns: 1 10-in columbiad

BELTZHOOVER'S COMMAND (SOUTHERN SECTOR)

Railroad Battery:
Location: 300 yards south-southwest of the Depot Battery
Elevation above mwl: 100 feet
Guns: 1 18-pdr rifle (Whistling Dick)
    1 20-pdr Parrott rifle

Brooke Battery:
Location: 700 yards west-southwest of the Depot Battery
Elevation above mwl: 40 feet
Guns: 1 6.4-in Brooke rifle

Marine Hospital Battery:
Location: 200 yards southwest of the Marine Hospital
Elevation above mwl: 40 feet
Guns: 3 42-pdr smoothbores
      2 32-pdr smoothbores
      2 32-pdr rifles

Widow Blakely Battery:
Location: 600 yards south of the Marine Hospital
Elevation above mwl: 130 feet
Guns: 3 32-pdr rifles
      1 7.44-in Blakely rifle (Widow Blakely)

South Fort:
Location: 1,800 yards south-southwest of the Widow Blakely Battery
Elevation above mwl: 170 feet
Guns: 1 10-in columbiad
      1 30-pdr Parrott rifle
      1 10-in mortar

Warrenton Battery:
Location: 5 miles south of South Fort
Elevation above mwl: approximately 50 feet
Guns: 2 20-pdr Parrott rifles
         2 30-pdr Parrott rifles

5

Decision
29 March 1863

FEDERAL PERSPECTIVE

Since the final week of December 1863, the Army of the Tennessee had floundered in the swamps of Mississippi and Louisiana, seemingly with nothing to show for its effort save swamp fevers and dissatisfaction. The northern public was beginning to believe that Grant belonged to the same dreary class of failures as McClellan, Burnside, and Buell, and agitation for his removal was intense. But, said Lincoln, "I can't spare that man. He fights."[1]

The armchair strategists all complained that Grant obviously was on the wrong trail, and so did most of his military associates, including his own corps commanders. The complaints as such meant nothing to Grant; he ignored them and bent his whole energy to the task of finding a chink in Vicksburg's armor. Four schemes were discussed at some length in his headquarters at Young's Point. First, the army could launch itself across the river in a direct amphibious attack on the Vicksburg batteries. Grant believed that this would end in slaughter and defeat, unless the Confederate River Defense batteries could be knocked out first. RADM Porter was not encouraging; he was confident that his ironclads could run past the batteries at any time that such a move became necessary, but even they could not withstand the pounding they would receive in a fort-versus-ship duel against the array of guns along the Vicksburg waterfront.

A second option was to return to Memphis and organize a new drive down the railroad toward Panola and Vicksburg, while Porter's ironclads and a small infantry force continued to threaten a frontal assault on the city. This scheme had the merit of violating no military maxims, and it was strongly recommended by MG Sherman. It was unacceptable to Grant. He feared that the national government would go down before the political winds generated by the appearance of a major retreat, following so closely upon the bloody Pyrrhic victory at Stone's River (31 Dec. 1862–2 Jan. 1863), and the disaster of First Fredericksburg (13 Dec. 1862). Further, in the back of Grant's mind was an almost instinctive reluctance to repeat a route already followed; even as a child, he had tried never to follow exactly the same route home from school.

The third proposal was to make one more determined effort to force a passage up the Yazoo River to Satartia, where troops could be put ashore out of range of the Snyder's Bluff defense complex. This plan was abandoned, in part because Porter had had enough of trying to force his big and precious ironclads through waters too small for them. Porter was reasonably certain that he could silence the batteries at Snyder's Bluff, but silencing them would not be enough; they would have to be occupied. Failure to do so would leave a powerful force in a perfect position to interdict the Yazoo River, which was the only practical supply route. Sherman's adventure at Chickasaw Bayou on 27–29 December 1862 had demonstrated the difficulty of occupying those fortifications.

The fourth possible alternative was to turn the Confederate left. This would require finding an overland route through Louisiana to some point south of Vicksburg where there was a good steamboat landing and enough dry ground to assemble most of the Army of the Tennessee before loading it on transports in preparation for a landing on the Mississippi shore. After such a place had been found, a site where the army could be safely landed on Mississippi soil would have to be selected. Once ashore, the army could drive northward toward Vicksburg and the Southern Railroad of Mississippi, which could then be cut somewhere between Big Black Bridge and Vicksburg, and the city invested. If this all worked, the fortress would fall, and quickly. Of course, this was all contingent upon Porter and the navy. They would have to run some of the ironclads past the Vicksburg batteries in order to provide gunnery support for a landing in Mississippi. Even more

daunting, somehow the Federals would have to get a transport fleet below
the city as well. Porter had no doubts about the ability of his ironclads to run
the batteries, but about transports he was not so sure.

Shortly after the Federal Army of the Tennessee had established itself at Milliken's Bend and Young's Point, patrols had pushed southward
and cut the Vicksburg, Shreveport & Texas Railroad (VS&TRR). They
had found a waterlogged countryside. During late March, the river was
rising toward the crest of its annual spring flood, and the only lands above
the level of the floodwaters were the narrow strips of the natural levees
along the major bayous. The water in the backswamps was so deep that
they were utterly impassable by anything except *pirogues*, the small, unstable canoes of the swamp dwellers. Grant's engineers did notice one
interesting fact; the water in the main channel of the Mississippi was several feet higher than the water in the swamps. The scouts also learned
that a road of sorts passed through the little town of Richmond, LA, and
followed the natural levees along Roundaway Bayou all the way to New
Carthage, on the Louisiana shore of the Mississippi twenty-five river
miles below Vicksburg. It was reported that there was a considerable
amount of dry ground around New Carthage.

Furthermore, Walnut Bayou, which passed close to the western side of
the camp at Young's Point, connected to Roundaway Bayou at Richmond.
It was lined with plantations, and they were connected by a road, albeit not
a very good one. Grant's engineers believed that the Walnut and Roundaway
bayous, while relatively shallow and grown up with bald cypress and tupelo,
might be made navigable, at least for barges and shallow-draft steamboats, all the way to New Carthage, provided the water level in them could
be raised. That, they said, would not be difficult. They would dig a canal
from Duckport Landing on the Mississippi to a point on Walnut Bayou near
J. C. Cooper's plantation, a distance of only a bit over two miles. Then they
would cut the levee at Duckport Landing, forming an artificial crevasse. The
flood pouring through the gap would scour out the canal and raise the
water levels in Walnut and Roundaway bayous. The engineers would clear
the trees out of the bayous, giving the army a navigable supply route all the
way to New Carthage. With luck, they might even get enough small steamboats through the waterway to provide Grant with the transport he would
need to cross the river.[2]

Many of Grant's officers believed that an overland march along the
skeletal Louisiana road network bordered on madness. They pointed out
that there was only a single road—if it could be dignified with that

name—running south, which meant that the army would be strung out marching in a thin column for many miles along it. The column would be terribly vulnerable to an attack from the west by GEN Kirby Smith's Confederate army in Louisiana.

Grant apparently knew better. The proposed route was guaranteed by Mother Nature against interference from the west as long as the river remained in flood. The roads to the south lay along natural levees. The natural levees themselves were open, cultivated, and dry; but they were bordered on one side by the heavily forested and deeply inundated backswamps, and on the other by the deep, swiftly flowing waters of the bayous. Kirby Smith's army would have to cross a six-mile-wide belt of flooded swampland to reach Grant's line of march. There were only two practical crossings. One was along the VS&TRR, and the other was a ridge of dry ground far to the south, below Lake St. Joseph. Grant easily could guard the railroad corridor by stationing a strong force at Richmond. He could do nothing about the Lake St. Joseph corridor, but at least a force coming up from the south could be met head-on.

As Grant saw it, his one real problem would be actually crossing the river. It would be senseless to move south unless he could manage to get enough hulls that would float—some combination of steamboats and barges—below Vicksburg to ferry his troops across to the eastern shore. If the Duckport Canal worked as advertised, he would have no serious problem; but if it did not, then Grant would have an army in position, but no way of ferrying it across to Mississippi. Flamboyant Porter was reassuring; the ironclads would be there when Grant needed them. However, warned Porter, once they are below the city, they will have to stay there. Getting downstream past the batteries is no problem, but it will be well nigh impossible to get them back upstream.[3] Be very sure, said Porter, that this is what you want to do before you start! Porter was not at all concerned about the safety of his precious ironclads once they were past the Vicksburg batteries, because all he had to do to reach a safe haven was sail down to the mouth of the Red River, where RADM David Farragut already had a small squadron engaged in interdicting Confederate use of the river between Natchez and Port Hudson. If he chose, he could even go on to Baton Rouge, which was already a Federal naval station, because the Union ironclad *Essex* and ram *Sumter* already were based there. Getting there was no problem, because the Grand Gulf and Port Hudson batteries were cakewalks compared to those at Vicksburg.

One further aspect nagged at Grant's mind: there was no hope whatever that a march through Louisiana could be concealed from the Confederates. After all, the maneuver would be through enemy territory every step of the way, which meant that every movement would be monitored by Rebel scouts or spies. Nevertheless, a certain amount of obfuscation was possible. A corps could be left behind at Young's Point and Milliken's Bend until the very last moment, posing a credible threat of a direct assault upon the city. Porter could leave enough of his strength above the city to support the fiction. Perhaps the Rebels would even believe that the Army of the Tennessee was being broken up, with a portion of it being sent south to aid Union MG Nathaniel Banks in his effort to reduce Port Hudson. After all, he suspected that his own masters in Washington had concluded that Port Hudson should be the next objective. What he did not know was that a letter from Halleck already was on its way to him, urging that very move.[4] It was an attractive option, because the strategic objective of the campaign was to seize control of the Mississippi, and the fall of either Vicksburg or Port Hudson would achieve that end. If Port Hudson went first, Vicksburg could not possibly be held.

It is possible that, when that letter reached Grant, he hoped that the views of Washington, far from being a handicap, actually might work to his advantage. The general lack of effective communications security was notorious, and thus there was every reason to expect that the Confederate high command would be aware of the basic content of the letter nearly as soon as he was. If so, then it was likely that Pemberton, until much too late, would interpret any southward move as directed toward Port Hudson.

Finally, Grant knew that it was imperative to get his army out of its camps and into an open field campaign as soon as possible. Like all other military men of the time, he knew (even if he didn't know why) that men in camp tended to get sick from dysentery and "camp fevers" far more often and more severely than men on campaign. Keeping his men in camp meant that his army gradually would shrink through death by disease. Perhaps even more serious threats were posed by malaria and yellow fever, which were endemic in the Lower Mississippi Valley. Because both were chiefly summer diseases, they could be avoided by the simple expedient of getting his army onto high ground before the onset of the summer "disease season." Yellow fever occurred as epidemics only at irregular and utterly unpredictable intervals, but when one occurred, it frequently depopulated whole regions. If yellow fever started in his camps, he soon would have no army left with which to fight!

Grant thought long and hard. A last, on 29 March 1863, he decided upon the fourth alternative; he would move the Army of the Tennessee through Louisiana to a staging area at New Carthage. Porter would run gunboats and transports past the Vicksburg batteries, and the Army of the Tennessee then would be put onto the Mississippi shore at Warrenton. A landing at that point would place the Federal army close to its objective, the city of Vicksburg, and eliminate the need for a long campaign to reach the town. He called in his corps commanders and issued his orders: McClernand's XIII Corps would lead the way, followed by McPherson's XVII Corps, while Sherman and his XV Corps would remain behind to continue threatening a direct assault on Vicksburg.[5]

CONFEDERATE PERSPECTIVE

By 25 March 1863, LTG John C. Pemberton, who commanded the Department of Mississippi and East Louisiana from his headquarters in Jackson, MS, was breathing a heart-felt sigh of relief. His forces had just turned back two powerful Yankee amphibious thrusts through the Delta waterways. The first had come through the Yazoo Pass and down the Tallahatchie (which is a northern extension of the Yazoo), but MG William Loring had stopped it at Fort Pemberton, just west of Greenwood, MS. Pemberton had been amused by the tale: Loring had stood on the parapet with his beard blowing in the wind, screaming, "Give them blizzards, boys!"[6] The second Union incursion had been an attempt to bypass the batteries at Snyder's and Haynes's bluffs via a circuitous route up Steele Bayou to Black Bayou, then up Deer Creek to the Rolling Fork, and from there into the Big Sunflower and so into the Yazoo several miles west of Satartia. It had been turned back after penetrating no farther than the Rolling Fork, but it had been worrisome, because there was an excellent steamboat landing at Satartia, from which good roads radiated into the interior, offering direct access to Vicksburg from the northeast. While the twin victories had demonstrated that the Confederate defenses of the Delta were holding, it was still possible that the Federals would try again to use their overwhelming naval power to force a passage through the region. Caution and vigilance were indicated.[7]

The Union camps at Young's Point, Milliken's Bend, and Lake Providence were not a serious threat, because the troops there could not be used except by first crossing the river. An alert defense of the Delta would prevent their employment in that direction, and the only other practical option open to them would be a direct amphibious assault on Vicksburg itself. Both of the senior commanders at Vicksburg, MG Martin L. Smith and MG

Carter Stevenson, feared that such an assault might well succeed, provided the Federal high command was willing to pay the butcher's bill. Carter Stevenson especially was fearful of such a move. The Yankees could occupy DeSoto Point any time they chose. The river was so narrow that Stevenson feared that the River Defenses could be put out of action by a combination of heavy guns mounted on DeSoto Point and naval artillery, making a landing along the waterfront feasible. Vigilance was the only practical response. The River Defenses were kept in a state of constant readiness. Pickets were placed across the river in the ruined hamlet of DeSoto, and small craft patrolled the river during the night, to provide the timeliest possible notice of any Yankee movements.

There was, of course, a possibility that Grant would move his army south through Louisiana in an attempt to vault the river somewhere below Vicksburg, but the consensus was that such a course of action was highly unlikely. In the first place, the floodplain was mostly under water, and the few roads were so poor and discontinuous that moving an army would be very difficult and supplying it well nigh impossible. In the second place, there was no place to land on Mississippi soil south of Vicksburg except at Warrenton or Grand Gulf. The thought was not particularly comforting to Pemberton and his staff. Legally, however, they could not do anything about a Federal movement in Louisiana, even had they wanted or had the resources to do so, because Louisiana was a part of the Department of the Trans-Mississippi, which was GEN Kirby Smith's responsibility. Any significant action taken in Louisiana would have to be approved by Richmond and coordinated with Kirby Smith, and both tasks were so daunting that nobody gave them serious thought.

Pemberton thought an amphibious assault on Warrenton highly improbable, because it was only seven miles from Vicksburg. The fort there mounted only four guns, which would not be enough to halt a determined attack, but a threat to land troops there would alert the Vicksburg garrison, which could march to the scene in ample time to deal with the situation.

Grand Gulf was a different matter entirely. It was thirty miles from Vicksburg and so could not be supported directly by the Vicksburg garrison. The obvious answer to that was to fortify it, so BG John Bowen and his Missouri infantry brigade were sent there for that purpose.[8] Big antiship guns laboriously were brought in and emplaced, just in case the Yankees brought the ironclad *Essex* up from Baton Rouge to provide gunnery support. Pemberton was not particularly concerned about the prospects of Farragut bringing his saltwater ships upriver again, because they had been so roughly handled by the Port Hudson batteries on the night of 13–14 March. This made it unlikely that he would pit his unarmored ships against fortress guns again, except as a last resort. However, Pemberton did retain a nagging suspicion that Union RADM Porter could slip another ironclad or two past the Vicksburg batteries if he were willing to pay a heavy enough price. Since Vicksburg was a prize worth almost any price, Porter might well be induced to try it.

Finally, given the abysmal state of the Louisiana roads south of Richmond, the Federal movement necessarily would be so slow that GEN Kirby Smith's Trans-Mississippi forces would have plenty of time to intervene. Pemberton had, of course, notified Kirby Smith of the Yankee presence and had suggested that the Department of the Trans-Mississippi ought to take some action, but so far nothing had come of that.[9]

All things considered, Pemberton considered it likely that Grant would withdraw the Army of the Tennessee to Memphis and resume the offensive against Vicksburg by coming down the railroads. There was so much steamboat traffic along the river that it was impossible to tell for sure, but the few reliable intelligence sources that were available were suggesting that a withdrawal had already begun. One problem was that the Federal control of the river meant that very large forces could be shuttled north to Memphis very quickly. It was possible that a large army could be assembled at Memphis before the Confederates could detect it. But it really didn't matter, because, based on past experience, he thought that it would take weeks for such a force to move southward down the railroads. There would be ample time to shift forces from central to northern Mississippi by railroad to counter it. After all, the Federal thrust down the Mississippi Central Railroad in 1862 had moved very slowly indeed.

In the meantime, the defense line across northern Mississippi seemed to be holding, although with some difficulty. The Yankees, who had occupied the M&CRR between Memphis and Corinth, MS, had launched raid after raid southward through the contested zone between the Tallahatchie River and the Tennessee border. While all had been turned back, the pressure had been such that Pemberton had felt it most unwise to withdraw any of the cavalry in the defense forces for use in Central Mississippi. He had appealed for cavalry reinforcements to both GEN Joseph E. Johnston, commander of the Department of the West and his nominal superior, and President Davis, but to no avail.[10] It was more than worrisome to Pemberton that virtually all his cavalry was tied up in that area. Still, it could be tolerated as long as Grant's infantry was confined to Louisiana.

Far to the south, MG Franklin Gardner's garrison at Port Hudson, the southern anchor of the stretch of the Mississippi still held by the Confederates, was being threatened by MG Nathaniel Banks's Army of the Gulf, but the pressure was slight and clearly not a cause for immediate worry. Pemberton was cautiously optimistic because, at least for the moment, the Vicksburg defenses were holding and the Confederate grasp on the Mississippi was secure.

6

From Milliken's Bend to Ione
31 March–17 April 1863

Maps: 2. Northern Sector
5. The Core Region
9. Northeastern Louisiana
26. Disposition of Forces in Northeastern Louisiana: 17 April 1863

FEDERAL PERSPECTIVE

At the time Grant made his decision to move southward through Louisiana, the XIII Corps, under MG John McClernand, was located at Milliken's Bend with four divisions: A. J. Smith's, Osterhaus's, Carr's, and Hovey's. Sherman's XV Corps headquarters were at Young's Point, with his three divisions: Blair's, Tuttle's, and Steele's. McPherson and his XVII Corps was at Lake Providence with three divisions: McArthur's, Logan's, and Sanborn's (later Crocker's). The XVI Corps, commanded by Hurlbut, had the equivalent of three infantry divisions and a cavalry division, but only BG Grenville Dodge's INF DIV at Corinth was completely organized and battle-worthy; the rest were distributed in penny packets across northern Mississippi and western Tennessee.

Grant set his plans in motion on 29 March 1863, ordering MG John A. McClernand to move his XIII Corps to New Carthage as rapidly as possible, building whatever roads he needed as he went.[1] McClernand's corps was chosen to lead the advance largely by accident; the shortest and best road from the river to Richmond started at Milliken's Bend. That was where McClernand's troops were located, so his corps was the logical choice.

At the same time that Grant ordered McClernand south, he wrote to RADM Porter, giving him an outline of his plans and asking him if it would be possible to run a squadron of ironclads past the Vicksburg batteries. Grant suggested that two advantages would accrue. First, the warships would provide needed gunnery support when the time came for crossing the river. Second, they would effectively sever whatever communications the Rebels still had with the Trans-Mississippi region.[2] Privately he also visualized a need for naval artillery if and when Kirby Smith came up from the south to dispute the Union movement. There were, Grant knew, four Confederate gunboats remaining in the Red River and its tributaries, including *Webb* and *Queen of the West* (the latter's Union crew had run her aground and abandoned her during the preceding winter, and the Confederates had refloated and restored her to service). If those vessels somehow could manage to slip past Farragut's blockade of the mouth of the Red, they could make real nuisances of themselves. Grant understood full well that infantry on the exposed natural levees could not survive ship-borne artillery.

Porter's reply came back to Grant the same day: "I am ready to cooperate with you in the matter of landing troops on the other side, but you must recollect that, when those gunboats once go below, we give up all hopes of getting them up again."[3] The Eads ironclads could make a sustained speed of about six knots. This, added to the speed of the current in the river close to the west bank of about four knots, meant that a vessel going downstream need stay under the Vicksburg guns for only about twenty minutes. Going upstream was a different proposition altogether; current speed subtracted from ship speed left a bare two knots, which meant that, even under ideal conditions, the boats would be under the guns for ninety minutes. Porter feared that not even the sturdy City Series ironclads would be able to withstand the battering for that length of time. Furthermore, once the ironclads were below the city, there would no longer be strength above the town to support a direct assault on the city. Porter was placing on the record his caution to Grant that his scheme had better work, because the passage of the gunboats irrevocably committed him to a crossing below the city.

Grant also had given serious thought to the prospect of supplying a large army below Vicksburg along a single wagon road passing along the natural levees bordering Walnut and Roundaway bayous. The roads would be unmetaled, and even a day of rain would turn them into an impassable quagmire. If at all possible, an alternate method of moving supplies to New Carthage had to be found. Grant was not optimistic about the prospect of success for the Duckport Canal, which his engineers had proposed, but he had few options, so he told them to go ahead. The first spadeful of earth was moved on 31 March; from then on, under the command of COL George Pride, work proceeded apace.[4]

McClernand received Grant's order to move south with a notable lack of enthusiasm. His problem was by no means simple. He assumed that the camp at Milliken's Bend was closely watched by Confederate pickets, so any large-scale movement to the south certainly would be reported to the Confederate high command in the Trans-Mississippi. The Rebels were likely to interpret such a move as an attempt permanently to sever the VS&TRR and, since one of the reasons for holding Vicksburg was to keep that line of communication open, McClernand reasoned that the Confederate response likely would be violent.

Even if the Federals did not run into trouble north of Richmond, there still was the problem of forcing a passage down Roundaway Bayou to New Carthage. Virtually everything was under water except the natural levees along the bayou, and there were reports that even these were breached in many places. The natural levees were only a few feet above water level, perfectly flat, and in some places only a few hundred yards wide. There would be a hundred opportunities for ambush-minded Rebels to construct lines of riflepits across the road. McClernand could visualize an endless succession of Thermopylaes. There would be no such thing as maneuver; it would be drive straight ahead and take whatever losses the Rebels could mete out.

The drive to the south began on 31 March. McClernand put his crony, BG Peter J. Osterhaus, in command of the movement.[5] Osterhaus assembled a task force consisting of COL Thomas W. Bennett's 69 IN INF, two companies of the 2 IL CAV, two mountain howitzers manned by a detachment from the 6 MO CAV, and Patterson's KY CO of Engineers and Mechanics. The force was light enough to be mobile, strong enough to discourage any force not equipped with artillery, and capable of building roads and bridges as needed.[6] McClernand, an inveterate politico, made a little speech after the task force was assembled; properly inspired, it marched down the road toward Walnut Bayou. At Oak Grove plantation, the force turned southwest on the direct road toward Richmond, and, to everyone's pleased surprise, there was no opposition from the Rebels. However, the roads were deep in mud, and it took the column until 1400 to cross the railroad and reach Roundaway Bayou, beyond which lay the little town of Richmond.

Patterson thoughtfully had brought along several small boats for just such an emergency, but when his men launched them in the chocolate

waters of Roundaway Bayou, a volley of small-arms fire from Rebels concealed in the houses across the stream drove everyone to cover. Bennett
deployed most of his infantry to keep the Johnnies occupied, meanwhile
sending Patterson and his boats upstream with two companies of infantry and the cavalry. They crossed unopposed, and, when the skirmish line
appeared on the flank of the defenders, the Rebels mounted up and gal-
loped away to the south.[7]

On the same day that the southward march began, 31 March, Grant and
his good friend Sherman cast about for a way to throw a bit of dust in Confederate eyes. They knew that Pemberton and his Vicksburg commander,
MG Carter Stevenson, were very sensitive to threats from the direction of
the Mississippi Delta, because the Army of the Tennessee already had made
three efforts from that direction: Sherman's effort, which had ended in his
defeat at Chickasaw Bayou; the Yazoo Pass Expedition, which ended in
defeat at Fort Pemberton; and the Steele Bayou effort, which ended only
with the fortunate extrication of five of Porter's ironclads from the maze of
waterways west of Yazoo City. Grant and Sherman reasoned that nothing was
more likely to attract Pemberton's attention than the threat of yet another
thrust through the Delta. Even better, they knew that the plantations along
Deer Creek, southeast of Greenville, were a major source of foodstuffs and
forage for the Southern armies in Mississippi. The destruction of those farms
and plantations surely would give Pemberton's commissary officers heart-
burn. So Greenville it was.[8]

Sherman wasted very little time. Steele's DIV left its camps at Young's
Point aboard a fleet of transports on 2 April and arrived at Smith's plantation, twenty miles below Greenville, on 3 April.[9] Steele's cavalry tried to find
a road to Deer Creek from that point, but everything other than the natural
levees along the Mississippi and Deer Creek was under water, and the roads
all were impassable. The next day, 4 April, the division went ashore unopposed at Greenville and by 8 April had penetrated as far down Deer Creek
as Percy plantation, within about twenty miles of Rolling Fork. There had
been skirmishes with a small Confederate force under LTC Samuel W.
Ferguson virtually all the way, but nothing really serious had occurred. At
Percy, however, Steele was pleased to discover that Confederate BG Stephen
D. Lee was at Rolling Fork with a reinforced infantry brigade; that meant
that the Confederates were taking the matter seriously, so one major purpose of the raid had been achieved.[10] Combined with Ferguson's men, Lee
would have a force nearly comparable in strength to Steele's, so Steele withdrew slowly to Greenville, where he arrived on 10 April. He had stripped
the plantations along Deer Creek of their food, forage, and cotton, and he

was convinced that he had put a serious crimp in the Confederate commissary arrangements.

On 2 April 1863, Grant went to see Porter and told him that he was now committed to a river crossing somewhere south of Vicksburg. His plan was to use New Carthage as the staging area for a landing at Warrenton, which would put his troops almost in Vicksburg's backyard. McClernand's XIII Corps, he said, soon would be at New Carthage, and, if they acted very promptly, McClernand's men could be ashore and established before the Confederates in Vicksburg could react. Therefore, said Grant, the navy should run the batteries as soon as possible.[11]

Meanwhile, Osterhaus's DIV moved slowly southward. COL Bennett and his task force reached Stansbrough's plantation, four miles south of Richmond, on 2 April. Here he stopped and sent out cavalry scouts. The scouts came back with a report that there were strong Confederate forces just south of Holmes's plantation, seven miles further south on Roundaway Bayou. This was too much for Bennett's nerves, and he retreated to Richmond. Meanwhile, Patterson and his Kentucky engineers had built a bridge 200 feet long across Roundaway Bayou at Richmond, making it possible for large forces to cross easily.[12]

When Osterhaus and McClernand discovered Bennett back at Richmond, it dawned on them that a little personal leadership was required. The next morning, 3 April, the corps commander and the division commander personally led Garrard's BDE down the road toward Stansbrough's. Sheldon's BDE of Osterhaus's DIV was left at Richmond to guard against interference from the direction of Delhi, even though there had been no hints whatever of a threat from the west.

By nightfall on 3 April, McClernand's advance had reached Pointe Clear plantation, at the junction of Roundaway Bayou and Bayou Vidal, only two miles north of New Carthage. Here they were dismayed to discover that only the roofs of the buildings in the hamlet were above water, and there were three wide crevasses in the levee between Pointe Clear and the village. The water was pouring through them in such volume that bridging was hopeless, and there simply were not enough boats to ferry more than a few men at a time across the gaps. A reassessment clearly was in order.[13]

Confederate sniping had grown slowly in intensity as the Union van pushed southward along Roundaway Bayou, and by afternoon of 4 April there was persistent rifle fire all around the perimeter of the Union camp at Pointe Clear. The country people told Osterhaus that the main camp of the Rebels was westward along Bayou Vidal, so the Prussian led a combat patrol in that direction along the north bank levee of the bayou to find and destroy the nest. The snipers fell back before the advance, but at Dunbar's plantation, six miles west of Pointe Clear, they suddenly vanished. The country people explained to Osterhaus that the Rebel camp was in the swamps to the east, near Bayou Bridgeman, and could be reached only by water. One look at the gloomy and sinister swamp was enough to persuade Osterhaus of the futility of trying to root them out. Frustrated for the second time that day by the lack of boats, Osterhaus left a vedette at Dunbar's and returned to Pointe Clear.[14]

That night an "intelligent contraband" (i.e., an escaped slave) told Osterhaus that there was a large scow hidden on Bayou Vidal several miles southwest of Dunbar's plantation.[15] This was just what Osterhaus needed. Early on the morning of 5 April, a cavalry patrol found the boat, which they poled back to Pointe Clear. Patterson and his engineers had arrived in the meantime, and they boarded the sides up with three-inch planks, cut holes for oars and others for gunports, and mounted a mountain howitzer in the bow. She was named *Opossum*, probably because she was a denizen of the swamp, and, on the morning of 6 April, she provided Osterhaus with the naval support he needed to occupy New Carthage.

Only the roofs of the town showed above the water, with no dry ground except the narrow tops of the artificial levees along the bank of the Mississippi and the surrounding bayous. Osterhaus took a patrol southward along the Mississippi River levee, and about a mile and a half below the village, he came to Ione plantation, surrounded by about twenty acres of dry ground. Trouble was, the Rebels had converted the gin house into a blockhouse which commanded the whole usable area. Osterhaus sent for his naval support, and soon a few shots from *Opossum's* howitzer forced the Rebels to give up and withdraw to the south.[16]

Joshua James, the owner of Ione, told Osterhaus the good news: the levee along the Mississippi extended without a break all the way to St. Joseph, and there were plantations here and there all along the levee, each with its patch of dry ground. But James also had bad news. The Confederate force that had occupied Ione consisted of MAJ Isaac F. Harrison's 15 LA CAV BN, 240 strong, supported by a six-gun battery of 6-pdrs. Later that day, the Yankees learned from the blacks on the plantation that two regiments of Cockrell's dour Missouri infantry also were on the west bank of the river. The Missourians were deeply respected, so this was bad news indeed.[17]

Here matters rested for several days. Osterhaus did not bring his entire division forward to Pointe Clear or Ione; instead, he positioned it in penny packets all along the long road from Milliken's Bend, ostensibly to protect the road from Confederate interference. There were garrisons at Richmond, Stansbrough's, Holmes's, Surget's, Pointe Clear, Montgomery's, Dunbar's, and Ione.[18] Supplies of food were a bit uncertain, so Osterhaus sent out patrols from Dunbar's to sweep up what food they could from the countryside. One such patrol liberated a skiff and managed to navigate Alligator Bayou as far as the Tensas River, taking a little Rebel outpost there completely by surprise. But the important thing was the confirmation that the whole country was under water and utterly impassable for troops in large numbers, which meant that McClernand's forces had no need to concern themselves about a threat from the direction of the Tensas River.

By 12 April, the Duckport Canal was progressing nicely. Walnut and Roundaway bayous had been cleared of major obstructions, and small boats at last were being used to transport supplies to the troops at Ione and Pointe Clear.[19] On 13 April, the Mississippi River levee at the head of the canal was cut, and water began pouring into the ditch. Four steam dredges, which had been brought down from the north for the purpose, immediately were moved into the canal and put to work. However, within twenty-four hours it was clear that the water level in Walnut Bayou was not rising as expected, and Grant began to suspect that the efforts had been in vain.[20]

Down at the tip of the advance, at dawn on the morning of 15 April, a strong Rebel infantry force crossed Mill Bayou, south of Dunbar's, and drove in the Union cavalry pickets. The 49 IN and 120 OH infantry were sent forward from Montgomery's plantation, and, in the face of steady infantry volleys, the Confederates withdrew.[21] The Rebels had been identified as Missourians, which meant that they were from Cockrell's BDE, which rumor said was at Grand Gulf. That was interesting, because it meant that they were from Pemberton's command and *not* from Kirby Smith's Department of the Trans-Mississippi. The implication was that Kirby Smith remained uninterested in Union activity in this part of Louisiana—a useful piece of information, if true.

With a suitable staging area secured at Ione by the evening of 6 April, Grant urged McClernand to move the rest of his XIII Corps southward; by 16 April, Carr's, A. J. Smith's, and Osterhaus's divisions were camped around Ione and Pointe Clear. Hovey's division, the last of McClernand's four divisions, had moved forward to Richmond, leaving the Milliken's Bend campgrounds free for McPherson's troops, which now were beginning to move down from Lake Providence in large numbers.[22]

CONFEDERATE PERSPECTIVE

Neither Pemberton in Mississippi nor Kirby Smith in Louisiana was particularly worried about the presence of Federal troops at Young's Point and Milliken's Bend. The eastern shore was very strongly held, although the defending units were scattered quite widely. Moore's and Tilghman's BDEs, both under the command of MG William Loring, were in garrison at Fort Pemberton, which guarded the northern approaches to Vicksburg via the navigable Coldwater and Yazoo rivers route. MG John H. Forney's DIV manned the fortifications at Snyder's, Drumgould's, and Haynes's bluffs, which guarded the northern flank of Vicksburg from any approach via the lower Yazoo River. Forney had a regimental combat team under the command of LTC Ferguson out on Deer Creek. The garrison of Vicksburg itself consisted of MG Carter Stevenson's DIV, MG M. L. Smith's DIV, and COL Edward Higgins's River Defenses. Green's BDE guarded the Big Black Bridge, nine miles east of Vicksburg, where the Southern Railroad of Mississippi crossed the unfordable Big Black River. The garrison at Grand Gulf, twenty-five airline miles south-southwest of Vicksburg, was commanded by BG John Bowen and consisted of Cockrell's MO BDE and Wirt Adams's MS CAV RGT. Buford's BDE was in Jackson, guarding that nexus of communication lines. Altogether the Confederate troops in the region east of the river numbered perhaps thirty thousand men.

Kirby Smith, as commander of the Confederate Department of the Trans-Mississippi, was the man responsible for keeping an eye on the Yankees at Lake Providence, Milliken's Bend, and Young's Point, but his only presence in the area consisted of BG Paul Hébert, whose headquarters were at Delhi, LA, and whose total force consisted of two cavalry battalions with perhaps five hundred men in all. COL Frank A. Bartlett's 13 LA CAV BN was watching Lake Providence, and MAJ Isaac F. Harrison's 15 LA CAV BN operated out of Richmond, LA. Harrison was a cool, thoughtful man; while technically he was responsible only to Kirby Smith, he realized that Pemberton was the man most concerned with the activities of the Yankees across the river from Vicksburg, and so, as a matter of courtesy, his reports flowed to Pemberton as well as to Kirby Smith. In practice, it was very difficult for him to communicate with Vicksburg, so his actual point of contact on the eastern shore was BG John Bowen at Grand Gulf.

The only real problem that having the Yankees in Louisiana had created was that they prevented the repair of the railroad between Delhi and DeSoto, but that was a minor and temporary irritation. To be a real threat, Grant would have to get the Army of the Tennessee across the river, and there was no obvious way he could do that. Eventually he would have to retreat to Memphis, and then the railroad perhaps could be put back into service. In the meantime, Harrison and Bowen would see to it that the Yankee camps were watched carefully, just to be sure that they did nothing unexpected.

Harrison placed his pickets far forward, just outside the perimeters of Milliken's Bend and Young's Point, with instructions to watch carefully but to withdraw if the Yankees came out; their mission was to observe, not to fight. For a long time, the pickets reported nothing other than the usual restless movements of small Federal cavalry patrols, but on the morning of 31 March, a regiment-sized task force with cavalry and artillery moved out on the Richmond Road. Harrison's pickets withdrew quickly and silently into Richmond and there awaited the arrival of the Yankees. Sure enough, in due course the bluecoats arrived and tried to cross Roundaway Bayou, but they were readily driven back by small-arms fire. Unfortunately, Harrison had too few men to hold the entire south bank, and it was not long before the Yankees had crossed the bayou beyond Harrison's western flank. There was no hope that Harrison's few cavalrymen would be able to stand against the Federal infantry, so there was nothing for him to do but retreat to the south, down the road toward New Carthage.[23] The Yankees followed cautiously as far as Stansbrough's plantation; then, for some inexplicable reason, they returned to Richmond.

Bowen was puzzled when this was reported to him but assumed that the Yankee incursion was only a raiding or foraging expedition. Nevertheless, he sent an account to Pemberton, who was at his headquarters in Jackson. Pemberton interpreted it as either a move to block the flow of commissary supplies from the rich plantations along Roundaway Bayou to Vicksburg, or else a transfer of forces from the Army of the Tennessee to MG Nathaniel Banks's Union army, which was threatening Port Hudson from Baton Rouge and driving Kirby Smith's small force up the Bayou Teche toward Alexandria. In either case, the movement posed no threat to Vicksburg.

Harrison retreated to Holmes's plantation. On 2 April, a Yankee cavalry force came down the road from the north, and there was a noisy but harmless firefight before the Yankees withdrew. Still, Harrison thought that the presence of Yankees so far from their bases at Milliken's Bend and Young's Point implied something other than foraging, so he asked Bowen for help. Bowen was willing but had no steamboats, so he had to tell Harrison that he was on his own. The very next day, 3 April, a strong Yankee infantry force, with cavalry and artillery, came down the road from Richmond; before the day was over, they had reached Dunbar's plantation on Bayou Vidal. There also was at least a brigade camped at Pointe Clear, and patrols had probed at New Carthage. Harrison thought it was not a mere raid or foraging expedition, but a major movement.

Bowen agreed but still couldn't help. Then, by chance, two little steamboats, *Hine* and *Charm,* appeared at Grand Gulf on 4 April. They had been up the Big Black River collecting commissary supplies. Bowen impressed them, loaded two regiments of COL Francis M. Cockrell's MO infantry and a section of artillery aboard, and sent them across to Hard Times. This was violating cherished military protocol, because Louisiana was Kirby Smith's responsibility and the move should have been coordinated, so Bowen was careful to keep Pemberton informed to avoid any misunderstanding.[24] There was a telegraph line from Grand Gulf to Vicksburg and on to Jackson, so Pemberton very shortly knew of Bowen's indiscretion, but he nevertheless approved of Bowen's initiative. He did not expect the Missourians to encounter any serious trouble. Pemberton had two good reasons for believing that the Yankee presence below Richmond was a mere raid. First, on 3 April, he had learned that MG Nathaniel Banks, the Union commander in New Orleans, had withdrawn most of his troops from Baton Rouge, and this seemed to remove any possibility that Grant was moving his army south to reinforce Banks for a joint attack on Port Hudson. Second, he also had received word that there was heavy steamboat traffic on the river above Milliken's Bend, and much of it seemed to be going north. Pemberton took this as evidence that Grant was shifting troops back to Memphis, which was what Pemberton had expected him to do all along, given the fact that Vicksburg was unassailable from the river side. That meant that the large force at Pointe Clear and Dunbar's probably was a raiding expedition sent to destroy the agricultural potential of the region prior to an evacuation of the Louisiana posts, or a diversion to cover a withdrawal to Memphis, or both. It was quite certain that the Northerners could not be intending to cross the river below Vicksburg, because they would need steamboats to do so, and there were none available below the city. The Vicksburg batteries would see to it that none ever became available.

After the Union occupied New Carthage and Ione plantation on 6 April, Bowen began to entertain serious doubts that there remained any direct threat to Vicksburg, or to Vicksburg's northern flank. Why would the Yankees occupy a long stretch of dry ground along the Mississippi unless they intended to use it as a staging area? No, it could only be the vanguard of a major movement to the south, though the immediate objective was not apparent. Whatever the intention was, the movement could bode no good, so he sent another regiment of Cockrell's Missourians across the river to interfere. Cockrell, with three regiments and a section of artillery, established a fortified line across the levee near Mrs. Perkins's plantation, just south of Bayou Vidal. The line could be attacked only by a frontal assault right down the natural levee, and Cockrell thought he could hold it against the whole Army of the Tennessee.[25]

Bowen was not quite so sanguine. He remembered that there was a formidable Union naval presence in the river below Vicksburg, if the Yankees wanted to use it. It consisted of two of Farragut's saltwater ships, *Hartford* and *Albatross;* ironclad *Essex;* and the ram *Switzerland,* which had been trapped below Vicksburg after running the Vicksburg batteries during the previous March. Bowen was not too concerned about Farragut's unarmored ships, because he doubted that the Federals would risk them against his guns, considering their recent experience against the Port Hudson batteries. The ram, too, was unarmored and therefore vulnerable. But ironclad *Essex* was another matter entirely. She was based at Baton Rouge, but Bowen had no illusions that the relatively weak batteries at Port Hudson (there were only twelve heavy guns in the river batteries, as opposed to thirty-four at Vicksburg), or even his brand new batteries at Grand Gulf, would be able to keep the ironclad below that point. If the Yankees sent *Essex* up the river, her huge guns would sweep Cockrell's infantry right off the levee. On 8 April, he telegraphed Pemberton, suggesting that it might be wise to remove his (Bowen's) entire force from Louisiana if the Yankees advanced in great force.[26]

Pemberton replied to Bowen's proposal by saying that, indeed, he ought to make provisions for getting his men back across the river in the event that *Essex* appeared; but, until she did, he should move the rest of his troops to Louisiana to resist the Federal advance to the south.[27] This was a new departure for Pemberton, because Louisiana was part of the Department of the Trans-Mississippi, and he really had no business organizing military actions there without the approval of the department commander, Kirby Smith. All Bowen's incursions into the Trans-Mississippi had been made without any coordination with Kirby Smith, but up to now Smith had made no objection, possibly because, by this time, he was busy with more pressing troubles of his own.

In the event, Bowen ignored Pemberton's proposal. His total transport fleet consisted of two unarmed transports, which would be incapable of removing his men in time if the Federal ironclad from Baton Rouge appeared on the scene.

Pemberton's opinion that the real threat would develop in the north was further reinforced on 9 April, when his commander in Vicksburg, MG Carter Stevenson, reported that he had sent BG Stephen D. Lee and a brigade of infantry to Rolling Fork to support Ferguson's combat team in the Mississippi Delta, because a major Union force, at least a division in size, had landed near Greenville, MS, and was probing inland toward Deer Creek. Pemberton immediately assumed that it was the vanguard of yet another attempt to get into the rear of the Vicksburg defenses, and immediately he ordered MG Loring, at Fort Pemberton, to send 1,500 men of Moore's brigade to Rolling Fork, there to combine with Lee and Ferguson. The rest of Moore's brigade was to move immediately to Snyder's Bluff to strengthen that garrison, because a Union attack through Rolling Fork presumably could come down the road along Deer Creek and hit the complex. Such an attack could readily be supported by Union naval forces coming up the Yazoo.

Bowen's man in Louisiana, COL Francis Cockrell, was a notably bellicose type, and on 8 April he tried to goad the Yankees at Ione into an attack on his position at Mrs. Perkins's. He took his two 12-pdr howitzers up to within 800 yards of the Federal lines at Ione and opened fire. The Yankees took shelter behind their earthworks and ignored him. They didn't even bother to reply with their own artillery. After forty-five minutes of wasting ammunition, Cockrell gave up in disgust and returned to his own lines. In the succeeding days, he kept probing the Union lines at both Ione and Dunbar's plantation, and by 12 April he knew the location of virtually every man in Osterhaus's DIV. Furthermore, he reported to Pemberton that the Yankees made no secret of the fact that their objective was to get below Warrenton and cut off the supplies that flowed into Vicksburg via the Mississippi. He also reported that the Yankees had no significant logistics problem, because they could move supplies readily by flatboats and skiffs down the Walnut Bayou–Roundaway Bayou waterway.

Cockrell's information that the Union movement to the south was dictated by a desire to cut off supplies flowing upriver to Vicksburg helped convince Pemberton that the Louisiana movement was not a significant threat. However, he had another, perhaps even stronger, reason for thinking this. He had seemingly solid information from BG Chalmers, who commanded the Confederate forces in northwestern Mississippi, that the Army

of the Tennessee was withdrawing upstream. Chalmers had been keeping
close watch on the Union forces withdrawing from the Yazoo Pass Expedition, and his scouts reported that when the convoys got to the Mississippi,
most of the troopships turned upstream toward Memphis.[28] Only one division had gone downstream, and rumor had it that it had landed at Greenville.
At the same time, Stevenson's scouts from Vicksburg reported that Steele's
Union division had landed at Greenville and that Quinby's Union DIV had
been seen at a point near the mouth of the Arkansas River. It, too, was
headed downstream, destination unknown.

Pemberton put these two reports together and undoubtedly assumed
that both Steele and Quinby were at Greenville. Greenville was not a good
place on which to base a trans-Delta attack on the northern flank of
Vicksburg, because at that point there was no navigable water connection
between the river and the navigable Delta bayous. Therefore, the reason for
the occupation of Greenville could only be to establish a fortified post to
guard the withdrawal of the Army of the Tennessee upstream. Given this
interpretation, the Federal troops in Louisiana at New Carthage and Ione
were a red herring, best ignored. If those forces were there to interdict
Confederate supplies coming up the river to Vicksburg from the south, they
were in for a surprise, because the Vicksburg forces drew almost nothing
from that direction!

Then, on 15 April, Pemberton's convictions were shattered. First
came a message from Chalmers at Panola, to the effect that a huge fleet
of sixty-four steamboats loaded with troops had left Memphis, headed
south.[29] Next came a message from Bowen, reporting first that the Yankees at Ione had established a battery capable of interdicting any supplies
being sent to Vicksburg via the river, and second that the countryside was
abuzz with rumors that the Yankees were going to run a gunboat fleet past
the Vicksburg batteries. Pemberton immediately wired to Stevenson, his
commander in Vicksburg, that all information suggesting that Grant was
withdrawing had been a ruse, and that Stevenson should expect an attack
soon.[30] No message went to Bowen, which suggests that Pemberton believed that the main attack was going to be an amphibious assault directly
on the city, and that the movement to the south was a feint.

No such interpretation crossed Bowen's mind. He was convinced that
the main body of the Army of the Tennessee was at Ione and Pointe Clear,
marshaling its forces for a thrust across the river somewhere south of
Vicksburg. He would do what he could to interfere: He ordered Cockrell to
attack the Federal forces in Louisiana and destroy them, if he could.[31] This

was a tall order, even for the Missourians, but Cockrell tried. On the morning of 15 April, he massed two of his three regiments opposite the Union lines at Ione, meanwhile sending the third to attack the position at Dunbar's plantation. His plan was to smash the cavalry outpost at Dunbar's and attack the camp at Pointe Clear. If the Yankees showed signs of panic, he then would attack the post at Ione, sweep it away, and join the assault on the big camp at Pointe Clear. If everything went exactly right, the Yankees actually might be persuaded to withdraw up Roundaway Bayou toward Richmond.

Things did not go exactly right. Against all expectations, the cavalry at Dunbar's fought bitterly and could not be broken. Within an hour, two blue-clad infantry regiments appeared in the lines, and not even the Missourians could make headway. Cockrell called off the attack and fell back to his fortified position at Mrs. Perkins's.[32]

Then, early on the morning of 17 April, the world turned upside down. Down the wires from Vicksburg came the chilling news that a fleet of seven Union ironclads and three transports had run the batteries and were safely below the city.[33] With both transports and ironclads below the city, control of the river had passed entirely to the Union, except for those short reaches within range of the guns of Port Hudson, Grand Gulf, and Vicksburg. Even more important, the Federals now had the means to cross the river at virtually any point.

7

Running the Batteries
16–17 April 1863

Map: 8. The Defenses of Vicksburg

FEDERAL PERSPECTIVE

When Grant made his decision to march southward through Louisiana with the Army of the Tennessee and cross the river somewhere below Vicksburg, he acted with full understanding that he would need naval support below the city. When his leading elements reached New Carthage on 6 April, he was certain that the movement through Louisiana was going to be a success, so he wrote to RADM Porter and told him that he was ready for the ironclads and some transports. Porter told him to expect the ironclads shortly, but that getting the transports downstream was a bit less certain. Porter moved his ships to a secluded anchorage just above the mouth of the Yazoo River and set to work to prepare for the trial.

Midway through the preparations, on April 11, he received a message from Secretary of the Navy Welles that changed everything, because it ordered Porter to "occupy the river below Vicksburg, so that Admiral Farragut can return to his station."[1] In other words, Welles wanted Porter to take over the task of patrolling the Mississippi between Port Hudson and Vicksburg, so that Farragut's blue-water ships could return to their proper duty of blockading the Gulf of Mexico shoreline of the Confederacy. Whether Welles understood what he was ordering is open to question, since the only places that could provide a base for the gunboats below Vicksburg were Baton Rouge and New Orleans. To obey his order, Porter would have to abandon the mission of providing gunnery support to the Army of the Tennessee, thus effectively locking Grant onto the western shore of the Mississippi. And that would end the effort to seize Vicksburg.

Certainly Porter understood the implications. Nevertheless, Welles's order had to be obeyed, or at least seem to be obeyed. So he showed Welles's letter to Grant, with the comment that now he would have to pass the Vicksburg batteries much earlier than he had planned. At the same time, he assured Grant that he had no intention whatever of abandoning him, but that he would greatly appreciate it if the army could arrange for some transports to accompany the fleet as soon as possible. This was necessary because the transport fleet, which comprised the vessels which would have to do the work of carrying Grant's troops across the river, was under army control. This proposal was no shock to Grant, who already had asked Porter about the practicality of getting some transports past the Vicksburg batteries. Thus it came as no surprise to Porter when Grant replied that the army would meet any timetable the navy set, and that, indeed, he would be very happy to have the navy assume responsibility, in view of their greater expertise in such matters.[2] There was enough truth in this flattery to make Porter swallow the bait, and he set to work with a will.

Everything was ready by late afternoon on 16 April. The fleet was to consist of seven ironclads: flagship *Benton,* giant *Lafayette,* four City Series gunboats (*Mound City, Pittsburg, Louisville,* and *Carondelet*), and the miserable *Tuscumbia.* Accompanying the ironclads would be the armed ram *General Price,* three army transports (*Silver Wave, Henry Clay,* and *Forest Queen*), and a tug, *Ivy.* Each of the three transports was loaded with stores and had an army barge filled with forage lashed to each beam, providing at least some minimal protection to their thin skins. Five more barges filled with forage and miscellaneous equipment were lashed to the starboard sides of the ironclads, and each of the seven gunboats had a navy barge filled with ten thousand bushels of coal lashed to its port side, for the dual purpose of providing fuel when the seven were below the city and giving additional protection to the hulls of the warships.[3]

Porter's operational plan was to maintain an interval of 50 yards, and each vessel was to steer a course slightly to port of the one just ahead. After rounding the tip of DeSoto Point, the boats were to hug the Louisiana shore. However, if they were seen and fired upon, all were to steer immediately for the Mississippi shore, primarily to take advantage of the fact that the Rebel guns could not be depressed enough to hit the water near shore, but also to take advantage of the fact that the current was faster near the Mississippi side. The gunners were not to fire unless the heavy ordnance of the fortress opened fire. If that happened, there was to be no attempt to knock out the big guns of the River Defense batteries. Instead, as soon as the fleet closed the Mississippi shore, they were to open fire with grape and shell, with the guns ranged for 900 yards. The only purpose of the bombardment was to disturb the aim of the Rebel gunners.

Lines were cast off at 2115, the appointed hour, and the ships assumed their positions in line. The six Eads gunboats came first, then the ram and the transports, with ironclad *Tuscumbia* bringing up the rear. Porter had placed her there, ostensibly to keep an eye on the transports and make sure that they did not put about and attempt to get back upstream when the guns began to shoot. However, Porter detested *Tuscumbia*, and there were those who uncharitably suggested that he placed her at the tail in the hope that, by the time she got opposite the batteries, the Rebel gunners would be fully aroused and sink her.

As soon as *Benton*, leading the column, reached the tip of DeSoto Point, she was peppered with small-arms fire, and it was obvious that Porter's hope of slipping past the city undetected had been frustrated. Then fires broke out on DeSoto Point and along the city waterfront, so the squadron was sailing through an avenue of light.[4] At first the fortress guns fired very slowly, but, as additional guns came into action, the tempo of fire gradually increased. At 2311, the ironclads of the fleet opened fire on the town.[5]

The neat line held by the Union fleet as it rounded DeSoto Point quickly degenerated into utter confusion. The smoke of burning buildings and tar-barrels, combined with dense clouds of powder smoke, was illuminated by flickering light coming from all directions, the bright muzzle flashes of the heavy cannon, and the dazzling flare of exploding shells. All this completely confused the pilots. In addition, the Eads ironclads were notorious for their cranky steering; faced with the added encumbrance of barges lashed to either beam and the unpredictable eddies of the unruly Mississippi, they were as cantankerous as so many wild elephants. The vessels turned first this way, then that, and sometimes turned completely around so that the ships were pointed upstream.[6]

Halfway past the city, a hit on the transport *Henry Clay* set her afire and knocked out her engines. The brightly blazing ship made an excellent target, and, all down the line, the Rebel gunners concentrated on her, hitting her again and again. Her pilot found a plank and deserted the flaming wreck. Incredibly, he was rescued from his plank later that night, but his boat was a total loss.

Meanwhile, ashore in Louisiana, the soldiers at Young's Point and Ione were awakened by a dull grumble, as of distant thunder. It grew steadily in volume until it became one long roll, and the sky over Vicksburg turned lurid. There could be only one interpretation: Porter's ironclads were running the batteries. All through the midnight hours, the dull roar of artillery continued, finally to die away to fitful individual explosions and then complete silence. About 0200, the artillery grumbled briefly again, but this time farther to the south, and the infantrymen grinned at each other through the darkness. That would be the guns at Warrenton, and it meant that at least some of the vessels had gotten past mighty Vicksburg.

The next morning, 17 April, the men of Osterhaus's DIV lined the shore at Ione, eagerly watching the river for signs of the gunboats. They groaned in dismay as the first boat came into view. It was *Henry Clay,* a transport reduced to a flaming wreck, drifting with the current. A few minutes later, three barges came down, quite obviously broken away from the fleet. The spirits of the infantrymen fell still lower as nothing more appeared, and it began to seem that the ironclads all had been destroyed. Then, a little before noon, their anxious eyes saw smoke upriver, and soon *Pittsburg* slid gently into the levee and tied up. Nothing had ever looked so beautiful to the soldiers as that grim and ugly ironclad. Within minutes, the whole camp knew that the rest of the fleet was safe, and hardly damaged. Morale soared. Stolid Grant said nothing, but he was as elated as any; he now had the means to cross the river almost at will, almost anywhere south of Vicksburg.

That same day, Hovey's DIV moved forward to Dawson's plantation. The entire XIII Corps was now in a position from which it could be launched across the river.[7] All that was needed was a place to land, and Warrenton was the obvious choice.

CONFEDERATE PERSPECTIVE

In the spring of 1863, the Confederate high command believed that the River Defense batteries had been improved so greatly since the time of Farragut's passage earlier in the year that any vessel attempting the feat would be destroyed. Nevertheless, Pemberton knew perfectly well that a major Union objective was control of the river, and that sooner or later RADM Porter would attempt to run some of his ironclads past the batteries. If he could do so, the ships likely would become a serious thorn in the flesh of the Confederacy, because they would be able not only to stop all traffic across the river, thus isolating the Trans-Mississippi, but also to probe the waterways west of the river and cause untold damage.

In principle, the Union already had that capability, based on the fleet at New Orleans and the ironclad *Essex,* which had slipped past Vicksburg the previous year. However, the reality of the situation was that, even though *Essex* was an ironclad, the Confederates well might be able to trap and capture or destroy her if she tried those narrow waters alone. Nor could she be supported by the ships at New Orleans, because they were mostly saltwater vessels with drafts too deep for effective operation in the shallow rivers and bayous west of the Mississippi. The key, therefore, was to keep Porter's ironclads above Vicksburg.

Accordingly, Pemberton told COL Higgins, commander of the River Defenses, to exercise every possible means to prevent the passage of the Federal ironclads. Higgins needed no urging. He figured that the attempt would be at night, so he had barrels of tar and other combustibles placed along the waterfront to provide light.[8] The hamlet of DeSoto was occupied, and combustibles were piled in all the buildings, so that they could be set alight at a moment's notice. He sent picket boats out into the stream near the tip of DeSoto Point to give warning. Of course, pickets watched from the shore as well. The signal station on Fort Hill was manned twenty-four hours a day.

It was even more difficult to keep a secret in 1863 than it is today, and on about 15 April Pemberton learned that there was feverish activity in the Union fleet.[9] The Rebel scouts could not tell exactly what was going on, because the major portion of the ironclad fleet had been moved to a secluded anchorage above the mouth of the Yazoo River, and the Yankees kept such a very close watch that nobody could get close. The general feeling was that they were preparing for a major attack on the River Defense batteries. If so, the attack would come during daylight, when visibility would be good. Vigilance at night was not by any means relaxed, but some of the tension faded.

In the city, life went on. The evening of 16 April was tranquil, with the fragrance of early honeysuckle drifting through the quiet streets. A few minutes before 2300, a remote crackling sound from upriver went unremarked. Then, a moment later, the unmistakably sharp crash of a field gun cut through the stillness. Those still awake at this late hour raised an eyebrow, wondering if some cannoneer had carelessly pulled a lanyard. And then, down from the north, came the deep-toned thunderous roar of a heavy gun, and then another. Stunned officers awoke and gazed at each other for an instant in horrified understanding and then broke for their posts.

Out in the river, the picket boats at the tip of DeSoto Point were alert and saw a line of blacked-out monsters sliding downstream. One of the boats rowed desperately for the Mississippi shore to warn the Confederate artillerymen. The others landed on the Louisiana shore near the hamlet of DeSoto, where the men fired the few buildings still standing and a line of tar-barrels thoughtfully placed along the bank, to light the river for the gunners on the other side.[10] In so doing, they not only ran the risk of capture, but also placed themselves directly in the path of the storm of shot that would be aimed at the Union fleet as it passed between the burning buildings and the batteries.

As the first of the ships passed DeSoto Point, the Confederates ashore on the point opened fire with small arms, in the hope not of hurting the invulnerable ironclads but of alerting people in the River Defenses. Sure enough, in a moment, one of the 12-pdr guns on Fort Hill boomed, and six minutes later, one of the big guns in the Water Battery opened fire.[11] Simultaneously, the barrels of combustibles along the waterfront were ignited, and the whole river lit up. Soon every gun that could bear was in action.

Despite every effort, however, the long line of warships swept past. Furthermore, the ironclads retaliated. A hail of grapeshot and heavy shell drove into the city, but it was clear that the Yankee gunners were firing more or less at random, and none of the forts was damaged. In an hour it was all over, and the last of the boats had vanished below the Warrenton Battery, clearly out of danger. So far as the Confederates could tell, none of the ironclads had been seriously damaged. Even the transports mostly had survived; only one of them had been hit hard. To the stunned Rebels, it was all too obvious that the River Defense Batteries had failed in their primary mission.[12]

The chilling news that a fleet of seven Union ironclads, a ram, and two transports had run the batteries and was safely below the city came to Pemberton over the wires from Vicksburg early on the morning of 17 April. The strategic situation on the Mississippi had been changed irrevocably. With both transports and ironclads below the city, control of the river had passed completely to the Union, except for those short reaches commanded by the guns of Port Hudson, Grand Gulf, and Vicksburg. Even more important, the Federals now had the means to cross the river at virtually any point.

But where would the crossing be made? Now powerful Federal navy and army forces stood both above and below Vicksburg. Because it would be relatively easy to coordinate an assault by using the Union Navy's semaphore signaling system, a very real possibility existed that the Yankees would make a direct assault on Vicksburg, with one thrust coming directly across the river from DeSoto Point and the other hitting the defenses from the direction of Warrenton. This was the possibility most feared by Carter Stevenson. However, the main assault might be at Warrenton, with the forces above the city used to create a diversion. Or the primary thrust might be at Grand Gulf. Or at Snyder's Bluff, with the forces below the city creating the diversion. It might be somewhere still farther downstream. It was even possible to imagine that Grant might take advantage of the huge transport fleet above Vicksburg to move the whole army suddenly back to Memphis and launch a conventional offensive down the railroad, meanwhile creating a diversion below Vicksburg with a division or two left behind for that purpose. It was even possible that Grant would move the bulk of the army via the river to combine with Banks's army for an assault on Port Hudson, meanwhile keeping a few troops behind to maintain a credible threat to Vicksburg. The possibilities were endless and bewildering.

And all this had been made possible by the simple act of running seven ironclads, a ram, and two transports past the Vicksburg batteries! It was a stunning demonstration of the use of naval power.

8

From Ione Plantation to Hard Times

18 April–28 April 1863

Maps: 1. The Theater of Operations
9. Northeastern Louisiana
27. Disposition of Forces in Northeastern Louisiana: 28 April 1863

FEDERAL PERSPECTIVE

On the morning of 18 April, Grant had two workable transports and a number of barges below the city, and Porter had seven ironclads to provide gunnery support, plus an unarmored ram and a tug. During the previous day, 17 April, Hovey's DIV had moved forward to Dawson's plantation, so that by morning of 18 April all four divisions of XIII Corps were in positions from which they could be launched across the river. In principle, Grant now had the means to put his troops ashore on the eastern bank. The basic question was: where?

All during the days of McClernand's march to Ione and Pointe Clear, Grant had assumed that Warrenton was the logical objective. However, now that he had a realistic picture of the geographic as well as the military situation, he had second thoughts. In the first place, Warrenton was seventeen river miles above Ione, the only practical staging area, and that meant an elapsed time of at least three hours for the transports. It might then take Porter's ironclads another couple of hours to silence the Warrenton battery.

There was no hope whatever that the movement could be concealed from Pemberton's scouts; with five hours of warning time, the Rebels easily could move large bodies of infantry and field artillery out of Vicksburg and have them waiting at Warrenton. Trying to land troops in the face of determined infantry resistance, even with the support of the ironclads' big guns, was not an inviting prospect. So Warrenton was not a viable option.

What Grant needed was a place where he could get at least a corps ashore unopposed by the main Confederate army, with time to get organized before the Vicksburg troops arrived on the scene. The obvious candidate was Grand Gulf, twenty-four river miles downstream from Ione.

On 18 April, Grant left Young's Point and went down to Pointe Clear to talk to McClernand about it. The ride along the Duckport Canal, across to Richmond, and down Roundaway Bayou was an eye-opener; it was probably the first time he fully appreciated just how vulnerable that single road was to both the vagaries of the weather and Rebel interference. He realized that supplying the entire Army of the Tennessee over that single road would be very difficult, perhaps impossible. The success of the Duckport Canal was in doubt; water was still pouring through the canal from the Mississippi, but the water level in Walnut Bayou had risen only a few inches, even after several days, and that was far too little to permit navigation by regular transport steamboats.

Somewhat to Grant's dismay, McClernand was less than enthusiastic about an attack on Grand Gulf. McClernand's profound dislike for Porter translated into a deep distrust of the navy. He argued that the army ought to be able to move independently of the navy, and he asked Grant to run several more transports past the Vicksburg batteries.[1] Grant knew that McClernand's concern about the navy was nonsense, but he agreed to see what he could do about providing more shipping. After all, the more vessels, the better. In the meantime, he would move McPherson's XVII Corps to within close supporting distance and send a pontoon train down so that the crevasses between Pointe Clear and New Carthage could be bridged, thus eliminating McClernand's dependence on small boats for moving troops and supplies from Pointe Clear to New Carthage and Ione. As he left for the return to Milliken's Bend, Grant remarked to McClernand that he hoped that, the next time they met, McClernand would be in Grand Gulf.[2]

Grant's fears about supplying the army were reinforced when he got back to Young's Point and was told that the water in the Mississippi was falling at the rate of six inches per day, and water was now beginning to drain out of the half-finished Duckport Canal. Even so, on 20 April, the little tug *Victor* and several barges managed to squeeze through the canal into Walnut Bayou. It was abundantly clear, however, that there would be no more such opportunities. The canal was a failure.[3] That long, single, tortuous road to the south would have to do.

McClernand, meanwhile, was faced with the problem of landing his four divisions at Grand Gulf. With only three operable steamboats—the ram could be made to serve as a transport—and a few barges, it would take many shuttle trips between Grand Gulf and Ione plantation to transfer all his troops to the eastern shore, which meant that the first troops ashore would be terribly vulnerable to a Confederate counterattack. If at all possible, he had to find a staging area much closer to Grand Gulf, in order to reduce the shuttle time between embarkation and landing points. His intelligence sources had told him that there really were only two places along the river above Grand Gulf where there were good steamboat landings and enough dry ground for the camps of substantial numbers of troops. One of those was Mrs. Perkins's plantation, about three miles below Ione, and the other was the plantation community of Hard Times, a mere five river miles above Grand Gulf. Unfortunately, neither of those places readily could be reached by land from Pointe Clear, the effective terminus of the road along Roundaway Bayou. There was solid ground along the natural levee between Ione and Mrs. Perkins's plantation, but the crevasses in the levee between Pointe Clear and New Carthage proved to be too deep and swift to be bridgeable, which made it impractical to move troops in large numbers to Ione and Mrs. Perkins's by that route.

There was reputed to be a road along the west bank of Bayou Vidal, which would make it possible to reach Mrs. Perkins's by a somewhat circuitous march, but there was no firm intelligence concerning it. Finally, it was known that there was a good road connecting Mrs. Perkins's plantation with Hard Times via the natural levee along the west bank of Lake St. Joseph. It was clear, therefore, that most of the army would have to reach Hard Times by way of the Bayou Vidal and Lake St. Joseph roads.

One comforting factor was the presence of the ironclad squadron; there was no longer any reason to fear the Rebel infantry which held Mrs. Perkins's plantation, because the naval guns would simply sweep them off the levee if they attacked. Safety assured, McClernand began to inch southward. On 19 April, his scouts reported that the route along Bayou Vidal was practical, albeit difficult, all the way to Mrs. Perkins's plantation.[4] However, to make it suitable for the movement of an army, sections of the road would have to be corduroyed and some rather long bridges built. One bit of good news, however, was that the Rebel infantry which had held Mrs. Perkins's plantation seemed to have evaporated. Life was bound to be simpler if those troublesome Missouri regiments did not have to be pushed away.

That same evening, 19 April, to McClernand's surprise, the steamboat *Forest Queen* and the tug *Ivy* arrived at Pointe Clear, demonstrating that there was a navigable channel between the river at New Carthage and Roundaway Bayou.[5] McClernand promptly pressed the two boats into service, and by nightfall on 20 April, Osterhaus's entire DIV had been carried by water to Ione. Carr's DIV followed the same route over the next four days.

Meanwhile, Porter had tidied up the damage to his ironclads and on 20 April took *Tuscumbia* and *General Price* down for a look at Grand Gulf. What he found was swarms of men working on a massive earthwork under Point-of-Rock, along with abundant other evidence of additional fortifications. Porter was impressed by their strength and realized that the fortifications rapidly would get stronger. He immediately notified Grant but suggested that the place could still be taken if the army moved promptly.[6]

The next day, 21 April, McClernand moved Hovey's DIV from its camp at Dawson's plantation to Dunbar's plantation and assigned it the task of building bridges and improving the road along Bayou Vidal. Hovey and his men started work in earnest on 22 April, and by nightfall of 26 April the job was finished. They had built three long bridges and constructed several miles of road through flooded forests.[7] At the same time, Osterhaus had pushed slowly down the levee along the Mississippi and occupied Mrs. Perkins's plantation. They had not seen a single Rebel.

However, McClernand's movements seemed too lethargic for the impatient Porter, and on 22 April he took his squadron down to look over the situation at Grand Gulf more carefully. The sight was discouraging; work parties were swarming all over the place. With the rest of his squadron hanging back, Porter took mighty *Lafayette* into artillery range and lobbed a few 11-in shells into the midst of the work parties, both to interrupt their work and to goad the Rebels into returning the fire, so that the calibers of the guns emplaced in the works could be determined. The shelling broke up the work parties, all right, but, to Porter's surprise, the guns that replied were emplaced in another fort several hundred yards downstream. Until it fired, the lower fort had been undetected. The size of the waterspouts raised by the shots indicated rifled 32-pdrs, big enough to be a problem.[8]

Porter immediately wrote to McClernand, telling him that, if left to themselves, the Rebels soon would make the place impregnable, but he went on to say that he would attack the place with his fleet in the morning. If McClernand would send down as many men as he could on the available transports and barges, they would be able to seize and hold the place until the rest of the army could be brought forward. Said Porter: "This is a case where dash will save everything."[9]

Little *Ivy* brought Porter's message to McClernand at his headquarters at Pointe Clear at 2300, and it acted as an elixir. He could see the headlines back home in Illinois. Within the hour, Osterhaus had been ordered to put his men aboard anything that would float and be prepared to cooperate with the navy to seize and hold Grand Gulf. McClernand also notified Grant as to what was afoot.[10] McClernand's morale was improved still further by a long roll of thunder from Vicksburg's River Defenses, at about the same time that *Ivy* docked at Pointe Clear. It meant that Grant was sending McClernand the additional transports that he had requested. When they arrived, McClernand would have enough shipping to transport another division to support Osterhaus.

Meanwhile Osterhaus, at Mrs. Perkins's plantation, had to make do with what he had, which consisted of tiny *Ivy*, the transport *Forest Queen*, the unarmored ram *General Price*, and a number of barges, some of which were barely seaworthy. Despite terrible crowding, Osterhaus had nearly his whole division—some 4,500 men, including two six-gun batteries of field artillery— loaded and ready to go by 1100 next morning, 23 April. It was all in vain; about noon Porter arrived from downriver with *Benton, Lafayette,* and *Tuscumbia* and explained that a Union sympathizer had appeared that morning with intelligence that the Grand Gulf garrison included 12,000 men, and that there were eighteen heavy guns already mounted in the works. Porter figured that it would take McClernand's entire corps to effect a landing and had called off his attack.[11]

McClernand was furious. He thought the admiral craven. He demanded a boat so that he and Osterhaus could see for themselves. Porter cheerfully loaned them *General Price*. The two soldiers anchored the ram two miles off Point-of-Rock, from which point neither he nor Osterhaus could see any signs of fortifications or big guns. Returning to Mrs. Perkins's, McClernand tried to persuade Porter to resume the attack, but the admiral would have none of it, so McClernand sadly ordered Osterhaus to debark his men.[12]

In the meantime, Grant had thought long and hard after he returned to his headquarters at Milliken's Bend on the evening of 18 April. That long and tenuous supply line worried him. However, on 20 April, he at last decided to go ahead with the plan to make his landing at Grand Gulf. Once

ashore, he would need every man he could put into the field, and that meant
bringing McPherson's XVII Corps and Sherman's XV Corps south as quickly
as possible. With this in mind, he issued Special Order 110, which ordered
all the readily available forces of the Army of the Tennessee to concentrate
at Pointe Clear as quickly as the divisions could be moved down that single
terrible road. Further, having made his decision, Grant then moved his headquarters forward to Pointe Clear on 23 April.

In response to Grant's special order, McPherson on 21 April started
McArthur's DIV on its way south by moving Ransom's BDE of McArthur's
DIV by steamboat from its camp at Lake Providence to Milliken's Bend.
Grant had not forgotten McClernand's request for more vessels, and on the
night of 22 April, six Army transports attempted to run past the Vicksburg
batteries. This time the Rebels were ready, and, without counterbattery
from armed ships to interrupt their aim, they hit the transports hard. One
was sunk, one had her engines destroyed and arrived below Warrenton as
nothing more than a floating hulk, and the remaining four were damaged
to some degree. Nevertheless, Grant now had a fleet of six operational transports, a tug, a transport hull that nevertheless could be used as a commodi-
ous barge, and lots of regular barges that could be used to transport troops.
There was also the ram *General Price* that could be pressed into service as
a transport if need be.

Porter visited Grant at his new headquarters at Pointe Clear on the
afternoon of 23 April, and, on the basis of his experiences at Grand Gulf
the previous day, tried to convince Grant that Grand Gulf was too strong
to make a frontal attack practical. Instead, Porter proposed that the army
march overland to some point below Grand Gulf, after which he would
run both ironclads and transports past the guns at Grand Gulf and ferry
the troops across onto Mississippi soil. Grant was noncommittal; a supply line running overland through Louisiana all the way to somewhere
below Grand Gulf seemed too tenuous a link with his bases at Milliken's
Bend and Young's Point to be practical. Before committing himself to
such a course of action, he thought he would like to see the situation at
Grand Gulf for himself.[13] Porter thought that reasonable enough, and
next morning, 24 April, the admiral and the general boarded fast and
handy *General Price* and went down for an inspection. Grant thought the
place was not as strong as Porter believed, but neither was it as weak as
McClernand would have it. He thought that if an assault in force could
be made within the next two days, the place could be taken.[14]

The real problem lay in assembling the force. The transport fleet that was available below Vicksburg was by no means enough to transport the complete army at one time, but it would have to do. Much more serious was the fact that there was not nearly enough dry ground at Mrs. Perkins's plantation to assemble more than two divisions. Grant calculated that he had to get at least a corps ashore very quickly, in order to beat off the inevitable counterattack that the Confederates would launch, if and when the Federals won a beachhead. The solution to the problem was to move the army to Hard Times, where Porter had established that there was not only an extensive area of dry ground, but also a good steamboat landing, so that, when the landing was finally made, the available shipping could make frequent and rapid shuttle trips to bring reinforcements into the bridgehead.[15]

With this in mind, Osterhaus on 25 April was ordered to reconnoiter the road that followed the natural levee north of Lake St. Joseph. Osterhaus left Mrs. Perkins's early that morning and found that, while the road was good, the Confederates had burned all the bridges across the bayous that entered the lake from the north and west, and they tried to interfere with the Union engineers when they rebuilt them. But there were too few of the Rebels to be effective, and on the morning of 28 April Osterhaus's van reached Hard Times.[16] Porter had been right; it was a substantial "plantation town" with enough dry ground around it to provide camping spaces for both McClernand's and McPherson's corps.

Meanwhile, additional units of the Army of the Tennessee were moving southward. McPherson moved Alexander's BDE of Sanborn's DIV from Young's Point to Richmond on 23 April. On 24 April, A. J. Smith's DIV of McClernand's XIII Corps marched from Holmes's plantation to Pointe Clear. Far up the river, Sherman started Steele's DIV of the XV Corps downstream from Greenville. On 25 April, Steele's men landed at Young's Point and prepared for the march south; Holmes's BDE of Sanborn's DIV moved from Richmond to Holmes's plantation; Boomer's BDE of Sanborn's DIV, and Logan's DIV left Milliken's Bend and marched all day and well into the night. Logan's DIV stopped at Richmond, but Sanborn, with Boomer's and Holmes's BDEs, marched on through the night to Holmes's plantation.[17]

By this time, Grant had discovered that infantry could move down the road from Milliken's Bend without much difficulty, but wagons and the artillery were having a trying time. On 25 April, he wrote to Sherman, whose headquarters were at Young's Point, asking him to stay behind and improve the road network. Sherman instantly put Tuttle's DIV to work building a road along the abandoned Duckport Canal, thus providing an alternate road from Milliken's Bend to the head of the Richmond Road.[18]

There being only a very difficult road along Walnut Bayou from Young's Point to Richmond, Sherman also moved Steele's DIV by water from Young's Point to Milliken's Bend, where it would be in a better position to move south when the time came.

Grant was having second thoughts about an attempt to force a landing at Grand Gulf, in the face of those steadily improving Rebel fortifications, so he cast about for an alternate landing place. On 26 April, he sent LT Wilson of the engineers and a strong patrol to reconnoiter Trasher's Point and Congo plantation, from which a road reputedly led to high ground.[19]

That same day, 26 April, Grant had visited Porter aboard mighty *Benton,* and Porter had made it quite clear that Grand Gulf already was very strong and was getting stronger by the hour. Grant then visited McClernand at McClernand's headquarters at Mrs. Perkins's plantation. This time it was Grant who wanted to plunge ahead and McClernand who dragged his feet. McClernand had been stubborn about the need for having his whole corps close at hand before an attempt was made. Perhaps his own scouts had convinced him that there really were a lot of Confederates waiting for him on the eastern shore and that he would need every man he could gather to ensure hanging onto a bridgehead, once made. Having been persuaded by Porter that haste was essential, Grant would have none of McClernand's newly acquired caution; he ordered McClernand immediately to embark both Osterhaus's and Carr's divisions, and to be prepared to land at Grand Gulf.[20]

Grant was not being quite so unreasonable as McClernand probably believed, because the bulk of the Army of the Tennessee was rapidly flowing down the roads from Milliken's Bend and Young's Point and soon would be within ready supporting distance. By nightfall of the same day that Grant and McClernand were having their discussion, Landram's BDE of A. J. Smith's DIV had reached Nigger Bayou on the Bayou Vidal Road, Burbridge's BDE of A. J. Smith's DIV was at Mrs. Perkins's plantation, Sanborn's DIV reached Pointe Clear, Logan's DIV was at Holmes's plantation, and McArthur's DIV of the XV Corps was at Richmond. To keep up with his troops, McPherson had moved his headquarters from Young's Point to Pointe Clear, right next to Grant's headquarters.[21]

Wilson returned from his reconnaissance of the eastern shore on the morning of 27 April and reported that he had explored the east bank all the way to Palmyra Bend. There was a tiny area of dry ground around Congo plantation, and indeed a road led eastward from it, but it was about three inches above water and barely wide enough for a single wagon. Moreover, after crossing two miles of flooded swampland, it led to McKay's Ferry across the unfordable Big Black River. Beyond the Big Black was an imposing line of bluffs, and atop the bluffs a lot of Confederates were busily throwing up fortifications.[22] Wilson also reported that there was another ferry, Thompson's, less than three miles farther upstream. In both cases, however, the ferryboats were barely large enough to carry a single farm wagon across the stream, far too small to support the movement of any significant military force. Grant sighed and concentrated on Grand Gulf.

His first move was to return to Mrs. Perkins's plantation to see how McClernand's embarkation of Osterhaus's and Carr's divisions was proceeding. What he found was that McClernand had completely ignored his order of the previous day. Grant was furious. He wrote a letter of harsh reprimand but put it in his pocket and calmly repeated his order to load the two divisions already on hand.[23] This time, with Grant standing by, McClernand obeyed, and by nightfall, despite periods of heavy rain, both Osterhaus's and Carr's divisions were loaded aboard the available transports and barges. It was horribly crowded, and the only horses were those needed to pull the guns of the artillery. Even Grant and the corps commanders were going to walk, at least until the bridgehead was firmly established.

The rest of the Army of the Tennessee tried to continue its movement southward, but heavy rain on 27 April turned the roads into quagmires. Even with the infantry to help the wagons and artillery along, Logan's DIV made only seven miles, to camp for the night just west of Pointe Clear.[24] Sanborn and McArthur stayed in camp, since there seemed no point in exhausting both men and horses for no purpose.

Grant was certain that the Confederates were aware of the movement to the south and feared that Pemberton would move the entire Army of Vicksburg southward to Grand Gulf, into position to oppose any landing the Federals might make. He needed a device to keep a large part of their forces locked in Vicksburg until he could get at least a corps ashore and secure. He had few options. However, he knew that the Confederates in Vicksburg were very sensitive to threats from the direction of the Delta, and he figured that a menacing move from that direction would persuade them to keep most of their maneuver forces in the city. Thus, early on the morning of 27 April, he sent a message to Sherman, who had Steele's and Blair's divisions at Young's Point and Milliken's Bend, suggesting that a demonstration in strength toward Snyder's Bluff would be very helpful.[25] However, he went on to say that he feared that such a move would be reported in the North as a real attack, rather than as a feint, and when the force was withdrawn, it then would be interpreted as yet another defeat. Grant left it to Sherman to decide what to do. Sherman was contemptuous of public opinion. The Northern newspapers had called him crazy when he told Lincoln early in the war that it would take at least 200,000 men in the West alone to suppress the rebellion. His instant response to Grant's suggestion was to launch the demonstration as soon as he could get a suitable fleet of transports together and coordinate the effort with the navy.[26]

The rain stopped early on the evening of 27 April, and by dawn the next day the roads were beginning to dry. With the dawn, the blue divisions resumed their march to the south. By nightfall of 28 April, Carr's DIV had been carried to Hard Times by water, where it had been put ashore so that the transports could return to Mrs. Perkins's to pick up Hovey's DIV. Hovey's DIV had marched from its campsite on Bayou Vidal to Mrs. Perkins's plantation, where it had been picked up and carried to the anchorage off Hard Times, next to the transports and barges carrying Osterhaus's DIV. Landram's BDE of A. J. Smith's DIV was near Dr. Bowie's plantation on Lake St. Joseph; Logan's DIV was at Mrs. Perkins's plantation, having marched along the Bayou Vidal Road; Sanborn's DIV was at the Fisk plantation; and McArthur's DIV had moved southward to Holmes's plantation and Pointe Clear.[27]

Grant now had three divisions (Osterhaus's, A. J. Smith's, and Carr's) at Hard Times, ready to cross the river, and three more divisions (Hovey's, Logan's, and Sanborn's) within a day's march or less of the staging area at Hard Times. A seventh division, McArthur's, was perhaps three days' march away but moving rapidly southward. He could do no more until the heavy guns in the new Rebel fortifications at Grand Gulf were silenced, and that was a job for the navy.

CONFEDERATE PERSPECTIVE

Early on 16 April, BG Louis Hébert, who commanded the brigade guarding Snyder's Bluff, sent word to MG Carter Stevenson that the barrier raft across the Yazoo just above Anthony's Ferry had been swept away by high water.[28] That same night, Stevenson watched in horrified dismay as a squadron of Union ironclads and transports ran past the Vicksburg batteries. By the next morning, he had realized that, if ironclads could pass mighty Vicksburg, the much weaker batteries at Snyder's Bluff would offer them no real challenge. With the barrier raft gone, there was nothing to prevent them from pushing up the Yazoo virtually at will, and the stage would be set for Stevenson's worst nightmare. He was fully aware that by no means all the Union ironclads had passed the Vicksburg batteries, because *De Kalb* and mighty *Choctaw* still swung at their anchors off the mouth of the Yazoo. In addition, a number of the deadly tinclads and plenty of transports were always around. Now that the Yankees had a fleet below the city, this array of naval power meant that they could attack simultaneously from three directions: one thrust could come up the river against Warrenton, launched by those troops at Ione; another could come directly against the city, launched from Young's Point and Milliken's Bend; while a third could come from a landing up the Yazoo above Snyder's Bluff.[29] In visualizing such a possibility, Stevenson realized that he might not be able to shift manpower around fast enough to reinforce a threatened spot.

Early on the morning of 17 April, he rode up to Hébert's headquarters to inspect the situation at first hand. There he discovered that there was no possibility of rebuilding the barrier raft in any reasonable length of time. Accordingly, he ordered the barrier raft at Yazoo City brought downriver to replace the one that had been swept away,[30] and that same night he sent a telegram to Pemberton, in Jackson, suggesting that a strategic reserve be assembled somewhere along the railroad east of Vicksburg.

Down at Grand Gulf, Bowen watched the steady advance of the Army of the Tennessee southward with increasing unease, especially now that the Federals had an ironclad squadron in the river between Vicksburg and Grand Gulf. Bowen could see only one purpose for that fleet, and that was to cover a landing on the Mississippi shore, probably at Grand Gulf.[31] The presence of those dreaded black warships also made it impossible for him to maintain a significant force in Louisiana, so on 17 April he brought Cockrell's three regiments back across the river on *Hine* and *Charm*. Harrison and his combat team belonged to Kirby Smith, so they were left behind to do whatever they could to delay the Federal advance.

Bowen thought that all his messages to Pemberton had fallen on deaf ears, but in fact that was not the case. To be sure, Pemberton still did not really believe that the Federal movement through Louisiana constituted a direct threat to Vicksburg. Just to be on the safe side, however, on 17 April he ordered Green's BDE, which was located at Big Black Bridge, to march for Grand Gulf with all deliberate speed. At the same time, he directed a force consisting of the 6 MS INF, 1 Confederate BN, and the Pettus Flying ARTY to march from Jackson for Grand Gulf.[32]

Green left Big Black Bridge the next morning, 18 April, but he left one regiment and a battery of artillery behind as a bridge guard. His men walked into Grand Gulf late that same night, dead tired after a march of more than thirty-five miles. Not even Stonewall Jackson's "foot cavalry" could have done better.

After thinking the matter over, Pemberton began to realize that a surprise Yankee landing somewhere in the vicinity of Grand Gulf might overwhelm Bowen before reinforcements could reach him from either Jackson or Vicksburg, especially since the only bridge across the Big Black River was the Big Black Bridge on the railroad between Vicksburg and Edwards. A force might be delayed for many hours at Hankinson's Ferry, because only one relatively small ferryboat was available. Accordingly, on 18 April, Pemberton asked Carter Stevenson to build a raft bridge across the Big Black River at Hankinson's Ferry, on the main road between Vicksburg and Port Gibson.[33]

Some days earlier, GEN Joseph E. Johnston, who commanded the Department of the West from his headquarters in Tullahoma, TN, and who nominally was Pemberton's superior, had asked Pemberton to send reinforcements to GEN Braxton Bragg's army in Tennessee, which was threatened by an advance by Union MG William S. Rosecrans, and Pemberton obligingly had sent Buford's BDE. Now, however, the growing sense of crisis in Mississippi had infected even Johnston, and on 18 April he sent a message to Buford, who had reached Montgomery, AL, ordering him to stop his movement toward Tennessee and await orders from Pemberton.[34] That caused a bit of confusion, because two of Buford's regiments already had passed through Montgomery and were en route to Atlanta and Chattanooga. A few days earlier, Pemberton also had decided that the large garrison at Fort Pemberton was unnecessary and had ordered Loring to send Tilghman's BDE to Jackson, MS. The brigade reached Jackson on the afternoon of 18 April.

Pemberton had a bold and resourceful scout operating in the area between Vicksburg and Grand Gulf, and on 19 April he managed to get close enough to Porter's squadron while it was anchored off Ione plantation to count and identify the vessels, and to see the huge tent city that had sprung up along the levee at Ione.[35] Pemberton believed this to be the first reliable information he had had, Bowen's reports notwithstanding. Both Pemberton and Carter Stevenson interpreted the buildup as aimed at Warrenton, and Pemberton immediately ordered Stevenson to send five thousand of his infantry to that point.[36]

The next day, 20 April, Pemberton ordered Buford to march immediately for Jackson, and by nightfall Buford and some of his troops had reached Selma, AL. On the same day, Pemberton ordered the establishment of an advanced supply depot at Big Black Bridge, a position from which food and ammunition could be sent readily to any threatened point along the Mississippi River between Snyder's Bluff and Grand Gulf.[37] The depot was guarded by a regiment and a battery at the bridge and by another regiment at Edwards.

Meanwhile, Carter Stevenson was trying desperately to think of ways to strengthen his positions at Vicksburg. On 21 April, he received a reliable report from his scouts in the Delta that the water in the Tallahatchie had fallen so low that the stream was no longer navigable. That meant that there was no longer a need for heavy artillery at Fort Pemberton, so he asked Pemberton for permission to move the guns to Vicksburg. Pemberton didn't think that was a good idea; after all, for all he knew, the water could rise again tomorrow.[38]

While Pemberton was not personally acquainted with the Mississippi River floodplain, there were men on his staff who were, and it was obvious that the huge buildup at Ione had to be supplied by a long and tenuous road from Milliken's Bend. That road simply had to be vulnerable. Pemberton had no way of getting to it, but GEN Kirby Smith, Confederate commander of the Department of the Trans-Mississippi, certainly did. Thus, on 21 April, Pemberton sent a message to Kirby Smith, asking him to attack the Union positions in Louisiana.[39] No direct telegraphic links existed between the two men, so it would take several days for a courier to make the journey.

Bowen was slightly encouraged by the arrival on 21 April of the small task force which Pemberton had sent from Jackson on 18 April. It brought Bowen's strength up to about 4,200 men. But when he compared that force with what he knew was moving south through Louisiana, his heart sank.

On 22 April, Pemberton was distracted by news that a major Union cavalry raid had penetrated the defenses along the Tallahatchie and apparently was moving southward through Central Mississippi, although its precise location was unknown.[40] It was easy to guess that the objective was the Confederate railroad network, but it was not so easy to predict exactly where the blow would fall; the Meridian–Tupelo line, the Jackson–Grenada–Panola line, or the Jackson–Meridian line all were equally likely targets. If the raid seriously damaged any of them, the effects would be serious indeed. And the worst aspect of the matter was that Pemberton was chronically short of cavalry, despite earnest pleas to both President Davis and Joe Johnston for cavalry reinforcements. The Yankees in Memphis and northern Mississippi had launched raid after raid southward into Confederate-controlled territory, and those raids had been so threatening that it had been impossible to detach cavalry forces from the commands defending the line of the Tallahatchie.

The result was that Pemberton was forced to defend Central Mississippi against this very deep raid with infantry. He sent Tilghman's BDE to Canton, where it was in position to move northward to defend the Jackson–Grenada–Panola line, and Buford's BDE was ordered to stop at Meridian, where it could move either northward along the Meridian–Tupelo line or westward along the Meridian–Jackson line.[41]

While all this was going on in the interior of Mississippi, Carter Stevenson at Vicksburg was preoccupied with his own problems. The more he thought about that Federal concentration at Ione, the more threatening it became. In Stevenson's view, it simply had to be aimed at Warrenton or at some point just to the south. Stevenson knew so little about the terrain to the south that he thought the Yankees might make a landing somewhere between Warrenton and the mouth of the Big Black River. If they did, his best response was to defend Vicksburg by blocking all the roads in that direction. With this in mind, on 22 April he moved his entire division, about 13,000 men, into position near Warrenton, from which point it could easily move to cover not only Warrenton but all possible avenues of approach from the south.[42]

Bowen knew better. On 22 April, he watched from his aerie on Point-of-Rock while a powerful Union ironclad squadron, accompanied by transports, slid downstream and anchored off Hard Times, barely five miles away. There could be only one objective: Grand Gulf.[43]

Late that night, the Confederate lookouts in DeSoto Bend sounded the alarm as a file of six steamboats loomed out of the dark and made a high-speed turn around the tip of DeSoto Point. The River Defenses awoke almost instantly, but the darkened steamboats were hard to see and even harder to hit. Even so, the batteries managed to sink one of them and damaged all the others, but in the morning it was all too clear that five of them had survived the gauntlet.[44] When Stevenson reported this disheartening news to Pemberton on the morning of 23 April, he also reported that it had proven impossible to build a bridge of any kind at Hankinson's Ferry, because the water was too high and the current too swift. Instead, he had ordered the barrier raft just below Big Black Bridge, which had been constructed as a defense against marauding Federal tinclads, to be cut loose and floated downstream to Hankinson's Ferry for use as a floating bridge.[45] It served admirably.

Even after the Union transports had run the batteries on the night of 22 April, Stevenson persisted in his belief that the primary attack would be a three-pronged attack on Vicksburg itself. After all, a powerful iron-clad squadron remained above the city; lots of men were in the big camps at Young's Point, Milliken's Bend, and Lake Providence; and numerous transports were moving about restlessly.

To meet this threat, he rearranged his defensive deployment. Tracy's, Barton's, Taylor's, and Reynolds's BDEs were positioned between Warrenton and South Fort; Martin L. Smith's DIV covered the Vicksburg waterfront; and Forney's two brigades held Snyder's and Haynes's bluffs. The remainder of his available manpower was formed as a mobile reserve.[46] In addition, Stevenson urged his interpretation of Union intentions on Pemberton, with the earnest plea that none of his men be sent on what he regarded as a wild goose chase to Grand Gulf.[47] Pemberton was not at all certain that Stevenson was correct, but on 23 April he promised not to reinforce Grand Gulf from Vicksburg unless absolutely necessary.

On 24 April, the telegraph to Meridian suddenly went dead, and a few hours later Pemberton learned that the Yankee cavalry force known to be in Central Mississippi had moved south and cut the Southern Railroad of Mississippi at Newton.[48] This was devastating news. Further, unless they were stopped, the raiders might turn east and cut the NOJ&GNRR somewhere south of Jackson, or move eastward to cut the M&ORR somewhere below Meridian. That had to be prevented at any cost. The difficulty was that almost the only effective cavalry Pemberton had was Wirt Adams's MS CAV. They were operating out of Grand Gulf, keeping watch over the river between Warrenton and Rodney, and making certain that the Yankees would be detected if they were to attempt a landing. Pemberton did not want to divert them from that task except as a last resort. Without cavalry, Pemberton's only option was to try to hunt the raiders down with infantry. It was all futile, of course, and the raiders vanished into the piney woods country south of the railroad, obviously headed for Baton Rouge. Almost the only thing Pemberton could do was to try to protect important places with infantry. Even that was a frail reed, because many of the units available for such an endeavor consisted of State Troops markedly deficient in both equipment and training.

Bowen, unlike many of his colleagues, had scouted the countryside for a considerable distance around Grand Gulf quite thoroughly and was all too aware of the country road that led from Congo plantation across McKay's Ferry to Ingleside. When it became clear that the Yankees were concentrating at Ione, it occurred to him that it was just possible that the Yankees might contemplate sending a couple of regiments and a battery to attack by that route. This would put an infantry force in the rear of his Grand Gulf fortress, and that would be more than an embarrassment; it would be a positive danger. Bowen reacted by sending the 1 MO CAV (DSMTD), a battalion of sharpshooters, and a four-gun battery of field artillery to throw up entrenchments on Thompson's Bluff, which commanded both McKay's and Thompson's ferries, purely as a precaution.[49] Sure enough, on 25 April, one of Wirt Adams's scouts, operating along the river to the north of Grand Gulf, reported to Bowen that he had seen a force of Yankee cavalry come ashore at Trasher's plantation and fan out to the east and north. They had found the McKay's Ferry Road but had turned back after reaching the Big Black River.

Bowen was receiving news from Harrison's combat team in Louisiana all through this period. On the evening of 26 April, Harrison sent him a message reporting that he had tried to hold the crossing of Clark's Bayou, which flows out of Lake St. Joseph near Ruthwood plantation, but had been forced back under considerable pressure as far as Choctaw Bayou, which flows out of Lake Bruin only five miles north of the village of St. Joseph. St. Joseph is separated from the Mississippi only by a man-made levee.

Bowen thought that the Union thrust toward Lake Bruin looked like a Union probe looking for a practical overland route to St. Joseph, which implied that the Yankees were willing to consider crossing places well below Grand Gulf. But where? He thought Rodney, a mere four river miles below St. Joseph, was the logical place. There was no doubt in his mind that Porter could run his gunboats and transports past the Grand Gulf batteries; if mighty Vicksburg could not stop them, then certainly Grand Gulf could not. Nothing would be simpler than for Grant to move his army farther downstream, load the transports at St. Joseph, and be across the river at Rodney within hours. However, Bowen couldn't be sure the landing would be at Rodney; and he knew very little about the country south of the mouth of Bayou Pierre. For all he knew, there might be other equally practicable landing sites.

If he marched south with the Grand Gulf garrison in an attempt to oppose a landing at Rodney and it actually took place somewhere north of that village, Bowen and his little army would be forced off to the south

and out of the game. In that event, Grand Gulf would be left utterly unprotected. If landing parties from the Union navy seized the place, Federal infantry and artillery would soon follow, and Vicksburg would be
outflanked. No, Grand Gulf had to be defended. He could only wait for
more information. And that information would have to come from Wirt
Adams's Mississippi cavalry, who were Bowen's only eyes and ears in the
country south of Grand Gulf.

Meanwhile, the Union raiders who had cut the Southern Railroad of
Mississippi at Newton had vanished into southern Mississippi without a
trace. They surfaced again by smashing into Hazelhurst, destroying a
mile-long stretch of the NOJ&GNRR, and then vanishing yet once more.
The raiders had to be run to earth before they did even more damage,
but for that task, only cavalry would suit. And now Pemberton was faced
with a terrible dilemma. The only cavalry he had was Wirt Adams's Mississippians, but they were Bowen's only source of information concerning a potential Union landing below Grand Gulf. Which was worse? A
devastated logistical system, or an unmarked landing?

On 27 April, Pemberton finally got another fix on the Union cavalry raid;
it was in the vicinity of Gallatin, about thirty-eight miles east-southeast of
Grand Gulf. Pemberton, not yet quite convinced that the Yankee army in
Louisiana was intending to force a crossing below Grand Gulf, made his
decision. To Bowen went a message: send Wirt Adams's cavalry regiment to
intercept and destroy the raiders.[50] Bowen sent Adams on his way with profound misgivings. Almost in despair, he told Pemberton about the enormous
concentration of shipping and men at Hard Times, and proposed that it was
directed at either Grand Gulf or Rodney. He was, said Bowen, reconnoiter-
ing a defensive position south of Port Gibson. The implication was that, with
Wirt Adams away chasing Union cavalry raiders, Bowen no longer had any
way of locating the landing site, so the only thing he could do was to wait
for the Yankees to attack him.[51]

The next day, 28 April, yet another message from Harrison arrived
in Grand Gulf, this one reporting that he had been forced to fall back
below Choctaw Bayou. This looked to Bowen as if the Union were continuing its southward movement, and he immediately sent a message to
Carter Stevenson, in Vicksburg, reminding him that Pemberton had
placed five thousand men of the Vicksburg garrison at his (Bowen's) disposal, and asking him to start the force immediately toward Grand Gulf.

Stevenson appealed Bowen's request to Pemberton, urging that no
troops be sent from Vicksburg because of the imminent danger of a direct

attack on Vicksburg. Pemberton, having no way to determine Yankee intentions with any certainty, wired Bowen: "Have you force enough to hold your position?"[52] The wording was unfortunate. Pemberton was asking Bowen if he could hold Grand Gulf against a direct attack, but Bowen interpreted it to be a query as to whether he could hold the Mississippi shore against a Federal landing. The question enraged Bowen; he had 4,200 men, and Pemberton knew it. Yet here was Pemberton asking him if he could prevent a landing anywhere along fifty miles of shore! Bowen did the only thing he could. He reiterated that most of the Army of the Tennessee was concentrated across the river and begged that every man and gun that could be found be sent to him.[53]

Pemberton was still not absolutely certain that Bowen's interpretation was correct, especially since it ran directly counter to Carter Stevenson's evaluation. He compromised. He ordered Stevenson to have five thousand men ready to march for Grand Gulf upon Bowen's request and told Bowen that he would send another three thousand from Jackson if needed.[54] True to form to the last, Stevenson replied that the force at Hard Times certainly was nothing more than a feint and that the main attack was going to hit Vicksburg directly.[55] Nevertheless, Stevenson told Tracy and Baldwin to have their brigades ready to march for Grand Gulf at a moment's notice. Tracy was near Warrenton, but Baldwin was camped north of the city and so would have at least another seven miles of marching.

The notice came from Bowen about 1600 on 29 April, and Tracy and Baldwin were on the road almost instantly.[56] Stevenson immediately informed Pemberton, going on to say that, within the last few hours, a large fleet of Union gunboats and transports had sailed up the Yazoo and at that moment was anchored off the mouth of Chickasaw Bayou. In other words, Stevenson was telling Pemberton that it didn't matter what Bowen thought he was seeing; the real attack was coming against Snyder's Bluff, just as he, Stevenson, had predicted all along.

9

Strategy in North Mississippi

Maps: 1. Theater of Operations
       2. Northern Sector

FEDERAL PERSPECTIVE

When Grant moved the bulk of the Army of the Tennessee from North Mississippi to Louisiana opposite Vicksburg in the winter of 1862–63, he left MG Stephen Hurlbut and his XVI Corps behind at Memphis, TN. Memphis, roughly halfway between Milliken's Bend and Cairo, IL, had become a vast supply depot by the spring of 1863. Its warehouses supplied not only the Federal forces defending western Tennessee, but also the garrison at Helena, AR, and all Grant's forces opposite Vicksburg. Memphis was also a major naval station, essential to the efficient operation of Porter's ironclad battle fleet and the tinclad squadrons that kept the supply line open down the Mississippi River.

In addition to ensuring the security of Memphis, Hurlbut was responsible for the defense of western Tennessee, which had been under Union control since the fall of Memphis on 6 June 1862. The tinclads of the navy effectively prevented major Rebel incursions from across the Tennessee River, and Hurlbut's posts along the Memphis & Charleston Railroad (M&CRR) protected the region from Rebel raids originating in northern Mississippi. Behind these screens, the land was returning to economic normality and held out the promise of becoming an important source of cotton for the mills of the North during the next growing season.

Hurlbut had perhaps 25,000 men to defend Memphis and western Tennessee. Of these, the only fully battle-worthy infantry division was that of the brilliant but erratic BG Grenville Dodge, at Corinth, to which was attached COL Florence Cornyn's cavalry brigade. BG Jacob Lauman's INF

DIV garrisoned Memphis and the posts eastward on the railroad as far as Grand Junction, TN. Attached to Lauman's command was the equivalent of a cavalry brigade, including a regiment commanded by a former music teacher, COL Benjamin Grierson. While Lauman's DIV was formally organized, its units had never worked together, and it was not considered completely battle-ready. The remainder, which consisted of a number of unattached regiments and detachments of various kinds, was scattered all over West Tennessee and as far afield as the post at Columbus, KY.

Such dispositions were fine to protect the railroad and western Tennessee against small-scale cavalry incursions, but if the Rebels were bold and clever, they could use their railroads quickly and secretly to assemble a powerful infantry and artillery army at Panola and strike directly up the Mississippi & Tennessee Railroad (M&TRR) toward Memphis. Only by the greatest good fortune would there be adequate warning to assemble the widely dispersed Union detachments into a force large enough to hold that critical supply depot, especially if the main thrust up the M&TRR were supported by a couple of cavalry raids that cut the M&CRR somewhere between Corinth and Grand Junction. The loss of the huge Memphis depot, even for a few days, certainly would dislocate, and perhaps permanently defeat, any plans that Grant might have.

Grant liked and trusted Hurlbut, and each kept the other informed of his plans and movements. So it was that, by early April, Hurlbut was aware that the maneuver forces of the Army of the Tennessee were moving southward through Louisiana, and that Grant intended to find a place below Vicksburg where he could cross unopposed. That was all very well, but to Hurlbut that meant that no reinforcements could be expected in the event that the Rebels struck at Memphis. He was on his own. His inclination was not to await the pleasure of the Confederates, but to take the war to them. Furthermore, if at all possible, the offensive should be carried out in such a way as to provide material support to Grant's efforts.

In the best of all possible worlds, the thing that would help Grant most would be to sever Pemberton's supply line to Atlanta and Richmond. That meant cutting the Southern Railroad of Mississippi (SRRM) somewhere between Meridian and Vicksburg. While that objective was not quite impossible, it certainly would be very difficult, considering that the railroad lay on the far side of 190 miles of enemy-held territory. The second most useful contribution to Grant's welfare would be to tie up or exhaust all the Rebel cavalry in northern Mississippi, so that it could not be sent to the aid of Pemberton, who was known to be desperately short of horsemen. Of course, the Confederate High Command might decide to detach some of Bragg's powerful cavalry forces from the Army of Tennessee and send them to Pemberton at Vicksburg, but Hurlbut could do nothing about that, because Bragg was MG Rosecrans's responsibility.

Eventually Hurlbut—in concert with Dodge, who had heard rumors of a Confederate buildup in northern Alabama—evolved a scheme consisting of two separate but related efforts. First, Dodge and Cornyn would strike southward down the Mobile and Ohio Railroad (M&ORR) and occupy Pontotoc.[1] This would attract the attention not only of Rebel BG Daniel Ruggles, who commanded the Confederate troops in northeastern Mississippi, but also of the Confederate forces in northern Alabama. Then, when the Rebels were nicely occupied, Dodge would launch Cornyn's CAV BDE southward to cut the Southern Railroad of Mississippi somewhere east of Jackson and the Mississippi Central Railroad south of Grenada. Hurlbut was willing; even if the whole cavalry force was lost, the strategic gain would be worth the price. This scheme was proposed to Grant (or perhaps Grant proposed it to Hurlbut; no one really knows for certain), and Grant agreed that it was worth a try.

Unbeknownst to either Grant or Hurlbut, there was yet another player in the game. Union MG Rosecrans, who commanded the Army of the Cumberland from his headquarters in Nashville, TN, was looking for a way to persuade Rebel GEN Braxton Bragg to withdraw from his position at Tullahoma, TN, and fall back to Chattanooga without a serious fight. The obvious way to do that was to cut Bragg's umbilical cord, the railroad that connected his Army of Tennessee with Atlanta. Rosecrans thought this might be accomplished by sending a large raiding force along the southern bank of the Tennessee River; across the mountains to Rome, GA; and then on to the vital Western & Atlantic Railroad at Kingston. However, shaking such a raid free in northern Alabama meant that Confederate COL Roddey's troops, who were responsible for the defense of northwestern Alabama, would have to be taken out of play. Old Rosie thought he had an answer to that; he would ask Dodge to help.

Thus it was that, during the second week of April, Dodge received a message from Rosecrans asking for his assistance.[2] Dodge dared not support Rosie's scheme without Hurlbut's approval, but he also understood that anything that kept Bragg's cavalry forces in Alabama occupied would prevent them from being sent south to Pemberton. So Dodge sent the request forward to Hurlbut.[3]

Machiavellian Hurlbut understood the implications even better than Dodge. Here was Rosecrans offering to do the very thing that Hurlbut had thought impossible: take some of Bragg's cavalry out of play! There was no question but that a raid across Alabama would suck some of those Rebel horsemen into the action, thus keeping them out of Grant's hair. Just as Dodge had expected, Hurlbut told Dodge to go ahead, and to do so with enough strength to make the Rebels take the effort seriously.[4]

To be sure, the diversion of Dodge to Alabama meant that the Rebel forces in northeastern Mississippi would not be properly occupied while the long-distance raid made its penetration, but perhaps that could be dealt with by beefing up the raiding force and using more elaborate deceptions. Thus, as the scheme finally took shape in Hurlbut's mind, it consisted of three parts: (1) Rosecrans's raid toward Kingston, which would start about 15 April; (2) a raid from Memphis and Grand Junction toward Panola and Grenada, which would start about 17 April and keep Rebel BG Chalmers, who commanded the Confederate troops in northwestern Mississippi, distracted; and (3) a deep-penetration raid toward the Southern Railroad of Mississippi, which would also start from Grand Junction about 17 April.

CONFEDERATE PERSPECTIVE

When the Union Army of the Tennessee shifted most of its forces from Corinth and Holly Springs to the Louisiana shore opposite Vicksburg, the Confederates moved the major portion of their infantry army to Vicksburg, which obviously was the critical point that had to be defended. A new defensive frontier was established that extended along the Tallahatchie River from Panola to New Albany, then across country to the Tennessee River near the mouth of Big Bear Creek. It was not a fortified line; the Tallahatchie simply marked the northern limit of effective Confederate control. The Tallahatchie had been chosen primarily because it flowed through swampy lowlands that were difficult to cross except at a very few places where important roads crossed the water-saturated ground. The area between the Tallahatchie and the M&CRR was a debatable zone, haunted by patrols of both Blue and Gray but controlled by neither.

Pemberton had little choice but to leave virtually all his cavalry behind to defend the Tallahatchie frontier. The defensive frontier was about two hundred miles long, and he had only about 4,500 men available to defend it. The only practical solution was to depend upon mobility—and that meant cavalry.

The frontier was divided into two principal commands. BG Daniel Ruggles commanded the First Military District of Mississippi, with headquarters at Columbus, MS. He had the equivalent of about three regiments of regular cavalry, a regiment of State cavalry, and about six independent cavalry battalions, some of them State Troops.[5] The horse soldiers were supported by three artillery batteries, probably eighteen guns. There were perhaps 2,600 men in all, the equivalent of a large brigade. BG James Chalmers commanded the Fifth Military District of Mississippi, with headquarters at Panola, MS.[6] He had McCulloch's four-regiment brigade of regular cavalry, plus assorted unattached battalions and companies, all supported by a single four-gun battery. His total strength was probably about 1,800 men.

Pemberton had retained direct control of only two cavalry regiments. One was LTC W. Ferguson and his regiment, which was on detached duty in the Delta, with the dual missions of watching the Delta for signs of Union incursions and harassing the Union supply line down the Mississippi. The other was Wirt Adams's MS CAV, which operated out of Vicksburg and Grand Gulf and served primarily as a scouting force to watch the Mississippi shore of the river. A number of other miscellaneous small detachments were scattered about the state, but they were mostly State Troops who could not be depended upon.

Thus, Pemberton had the approximate equivalent of a small cavalry division under his command. The problem was that he dared not move the bulk of it away from the Tallahatchie frontier, because to do so would open all of northern Mississippi to marauding Yankee scouting and foraging parties. Even worse, it would open the Mississippi railroad network to destruction by deep-penetration raids, to which Pemberton would have no effective counter. In effect, this left the Vicksburg army with only a single cavalry regiment, Wirt Adams's Mississippians, to serve as its eyes and ears.

Of course, the Confederate defensive arrangements extended eastward into Alabama, but the forces there were led by BG Philip Roddey, who commanded the District of Northern Alabama from his headquarters at Tuscumbia, AL.[7] Roddey reported not to Pemberton but to GEN Braxton Bragg, who commanded the Army of Tennessee, with headquarters at Tullahoma, TN. Roddey had only about 3,100 men, mostly cavalry, but in an emergency he could ask Bragg for help from MG Earl Van Dorn's CAV Corps at Spring Hill, TN. One of Van Dorn's brigades was led by BG Nathan Bedford Forrest, the most highly respected cavalry commander west of the Appalachians.

10

Raids from the North 15 April–3 May 1863

Streight versus Forrest: The Raid toward Kingston 10 April–4 May 1863

Map: 2. Northern Sector

FEDERAL PERSPECTIVE

Rosecrans formed a provisional brigade at Nashville to conduct his raid across North Alabama, putting clever and tenacious COL Abel Streight in command. The plan was complex, like so many of Rosecrans's schemes. Streight would move his men by river boat from Nashville to Palmyra, TN, and then march overland to the Tennessee, where they would be met by a steamboat flotilla which would take them to Eastport. Here they again would disembark and march southward to join Dodge and Cornyn at Big Bear Creek, just east of Iuka, which was the effective frontier between Blue and Gray in that area. The combined force then would strike eastward toward Decatur. At some opportune moment, Streight and his raiders would sneak away from Dodge's force, loop southward through Moulton, Blountsville, Gadsden, and Rome, and eventually cut Bragg's key source of support, the Western & Atlantic Railroad (W&ARR), at Kingston.[1] In other words, the raid was to travel some two hundred miles across enemy territory before reaching its objective.

But instead of cavalry, Old Rosie gave Streight only infantry! Recognizing the futility of attempting a long-distance raid with infantry, Streight asked Rosecrans if he could mount his troops. Considering that most of the raid would be through the mountains of northern Alabama and Georgia, Streight thought mules might well be superior to horses. Rosie agreed, but it turned out that the Nashville depots contained enough animals for only about half the men, so Streight was forced to plan on "liberating" the rest from the countryside.[2] As soon as he tried that ploy on the leg from Palmyra to the Tennessee River, word ran ahead that the Yankees were stealing horses and mules, and beasts of any kind became very hard to find.[3]

What with one thing and another, Streight did not reach Eastport until 18 April, three days late.[4] By that time, Dodge and Cornyn were already camped on the west bank of Big Bear Creek and growing a mite impatient. At last united, the combined force moved eastward against bitter Confederate resistance,[5] with Dodge doing all the fighting and Streight's men bringing up the rear. Dodge occupied Tuscumbia on 24 April;[6] during the next three days, Cornyn and his cavalry brigade pushed on toward Decatur. On 27 April, the Federal scouts heard that BG Nathan Bedford Forrest was at Town Creek with his brigade of veteran cavalry.[7] At the very least, this meant that there would be a stiff fight for Decatur. The next day, Dodge and his infantry forced their way across Town Creek but halted abruptly a short distance beyond, when a courier arrived with word that the Rebels were threatening to cross the Tennessee at Tuscumbia. The thought of a force across his line of communication with Iuka and Corinth was too much for Dodge, and he hastily withdrew to deal with the threat.[8]

Meanwhile, on the night of 27 April, in a downpour, Streight and his two thousand raiders had left Tuscumbia and headed for Moulton.[9] The torrential rain, plus the fact that only about two-thirds of his men were mounted, slowed the pace to a crawl, and he was overtaken by Forrest at Days' Gap on 30 April.[10] Here Streight lured the impetuous Forrest into an ambush and hurled him back with many casualties, before continuing toward Blountsville.[11] At Hog Mountain, Forrest tried again and again was mauled by Streight's infantrymen. And now the chase became one long succession of skirmishes, with both Billie Yank and Johnny Reb growing so tired that men fell out of the saddle.

At last, on 3 May, Streight and his desperately tired command reached Straight Neck Precinct, twenty miles west of Rome. Here they found an easily defensible hilltop and stopped to rest, with men falling asleep on their rifles, while Streight sent a scout forward to Rome. When the scout returned some hours later, he reported that the town was aroused, the local militia had been called out, and the planking removed from the bridges across the deep and unfordable Oostanaula River.[12] By this time, Forrest had reached the scene and surrounded the hilltop, so there was nothing to do but surrender.[13]

It was several days before the fate of the expedition reached Union

ears. When it did, Rosecrans regarded the raid as a failure. But subtle
Hurlbut smiled in satisfaction: No cavalry from Bragg's army would be
sent to Vicksburg!

CONFEDERATE PERSPECTIVE

The Big Bear Creek frontier had been relatively quiet for some time when
suddenly, on 15 April, a powerful combined arms force moved eastward
from Iuka. BG Roddey had no idea what the Yankees intended, but he
did his best to stop them. When he realized that the force consisted of
an infantry division plus a cavalry brigade, he knew he was in trouble and
yelled for help. Bragg, at Tullahoma, was not terribly interested in skirmishing on his Mississippi–Alabama frontier, so it was not until 23 April
that he finally wired Van Dorn, who commanded his cavalry forces, to
send Forrest, who was at Spring Hill, TN, to take care of the problem.[14]

Forrest's forte was speed. By the night of 27 April, he was at Brown's
Ferry on the Tennessee, and by dawn on 28 April, he had joined forces
with Roddey, who was holding the east bank of Town Creek against a
Union force that was pushing slowly but steadily eastward.[15] But not even
Forrest and Roddey together could stop an infantry division, and during
the day, the Confederates lost their hold on the stream crossings.[16]

About midmorning, while the skirmishing for the crossings over Town
Creek was in full swing, a scout came into Forrest's camp with the news that
a powerful Yankee cavalry force was well south of Tuscumbia and headed
southeast.[17] Forrest assumed that it was simply a foraging expedition and
ignored it. Late that afternoon, however, he learned that the Yankee cavalry
had passed through Mount Hope and was heading east toward Moulton.
This news convinced Forrest that the bluecoats had bigger game in mind
than commissary supplies, but he still had no idea of their final objective.

He was faced with a dilemma: try to keep Dodge from occupying
Decatur, or try to stop what clearly was a major raid. At this moment, like
a gift from the gods, his problem was solved by the sudden withdrawal
of the Union infantry that had just forced its way across Town Creek.
Leaving Roddey to keep pressure on the withdrawing Federal infantry,
Forrest rode south with his horsemen to intercept the Union raiders.[18]

Before long, it became clear that the damned Yankees really were
heading eastward, and Forrest realized that they must be aiming for Bragg's
lifeline, the W&ARR somewhere east of Rome, GA. That had to be prevented at all costs. Forrest caught up with the Yankee raiders at Day's Gap.[19]
Convinced that they were Union cavalry (after all, no one would be so

foolish as to send infantry on a deep-penetration raid), he drove right in, expecting to sweep them away at the first charge. To his dismay, his men rode into sheets of rifle fire that emptied many saddles and sent his men reeling back for the better part of a mile before they could rally.[20]

He caught up again at Hog Mountain and again was punished so badly that he at last realized he was facing infantry.[21] From this point on, the pursuit was pressed more circumspectly, but it nevertheless was pressed. It went on and on, with the men of both Forrest's and Streight's commands so exhausted that many no longer could stay in their saddles. At last, twenty miles west of Rome, Forrest found the raiders deployed in a strong defensive position. By this time, Forrest had only five hundred men with him; the rest had dropped out of the chase through sheer exhaustion.[22] With his men so weary that they were unable to attack, Forrest sent a scout forward to warn the authorities in Rome of the presence of the Yankee raid; but the scout discovered that the townspeople already had removed the planks from the bridge across the Oostanaula River and were preparing defenses to hold Rome against the expected Yankee attack. With this news to buttress him, Forrest demanded that Streight surrender his command;[23] after protracted negotiations, Streight did so.[24]

Bragg and Johnston breathed a sigh of relief; the raid had failed, and the Confederacy had increased its bag of Union prisoners by nearly two thousand. To be sure, Forrest's CAV BDE was so exhausted that it would not be fit for service for at least two weeks, but that seemed a small price to pay for having saved Bragg's vital railroad link with Atlanta.

Bryant and Sooy Smith versus Chalmers: The Raid toward Panola 17 April–24 April 1863

Maps: 2. Northern Sector
      3. The Region between Abbeville and Tupelo

FEDERAL PERSPECTIVE

Hurlbut knew that most of the Confederate troops in northwestern Mississippi were at Coldwater, although the district headquarters were at Panola. He also knew that Chalmers, their leader, thought of himself as a dashing field commander and that he spent most of his time in the field with his "army," leaving his chief of staff to run his headquarters. Hurlbut proposed to take advantage of this situation by attacking the Coldwater position with a column out of Memphis, meanwhile sneaking a force based at La Grange in behind it. If everything went perfectly, the La Grange force would pin Chalmers against the Memphis column. It was possible that the entire Rebel force might be captured. Hurlbut was much too experienced a soldier to expect that to happen, but at worst he expected that his strategic purposes would be served, because Chalmers would be kept too busy to interfere elsewhere.

Furthermore, perhaps the La Grange column could destroy the Mississippi Central Railroad (MCENRR) bridge across the Tallahatchie River just north of Abbeville. That would seriously inhibit the Southerners' ability to use the railroad to build up forces for raids on the M&CRR, and that would be an important fringe benefit. Still further, if the La Grange column rebuilt the railroad, perhaps as far as Holly Springs, the Rebs might be convinced that a major Union offensive was in the making, and that thought might even suck some of Ruggles's troops in from northeastern Mississippi, making it easier for the deep-penetration column to slip through the cordon.

Hurlbut asked MG Jacob Lauman to put BG Sooy Smith, one of his brigade commanders, in charge of the eastern wing of the pincers. On the jump-off date, 17 April, Sooy Smith started south with his men aboard a train, but every mile or so a rail had been removed from the tracks as a precaution against surprise train-borne penetrations. Each break had to be repaired, so the expedition did not reach Holly Springs until the evening of 18 April.[25]

Below Holly Springs, the railroad could not be repaired with the limited resources available, so Sooy Smith and his men continued on foot as far as Waterford. Here Smith was surprised and gratified to learn that the Rebels graciously had achieved one of his missions for him; they had burned the MCENRR bridge over the Tallahatchie River. At Waterford, he turned toward the southwest, and by late the next afternoon, 20 April, he occupied Sardis.[26] He was astride the M&TRR, which connected the Rebel forces along the Coldwater with their base at Panola. They had scarcely seen a Rebel the whole time.

The Memphis arm of Hurlbut's pincers, which left Memphis on the morning of 18 April, consisted of COL George Bryant's INF BDE of Lauman's DIV, supported by some small cavalry formations. The advance guard encountered Confederate pickets at Nonconnah Creek, only four miles south of Memphis, and from then on the gray-clad horsemen launched one savage little attack after another. That night at Hernando, five or six hundred Rebels attacked Bryant's camp with such determination that they broke through the cavalry screen, and Bryant had to use his infantry and artillery to drive them off.

Next morning, the march was resumed amid the crackle of sniper fire from all directions. The Coldwater River, eight miles south of Hernando, was swollen by recent torrential rains, and Rebel resistance was so effective that Bryant dared not attempt a crossing.[27] He managed to get scouts across the stream, and they penetrated a mile or so further south but found no trace of Sooy Smith, who was supposed to be closing from the direction of Senatobia. That was too much for Bryant's already shaky nerves, and he pulled back to a camp two miles south of Hernando. The next day, 20 April, he withdrew to Hernando, so the anvil against which Sooy Smith's hammer was to crack Chalmers's little army had evaporated.[28] The next day, 21 April, still without any knowledge of Sooy Smith's position, Bryant withdrew to Johnson's farm, thirteen miles south of Memphis.[29]

Hurlbut was horrified when he learned of Bryant's action; he had visions of Sooy Smith being trapped and destroyed south of the swollen Coldwater. There were rumors that the Rebel garrison at Fort Pemberton, near Greenwood, was sending reinforcements to Chalmers.[30] If true, that was bad news; those troops would be regulars of the Confederate army and not to be taken lightly. To save his carefully planned scheme from total ruin, Hurlbut sent a two-regiment task force under COL Benjamin Dornblasser to add spine to Bryant. Dornblasser also carried a letter from Hurlbut to Bryant: Sooy Smith is south of the Coldwater, and no excuse for failing to cross the Coldwater and join him will be accepted.[31]

This persuaded Bryant to reoccupy Hernando on 22 April, but that was as far as he got. He threw out scouts as far as the Coldwater, but they found no trace of Sooy Smith, so Bryant concluded that there was no point in going farther and slowly withdrew to Memphis, arriving on 24 April. He brought with him eighty prisoners, two hundred horses and mules, and twelve thousand pounds of bacon. He was especially proud of the bacon.[32]

Meanwhile, Sooy Smith had started north up the M&TRR on the morning of 21 April, destroying bridges and culverts as he went, but every creek was a flooded torrent, and progress was so slow that he had to stop at Senatobia for the night.[33] There was no word from Bryant and, oddly enough, no contact with Rebels. During the night, scouts fanned out in all directions, and at dawn Sooy Smith knew that there was a concentration of

Confederates at Looxahoma, ten miles to the east, and that it was commanded by Chalmers. Since the Southerners obviously had escaped the trap, Sooy Smith's sole concern was how to get safely out of Confederate territory. The first step was to persuade Chalmers's force not even to think of following on his rear while he moved north toward the Coldwater, so he turned menacingly in their direction. The Southerners fell back readily enough, and Sooy Smith followed them as far as Buck Snort, where he suddenly lost contact. It was now late on 22 April, and any hope for a juncture with Bryant was gone. In any event, Chalmers quite evidently had escaped the pincers by fleeing south, so Sooy Smith continued on to Byhalia, spent a quiet and uneventful night, and the next day reached the M&CRR at Collierville.[34] He immediately telegraphed Hurlbut that he was safely out of "Secessia," which greatly relieved the worried corps commander, who had had no word of Sooy Smith's movements since he had passed through Holly Springs four days earlier.

Hurlbut was not distressed by the failure to trap and destroy Chalmers's little army. It didn't matter, because the principal objective, which was to tie up the Confederate forces in northeastern Mississippi, had worked to perfection.

CONFEDERATE PERSPECTIVE

BG Chalmers, in the field with his little army on the morning of 17 April, was thinking of organizing a raid on the M&CRR, but that afternoon his scouts reported that the Yankees in Grand Junction had loaded a lot of troops on a train and started south. He interpreted that to mean that the force was heading for Grenada, where the MCENRR met the M&TRR. Since the Yankees had started out by rail, Chalmers assumed that they intended to repair the railroad all the way to Grenada.[35] Knowing that the railroad had been destroyed between the Tallahatchie River and Holly Springs, he figured that he had plenty of time to prepare a countermove.

On the morning of 18 April, Chalmers's scouts picked up a very strong infantry-artillery-cavalry force moving southward out of Memphis. It seemed to be too strong to be a mere raid, so Chalmers decided to oppose it with his whole strength, meanwhile stopping the Union drive on Grenada by the simple expedient of burning the railroad bridge across the Tallahatchie River three miles north of Abbeville. The MCENRR was, after all, of no use to the Confederates, since it led only to the Union base at Grand Junction. Decision made, he put the Grand Junction force completely out of his mind.

All through 18 April, Chalmers's cavalry struck again and again at the column marching south from Memphis along the line of the M&TRR. By the time the Federals camped for the night at Hernando, Chalmers had enough men on the scene to risk an engagement, so he attacked the Yankees as they were cooking dinner. It was a mistake. The bluecoats left their food uneaten, deployed smoothly, and two hours later Chalmers drew back, leaving thirty dead and wounded on the field and seventy-two men missing.[36] That experience convinced Chalmers that he could not fight infantry in the open field with his cavalry and State Troops, so he fell back behind the Coldwater River, leaving only strong vedettes north of the stream.

By 0900 the next morning, 19 April, the Unionists reached the Coldwater. They made a few halfhearted attempts to cross but were easily discouraged, and about midafternoon the whole force inexplicably withdrew to a campground two miles south of Hernando.[37] Chalmers didn't know quite what to make of such behavior, since it was clear to him that the Federal infantry easily could have forced their way across if they had been serious about doing so.

The next morning, 21 April, Chalmers's scouts north of the Coldwater reported that the Union column had withdrawn to Johnson's farm and that there it had been reinforced by several regiments of infantry and a battery of artillery. Obviously the Northerners were going to continue their offensive to the south, so Chalmers spent the morning strengthening his positions on the southern bank of the Coldwater.

Then, at noon, the roof fell in. A courier from the south told him that a powerful Union taskforce had occupied Sardis the previous night and even now was moving northward up the M&TRR. Chalmers clapped his hand to his head as he remembered the Federal force on the MCENRR south of Holly Springs; the tricky devils had not stayed on the railroad, as he had expected, but instead had marched overland into his rear. He told his unit commanders to get their men out as best they could and to rendezvous at Looxahoma, ten miles east of Senatobia.

By late that evening, much of the little army again had coalesced at the rendezvous.[38] There he learned that the Yankees had occupied Senatobia and that there were blue-clad patrols all over the countryside. Stragglers came in all night long; the next morning, long before he was prepared for action, the Yankee troops at Senatobia moved eastward in his direction. There was nothing to do but withdraw farther to the east before turning southward to escape. The Federals followed as far as Buck Snort, then evidently tired of the game and turned north. Chalmers continued to ride all night, arriving in Panola the next morning, 22 April, with men and animals so exhausted they were unfit for further action.[39] He congratulated himself on escaping the trap, but he had little hope of being able to defeat the huge Yankee task force moving south on the M&TRR.

Then, like an answer to a prayer, a courier arrived with word that the Yankee force, instead of advancing, had turned around and headed back for Memphis. Chalmers breathed a sigh of relief, even though the Yankee behavior made no sense at all.

Grierson: The Deep-Penetration Raid 17 April–3 May 1863

Maps: 2. Northern Sector
        3. The Region between Abbeville and Tupelo
        4. Southern Sector

FEDERAL PERSPECTIVE

The diversion of Dodge and Cornyn to support Rosecrans's raid toward Kingston unfortunately meant that there was little Hurlbut could do to entertain BG Ruggles, who commanded the Rebel forces in northeastern Mississippi. This meant that his deep-penetration raid would have to get through the Rebel cordon by their own efforts. Still, the fact that the raid would go right down the seam between Ruggles's and Chalmers's districts was a significant advantage, because both the Rebel commanders might well assume that dealing with the raid was the other's responsibility.

Grant had heard good things about COL Benjamin Grierson, the music teacher turned horse soldier; and Grant, in a dispatch dated 9 March 1863, suggested Grierson as perhaps the best leader for the deep-penetration raid. That was fine with Hurlbut, so COL Grierson found himself in command of a provisional brigade consisting of two Illinois cavalry regiments (6 IL CAV and 7 IL CAV) plus COL Edward Hatch and his 2 IA CAV, and an artillery battery, with instructions to leave La Grange in the predawn darkness of 17 April. His primary objective was to cut the SRRM somewhere between Meridian and Jackson. En route, he was to cut both the Mobile & Ohio Railroad (M&ORR) and the MCENRR if he could.[40] Hurlbut suggested that he would be able to get out by swinging wide to the east and returning through Alabama, though he very carefully did not specify exactly how this was to be accomplished. As he rode back to his camp, Grierson reflected in wry amusement that nothing in his previous profession had prepared him for anything like this.

Grierson also was pretty certain that he had not been told the whole story. Everybody knew that Grant was in Louisiana opposite Vicksburg, trying to get across the river, so it was fairly obvious that cutting the railroad east of Jackson was supposed to help Grant by interfering with Pemberton's communications with the interior of the Confederacy. In other words, this raid might make the difference between success or failure for Union strategy in the Mississippi Valley, and perhaps for the war as well! It was a daunting but exhilarating prospect.

Grierson knew that Chalmers's Rebel forces in northwestern Mississippi were being entertained by forces commanded by Sooy Smith and Bryant, and that BG Roddey in northwestern Alabama was being kept occupied by Dodge's thrust toward Decatur. He also knew that nothing was being done to divert Confederate BG Ruggles's forces in northeastern Mississippi, so he would have to get past Ruggles all by himself. He thought he knew how it might be done.

He led his 1,700-man PROV CAV BDE out of La Grange just at dawn and rode steadily southward.[41] At Ripley next morning, Grierson sent Hatch and his 2 IA CAV southeastward, as if aimed at the M&ORR at Baldwyn, while he continued on south toward New Albany with his main body. He hoped that the Rebels would believe that Hatch's force was the main effort and rally to oppose it, leaving open a path for himself and the main body.

At 1100 on 18 April, Grierson captured the bridge across the Tallahatchie at New Albany.[42] The next night, 19 April, the raiders camped on Chiwapa Creek, five miles south of Pontotoc. They now were well through the Tallahatchie River frontier, and still no significant Rebel resistance had presented itself. COL Hatch and his Iowans likewise had encountered no resistance and had rejoined the main column during the day.

During the night, Grierson learned that the MCENRR bridge across the Yacona River near Water Valley never had been repaired, and he interpreted that to mean that he could safely ignore Hurlbut's orders to raid that railroad. He found it very hard to understand why there had been no Confederate reaction to his presence as yet, and he assumed he was having a run of unbelievably good luck. If so, it could end at any moment. In an attempt to extend the run with a little deception, the next morning he sent MAJ Hiram Love with 175 men and an artillery piece back to La Grange, marching as obviously and noisily as possible, hoping that the Rebel scouts would interpret the move as evidence that the raid had turned back.[43]

Day after day, Grierson rode south, throwing out patrols and diversions as he went, in continuing attempts to keep the Confederate command confused as to both current location and future objective. On 20 April, Grierson reached Dr. Kilgore's plantation, eleven miles southeast of Houston,[44] where he again detached Hatch, this time to strike at the M&ORR bridges across the Noxubee River, after which he was to return to La Grange. If all went well, Ruggles would follow Hatch, leaving Grierson and the main body to continue unmolested to the south.

The next night, Grierson was four miles southwest of Starkville;[45] the next night, 22 April, he was at the Estes farm, seventeen miles north of Philadelphia. The next morning he seized the Pearl River bridge before it could be burned and marched on, hour after hour, with only the briefest pauses for rest. It was about 0700 on 24 April when he stormed into Newton, on the SRRM. He sent a party eleven miles to the east to burn the bridges across Chunky River, and westward nearly to Lake, burning bridges and culverts, destroying water towers, ripping up track, and rolling up and carrying away the telegraph wires.[46]

Grierson gathered his tired men together about 1400 and marched southeast toward Enterprise, on the M&ORR ten miles south of Meridian.[47] Once out of sight of Newton, however, he turned sharply south and headed for Garlandville, deep in the rolling wooded hills of Central Mississippi. He stopped to rest and to think only 4.5 miles south of Newton.

Meanwhile, after Hatch and his 2 IA CAV separated from Grierson and the main body early on the morning of 21 April, Hatch had continued on to the southeast toward Palo Alto, marching slowly and with no attempt at secrecy. Sure enough, at 1030, two miles northwest of Palo Alto, Hatch's rear guard was fired upon by a force of Confederate cavalry, obviously hot on their trail. Hatch formed a battle line near Palo Alto Church and waited for the Confederates to attack. Hatch was delighted, because every moment that he was able to keep the Rebels diverted was another moment of precious time earned for Grierson and the main body.

About 1300, his scouts informed him that the Rebels had divided their forces, with the main body going on a wide swing obviously intended to get into the rear of the Federals, while leaving a force of State Troops to keep the Unionists locked in place. This was a situation made for Hatch. On his signal, his entire force suddenly charged the State Troops to their front. The Confederate line disintegrated. Hatch broke off and headed north for Cox's Bridge across Chookatonchee Creek.

He and his Iowans penetrated the notorious Chookatonchee swamps without a flaw, and the next afternoon, 22 April, occupied Okolona. They burned the ordnance depot and the barracks of the State Troops;[48] continued on northward, marching at a leisurely pace; and, late on the afternoon of 26 April, arrived safely back at La Grange, TN.[49]

Grierson had captured the Confederate mails in Newton and had learned that large forces were being gathering in North Mississippi to oppose his return to La Grange. That left three possibilities: circle through Alabama, as his orders had proposed; go to Natchez, where the inhabitants were known to be friendly and where he probably could make contact with Union naval forces; or go to Baton Rouge, which was held by a Union garrison. He decided against Alabama, mostly because he didn't think his tired troopers would be able to keep going for the two weeks or more that would be required. For the moment, he would continue on to the southwest and decide later whether to try for Natchez or Baton Rouge.

Grierson left the camp south of Newton about 1830, heading southward, and stopped for the night at the Bender farm, two miles southwest of Montrose.[50] He had not seen a Rebel soldier since leaving Newton. The raiders rode slowly and steadily southwestward for the next two days. The country people were buzzing with rumors that there was going to be a battle near Port Gibson. Details were scanty and confusing, but it seemed to mean that Grant and the Army of the Tennessee were already across the river or were about to make the crossing. If so, then the obvious thing to do was to head for Port Gibson and join the fun.

Decision made, Grierson headed straight west. Late on the night of 26 April, he captured the vital Pearl River ferry east of Georgetown; and late on the afternoon of 27 April, he reached Hazelhurst on the NOJ&GNRR.[51] When he left the town later that same evening, the railroad in both directions was a complete ruin. A mile west of Gallatin, his men captured a Rebel ordnance train carrying a 65-pdr Brooke rifle, a prefabricated gun carriage, and lots of ammunition. When Grierson discovered that the train was heading for Grand Gulf, he realized that meant that Grant was not yet across the river. If he continued on his present course, he likely would run into the Rebel forces who must be gathering to oppose Grant's landing.

There was now nothing to do but to turn southwest toward Natchez. By noon on 28 April, Grierson was two miles northeast of Union Church, on the direct Natchez road. And here, for the first time since leaving Newton, his advance guard was fired on.[52] Grierson instantly attacked. He drove the Rebels through Union Church and stopped for the night in line of battle on a commanding hill three miles west of the hamlet.[53] During the night, Grierson reflected that the Rebels would have plenty of time to assemble strong forces on the Natchez road, and he concluded that Natchez no longer was a viable objective; now it was Baton Rouge or nothing.

Next morning at dawn, Grierson launched a brisk little attack on the Confederates to the west of him with a couple of squadrons, then disengaged and rode rapidly away to the east.[54] At noon, he occupied Brookhaven, burned all the public property, and rode southward along the railroad, burning every bridge, trestle, culvert, and water tower as he went.[55] At noon the next day, 30 April, he entered Summit, discovering to his surprise and delight that the local people were friendly.[56] His men and animals were fed and rested and treated most kindly. The townspeople gave him explicit directions concerning the roads to the southeast, and when he left the town two hours later, they wished him a fervent Godspeed. Grierson and his men camped that night nine miles east of Liberty.[57]

Next morning, Grierson turned south; captured Wall's Bridge across the Tickfaw River after a sharp skirmish;[58] dispersed another Confederate force after a little skirmish on Crittendon's Creek, nine miles south of Wall's Bridge; and, about 1530 on 1 May, crossed to the west bank of the Tickfaw at Edwards's Bridge, two miles east of Greenburg.[59] At close to midnight, Grierson's van captured Williams's Bridge across the deep and unfordable Amite River, the last serious water barrier before Baton Rouge.

At 0500 on the morning of 2 May, the raiders forded Sandy Creek at Burlington's Ferry; captured and burned the camp of Hughes's BN of Partisan Rangers at Greenwell Springs; and finally, at 0800, so tired that neither men nor animals could continue, stopped for food and rest four miles west of Roberts Ford on the Comite River.[60] And here a patrol from MG Christopher Auger's Baton Rouge garrison found them. They were too tired to care very much. But when they rode through the Union lines into Baton Rouge at noon, pride pulled them erect in their saddles.[61] They had ridden 475 miles in sixteen days, put two of the Confederacy's major rail links out of action, and seriously dislocated Confederate military dispositions in Mississippi. For this, the price had been four men killed, sixteen wounded, and seventeen left behind.

Hurlbut, not surprisingly, was pleased.

CONFEDERATE PERSPECTIVE

Ruggles, who commanded the Fifth Military District of Mississippi, was acutely aware of the Union infantry division at Corinth, as well as of the strong Yankee forces at La Grange and Grand Junction, and he kept them under constant surveillance by means of wide-ranging cavalry patrols. Those patrols were a part of LTC Clark Barteau's command, the principal maneuver force of Ruggles's command. That force consisted of two regiments of regular cavalry, one regiment of State Troops cavalry, and two independent battalions of State Troops cavalry. Other detachments were located at various places throughout the district, with especially strong posts at New Albany and King's Bridge to defend the line of the Tallahatchie River, and at Chesterville, six miles west-northwest of Tupelo, where the State Troops had their base and a Camp of Instruction. Barteau's headquarters were at Verona, on the M&ORR, four miles south of Tupelo.[62]

It was no surprise when, early on the morning of 18 April, one of those patrols encountered a powerful Union cavalry force at Molino, eight miles northeast of New Albany. Barteau, in Verona, learned of the contact a couple of hours later and immediately notified LTG John Pemberton, in Jackson, but he did not inform Ruggles, his immediate superior, mostly because he didn't know where he was! Things had been so quiet during early April that Ruggles had left his headquarters at Columbus and gone on a wide-ranging inspection tour of his widely scattered units.[63]

Barteau assumed that the Yankee objective was the Camp of Instruction at Chesterville. He thought that gave him plenty of time, so he waited until about 1000 the next morning, 19 April, before beginning his march toward Chesterville. He arrived about noon, calmly deployed his troops in ambush, and awaited the Yankee's arrival. Finally, at 2200 another scout came in, this one reporting that the Yankees were camped at Pontotoc, eleven miles to the west-southwest![64]

Confidence completely unshaken, Barteau now decided that the Federal objective was the M&ORR at Okolona, and he rode south through the night to get across the Pontotoc–Okolona road. He arrived at a point on the road about eight miles northwest of Okolona about 0830 the next morning, 20 April, but found no sign of Yankees. He had learned from the lesson at Chesterville and this time did not wait in ambush; instead, he rode toward Pontotoc, hoping to surprise the raiders in camp.[65]

At about this same time, on the morning of 20 April, BG Ruggles was returning from his inspection trip. He was fourteen miles from his headquarters at Columbus when he learned, for the first time, that Yankee raiders were at large in his district and that they already had passed through Pontotoc and were headed south. Three hours later, when he arrived at Columbus, he found a message from Pemberton awaiting him: Federal raiders are approaching Pontotoc, and what are you doing about it?[66] It was in this fashion that Ruggles learned that his subordinates were sending messages directly to Pemberton without bothering to send copies to their own commander.

By noon of 20 April, confusion was spreading widely through

Pemberton's command. Everything seemed to be happening at once. He was threatened by three corps of the Army of the Tennessee opposite Vicksburg; there was at least a Union division at Greenville in the Mississippi Delta threatening Yazoo City; there was the constant threat of a Federal thrust up the Yazoo River; there was a powerful infantry force moving southward from Memphis; there was a raid heading south in Central Mississippi. His impression was that the damned Yankees were trying to force him to divert troops from the Vicksburg front to northern Mississippi. At this juncture, Pemberton, in his headquarters at Jackson, received an urgent message from GEN Joseph Johnston, requesting that Pemberton send help to Roddey,[67] who was trying to repulse a Federal offensive that was moving eastward along the south bank of the Tennessee River toward Decatur, AL. To be asked for help for an affair in Bragg's theater of operations was the last straw for John Pemberton. In total frustration, he not only refused, but replied by asking Johnston to send a force toward Abbeville, where the MCENRR crossed the Tallahatchie River.[68]

From this point on, matters only grew worse. Barteau followed the raiders southward from Pontotoc. Since they had not headed for Okolona, as he had expected, their objective could only be the long railroad trestle across Tibbee Creek south of West Point. Thus, when he arrived at Montpelier about 1000 on 21 April, he followed a trail leading eastward, assuming that a second trail leading southward was only a feint. Sure enough, a mile or two west of Palo Alto, he caught up with the Yankee rear guard. Just as he hoped, the bluecoats turned to fight. He circled widely with his 22 TN CAV (regulars, and his only truly reliable troops) to get behind the Yankees and across the road to West Point, leaving his State Troops to keep the Federals entertained. It was a mistake. The moment he was out of sight on his flanking march, the Yankees charged, scattering his State Troops to the winds, and headed northward toward Cox's Bridge and Okolona.

Barteau was disappointed but consoled himself with the fact that the Yankees had been turned back from their objective and obviously were in flight back to their base. He pursued, but not very diligently; got lost in the Chookatonchee Creek swamps near Cox's Bridge;[69] and at last, on the afternoon of 24 April, abandoned the pursuit after the Federal force fell back across Camp Creek, a mile northwest of Birmingham, and burned the bridges behind them.[70] Barteau was not displeased. To be sure, he had not captured the pesky raiders as he had hoped, but at least he had turned them back before they reached their presumed objective, the Tibbee Creek bridges on the M&ORR. His satisfaction lasted until the following day, when he learned that Yankee cavalry had occupied Newton and destroyed the SRRM track for several miles in both directions. Only then did he remember the trail leading south at Montpelier, which he had assumed was a feint covering the force he had elected to pursue.

Meanwhile, about midmorning on 22 April, Pemberton learned that the Yankee raiders had occupied Starkville and were headed south.[71] He assumed the objective to be the long and high M&ORR bridge across the Noxubee River at Macon, and he began shifting troops to protect that point. With no cavalry, he was forced to make do with infantry.[72] That evening, the telegraph brought word of a strong Union cavalry force just west of Macon, which confirmed his view that the Noxubee River bridge was the objective.

About noon on 23 April, Pemberton breathed a sigh of relief when a message from Ruggles arrived, telling him that the raiders were in full retreat. His satisfaction lasted until 0700 the next morning, 24 April, when the telegraph brought him the news that Federal cavalry was in occupation of Newton and was busily at work destroying the SRRM tracks.[73] He could not imagine how they could have reached so far south without being detected. There were no Confederate troop units of any significance between Meridian and Jackson, so Pemberton assumed that the raiders would march westward, destroying the railroad as they went, until, somewhere near Jackson, they would turn south and head for Baton Rouge,[74] which was occupied by a detachment of MG Banks's Union army.

With this in mind, Pemberton hastily organized a force to move eastward along the railroad, hoping that the raiders would blunder into an ambush. At the same time, he telegraphed MG Gardner at Port Hudson to intercept the raiders north of Baton Rouge.[75] Meanwhile he repositioned his own forces north of the SRRM to catch the raiders in the unlikely event that they tried to escape toward the north.

On the morning of 25 April, a Yankee force numbering more than a thousand men was reported at Kosciusko. That seemed to mean that the Federals had split their forces somewhere near Louisville and sent one wing to destroy the SRRM, while the other struck for the large and critical MCENRR bridge across the Big Black River at Way's Bluff. Of the raiders south of the SRRM, there was no word whatever; they seemed to have vanished into thin air. Late that afternoon, however, the telegraph between Jackson and Meridian was restored, and virtually the first message to come over the wire was from "Old Blizzards" Loring, who reported that the Yankee raiders were just west of Enterprise. That made a good deal of sense, because destruction of the M&ORR south of Meridian would disrupt one of the two remaining rail links between Meridian and the East Coast. Pemberton rather hoped the raiders would try that gambit, because Loring was at Enterprise with two regiments of infantry, more than enough to deal with any conceivable number of cavalry. The hope was dashed late that night, 25 April, when Loring wired that the Yankees had evaded his ambush and were now at Garlandville.[76]

By this time, there were Yankees everywhere. BG John Adams reported on the morning of 26 April from Lake that the raiders had six hundred men, that they were fifteen miles to the south, and that they were going to attack either Lake or Forest. Pemberton discounted this report, because there seemed no reason why the raiders would remain inactive so close to the railroad. He was right, because at 1030 the next morning, 27 April, he learned that the bluecoats had crossed the Strong River near Westville and were near the Pearl River at Georgetown.[77]

This was bad news indeed. Far from heading south, they seemed to be heading west, toward Grand Gulf, Big Black Bridge, or Natchez. Pemberton warned both BG John Bowen at Grand Gulf and MG Carter Stevenson at Vicksburg to be on the alert.[78] Even worse, to get to either place, the Federals had to cross the NOJ&GNRR, probably somewhere near Hazelhurst. Unless they could be stopped, that meant yet another ruined railroad and further isolation of the Confederate forces at Jackson and Vicksburg.

Pemberton was now desperate. It was a military truism that the only way to deal with cavalry raiders was to hunt them with cavalry. The only sizable Confederate cavalry commands which consisted of reliable troops—that is, regulars—were Wirt Adams's MS CAV at Grand Gulf and Barteau's two regiments, 22 TN CAV and 2 AL CAV, which by this time had returned to their base at Verona in northern Mississippi. Given that it was worthwhile to hunt the raiders down, Pemberton did the only thing he could: he ordered Bowen to send Wirt Adams eastward to meet the enemy[79] and directed Barteau to move to Hazelhurst. He also wired Johnston that he was stripping North Mississippi of cavalry, which would leave the area dangerously exposed.

Down at Port Hudson, Gardner was trying hard to make certain that the raiders did not slip through to safety at Baton Rouge. He tried to place a blocking force on every major road leading south. By the evening of 28 April, there were forces at Centreville, MS; Woodville, MS; Clinton, LA; and Tangipahoa, LA.[80]

Early on the evening of 27 April, Pemberton's fears were confirmed, when he learned that the Yankee raiders had occupied Hazelhurst and demolished the railroad. The only good thing was that he now knew exactly where they were. He organized a "Killer Group" of mounted infantrymen and sent them south to follow the raiders to the death. The problem was that the Confederates could find horses for only three companies,[81] so the effort was pretty much a forlorn hope from the very beginning.

Late on the afternoon of 28 April, Pemberton learned that Wirt Adams had blocked the raiders three miles west of Union Church. That meant that they could no longer hope to reach Natchez and would have to head south for Baton Rouge, so Gardner began shifting troops toward Woodville and Centreville, to intercept them[82] in the event that they somehow escaped from their predicament.

It was about 1000 the next morning, 29 April, when a message from Bowen told Pemberton that the raiders somehow had managed to disengage from Wirt Adams's cavalrymen and vanish into the hills of southern Mississippi. Adams thought that they were heading for Meadville and Liberty, and set out in pursuit. Early in the afternoon, Pemberton learned the devastating truth; the raiders had turned back to the east and had occupied Brookhaven, shattering a force of five hundred militia in the process. No one knew where they had gone after occupying the town, but the logical course for them to follow would be toward Homeward and Liberty.

Pemberton's mind suddenly was drawn to other matters on the morning of 30 April, when a message from Bowen, written on the morning of 29 April, informed him that Grand Gulf was under heavy attack by the Union ironclad fleet. The message had been long in coming, because the telegraph between Grand Gulf and Vicksburg had failed,[83] and it had taken a courier many hours to get to a telegraph station.

Wirt Adams reached Liberty late on the afternoon of 30 April, where he joined forces with COL Wilbourn, commanding a taskforce consisting primarily of Hughes's MS Partisan BN of Gardner's Third Military District of Louisiana. They expected the raiders to come down the road from Homeward at any moment. During the night, COL Gantt and his 9 TN CAV BN arrived at Liberty, giving the Confederates more than enough strength to deal with a few hundred cavalrymen.

Early the next morning, 1 May, the combined force moved confidently eastward toward Summit, expecting to meet the raiders at any moment. They met nothing at all until they reached the Spurlark plantation, where a courier from COL Richardson, the commander of Pemberton's special "Killer Group," found them. Here they learned the terrible truth: the damned raiders had marched straight south along the railroad, as far as Summit, burning and wrecking as they went. The townspeople in Summit had told Richardson that the raiders had headed for Magnolia and had directed him along a shortcut that they said would get him to Magnolia ahead of the raid. Richardson, now in Magnolia and expecting the raiders momentarily, wanted help in ambushing them. The combined force immediately turned toward Magnolia.

A Confederate patrol arrived at Magnolia about 1400, and it brought discouraging news. Earlier that day, the Yankee raiders had forced a crossing of the Tickfaw River at Wall's Bridge, which was fifteen miles southwest of Magnolia, and they were marching south down a road on the west bank, evidently headed for Edwards's Bridge, near Greensburg. By this time, they surely would be across, and that meant that they already had penetrated the cordon that was supposed to keep them out of Baton Rouge. The only hope was to overtake them, and this the combined force set out to do. But it was all in vain. Late that evening, Wirt Adams was overtaken by a courier with an order from Pemberton: the Federal army is across the river; therefore, abandon pursuit of the raiders and operate on the army's flanks in the vicinity of Port Gibson.[84]

Early the next afternoon, the pursuing force was met by a courier who told them that the raiders had entered the Union perimeter of Baton Rouge about noon. The chase was over. Pemberton reflected ruefully that the raid had been a devastating success; it had ruined long stretches of two of his three vital railroad links and had scattered his forces in Central Mississippi to the four winds. Worse, it had pulled his eyes and ears away from the river; in that interval, the Federal army had leaped the barrier and landed safely on the east bank.

Hatch and Cornyn versus Chalmers: The Supporting Raid 29 April–8 May 1863

Maps: 2. Northern Sector
      3. The Region between Abbeville and Tupelo

FEDERAL PERSPECTIVE

Once Grierson's raiders were well on their way, there was little Hurlbut could do to help. Then, on 28 April, Sooy Smith reported that the countryside was buzzing with stories that the SRRM had been cut at Newton on 24 April, and that the raiders were heading north in an attempt to return to La Grange. Furthermore, there were reports that Rebel BG Chalmers had left Oxford on 26 April with 1,500 men en route to Okolona. Hurlbut had no idea where Grierson and his raiders were; as far as he knew, they might be trying to return to La Grange. If so, then Chalmers's move could be interpreted as an attempt to block the roads leading to the bridges across the Tallahatchie River in the vicinity of New Albany.

Out at La Grange, Sooy Smith saw the pattern just as clearly as Hurlbut and proposed that COL Hatch be sent with a provisional cavalry brigade to break up Chalmers's concentration. Also, he said, the scheme would work much better if Dodge launched his cavalry southward toward Tupelo, where they could join up with Hatch.[85] The combined force would be invincible. Hurlbut instantly agreed with Sooy Smith's plan, but he reminded Smith that Dodge's cavalry currently was involved in an offensive into Alabama and would not be available until 1 May at the earliest.[86] Hatch left La Grange in the predawn darkness of 29 April with a provisional cavalry brigade of 1,300 men and a four-gun battery of 10-pdr guns. He marched steadily but slowly all that day, scouts spread widely in all directions, and camped for the night one mile south of Ripley.[87] There had been no opposition, but Hatch felt certain that his march had not gone unobserved.

Early next morning, Hatch knew that Chalmers was at New Albany, that Chalmers already knew of the Yankee raid, and that he intended to hold the Tallahatchie River bridges in that area.[88] That was fine with Hatch; he sent a detachment forward to amuse the bridge guards, while he circled through Lee's Mills with his main body. The small Rebel detachment at Lee's Mills was overwhelmed, but when he got to New Albany, he discovered that Chalmers had withdrawn to the north bank of the Tallahatchie and had burned the two New Albany bridges behind him.[89]

Hatch now was faced with a dilemma. His orders were to break up Chalmers's concentration, but it was pretty clear that he could chase the Rebels forever without achieving that laudable goal. After meditating for some hours, Hatch decided that his real objective was to get Grierson safely out of "Secessia," and the scheme most likely to work was to drive southward hoping for a junction. If Chalmers followed, so much the better.

The weather was terrible. The creeks all were flooded from intermittent heavy rains, and the roads were quagmires through which it was difficult even for horses to move. Hatch slogged southeast toward Tupelo, occupied and burned the Camp of Instruction operated for Mississippi State Troops at Chesterville, and at nightfall camped in sodden fields two miles south of Tupelo, next to the tracks of the M&ORR. The force hadn't seen a

Rebel soldier all day long. Neither had they seen or heard from Union COL Cornyn, who was supposed to join forces with Hatch at Tupelo.

The next day, 2 May, the Federal raiders marched slowly southward along the M&ORR tracks as far as Chiwapa Creek. Hatch looked across the angry yellow waters and decided not to cross, lest he be trapped on the southern bank. After all, Confederate BG Ruggles was down there somewhere, and by this time he undoubtedly was alert and waiting. Hatch turned northwest, marched up the low ridge of comparatively dry ground between Chiwapa and Coonewah creeks, and camped for the night near the hamlet of Coonewah, eight miles east of Pontotoc.[90] An hour later, it began to rain in torrents. There had been no sign of Confederates.

Next morning the roads were in such terrible shape that Hatch decided to remain in camp rather than attempt to haul his artillery through the belly-deep mud. Early in the evening, one of his scouts reported that Chalmers had recrossed the Tallahatchie River at Rocky Ford and was in camp near La Fayette Springs, twenty-four miles to the west. It was a long way to march through such abominable weather, but it was the opportunity Hatch had been waiting for. His men were on the road within the hour, but he had covered only a couple of miles when another of his scouts came in with bad news. Chalmers suddenly had withdrawn from La Fayette Springs and was moving in the direction of Oxford.

Hatch realized immediately that, while he had not seen any Confederate scouts, they had seen him, and that Chalmers was deliberately avoiding contact. He promptly gave up the hopeless chase and camped about six miles east of Pontotoc.

The next morning, 3 May, the roads were beginning to dry a bit, and Hatch had his horsemen in their saddles bright and early, marching for La Grange by the shortest route. He was not molested in any way. That night, 3 May, an hour after Hatch went into camp, a mud-spattered and dog-tired Union courier found him with a message from Hurlbut: Grierson had arrived safe and sound at Baton Rouge on the previous day, 2 May![91] Hatch rode safely into the La Grange perimeter late on the afternoon of 5 May.

Meanwhile, COL Cornyn and his cavalry brigade had reached Burnsville, MS, on 1 May,[92] where he was handed Hurlbut's order to move south to Tupelo, where he would join Hatch. Cornyn's men and horses were tired after fifteen days of campaigning in North Alabama, so Cornyn gave them a day of rest before starting south. Even so, his men were in the saddle at dawn on 3 May. At noon the column passed through Jacinto, late in the afternoon rode through Booneville on the M&ORR, and well after dark stopped for the night at Baldwyn, seventeen miles north of Tupelo. Unbeknownst to Cornyn, Hatch at this time was camped six miles east of Pontotoc and was on his way home.

Next morning, 4 May, Cornyn's advance hit Confederate pickets at Guntown. The Rebels were not strong enough to be more than an inconvenience, but the streams all were in flood, so Cornyn could not get into Tupelo.[93] There was no word of Hatch.

On the morning of 5 May, Cornyn moved slowly southward, paralleling the east bank of Oldtown Creek; stormed Reece's Bridge; and met stiff resistance on the west bank. Cornyn figured that the Rebels were trying to prevent him from joining Hatch, who must be in Tupelo as per the plan. A little pressure on the Rebel line revealed that it was very short, so Cornyn entertained the Confederates with a skirmish line, while he took the main body and looped to the right. Within a few minutes, he was across the Verona–Tupelo road, between Tupelo and the force that had tried to defend Reece's Bridge. He called in his skirmishers and rode into Tupelo, only to find the town vacant of troops, Union or Confederate. He soon discovered that no Yankees had been through the town, so he had no idea what had happened to Hatch.

Cornyn had learned some lessons about cavalry warfare while in Alabama, and one thing he had learned was the value of wide-ranging patrols. While he was thinking over his next move, one of his patrols came in to report that a strong Rebel cavalry force was marching rapidly up the Verona–Harrisburg road. Cornyn calmly emplaced his artillery overlooking King's Creek, an inconsiderable stream one mile west of Tupelo, and placed his men in ambush on the east bank. A few minutes later, the Rebels carelessly rode into the trap. They broke under the unexpected fire; thirty minutes later, some were fleeing toward Chesterville, and the remainder were in flight toward Harrisburg and Verona.[94]

Cornyn now realized that the planned juncture with Hatch had gone glimmering. He withdrew into Tupelo and then marched north toward home. He rode all night, very slowly and methodically, as if daring the Rebels to interfere. They did not, and on 8 May his troopers rode safely into the Corinth lines.[95]

Hurlbut was more than satisfied. Although Grierson had not needed assistance, the raids had kept every Rebel cavalryman in North Mississippi fully occupied, and that meant that none had been available to assist Pemberton in the south, at a time when that gentleman desperately needed horsemen. After all, Grant and the Army of the Tennessee were ashore and loose in the interior of Mississippi. Without cavalry, Pemberton would be half-blind.

CONFEDERATE PERSPECTIVE

BG Chalmers had arrived at Panola on the morning of 23 April after an all-night ride. Many of his men were still scattered through the woods and fields of northwestern Mississippi after their narrow escape from the trap sprung by Union BG Sooy Smith. Small parties were still coming in the next morning, when he was handed a telegram from Pemberton, informing him that Federal cavalry raiders had cut the SRRM at Newton and directing him to take all his available men and move immediately to a position suitable for intercepting the raiders, should they attempt to return to Tennessee.

Tired and disorganized as his men were, Chalmers nevertheless managed, by the evening of 26 April, to get them into position at Pontotoc, which stood at the center of a web of roads commanding all the country between the M&ORR and the MCENRR. Then, on the afternoon of 29 April, a scout reported that a powerful Yankee cavalry column under the command of COL Hatch, a notably competent Federal cavalryman, had left La Grange that morning, heading south. To Chalmers, that meant that the Federals were sending a force to join with the returning raiders. If the two were permitted to join forces, they certainly would be too strong to handle. He had to prevent a juncture.

After informing Pemberton (but not Ruggles, who was responsible for the defense of the eastern half of northern Mississippi), Chalmers moved every man he could muster to New Albany,[96] where he positioned them all on the north bank of the Tallahatchie, to prevent the force moving south from La Grange from crossing the stream. In Jackson, Pemberton was near despair. Another major raid from the north would so dilute his cavalry resources that the enemy would be free to roam more or less at will through Mississippi. He sent a desperate wire to President Davis, pleading for more horsemen.

Alas for Chalmers's hopes. About midmorning, a large Union force overwhelmed the crossing guards at Lee's Mills, five miles upstream from New Albany, and drove on New Albany. Chalmers could not move his men back across the New Albany bridges rapidly enough to construct a defensive position on the south bank, so there was nothing he could do but burn the Tallahatchie River bridges behind him. For good measure, he also burned King's Bridge, six miles downstream.

This meant, of course, that the Yankee forces now were free to combine, unless Chalmers could pull a rabbit out of the hat. After some thought, he decided that the only constructive thing he could do was to launch a counterraid into western Tennessee, hoping that it would draw Hatch's force into a pursuit.[97] If that could be done, perhaps Ruggles and Barteau would be able to intercept the Yankee raiders who were coming up from the south. However, the rains of the last several days had so ruined the roads that not even cavalry could operate freely, and moving artillery was hopeless. By nightfall, Chalmers had given up the notion of raiding Tennessee; the roads simply would not support rapid movement.

Pemberton's appeal to Davis was answered when Davis wired GEN Joseph Johnston in Tullahoma, pointing out that, unless Pemberton had more cavalry, he would not be able to prevent the Federal cavalry raids.[98] Johnston had overall command of all Confederate forces between the Appalachian Mountains and the Mississippi River, and thus both Bragg in Tennessee and Pemberton in Mississippi presumably were under his orders. Johnston had a ready reply: Forrest and Roddey were fully occupied in coping with a Union offensive into northeastern Alabama that clearly was intended to sever the W&ARR, and no other cavalry forces could be spared from Bragg's army. Johnston then went on to ask why Chalmers could not join with Barteau to prevent the raids.[99] This was a not-so-subtle slap at Pemberton, because it implied that Pemberton had the necessary resources but was not using them properly.

Ruggles at last learned, on the evening of 1 May, of the Hatch raid.[100] His instant response was to ask Pemberton for help. Pemberton, having nothing to send him, refused. He also sent a message to Johnston, pointing out the obvious: if the raids were not prevented, the Yankees had the power to cripple the railroad system.[101]

Ruggles's second response was to lend what aid he could to Chalmers. By this time, he knew that the Yankee raiders who had cut the SRRM at Newton were heading for Baton Rouge, but he made no move to inform Chalmers of that important fact. However, the news meant that he was free to use his men against the new raids coming down from the north. He alerted Barteau, who was at Tupelo, and on 1 May Ruggles moved from Columbus, MS, to Okolona to take personal command.[102] Late that night, one of Ruggles's scouts reported a strong Yankee force at Camargo, eight miles to the northeast of Okolona and on the far side of flooded Oldtown Creek. On the assumption that the Yankees were striking at either Okolona or Aberdeen, he moved his forces out a mile northeast of Okolona and deployed them to await the Yankee attack.

Meanwhile, late on the night of 1 May, a mud-spattered scout informed Chalmers, who was at New Albany, that Hatch and his bluecoats had destroyed the Mississippi State Troops' Camp of Instruction at Chesterville and were camped south of Tupelo on the M&ORR. This no longer looked like an attempt to link up with the raiders from the south, but instead looked like a conventional raid to destroy Confederate resources and communications. Since the Federals were near Tupelo, which was LTC Barteau's territory, surely Barteau was in action against them. If he (Chalmers) could engineer a junction with Barteau, the two Confederate forces together might be able seriously to discomfit the Yankee column.

Early next morning, 2 May, Chalmers marched downstream to Rocky Ford, crossed to the south bank of the Tallahatchie River, and by nightfall was camped at La Fayette Springs. He intended to move eastward the next morning, onto the rear of Hatch's column, which Chalmers assumed would continue to move southward along the railroad.

On this same day, near noon, Ruggles learned that there had been no Yankees at Camargo after all. Late that night came the news that a large Federal cavalry force had been sighted about midday on the northern bank of Chiwapa Creek, only seven miles to the north. Early the next morning, 3 May, Ruggles began moving slowly northward for a confrontation.[103] When he reached the southern bank of Chiwapa Creek, he learned that the Yankees were camped at Coonewah, and that Chalmers was at La Fayette Springs and moving eastward in expectation of joining with Barteau's troops. The Yankees had destroyed the telegraph between Tupelo and Okolona, so there was no word from Barteau, who presumably was at Tupelo and, Ruggles hoped, operating on the Yankee rear.

Ruggles was not enthusiastic about crossing flooded Chiwapa Creek and attacking the Federal raiders; he sent a message to Pemberton citing his inferior numbers. What he needed was a junction with both Barteau and Chalmers. However, because the Yankees were between Chalmers and himself, Chalmers would have to detour to the south to effect a meeting. The thing to do was to move north to Verona, where he presumably could make contact with Barteau, and there await the arrival of Chalmers. He camped that night, high and dry, two miles south of Vernon.

Unfortunately for Ruggles's hopes, early that afternoon Chalmers had learned that Hatch had turned west and was near Coonewah. At this point, the last thing that Chalmers wanted was a head-on battle, so he withdrew toward Oxford, meanwhile sending a courier to Ruggles. The courier reached Ruggles early the next morning, 4 May, at his camp south of Verona. At the same time, one of his own scouts reported that the Yankees were moving north, obviously returning to Tennessee. It was just as well, because, that same morning, a messenger from Barteau had arrived with the news that yet another Yankee cavalry column was at Guntown, thirteen miles north of Tupelo, and moving south.[104]

Barteau was not seriously concerned about a direct attack upon Tupelo, because Oldtown Creek was in flood, but he thought that the Yankees might try to cross at Reece's Bridge, a few miles south of the town. He sent CPT Mann's BN to destroy the bridge,[105] but before they could manage it, they were submerged by a flood of Union horsemen.[106] Mann was forced back to Verona, but the Yankees kept shifting to the left, and before long Mann's line faced north, leaving the Yankees between him and Tupelo. In this situation, he was joined by Barteau's main body, which had ridden a circuitous route and thus avoided the Federals. A few minutes later, LTC Cunningham and his 2 AL CAV also arrived.[107]

Cunningham saw the situation as an opportunity to wipe out the pesky Yankees. He left Mann to hold the Yankees in position, while he took the main body toward Tupelo via Harrisburg. This would put him squarely on the rear of the Yankees facing Mann. As he crossed King's Creek one mile west of Tupelo, the woods and fence lines to his flanks and front erupted in flame, and a battery concealed on the hill east of the creek raked his ranks with canister. His column disintegrated in chaos. Barteau's men fled westward to Harrisburg, and Cunningham, with only eight companies of his 2 AL CAV, escaped toward Chesterville;[108] the remainder of his troops fled south toward Verona.[109] Late that evening, cautious scouts probing toward Tupelo discovered that the Yankees were gone, heading north toward Baldwyn.

Ruggles was unaware of the debacle, and at 0200 the next morning, 6 May, he led his strategic reserve out of Okolona toward Verona. At 0500, Barteau began moving slowly and carefully toward Harrisburg, where Ruggles overtook him a couple of hours later. Ruggles had had enough; he terminated the "pursuit" and sent everyone back to camp to recuperate.

11

Demonstration at Drumgould's Bluff 28 April–1 May 1863

Map: 9. Northeastern Louisiana

FEDERAL PERSPECTIVE

Sherman's timing was almost perfect. After reading Grant's letter of 27 April, which suggested a distracting demonstration against the Confederate fortifications on the Yazoo above Vicksburg,[1] he and CDR Breese, who commanded the naval squadron above Vicksburg, had scraped together a fleet of ten transports by the morning of 29 April. That same morning, the little flotilla picked up Sherman, Blair, and ten of Blair's best regiments at Young's Point and, about noon, headed up the Yazoo River, convoyed by the ironclads *Choctaw* and *De Kalb;* the "timberclad" gunboat *Tyler;* tinclads *Linden, Signal, Romeo,* and *Petrel;* and huge *Black Hawk,* flagship of the fleet. They took along three mortar scows, each carrying a huge 13-in siege mortar.[2] The mortars weren't very accurate, but they threw 220-pound shells. Sherman hoped that the Rebels would think that a force that employed such heavy guns was intent on serious business.

By 1630, the convoy had anchored near the mouth of Chickasaw Bayou, within sight but just out of range of the Confederate heavy guns mounted at the base of Drumgould's Bluff.[3] Considering that Grant, with the main army below Vicksburg, had only six operational transports with him, Sherman figured that a fleet of ten transports and eight fighting ships was bound to attract attention.

A little careful reconnaissance revealed that there were three principal strongpoints along the line of bluffs. The northern fort was at the base of Haynes's Bluff; the middle fort was just above the mouth of Skillikalia Bayou, at the foot of Snyder's Bluff; and the southernmost earthwork mounting heavy guns was near the top of Drumgould's Bluff. There were riflepits and field-gun emplacements all along the base of the bluffs from Snyder's Bluff to south of Drumgould's Bluff. To call the Rebel works formidable was something of an understatement.

CDR Breese was a cautious man who, above all else, wanted to avoid a repeat of the incident the previous year when a Rebel mine had sunk the ironclad *Cairo* in these very waters. It was a problem, because the Yazoo River was so narrow that it gave him very little room to maneuver. The next morning, 30 April, he sent *Petrel* downstream to anchor in the mouth of Old River, so that the Rebels could not enter the Yazoo and plant the devilish devices behind the fleet.[4] He was worried about giant *Choctaw*, because her 260-foot length made it very difficult to turn her around in the narrow stream without running aground. Fortunately, while the height of the spring flood had passed, the water remained deep enough to make it possible, if only barely.

The fleet moved forward at about 0900. *Choctaw* and *De Kalb* anchored near Anthony's Ferry and immediately opened a deliberate fire on the earthworks protecting the Confederate heavy guns at the base of Drumgould's Bluff.[5] Being far more vulnerable to fire, *Tyler* and *Black Hawk* anchored farther downstream and opened fire on the Rebel field-gun emplacements near the base of Drumgould's Bluff. Still farther downstream, the mortar vessels moored next to the bank and opened fire on the Rebel earthworks.[6]

About midafternoon, the troop transports moved up to Blake's lower plantation and unloaded Blair's regiments. The infantry immediately began to push inland toward the bluffs but were opposed by a strong Confederate skirmish line. The water in the backswamps between the Yazoo channel and the base of the bluffs mostly had drained away, but the ground was still so soft that movement was difficult. As soon as the Federal advance reached within easy range of the Confederate artillery, the Rebels opened fire and quickly brought the advance to a stop. Blair and Sherman began to withdraw the infantry almost immediately, and by 2000 all the troops were back aboard their transports.[7] Meanwhile, the ironclads had spent the afternoon intermittently shelling the Confederate works, without noticeable effect.

Far to the south, the main body of the Army of the Tennessee was ashore at Bruinsburg and marching inland, but Sherman, Blair, and Breese knew nothing of that.

Early the next morning, 1 May, Blair landed a regiment on the west bank of the Yazoo and probed upstream until the infantrymen were turned back by fire from the big guns in the Snyder's Bluff work. Another two regiments were put ashore at Blake's lower plantation. They probed cautiously toward Drumgould's Bluff, as if searching for practicable routes through the partially flooded lowlands along Chickasaw Bayou.[8]

At 0800, a dispatch boat came hurrying upstream to deliver a letter from Grant. Written on 30 April, it told Sherman of Porter's defeat at Grand Gulf on the previous day but went on to recount how the fleet had run the batteries that same night. The army was moving still farther south down the Louisiana shore, the missive reported.[9] Grant was confident of getting ashore in Mississippi and ordered Sherman to bring two of his divisions immediately to Mrs. Perkins's plantation, but to leave the third at Young's Point and Milliken's Bend to protect and maintain the roads to Richmond. Of course, Sherman realized that he could not possibly move two of his divisions south in time to be of any assistance in the river crossing. The only aid he could extend would be to try to keep the Rebels from sending reinforcements south to oppose the Federal landing.

The fortifications were much too strong to assault with infantry, but perhaps the navy could make life a bit difficult for the Rebels. Breese accommodatingly took *Choctaw, De Kalb, Tyler,* and *Black Hawk* back upstream at about 1500 and opened a sustained and savage bombardment of the earthwork at Drumgould's Bluff.[10] After an hour, the fort was silenced. The Federal gunboats then shifted fire to the field-gun emplacements and riflepits. The bombardment went on and on until nightfall, with the Confederates unable to reply with anything more potent than small arms.

The infantry were called back to their transports, and about 2000 the fleet dropped back down the Yazoo. The troops were ashore and asleep at Young's Point by midnight.[11]

CONFEDERATE PERSPECTIVE

BG Louis Hébert, who commanded the Confederate fortifications at Snyder's and Drumgould's bluffs, was informed of the presence of a large Union fleet in the Yazoo River near 1700 on 29 April. He hastily alerted his men and, as a precaution, manned the riflepits and forts along the foot of Drumgould's Bluff.[12] When the fleet anchored off the mouth of

Chickasaw Bayou, Hébert was able to count ten transports carrying infantry of Sherman's corps, two ironclads, six other gunboats, and three mortar scows. There were enough vessels to carry a division of infantry and enough firepower to give his heavy artillery a real challenge. He immediately notified Carter Stevenson in Vicksburg that there was a large fleet in the Yazoo threatening Snyder's and Drumgould's bluffs but that no attack had yet developed.

Hébert's message was one of Stevenson's nightmares come true; here was one arm of the long-awaited direct assault on the defenses of Vicksburg. He promptly notified Pemberton of the fleet, told him that it undoubtedly was the prelude to a major attack, and then reminded Pemberton that he had just sent two of his best brigades, Baldwin's and Tracy's, to Grand Gulf. He also alerted MG Forney to move his division into the defense complex at Snyder's and Drumgould's bluffs.

At dawn on 30 April, Forney moved COL Ashbel Smith's 2 TX INF into the riflepits at Snyder's Bluff,[13] sent the 3 LA INF forward into the floodplain toward Blake's lower plantation to oppose any Yankee probe toward the bluffs,[14] and occupied Redwood plantation, which stood on a strategic location on the bank of the Yazoo River near the mouth of Skillikalia Bayou, with a strong infantry force.

It was close to 1000 when the Federal gunboats inched upstream and opened fire on the earthworks on Drumgould's Bluff and the mouth of Skillikalia Bayou. Hébert returned the fire, concentrating on the huge ironclad *Choctaw*.[15] He could see the shells hit her armor and glance off in showers of sparks, but she suffered no perceptible damage. After an hour, for no obvious reason, the gunboats withdrew downstream out of range, but the transports pulled into shore at Blake's lower plantation and began unloading troops. Before long, large numbers of blue-clad infantrymen began moving eastward toward the base of Drumgould's Bluff. They gradually pushed 3 LA INF back, but when they came within easy range of the big guns in the earthworks on Drumgould's Bluff, Hébert opened fire, and the advance stopped as if it had run into a wall. Soon the Yankee infantry withdrew to the safety of the ships.[16]

Without the fire of the gunboats to interfere, Hébert put parties to work on his parapets to repair the damage done by the morning's bombardment.[17] To everyone's surprise, it was minor.

That evening, Forney reported to Carter Stevenson that the attack had been very weak and almost certainly was nothing more than a mere demonstration.[18] Stevenson was unconvinced. He thought it likely that the Federal actions had been a reconnaissance in force, and that tomorrow would see a determined assault on Drumgould's Bluff.

Sure enough, early next morning the Yankees were astir. There were infantry probes up both banks of the Yazoo early in the morning.[19] They were turned back by gunfire from the forts, but that meant nothing, because reconnaissance forces would not engage in a fight if it could be avoided. Then, about midafternoon, the two ironclads and two other large gunboats moved up and opened a devastating fire on the fortifications of Drumgould's Bluff. The heavy guns on Drumgould's were silenced in an hour, and the rest of the earthworks subjected to a terrible mauling. Forney and Hébert withdrew their men to safety behind the bluffs, so few lives were lost, but the earthworks were pounded into ruins; not an artillery piece could fire in return.[20] Even so, Hébert and Forney noticed that the infantry stayed well back and in fact, late that afternoon, returned to the transports. So the whole affair was a feint, intended to draw attention away from some kind of action elsewhere. If only they knew what and where!

12

Battle of Grand Gulf
29 April 1863

Maps: 9. Northeastern Louisiana
      10. The Region between Vicksburg, Bruinsburg, and Raymond

FEDERAL PERSPECTIVE

By nightfall of 28 April, Grant concluded that he had adequate forces on hand, or within ready supporting distance, to make a landing on the Mississippi shore. Virtually all of McClernand's XIII Corps was concentrated at Hard Times. Osterhaus's and Hovey's men were still aboard the transports and barges anchored offshore and were getting mighty tired and restless from their confinement. Carr's DIV and Landram's BDE of A. J. Smith's DIV were encamped at Hard Times, and Burbridge's BDE of A. J. Smith's DIV was on barges at Mrs. Perkins's plantation. McPherson's XVII Corps was fast closing up, and much of it was within a day's march of Hard Times or Mrs. Perkins's plantation, where steamboats easily could pick them up and carry them to any bridgehead which McClernand's corps might establish. Far upstream, Tuttle's DIV of Sherman's XV Corps had finished the new road along the Duckport Canal and built a bridge across Walnut Bayou near Oak Grove, thus providing a second road connecting Milliken's Bend with the Richmond Road. This addition would help to speed Grant's divisions southward when the time came.

    Grant also knew that red-bearded Sherman was about to launch a demonstration against Snyder's Bluff; given the known sensitivity of the Confederates to threats of attack from the Delta, that was bound to confuse the defenders for at least a few hours. With luck, it would persuade

Carter Stevenson to hold all his field forces in Vicksburg until the Army of the Tennessee was safely ashore in Mississippi.

Even though Grant was optimistic about his chances of effecting a landing at Grand Gulf, the possibility existed that it would prove too tough a nut for the navy to crack. As a hedge, he ordered his cavalry to scout the Louisiana shore to the south as far as St. Joseph, not only to determine the nature of the land, but also to see if any solid information could be picked up about conditions on the eastern shore. Regardless of the state of readiness of the army, at this moment the entire game was in the hands of the navy. If the Army of the Tennessee were to be put ashore at Grand Gulf, Porter's ironclads first must suppress the Confederate heavy artillery.

Porter had looked very carefully at the fortifications and realized that the task definitely was not trivial.[1] There were two major forts, one nestled just above water level right on the bank under Point-of-Rock and the other about 1,500 yards farther downstream, on a low terrace about 200 yards back from the river bank. He knew that both works mounted big guns, but he knew neither calibers nor numbers of pieces. Only one gun, a rifled 32-pdr, actually had fired on his ironclads, but he knew that there were many more.

At 0700 on 29 April, the ironclad fleet moved slowly out of its anchorage off Hard Times and headed downstream to try the Grand Gulf forts. LT William Hoel, commanding *Pittsburg,* had been a river pilot before the war and knew the river like no one else in the fleet, so Porter had given him the honor of leading the battle line.[2] Behind *Pittsburg* came *Louisville, Carondelet,* and *Mound City.* They opened fire on the fort beneath Point-of-Rock as they came within range, but it did not deign to reply until 0815, when the ironclads were close enough to offer the Rebel gunners a reasonable chance of hitting a moving target. The Confederate fire was rapid but not particularly accurate, and Hoel's four-ship squadron slid past without damage and took up position opposite the lower fort, with bows upstream. The City Series ironclads were steady as rocks when pointed upstream, and from the stable gun platforms thus afforded, they sent broadside after broadside into the earthen parapets of the lower fort.[3]

The remaining three ironclads, under Porter's personal command, formed a group some distance behind Hoel's squadron. *Benton* and *Tuscumbia* took up a position in midstream directly west of the upper fort, but huge *Lafayette* steamed northward and took up a position in the Grand Gulf northwest of the earthwork, from whence she could partially enfilade it with her 100-pdr Parrott rifles.[4]

Well behind the warships, the transport fleet dropped downstream, but they stayed just out of range of the guns in the Rebel forts. Grant, in little *Ivy,* moved in closer to observe the effects of the bombardment. In the army transports and barges, the infantrymen listened as the cannonade went on and on, with no sign whatever that the fire from the forts was slackening.[5] The thought of attempting a landing in the face of those guns was enough to shrivel the most dauntless heart.

By 1000, however, Porter's experienced ear could tell that the fire from the lower fort was growing ragged and slow, and he signaled *Lafayette* to go down and help Hoel administer the finishing touches. With the guns of *Lafayette* added to those of the four City Series gunboats, the fire of the lower fort gradually dwindled. The last shot was fired about noon.[6]

The upper fort was a different matter entirely. At about 1010, a heavy shell smashed through the armor of *Benton's* pilothouse, shattering her steering gear and wounding the pilot. The flagship sheered wildly out of control and ran aground right under the parapet of the upper fort. At this point, *Benton's* crew members discovered, to their amazement and delight, that the fort's parapets were so thick that the guns could not be depressed enough to hit them. They calmly effected repairs and then backed out into the river to resume action.[7]

Benton was not the only Union vessel hit hard. The Rebel gunners seemed to concentrate on *Tuscumbia.* She had a weird design; her port engine drove a paddlewheel, and her starboard engine drove twin screws. Neither engine alone could push her at more than about four knots. About 1230, a Rebel shell penetrated her casemate and shattered her port engine. Unable to maintain her place against the current, she was forced to drop down below the forts, where her crew managed to get close enough to the Louisiana shore so that she could be anchored.

By 1250, Porter realized that his ammunition was beginning to run low. He went back to talk to Grant, and they agreed that it was madness to even think about trying to land troops in the face of the still-active guns of the upper fort. The riflepits and field-artillery positions between the upper and lower forts, as well as on the hills above the ruined town, were not damaged at all, if for no reason other than that the ships had been forced to concentrate exclusively on the two forts.

Unable to force a landing at Grand Gulf, Grant had only two options remaining. He could give up and march back to his bases opposite Vicksburg; or he could march his men farther south through Louisiana and seek an unopposed landing somewhere below Grand Gulf.[8] At 1315, he signaled the transport fleet to go back to Hard Times and unload the troops. At the same time, Porter signaled his ironclads to break off their action, and by 1430 everything that would float, except for *Tuscumbia*, was back at the Hard Times anchorage.

Later that afternoon, Porter noticed that repair parties were swarming over the works, so he sent the virtually invulnerable *Lafayette* down to discourage them. The huge ironclad anchored out in the middle of the Grand Gulf, the baylike expansion of the river northwest of Point-of-Rock, and planted a 100-pdr shell in the works every five minutes, regular as a metronome, until 2000. The Confederates replied just often enough to make it clear that they were alert.[9]

When Porter added up the damage late that afternoon, he found that the defeat had cost him dear. The fleet had eighteen dead and fifty-seven wounded. *Benton* had been hit forty-seven times and pierced repeatedly; *Pittsburg* had been hit thirty-five times; and *Tuscumbia* had been hit eighty-one times, her casemates were in ruins, and one of her engines was almost beyond repair.[10] Oddly enough, the other vessels had hardly been touched. It was clear to Porter that the Rebels had concentrated on only three ships, and their choices were interesting: *Benton* was the flagship, *Pittsburg* was the leader of the lower squadron, and *Tuscumbia* was the weak sister.

Porter had learned a lesson that undoubtedly was good for his soul: he could run his armored warships past any array of guns on the planet, but battering a strong and modern earthwork into submission was a different breed of cat entirely. This one could claw even after the Federal fleet had spent five and a half hours and seventy-five casualties.

While Porter's ironclad squadron had been dueling with the Grand Gulf batteries, McPherson's XVII Corps had been marching southward in support. Logan's DIV trudged into Hard Times about 1600 to discover, to their consternation, that Porter had been fought to a standstill. With the roads and campgrounds around Hard Times crowded with McClernand's men, McPherson could go no further, and he told Logan to camp his men where they were, strung out along the Lake St. Joseph Road. They slept the sleep of exhaustion, scarcely disturbed by the thunderous cannonade as the fleet ran the Grand Gulf batteries that night.

CONFEDERATE PERSPECTIVE

From his aerie on Point-of-Rock, BG John Bowen had noted the arrival of the Federal ironclad squadron at Hard Times and watched with steadily deepening unease the growing concentration of blue-clad infantry in the open areas around the plantation town. By 26 April, Bowen was absolutely certain that the main body of the Yankee army was being marshaled in Louisiana opposite Grand Gulf and that he was its target. He was frustrated to the point of fury by his inability to convince Pemberton of that fact. Then, on 27 April came an order from Pemberton: call in Wirt Adams's cavalry and send them toward Brookhaven to intercept and destroy a Federal cavalry raid that was operating in that area. It was the final blow. Without cavalry, Bowen would have no eyes and ears south of Grand Gulf, which meant that the Yankees could cross anywhere below his position without either opposition or detection. Pemberton was either mad or traitorous to order such an action. To be sure, Yankee cavalry loose in the middle of Mississippi was serious, but an unopposed landing by the Army of the Tennessee might be deadly. Nevertheless, like a good soldier, he passed the word on to Wirt Adams; and a few hours later, Adams was busy concentrating his men in preparation for a move toward Union Church.

Since Bowen's arrival in Grand Gulf in mid-March, he had had his men working like the proverbial beavers, so that, by 29 April, when the Union blow finally fell, he had managed to carve out a defensive complex of great strength. It was organized around two main positions, Fort Wade and Fort Cobun. Fort Cobun was dug into the base of Point-of-Rock and commanded the swirling waters of the Grand Gulf, which extended north and west in a broad sheet from the very base of the precipitous hill. This fort mounted two 32-pdr rifles (the shells actually weighed about 58 pounds), one 8-in Dahlgren shell gun, and a 30-pdr Parrott rifle, all firing through narrow embrasures in a massive parapet forty feet thick and some forty feet above the water level. If Cobun had weaknesses, they were the limited traverses afforded the guns by the extremely small embrasures, and the impossibility of bringing the guns to bear on the river close to the base of the bluff.

The second strongpoint, Fort Wade, was located about 1,500 yards below Fort Cobun. At this point, the river bank was about 200 yards from the base of the bluff. Fort Wade was located at the base of the bluff, on a narrow terrace about 20 feet above the ruined town. It mounted one 100-pdr Blakely rifle, two 32-pdr rifles, and an 8-in Dahlgren shell gun, all mounted behind parapets similar to those of Fort Cobun.

A double line of riflepits running along the base of the bluffs connected the two forts, and another line of riflepits, with earthworks for several field artillery batteries, crowned the hills above the town.[11] Bowen also had a wooden tower atop Point-of-Rock, from which he could look far and wide across the floodplain to the west. Hard Times was only five miles away and was readily visible.

Bowen was more than a little worried about the possibility that the Federals would send a tinclad or two up the navigable Big Black River, the mouth of which entered the Grand Gulf about 2,300 yards northeast of Fort Cobun. Many of Bowen's commissary supplies came down that river, and a Union tinclad in the river would be a real inconvenience. To guard against such an eventuality, Bowen had a barrier raft constructed at the foot of Winkler's Bluff, just upstream from the mouth, and guarded it with a battalion of infantry and two 12-pdr field guns. Bowen harbored no illusion that the light guns would be effective against a tinclad, but he thought they might discourage a landing party put ashore to cut the raft loose.

Since Bowen had detached six pieces of field artillery to McKay's Ferry and the barrier raft at the mouth of the Big Black River, he was left with only five field pieces to deploy for the defense of Grand Gulf itself. As a result, not all the field-gun battery positions in the Grand Gulf defenses could be occupied at any one time.

Grand Gulf also had a vulnerable southern flank. Bayou Pierre discharged into the Mississippi about eight miles below Grand Gulf, and it was navigable for small steamboats during periods of high water. This meant that the Union could send a transport or two upstream at least as far as the base of the bluffs. The only practical landing point was opposite Coon Island Lake, where a dilapidated little ferry carried traffic on the Bruinsburg–Grand Gulf road (it was scarcely more than a track along the base of the bluffs) across the stream. On 28 April, when Bowen saw the huge concentration forming at Hard Times, he recalled the 1 MO CAV (DSMTD) from Thompson's Bluff and sent them to guard the Coon Island Ferry landing place. He had no more field guns to send, so the Missourians went without artillery support.

On the morning of 29 April, Bowen, from his lookout on Point-of-Rock, saw the Union ironclad squadron, followed by a fleet of transports and barges, leave the anchorage at Hard Times and head downstream toward Grand Gulf. He immediately sent the infantry of his little army, which consisted primarily of COL Francis Cockrell's and BG Martin E. Green's brigades, behind the line of bluffs, where they would be safe from the artillery storm that he knew was coming.[12] The commanders of forts Wade and Cobun were alerted and told to open fire at their discretion.

Bowen also tried to send a telegram to Vicksburg, informing Carter Stevenson of the impending attack, only to discover that the wire no longer worked. Bowen knew only too well that a major Union cavalry raid was in progress somewhere in the interior to the east of him, and visions of blue-clad horsemen roaming the countryside between Grand Gulf and

Vicksburg danced through his head. A few hours later, it turned out that the break was just a normal malfunction, and he breathed a heart-felt sigh of relief. Oddly enough, he did not send a courier, probably because he assumed that, by the time a courier got to Vicksburg and aid marched back, the issue would have been decided long since.[13]

The Rebel gunners watched as the black ironclads separated into two squadrons. The first group, which consisted of four City Series gunboats, slid downstream past Fort Cobun, dealing out a few quick broadsides as they passed; and for a few minutes Bowen thought they were intent only on running past the Grand Gulf batteries. But then, directly in front of Fort Wade, they rounded to and, with bows upstream, began a deliberate and intense bombardment of the earthwork. The Confederate guns instantly replied, concentrating their fire on the squadron leader. Shells were observed to hit her again and again, but most glanced off her seemingly impenetrable armor.

To the almost immediate dismay of the Confederate defenders, the earthwork was proving far from invulnerable. The big shells from the naval artillery drove deep into the fresh soil, exploded, and threw immense masses of earth over everything. Soon the guns could no longer be brought back into battery, and even the firing mechanisms and the bores of the guns became clogged with earth. The fire grew increasingly ragged; by 1000, both the 32-pdr rifles in Fort Wade had been dismounted, and the remaining two guns could be fired only by dint of great effort. Sometime during the morning, a shell splinter struck and killed COL William Wade, who had understood artillery as no other man in the Grand Gulf garrison. About 1030, huge *Lafayette,* which had been pounding Fort Cobun from a position out in the Grand Gulf, came sliding ominously down the river and took position off Fort Wade. Her enormous 100-pdr shells, added to those of the four gunboats already pounding the parapets into ruin, were too much, and by noon Fort Wade no longer could fire a gun. Other than the dismounted 32-pdrs, the guns were not really damaged; they were only so covered with earth that they could not be served.

Fort Cobun was faring much better. The immensely thick parapets protected the guns from direct damage, and the walls were just high enough so that all the Yankee shells that hit the fort struck directly into the face, where they did but little damage. Those that failed to hit went shrieking over the top of the parapet to bury themselves harmlessly in the steep face of the bluff behind the fort. The other side of the coin was that the fort's shells seemed to be scarcely more effective against the ironclads. The embrasures were so narrow that it was hard to keep the guns trained on the restlessly moving vessels. However, a bit after 1000, *Benton* suddenly went out of control and grounded under the parapet. To the immense frustration of the garrison, the guns could not be depressed enough to hit her, even though the gunners could clearly hear the shouts of the Yankee sailors as they made repairs. Soon the big ironclad backed off and resumed firing, as if nothing had happened.

Tuscumbia's reputation had reached even into the Confederate service, and the gunners in Fort Cobun concentrated on her, in an attempt to sink her. By late morning, she was clearly in trouble; she dropped out of place and drifted downstream to an anchorage well out of gun range.[14] However, the rest of the ironclad fleet was made of sterner stuff and resisted all efforts made by the Confederates until about 1315, when the ships suddenly ceased firing and withdrew upstream to their previous anchorage off Hard Times.

The men in the ranks were euphoric at the thought that they had defeated the terrible ironclads, but Bowen knew better. He remembered that Harrison had been driven back to St. Joseph. He knew, too, that there was nothing to prevent the Yankee army from marching overland to the south, and that the ironclads and transports could run past his batteries virtually at will. After all, the boats had easily survived five and a half hours of the best the batteries could deal out, while running past them would take only a few minutes.

Still, Bowen would do what he could. He put his men to work repairing the parapets and getting the guns of Fort Wade back into action. About midafternoon, the Yankees noticed the activities and sent the invulnerable giant, *Lafayette*, down to interfere. She stood out in the Grand Gulf and threw a 100-pdr shell into the works every five minutes or so, which made it virtually impossible to effect any extensive repairs on the exteriors of the parapets.[15]

By late afternoon, the telegraph to Vicksburg had been repaired, and Bowen sent a message to Pemberton, informing him of the days' events and asking for cartridge bags and shells for his big guns.[16] As soon as Pemberton got the news, he sent a peremptory wire to Carter Stevenson: "Hurry forward reinforcements to Bowen to-night."[17] Only then did Stevenson order Tracy's and Baldwin's brigades to hit the road for Grand Gulf.

When Bowen added up the damage late that afternoon, he found it remarkably light: three men killed and eighteen wounded.[18] He had won a famous victory. But he knew that it was a shadow victory, since the Yankees remained entirely free to move where and when they willed.

13

Landing at Bruinsburg
30 April 1863

Maps: 9. Northeastern Louisiana
  10. The Region between Vicksburg, Bruinsburg, and Raymond
  28. Disposition of Forces in Northeastern Louisiana: 30 April
    1863

FEDERAL PERSPECTIVE

During the afternoon of 29 April, after the unsuccessful attempt by Porter's ironclad squadron to suppress the forts at Grand Gulf, the transport fleet returned to Hard Times and immediately began debarking troops. To no one's great surprise, McClernand's corps was assembled in some haste and marched off directly southward across the base of Coffee Point, along a line of march that was barely out of range of the Confederate big guns in the Grand Gulf forts. By evening, the advanced elements had reached Disharoon's plantation, three airline miles south of Hard Times. The plantation occupied an especially high natural levee, almost all of which was under cultivation, so there were cleared fields and lots of nice dry ground to camp on. There was also a good solid bank, almost like a wharf, where steamboats could tie up. Both Grant and McClernand arrived about sundown.

At this point, neither Grant nor McClernand had a clear idea of either the road network or the nature of the terrain on the east bank. The maps available to the Union commanders were few and poor, but such as they were, they indicated that Rodney, which was known to have a good steamboat landing, was the nearest practical landing point on the eastern shore.

It was connected to Port Gibson by a good road, and Port Gibson was a sort of regional communications center, from which major roads fanned out in all directions, including to Vicksburg and into the rear of Grand Gulf. That was important, because control of Grand Gulf would have to be the first objective after the beachhead itself was secured.

Once the fleet of transports required to ferry the army from the Louisiana to the Mississippi shore was concentrated below Grand Gulf, it was clear that the Rebel batteries would prevent them from returning upstream. Thus, failure to secure Grand Gulf would mean that supplies would have to be brought south by wagon all the way from Milliken's Bend to Disharoon's, a nearly impossible task. Thus, the only practical course of action was to seize Grand Gulf as soon as possible, so that it could be used as the main supply depot on Mississippi soil. With the Army of the Tennessee in control of Grand Gulf, the transport fleet would have freedom to move anywhere on the river south of Vicksburg, which meant that supplies could be picked up at Mrs. Perkins's and delivered directly to the bank at Grand Gulf. This would so simplify the logistical problem that the remaining difficulties could be accepted with some equanimity.

Rodney, then, was the logical place to effect a landing. But first, of course, Porter had to run his ships past the Grand Gulf batteries. Grant need not have been concerned. At 1945 that evening, 29 April, the fleet, transports as well as ironclads, cast off from the Hard Times landing and headed purposefully downriver, flagship *Benton* in the lead. *Lafayette* joined the squadron as it swept by her station in the Grand Gulf. This time the ships paused only briefly in front of the forts, dealing out rapid broadsides as their batteries bore first upon Fort Cobun and then upon Fort Wade. The forts struck back savagely but harmlessly.[1] Covered by the fire of the gunboats, the transports slipped past by hugging the Louisiana shore. Once the transports were out of range, the gunboats slowly followed. The transports were unscathed; the gunboats had a few more dents in their armor. The whole fleet tied up at Disharoon's plantation landing, where they were welcomed enthusiastically by the advance elements of McClernand's corps.

Late that night, an "intelligent contraband" was brought to Grant's tent. He told the stolid general some very interesting things. First, there were no Confederate troops on the Mississippi shore south of the mouth of Bayou Pierre, and even the cavalry that normally kept the shoreline under observation had been withdrawn to hunt for Yankee raiders in the interior of Mississippi. This was intriguing information, because it implied that Grierson and his horse-soldiers must have achieved their objective of cutting the

Southern Railroad of Mississippi somewhere east of Jackson. Second, there was a good road leading inland from the plantation settlement of Bruinsburg to Windsor plantation, where it joined the main Rodney–Port Gibson Road. Third, Bruinsburg had a good, solid bank with enough space for a lot of steamboats. And fourth, Bruinsburg was only five miles downstream. That was important, because it meant that the transports would need only an hour to make a shuttle trip. By contrast, Rodney, which was nearly eleven miles downstream, would require three hours at least. Grant instantly made up his mind: the landing would be at Bruinsburg.[2]

Now virtually certain that his landing would be unopposed, Grant immediately decided to commit his entire strength to the effort. To Sherman, who was masterminding a demonstration in the Yazoo River against the Snyder's Bluff defense complex, went a message: immediately send two divisions of your XV Corps to Mrs. Perkins's plantation as fast as they can march, and deploy the third to protect and maintain the absolutely vital roads connecting Young's Point, Milliken's Bend, and Richmond.[3]

Unlike the movement of supplies, communications both upstream and downstream were easy, because the navy communicated by semaphore, which would operate wherever a line of sight could be obtained. Thus, strategically located semaphore teams, stationed either on the banks or aboard naval craft, could get a message between Grant and Sherman within an hour or two, even though they were thirty airline miles apart and even farther as the river ran.

April 30 dawned clear and hot on the tents of McClernand's corps in the fields around Disharoon's plantation. Through the pale light of early morning, the soldiers could see dark bluffs rise menacingly beyond the river. In the Mississippi, seeming to float in the airy morning mists rather than the brown waters of the river, lay the battered ships of RADM Porter's squadron. The transports and barges had gaping holes where Vicksburg's shells had torn through; the ironclads were stained and dented from much hard usage and few repairs. The fighting men filed aboard transports, barges, and gunboats alike in thoughtful silence, until the vessels lay low in the water, crowded to the gunwales with blue-clad soldiery.[4] The only horses taken aboard were skeleton teams for the artillery. Not even Grant's horse was loaded. Even the ambulance wagons were left behind; every available inch was devoted to the fighting men.

At 0800, the fleet cast off and chuffed slowly downstream. The men were nervous and subdued, each thinking of the slaughter to come if those huge bluffs to the east held a Rebel army. It took but little imagination to visualize what would happen aboard the packed transports if artillery shells came crashing into the press of bodies. Standing beside Porter in the pilothouse of mighty *Benton,* Grant noticed the tension and signaled to the ship's band.[5] It took the startled soldiers only a moment to understand that the general was telling them, with the ringing notes of "The Red, White, and Blue," that there was no reason for secrecy or silence and that there was nothing to fear. A tremendous wave of cheering swept the fleet, and the strained spirits of the men rose giddily.[6] Grant and Porter glanced at each other in complete understanding; such trickery sometimes was necessary to keep the soldiers' morale in order. For the commanders, the deadly worry continued, since there was no way to know what lay behind that forbidding line of hills to the east.

Opposite the little cluster of buildings at Bruinsburg, the fleet swung slowly into shore. *Benton* grounded first, and over her capacious bow poured LT Thomas A. Howes and the infantrymen of Companies A, B, and C of the 46 IN, proud to be the first to reach the soil of rebellious Mississippi. They were followed seconds later by the 24 IN. It was about 0930. The skirmish lines formed like magic and raced inland, to find that the sole witness was a farmer who seemed too confused to flee. They sent him back under guard to *Benton,* on the odd chance that he might be a Rebel spy, but instead he turned out to be one of Grant's scouts. Within moments, Grant knew that there were no Rebels anywhere in the vicinity and that a complex of roads led inland from Windsor, the stately plantation home of the Daniels family, which stood on the bluff only 350 yards from where the Bruinsburg Road joined a road to Rodney.[7]

Of course, Grant was not content to wait inside his skirmish lines without attempting to acquire information about what awaited him on the bluffs to the east, so he sent out small infantry patrols. They probed cautiously northeastward up the Rodney Road toward Port Gibson, and southward toward Bethel Church. There were no traces of Rebel forces.

By noon, almost all McClernand's 17,000 men were ashore, and the picket line had been pushed to the base of the bluff, about a mile to the east. Grant moved among his troops with continuous admonitions to hurry; until the tops of those great bluffs hanging over their heads had been secured, there was no safety for anyone. Near noon, just as he was about to give the order to march, his aplomb was shattered by the discovery that McClernand and his division commanders had forgotten to issue rations to their men. Because it obviously would be impossible to land them with the combat troops, the wagons had been left at Disharoon's plantation. In circumstances such that the combat troops had to operate away from the trains, it was standard procedure to issue the men three days' rations. It probably never occurred to Grant that a corps commander could overlook so elementary a bit of housekeeping. But McClernand and his division commanders *had* overlooked it, and four desperately needed hours had to be taken while rations of hardtack and salted meat were collected and ferried across the river to the waiting troops.[8]

The moment the ration boxes were ashore, Grant ordered the march inland to begin, so the grumbling soldiers had to carry the unopened boxes on their shoulders as they started up the long hill toward Windsor.[9] Carr's DIV led the way, followed by Osterhaus, Hovey, and A. J. Smith. By the time the van reached the top of the hill, bands were playing, and the men were singing.[10] Almost everybody except the artillery was on foot. BG A. J. Smith, in defiance of Grant's specific orders, somehow had managed to squeeze two horses onto the transports. When he discovered that even the army commander was walking, he sent one of them to Grant.[11] Grant accepted the gift, even though he must have wondered how A. J. Smith had come by it. As the afternoon wore on, other officers found mounts by the simple expedient of "requisitioning" them from the countryside. Carr's animal turned out to be a big white mule, but riding it was better than walking.

Now that petty housekeeping details like rations for his men had been taken care of, McClernand was in a tearing hurry. In the shade of the twenty-two immense Corinthian columns of Windsor, McClernand told Grant that it was important to surprise the enemy and if possible prevent him from destroying the bridges across the Bayou Pierre. McClernand proposed to push on in a night march.[12] Nobody reminded him of the four hours lost at Bruinsburg.

When the march resumed after a brief rest at the top of the hill, the soldiers were surprised and disappointed to discover that the direction of march was south rather than north. Rumors that the army was going to help MG Nathaniel Banks swept the marching columns, and spirits sank at the prospect of the endless days of marching required to get to Port Hudson. After about an hour's march, an officer standing in the middle of the road silently directed the head of the column into an eastward-leading road which turned off the main north-south highway just beyond little white Bethel Church. Spirits rose, because everyone knew that Port Gibson lay somewhere to the east. The soldiers nodded wisely to each other: wily old Sam Grant simply had moved inland to give himself maneuvering room in the event that the Rebels contested the advance.

Once the force had scaled the bluff at Windsor, the road had proven to be quite flat, but the terrain was a tactician's nightmare. The roads followed the crests of sinuous ridges which only here and there widened into flat-topped plateaus large enough to be cleared and farmed. More commonly, the ridges were so narrow that there was barely space for the road on top. The ridge sides were astonishing; in many places they were so steep that they could not be climbed without using both hands and feet, and in some places they were nearly vertical. Often the ravines were more than 100 feet deep, and their sides were covered with timber and impenetrable tangles of grapevines, greenbrier, honeysuckle, cat's-claw, and poison ivy. The bottoms of the larger ravines were even worse, if that were possible. They were flat, boggy, and, in those places not covered by the usual tangle of trees and vines, filled with canebrakes so dense that a man could not see a companion ten feet away. The whole landscape formed a maze in which it was impossible to keep a sense of direction.[13]

The skirmish line that led the way found it almost impossible to retain cohesion as it struggled through the nightmarish terrain, so halts were frequent as the army felt its way forward. It was getting dark by the time the Federal van started down the long hill leading to James Creek, about 1.5 miles northeast of Bethel Church. At this point, Carr decided that the skirmish line was impractical. He called it in and replaced it with a sixteen-man patrol, which he instructed simply to follow the road until fired upon.[14]

While McClernand's corps seized the Bruinsburg bridgehead and marched eastward toward Port Gibson, McPherson's XVII Corps marched steadily southward in support. Logan's DIV had started early from Hard Times, and that afternoon both J. E. Smith's and J. D. Stevenson's BDEs of Logan's DIV had arrived at Disharoon's plantation, been picked up by the shuttling transports, and carried across to the Mississippi shore. Because of the delay caused by the rations fiasco in McClernand's corps, Logan's two brigades were able simply to fall in at the rear of McClernand's column.[15]

All that night, the busy transports shuttled back and forth between Bruinsburg and Disharoon's, moving the artillery, horses, wagons, and mountains of supplies to the eastern bank. About 0300 on 1 May, *Moderator* collided with *Horizon,* and fragile *Horizon* sank, carrying with her the guns, horses, and equipment of BTRY G, 2 IL ARTY.[16] The loss of *Horizon* and the damage to *Moderator* seriously disrupted the Federal timetable; as a result, E. S. Dennis's BDE of Logan's DIV did not cross until midmorning.[17] Nevertheless, the Federals had succeeded in landing 22,000 men in Mississippi in twenty-four hours—the greatest amphibious operation in American history up to that time. The record was not broken until the American landings in North Africa in 1942.

It was near midnight when the patrol climbed the long slope leading out of the deep valley of Widow's Creek.[18] The men had been expecting opposition all night long and were moving slowly and carefully. The moon had set, and the blackness was so complete that often it was hard to see the road. Shortly after they reached the top of the ridge, they could hear confusing, muted noises coming from their front. While the sounds did not seem to be those which a military unit would make, the men in the advance patrol nevertheless grew exceedingly edgy as they continued eastward along the road.

Meanwhile, Grant had stayed behind in the bridgehead for some time. The overwhelming importance of getting as large a force of battle-worthy infantry ashore as quickly as possible had dictated that no supply train of any kind would be taken across the river until every fighting man had been brought across. Nevertheless, Grant knew full well that the army could not exist for any length of time without a supply train, because a single brief engagement would exhaust the supply of ammunition that could be carried by the individual soldiers. While he did not care much for the implications, he nevertheless ordered his men to seize everything with wheels or four legs from the surrounding farms and plantations. The blue-clad soldiers took him at his word, and soon a military train unlike anything previously seen wound along the roads from Bruinsburg. It consisted of horses, mules, oxen, farm wagons, ladies' carriages, two-wheeled donkey carts—anything and everything that could carry a few pounds.[19] And every vehicle was loaded to capacity with ammunition and stores from the mountains of supplies that the shuttling transports were dumping helter-skelter on the shore at Bruinsburg.

Despite everything, the landing had gone well, and Grant had an army on the Mississippi shore. His first priority now was to gain control of enough territory to make maneuver possible; he dared not allow himself to be locked into a restricted bridgehead.

On 30 April, while McClernand's XIII Corps of the Army of the Tennessee was crossing the river and establishing itself on the Mississippi shore, and McPherson's XVII Corps was moving rapidly down the roads toward Hard Times, the bulk of Sherman's XV Corps lay waiting at Young's Point. All, that is, except the ten regiments of Blair's DIV who were aboard a fleet of transports in the Yazoo River, pretending that they were preparing to make an attack on the Snyder's Bluff defense complex north of Vicksburg.

CONFEDERATE PERSPECTIVE

Bowen watched the Union fleet run by his batteries on the night of 29 April with a feeling of bitter helplessness. From his ringside seat in the riflepits on the crest of the bluff behind the fortress, he could see the transports race past without a light showing, hugging the Louisiana shore, while the ironclads savagely shelled the batteries to cover their passage. There was no question that the Yankees could land a strong force on the Mississippi shore somewhere to the south. If only he knew where! With Wirt Adams's horsemen gone into the interior to hunt Federal raiders, there remained no screening force whatever along the river bank. Nevertheless, he could not do without intelligence, so he mounted a few of his infantrymen and sent them to scout the area west and south of Port Gibson.

Having sent out his scouts, Bowen's next impulse was to take every man of the Grand Gulf garrison and march south to find and oppose them. After a moment's thought, however, he realized that he dared not, because he was not absolutely certain that sending the ships south was not a feint; if he sent his whole garrison south on the assumption that the main body of the Yankee army was with them, Grant might simply return with his armored gunboats and make a direct assault on the fortress with troops left at Hard Times.[20] He would not possibly be able to march his troops back in time. Those damnable steamboats gave the Federals a mobility that he could not match.

If the movement of the fleet was not a feint, then the most likely place for the Yankee landing was Rodney, where there was a good steamboat landing and good roads fanning out into the interior. Bowen laid his plans accordingly. He would divide his garrison, sending one brigade south to act as a delaying force, while keeping the second in Grand Gulf to guard against surprise. He knew that two more Confederate brigades were on the road from Vicksburg; if they arrived in time, it still might be possible to hold the Yankees to a bridgehead south of Port Gibson. He was very confident that, once ashore, the first Yankee objective would be Port Gibson and Grand Gulf, because he could visualize the enormous supply difficulties that the Yankees must be having. After all, they had to carry their supplies overland from Milliken's Bend to some point on the river, such as New Carthage, then put them on steamboats as far as Hard Times, and then offload them and put them on wagons as far as Disharoon's plantation, and then put them back on steamboats once again to get them to the Mississippi shore. It was perfectly clear to Bowen that they could not tolerate that for long, so they would try to force the Confederates out of Grand Gulf, because using Grand Gulf as a supply depot would reduce their logistics problem to a tolerable level.

This reasoning dictated a march against Port Gibson via the Rodney–Port Gibson road, so, at about 0100 on 30 April, Bowen ordered BG Martin L. Green to march his brigade at once to Port Gibson, and to occupy a position across that road at a suitable place west of the town.[21] He dared not send them farther south, because to do so would place them beyond ready supporting distance of the Grand Gulf garrison. He told Green that he soon would be reinforced by the 6 MS and the Pettus Flying ARTY. It took Green awhile to get organized, so it was about 0700 when he marched off, and about 1030 when he arrived at the junction of the Bruinsburg and Rodney roads, about a mile west of Port Gibson. At that point he was met by some excited farmers who told him that Yankees were coming up both the Rodney and the Bruinsburg roads. Since he did not have the strength to block both roads (his brigade numbered perhaps 900 men), he decided to deploy just east of the road junction, while he sent patrols forward to reconnoiter both roads as far as Widow's Creek. Despite the farmer's reports, he still believed that the main thrust would come up the Rodney Road, so he decided on a strong position near Magnolia Church, where a commanding ridge crossed the Rodney Road about 800 yards east of Shaifer's farm. Later that morning, the 6 MS and the Pettus Flying ARTY arrived, just as Bowen had promised.[22] They brought Green's strength up to perhaps 1,200 men. The Mississippians and artillerymen were feeling great; the ladies of Port Gibson had treated them to a sumptuous breakfast as they passed through the town.

That afternoon, 30 April, about 1600, Tracy's AL BDE and the Botetourt ARTY from Vicksburg arrived at Ingleside, four miles east of Grand Gulf. The Alabamans had left Warrenton at 1900 the previous night and marched all night and all day; they were utterly jaded. They had no provisions, and they had left stragglers all along the road between Ingleside and Hankinson's Ferry. Bowen's staff managed to find food for them, and Bowen told them to cook, eat, rest, and wait for their stragglers to rejoin. When Tracy felt his men could resume the march, he was to go directly to Port Gibson and report to Green.[23]

Late in the afternoon, one of Bowen's scouts arrived in a state of near-exhaustion and reported that he had seen a Yankee force of about 3,000 men turning eastward on the Rodney Road at Bethel Church. That was what Bowen needed to know. He mounted up and rode down to Port Gibson, where he arrived at Green's headquarters near the road junction at 1900. He told Green that Tracy's powerful brigade of about 1,500 men was nearby and soon would be joining up. He also passed on the information about the Yankee force at Bethel Church, which implied that the Federals were concentrated on the Rodney Road. This in turn meant that they would not have to split their forces between the two roads. Together the two rode out to inspect the position Green had selected near Magnolia Church. Bowen approved, and he directed Green to bring his whole brigade forward, leaving no more than three companies as a roadblock on the Bruinsburg Road.[24]

Despite everything, Bowen still was not quite certain that the Yankee force on the Rodney Road was the only effort. He well knew the tendency of scouts to exaggerate, so the 3,000 men that had been reported at Bethel Church might well be no more than a brigade making a demonstration or a reconnaissance in force. The real blow still might fall on Grand Gulf, and, if so, that was where he belonged. By about 2000, he was satisfied that he had done all he could, and he left for his fortress on the river.

Within minutes of Bowen's departure, one of Green's scouts reported that there was a major Union force advancing up the Bruinsburg Road.[25] He was very positive about it. Fortunately, at almost the same time, Tracy's van came down the road from Port Gibson. Green breathed a sigh of relief and sent Tracy and his big Alabama brigade out to take a position on the Bruinsburg Road near Andrews' farm, while he took his own brigade out to occupy the position previously selected near Magnolia Church.[26]

By this time, it was nearly 2200. While Green did not believe that the Yankees would march through unfamiliar countryside during the night, he was not one to take chances. He sent a small patrol out about 300 yards in advance of his position, telling its members to stay alert. The patrol moved westward through the inky night and found a position in the northern corner of the Shaifer's kitchen garden, where the men had an unobstructed view of the road for 200 yards or so.[27]

Bowen arrived back in Grand Gulf at about 2230, to be met by excited staff officers who told him that there were four Federal gunboats probing up Bayou Pierre. Bowen didn't have time to check the reports, but he was certain they could not be ironclads, because the water was far too shallow. Still, there was no reason why they could not be tinclads, although how the Yankees had gotten them into the Mississippi below Vicksburg was pretty mysterious. Bowen really had no choice. Shallow-draft gunboats could penetrate Bayou Pierre nearly as far as Port Gibson, and if they managed to knock out the railroad and highway bridges on the Port Gibson–Grand Gulf roads, then Green's and Tracy's BDEs were as good as lost.[28] He instantly detached 1 MO from Cockrell's BDE and sent it, accompanied by Wade's MO ARTY, to reinforce the infantry force he already had posted at the Coon Island Ferry. Wade's guns, four 10-pdr Parrott rifles, were the only ones that stood a chance against gunboats. The reinforcement raised the Coon Island Ferry force to about 700 men, big enough to create a problem for the Yankees if they tried to make a landing.[29]

The rest of Cockrell's BDE, which consisted of three regiments of Missouri infantry and two batteries of artillery, was placed on alert on the hills east of Grand Gulf, ready to march for Port Gibson on a moment's notice.

Nearly sixty miles to the northeast, at Jackson, Pemberton had organized a small taskforce under the command of BG Lloyd Tilghman and sent it by rail from Jackson to Big Black Bridge, where it arrived late on the afternoon of 29 April.[30] Pemberton also had sent orders to his detachments at Grenada, Columbus, and Meridian, instructing them to concentrate at Jackson. He realized that the center of action had shifted away from Jackson, and on the afternoon of 30 April he moved to Vicksburg to take personal command of the Army of Vicksburg.[31]

Far to the north of Grand Gulf, Baldwin's BDE had left the northern end of the Vicksburg defenses at 2100 on the evening of 29 April. The men had marched all night and had arrived and gone into camp on the southern bank of the Big Black at Hankinson's Ferry at 1300 on 30 April. Stevenson had informed Bowen by telegraph, so one of Bowen's couriers had found Baldwin at Hankinson's Ferry around 2030 that night, with orders to join Green west of Port Gibson as fast as he could march. Baldwin was on the road within minutes and, shortly after midnight, finally stopped for much-needed rest in the fields just north of Grindstone Ford,[32] seven miles east-northeast of Port Gibson on the main Port Gibson–Vicksburg road.

MG Carter Stevenson, Confederate commander in Vicksburg, had released Baldwin's and Tracy's BDEs much against his will. He was convinced that the Union fleet of gunboats and transports anchored off Chickasaw Bayou in the Yazoo River below Snyder's Bluff was the prelude to an assault on the defenses of his northern flank. He told Pemberton as much, in a long dispatch sent after Baldwin's BDE had marched out of its camps at the north end of the city.[33]

14

Battle of Port Gibson
1 May 1863

Maps: 10. The Region between Vicksburg, Bruinsburg, and Raymond
     11. The Battlefield of Port Gibson
  29–32. The Battle of Port Gibson

FEDERAL PERSPECTIVE

It was just past midnight, 1 May 1863, and the sixteen-man patrol leading the advance of the Army of the Tennessee suddenly realized that the top of the ridge broadened into an open field, and that odd sounds were coming from the velvety darkness in front of them. Puzzled, the patrol grew very cautious indeed. Then, when they were halfway across the open area, a rifle shot rang out from the edge of the woods beyond the clearing. Almost reflexively, the Federal infantrymen fired a volley in the general direction of the trees and dove for cover. A spattering of fire came back, making it clear that at last they had made contact with the Rebels. COL W. M. Stone, who commanded the lead brigade of Carr's DIV, pulled in his patrol and deployed a skirmish line which pushed slowly forward.[1] A little pressure, and the Confederate picket yielded slowly, then vanished.

When the Union advance encountered no more resistance, Stone assumed that the Confederates had been members of a patrol well in advance of the Rebel position and confidently ordered his skirmishers forward. They passed the Shaifer house, which was dark and silent, then the Magnolia Church, which they could see silhouetted against the sky on their right. As they approached the next ridge (Foster Ridge), a fierce volley lashed out from no more than 50 yards in front of them.[2] It was too dark for marksmanship, so no one was hurt, but the Federals recoiled and, fearing an ambush, pulled back to the Shaifer house, leaving Magnolia Church Ridge unoccupied.[3]

As the lead regiments of Stone's BDE of Carr's DIV arrived at the scene, a skirmish line was formed and pushed out, but it was too dark to see anything. Fearing a trap, the Unionists did not attempt to press hard. They brought up the six guns of the 1 IA BTRY, which dueled fiercely with four Rebel guns emplaced beside the road on a ridge about 350 yards east of the Magnolia Church Ridge. The Southerners proved to be very good at firing at muzzle flashes, and the Federal artillery began to lose both men and horses, so, like the infantry, they withdrew to the ridges near the Shaifer house.[4] By 0300, the firing had tapered off into virtual silence. Carr tried to get a picture of the terrain, but the ravines were so confusing, and the darkness so intense, that finally he gave up and waited for daylight.

Dawn revealed to the Federal commanders an almost surreal landscape. It was a maze of ridges, each more or less flat-topped and of equal height, but varying in width from a few yards to a hundred or so. The ridges ran in all directions, and each was separated from its neighbor by a steep-sided ravine filled with an unbelievable tangle of trees, vines, and almost impenetrable canebrakes. Only here and there, chiefly around farm buildings, were there groves of trees on the tops of the ridges; otherwise, almost without exception, the hilltops were cultivated. Visibility was excellent from ridgetop to ridgetop, but down in the ravines, the jungle closed tightly around, so that each man's world became a green-walled room only a few yards across.

McClernand and Grant arrived on the scene at dawn. From his position on the little knoll east of the Shaifer house, McClernand could see a Southern battle line along a ridge trending east-west some 1,500 yards to the north. One of those "intelligent contrabands" who always seemed to show up in the Union lines at critical moments told him that the Bruinsburg Road ran along that ridge, and that the Shaifer Road, which led off to the north from the road junction just east of the Shaifer house, connected with it. McClernand also could see clearly the Magnolia Church Ridge, which he assumed to be occupied by a Confederate battle line, although he could see no trace of it. Since the terrain between the Rodney Road and the battle line to the north seemed impassable, he decided to ignore it and concentrate on the force to his immediate front.[5]

McClernand was not a subtle general; his tactics consisted primarily of assembling an overwhelming force and driving straight ahead. With

daylight, as troops came up, he tried to deploy them along the short transverse ridges in the vicinity of the Shaifer house, but the terrain was so
rough that there was not enough room. The Union regiments became
more and more crowded together as the morning wore on. In the meantime, dawn also had revealed that the "intelligent contraband" had been
right about the Shaifer Road; it ran north along a ridgetop that connected
with the ridge to the north, which was occupied by a second Confederate battle line. That worried Grant, because he realized that the Rebel
battle line to the north could march right down that road onto
McClernand's rear. Shortly after dawn, he ordered Carr to push a force
out along the Shaifer Road strong enough to delay any Confederate advance along it, and Carr quickly sent a four-company taskforce from
Benton's BDE. The taskforce deployed as skirmishers and moved northward along the road, only to run into concentrated rifle and artillery fire
after they had gone less than 1,000 yards north of the Shaifer house.[6]
McClernand and Carr now were in the unenviable position of having an
enemy battle line both ahead of and behind them.[7]

By about 0530, Garrard's BDE of Osterhaus's DIV was beginning to
arrive, so McClernand sent him up the Shaifer Road with orders to disperse the force on the Bruinsburg Road. Like Carr's skirmish line before them, they ran into intense fire 1,000 yards north of the Shaifer
house, which brought them to a stop.[8] Despite the firefight, McClernand
was confident that Garrard's BDE had sealed off any threat to the troops
on the Rodney Road, so, from that time on, he ignored the action along
the Bruinsburg Road.

McClernand personally was in charge on the Rodney Road, and things
moved slowly. He had organized a formal assault on the Magnolia
Church Ridge, believing it to be the main Confederate line. When the
Union line at last moved forward, it soon became clear that there was
nothing but a thin skirmish line there, and, despite the terrain, the ridge
was firmly in Union possession by about 0700.[9] However, as soon as they
crested the ridge they realized the true situation; between them and the
main Rebel line was a very deep ravine filled with the usual tangle of cane-
brake, trees, brush, and vines.

Meanwhile, Hovey's DIV began the long climb from Widow's Creek
at about 0530. The men had not yet had time to deploy when, about 0845,
the right flank of the Confederate line on the Rodney Road suddenly
surged forward in an assault on Stone's BDE, which held the Union line
opposite. As soon as their battle line left the shelter of their ridge, the

same terrain that was giving the bluecoats such problems destroyed the cohesion of the assault, and Stone's steady regiments had no trouble beating the Rebels back.[10] Stone did not attempt to counterattack, because he knew that the same thing would happen to him if he tried it.

With the attack safely defeated, Hovey began to deploy, and behind Hovey came A. J. Smith's DIV. By 1000, there were so many Federal troops on the scene that there simply was not room for them all to deploy. Regiments were stacked up two, three, and sometimes four deep all along the Magnolia Church Ridge. Furthermore, the terrain was so rough and confusing that not even regimental alignments could be kept, let alone brigade. Flat ground suitable for artillery was especially hard to find, and the Federal forces never did succeed in getting more than three batteries into action.

McClernand tried to move his entire three-division battle line forward in a formal attack, with everything lined up neatly. The terrain ruined that in the first five minutes. Instead, the advance became almost fluid, with each regiment, and sometimes each company, trying to find a way forward through the tangle. But move forward they did, though the Confederates did their best to stop them with sheets of musketry fire. In the middle of the line, where the Rodney Road penetrated the Confederate position, a battery of Rebel artillery was especially trying.

Shortly after 1000, the Union forces had pushed forward, in some places, to only 80 yards from the Confederate lines.[11] At this point, Hovey's patience ran out. His two brigades straddled the Rodney Road, which was more or less the center of the Union line, and he launched his troops in a direct assault. Carr's brigades instantly followed suit. It was as if a dam had broken. The blue flood poured forward and over the Rebel line, shattering it completely. They took two guns of the famous Botetourt ARTY and two hundred prisoners.[12]

The Union forces were in such disarray after the attack that there was no hope of organized pursuit. McClernand and his division commanders stopped to sort things out and, although they took their own sweet time about it, eventually started to move forward again.[13] Skirmish lines tried to penetrate the tangled ravines along both sides of the road, and so the going was excruciatingly slow. Most of the troops simply were brought back to the road, where they reformed in march column and moved slowly forward behind the skirmish lines.[14]

About 500 yards east of the position that the Confederates had occupied, the Union force came to a road junction. The right arm led east-southeast, and some of the Confederates had retreated in that direction. The left arm was the main Rodney Road, and it led northeast toward Port Gibson, and most of the retreating Southern force clearly had gone that way. McClernand decided that the few who had gone to the right were simply escaping, and he chose to let them go; he would follow the main Rodney Road right into Port Gibson.

After about 1,500 yards of cautious advance along the Rodney Road, the Union skirmishers came under fire from a Confederate skirmish line in the creek bottom to their right and front. Farther to the east, a battery of artillery opened, and it was clear that it dominated the entire ridge along which the Rodney Road ran. McClernand and his division commanders stopped to consider; the whole situation looked like a trap.[15]

Still, there was no help for it, so the Federal divisions deployed along the Rodney Road Ridge, facing east, and moved slowly into the White Branch ravine to their front, pushing the Rebel skirmishers up and over the ridge behind. Then, as the Union battle line crested the ridge, the reason for the strange Confederate behavior became clear. The advancing line was blasted by savage volleys from gray-clad infantry in the woods at the base of the slope beyond the Irwin Branch, and raked by artillery from batteries on the hills beyond. The Federals took what shelter they could in the little subsidiary ravines, and for ninety minutes a bitter firefight raged all along the front, with the Yankees getting very much the worst of it, since they were in the most exposed position by far.

After a while, McClernand realized that his men were getting nowhere, so he decided to repeat the tactic that had been successful that morning; he would bring up every man he had and simply smash straight through by sheer force of numbers. When his deployment was completed, he had twenty-one regiments compressed into a front barely 800 yards long, or something like 38 yards per regiment. Needless to say, things were a bit crowded.

While McClernand was assembling his assault forces, Hovey noticed a Confederate column moving to the right across his front in the next ravine to the east. Instantly he divined that they were en route to a position from which they would be able to strike the Federal right flank.[16] There was no time to get infantry into position, so he took every gun in his division and deployed them all in a massive battery on a nose of ridge overlooking the White Branch.[17] Scarcely had the guns gotten into position than the Rebels came over the ridge 300 yards to the right and struck Slack's BDE in flank like a tidal wave. It was about 1530. Hovey's twenty-four guns opened like a clap of thunder, ripping at the Confederate line with shell and canister. Slack's flank crumbled, but the regiments farther down the line managed to change front, since the charge was being slowed by Hovey's guns. Soon additional Union regiments came up, and after about an hour of fierce fighting, the Rebels began to drift back, unable to stand against both infantry and artillery in such numbers.[18]

Interestingly enough, while the Confederate flanking attack did not accomplish its objective, it did in fact dislocate the Union plan. Much of McClernand's reserve had been pulled into the fight, and McClernand simply did not know what to do next. As a result, he did nothing. During the time the Union right flank was under attack, however, the tremendous firefight in the middle and left of the Union line had raged on, and finally the Confederate line began to give. A couple of Southern regiments moved forward against the left flank of the Federal line, in what was clearly intended as a counterattack, but the Rebels were thrown back effortlessly.[19] After all, they were outnumbered perhaps five to one. Then, a few minutes later, both Union flanks began to inch forward, not in a charge but in a slow and relentless application of pressure. The Confederate line began to yield, and soon both its left and its right flanks had been forced back so far that the Federals thought briefly that they might bag the whole force. Suddenly, about 1800, all resistance vanished, and in a few moments it was clear that the Rebel force had broken contact and withdrawn.[20] There was no semblance of a Union pursuit.

All this time, a completely independent battle was raging to the north, along the Bruinsburg Road. Soon after Garrard's BDE of Osterhaus's DIV had stabilized a front across the Shaifer Road, the rest of Osterhaus's DIV came up, and McClernand fed it into the battle. Slowly the division began to forge ahead, pushing the Rebel skirmish line ahead of it, until it hit the main Confederate battle line along the Bruinsburg Road. Here everything ground to a halt.[21] It was not entirely Osterhaus's fault. The smoke of battle and the confusing maze of ravines, each filled with a wild tangle of brush, cane, and brambles, caused regimental alignments to disintegrate after an advance of only a few yards. A four-gun battery of Rebel artillery was particularly annoying, and Osterhaus brought up his own artillery to provide counterbattery, but even that was not enough.

Well, if the terrain would not permit a formal assault, Osterhaus would try something different. He established a skirmish line and gradually built it up until the Confederates were overwhelmed by sheer volume of fire. By this time, the deadly Union artillery also had begun to take effect, and the combination proved irresistible. The Confederate line on the Bruinsburg Road began to drift slowly back, fighting viciously but badly outgunned by the far more numerous blue-clad hordes. By 0930, Osterhaus was in possession of the junction of the Shaifer Road and the Bruinsburg Road. But here his attack encountered even more determined Confederate resistance and stopped moving forward.[22]

The terrain was so impenetrable that Osterhaus finally decided it was hopeless to try to organize a proper assault on the Confederate line anywhere except in the center, where some open fields at least made it possible to see what one was shooting at.[23] To get set, he shifted regiments from both flanks; finally, about 1500, he was ready. But at that point, with at least a three-to-one superiority in manpower, he decided that he needed reinforcements.[24] Osterhaus was nothing if not cautious. As it turned out, reinforcements were close at hand, in the form of Logan's DIV of McPherson's XVII Corps.

Logan's DIV did not get across the river until the morning of the battle. However, once ashore, Logan hurried to the sound of the guns and, at about 1400, arrived on the battlefield with two brigades.[25] Here he ran into a controversy. McClernand wanted to use both brigades for his attack up the Rodney Road, but Grant said that there was no room to deploy them, so they ought to be used elsewhere. McClernand stormily insisted, and Grant finally let him have John Stevenson's BDE, but he sent J. E. Smith's to Osterhaus.[26]

By this time, the Confederates on the Bruinsburg Road gradually were withdrawing, but fighting every step of the way. By 1500, their line ran from the bank of Bayou Pierre to a point on the Bruinsburg Road about 500 yards east of the road junction, and then eastward more or less parallel to the Bruinsburg Road for a distance of about 1,500 yards. That portion of the line that paralleled the road formed a huge arc, concave toward the Union advance. What this meant was that, every time a Union advance thrust forward, it was met by converging fire from the entire Confederate line. The terrain was as difficult as elsewhere on the field, and this converging fire from the defenders, coupled with the disorganization produced by the terrain, combined to slow Union progress to a crawl. By this time, however both Osterhaus and J. E. Smith had realized that the long Rebel line was very thin, in many places scarcely more than a strong skirmish line.

The terrain made a formal assault impractical, so once again Osterhaus, now reinforced by J. E. Smith's BDE of Logan's DIV, was forced to form skirmish lines and keep feeding men into them until they forced the Confederate line back by sheer firepower. J. E. Smith's BDE was deployed on the Union left and given the mission of forcing the Confederates back from the section of line between the Bruinsburg Road and Bayou Pierre. Here the terrain was absolutely incredible; the ground slanted downward from the road to the bayou in a slope so steep and broken that no semblance of a formal battle line could be maintained. Nevertheless, J. E. Smith pushed stolidly ahead, and the Confederates gradually gave before his attack. The whole right flank of the Confederate line swung like a gate hinged at the Andrews house, which sat on a commanding knoll north of the Bruinsburg Road and about 900 yards east-northeast of the road junction.

By 1600, relentless pressure from J. E. Smith's BDE of Logan's DIV and Garrard's BDE of Osterhaus's had forced the Confederates back to a line about 2,300 yards long that ran almost north-south. Its right flank was about 1,000 yards north of the Andrews house and continued along the narrow ridges projecting southward from the Bruinsburg Road into the valley of Centers Creek.[27]

Logan himself now was on the scene, and he and Osterhaus, concluding that the thin Rebel line must imply a limited amount of manpower, ordered both Sheldon's BDE (on the Union right flank) and J. E. Smith's BDE (on the left) to extend their lines in an attempt to find the Rebel flanks. The terrain was far worse than the Confederate resistance; at one point a Union regiment descended into a ravine filled with cane and emerged to find a battle line on the ridge above them. They opened fire, only to discover a few moments later that it was a Union battle line. They had made a complete 180-degree turn while hidden in the cane.

Despite all such obstacles, the Union pressure grew and grew, and again the Confederate lines began to swing like gates hinged at the Andrews house. By 1700, the southern line was a salient, with the point at the Andrews house and both flanks bent sharply back. The rate of advance was accelerating gradually, when suddenly, about 1800, the Confederates vanished.[28] Sheldon's men were in the best position to follow, and they discovered that the Confederate army had withdrawn in good order along a country road that followed a long, rounded ridge leading northeast from the Andrews house. A little inquiry revealed that it joined the main Grand Gulf–Port Gibson road about 2.3 miles to the northeast. There was no significant attempt at pursuit; the Federal regiments were so disorganized and took so long to assemble that the Confederates were long gone before an organized Union effort could be mounted.

The Army of the Tennessee had broken out of its bridgehead and now was free to maneuver at will in the interior of Mississippi.

CONFEDERATE PERSPECTIVE

By midnight, 30 April 1863, Bowen had concentrated most of his available force in positions in the vicinity of Port Gibson. Green's BDE was deployed along Foster Ridge, which crossed the Rodney Road about 800 yards southeast of the Shaifer house. Tracy's Alabama BDE was formed on a ridge transverse to the Bruinsburg Road, which at this point was almost 2,000 yards directly north of the Shaifer house; and Baldwin's BDE was in bivouac at Grindstone Ford, six airline miles east-northeast of Port Gibson. Cockrell's Missouri BDE, the best troops in either army, was being held at Grand Gulf in case the Federals tried a direct assault on that fortress.

To Green, the very silence was sinister. The last reliable word he had was that there had been Yankees at Bethel Church, some eight miles to the west. He had been told by some locals that there also were Yankees on the Bruinsburg Road, but he could not be confident of either report.[29] He did not think the Yankees would march along unfamiliar roads at night, but one never knew about Yankees. All he could do was wait. Early in the evening, 30 May, he sent a small picket out to a point on the Rodney Road 100 yards or so west of the Shaifer house, some 800 yards in advance of his line, since that was the most likely avenue of approach for the Federal army.[30]

About 0030 on the fateful morning of 1 May, his nerves could take no more, and he rode forward to check on his picket. At the Shaifer house, he found a small segment of chaos. Mrs. A. K. Shaifer had heard rumors that the Yankees were coming, and she and the other women of the household were trying frantically to load their possessions into a wagon for removal to safety in Port Gibson. Green calmly told them to take their time; the Yankees could not possibly arrive before daybreak.

Hardly had the words passed his lips than the sharp report of a rifle sounded from west of the house, followed almost instantly by a crashing volley. One ball smashed into the wall of the house, and another struck the load of furniture.[31] Without further ado, the ladies and their two servants grabbed the tongue of the wagon and headed in the direction of Port Gibson. The Yankees had arrived ahead of schedule.

Green hastened back to his men and told them to hold their fire until the Federals were within 50 yards. They had only a few minutes to wait. The Unionists were talking among themselves as they advanced, a foolish thing to do; when Green judged them close enough, he ordered his men to fire.[32] One crashing volley was enough; the Federals vanished back down the road, and silence reigned over the fields once more. But not for long.

Now that he knew where the Yankees were, Green pushed a skirmish line forward, and in a relatively short while they had occupied the Magnolia Church Ridge. Soon a blue-clad skirmish line probed forward, but it was so dark that the men were reduced to firing at muzzle flashes. The Yankees brought up artillery and opened fire, but Green had anticipated that and placed his four guns to sweep the road and adjacent fields, and soon even the Federal artillery gave up and pulled back to the Shaifer House Ridge. By 0300, the firing had dwindled to silence.

Meanwhile, on the Bruinsburg Road, Tracy had heard the sound of firing and, having no idea what was going on, redeployed facing the sound of the guns.[33] His new line was almost parallel to, but a few yards south of, the Bruinsburg Road, with his right flank across the Shaifer Road, which linked the Bruinsburg and Rodney roads.

As soon as it was light enough to see, Green saw the massing of forces opposite him and realized that he could not possibly hold. He sent a messenger to Tracy, whom he knew to be unopposed at this point (he could, after all, see his battle line on the ridge to the north, beyond Centers Creek), asking for help.[34] Tracy was less than enthusiastic about giving up any of his men, but nevertheless he sent one regiment and a battery of artillery.[35] To get from his position to Green's, they had to go all the way back to the road junction and then out the Rodney Road, a distance of some eight miles. Needless to say, it took a while to make the transfer.

Bowen arrived at Green's headquarters on Foster Ridge at about 0730.[36] He took one look and realized that he had made a mistake in approving the position Green had selected along Foster Ridge, because that portion of the ridge south of the Rodney Road was dominated by the Magnolia Church Ridge, only 300 yards away to the west. There was little he could do about it at this point except make the best of a bad situation; an attempt to occupy Magnolia Church Ridge would take far too much time. More than anything else, Bowen needed more men. And now that he knew where the Yankees were, he felt free to strip Grand Gulf of infantry, so he immediately sent for Cockrell's three regiments of Missourians.

With daylight, Tracy, from his headquarters near the Andrews house on the Bruinsburg Road, could see the battle developing to the south of

him along the Rodney Road, and he looked for a way to participate. He
soon discovered that the Shaifer Road, which passed through his right
flank, led south and seemed to head directly into the rear of the Union
battle line that was facing Green. This seemed like a God-given opportunity, but he dared not leave the Bruinsburg Road unguarded, so he sent
a single regiment out to explore the road leading south. The men got as
far as a transverse ridge about 500 yards south of the Bruinsburg Road
and there ran into a Yankee skirmish line moving slowly northward.[37]

Tracy had no trouble bringing the blue skirmishers to a stop, but
before long they were strongly reinforced. Although they made no direct
attack, they nevertheless began to push slowly forward, forcing the Southerners back by sheer numbers and volume of fire. Tracy made the mistake of going forward to assess the situation and was promptly killed by a
Union sniper. COL Isham Garrott assumed command. Tracy had been a
strange, secretive man. As was his custom, he had confided his battle plan
to no one. As a result, Garrott had not the foggiest notion what kind of
battle he was supposed to be fighting. He asked Green for guidance, but
it took two hours for the messenger to get to Green and back, and when
the courier finally arrived, all Green had to say was "Hold at all costs."[38]
Not very helpful, under the circumstances.

Still, reinforcements were on the way. Baldwin's BDE had been hurried forward from Grindstone Ford and arrived at the Rodney Road–
Bruinsburg Road junction by about 1000. Not far behind Baldwin came the
last of the Grand Gulf garrison, Cockrell's three regiments of Missourians.[39]

On Green's front, about 0630, a powerful blue battle line moved forward and pushed the Confederate skirmish line off Magnolia Church
Ridge.[40] The Unionists immediately brought up artillery and began to
shell the Confederate positions, in some cases from distances of less than
300 yards. As always, the excellent Yankee artillery hurt, and Bowen
looked for a way to discomfit them. Bowen thought he might be able to
reoccupy at least a part of Magnolia Church Ridge if he launched an attack on what seemed to be the Federal right flank; it appeared to be
lightly held. In the resultant confusion, maybe an infantry force could at
least seize the high ground where Magnolia Church Ridge crossed the
road. The threat to their flank might make the Federals draw back to the
Shaifer house ridge, nearly 900 yards to the west. The attack was launched
at 0900 with two regiments and a battalion, and it failed in the face of
sheets of musketry fire from what by that time was a solid blue battle
line.[41] By 0930, Bowen realized that all was lost unless he could assemble

a larger force, so he rode back to find Baldwin's BDE, which he hoped was, by this time, very near.[42]

By 1000, the Federal line had pushed forward in some places to within 80 yards of Green's defensive line. Shortly after 1000, the Federals suddenly surged forward in irresistible strength and rolled right over the center of Green's line, capturing two guns of the Botetourt ARTY and shattering the infantry line.[43] The regiments broke up and fled to the rear, some along the Rodney Road and some through the ravines to the north and south. About a mile back, they encountered Baldwin's BDE, which was deploying rapidly but calmly across the road.[44] Bowen realized that it was hopeless to attempt to rally Green's defeated troops without a period for reorganization, so he told Green to assemble them at the road junction and then take them out the Bruinsburg Road to assist Garrott. He assumed, correctly, that the long march would give Green time to get his men sorted out.[45]

Bowen had learned on Foster Ridge that a ridgetop is not necessarily the best defensive position in terrain such as this, because the bare ridgetops could be swept so readily by both artillery and musketry fire, while the attacking force, more often than not, was concealed in the jungle-choked ravines. So this time he deployed his men in a ravine bottom, hoping to spring a tactical trap on the Yankees. He deployed Baldwin's four regiments behind Irwin's Branch of Willows Creek, and sent a line of skirmishers forward into the bottom of White Branch of Willows Creek, which flows more or less parallel to the Irwin Branch but is separated from it by a steep ridge.[46] When the Yankees pushed that skirmish line back, they would come up over that bare ridge and into the artillery and musketry of the Confederate troops in the ravine bottom to the east.

Before very long, right on schedule, a Yankee skirmish line appeared on the Rodney Road, followed in short order by a massive battle line. Bowen was less concerned about the buildup on his front than about the fact that the Yankee regiments on his left evidently were feeling for his flank. The danger was that they would discover that the Natchez Road was only 1,200 yards away in that direction. If they found it, they could pour a division or so into Port Gibson and take his whole force in rear.[47]

Bowen had held two regiments of Cockrell's Missourians in reserve for just such an eventuality.[48] Bowen marched them up the Irwin Branch, where he hoped the thick timber would conceal them until they were hidden from Yankee eyes by a knoll beyond the Union right flank. Here Cockrell formed his men into a massive assault column. His mission was to hit the Federal right flank and roll it up.[49] If all went well, the Union attack would be dislocated and possibly even defeated, although that was a lot to hope for. If things did not go well, the attack at least would prevent the Yankees from finding the Natchez Road.

Cockrell and his men soon passed beyond the Federal right flank, turned, and launched themselves in an all-out charge into the flank regiments. But as they emerged from cover, a concentration of Union artillery on the ridge to the southwest opened up with dreadful effect.[50] The Confederates had no artillery of their own. Despite the shelling, Cockrell's men struck the Union flank and crumpled it. In a very few minutes, however, still more Union regiments appeared on the scene, and the combination of infantry fire and shelling from the Yankee guns was too much. The attack stalled, and then the men began to drift back.[51] The counterattack had failed.

Furthermore, during the time Cockrell was attacking the Union right flank, a tremendous firefight was raging all along the rest of the line and soon began to take its toll. The Confederate infantry was beginning to run out of ammunition, and here and there a man could be seen drifting to the rear—a sure sign of ebbing morale.

Still, when 1530 came and went with no sign of a Union assault, Bowen began to worry that the Federals had discovered the Natchez Road despite Cockrell's effort. The troops now in his front might be simply a holding force to rivet his attention while the major force slipped off and into Port Gibson on his rear. To test the theory, Bowen asked Baldwin to launch an attack against the Union left flank.[52] The Southern line had gone no more than a dozen paces when it was smashed back by the concentrated fire of a score of Union regiments. Bowen's mind was set at rest; the Federals had not divided their forces.[53]

A few minutes later, both Union flanks began to inch forward, not in a charge but in a slow and relentless application of pressure. The tired Confederates began to yield, and soon Bowen's whole position was in peril. Finally the pressure became too great, and Bowen pulled out while he still had control. It was an orderly withdrawal, with no threat of Union pursuit.[54]

Meanwhile, out on the Bruinsburg Road, Garrott found his right-flank regiments, which extended across the Shaifer Road 500 yards south of the Bruinsburg Road, under increasing pressure from a Yankee skirmish line supported by artillery. There was nothing that could be called an assault, but the musketry fire grew in intensity, and when the blue-clad line began to lap around his right flank, Garrott slowly yielded control of the road junction and withdrew to a position about 300 yards east, where he could rest his right flank on the Bayou Pierre.[55] However, Garrott soon discovered that the terrain between the Bruinsburg Road and the bayou was so incredibly steep and jungle-covered that it was impossible to establish a battle line. Thus he contented himself with a skirmish line, assuming that the Yankees would have the same problem he did.

As it turned out, they did. But they also had more manpower, and they reinforced their skirmishers to the point where Garrott's right flank was forced back by overwhelming numbers. Fearing that his skirmishers would break up completely in the frightful terrain, Garrott pulled them out. About 1400, he formed a formal battle line along the Andrews house ridge, which commanded everything to the west of it. The line was about 2,200 yards long, far too long for his few men, and Garrott knew he could not hold it for long. Then, about 1430, just as pressure was beginning to build, Green's regiments, plus one of Cockrell's, came hurrying down the Bruinsburg Road from the direction of Port Gibson.

Green quickly told Garrott what had happened on the Rodney Road, and Garrott, realizing that Green's men were in no shape to resist a strong attack, put them in on his left flank, which was relatively quiet. However, his people were beginning to run out of ammunition, everybody was desperately tired, and the Yankees kept increasing the pressure, even though they did not actually make an assault. By 1530, the pressure was becoming intolerable, and both Garrott's flanks began to give ground, so that both wings of his battle line swung slowly back, with the strongpoint afforded by the Andrews house acting as a hinge.

About 1600, Garrott realized that he was in serious danger of complete encirclement, and abruptly he pulled his regiments out of line, formed them on the farm road that ran from near the Andrews house to a junction with the Grand Gulf–Port Gibson Road, and marched rapidly away and out of danger.[56] The force turned north onto the Grand Gulf Road at 1630, crossed and then burned the Bayou Pierre bridges, and turned to defend the crossings against the expected Yankee pursuit. There was none.[57]

Bowen and his army had been defeated, but not by superior tactics or gallantry. He had been defeated by sheer weight of numbers. It was no consolation. He had failed to contain the Federal bridgehead, and the Union army now was free to maneuver in the interior of Mississippi.

During the same day when Bowen was fighting so hard to stem the Federal advance west of Port Gibson, Pemberton and his headquarters staff had moved from Jackson to Vicksburg. The commanding general now was on the scene and in tactical command of his field army.

15

Advance to the Big Black River 2 May–3 May 1863

Maps: 10. The Region between Vicksburg, Bruinsburg, and Raymond
33. Disposition of Forces in the Region between Vicksburg, Bruinsburg, and Raymond: 1200, 2 May 1863
34. Disposition of Forces in the Region between Vicksburg, Bruinsburg, and Raymond: 1200, 3 May 1863

FEDERAL PERSPECTIVE

By 1800 on the afternoon of 1 May, Grant was certain that he had won the battle for Port Gibson handily, and that his bridgehead on Mississippi soil was secure. The next objective was to secure a place on the east bank of the Mississippi that could be converted quickly and easily into a major supply depot. Bruinsburg would not do, if for no other reason than that it lay at the end of a long, complicated, and tenuous supply line. A box of hardtack delivered at Bruinsburg landing first had to be brought down the river from Cairo to Milliken's Bend by steamboat, offloaded and carried by wagon over that long and difficult road down Roundaway Bayou, Bayou Vidal, and Lake St. Joseph to Hard Times and across Coffee Point to Disharoon's plantation, where it could be loaded on a ship and carried across the river. Small boats and barges moved by oars and poles along Walnut and Roundaway bayous helped a bit, but the route still demanded far too many horses, wagons, and men to be tolerable for any length of time.

The logical alternative was Grand Gulf, which at least would eliminate the long wagon haul along Lake St. Joseph and across Coffee Point to Disharoon's; with the fall of Grand Gulf, his steamboats could return to the reach above Grand Gulf and serve as ferries to transport the goods from Mrs.

Perkins's plantation to Grand Gulf. Further, Grand Gulf was easily defensible, stood well above flood level, and was served by a good road which led away into the interior. On the morning of 2 May 1863, Grant's problem was to eject the Confederates from the place without undue delay.

Given that Grand Gulf was the primary objective, Grant had two obvious courses of action open to him as soon as the Battle of Port Gibson had been won. First, he could drive straight along the railroad and try to take the fortress by brute force, before the Confederates could get set. There were some disadvantages. First among these was the fact that Grand Gulf lay north of the unfordable Bayou Pierre. Grant had no illusions that the morale of the Confederate forces whom he had defeated at the Battle of Port Gibson had been seriously damaged; after all, they had disengaged cleanly and gotten away with organizations intact. This meant that they would burn both highway and railroad bridges and undoubtedly would strongly oppose any attempt by the Federals to cross. The thought of crossing an unfordable stream in the face of determined resistance held few charms. Especially since the navy could not be there to help.

Further, even if, by good fortune, the Army of the Tennessee could vault the Bayou Pierre before Bowen's forces could get organized for its defense, his army could be expected simply to retreat into the town, which was known to be heavily fortified. The landward defenses of Grand Gulf were in terrain similar to that west of Port Gibson, and this alone was enough to give pause. Fighting from prepared defenses in terrain like that at Port Gibson, the Rebels could be expected to exact a dreadful price for capture of the fortress—if, indeed, the place could be taken at all.

If an immediate assault did not succeed, then the Union army might be in serious trouble. It was a given that Pemberton would assemble a field army to contain the Union bridgehead, which would mean that the Army of the Tennessee would have to fight to defend Bruinsburg and the roads connecting it to his army, while the latter was investing Grand Gulf, with every pound of supplies coming down that long and impossibly complicated supply line from Milliken's Bend. It was a daunting prospect.

Furthermore, even if the fortress fell relatively quickly, a powerful Rebel force might assemble, and then the Army of the Tennessee would again have the problem of breaking out of a bridgehead, but this time the freedom of maneuver would be restricted by two unfordable streams, Bayou Pierre and Big Black River. Clearly, capturing only Grand Gulf was not enough; an equally important requirement was to enclose as much territory as possible in the bridgehead.

That second requirement was the key to Grant's second option: drive straight up the Vicksburg–Port Gibson road, seize Hankinson's Ferry, and, if at all possible, occupy Rocky Springs. Rocky Springs was the cork controlling the peninsula between the Big Black and Bayou Pierre. Once in control of the road junction there, maneuvering to the east and northeast would be easy, should that become necessary. If Hankinson's Ferry and Rocky Springs could be occupied, the Confederates would be forced to evacuate Grand Gulf or else be cut off and eventually captured. Such a move would also secure the only practical crossing of the Big Black River; McKay and Thompson's ferries were scarcely large enough to hold a farm wagon and could not be used to support the movement of large bodies of men and masses of equipment. Furthermore, this plan would provide a defensible frontier while the remainder of the army moved up. After all, some of McPherson's corps, and all of Sherman's, were strung out through Louisiana all the way back to Milliken's Bend. It would take some days for all of them to be brought forward, even after Grand Gulf became available.

Grant chose the second option. The main highway to Vicksburg first crossed the Little Bayou Pierre on a suspension bridge just north of the town, then turned almost due east for eight miles. At this point it crossed the Big Bayou Pierre on a second suspension bridge at Grindstone Ford. Both streams were reputed to be unfordable. Beyond Grindstone Ford, the road went nearly straight north for two miles, where it crossed the Grand Gulf–Rocky Springs Road at the strategic road junction of Willows. Seven miles farther to the north, the road crossed the unfordable Big Black River at Hankinson's Ferry. The country people said there was no bridge, only a ferry. That might prove to be an advantage, since the necessity of ferrying large numbers of troops across the Big Black certainly would slow the movement of Confederate reinforcements for Bowen's Grand Gulf field army.

The peninsula between the Big Black River and Big Bayou Pierre is no more than a single huge ridge, with many sharp spurs dropping to the Big Black on the north and Big Bayou Pierre on the south; and the only continuous east-west road, the Grand Gulf–Rocky Springs Road, runs right along the watershed. Thus, whoever controlled Willows effectively controlled the road network of the entire peninsula. To be sure, the Kenison Creek Road, which more or less directly connected Ingleside with Hankinson's Ferry, could be used to bypass Willows, and that might pose a problem. Nevertheless, once the Federal army was in possession of Willows, the Confederates almost certainly would be forced to evacuate Grand Gulf or be trapped there. Grant was pretty certain they would evacuate. If he were very lucky and the Rebels waited too long to begin their evacuation, at least some of them might be cut off before they could reach Hankinson's Ferry.

They would be trapped against the Big Black, unable to escape across a river crossed only by the tiny ferryboats at McKay's and Thompson's ferries.

As soon as Grant realized that the Confederates had withdrawn from the battlefield, he ordered McClernand to pursue until dark and to take up the chase at dawn. With luck, the blue infantry might occupy Port Gibson and seize the suspension bridge across Little Bayou Pierre before the retreating Rebels could manage to destroy it. But McClernand, always the politician, simply ignored his commander's order and let his tired men rest on the battlefield. Oddly enough, Grant did not demur. Perhaps he realized that his soldiers had done enough for one day. After all, most had had no sleep since they left Disharoon's plantation on the morning of 30 April, some forty hours earlier. During the night, Sanborn's DIV of McPherson's XVII Corps arrived on the scene, giving Grant five full divisions.[1]

The men were so tired that it was hard to get them moving in the morning, so it was not until about 1000 on 2 May that the leading elements entered Port Gibson.[2] To Grant's disgust, they found the suspension bridge across unfordable Little Bayou Pierre, on the northern edge of town, in flames from end to end. The troops were unable to put it out, and the bridge was utterly destroyed.[3]

Grant gave the problem of getting across the stream to CPT Stewart Tresilian, his chief engineer.[4] It was clear that building a bridge was going to take a while, and Grant worried about what would happen if Bowen decided to contest the crossing with a battery of artillery and a couple of regiments, so he asked McPherson to see if he could find a ford somewhere upstream where a brigade could be put across.[5] With luck, the infantry could take a position that would secure the crossing site while the bridge was being built. McPherson thought maybe one brigade would not be enough, so he sent both J. E. Smith's and Dennis's BDEs of Logan's DIV. They found Askamalla Ford only four miles upstream from the bridge, and it was unguarded. By noon, Logan's two brigades had taken up a position at Humphrey's plantation, 2.5 miles east of Port Gibson, where they blocked all approaches to the bridge site from the east.[6]

At the same time that McPherson sent out Dennis and J. E. Smith, he dispatched Logan with Logan's third brigade, J. Stevenson's, to check out the railroad to Grand Gulf.[7] Not only were both the railroad bridge and the parallel highway bridge gone, but extremely belligerent infantry and artillery occupied the far shore. Logan had no intention of trying to force a crossing, but he thought it might be useful to hold as much of the Rebel army as possible here, while the main body of the Army of the Tennessee built a bridge at Port Gibson and struck for Grindstone Ford.

After all, the fewer Rebels trying to hold the ford, the better for Grant. So he encouraged an extremely noisy but completely harmless firefight across the bayou for several hours until finally, about 1630, he withdrew and returned to Port Gibson.[8]

Meanwhile, Tresilian went to work with a will. He found some handy cotton gins to disassemble, and by noon a raft bridge had been constructed near the burned suspension span. The infantry officers didn't think much of it, so they tried it out with an artillery piece drawn by a team of mules before trusting their precious men to it. Sure enough, it flipped over and dumped gun and mules into the river. "It was rather an expensive trial," said one of the infantrymen, "but better than a column of infantry."[9] The next effort was better. It was finished by 1600, and Crocker's DIV (it had been Sanborn's until that morning) immediately began to cross. J. Stevenson's BDE of Logan's DIV followed an hour later.

The next intermediate objective was the suspension bridge at Grindstone Ford, where the main road to Vicksburg crossed the Big Bayou Pierre. Crocker and Logan, with Stevenson's BDE, marched rapidly toward Grindstone Ford, hoping to seize the bridge before it, too, could be destroyed. Dennis and J. E. Smith fell in at the tail of the column as it passed Humphrey's plantation.[10]

The advance guard reached Grindstone Ford about sunset, only to find the far end of the bridge in flames. But engineer Tresilian, who was marching with the advance guard, organized firefighting parties and managed to put out the blaze.[11] Tresilian and his men worked like demons all night to repair the damaged span; and by 0530, 3 May, Logan's DIV crossed and started the march toward the strategic road junction at Willows.[12]

An old man sitting on the porch of Buena Vista plantation, on the lower slopes of the long hill leading up to Willows, assured Logan's advance guard that there were no Rebels anywhere about. Halfway up the hill, the advance guard scrambled for cover as a salvo of shells from a battery of Rebel guns on the hilltop to the north whistled down the road and exploded near the head of the column. The blue-clad infantry quickly formed a skirmish line and pushed on, encountering no further opposition until they reached Willows. Here, around 0830, they found the hamlet unoccupied, but they quickly ran into Confederate battle lines on both the road going westward toward Ingleside and Grand Gulf, and the one heading north toward Hankinson's Ferry.

When McPherson saw the disposition, he turned Logan's DIV westward against the roadblock on the Ingleside Road and sent Crocker, whose division was marching close on Logan's heels, to the north to deal with the

Rebels on the Hankinson's Ferry Road. Logan drove strongly, and, after only a few moments, the Confederate line abruptly collapsed and fled down the Ingleside Road toward Grand Gulf.[13] Logan followed as rapidly as he dared, and when he reached the road junction about 2,000 yards east of Ingleside, where the Kenison Creek Road diverges to the north, the condition of the road clearly indicated that a very large body of Confederate troops, accompanied by wagons, had passed a short time before.

Grant, marching with Logan, realized instantly (and with intense satisfaction) that this meant the evacuation of Grand Gulf; the entire Confederate field army must be in flight toward Hankinson's Ferry and Vicksburg. It was shortly after noon. Throwing caution to the winds, Logan marched as rapidly as he could to the northeast along the Kenison Creek Road, hoping that he could catch the Rebels astride the Big Black River. In the next couple of hours, his men picked up 154 stragglers, but they couldn't catch the main body.[14]

While Logan turned northeast toward Hankinson's Ferry, Grant and twenty cavalrymen continued on toward Grand Gulf. When he rode down out of the hills into the ruined town about 1800, he found the place swarming with Porter's bluejackets.[15] Porter himself was gone. However, he had left LCDR Elias Owen, with *Louisville, Mound City,* and *Carondelet* behind as a welcoming committee. Owen told Grant that poor *Tuscumbia,* which by this time had been repaired, had been left at Bruinsburg, and that the admiral had gone south down the river with the rest of the ironclads![16] Owen gave Grant some fresh underwear and a good dinner, and let him rest in peace on *Louisville's* spar deck.

Meanwhile, Crocker, on the Willows–Hankinson's Ferry road, had run into something of a problem. The Federals had encountered gray-clad skirmishers about 1,000 yards north of Willows, and at first the Southerners had fallen back readily enough. Still, Crocker was forced to deploy, and moving a battle line forward through ravines resembling those at the Port Gibson battlefield was slow and exceedingly difficult. Then, as the infantry were struggling through the canebrakes in the Kenison Creek bottoms about 2,500 yards north of Willows, they were subjected to a deliberate, accurate, and heavy fire from a battle line on the ridge to the north.[17] When Crocker identified the battle flags as belonging to the Alabama BDE that had fought so well at Port Gibson, he grew cautious. These were not troops to be taken lightly.

Crocker halted, deployed his division, and started forward. His battle line overlapped the Rebel line on both flanks; thus threatened, the Southerners drew slowly back, covering their withdrawal with savage volleys.

At last they came to a stubborn stand on a ridgetop about 2.5 miles north of Willows.[18] About this time, Crocker noticed that the Rebel line now also flaunted the battle flags of Cockrell's deadly Missouri brigade, and matters began to look serious indeed. However, Crocker maintained his pressure and had begun lapping around both flanks of the Rebel position, when suddenly all resistance evaporated.[19]

Crocker marshaled Dennis's BDE and the 8 MI BTRY on the road and marched with all speed for Hankinson's Ferry. As they came in sight of the river about 1445, they were surprised to find all the Rebels safely across the stream, with the exception of a working party which was trying desperately to destroy a sturdy raft bridge. The 8 MI BTRY deployed like lightning, and the first salvo sent the Rebels scurrying.[20]

Crocker's first move to consolidate his position was to send an infantry combat patrol to occupy the strategic road junction of Rocky Springs,[21] through which any Rebel force coming from the direction of Jackson or Edwards would have to pass. With Rocky Springs occupied, the Army of the Tennessee was in firm control of Grand Gulf and everything south of the Big Black River, as well as of a good bridge on the direct road to Vicksburg. The second major objective of the campaign had been achieved.

Perhaps the most striking thing about all these maneuvers is that the Union forces moved so unerringly through the road network south of the Big Black River. The existing maps were miserable—they tended to be more schematic than realistic—and yet the Federal commanders seemed always to know exactly where each road went and how far it was to the next road junction. It is difficult to escape the conclusion that the country people were guiding them, and with great care.

CONFEDERATE PERSPECTIVE

When Bowen's little army had withdrawn from the Port Gibson battlefield late on the afternoon of 1 May, Green's, Garrott's, and Cockrell's BDEs crossed to the north bank of Bayou Pierre at the railroad bridge some 2.8 miles northwest of Port Gibson.[22] Baldwin's BDE had withdrawn along the Rodney Road, passed through Port Gibson, crossed to the north bank of Little Bayou Pierre on the suspension bridge north of town, marched eastward on the Vicksburg Road, and crossed to the north bank of Big Bayou Pierre at Grindstone Ford about midnight, not forgetting to set fire to the bridge after crossing it. Marching north to Willows, then west through Ingleside, Baldwin's troops reached Bowen's headquarters on the north bank of Bayou Pierre, at the railroad bridge, about 0900, 2 May.

It was obvious to Bowen that Grant's next objective would be Grand Gulf, and he thought it likely that the blow would come right up the railroad from Port Gibson. Accordingly, he destroyed the railroad bridge and the parallel highway bridge and deployed his available troops to defend the crossing. He also ordered patrols to destroy the ferry across Big Bayou Pierre on the Port Gibson–Ingleside Road, as well as the suspension bridge at Port Gibson, in an effort to lock the Federal army south of the Big Bayou Pierre. The previous night (i.e., on the night of 1 May, after the Battle of Port Gibson), Bowen had received a dispatch from Pemberton, now in Vicksburg, to the effect that MG William Loring was en route to Grand Gulf with two brigades.[23] Loring's two brigades would raise Bowen's strength to nearly 7,000 men, and Bowen figured that, with that number, he could hold Bayou Pierre between Port Gibson and the Mississippi River against almost anything, at least for a few days.[24] That would give Pemberton time to move the Vicksburg army southward in support.

When a Union brigade showed up on the south bank of Bayou Pierre at the railroad bridge at about 1000, pushed a skirmish line up to the river bank, and opened fire as if they were getting ready to cover a crossing, Bowen was certain that he had divined Grant's intentions; and he settled down to await the arrival of Loring and his two brigades.

Alas for Bowen's hopes! In the first place, the two brigades did not exist. When Loring arrived at Rocky Springs about 0800 on the morning of 2 May, he was accompanied only by BG Lloyd Tilghman and his demi-brigade. That is, only two regiments arrived; somehow Pemberton's message had been garbled, transforming two regiments into two brigades. At Rocky Springs, Loring learned that a massive Yankee column was driving on Grindstone Ford. If that force got across Big Bayou Pierre and across the road junction at Willows, Bowen's entire force would be in a trap. He put Tilghman's demi-brigade under the command of COL A. E. Reynolds and started it on its way to Grindstone Ford, with orders to hold at all hazards.[25] He also sent a courier galloping ahead with a message telling Bowen what he had done. Then, at a more sedate pace, he and Tilghman rode on toward Grand Gulf to find Bowen.

Loring's courier arrived at Bowen's position at the site of the railroad bridge about 1515. When Bowen heard that Loring had brought only two regiments instead of two brigades and that the Yankees were driving for Grindstone Ford instead of the railroad bridge, he was close to despair. His only thought at this point was to get his men out of the trap before it closed.[26] Even though the Yankee force at the railroad bridge now had been revealed as a feint, he dared not leave the crossing unguarded. As soon as

the Yankees marched away toward Port Gibson, however, he started
Baldwin's, Green's, and Garrott's brigades on the road to Ingleside, leaving
only Cockrell's troops to guard the railroad bridge. He also ordered everything movable at Grand Gulf to be loaded on wagons and sent to Hankinson's
Ferry. The magazines at Fort Wade and Fort Cobun, and everything else
that could not be moved, were to be prepared for destruction.[27]

However, Bowen did not yet order the fuses lit. After recovering from
his initial shock at the discovery that Loring's two brigades had shrunk to
two regiments, he concluded that he might yet salvage something from
the situation. This optimism was based on a message from Carter
Stevenson that arrived at about 1900, informing him that A. W. Reynolds's
BDE of Stevenson's DIV had left Vicksburg for Grand Gulf at about 1800
on 2 May. If they marched all night, they would arrive sometime in the
wee hours of 3 May. Of course, he realized that A. E. Reynolds's demi-
brigade could not stop the Union hordes, but if A. W. Reynolds's BDE
could be brought into play before the Yankees on the Vicksburg Road
reached the bridge at Grindstone Ford, the Union column might well be
delayed for a considerable time and perhaps even stopped until larger
forces could be brought down from Vicksburg. At worst, the combined
force should be able to hold until everything useful was safely out of
Grand Gulf. Thus Bowen delayed ordering the demolition of Grand Gulf.

Loring and Tilghman arrived at Bowen's headquarters near the railroad bridge about 2300, 2 May; and Bowen immediately offered command to Loring, who was his senior. Loring refused to accept but instead
"requested" that Bowen give the order for the evacuation of Grand Gulf.[28]

As the night wore on, Bowen realized that, even with the help of A. W.
Reynolds's BDE, he would never be able to hold the line of Bayou Pierre
against a force as large as the Army of the Tennessee and at the same
time protect Grand Gulf against an amphibious landing. After much soul-
searching, he reluctantly gave the order to evacuate his stronghold. It was
about 0200, 3 May 1863.[29]

Sure enough, A. W. Reynolds and his brigade arrived, tired and foot-
sore, about 0300 on the morning of 3 May. Bowen instantly sent them off
to reinforce A. E. Reynolds, who by this time presumably was in position
at Grindstone Ford.[30] Loring then started his force north of the railroad
bridge toward Ingleside and Hankinson's Ferry. He and Tilghman rode
along with the van. Now that the order to evacuate Grand Gulf had been
given irrevocably and the army started on its retreat, chivalrous Loring
assumed command of all Confederate forces in the area.[31]

A mile or so east of Ingleside, who should they meet but A. W. Reynolds, marching at the head of his brigade. He had lost his way on the twisting Mississippi roads and never had located either the road to Grindstone Ford or A. E. Reynolds and his demi-brigade.[32] Marching with A. W. Reynolds was BG Stephen D. Lee, whom Pemberton had sent to take command of the AL BDE, which had fought so nobly at Port Gibson under COL Garrott's command.

In the meantime, A. E. Reynolds's demi-BDE had arrived on the hills above Grindstone Ford shortly after midnight, 3 May. He saw men, obviously Union soldiers, laboring by torchlight, like demons from the Pit, on the bridge. The sight of the sea of campfires on the south bank of the bayou convinced him of the futility of trying to hold the line of the river. Instead, he deployed his two regiments across the road near the top of the hill and awaited developments.[33] Shortly after dawn, a powerful Federal force poured across the Grindstone Ford bridge and started up the hill toward Willows. At the sight of the masses of infantry and artillery winding its way up the road, A. E. Reynolds panicked. His artillery fired a single long-range salvo, and then both infantry and artillery withdrew toward Willows.

When Loring met A. W. Reynolds and his brigade, he realized that A. E. Reynolds and his two regiments (i.e., Tilghman's demi-BDE) never would be able to hold Grindstone Ford. Thoroughly alarmed and thinking that, despite all his precautions, he still might be blamed for the disaster, Loring sent his good friend Tilghman to take the Alabama BDE, now under the command of S. D. Lee, to support A. E. Reynolds.[34] Tilghman, with Lee and his brigade, rapidly marched off toward Willows by the most direct road.

Tilghman and Lee met A. E. Reynolds at the strategic Willows crossroad, but instead of trying to hold the crossroad by deploying south of it, Tilghman (having resumed command of his demi-brigade) deployed his two regiments across the Ingleside Road west of the crossroad, while Lee and his brigade established a block across the Hankinson's Ferry Road about 1,200 yards northeast of the hamlet, leaving the road junction itself unguarded.[35]

As Loring turned onto the main Willows–Hankinson's Ferry Road, he grew more and more worried that the Federals would break through Lee's roadblock and cut his retreating column in two. As a precaution, he peeled Cockrell's Missouri BDE off the column and sent it toward Willows to reinforce Lee.[36] This would, he hoped, secure the flank and rear of the retreat until it had safely crossed the Big Black River.

The telegraph line from Port Gibson to Vicksburg crossed the Big Black River at Hankinson's Ferry. At last safe on the north bank at about 1030, 3 May, Loring sent a message to Pemberton in Vicksburg: "Shall I immediately withdraw to Vicksburg, or shall I try to hold the line of the Big Black?"[37] He did not wait for a reply. Instead, he put most of his troops in motion, not toward Vicksburg, but toward Big Black Bridge.

When the Yankee van reached the Willows junction, one division turned west toward Ingleside, while another continued north, heading for Hankinson's Ferry. Tilghman, again in command of his own demi-brigade, lost his nerve in the face of an impending attack by a Federal division and immediately retreated west along the Ingleside Road[38] as far as the junction with the Kenison Creek Road, turned north on the latter, and marched with all possible speed toward the ferry. By this time, all the troops in the Grand Gulf force had passed, so Tilghman was bringing up the rear of the retreat.

Back at Willows, Lee saw a Union division deploy and move toward him. He fell back slowly, hoping for the best. The terrain was frightful, all broken ravines, canebrakes, and knife-edge ridges, so the Yankee advance was slow and painful. Nevertheless, they came on relentlessly, until at last Lee was forced back to the ridge north of Kenison Creek. Here, like the answer to a prayer, Cockrell and his Missourians arrived, and the two commanders quickly formed a solid battle line along the ridge. The Yankee advance came to an abrupt stop.[39]

But only for a moment. More blue-clad regiments came up and deployed, and before long, their line extended well beyond the Confederate flanks. At this point, Lee ordered Cockrell to cover his withdrawal to Hankinson's Ferry. As soon as Lee was well under way, the Missourians fell slowly back, covering their grudging withdrawal with savage volleys until their battle line was almost along the Ingleside–Hankinson's Ferry Road. Cockrell was not one to overlook details; he had sent scouts out to the west on the Ingleside–Hankinson's Ferry Road, and when they detected the advance guard of a large Yankee force hurrying eastward along it, he disengaged cleanly and crossed the raft-bridge at Hankinson's Ferry without interference.[40] Cockrell put a demolition team to work destroying the bridge, but they hardly had started when a Federal artillery battery opened fire, and they were forced to flee.[41]

The Grand Gulf army was safe on the north shore of the Big Black, but the Yankees definitely had won the first round. They controlled everything south of the Big Black River, they had a good bridge on the highway to Vicksburg; and, even more important, the occupation of Grand Gulf gave them a good supply depot on the river below Vicksburg.

16

Logistics, Communications, and Reinforcements 30 April–19 May 1863

Maps: 1. The Theater of Operations
  2. Northern Sector
  4. Southern Sector
  9. Northeastern Louisiana

FEDERAL PERSPECTIVE

On 30 April, with most of McClernand's corps already safely ashore and two divisions of McPherson's corps in close support, Grant was confident that he would be able to maintain a bridgehead in Mississippi. He assumed that the surprise of his landing at Bruinsburg would not last long and that, within a day or two, substantial Confederate forces would be concentrating against him. He would need every fighting man who could be brought into action to keep his bridgehead secure and to provide the strength for a move against Vicksburg. The only troops he had which could be brought to the scene of action quickly were McArthur's DIV of McPherson's XVII Corps, and the three divisions of Sherman's XV Corps, which were at Young's Point and Milliken's Bend. McArthur's troops were not really available, because they had been assigned the duty of guarding and maintaining the long road down Roundaway Bayou, Bayou Vidal, and Lake St. Joseph.[1] That left Sherman.

From Bruinsburg, Grant wrote to his red-bearded friend, ordering him to send two of his three divisions southward as rapidly as possible, but he was so concerned about the supply line through Louisiana that he ordered Sherman to keep one division at Milliken's Bend to build and maintain the roads from Milliken's Bend and Young's Point to Richmond.[2] The message reached Sherman on 1 May, while he was in the Yazoo with ten of Blair's regiments, demonstrating against Drumgould's Bluff. The remainder of Blair's regiments were at Young's Point, working on the road from Milliken's Bend to Walnut Bayou. The Drumgould's Bluff expedition arrived back at Young's Point about 2200 that same night.[3] Sherman immediately ordered Steele's and Tuttle's DIVs to prepare for the long march to Hard Times. Blair's DIV was the unlucky one; it was to be left behind to work on the roads.

By 5 May, Sherman, with both Tuttle's and Steele's DIVs, was at Mrs. Perkins's plantation, having reached there by a long march around Bayou Vidal.[4] On 6 May, Sherman and Steele marched all the way to Hard Times and by dark were loading on the transports, ready for the ride across the river to Grand Gulf. Tuttle's men, however, were forced to stop for the night just south of Clark Bayou, seven miles short of Hard Times.[5] The next day, 7 May, Tuttle's men moved into Hard Times, while Steele's men, with Sherman, were ferried across to Grand Gulf. The boats immediately returned to Hard Times and loaded Tuttle's men, and by nightfall they, too, were resting beneath the frowning bluffs of Grand Gulf.[6]

Sherman was late for his appointment at Hankinson's Ferry, so next morning, 8 May, he and Steele's men were on the road by 0500. The day was very hot and sultry, and, though it was a march of only sixteen miles, the troops were weary to the bone when they tramped into Hankinson's Ferry late that afternoon. Tuttle's men moved out of the Grand Gulf camps a bit later and camped for the night at Willows, the only place along the road between Grand Gulf and Rocky Springs where there was enough water for the men and animals.[7]

While Grant was resting aboard *Louisville* at Grand Gulf on the night of 3 May, he had time to reflect on ways to deal with three critical problems. The first and most pressing was the need for manpower. The Battle of Port Gibson had taught him that the terrain in this region fought hard on the side of the defender, so a campaign against Vicksburg would require every man he could assemble. A message went upriver to MG Stephen Hurlbut, commander of the XVI Corps, in Memphis, directing him to send four regiments to Milliken's Bend, so that Grant's last remaining battle-worthy unit, Blair's DIV, could move south in support.[8]

Now that Grand Gulf was available as a depot in Mississippi, it was possible to address the task of simplifying his logistical system. With Grand Gulf in his hands and much of his army of maneuver now on the Mississippi shore, the steamboats below Vicksburg could be devoted primarily to the job of transporting food, fodder, and war materiel. This meant that the wagon roads south of Mrs. Perkins's plantation could be abandoned. It would be nice if the long road from Richmond down Roundaway Bayou and Bayou Vidal could be left behind as well. The security of that long wagon road was beginning to weigh more heavily on Grant's mind, because the water level in the river was falling rapidly and the backswamps were beginning to drain. That trend was certain to continue, so the swamps soon would become passable for infantry and artillery. That meant that Kirby Smith's Trans-Mississippi forces would be able to reach the area via steamboats on the Tensas River. There was a road of sorts between Buck's plantation on the Tensas River and Bayou Vidal, so a few miles of marching through the swamps would put those troops astride the Union supply road down that bayou, and that would be that. An added benefit to the abandonment of the overland route to Hard Times was that it would free McArthur's DIV for duty with the army of maneuver in Mississippi. And there was a way in which this all might be accomplished!

Grant wrote to BG Jeremiah C. Sullivan, who commanded the District of Northeast Louisiana from his headquarters at Young's Point, directing him to build a new road from Young's Point to Bowers' Landing as soon as the swamps had drained enough to permit it.[9] Such a road would mean that supplies could be offloaded at Young's Point and carried by wagon directly to Bowers' Landing, which was just below Warrenton on the river. There the transport fleet below Vicksburg could pick them up and carry them all the way to Grand Gulf.

When Grant's message arrived at Young's Point, the water in the swamps between Walnut Bayou and Bowers' Landing was still too deep to permit the construction of the road. However, by 9 May, the river had fallen and the swamps had drained enough so that BG Sullivan judged that construction of the Bowers' Landing Road could begin. He ordered CPT William Jenney, Sherman's chief engineer, to survey a route and begin construction the next day.[10]

There was one small potential problem. Bowers' Landing was within range of the 30-pdr Parrott rifles in the Confederate battery at Warrenton, and both Ewing and Sullivan worried about what those big guns would do to thin-skinned transports if they attempted to tie up at Bowers' Landing. It clearly was a job for the navy. Thus, at 0910 on 10 May, squat, deadly *Mound City* slid up and calmly anchored directly in front of the fort. The gunboat blasted the battery for an hour but elicited no response from the Confederates, so a naval landing party was put ashore. They found Confederates alive and well in the fort and hastily retreated to their ships, whereupon the navy gunners shifted to incendiary shells. The wooden backing for the armored battery was completely destroyed, and that ended the threat. Much comforted, Sullivan and Ewing ordered construction of the road to begin immediately.[11]

A good road already existed from Young's Point to Hecla Place, a distance of three miles, but a completely new road about six miles long had to be constructed across the swamp between Walnut Bayou and Bowers' Landing. Manpower came from Ewing's BDE (Blair's DIV, XV Corps), which had been left behind expressly to guard, build, and maintain the roads around Milliken's Bend and Young's Point. They were at work by noon on 10 May; by the evening of 11 May, a right-of-way had been carved through the woods and a series of trestles had been built over the worst of the swamp.[12] But the first wagons to try the "road" sank nearly out of sight in black, sticky, slippery, bottomless mud. The solution was to corduroy the entire six miles from Hecla Place to Bowers' Landing. By 15 May, the road was functioning, and wagon trains were delivering huge quantities of supplies to Bowers' Landing, where the steamboat fleet below the city picked the material up and transported it to Grand Gulf.[13]

Grant left Grand Gulf in the wee hours of 4 May and breakfasted later that morning at McPherson's headquarters at Hankinson's Ferry. As the day passed, Grant heard reports of the formidable strength of the Vicksburg defenses and learned that great numbers of infantry were concentrating north of the Big Black River. By 5 May, he began to worry that he had underestimated his need for fighting men, so he again wrote to Hurlbut, this time ordering that BG Jacob Lauman's DIV be sent downriver as soon as possible. Grant knew that Lauman's departure would strip Memphis of its defenses, so he authorized Hurlbut to call on BG Alexander Asboth, commander of the Post of Columbus, KY, for reinforcements. He also wrote to MG Benjamin Prentiss, who commanded the District of Eastern Arkansas, to send three regiments from the Helena garrison to Memphis.

The messages Grant had written on 3 and 5 May reached Memphis on 8 May, and loyal Hurlbut took action instantly. BG James Veatch, commander of the Memphis garrison, had four infantry regiments ready to leave for Milliken's Bend the next day. It took a while to collect enough steamboats to send Lauman's DIV, but BG Bryant's BDE left on 11 May, COL Cyrus Hall's on 13 May, and COL Isaac Pugh's BDE on 16 May. Veatch's four regiments landed at Milliken's Bend on the afternoon of 11 May, and Lauman's three brigades arrived in sequence: Bryant's on 13 May, Hall's on 16 May, and Pugh's on 19 May. By that time, of course, there was no longer any need for them in the interior. Bryant's and Cyrus Hall's BDEs were sent to Grand Gulf to garrison the place, and Pugh's BDE eventually was sent to Snyder's Bluff, which by that time was under Union control.

Back at Hankinson's Ferry on 6 May, Grant was out of touch with conditions in the swamps of Louisiana and assumed that the road he had ordered built to Bowers' Landing was well under construction. On this assumption, he asked McPherson to bring McArthur's DIV, which had been assigned the task of guarding the long road down through Louisiana, across the river as rapidly as possible. William Hall's BDE guarded the road along Roundaway Bayou between Richmond and Pointe Clear, while Ransom's BDE held posts all along Bayou Vidal. Ransom was restless and impatient with his seemingly trivial task, so he whiled away the time by building bridges across the crevasses between Pointe Clear and New Carthage.[14] They all were finished by 8 May. On 9 May, Grant's order, relayed through McPherson, reached Ransom and William Hall, who were only too happy to obey.[15] They began to move out of their camps along the Roundaway Bayou–Bayou Vidal road even before the Bowers' Landing Road was completed!

William Hall and his brigade left Holmes's plantation on Roundaway Bayou on 11 May, marched via Ransom's new bridges to New Carthage and thence down to Mrs. Perkins's plantation, where they arrived late the same afternoon. The next day, 12 May, they were ferried across to Grand Gulf. Ransom's BDE left Pointe Clear on 11 May, marched via the new bridges to New Carthage, and on 12 May was ferried from Mrs. Perkins's plantation to Grand Gulf by the hard-working transports. For all practical purposes, the roads along Bayou Vidal and Lake St. Joseph had been abandoned. That was no loss, because Ransom's bridges made it possible to march overland from Richmond, down Roundaway Bayou to Pointe Clear, then across to New Carthage, and then down the levee to Mrs. Perkins's plantation. One of Ransom's regiments was left behind at Mrs. Perkins's to maintain the campground, in case it should be needed in the future.

CONFEDERATE PERSPECTIVE

LTG Pemberton was growing steadily more disturbed by the news coming from Bowen at Grand Gulf during the final days of April. By 30 April, it was clear that Grant and his army were going to be able to make a landing in Mississippi somewhere south of Grand Gulf and that Bowen would be unable to prevent it. That meant that the Confederacy would have to fight a field battle to contain the bridgehead, and for that Pemberton would need every man who could be assembled. On 1 May, Pemberton sent a message to MG Franklin Gardner, commander of the garrison at Port Hudson, to send BG John Gregg's BDE to Jackson as soon as possible.[16] He specifically asked for John Gregg because Gregg had a reputation as a fighter.

Gardner wasted not a moment; Gregg and his brigade were on the march for Osyka, on the New Orleans, Jackson & Great Northern Railroad, early the next morning, 2 May. Gregg wasted no time, either. He arrived at Osyka at about 1800, only to find that no trains were running. He quickly determined that there would be no trains anytime soon, because Grierson's Union cavalry raiders had made a shambles of the railroad between Osyka and Brookhaven. The only good thing was that one of his regiments, 7 TX INF, which had been detached to hunt the pesky raiders, was at Osyka. Gregg added the Texans to his force; and, over the agonized protests of the local populace, he seized everything with wheels or four legs in the vicinity to carry his gear. Next morning, 5 May, he started marching up the railroad line toward Jackson.

Gregg reached Brookhaven, at the northern end of the gap Grierson had torn in the railroad, at about 1600 on 7 May. He promptly put his men aboard the trains he found there. The next day, 8 May, he arrived triumphantly in Jackson and went into camp about three miles east of the city.[17]

17

Making Trouble in the Trans-Mississippi 2 May–13 May 1863

Maps: 1. The Theater of Operations
     4. Southern Sector
     9. Northeastern Louisiana

FEDERAL PERSPECTIVE

On the evening of 1 May, RADM Porter, aboard mighty *Benton,* anchored off Bruinsburg, received news that the Army of the Tennessee finally had beaten the Rebel army defending Port Gibson after an all-day battle. Porter breathed a heart-felt sigh of relief at the thought that Grant and his blue-clad soldiery no longer were in imminent danger of being thrown back into the river. However, the Federal army was not yet completely out of the woods, because the Rebels certainly would try to hold the line of Bayou Pierre and thus retain their grasp on Grand Gulf. If they could do that until the Vicksburg army moved south into position, Grant and his troops would be completely dependent upon the supply line through Louisiana. That line was simply too long and tenuous to be made secure, especially now that the crest of the spring flood had passed. The water in the river was dropping daily, and the backswamps were draining rapidly. Soon there would be no protective shield of flooded swamps between the Tensas River and the Mississippi. As soon as those swamps became passable, it was very likely that GEN

Kirby Smith, who commanded the Confederate Department of Trans-Mississippi, would launch an effort to cut the major supply line connecting the Army of the Tennessee with its bases at Milliken's Bend and Young's Point.

Grand Gulf was the key. Until the Rebels could be ejected from that fortress, Grant and his men remained in terrible danger. With Grand Gulf in Union hands, the supply line still would be far too long for comfort, but at least it would involve only one overland leg, from Milliken's Bend to Ione and Mrs. Perkins's plantation. The army transports could ferry the goods by water from that point.

Furthermore, if Grant were to be held south of Bayou Pierre for more than a very few days, there remained a real danger that the Rebels would be able to marshal an army, defeat him, and perhaps force him to evacuate his bridgehead in Mississippi. Thus, Porter decided to keep the ironclads at Bruinsburg, where they could cover a bridgehead with their big guns, just in case. In the meantime, there was nothing to do but keep steam up and powder dry.

Porter fretted through the next day, 2 May, and late that afternoon was diverted by the arrival of the ram *Switzerland,* carrying dispatches for Grant from MG Banks,[1] who commanded the Federal Army of the Gulf from his headquarters at New Orleans. From the ram's captain, Porter learned that Banks had launched an offensive up the Bayou Teche, with the objective of occupying Alexandria, LA. The captain also told him that he was unlikely to make it, one reason being that Farragut had only wooden ships which had been designed for saltwater operations. They were not at all suitable for river operations; even worse, they were not armored. Getting past Confederate fortifications, such as those at Fort de Russy, twenty miles below Alexandria on the Red River, was likely to pose a serious problem. Porter reflected that, regardless of its success, Banks's offensive was a blessing, because it would keep the Rebels in Louisiana so occupied that they would have neither time nor resources to do anything much about Vicksburg.

There was no word from Grant. That night Porter slept fitfully. Then, at 0400 on the morning of 3 May, the thunder of three huge explosions rolled down from the north.[2] Those explosions could mean only one thing: the Rebels had detonated the powder magazines at Grand Gulf. And that meant that they had evacuated it; the Army of the Tennessee, was not only safe but across Bayou Pierre. Porter had his squadron steaming north almost within minutes, all but miserable *Tuscumbia,* which was left behind on guard duty.

Benton arrived off the town at 0600. There was no sign of either

Confederate or Union troops, so Porter put a naval landing party ashore to take possession.[3] Thus it was that, when Grant arrived later that same day, the town and its ruined forts already were solidly in Union hands.

With the Federal bridgehead in Mississippi now secure, the big guns of the navy were no longer needed, and Porter turned his attention to other concerns. First, of course, was the matter of Welles's letter ordering him to assume responsibility for patrolling the Mississippi between Vicksburg and Port Hudson, so that Farragut could get back to his blockading duties. There was no longer any reason why that should not be done, so the obvious thing to do was to head south, contact Farragut, and with him work out whatever arrangements seemed appropriate. Moreover, such a move could be made to serve a second, and in Porter's mind much more important, purpose: making sure that there were no Rebel incursions from the west against Grant's supply line.

The logic was straightforward. The supply line from Milliken's Bend remained very long and vulnerable, but the Confederates still would find it difficult to get into position to attack it. Given the fragmentary nature of the Louisiana road network, it seemed clear that they would have to bring their forces into the area by water. They had only two options. The first was to bring troops north from Kirby Smith's forces at Alexandria. There was navigable water almost all the way, enabling a force to move up the Tensas River to a point opposite Mrs. Perkins's plantation. The Tensas and the Mississippi were less than ten miles apart at that point, and, now that the waters in the backswamps were drying, they would be able to use the road which reportedly connected Buck's plantation on the Tensas with Bayou Vidal. Such a movement could be accomplished very quickly. This, of course, presupposed that Kirby Smith would risk detaching a force while engaged with Banks on the Bayou Teche. However, if the captain of *Switzerland* were right, that affair might end at any time. If Banks withdrew to Berwick Bay, Kirby Smith surely would strike in support of Vicksburg, the lock that prevented Union use of the Lower Mississippi and kept the Confederacy stitched together.

Kirby Smith's second possible course of action was to shift troops from the Army of Arkansas down to Monroe, LA. They then would have the option of going by steamboat down the Ouachita to its junction with Bayou Macon, and back up that stream to Delhi; or they could come by railroad across country from Monroe to Delhi. Delhi was still twenty-five miles from Milliken's Bend, and that would be at least a two-day march over a single miserable road. Porter thought that an unlikely course of action. Much more likely, he thought, would be to bring the troops by steamboat down the Ouachita from Monroe to the mouth of the Tensas and then back up the Tensas to Buck's plantation opposite Bayou Vidal. That would put them at the head of the road to Bayou Vidal and Mrs. Perkins's plantation on the Mississippi. From there they could strike at New Carthage, severing the supply line that supported Grant's army in Mississippi.

The weakness of all these Confederate plans was that they would depend upon boats using waterways that connected to the Red River. Porter could push naval forces up those streams and disrupt any moves that the Rebels might be either making or contemplating. If a squadron could get as far up the Ouachita as Monroe, it would end any threat posed by Rebel troops from Holmes's Army of Arkansas. Furthermore, Porter could provide some ironclads to deal with the Confederate forts on the Red River, such as Fort de Russy, which the captain of *Switzerland* had told him was holding up Farragut's wooden gunboats. With Fort de Russy knocked out, Banks's army would be assured of the Red River as a supply route, and that would enormously enhance its chances of success. Too, that would mean that Kirby Smith's Rebel army in Louisiana would be unable to detach troops for an effort against Grant's supply line. It was perfect!

For Porter, the thought was never far from the deed. At 1100, he was on his way to the mouth of the Red River with *Benton, Lafayette, Pittsburg, General Price, Switzerland,* and handy little *Ivy*. He left LCDR Owen in command at Grand Gulf with *Louisville, Mound City,* and *Carondelet. Tuscumbia,* being useless for serious work, was left at Bruinsburg.[4]

Porter's squadron arrived at the mouth of the Red River on the morning of 4 May. There he found Farragut in his big saltwater flagship *Hartford*.[5] Farragut was delighted; with the ironclads, there was little doubt that Alexandria could be occupied. With Farragut's blessing, Porter steamed up the Red River, and that same afternoon he met CDR Hart, with *Estrella* and *Arizona,* two of Farragut's wooden saltwater gunboats, lying near the mouth of the Black River.[6] Hart's task was to support Banks's infantry, which was moving up Bayou Teche in an offensive against Alexandria. He had gotten into the Red by subduing Rebel Fort Burton, at Butte-a-la-Rose on the Atchafalaya, a few days previously and steaming on up that river to its origin, thus bypassing Port Hudson.

Hart told Porter that he had tried to force his way past Fort de Russy but had found it defended by a pair of very determined Rebel gunboats, as well as by a raft across the river which made it impossible to go beyond the fort. His wooden ships simply were not suited for such work.

Late the same day, 5 May, Porter and his combined squadron arrived at Fort de Russy, only to find the Rebel gunboats gone and the fort deserted.[7] *General Price* made short work of the barrier raft, and, with no opposition of any kind, the fleet anchored for the night at Grand Bend, nine miles below Alexandria. Convinced that the Southerners had evacuated the region, he sent *Arizona* on ahead, in the hope that the Rebels had left some shipping behind at Alexandria. The anchorage was deserted, however, and there was not a Rebel soldier in sight.[8]

Hoping to eliminate any threat from Fort de Russy once and for all, Porter set the crew of *Benton* to the task of razing it, meanwhile sending the rest of the fleet upriver to occupy Alexandria. That same afternoon, 6 May, Banks's infantry arrived and occupied the town without firing a shot. That took care of the first objective.[9]

Leaving CDR Walke and mighty *Lafayette* behind to provide Banks with some heavy-duty gun support in case he needed it, Porter dropped back downstream with the rest of his squadron and sent CDR Selim E. Woodworth, of *General Price,* up the Black (Ouachita) with *Pittsburg* and *Switzerland. Arizona* was sent along, not because Porter thought she would do any good, but mostly just to keep Farragut's men involved in affairs in what was, after all, their hunting ground. He thought they might have some excitement, for he had heard rumors that a large Rebel force was coming down the Ouachita from Arkansas.

Woodworth moved very slowly and cautiously, so it was not until about 1400 on 10 May that he anchored his little squadron at the mouth of Bushley Bayou, about two miles south of Harrisonburg. He had learned that there was a Rebel fortification, Fort Beauregard, just below the town, and he wanted to take a look before engaging it. He tried to bluff the fort's commander, LT Logan, into evacuating, but Logan would have none of that.[10] Woodworth had only one vessel, ironclad *Pittsburg,* suitable for this kind of work, but he moved up and engaged. The fort replied in kind. It was a standoff, neither inflicting any significant harm on the other. Woodworth tried again the next day, with no better success, so he gave up and dropped back down to the Red River.[11]

Porter was philosophical about the defeat. It didn't really matter. What mattered was to prevent the Rebels from using the Ouachita and Black rivers, and that clearly had been achieved. However, he now had been away from the Mississippi River for nine days, during which time he had received no news whatever from that front. Anything could have happened in his absence. It was time to go back. He sent *Switzerland,*

Estrella, and *Arizona* back up the Red to reinforce Walke (*Switzerland* was fast, and thus useful for carrying dispatches up and down the river, and the other two ships actually belonged to Farragut), and headed for the Mississippi.[12] He reached the river the same afternoon, transferred to speedy *General Price*, and headed upstream for Vicksburg. *Benton* would struggle back upstream at her usual snail's pace, but he loaned Farragut *Pittsburg* and *Ivy* to use against Port Hudson.

Porter arrived at Grand Gulf on 13 May[13] and learned that, so far as anyone knew, the Army of the Tennessee was far inland but safe. Next day he moved on up to Bowers' Landing, to find that the army was building a new road connecting it with Hecla Place on Walnut Bayou. It would be ready for wagons in a couple of days, and that would make it possible to evacuate the depot at Mrs. Perkins's plantation. Porter was delighted: for all practical purposes, the only way the Confederates now could interrupt the Federal logistical system would be to mount a major attack on the fortified posts of Milliken's Bend and Young's Point. That would require elaborate preparations, so the possibility could be ignored, at least for the time being. Trading his boat for a horse, the admiral the next day rode up the new road and rejoined the upper squadron, which was lying peacefully at the naval anchorage off the mouth of the Yazoo River.[14] He had been gone for twenty-eight days. *Benton* straggled into Grand Gulf on 16 May.

CONFEDERATE PERSPECTIVE

GEN Edmund Kirby Smith was new to his job. He had arrived at Alexandria as commander of the Trans-Mississippi Department on 1 March 1863 and had hardly had enough time to memorize the names of his senior commanders before the roof fell in.

On 1 May, he had about 35,000 combat troops under his command, but they were scattered in packets of division sized or smaller from Jacksonport, AR, to Franklin, LA. With this force, he was expected to defend the entire Trans-Mississippi, which in practice meant everything west of the Mississippi that remained in Confederate control. It was not an unimportant task. The states west of the Mississippi River were important sources of commissary supplies for the Confederate armies east of the river, and they were important sources of manpower as well. They always could be counted on to provide effective combat troops for service east of the river in an emergency.

Furthermore, by 1863, significant amounts of European war materials

were being offloaded at Matamoros, Mexico, sent up through the sounds of
the Texas coast, and then transported through the Louisiana waterways to
the Mississippi.[15] An important alternate route led up the Ouachita to Monroe and then, via the Vicksburg, Shreveport & Texas Railroad, to Delhi, LA,
from whence materials could be ferried across the Mississippi to Vicksburg.
Of course, Grant's occupation of Milliken's Bend and Young's Point effectively severed that latter route. To the Confederate authorities, however, that
situation was a temporary inconvenience; service would be restored when
the Yankees were forced to evacuate those posts and return to the North.
As of March 1863, considerable amounts of goods still were reaching the
river and being carried across between Port Hudson and Grand Gulf, despite the fact that Farragut, the Union naval commander in New Orleans,
beginning on 15 March 1863, developed a nasty habit of patrolling the river
with ships from his Gulf Coast Squadron.

These patrols had become feasible because they no longer had to pass
the Port Hudson batteries. Banks's Union army had occupied Brashear
City in January 1863, giving the Federals control of the mouth of the
Atchafalaya. Then, on 11 April, the Yankee army unexpectedly launched
an offensive up Bayou Teche, obviously aimed at Alexandria. Kirby
Smith's forces on the Bayou Teche, under LTG Richard Taylor, amounted
to less than 5,000 men; they could not hope to hold against the blue-clad
hordes, so they withdrew to Opelousas. The Yankees promptly pushed a
squadron up the Atchafalaya and captured the Confederate fort at Butte-
a-la-Rose on the Atchafalaya. That gave them a navigable route to the Red
River, which in turn connected to the Mississippi a few miles above Port
Hudson.[16] The route completely bypassed the batteries of Port Hudson,
which had been designed specifically to prevent Union naval access to the
river between Vicksburg and Port Hudson.

In the meantime, a letter from Pemberton had reached Alexandria,
asking Kirby Smith to intervene in the defense of Vicksburg by attacking the
Federal troops in Louisiana. But Kirby Smith had his own troubles, namely,
the Yankee offensive in southern Louisiana. To Kirby Smith, the Yankee
operations looked very much like a major effort to occupy Louisiana and thus
close the supply line to Matamoros. Given the numerical disparity between
Taylor's troops and those of Banks, Kirby Smith saw no reason why Banks
could not drive all the way to Shreveport, especially since he would be able
to supply his troops by means of transports on the Red River. Assuming, of
course, that the Federals could take Fort de Russy.

Viewed in this light, the Federal operations opposite Vicksburg might well be preparations for a thrust westward toward Monroe and Shreveport in coordination with Banks's offensive up the Red River. Anticipating the loss of Alexandria, Kirby Smith planned to retreat up the Red River to Shreveport. This would give him time to collect an army large enough to deal with the matter. Accordingly, he ordered MG J. G. Walker to move his Texas Division from Hamburg, AR, to Camden, AR,[17] where he would be in a position to effect a junction with Taylor somewhere in the vicinity of Shreveport. However, he did not see fit to explain his reasoning to Walker.

Walker, of course, knew the Union army was opposite Vicksburg, and he had heard of Banks's offensive westward from Berwick Bay. Thus he assumed he was being ordered southward to join the fight against either Grant or Banks. Given that assumption, a move to Camden made no sense whatever, and Walker assumed that it was an error. Instead, he more or less marched toward the sound of the guns.[18] Upon inquiry, BG Paul Hébert, commander of the District of NE Louisiana, promised him transports on the Ouachita near the mouth of Bayou Bartholomew, so he would be able to go by water either to Monroe, to be used against Grant, or further south, to be used against Banks on the lower Red River.

Walker's Texans reached the Ouachita near the mouth of Bayou Bartholomew, about twenty miles above Monroe, on 1 May. There they found twelve transports awaiting them, just as Hébert had promised. Walker loaded his men and moved down to Monroe, reaching there on 2 May. He promptly sent a message to Kirby Smith notifying him of his whereabouts.

At Monroe, Walker discovered that Hébert had his own agenda. Hébert was convinced that the big Union army opposite Vicksburg was a serious threat to the Confederacy itself, because its objective was Vicksburg. If Vicksburg fell, the Confederacy would be cut in two and doomed to eventual extinction. He pressed this view on Walker, arguing that Walker should stay at Monroe and make preparations to attack the Union forces at Milliken's Bend.[19] He figured that the Louisiana posts had to be lightly held, because the damned bluecoats were stretched out all the way from Lake Providence to Hard Times. The water in the backswamps now was so low that the road between Delhi and the Mississippi was passable, albeit still a bit difficult.

Walker was sympathetic but refused on the grounds that he could not disobey a direct order from Kirby Smith. Sure enough, when Kirby Smith got Walker's message on 3 May, he was furious. His reply to Walker denounced his actions in scathing terms and concluded by telling him to get ready to move to Alexandria. In a last-ditch effort to assemble a force large enough at least to make itself felt against the Yankees, Hébert pleaded with Walker to leave a brigade behind; that force, coupled with his own cavalry (which amounted to a small brigade composed mostly of State Troops), at least would be able to harass the Yankee supply lines. Walker, still smarting from Kirby Smith's scolding, refused. But he did promise to talk to the commander when he got to Alexandria.

During all this time, the Union infantry was moving slowly but steadily up Bayou Teche toward Alexandria. On 4 May, a pair of Yankee gunboats tried to knock out Fort de Russy but were beaten off by CDR Kelso's little squadron of cottonclads.[20] That was a temporary and meaningless victory, because Kirby Smith had learned that RADM Porter was in the Red River with a squadron of those damnable ironclads, and neither Kelso nor Fort de Russy (which was mostly under water because of a flood crest on the Red) would have the slightest chance of stopping them. He ordered Taylor to withdraw to a position northwest of Alexandria and sent Kelso back to Grand Ecore. Sure enough, Porter's gunboats arrived at Alexandria early on the morning of 6 May, and Banks's infantry tramped into town that same afternoon.[21] However, to Kirby Smith's surprise, they made no move whatever to press on up the Red River.

Walker, at Monroe, had a problem. There were not enough transports available to carry his men, guns, and wagons, so on 8 May he started his wagon train overland toward LeCroix Ferry on the Little River, twenty-two miles north-northeast of Alexandria. The next day he started down the Ouachita with his men aboard Hébert's twelve transports. That afternoon his little fleet reached Harrisonburg, where it was intercepted by a courier from Kirby Smith, bringing the news that Alexandria had been evacuated. That was bad enough, but far more chilling was the news that the Yankee RADM Porter was in the Red River with his gunboats. Walker knew all about Porter and assumed that a squadron of his deadly ironclads very soon would be in the Ouachita. Within the hour, the little fleet was heading back toward Monroe at full steam, with his men looking apprehensively downriver, expecting to see tell-tale plumes of smoke from the gunboats at any moment. No one had the slightest faith that Fort Beauregard, just below Harrisonburg, would delay the ironclads for more than an hour or so.

Somewhere along the river, Walker was intercepted by another courier from Kirby Smith, this one ordering him to march his men overland to Natchitoches, on the Red River seventy-five miles away to the southwest.[22] Kirby Smith had ordered this move with the intention of uniting

Walker with Taylor and using the combined force to drive Banks back to Berwick Bay.

A letter from Pemberton arrived in Kirby Smith's headquarters on 13 May with the news that Grand Gulf had fallen and that an attack on Vicksburg was expected at any moment. The missive also contained a plea that Kirby Smith strike at Grant's supply line in Louisiana, which Pemberton knew to be very long, tenuous, and vulnerable.[23] Kirby Smith ignored the plea. In fact, he scarcely could do otherwise. Taylor's division was now near Grand Ecore, and, with the Union navy controlling the waterways, there simply was no way in which Kirby Smith's troops could be moved quickly into a position for a strike against the Yankee supply line opposite Vicksburg. Walker's Texas division was similarly out of play, somewhere between Monroe and Natchitoches. Under the circumstances, the best thing would be to proceed with his plans to push Banks back to Berwick Bay.[24] With luck, the Yankee gunboats would then withdraw to the Mississippi, and that would make it possible to move a force by water from Alexandria to the Tensas River, where it would be in a position to strike at Grant's supply line.

On 15 May, it looked as if the gamble had paid off even more quickly than Kirby Smith had hoped, because the bluecoats were withdrawing from Alexandria, even though they were not yet under any pressure from Taylor. It was time to start thinking about a plan for assisting Vicksburg.

18

Toward Edwards and the Railroad
4 May–6 May 1863

Maps: 6. Physiographic Regions Significant to the Vicksburg Campaign
      9. Northeastern Louisiana
    10. The Region between Vicksburg, Bruinsburg, and Raymond
    35. Disposition of Forces in the Region between Vicksburg,
        Bruinsburg, and Raymond: 1200, 5 May 1863

FEDERAL PERSPECTIVE

When night fell on 3 May 1863, the Army of the Tennessee was in firm control of the region between the Big Black River and Bayou Pierre as far east as a line roughly connecting Grindstone Ford, Rocky Springs, and Hankinson's Ferry. Late that night, a courier from the infantry patrol sent to occupy Rocky Springs reported no trace of Rebels in that direction, and that was a surprise, because it had been assumed that the Southerners at the very least would try to block the roads to the east. No Rebels at Rocky Springs meant that all the Grand Gulf force had retreated across the bridge at Hankinson's Ferry. Grant was pleased, because it meant that he would not have to guard against a counterattack from the east.

As Grant ate his breakfast in McPherson's headquarters on the morning of 4 May, he must have felt a vast sense of triumph as he reflected on the achievements of the last several days. The left flank of Fortress Vicksburg had been crushed in, and the Army of the Tennessee had secured a convenient forward base at Grand Gulf. Sherman's divisions were hurrying to catch up and would arrive in a few days at most. However, until they appeared, Grant had time to think. It is clear that much of his thinking was strongly influenced, perhaps even was dominated, by terrain considerations.

There were two possible approaches to Vicksburg. First and most direct would be to storm across the Big Black River at Hankinson's Ferry and drive straight up the Vicksburg Road. But there were reports that the Rebels were digging in along a line extending east from Warrenton. To strike directly for Vicksburg might be to risk cracking the knuckles of his army in a slugging match on ground of the Rebels' own choosing. Furthermore, even though the railroad had been broken by Grierson's raiders between Vicksburg and Meridian, Pemberton's army still would be supported by unlimited supplies and reinforcements flowing in over the Southern Railroad of Mississippi from the depots around Jackson. As long as the railroad between Jackson and Vicksburg was intact, Pemberton would retain the strategic advantage of interior lines.

The second possible course of action was to hold the line of the Big Black while swinging to the northeast in a flanking move designed to break the railroad somewhere between Big Black Bridge and Jackson. That would eliminate the railroad. Even better, if the Southerners came out to fight to protect it, the battle would be fought in the more open and gently rolling terrain of the Mississippi interior, where the superior Union artillery could be used to best advantage. And there was yet another potential advantage in moving against Edwards, perhaps greater than all the rest, and that was conferred by the presence of RADM Porter and his warships. Grant was reasonably certain that Pemberton did not know that the Louisiana posts had been almost stripped of troops. Thus, as long as the navy remained in the river, there was a creditable threat of a direct Federal amphibious assault on the city. Pemberton's only possible response to an offensive against Edwards would be to leave enough men in the city defenses to deal with the amphibious threat and at the same time send a major portion of his army to defend Edwards and Big Black Bridge. Forcing an opponent to divide his forces on the eve of battle is the dream of every strategist. In contrast, a direct attack on the city would permit Pemberton to concentrate his forces.

Grant could not make a firm decision until he had a clearer picture of both the terrain to the north and east, and the distribution of the Confederate forces. For all he knew, Pemberton's entire army of maneuver might be poised just across the Big Black River. If Grant moved the bulk of his army eastward, Pemberton might attack his rear or, even worse, strike at and reoccupy Grand Gulf. If that happened, the Army of the Tennessee would be trapped in the interior without access to the river and the essential supplies that it provided, and its doom would be sealed. On the other hand, if he launched the Army of the Tennessee across the Big Black at Hankinson's Ferry, Pemberton might use Bowen's troops, probably reinforced by this time with troops from the Vicksburg garrison, to hit him while he had one foot on either bank. Again, the result was not hard to predict.

So the first priority was to find out, if possible, whether the Confederate army had moved out of Vicksburg; and, if so, whether it was concentrated somewhere between Hankinson's Ferry and Vicksburg, or at some point along the railroad to the east of Vicksburg, such as Big Black Bridge. Accordingly, McPherson was ordered to probe northward toward Vicksburg, and McClernand northeastward toward Edwards.[1]

McClernand as yet had no cavalry, but Osterhaus had advanced infantry elements in Rocky Springs, and he used them to patrol aggressively northeastward toward Reganton. They found no Rebel formations, but they did pick up a deserter who tattled that there were four steamboats at Hall's Ferry on the Big Black River. This tale got McClernand's attention. With the arrival of COL Clark Wright's 6 MO CAV on 4 May, McClernand at last had a strong mounted force at his disposal, and, on the morning of 5 May, he sent three companies of them, supported by Osterhaus's infantry division, up the road toward Reganton and Cayuga, hoping to seize those boats. Alas for his hopes. Just north of Big Sand Creek, the cavalry was fired upon by a Confederate cavalry patrol. LT Isaiah Stickel led a thundering cavalry charge that rolled right over the Rebels, killing twelve and capturing thirty of them.[2] It was a hollow victory, however, as it meant that the element of surprise was lost. With all hope of capturing the steamboats gone, Osterhaus camped for the night in the bottoms of Big Sand Creek. The skirmish north of Big Sand Creek also told Grant that the Confederates once again had made contact with his right flank, and that any movement in that direction could not be made in secret.

Meanwhile, McPherson had taken his reconnaissance duties seriously. Early on the morning of 5 May, he personally led a combat patrol toward Vicksburg. It consisted of three companies of Wright's 6 MO CAV, which had arrived at Hankinson's Ferry late the previous afternoon; two regiments of Boomer's BDE; and a section of artillery—enough force to make the Confederates take it seriously, but not enough to be unwieldy. The patrol hit a Confederate picket line two miles south of Redbone Church, and there were glimpses of strongly-manned fortifications just beyond. Boomer threw out skirmishers and pushed a bit, but the Rebels did not seem disposed to move, so McPherson disengaged and returned to Hankinson's Ferry.[3]

McPherson's report was enough to give Grant pause. First, and in some ways most worrisome, was the fact that there had been no trace whatever of Bowen's force which had retreated across the Big Black at Hankinson's Ferry. Almost certainly, that meant that Bowen had withdrawn not toward Vicksburg, as Grant had more or less expected, but toward Big Black Bridge. The second bit of unsettling information was that hills and ravines like the battlefield of Port Gibson went all the way to Vicksburg. Third, the Rebels had a prepared defense line near Redbone Church, which was nine long miles from Vicksburg. Those three facts, taken together, were disquieting. It had taken the Army of the Tennessee in overwhelming force almost all day to force Bowen's little army out of unprepared positions at Port Gibson, and it was all too easy to imagine what it would be like to attack a much larger force in prepared positions in the same kind of terrain.

The implications were obvious. A thrust directly toward Vicksburg would impact against the fortified positions south of Redbone Church, at which point the force which was clearly concentrating at or near Big Black Bridge would strike the Federal right flank. If that happened, the position of the Army of the Tennessee would be precarious indeed. The only bit of good news that could be wrung from McPherson's report was that the Rebels seemed content to dig in near Vicksburg, which effectively removed any threat to Grand Gulf or the rear of the Army of the Tennessee, if Grant decided to turn to the northeast. Given this insight, Grant took but little time to decide not to put his head in that particular noose, but instead to strike for the railroad at the most convenient point east of Big Black Bridge, which would be Edwards. If Pemberton did not fight for the railroad, he eventually would be forced to evacuate Vicksburg, simply because the city could not possibly be held for long without the supplies carried by the railroad. Therefore, Pemberton almost certainly would concentrate a field army at Edwards in preparation for a fight to the death to preserve his umbilical cord.

Grant had noted the character of the Big Black River floodplain. It could be crossed only at a very few special places, such as Fisher's Ferry, Hall's Ferry, and Baldwin's Ferry. Furthermore, Grant knew the water was deep as far upstream as Amsterdam, well north of the railroad, because it was navigable by steamboats. In a word, it was a major military obstacle which could be used to secure his left flank as he moved northeast. McClernand's reports also indicated that an excellent road ran more or less directly from Grand Gulf to Edwards. The Federal wagon trains would have no problems with such a route. Assuming that he won the battle when the Confederates came out to fight for the railroad, Grant then could cut Vicksburg's supply line, and that would mean either the evacuation of Vicksburg or the investment of the Rebel army in the city. Grant would be satisfied with either of these two possibilities. He would turn to the northeast, in the full expectation that he would be met by Pemberton's army of maneuver somewhere south of Edwards. That was fine, but to give any reasonable hope of success in the battle that would be fought there, he needed Sherman's troops. And Sherman had not yet arrived.

While awaiting the arrival of tardy Sherman, Grant ordered Osterhaus to continue his probes toward the northeast, in the direction of Edwards, hoping to obtain information on the location of Pemberton's field forces. On the morning of 6 May, Osterhaus sent strong infantry patrols up the road toward Edwards. One of them reached the Big Black River at Hall's Ferry without seeing a single Rebel. Another probed up the main Rocky Springs–Raymond road through Cayuga and Auburn, and before nightfall it was able to establish an observation post on a hilltop near the Telegraph Road, only about 2,500 yards south of Fourteenmile Creek. The men could see small Confederate units moving restlessly on the slopes north of the creek, and local farmers told them that there was a large Confederate force in Edwards.[4] Osterhaus could not quite believe that there were no strong Confederate forces to the east, even though there had been no contacts in that direction. As a precaution, he used his cavalry to picket the roads east and south of Cayuga; Cayuga was on the main road to Raymond and was the most likely axis of advance of any Confederate forces that might be gathered at Jackson.

By the evening of 6 May, scout reports and patrol contacts indicated that there were major Confederate concentrations at Warrenton and in the Edwards-Big Black Bridge area, with possibly another very minor concentration at Jackson. Steele's and Tuttle's divisions of Sherman's XV Corps were at Hard Times and would begin to come ashore at Grand Gulf on 7 May. It was time for Grant to move. His plan called for McClernand's corps to advance through Rocky Springs and Cayuga to Edwards, following the roads closest to the Big Black River. McPherson's corps would diverge at Reganton, turning south and then eastward to Utica, thence proceeding up the turnpike to Raymond. Sherman's corps would follow McClernand as far as Cayuga and then turn northeastward up the road to Auburn, midway between the two flanks. It was a plan

borrowed from Napoleon: three parallel columns moving within supporting distance of each other. But it was also dictated by harsh circumstances; subsistence farms have small food surpluses. Further, it was
spring, when the larders of most farm families are nearly empty. He had
to spread his men out so they could subsist.

Meanwhile, Grand Gulf was becoming a hive of activity, as the Federal forces converted it into a major supply depot. The Rebels evidently
were not unaware of this, because their cavalry tried to interfere with the
supply trains that by this time were crawling along the road from Grand
Gulf through Willows to Hankinson's Ferry and Rocky Springs.[5] However,
both the 6 MO CAV and 2 IL CAV had landed at Grand Gulf on 4 May,
and they were able to drive the Rebel horsemen south of Bayou Pierre
and keep them there.[6] Since there were no reports of significant Confederate infantry forces to the south, the southern flank seemed secure.

CONFEDERATE PERSPECTIVE

Pemberton had received the dreadful news of Bowen's defeat at Port
Gibson late on the evening of 1 May at his new headquarters in Vicksburg.
He knew that Bowen's force had fallen back to the north bank of Bayou
Pierre in good order, and he thought it likely that Loring would be able
to hold the line of Big Bayou Pierre at least until Barton's, Taylor's, and
A. W. Reynolds's brigades from Vicksburg got there. With those three bri-
gades, plus Tilghman's demi-brigade, Loring would have something like
17,000 men. With such a force, it should be possible to hold the line of
Bayou Pierre for several days at a minimum.

Pemberton understood that, if Grant were able to seize control of Grand
Gulf and the peninsula between the Big Black River and Bayou Pierre,
Grant would have at least two possible courses of action open to him. He
could strike straight for Vicksburg, or he could strike northeast in an attempt
to cut the railroad by capturing or destroying the Big Black Bridge.
Pemberton had to defend both. The answer was a concentration at Big Black
Bridge, from which point forces could be moved either east or west as
needed. Featherston's BDE, from Fort Pemberton, was placed at the bridge
on 3 May, along with several hundred miscellaneous troops.[7]

Loring's message, sent from Hankinson's Ferry at 0500 on the morning
of 3 May, ended the hope that the Yankee bridgehead could be contained
to the area around Port Gibson. It must have come as something of a shock
to discover that Loring was giving up the line of Big Bayou Pierre without a
struggle and that Grand Gulf was being evacuated. That meant that the Big

Black River was the only remaining water barrier between the Army of the Tennessee and Vicksburg. All through 3 May, Pemberton had no clear idea where Loring was or what was happening to him.[8] Loring's message had implied that he was withdrawing toward Vicksburg, but there had been no confirmation, so it was possible that he might have withdrawn to the northeast, toward Big Black Bridge. It was even possible that part of the force had gone one way and part another. Even worse, the news had been sent before all Loring's troops were across the Big Black, so it was possible that some of them had retreated to the east via Rocky Springs.

What Pemberton did not know was that Bowen and Loring had had few options late on the afternoon of 3 May. They had been forced to withdraw their entire army across the Hankinson's Ferry bridge to the north bank of the Big Black River, because the Union advance had occupied the strategic road junction at Willows before the Confederate main body got there. They had not dared attempt an escape through Rocky Springs by using the Hankinson's Ferry–Rocky Springs road, for fear that the Federal divisions would cut the retreating column in two by an advance directly toward Rocky Springs from Willows. As a result, on the night of 3 May, Loring found himself on the north bank of the Big Black with an army that consisted of seven BDEs (Cockrell's, Green's, Baldwin's, Taylor's, S. D. Lee's, A. W. Reynolds's and Barton's) and a demi-BDE (Tilghman's), a total of perhaps 17,000 men.

Loring completely lost contact with the Federal army when he was forced across the Big Black on the afternoon of 3 May. At that point, he believed that the Yankees had only one practical course of action open to them, and that was to launch a direct assault upon Vicksburg. Badly unnerved by the experiences of the previous forty-eight hours, he decided that he could not hope to hold the line of the Big Black River with an army he knew to be greatly outnumbered. As he saw it, the only practical course of action was to withdraw from the line of the Big Black and retreat to a much shorter defensive line that ran from Warrenton via Lanier's plantation to Big Black Bridge. The terrain was eminently defensible, and it was much closer to the supply depot at Vicksburg. The fact that he was giving up the last unfordable water barrier between the Federal army and Vicksburg, without even the semblance of a fight, seemed unimportant to him.

Furthermore, he gave up all opportunity to use his army as a single cohesive instrument by immediately dispersing it. Early on 4 May, he started John Bowen, with Cockrell's, Green's, and Taylor's BDEs, toward Big Black Bridge, while he withdrew the rest of his force to Hubbard's farm, perhaps because it was close to Baldwin's and Hall's ferries. He did not inform Pemberton of his actions. He did, however, send him a message telling him that the Yankees were moving on Rocky Springs.[9] This message seems to have had no basis other than the fear that the Yankees would quickly occupy Rocky Springs and Reganton and so gain access to two additional crossings of the Big Black: Campbell's Crossing, two miles upstream from Hankinson's Ferry; and Fisher Ferry, some seven miles farther upstream as the crow flies. If the Federals moved quickly, they could put a couple of divisions across the river and get astride Bowen's march route to Big Black Bridge. In other words, he feared that he was not yet completely out of the box.

This was the last message for some time, because the telegraph line from Hankinson's Ferry to Vicksburg followed the main road, and the move toward Hubbard's farm and Big Black Bridge took them into a region not served by wires. Loring did not try to compensate by using couriers to the telegraph station at Bovina, so, as far as Pemberton was concerned, Loring and 17,000 men had vanished from the face of the earth.

On the morning of 4 May, Loring did his best to regain contact with the Federal army, and he succeeded beyond his wildest expectations. He was desperately short of cavalry, but he assembled a scratch force under LT W. L. Cromwell and sent it across the Big Black, probably at Baldwin's Ferry, with orders to probe toward Rocky Springs. Sure enough, early on the morning of 5 May, just north of Big Sand Creek, Cromwell's patrol met a Union force moving rapidly north. There was a brisk skirmish, with Loring's scratch riders being overwhelmed by the veteran Federal cavalry.[10] LT Cromwell escaped and quickly reported to Loring, who interpreted the news as support for his worst fear: that the Yankees were moving in strength toward Fisher Ferry, no doubt with the intention of crossing. Curiously, Loring did not report this action to Pemberton, although by this time he had access to the telegraph station in Bovina, which was in direct telegraphic contact with Vicksburg via the line which paralleled the Southern Railroad of Mississippi.

Meanwhile, all through 3 May, Pemberton had no idea where Loring was. Finally the question seemed to be resolved on 4 May, when Loring's message arrived with the news that the Yankees were moving on Rocky Springs.[11] The message was ambiguous, but the wording clearly implied that Loring was located at Rocky Springs. Not unreasonably, Pemberton assumed that the bulk of Loring's forces must have withdrawn through that village, and that the Union army was marching to attack Big Black Bridge, having been drawn in that direction in pursuit of Loring's retreating force. This all made perfect sense to Pemberton, because the Union generals surely would regard the bridge as a worthwhile objective, since its capture would effectively isolate Vicksburg. Furthermore, a Federal march line that ran up the Rocky Springs–Auburn road would mean that their left flank would be protected by the unfordable Big Black River from interference by Confederate forces in and around Vicksburg.

Believing that Loring's force was near Rocky Springs, Pemberton instantly sent a dispatch ordering him to move his troops to Big Black Bridge.[12] His motive obviously was not only to protect the bridge, but also to move Loring out of danger until a concentration large enough to fight the Federals on something like even terms could be achieved. The courier, of course, ran into the Yankee pickets north of Rocky Springs. He managed to escape, but it was the next morning, 5 May, before he could deliver his message to "Old Blizzards," who by this time was already at Hubbard's farm, on the Baldwin's Ferry Road about eight miles southeast of Vicksburg. When Loring at last read the order, he professed to be much perplexed. He sent a message back to Pemberton, suggesting that he might be forced to fight a battle where he stood and also that supply difficulties might force the Yankees to move on Warrenton by water. Almost as an afterthought, he told Pemberton that Cockrell, Green, and Taylor already were marching toward Big Black Bridge.[13]

When Pemberton got Loring's message, later on 5 May, he finally realized that Loring and his army not only had withdrawn to the north bank of the Big Black River but also had abandoned the line of the Big Black River. There was little he could do to retrieve that situation, and indeed the withdrawal toward the Big Black Bridge was not all bad, because it was at that point that an army would have to be concentrated in order to defend Edwards and the bridge. He sent a message off, authorizing Loring to deal with the situation at Hankinson's Ferry as he thought best. The courier got lost, so Loring did not receive the communication until the next morning, 6 May, by which time he had evacuated the entire area south of Hubbard's farm.[14] There was no longer any hope whatever of containing the Army of the Tennessee south of the Big Black.

In the meantime, Pemberton had decided that Buford's BDE was being wasted in Jackson, so, on 4 May, it was brought forward to Big Black Bridge.[15] Thus, with the arrival of Bowen with Cockrell's, Green's, and Taylor's BDEs on 5 May, Pemberton had a significant concentration on the scene with which to defend the bridge, should that become necessary.

Pemberton's conviction that Big Black Bridge was the next Union objective was somewhat shaken on the afternoon of 5 May, when Carter Stevenson reported from Vicksburg that a powerful Yankee force of cavalry, infantry, and artillery had attacked his lines just south of Redbone Church. This seemed to imply that perhaps Vicksburg was the objective after all, in which case the force at Rocky Springs was a feint and possibly nothing more than a strong flank guard. Since Loring already had abandoned the line of the Big Black, thus eliminating any possibility of catching the Federals half on the north bank and half on the south, there was nothing to do but occupy the long-planned defense line that extended from Warrenton through Lanier's farm and on to Big Black Bridge. Pemberton took the opportunity afforded by the redeployment to organize most of the unattached brigades into two new divisions. Bowen was given command of one, consisting of Cockrell's and Green's BDEs, and Loring was placed in command of the other, consisting of Tilghman's, Buford's, and Featherston's.

By the morning of 5 May, Bowen's men were camped on the flats along Clear Creek, less than a half-mile north of Big Black Bridge, but their commander reported that they were so exhausted they would not be fit for active service for at least twenty-four hours. By this time, Loring had moved Tilghman's BDE and his headquarters back to Lanier's farm, three miles south of Mt. Alban.[16] Of his other two brigades, Featherston's was at Big Black Bridge, and Buford's was at Edwards. Carter Stevenson, with A. W. Reynolds's and Barton's brigades, was at Barnes's plantation, three miles northeast of Warrenton. Taylor's brigade held the intersection of the Hall's Ferry and Warrenton roads, with patrols thrown out to cover Hall's Ferry. Later that afternoon, Barton's BDE was sent into Vicksburg. COL Waul, whose Texas Legion had been left to garrison Fort Pemberton, was ordered to leave 300 men to hold the fort and bring the rest of his men to Snyder's Bluff. Pemberton was as ready as he ever would be to defend either Vicksburg or Big Black Bridge.

All through the confusing events of April, Pemberton had remained in Jackson, primarily because it was the only place which had good communications in all directions. Telegraph lines ran north along the railroads to the vital positions along the Tallahatchie River in northern Mississippi, south to the fortress of Port Hudson, and west to Vicksburg. Pemberton could still exploit that network from Vicksburg, because the line from Vicksburg to Jackson was quite reliable. However, the only telegraph line from Vicksburg to the south led to Grand Gulf and Port Gibson, and that was no longer helpful. The only effective communications with troops south of the railroad were by couriers, and, as the events of the last few days had amply demonstrated, they were slow and uncertain.

Even more serious, perhaps, was the chronic shortage of cavalry. There were lots of horsemen in the department, but nearly all were committed to defending the line of the Tallahatchie River, and the almost continual Federal probes at that line made it impossible to shift any of them to Central Mississippi. Throughout the campaign, Pemberton had pressed both Jefferson Davis and Joseph E. Johnston for more horsemen, to little avail. The only truly effective cavalry available to Pemberton in the Vicksburg-Jackson area was Wirt Adams's regiment of Mississippians. After Grierson's raiders had escaped to Baton Rouge, Wirt Adams quickly returned to duty on the southern flank of the Yankee penetration, and on 6 May he made his presence felt by strikes at the Federal wagon trains in the Port Gibson–Ingleside area.[17] It was too little and too late; by that time, the Federals had brought large cavalry forces of their own across the river, and Adams was forced back south of Bayou Pierre, where he was effectively neutralized.[18] Realizing that, and driven by his desperate need for eyes and ears for his main maneuver forces defending Vicksburg, Pemberton ordered Adams to move to Edwards as quickly as possible.

Despite the shortage of cavalry, Pemberton was able to maintain a scouting force that covered the roads southwest of Cayuga and Utica. Oddly enough, he was receiving no information whatever from the country people. However, on 5 May, his scouts reported a strong force moving northeast up the Rocky Springs–Reganton road. He was now on the horns of a dilemma, because the main Federal thrust might be toward either Vicksburg or Big Black Bridge, and he simply did not have enough information to be able to decide which was the case.

Furthermore, he was faced at this point with a far deeper dilemma. Pemberton had been sent west to defend Vicksburg at all costs. Simplistically, that meant the city. But the reason for holding Vicksburg was that Vicksburg was the northern anchor of a segment of the Mississippi, the other end of which was held by Gardner at Port Hudson. Together, the two fortresses held open the door which maintained communication with the Trans-Mississippi, with all that that implied in the way of human and material resources, as well as access to European war materials. If either anchor were lost, Confederate control of the Mississippi would be reduced to only that tiny segment of the river that could be commanded by the guns of the remaining fortress. To be sure, that would still be an inconvenience to the North, since it would deny the Yankees open utilization of the river, but the Confederacy nevertheless would be cut in two; Federal warships would prevent any significant transfer of goods, commissary supplies, or manpower from one bank to the other. Thus, the real question was not whether to hold Vicksburg, but rather how to maintain control of the river segment between Port Hudson and Vicksburg.

Vicksburg might well be held, at least for a long while, by concentrating all the armed might in the vicinity of the city and holding the Warrenton–Lanier plantation–Big Black Bridge line, plus an extension that followed the Big Black to the north. The Big Black south of Big Black Bridge could not be held, since the Yankees were free to cross at will at Hankinson's Ferry. Indeed, as far as Pemberton knew, they might well have done so already. The problem was that withdrawal into that defensive perimeter would give the Federal armies freedom to roam at will over Central Mississippi. Such freedom automatically meant the loss of Jackson, which was the vital communications hub upon which the defenses of northern Mississippi ultimately depended, and the loss of the railroad which supplied Vicksburg itself. Permanently deprived of that railroad, Vicksburg eventually would have to be abandoned, just as Memphis had fallen after control of the Memphis & Charleston Railroad had been lost after the evacuation of Corinth on 30 May 1862.

Furthermore, the Yankees had demonstrated that they could run even unarmored steamboats past the Vicksburg batteries, so there would be nothing to stop them from sending a corps or two by water to Port Hudson. If that happened, Port Hudson would be overwhelmed, and Confederate control of the river would instantly collapse to the area bounded by the range of the cannon in the Vicksburg River Defenses. In other words, the Confederacy would be cut in two.

Even further, without an effective Confederate force east of the river, there simply was not enough manpower to defend every point on the long line from Warrenton to, say, Cox's Ferry (on the Big Black River fifteen airline miles northwest of Amsterdam) in such strength as to prevent a Federal penetration somewhere along the line. Thus, there would be little to stop the Yankees from forcing a crossing of the Big Black somewhere to the north, perhaps at Bush's Ferry or Cox's Ferry, and driving westward to the Yazoo River. This would cut off the roads to the Delta, along with the commissary supplies upon which the Vicksburg army depended. In effect, Vicksburg would be besieged, even though the city itself would not be closely invested.

The obvious—indeed, the only—practical solution was to defeat the northern army in the field and force it back to a small bridgehead, perhaps around Grand Gulf, which could then be contained indefinitely. However, arranging that defeat required a bit of subtlety. Pemberton's troops had been in essentially static defensive positions for so long that he feared they would not be able to sustain the rigors of an extended campaign of maneuver. The only reasonable choice remaining was to interpose the Vicksburg army between the bluecoats and one of their major objectives, forcing the Yankees to attack the Confederates in a position of their own choosing. Edwards and Big Black Bridge were the obvious objectives if the Yankees moved north on the roads east of the Big Black River, and the terrain just south of Edwards was well suited for defense. Therefore, Pemberton decided to move the army to Edwards and fight the crucial battle on the ridges just south of the town. In the interim, while awaiting developments, he put a picket line well out to the south of Edwards to give ample warning of a Federal approach from that direction.

Pemberton also decided to hedge his bets by leaving strong forces to defend the Warrenton–Lanier's farm–Big Black Bridge line, in case the Yankees attacked in that sector in force. The terrain made that approach easy to defend, and the railroad and the Jackson Road would make it possible to shift forces quickly between Edwards and the defense line south of Vicksburg. After thinking about the matter for a brief time, Pemberton decided that he could further hedge his bets by fortifying the approaches to Big Black Bridge.[19] If by some chance he lost the battle south of Edwards, a fortified bridgehead would provide time for the defeated troops to fall back across the Big Black and assume a position from which to defend the line of the Big Black. On the afternoon of 5 May, he put his engineers to work building a fortified line just east of the Big Black Bridge,[20] and ordered Bowen to move his division to a point about three miles south of Smith's farm, on the road connecting Smith's farm with Montgomery Bridge. Bowen was also directed, once there, to place a strong regiment in Edwards and picket the line of Fourteenmile Creek. Bowen's men still were very tired, but he moved as directed and sent COL Elijah Gates and his 1 MO CAV (DSMTD), supported by a section of artillery, to Edwards.[21] Pemberton also strengthened the Warrenton–Big Black Bridge line by ordering Baldwin's BDE in Vicksburg to move to Lanier's farm.[22]

Early the next morning, 6 May, Pemberton finally learned about LT Cromwell's skirmish north of Big Sand Creek. This looked like the beginning of the expected offensive against Edwards and Big Black Bridge, but he could not yet be certain, because it might be a feint to cover a movement across Hankinson's Ferry and aimed directly at Vicksburg, or perhaps at Lanier's farm, which would take Big Black Bridge in rear. The obvious response was to position troops so that they could move readily in either direction. Accordingly, he ordered Buford's and Featherston's BDEs (of

Loring's newly formed division) to remain at the bridge, and ordered Loring, who was at Lanier's farm, to bring Tilghman's BDE to Big Black Bridge as well. However, "Old Blizzards" had had second thoughts about the force that had overwhelmed LT Cromwell; he now professed to believe that it had consisted of only a few cavalry and that everything else was a figment of Pemberton's imagination.[23] He simply *knew* that the Yankee attack was going to come across the Big Black River at Fisher Ferry or Hall's Ferry, or both. As a result, he deliberately disobeyed Pemberton's orders, and about 1000, 6 May, he started Buford's and Featherston's BDEs, as well as BTRY A, Pointe Coupée ARTY, toward Lanier's farm.

That same morning, Carter Stevenson, accompanied by Barton and BG S. D. Lee, inspected the Warrenton front. True to form, Stevenson sent a message to Pemberton, telling him that he could not possibly defend the nine-mile-long front without strong reinforcement. Stevenson was so worried that he brought Moore's BDE down from Vicksburg and placed it near Warrenton. At this point, the Confederates had about 31,000 men manning the Warrenton–Big Black Bridge line: Stevenson's DIV and Moore's BDE at Warrenton, Loring's DIV and Baldwin's BDE at Lanier's, and Bowen's DIV southeast of Big Black Bridge. Hébert's BDE at Drumgould's Bluff, Vaughn's BDE north of the city, Shoup's BDE in the city itself, and Higgins's River Defense force along the waterfront[24] added another 9,000 men available in the Vicksburg area.

Sometime during the afternoon of 6 May, Pemberton received a message from President Davis containing a categorical order to hold both Port Hudson and Vicksburg at all cost.[25] The good news was that GEN Beauregard was sending 5,000 men from the southeastern coast. Pemberton knew they would be a long time coming. In the meantime, he badly needed manpower, so, despite Davis's order, he asked Gardner to send BG Samuel Maxey's brigade to Jackson. After all, no one was seriously threatening Port Hudson at this time, and, if Vicksburg fell, Port Hudson would fall like an overripe plum.

Additional scout reports began to confirm the presence of powerful Federal forces moving northeastward on the Rocky Springs–Cayuga road, and so, late that afternoon, Pemberton informed his generals that Big Black Bridge was the Yankee objective. He thought that Jackson might be raided and sent a message to Governor Pettus and his commander in Jackson, BG Adams, to send everything useful toward Alabama for safety.[26]

19

Aiming for the Railroad
7 May–12 May 1863

Map: 10. The Region between Vicksburg, Bruinsburg, and Raymond

FEDERAL PERSPECTIVE

Having made his decision to strike for the Southern Railroad of Mississippi somewhere in the vicinity of Edwards, Grant was faced with something of a dilemma. It stemmed from the limitations of that long and fragile supply line that led through Grand Gulf to his depots in Louisiana at Milliken's Bend and Young's Point. There simply was no way in which the forty thousand men and thousands of horses of his eight-division maneuver force could be fully supplied with food and forage brought over that route. Any move into the interior of Mississippi automatically meant that his army would have to subsist, at least in part, by foraging in the countryside.

But that presented still another problem. A foraging army may be visualized as a solid core of infantry and artillery, surrounded by a haze of foragers gleaning everything edible from the farms and plantations of the region. It was simple enough in theory, but it was already evident that the country east of the Big Black River was not the rich plantation country that most expected, but instead was a patchwork of relatively small subsistence farms. Spring traditionally is "starvation time" in subsistence-farming communities, because the autumn harvests have been consumed through the winter, and the new crops are not yet in, so the foraging parties would soon strip them of the little they had. Forage for the thousands of horses and mules that pulled the wagons and guns of the army was in especially short supply. The landscape was green with early summer grass, but that didn't help much, because an army on the march cannot stop to let its animals graze.

Foragers cannot wander more than three or four miles from the parent column, because their sole function is bringing home the bacon; if they wander too far, they cannot make the round trip in time. Thus, a marching column "harvests" a strip of countryside only six or eight miles across. In the subsistence-farm landscape east of the Big Black, that meant that the lead division or two would do fairly well, but the follow-on divisions would find very slim pickings indeed. The only practical solution would be to advance in parallel columns, so that each column could glean from fresh countryside. It was a tactic that Napoleon had used, and what better model could one imagine?

West of Rocky Springs, the army had been confined to the narrow peninsula between the Big Black River and Bayou Pierre, but east of Rocky Springs the country opened out, so that each of the three corps could follow a different road to the northeast. In fact, there were four roads that could be used, and that was convenient, because it meant that no more than two divisions need move on any one road. One road ran more or less parallel to the Big Black from Cayuga to Montgomery's Bridge on Fourteenmile Creek; another ran from Cayuga northeast to Auburn and then north to Whittaker's Ford and Edwards; a third branched off at Auburn and trended northeast to Dillon's farm and then north on the Turkey Creek Road toward Champion Hill; and the fourth branched off at Reganton and ran east to Utica and then northeast to Raymond and Bolton.

Early on the morning of 7 May, Grant left Hankinson's Ferry and moved to Rocky Springs,[1] where he would be near the leading elements of his proposed advance toward Edwards. During the day, he was notified that Steele's DIV of Sherman's XV Corps was ashore at Grand Gulf, and that Tuttle's DIV would be landed before nightfall. Thus, he had eight of his ten battle-worthy divisions in hand for the coming offensive. Only McArthur's DIV of McPherson's corps and Blair's DIV of Sherman's corps remained in Louisiana. Grant assumed that additional troops were en route down the river from Memphis, but he knew they would be many days in coming. Grant arrived at Rocky Springs about noon and immediately ordered McClernand to move his corps forward, with one division occupying Auburn and the other three halting along the line of Maxey Creek.

During the day, Osterhaus probed toward Utica, Auburn, and the crossings of the Big Black River with strong cavalry and infantry patrols. McPherson, marching with Logan's DIV, moved forward from Hankinson's

Ferry to Rocky Springs, but he left Crocker's DIV behind to await the arrival of Sherman, who was expected that evening.[2] Carr's DIV moved up from Willows and camped beside Osterhaus's men in the bottoms of Big Sand Creek. Carr sent a regiment and the 30-pdr Parrott rifles of the 1 US INF forward to Reganton to command that strategic road junction. Sturdy A. J. Smith moved his division forward from Willows as far as Little Sand Creek, and sent out pickets to guard the Utica Road. Hovey and his men had a day of rest at Rocky Springs.

Late that afternoon, Clark Wright sent word that he and his 6 MO CAV had skirmished sharply with Confederate cavalry (and they were regulars, not State Troops) about six miles south-southeast of Reganton, but he had been able to force them back across Big Bayou Pierre.[3] This gave Grant momentary pause, because regular cavalry might imply infantry as well. Still, Wright had reported no infantry, so the force probably was nothing more than a few squadrons who happened to be in the area.

One item of really good news was that a 200-wagon supply train, loaded with food and ammunition, arrived from Grand Gulf on the afternoon of 7 May. That meant that the supply line was at least working.[4]

As soon as Sherman was on the scene, Grant planned to move McClernand's corps up the road through Cayuga to Montgomery's Bridge and so into Edwards, while Sherman's corps would diverge to the northeast at Cayuga, pass through Auburn, and turn north at Dillon's farm, to strike the railroad somewhere between Bolton and Edwards. McPherson's corps would diverge to the east at Reganton, pass through Utica, and drive up the turnpike to Raymond. If there had been no serious resistance up to that point, all three corps then would concentrate at Edwards and drive westward toward Big Black Bridge.

About nightfall on 8 May, couriers arrived at Grant's headquarters at Rocky Springs with word that Sherman was at Hankinson's Ferry with Steele's DIV, and that Tuttle's DIV of Sherman's corps was safely encamped at Willows. Earlier in the day, McClernand, who had been so careless about rations for his men at Bruinsburg, had told Grant that he dared not move forward as ordered, because his men did not have rations enough![5] That problem more or less cured itself, for that very evening a big wagon train arrived at Big Sand Creek with hardtack and coffee. Grant ordered the advance to begin the next morning.

As it happened, however, McClernand had an important visitor traveling with him on 9 May: Governor Yates of Illinois. So, instead of leading the offensive to the northeast, as Grant had intended, McClernand held a formal review of three of his four divisions. Both McClernand and the governor made speeches to the troops, though nobody remembers what they said. Grant also listened, stoic as ever.[6]

Perhaps Grant took some consolation in the fact that Crocker left Hankinson's Ferry that morning, marched through Rocky Springs, and stopped for the night at the Meyer farm, 2.5 miles southeast of Reganton on the Utica Road. Logan had fallen in behind as Crocker marched through Rocky Springs, so by midnight McPherson had both his divisions concentrated and well on the road to Utica, just as Grant had asked. Back at Hankinson's Ferry, Steele took over the task of defending the raft bridge across the Big Black. Tuttle, whose division spent the night at Willows, moved forward to Rocky Springs. The weather was unseasonably hot and dry, and water was beginning to be a serious consideration, because water sufficient for a division was to be found only in the major creeks and in copious springs like those at Rocky Springs and Willows.

Sherman had just come down the long road from Milliken's Bend and had been appalled by the thought of trying to supply the army over it. He wrote to Grant from Hankinson's Ferry on the morning of 10 May, recommending that COL William Hillyer be appointed as a "transportation czar," with power to do whatever was necessary to organize the logistics system.[7] Grant immediately accepted the recommendation but told Sherman that he did not expect to supply all the needs of the army by wagon train. The wagons would bring up the ammunition, and the men would get hardtack and coffee, but fresh food and forage would be gleaned from the countryside.[8]

McPherson's corps moved slowly forward through Utica on 10 May and camped for the night at the Weeks' farm, four miles east of Utica.[9] The only water was in Tallahala Creek, a mile to the south. Rebel cavalry had been encountered all across their front all day, but the Southerners had fallen back without much pressure from Wright's 6 MO CAV. That afternoon, Wright told McPherson that 150 Rebels were holding the bridge across Tallahala Creek two miles southeast of Utica, on a road that led to Crystal Springs, on the New Orleans, Jackson & Great Northern Railroad. McPherson jumped to the not unreasonable conclusion that the Rebels were holding it so that an infantry force, probably from Port Hudson, would be able readily to cross the creek and either hit his column in flank, or go on to the northwest and interdict the Union supply line, which extended back to Grand Gulf. McPherson told Wright to take his whole regiment, capture the bridge, and then raid the railroad at Crystal Springs, just to be certain that the Rebs were up to no mischief.

McClernand, vanity satisfied and with his men's ration boxes filled, at last moved ponderously northward with his four divisions. By nightfall on 10 May, Osterhaus's and Hovey's divisions were at Five Mile Creek on the Cayuga–Auburn Road, Carr's division was at Five Mile Creek on the Montgomery's Bridge Road, and A. J. Smith was at Cayuga in support. There had been cavalry bickering all across the front all day, so it was clear that Pemberton was aware of the movement.[10] Furthermore, the Army of the Tennessee presumably was marching through enemy countryside, where every farmer could be expected to carry tales to the Confederate scouts. Therefore Grant was confident that Pemberton knew not only the locations of the units, but their numbers as well. There being no hope of surprise, Grant had no choice but to press on, hoping that speed would substitute for subtlety.

Sherman, with Steele's DIV, spent the night of 10 May at Big Sand Creek.[11] The troops had dismantled the raft bridge at Hankinson's Ferry before they left, leaving only a company of cavalry to guard the crossing. Tuttle's DIV remained in camp at Rocky Springs, conducting church services, as was its custom on Sundays.

Hillyer's appointment was felt almost immediately, as the supply system began working with astonishing efficiency. Every day a train of anywhere from two to three hundred wagons, loaded with food, ammunition, and all the paraphernalia of war, arrived behind the lines. Another blessing was that the yeoman farmers of the region owned very few slaves, so the army was spared the task of feeding and managing the hordes of "contrabands" who often accumulated around Union armies.

Grant wanted to hit the railroad about the same time with all three columns. Since Sherman's and McPherson's corps had much farther to go, that meant that McClernand's corps had to mark time on May 11. However, while waiting for the other two corps to get into position, Osterhaus sent patrols forward all across his front. One occupied the road junction two miles northeast of Auburn to keep the road clear for Sherman; another probed up the Telegraph Road until it ran into a strong Confederate picket line about a half-mile south of Fourteenmile Creek. The Rebels refused to budge, and the local blacks told the Yankees that the Southerners intended to hold the crossings of the creek, no matter what. Still a third patrol penetrated to Fourteenmile Creek on the Auburn–Raymond Road, but not without a brisk skirmish with a strong Confederate cavalry detachment. Shortage of water was beginning to inhibit operations, since Fourteenmile Creek was the only source of quantities large enough for an army.[12]

While McClernand rested, Sherman waited for Tuttle to catch up and then marched forward with both Steele's and Tuttle's divisions to Auburn, where there was a pond large enough to supply his men and animals with water.[13] As usual, Grant marched with his friend Sherman. As the column passed through Cayuga, Sherman had detached COL William McMillen and his 95 OH INF to reconnoiter Hall's Ferry, where scouts had reported Confederate activity. As McMillen approached the river, he was fired on by Confederate pickets on the east bank. He deployed his men and drove forward, and the Southerners withdrew across the river after a sharp little firefight. At this point, McMillen discovered that he was not at Hall's Ferry at all, but at Baldwin's Ferry. Still, the force on the west shore looked so threatening that he decided to stay where he was to discourage them from crossing and making trouble in the rear of the army.[14]

As Grant and Sherman passed through the hamlet of Cayuga, Mrs. Jane Fisher Smith confronted the commanding general and demanded protection for her property. In her view, Grant owed her one, because she had provided a Federal cavalry patrol with useful information the previous day. Grant immediately granted her request.[15] The question is: from whom was she demanding protection? After all, had her neighbors been hostile, her house would have burned the moment the Yankee army was out of sight. In fact, it long survived the war. It was Union foragers whom she feared, not the townspeople; many, and perhaps most, of the country people were, if not pro-Union, at least neutral.

Way out on the right flank, McPherson was having trouble finding water for his troops and barely inched forward during the day, from Weeks' farm to Roach's farm, only 1.5 miles farther east.[16] Beyond that, the first adequate supply of water would be in Raymond. Unknown to Grant, COL Wright had given McPherson some good news during the day, when he reported that his expedition to Crystal Springs had found the town unguarded. His men had torn up a mile and a half of the railroad, just to make matters difficult for any force moving northward up the line.[17] The break wouldn't stop an infantry force, but it certainly would add to their problems.

On 12 May, the Union divisions lunged forward against increasingly stiff resistance. On the left flank, A. J. Smith's division of McClernand's corps moved forward so quickly and in such force that they captured Montgomery's Bridge across Fourteenmile Creek intact. They seized a bridgehead on the north bank, but the bulk of the division went into bivouac on the south bank.[18] On the Telegraph Road, Hovey, followed by Carr and Osterhaus, ran into a powerful skirmish line about one-half mile south of Whittaker's Ford on Fourteenmile Creek. This was no normal cavalry outpost; the line was supported by artillery and fought viciously and tenaciously. But Hovey forged ahead, eventually forcing the Confederates back across the creek. Hovey's crossing was briskly contended, but eventually the Rebels gave way and retreated to the shelter of a gray-clad infantry battle line on a ridge transverse to the road about two miles south of Edwards. Hovey stopped at Mt. Moriah, a mile south of the Confederate line, and the three divisions that already had crossed to the north bank (Hovey's, Carr's, and Osterhaus's) withdrew to the south bank, leaving only a skirmish line to keep the Rebels under observation.[19]

Sherman, Grant, and Sherman's two divisions advanced eastward along the Auburn–Raymond road, with Steele's division in the lead and screened by LTC Simon Swan's 4 IA CAV.[20] The Confederates bitterly contested the Fourteenmile Creek crossing, and Steele had to deploy two of his infantry brigades before he was able to force his way across the stream. Of course the Rebels had burned the bridge, and, while the water was scarcely ankle-deep, the banks were so steep and high that the creek formed a significant obstacle. Even after the division crossed, the Confederate resistance persisted, but eventually Steele occupied the junction of the Raymond–Auburn and Turkey Creek roads, about a mile east of Dillon's farm and six miles west of Raymond. Sherman's second division, Tuttle's, camped at Dillon's farm, at the junction of the Mt. Moriah and Raymond–Auburn roads, a mile west of Steele's position.[21]

There was no word from McPherson, whose two divisions were supposed to be marching up the Utica–Raymond Road, less than four miles away to the southeast. Grant was not worried, because he was quite certain that there was no substantial body of troops in Jackson, and the few who were there certainly would not attempt an attack on a force as large as two divisions. Earlier in the day, McPherson had reported cavalry clashes across his front, so the Confederates knew he was there. Grant assumed that the country people, if not Wirt Adams's horsemen, long since had counted their numbers and reported them to Pemberton.

CONFEDERATE PERSPECTIVE

By 7 May, it was evident that but little help was coming from elsewhere, so Pemberton tried hard to find additional manpower within his own department to strengthen the defenses of Vicksburg. He had conflicting requirements. First, with a large Federal army loose in the rear of the city, the first requirement was to form an army of maneuver with which to oppose it. Second, the city itself had to be defended against the possibility of a direct assault. That second threat was very real, because a significant force of Federal ironclads and tinclads remained above the city, as well as transports by the score. Pemberton was all too aware that several divisions of Federal infantry were dispersed along the Memphis & Charleston Railroad, and the presence of the transport fleet on the Mississippi meant that two or three of those divisions could be delivered to the Yankee bases in Louisiana opposite Vicksburg in a matter of days. In combination with the troops already there, that meant that a force of three or four infantry divisions, adequately supported by naval artillery, could be thrown against the River Defenses on very short notice. Thus, Pemberton had no option but to retain a large defensive force manning the defenses of the city, even though that restricted the size of the army of maneuver which he was trying to concentrate in the vicinity of Big Black Bridge.

Other than the Vicksburg garrison, Pemberton had no regular troops available, but a lot of Mississippi State Troops were scattered about. They guarded bridges and depots, patrolled railroads, and did the multitudinous other small tasks normal to military operations. They were mostly in the northern part of Mississippi, where the threat of Union cavalry raids was greatest. Pemberton ordered them concentrated, and by 7 May he had a force of about 700 at Columbus, under the command of BG Jeptha Harris. Once concentrated, they were directed to move to Jackson.[22] When they arrived, they were sent on to Warrenton, where they were attached to Moore's BDE.[23]

On 8 May, Gregg and his brigade arrived in Jackson, and that was a comfort.[24] Gregg couldn't be expected to fend off an army, but he could at least discourage raids.

There always was the chance that the Union offensive would not strike directly at either Edwards or Big Black Bridge; Grant might attempt to cross the Big Black at either Fisher Ferry, Hall's Ferry, or Baldwin's Ferry and strike northward toward Mt. Alban or Bovina, thus taking the defenses of Big Black Bridge from the rear. Pemberton guarded against this possibility by ordering Loring to place strong guards at all the potential crossing sites. The most likely was Hall's Ferry, and Loring placed Tilghman's BDE and a battery of artillery there.

By 6 May, Pemberton had scouts and patrols out in the area east of the Big Black River and south of Fourteenmile Creek, and by 8 May they were steadily being pushed back by strong Union cavalry forces. This confirmed

Pemberton in his belief that the main Federal thrust was coming up the east bank of the Big Black River toward Edwards, after which the Federals would wheel to the left and attack Big Black Bridge. To Pemberton, the odd thing was that the advance seemed to be on a front that extended all the way from the Big Black River to Tallahala Creek. None of the reports included estimates of numbers, and in the absence of hard data, he assumed that Grant would keep his major force concentrated, in accord with conventional wisdom, and that meant that the bulk of his force would be on the main Rocky Spring–Cayuga–Edwards road. The contacts farther to the east, toward Auburn and Utica, were nothing more than flank guards, probably cavalry supported by a regiment or two of infantry.

Reinforcements were still flowing in, albeit slowly. The first units of Walker's BDE arrived in Jackson on 9 May, with the rest due shortly.

On 9 May, Loring, who on 3 and 4 May had withdrawn from the north bank of the Big Black River at Hankinson's Ferry in near panic, now proposed to Pemberton that the Confederates assume the offensive.[25] His plan envisioned the Jackson force striking southwestward from Clinton, Bowen's DIV at Edwards striking south along the Telegraph Road, and Stevenson's DIV forcing a crossing of the Big Black River at Hall's Ferry, while Loring's DIV would attack across Baldwin's Ferry. Pemberton recognized it for what it was: a plan for a converging attack on a grand scale, conducted by four separate commands operating on a front some twenty-five miles long. He also recognized that the tenuous Confederate communications would make it impossible to coordinate such a venture and simply ignored Loring's proposal. Nevertheless, he was aware that the Yankees had the initiative, and until he could find a way to force the Northerners to react to Southern moves, the South was at a profound disadvantage. However, before that could be done, a maneuver force approximately equal in size to the Union army would have to be assembled. And that was a problem, considering that there remained the very real threat of a direct assault on Warrenton or even Vicksburg itself.

By 10 May, Confederate scouts were reporting that Union cavalry, supported when necessary by infantry, had pushed northeast to Five Mile Creek, Auburn had been occupied, and there was even a strong force at the Weeks' farm, twelve miles southwest of Raymond on the Utica Road. The Union cavalry screen was so effective that there were no estimates of the sizes of the forces, nor were there reports of any kind from the country people. The forces at Auburn and Weeks' farm were so far out on the wings that they could be nothing more than flank guards.

Bowen, whose division was responsible for what was assumed to be the principal target of the Union offensive, was worried, and about noon on 10 May he asked Pemberton whether he should fight at Edwards or withdraw into the Big Black Bridge fortifications.[26] Pemberton still was not entirely sure that the force south of Edwards was anything more than a feint, designed to draw attention away from the Warrenton sector. He had no certain knowledge of its size, and, for all he knew, powerful forces might still be in Louisiana. If it was a feint, he didn't want Bowen's DIV locked uselessly in place, and if it was the main Yankee effort, he didn't want Bowen's veterans chewed up before the rest of the army could come to his aid. His solution to the dilemma was to instruct Bowen to withdraw to the fortifications east of Big Black Bridge if the Federals advanced in great force.[27]

While Pemberton was not yet confident that Edwards and Big Black Bridge were the immediate objectives of the offensive, he was convinced that there was a substantial infantry force east of the Big Black River and south of Edwards. That being the case, M. L. Smith's and Forney's DIVs should be adequate to hold the Vicksburg–Warrenton area, and it therefore would be safe to move Carter Stevenson's powerful division from Warrenton to the Big Black Bridge–Edwards sector. Accordingly, Pemberton sent a message to Stevenson, directing him to leave Moore's, Baldwin's, and Harris's BDEs, plus Waul's Texas Legion, to man the Warrenton line, and to move with all the rest of his troops to Lanier's farm and Mt. Alban, where they would be within close supporting distance of Big Black Bridge and Edwards.[28]

These moves had been dictated by consideration of what a modern commentator would call a "nightmare scenario." If all Confederate maneuver forces were concentrated at Edwards in anticipation of a Union blow directed from the east at Edwards and Big Black Bridge, and the bulk of the Army of the Tennessee was south of Edwards, it would be possible for Grant to feint at Edwards with small forces and cross the Big Black at Baldwin's Ferry and Fisher's Ferry with his main army. The Yankees then could wheel north, seize Bovina and attack the Big Black Bridge from the west with a part of the army, meanwhile striking directly at Vicksburg with the remainder. Because the Big Black Bridge had only limited capacity, the Confederates might not be able to get their army back across the Big Black in time to counter such a move. Pemberton had no choice but to hold substantial forces on the west bank of the Big Black until he was certain that the Federals were aiming their offensive at Edwards.

Late that evening, 10 May, Pemberton decided that he had the means to strike a telling blow, even if the Yankee force south of Edwards were no more than a feint. With the arrival of Walker's vanguard in Jackson, Gregg's strong brigade could be employed for something other than garrison duty. Thus he wrote to Gregg, directing him to march immediately to Raymond, brush aside the flank guard that was marching up the Utica Road toward Raymond, and then turn and strike into the flank of the Federal force at Auburn, which Pemberton assumed to be no more than a strong combat patrol.[29] He assumed that the Auburn force would have continued to move east-northeast along the Auburn–Raymond Road, so Gregg would hit it somewhere near Dillon's farm. After smashing the Auburn force, Gregg would continue to the west and attack the flank of the main body, which would be marching up the Telegraph Road south of Edwards. Whatever else Gregg did, he certainly would dislocate the Union movement, at the very least forcing it to disclose its strength.

Gregg marched for Raymond with the dawn on 11 May and arrived about 1600 to be welcomed as a savior. The townspeople knew that a Yankee force was marching up the Utica Road, and the only thing available to oppose it had been a score or so of State Troops. Gregg cringed at the thought of the graybeards and striplings of the State Troops attempting to stop the veterans of the Army of the Tennessee, but he nevertheless sent them out to scout the Yankee advance.[30]

The same day that Gregg arrived in Raymond, 11 May, Pemberton got a critical bit of intelligence, when one of Tilghman's patrols reported that the bridge at Hankinson's Ferry was gone and there was only a small Union cavalry patrol on the south bank of the Big Black River.[31] That indicated beyond reasonable doubt that the main blow was coming up the east bank of the Big Black River, almost certainly up the Telegraph Road toward Edwards. Had the Yankees intended to move their main body to the west side of the Big Black, they certainly would have kept the Hankinson's Ferry bridge intact, since it would have been a critical link in their supply line to Grand Gulf. At this point, Pemberton realized that Gregg was going to be striking into the flank of the entire Army of the Tennessee, a task for which one brigade clearly was inadequate, so he ordered Walker to march as soon as possible for Raymond to support Gregg.

Pemberton also began to shift his troops eastward to meet the threat to Big Black Bridge. Loring was to send Buford's and Featherston's BDEs to the bridge, and Stevenson was ordered to shift still farther eastward.[32] At this point Pemberton dared go no farther, because there remained the possibility that Grant would force a crossing of the Big Black River at Baldwin's or Hall's ferries and strike either the rear of the Big Black Bridge defenses, directly at Vicksburg from the southeast, or both.

By 12 May, there was no longer any doubt. Strong blue-clad infantry and artillery forces had attacked the Confederate lines south of Fourteen-mile Creek and forced them back across the stream.[33] There were Federal divisions at both Montgomery's Bridge and Whittaker's Ford, and both forces had established strong bridgeheads on the north bank. Bowen had occupied a low ridge across the Telegraph Road about two miles south of Edwards, and there the Yankee advance had come to a stop. At last Pemberton felt that he knew exactly where the Federal main body was. He looked at the situation with some equanimity. The Federal forces to the east, who by this time had advanced to Dillon's plantation, seven miles west of Raymond, and up the Utica Road to within a few miles of Raymond, would be taken care of by Gregg and Walker. The Gregg-Walker force then would strike into the flank of a Union army fully committed to a full-scale engagement with Bowen and Loring.[34] Once Pemberton was certain that the main force of the enemy was committed south of Edwards, Stevenson's powerful division could be moved out of Mt. Alban and Bovina and brought east to Edwards. In anticipation of the coming battle, Pemberton moved his headquarters to Bovina, a hamlet two miles west of Big Black Bridge, and personally took command of the Vicksburg army.[35]

20

McPherson's Approach March to Raymond 12 May 1863

Maps: 10. The Region between Vicksburg, Bruinsburg, and Raymond
      12. The Vicinity of Raymond

GEOGRAPHY AND METEOROLOGY

The modest town of Raymond lies in a well-cultivated countryside. In 1863, most of the farms were subsistence-type enterprises, too small to warrant the holding of slaves. There were, however, a number of large slaveholding plantations in the general area; as a result, sympathies were sharply divided between pro-Union and pro-Confederate. The towns-people tended to be pro-Confederate, while many of the countrymen tended to be pro-Union.

A very large proportion of the land was under cultivation. Only the swampy floodplains of the major creeks, the slopes of the occasional ravines that scarred the sides of the higher hills and ridges, and the occasional rugged hilltop remained covered with timber. The timber patches often were very brushy and tangled with grapevines, cat's-claw, and the ever-present honeysuckle and poison ivy. Visibility was very limited inside such patches and movement even more so.

The landscape undulated gently. The vertical distance from creek bottom to adjacent hilltop rarely was more than 150 feet and in most instances was only 50 or 60 feet. As a result, the slopes were gentle and often almost imperceptible. In contrast, the creek channels often were deep and sinuous, with intricate meander loops. Banks were often vertical, being from 4 to as much as 10 feet high in places. During dry weather, the creeks were everywhere fordable; but the steep and high banks made them impassable to artillery and wagons and very difficult for cavalry. Even infantrymen were forced to search for places where crossings could be made.

The Confederates had placed a commissary depot at Raymond, because it stands at the nexus of a strategic pattern of roads. Good roads led to the state capital at Jackson, fourteen miles to the east; to Edwards on the Southern Railroad of Mississippi (SRRM), twelve miles to the northwest; to Gallatin, on the New Orleans, Jackson & Great Northern Railroad, fifteen miles to the southeast; and to Utica, sixteen miles to the southwest. Other slightly less well-traveled roads led north to Bolton on the SRRM and west to Auburn. A spur railroad also connected Raymond with the SRRM at Bolton.

In early May of 1863, the weather had been unseasonably hot and dry. The small creeks were all bone-dry, and even the larger streams, such as Fourteenmile Creek, which crossed the Utica–Raymond Road about 3,000 yards from the center of Raymond, held only a trickle of water. The roads were unsurfaced, and an army moving along them raised immense, choking clouds of dust. The agricultural fields all had been newly planted, so the soil was loose and easily disturbed. The muzzle blast of a cannon raised a huge and stifling orange cloud. Even a small arm fired close to the ground was enough to raise a puff of dust into the air.

The morning of 12 May was windless, hot, and oppressive. The sky was brazen rather than blue; people felt that a storm was coming. Today we would recognize the symptoms of an inversion layer, in which the condition of the atmosphere prevents dust or smoke from rising very far into the sky. It was as if an intangible lid had been placed on the landscape.

FEDERAL PERSPECTIVE

The heat was already oppressive at 0430, when McPherson's men formed in the road at the Roach farm for their march toward Raymond on 12 May. The weather had been abnormally hot and dry for the past several days, and McPherson was seriously worried about water supplies. His 12,500 men, plus the numerous horses of the artillery and cavalry, needed a large supply of water, and only the largest streams still retained any significant amounts. His camp at the Roach farm had been dictated by the fact that Tallahala Creek still flowed, and it was less than a half-mile to the south. The next reliable source of water would be the wells of the village of Raymond, eleven miles to the northeast. There would be no stopping until they got there, so it was going to be a long, hot, dusty day.

The good news was that the town of Raymond was rumored to have a large Confederate commissary depot, which the XVII Corps had been directed to capture and use to supplement the increasingly slender supplies of rations reaching it via the supply road to Grand Gulf, or "liberated" from the surrounding countryside by foraging parties.

The march had scarcely started when the cavalry screen came under fire.[1] Forward movement slowed, and by 0900 the resistance had become so intense that not even CPT John S. Foster's veteran cavalrymen could make progress. McPherson told the horsemen to move off to the side and guard the flanks so that an infantry skirmish line could clear the way.[2]

The dust was incredible. Dennis's BDE, which led the way, raised such clouds of the stuff that J. E. Smith's and Stevenson's brigades, marching in Dennis's wake, were virtually smothered. In an effort to make breathing easier, they allowed a large gap to develop between the tail of Dennis's column and the head of the theirs. Crocker, whose division brought up the rear of the column, followed suit, so that, by 0930, large gaps separated the brigades, and an even larger gap existed between the two divisions.

McPherson looked in some dismay at the towering dust clouds raised by his marching men. Given those huge plumes, one for each brigade, there was no way whatsoever to conceal the strength of his column. Furthermore, every farmer rocking on the porch and watching the column go by was a potential spy, so he assumed that the Rebels knew precisely how many men he had, as well as precisely where he was. The tenacity and belligerence of the Confederate cavalry looked very much like the prelude to a battle, but at the same time McPherson was reasonably certain that there were no large forces to his front. To be sure, there was rumored to be a concentration at Jackson, but it could not possibly be more than a brigade or two. Surely a force of that size would not contest the advance of two divisions. The situation was puzzling in the extreme.

Nevertheless, the march was going well, albeit slowly. By a little before 1000, the skirmish line leading the advance started up a gentle slope leading to the crest of a low ridge overlooking the shallow valley of Fourteenmile Creek, only two miles southwest of the village of Raymond. Suddenly the Confederate cavalry to the front evaporated, and everyone fingered his rifle nervously, wondering what that portended.

McPherson was all too aware that his two divisions were relatively isolated. Contact with Grant, who was en route to Dillon's plantation with Sherman, had been maintained until McPherson left the Roach farm, but after that communications had ceased. Even though the distance between Sherman's corps and McPherson's corps was only about four airline miles, the courier route was significantly longer. It ran back to Roach's farm, then northwest to Auburn, and then northeast to Dillon's—an overall distance of about sixteen miles. Even a well-mounted courier could not cover that distance in less than about three hours during such oppressive weather. Since there had been nothing significant to report for some hours after McPherson left the Roach farm, neither Grant nor McPherson had knowledge of the other's situation. Both were acting on the basis of information concerning Confederate dispositions garnered at least thirty-six hours prior to the morning of 12 May. If that information turned out to be wrong and there was a large force in front of him, McPherson might be in serious trouble. McPherson was by nature a cautious man, and this situation was enough to reinforce the trait.

So it was that McPherson asked MG Logan to deploy two regiments, one on either side of the road a few hundred yards behind the skirmish line, as insurance against an ambush. Logan passed the word on to Dennis, whose brigade led the advance, and Dennis, who also felt a vague sense of unease, went even further; he brought the six guns of the 8 MI ARTY forward and put them on the road immediately behind the two deployed infantry regiments.

At 1000, the skirmish line leading the advance crested a gentle ridge with cultivated fields on both sides of the road and started down a long open slope, across a pasture covered with knee-high grass, toward a belt of woods that crossed the road 300 yards away. There was not a sound. Then, when the advance reached within about 100 yards of the belt of trees, the silence was suddenly broken by the crash of a musketry volley from just inside the tree line. At the same moment, three shells came screaming across the valley to explode just in front of the blue line.

The battle for Raymond had begun.

CONFEDERATE PERSPECTIVE

When BG John Gregg marched his dusty regiments into Raymond on the afternoon of 11 May, the village seethed with rumors that the Yankees were coming up the Utica Road, but facts were as scarce as hen's teeth.

Gregg immediately asked for Wirt Adams, who was supposed to be there to meet him, but there had been a mix-up and Adams wasn't there. In fact, there were exactly five men of Adams's cavalry regiment in the town. Other than those five men, the only cavalry available were forty men of the local company of Mississippi State Troops, and they were all out patrolling the southern approaches to the village. Gregg was more than a little surprised to learn that they seemed to have done well up to this point, because they were able to tell him that the Yankee column had spent the night about ten miles to the south on the Raymond–Utica road. What they could not tell him was the size of the force, because the Yankee cavalry screen was impenetrable. He ordered them to slow the Yankee advance when it resumed in the morning but, even more important, to determine the numbers and composition in the advancing column.[3]

Very early on the morning of 12 May, a fifty-man patrol of Wirt Adams's cavalry rode in. Adams had sent them from Edwards the day before, when he realized that he had misinterpreted a message from Pemberton and inadvertently had left Raymond devoid of regular horsemen. The news they brought was very troubling. They had tried to ride down the Mt. Moriah Road to Dillon's, intending to follow the Auburn–Raymond road into Raymond. However, northwest of Dillon's, they had run into a strong Federal infantry-cavalry-artillery force which had forced them to detour across country to the north. Eventually they reached the direct Edwards–Raymond road and so came into Raymond from the northwest.[4] This news was a shock to Gregg, because he had been led to believe, first, that the Yankee advance in that direction had only reached New Auburn; and second, that it was no more than a cavalry patrol, whereas Adams's men had encountered an all-arms taskforce. If that force were a flank screen for the main body, which was advancing on Edwards, then it seemed likely that it would continue moving north toward the railroad. However, if, during that march, the bluecoats learned of the Confederate presence in Raymond, they might turn east on the Edwards–Raymond road and fall on the rear of Gregg's men while the latter were engaged with the Yankee force coming north from Utica. That would be dangerous, even if the attacking force consisted of no more than a couple of regiments.

Gregg had no proper response to that, but he did the best he could by sending Wirt Adams's newly arrived fifty-man cavalry detachment out to picket the roads leading into Raymond from the west and north.[5] Of course, that made the horsemen unavailable for use to the south, but Gregg didn't worry much about that, because he thought he already knew pretty much what was down in that direction. Recalling Pemberton's interpretation of the Federal movements, Gregg assumed that the Federal force on the Utica Road consisted of no more than a Union brigade, if that. It probably was screened by an abnormally strong complement of cavalry to give the illusion of strength. Cavalry could be ignored in a battle; who ever saw a dead cavalryman?

As the morning of 12 May wore on, Gregg realized that he had greatly underestimated those striplings and graybeards in the State Troops. Their couriers reported all through the morning, and soon it became evident that they had been chipping away at the Yankee cavalry screen to such effect that the Yankees had been forced to deploy infantry to support their cavalry in order to force their way forward. However, despite their best efforts, they had not been able to break through the Yankee cavalry screen, so there still were no estimates of numbers. Their own strength was insufficient to make a thrust in strength at the flanks, and the damned blue-bellies had foraging parties out, and these served as an effective screen against small groups or single scouts. Nevertheless, despite all the Southerners could do, the advance came on inexorably, albeit slowly.

While the countryside buzzed with rumors, nothing could be confirmed. It was very strange, but the country people all were being singularly uncooperative. The best that Gregg could do was monitor the Federal advance and use his infantry to guard against surprise by putting out strong pickets on the roads leading south.

About midmorning, one of Gregg's scouts came in and reported that he had slipped past the Federal cavalry screen and counted an infantry column of 2,500 to 3,000 men. Well knowing the tendency of scouts to double numbers, Gregg took this as confirmation of his initial estimate that the Yankee force consisted of no more than a single brigade of infantry, perhaps 1,500 men, with a strong screen of horse soldiers.[6]

That being so, Gregg believed he had nothing to fear. He would ambush the Yankees well southwest of town and send them reeling back in disorder toward Utica. That would free him to return to Raymond, where he would meet Walker, who by that time surely would have arrived. The two Rebel brigades then would march west, where the combined force would slap the Union detachment at Dillon's farm aside and proceed on into the flank of the main Union force along the Telegraph Road south of Edwards. It seemed to Gregg that Pemberton's plan was working well.

The only thing that really troubled him was that his little taskforce was relatively isolated. His department commander, John Pemberton, was in Bovina, two miles west of Big Black Bridge. The bulk of the Vicksburg army was concentrated on a line running from Warrenton through Big Black Bridge to Edwards. Between Edwards and Raymond there was virtually nothing, not even a cavalry screen. Walker's BDE presumably was somewhere on the road between Jackson and Raymond, but he didn't know exactly where. Furthermore, there were no direct telegraph communications between Raymond and either Jackson or Bovina. Telegraph lines tended to follow the railroad lines, but the Raymond–Bolton line was unreliable, so most communication was by courier, which tended to be slow but relatively certain. A message from Gregg to Pemberton would have to go by courier to Bolton, seven miles to the north, where it could be put on the wires for Bovina. A round-trip communication would take at least four hours and probably more. Pending the arrival in Jackson of GEN Joseph E. Johnston, who at least nominally was the overall commander of all forces in the region, no one was in command in Jackson. Gregg, a brigade commander, was the senior officer in the Jackson area, and he was in the field with his own brigade. And Johnston was still thirty-six hours away. Gregg reflected that, if he got in trouble, he would have to get himself out of it, because no one would be close enough to help.

Nevertheless, Gregg felt completely confident. His own force numbered some three thousand men, almost certainly overwhelmingly superior to the Federal force coming up from the southwest. The only real flies in the ointment were two reports of contacts with Yankees in unexpected places. First, a large Federal cavalry force had occupied Crystal Springs the previous day, and it was possible, albeit unlikely, that it would march up the road from Crystal Springs, through Gallatin, and so into Raymond directly from the south. The second disturbing factor was the strong Union force which seemed to be heading toward Dillon's farm, seven miles to the west, as reported by Wirt Adams's horsemen. If, against all logic, that force marched directly on Raymond, it necessarily would come in on the Auburn Road, which branched off the Utica Road about a mile southwest of town. Taking these two reports into consideration would make his dispositions more complicated than Gregg liked, but he would do the best he could with what he had. What he had was five veteran infantry regiments, an independent infantry battalion, a three-gun battery of artillery, and a squadron of cavalry. Fortunately, he had been given time to scout the area southwest of Raymond thoroughly and to make his plans accordingly.

Promptly at 0900, Gregg moved out of Raymond to set his trap.[7] He deployed one regiment across the Utica Road just south of the junction with the Auburn Road, in position where it could readily change front to block the Auburn Road, if required. Another regiment was placed across the Gallatin Road, about 1,000 yards to the east. A third regiment was placed about 800 yards farther south along the Gallatin Road. If no threat developed on that road, the troops would be in position to turn west, cross the upper reaches of Fourteenmile Creek, and strike the flank of the Union force on the Utica Road. Gregg placed his artillery on a little knoll just north of the junction of the Utica and Auburn roads, and deployed MAJ S. H. Colms's 1 TN INF BN in support of the guns. A fourth regiment was kept in close reserve just south of town, and a fifth regiment remained in the town itself, to guard against the unlikely possibility that the Yankee force at Dillon's farm would swing around to the north and come in from that direction.[8] Finally, he pushed a strong line of skirmishers out to the south edge of the belt of woods along Fourteenmile Creek and settled down to wait.

At 1000, a blue-clad skirmish line, which extended for some distance on either side of the road, came steadily over the crest of a low ridge about 300 yards south of the edge of the woods and started down the long, smooth slope. Gregg's skirmish line let them come to within 100 yards of the edge of the woods and fired a single volley. At the same instant, the artillery on the knoll back near the road junction opened fire, and three shells screamed across the valley to burst in front of the Yankee line.

The Battle of Raymond had begun.

21

Confusion Compounded: Battle of Raymond 12 May 1863

Maps: 10. The Region between Vicksburg, Bruinsburg, and Raymond
  12. The Vicinity of Raymond
  36–42. The Battle of Raymond

FEDERAL PERSPECTIVE

MG Logan was marching with BG Dennis near the front of Dennis's BDE as it moved slowly up the Utica Road, when the crash of gunfire came from the north. McPherson and his staff were marching with J. E. Smith's BDE of Logan's DIV, which was more than a mile behind Dennis, trying to keep out of the dust raised by the leading brigade. It was 1000, and the two deployed regiments had just reached the crest of the low ridge 400 yards south of Fourteenmile Creek.

Hearing the sound of artillery, McPherson instantly spurred forward, to find Logan and Dennis on the ridgetop, directing the deployment of Dennis's four regiments. The 8 MI ARTY was already unlimbered and in action.[1] To McPherson's dismay, the muzzle blasts raised immense clouds of dust. These, mingled with the powder smoke, hung in the windless air like great impenetrable balls of dirty cotton. Within moments, it had become difficult to see across the valley. Nevertheless, before the veils closed completely, McPherson saw a gray battle line on a ridge some 1,500 yards away to the northeast, and another near the Confederate guns, almost due north and about the same distance away. There also was a skirmish line in the edge of the timber along the creek. There were too many trees and too much smoke and dust to be certain, but McPherson guessed that there were four or five thousand Confederates in position.

McPherson's corps had been marching for many days through presumably hostile countryside, so he quite understandably assumed that the composition of his force was well known to the Confederate commander. The minimum number of men required for hope of a successful defense of Raymond was perhaps 5,000, in opposition to his own 12,500. With the Confederates in a defensive position of their own choosing, and with a Federal numerical advantage of more than two to one, McPherson would be cautious; at the same time, he could be confident of success. He sent couriers racing back down the road, telling his commanders to put the wagons in the ditches, if necessary, and to get the infantry and artillery forward as quickly as possible.[2]

The first task was to make firm contact, to see just what the Yankees were facing. Dennis waved his men forward as soon as his four regiments were deployed. They swept down the long, gentle slope and into the woods, pushing the Rebel skirmishers in front of them. There was no trace of a Confederate battle line, and the Rebel skirmishers abruptly vanished. Since there was no opposition, the men in Dennis's battle line stopped just inside the wood, stacked arms, and lay down to rest in the cool shade while their own skirmishers went forward to the northern edge of the belt of timber, some 200 yards north of the creek.[3] The skirmishers discovered in the process that Fourteenmile Creek was less than ankle-deep but that it flowed in a deep, meandering trench with vertical banks four to five feet high.

As soon as J. E. Smith's five regiments arrived, Logan deployed them in line of battle to the right of Dennis, sending them forward into the belt of timber along the creek. Here the wood was an utter tangle, and the creekbed in some places was as much as fifteen feet deep. Four of Smith's five regiments became so lost and disorganized that eventually they stopped and returned to the open field south of the woods, where they reformed. The fifth, the 23 IN, found a place where it could cross the creek and advanced to the north edge of the belt of timber. It was, of course, all alone in the world.

McPherson was puzzled by the lack of resistance, because, from what little he could see and from the reports of his skirmishers, Fourteenmile Creek would have been an ideal place for an inferior force to defend against superior numbers. He began to suspect a tactical trap and grew even more cautious. Furthermore, the fact that Fourteenmile Creek bent around his right flank had not escaped him, so when Stevenson's brigade of Logan's DIV came panting up, he deployed them on the right of J. E. Smith's men, who were just reforming in the open field south of the woods after their adventure in the tangle.

This extension of his line was only just under way when suddenly a solid gray battle line came sweeping across the fields north of the creek and into the woods. This took Logan and McPherson completely by surprise. The Rebels were not defending, but attacking! The only reasonable explanation was that they had far greater numbers than had been estimated, because no one in his right mind attacks a force twice as large as his own. The left flank of the Rebel assault drove through the belt of woods along Fourteenmile Creek and came out into the open on the south side. But here the Confederate attack was stopped by savage close-range volleys from the eight Union regiments now arrayed in the open field.[4] Even in the smoke and confusion, the Rebel regiment was recognized as the 7 TX, which had boasted that it had never been forced to retreat. The Texans were a part of Gregg's BDE, so at least a part of the Rebel army had at last been identified.

The right flank of the assault had less success, because the Union troops for 100 yards or so east of the road took shelter in the bed of Fourteenmile Creek and used it as a trench. The Texans were stopped, and the result was a Union salient projecting far into the flank and rear of the Confederate line. The Confederates could not deliver enfilade fire into the natural trench, because the creek bed made a sharp turn which formed a natural refused flank. Nature had designed it for defense.

Just about this time, a courier arrived at McPherson's position on the ridge beside the guns, to tell him that a large Rebel infantry force was coming through the woods bordering the creek on the right flank. Having more or less anticipated this, McPherson ordered Stevenson's brigade to deploy facing east and get ready to welcome the Confederates when they came out in the open.[5] Sure enough, in a few minutes Confederate skirmishers appeared in the edge of the trees, but they came no farther. In a little while, Stevenson became curious and sent a skirmish line of his own into the trees. There were Confederates there, but they were pulling back so rapidly that the blue-clad skirmishers could barely keep up. Since there was no hope that a battle line could move through the wilderness fast enough to catch them, Stevenson made no effort to do so.

While the infantry was deploying and stopping the Confederate assault east of the Utica Road, the Union artillery was arriving. And that was a problem. McPherson dared not move them forward to the infantry line, because they would be so close to the edge of the woods that a surprise Rebel thrust might overrun them. Visibility was so bad that they would have only a few seconds' warning. The only remaining option was to keep the artillery on the ridgetop, even though the only targets they had were the Rebel guns 1,100 yards away to the north. These Rebel guns were so obscured by smoke and dust that there was little hope of hitting them. Nor could the artillery be used in direct support of the infantry, because those same infantry masked the Confederate lines in the edge of the woods. By 1330, there were four batteries, with twenty-two guns, lined up on the ridgetop, firing blindly across the valley in a vain attempt to knock out the Confederate guns.[6] The only good thing about this situation was that the Confederate gunners were in an identical quandary. As a result, the guns fired during much of the afternoon but, so far as anyone could tell, failed to hit anything.

With the Confederate attack stalled at the southern edge of the woods along Fourteenmile Creek, McPherson took his time about reorganizing. At this point, he was uncertain whether he was going to have to fend off an attack by a strong Rebel force or be able to go on the offensive soon. By 1315 it was clear that, at least for the moment, no more Confederate attacks were going to be launched, so he began a slow but general advance toward Raymond. The Confederates in the trees resisted bitterly for a short time, and then the pressure of eight Union regiments concentrated on a front of only about 500 yards became irresistible, and the Confederate line in the woods abruptly broke. McPherson was elated when the Union advance surged across the creek and right to the far edge of the timber belt, some 200 yards north of the creek.

Everything seemed to be going well, when suddenly another long gray battle line appeared on the left rear of the Confederate line, and the Union advance came to an abrupt halt. McPherson still had no clear idea as to how many men were in the Confederate force. Everything was confusing. On his right flank, where Fourteenmile Creek flows generally northward before turning northwest, the powerful Confederate force detected there earlier in the day seemed to have vanished. He had no idea how to interpret that, and, in an effort to obtain information, a single regiment was detached to see if it could reestablish contact.

In the meantime, Sanborn's sturdy regiments had arrived on the field. Instead of committing them as a unit, McPherson parceled them out as reinforcements for portions of Logan's line which seemed to need strengthening. By 1400, the reinforcements were complete, and the Union line again surged forward. This time, the Confederate line east of the Utica Road shattered completely. The Texans fled in rout and were not seen again. The 3 TN was forced back and back, and eventually they, too, vanished from in front of the victorious Union regiments. However, at just about the place where Fourteenmile Creek makes its turn from flowing northward to flowing northwest, two powerful Confederate regiments appeared on the slopes of the hills north of the creek. The Union regiments facing them attacked, were repulsed, rallied, and attacked again. McPherson received only the most fragmentary reports of these actions; he knew they were going on, because he could hear the noise, but smoke, dust, and obscuring trees prevented him from getting a reasonably accurate view of what was happening. Each regimental commander was fighting anything that appeared on his front, essentially without regard to what was happening elsewhere. And it took so long for couriers to penetrate the belt of woods and cross the deeply entrenched creekbed that orders from the commander were obsolete by the time they arrived. It was a battle fought almost entirely on the initiative of the individual regimental commanders.

At last, about 1530, a breathless messenger arrived from the far right flank. The 32 OH, the regiment McPherson had sent out as a patrol to find out what had happened to the threat to his right flank, had encountered a Confederate regiment on a hilltop and been smashed back into the trees along Fourteenmile Creek. McPherson thought that might mean that the Confederate commander still was attempting to turn his right flank, perhaps by using troops withdrawn from the Utica Road front and sending them around to the eastern flank, where they could use the Gallatin Road to get into position for a new assault from an unexpected direction. Nevertheless, he dared not significantly reduce his strength on the Utica Road, since he had no idea what was transpiring in the direction of Raymond. The size of the Confederate force remained a complete mystery; for all he knew (after all, he really couldn't see anything), the Confederates might be preparing another strike in that sector.

McPherson's solution was to send two regiments of Sanborn's brigade on a wide sweep to the south and east, both to garner information and possibly to outflank the outflankers.

By 1600, a lull had fallen on the battlefield, and the smoke and dust were slowly dissipating. All along the line, the Union regiments were north of the belt of timber along Fourteenmile Creek, and it suddenly became clear that all resistance had evaporated, except for a single Rebel regiment on a hillside northeast of Stevenson's brigade, and they were clearly pulling back, screened by a cloud of skirmishers. By 1700, all trace of them had vanished, and McPherson was left in possession of the field.

McPherson was in no condition to pursue; his brigades were mixed and scattered from the Utica Road to the Gallatin Road, and he didn't know where many of them were. Stevenson's two regiments on the right flank seemed to have vanished into thin air. By the time the Federals got sorted out and into march column, the last Confederate skirmisher had vanished to the north, never to be seen again that day.[7] McPherson had won his battle, but he still didn't know exactly who he had been fighting or how large the force had been.

CONFEDERATE PERSPECTIVE

At 1000, when the Confederate skirmish line in the trees south of Fourteenmile Creek opened fire, Gregg was standing on the low ridge just east of the junction of the Auburn and Utica roads, 800 yards north-northeast of the bridge where the Utica Road crossed Fourteenmile Creek. He watched as the smoke from the muskets of his infantry bloomed like cotton bolls, and at first he did not realize that they were not dissipating as they usually did. The three guns of Bledsoe's MO ARTY, just to his right, opened fire simultaneously, and the gunners were irritated and dismayed to discover that not only did the smoke not dissipate, but also the muzzle blast raised huge clouds of orange dust, and it too hung in the air like a pall. After a few minutes of firing, the gunners no longer could see their targets, but they continued to fire in the general direction of the enemy, not knowing what else to do.

In a few moments, Gregg, off to the side of the artillery and therefore not yet blinded by smoke and dust, saw a six-gun battery of artillery appear on the ridgetop south of Fourteenmile Creek. They deployed on either side of the road, opened fire, and instantly vanished in huge clouds of smoke and dust. Now and then a gap appeared in the clouds, and through them Gregg could see shadowy blue lines of infantry deploying both to the east and west of the road, but the smoke and dust were so thick that he could not be certain of their numbers. He thought that there might be a brigade of infantry, which was not unexpected, given the scouts' reports earlier in the day. It was not a matter for serious concern, since he still would have something like a two-to-one advantage in numbers. Gregg was not in a hurry; he wanted the

Yankees to complete their deployment and fully commit themselves before he initiated his battle plan.

A little before 1100, the Union infantry advanced toward the line of trees along Fourteenmile Creek, pushing the Confederate skirmish line back, but then halted inside the tree line on the north side of the creek, even though there was no Confederate resistance whatever. Gregg was content; there was no sign of Federal activity on any of the other roads, and the Unionists deployed across the Utica Road obviously were not pressing an attack. By 1100, he was certain that the only Union force in the vicinity was the one on the Utica Road, and it was small, else it would not have stopped where it did. It was perfect.

Gregg's plan was to pin the Yankees in place with a frontal assault, meanwhile striking and perhaps enveloping their right flank with the two regiments placed on the Gallatin Road for that purpose. If luck was with him, his troops might get in behind the Federal lines, capture the guns on the ridge south of Fourteenmile Creek, and maybe capture the whole Yankee force.

At noon, Gregg began the first movements of his attack. The forward regiment on the Gallatin Road, the 50 TN, was moved down off its ridge and into position on the edge of the trees along Fourteenmile Creek, facing southwest. The regiment which had been placed farther back along the Gallatin Road (the 10-30 TN) was moved forward and went into line to the left of the 50 TN.[8] Both of the two Tennessee regiments were large, so Gregg had a striking force of perhaps twelve hundred infantrymen in position off the right flank and rear of the Union line. The 3 TN was brought up from its position near a graveyard and placed on the left flank of the 7 TX; and the two regiments, numbering perhaps a thousand men, were ordered forward to attack the Union infantry in the woods astride the Utica Road.[9] The Texans were to start the assault, to be continued right to left along the Confederate line. The idea was simple and direct; the troops attacking down the Utica Road would attract the full attention of the Yankees, whereupon the two regiments out to the east would strike into their flank and rear.

At first everything went well. The Texans and 3 TN drove into the woods, and only their right-flank companies were effectively stopped at the creek, because the Yankees took shelter in the streambed and used it for a trench. The Texas left flank kept right on going to the far edge of the woods, as did the Tennesseans on their left flank. But at this point Gregg lost control. Because of the smoke and dust, he no longer could see what was happening; and his left-flank regiments, 1,200 airline yards away, were beyond either vision or control. From here on until nearly 1600, the Confederate regiments fought almost completely independently, and of course they re-acted only to the situation in their immediate vicinity. After all, like Gregg, they could see very little.

Out on the Confederate left flank, the two Tennessee regiments heard the sound of firing and moved forward through the tangled woods, losing cohesion and direction in the process. Halfway through, they ran into a few dismounted blue-clad cavalrymen, who fled after a few shots. One of the two Rebel regiments finally emerged into the open, to find themselves, just as planned, on the right flank of the Union force. They had thus far scarcely fired a shot, and where they were, way off on the eastern edge of the battle, the smoke was not so bad. What they saw when they emerged from the trees was a massive blue battle line. It looked like at least a division and maybe more, and it was supported by at least two six-gun batteries of artillery. Furthermore, it was all too clear that the Yankees knew they were coming, because the right flank of the Union deployment was refused, and the Confederates were faced with a solid blue line perfectly positioned to receive them.

The southerners knew better than to try; they fell back into the tim-ber and managed to find a route, more or less, back the way they had come, pursued by an extremely aggressive Union skirmish line. A cou-rier was sent to Gregg but was unable to find him.[10] Gregg, however, knew that something had gone wrong, because he listened in vain for sounds of battle from his left wing.

At the same time, things were going wrong on the Utica Road as well. Most of the Confederate line pushed across Fourteenmile Creek and through the woods to the south side, but when they emerged into the open, they were met by sheets of musketry from a continuous blue battle line that went out of sight in both directions. They recoiled into the woods and sent to Gregg for orders.

Gregg had little choice. When messengers from the Utica Road front eventually found him, they told him that the Union force was far larger than he had assumed, but he still did not know just how large. The lack of sounds of combat from his left flank indicated that something drastic had happened to his flanking force. Knowing that the two commanders out on the left flank were veterans, he assumed they had only been de-layed, and he decided to commit his reserve, the 41 TN, which by this time had moved forward to the graveyard. It took awhile for the courier to get to them and even longer for the reserve regiment to reach the battlefield. In that interval, things changed drastically.

Remarkably, the Texans on the right flank, who had been stopped short at Fourteenmile Creek, still thought that they were faced with only a single Yankee brigade.[11] About 1330 they realized the truth, when a massive blue-clad battle line smashed into the woods. It was too much; the whole Texas line gave way, as did the Tennessee regiment to its left.[12] Both units fell back in disorder to the hilltop where the Confederate artillery continued in action.

Gregg watched this retreat in complete dismay. Those two regiments together numbered more than a thousand men, all veterans noted for their fighting ability. Yet they had been routed.[13] Union regiments at this time and place usually numbered about 350 men. Gregg was absolutely certain that the Texans and Tennesseeans would not have been defeated by anything other than greatly superior numbers, and that meant that they must have been attacked by at least four Union regiments. There were reports from his skirmishers on the extreme right of his line that there was a Yankee battle line extended beyond the right flank of the Texans, which meant still more Yankee regiments. And that meant that he was opposed by at least a division.

Only at this point did Gregg understand that he was opposed by a Yankee force much more powerful than he had assumed. He still did not know how large it actually was, but it was clear that he was badly outnumbered. When he realized that the hunter had become the hunted, he also understood that all he could do was to try to stabilize the situation long enough to extricate his troops from what might turn into a trap. By this time, the 41 TN had come up, and Gregg placed them on a ridge off the left flank of the two regiments along the Utica Road. He had two motives. First, he thought that the troops retreating from that front would rally on the reserve regiment. Second, he was fearful that the Unionists would find the gap between the Utica Road force and his two left flank regiments, which he thought were still out there somewhere, even though he had heard nothing from them since noon.

Gregg felt a certain satisfaction when a Yankee regiment came out of the woods south of the 41 TN and charged, only to be beaten back.[14] Gregg had sealed the gap just in time. Unbeknownst to Gregg, the two left flank regiments had fallen back to the Gallatin Road, where one of them (10-30 TN) stayed as a road guard, while the other drifted off to the west, eventually coming out on the flank of the 41 TN shortly after the latter had taken its position on the ridge.

At this juncture, a courier came in and reported that the Gallatin Road was unguarded and that there was Yankee activity in that direction.

Gregg necessarily took the message at face value. If the Yankee battle line extended from the Utica Road to the Gallatin Road, as this message seemed to imply, then he was faced with more than a division, which was disquieting indeed. On the other hand, it more likely was only a cavalry force, possibly the one that had raided Crystal Springs the previous day. In any event, it seemed to mean that his two left-flank regiments had themselves been outflanked, and that meant that a Federal force could drive up the Gallatin Road into his rear. He had no idea what had happened to his left-flank regiments, and he had no reserve. The best he could do was to order the relatively fresh 41 TN, which had just beaten off a Yankee attack, to pull out of line and march north to block the vital Gallatin Road. Gregg did not know that the Gallatin Road already was blocked by one of his two left-flank regiments, the 10-30 TN.

This led to a truly bizarre situation. The 10-30 TN, the regiment on the Gallatin Road, had heard the sounds of battle when 41 TN beat off the Union assault; being idle where they were, they marched toward the sounds of the guns. The two regiments traded places! As they passed each other, neither stopped to ask what the other was about.

It was now near 1600, and a lull had fallen on the battlefield. The smoke and dust were beginning to drift away, and Gregg now was able to see across the valley. The ridge south of Fourteenmile Creek was crowned with four batteries of Union artillery, and still more Federal regiments were moving restlessly in the open fields below the ridge. This was Gregg's first real confirmation that he faced an entire Yankee corps.

There was nothing to do but retreat.[15] Fortunately, the left-flank regimental commanders came to the same conclusion at roughly the same time, with the result that the brigade coalesced in Raymond. Gregg marched on through the town and retreated eastward on the Mississippi Springs Road. He expected pursuit, but there was none, not even by cavalry. During the night. these troops met Walker's brigade, adding perhaps a thousand men to Gregg's force. They were not enough to warrant trying the game again.

22

The Approach to Jackson
13 May–14 May 1863

Maps: 13. The Region between Edwards, Canton, and Jackson
    14. The Battlefield of Jackson
    43. Disposition of Forces in the Region between Vicksburg,
        Bruinsburg, and Raymond: 2000, 12 May 1863
    44. Disposition of Forces in the Region between Edwards,
        Canton, and Jackson: 2000, 13 May 1863

FEDERAL PERSPECTIVE

Grant was just settling down on the evening of 12 May at Dillon's farm, seven miles west of Raymond, when a sweat-stained courier arrived and poured out the news that McPherson's XVII Corps had just won an all-day battle two miles southwest of Raymond against a Rebel force estimated at two brigades and commanded by BG John Gregg. McPherson now was in firm possession of Raymond and was awaiting instructions.[1]

To Grant, this was startling news. He had not anticipated that McPherson would encounter serious resistance. The fact that a battle had been fought was disquieting. Like McPherson, he had assumed that the long march through presumably enemy country would have given the Rebels plenty of opportunity to determine the size of the force marching up the Utica–Raymond Road. The implication was that the Rebel force had been quite large, as it seemed unlikely that the Confederates would pick a fight unless they had something approaching equal numbers. Grant was quite prepared to accept McPherson's statement that he had encountered two brigades and probably was a little surprised that there hadn't been more, considering that the Rebels had taken the initiative.

However, Grant knew of Gregg's brigade and knew its approximate strength. Two such brigades plus attached cavalry would total six thousand, and perhaps as many as seven thousand, men—at least the equivalent of a Union division. That would be enough to fight a serious delaying action, perhaps to gain time for still larger forces to gather at Jackson. And Grant was certain that more were on the way. Suddenly the rumored concentration in Jackson began to seem entirely credible. To make matters worse, there were reasonably solid reports that GEN Joseph E. Johnston, commander of the Department of the West and reputedly the best general in the Confederacy after Robert E. Lee, was due to arrive in Jackson at any moment.[2] If a man like Johnston had as many as ten thousand men in Jackson, then it would be dangerous in the extreme to perform the planned wheel to the west against Edwards and Big Black Bridge, while such a combination existed in his rear.

The problem was that, on the face of it, it would be equally dangerous to wheel to the east toward Jackson, because the troops whom McClernand had encountered south of Edwards had been identified as belonging to John Bowen's DIV. Grant had good reason to respect Bowen's abilities. However, a decision to attack Grant's rear would be made not by Bowen, but by Pemberton; and Grant knew Pemberton to be cautious, as well as conservative. Cautious Pemberton could be counted on to restrain bellicose Bowen, so there was at least a reasonable chance that McClernand's four divisions south of Edwards could be disengaged and well on their way toward Jackson before Pemberton could bring himself to leave his prepared defenses and risk a campaign of maneuver.

A move against Jackson had other virtues to commend it. If the city could be taken, its value as a communications and supply center could be nullified. This would be far more useful than simply ripping up a few miles of railroad track between Clinton and Big Black Bridge, which is all Grant could hope to accomplish with the planned attack on Big Black Bridge. After all, Jackson was a crossroads through which war materials and troops poured not only westward toward Vicksburg, but also northward toward the defenses along the Tallahatchie River in North Mississippi, and southward to Port Hudson. Certainly, if Vicksburg ever were besieged, the destruction of Jackson and its railroad and telegraph lines would make the task of taking the river city a good deal easier. It would even help to reduce the war-making potential of the entire Confederacy, because Jackson was an industrial city with an arsenal, railroad yards and shops, spinning mills, foundries, tanneries, and food depots. The destruction of those industries would be felt deeply by the Confederate government.

Grant made his decision within the hour. He was certain that McPherson's corps alone would be inadequate to capture the place. It was reported to be fortified, and if Johnston had ten thousand men in the city, McPherson's remaining twelve thousand (he had lost 502 at Raymond) never would succeed. To be certain of success, Grant might have to use his whole army.[3]

His order directed McPherson to leave Raymond at first light next morning and march on Jackson via Clinton. Sherman was directed to take his XV Corps out of the camps around the Dillon's farm and advance on Jackson via Raymond and Mississippi Springs.[4] McClernand had by far the most difficult assignment. His task was to disengage from Bowen before Bowen discovered his intentions. The three divisions camped around Whittaker's Ford, south of Mt. Moriah, would march to Raymond on the road between Mt. Moriah and Dillon's farm, while A. J. Smith's DIV, camped at Montgomery's Bridge, would march first to Auburn. There, with any luck, he would meet Frank Blair's DIV of Sherman's corps, which was protecting the first of three big supply trains that were crawling up the road from Grand Gulf.[5] If necessary, both divisions then would continue to Raymond. If serious trouble developed at Jackson, all five divisions would be in position to join Sherman and McPherson in dealing with it on the following day.

While McPherson and Sherman were knowledgeable and experienced military leaders, they were more than a little surprised by Grant's orders for a converging attack on Jackson, even though they understood fully the reasons for it. Grant did not know enough about the situation in Jackson to be able to predict what the Rebel commander, whoever he was, would do. If the Union army were concentrated for a single attack along the Raymond Road, the Southerners might well hold the force in place with a stand somewhere southwest of Jackson, move their main Jackson army out toward Clinton, and then strike the flank of the Union army strung out along the Raymond Road. Alternatively, if the Clinton Road were to be used as the axis of advance, the same game could be played, but in reverse. The obvious, if unconventional, answer was to strike via both roads, despite the difficulty of coordinating a converging attack with two widely separated columns.

Next morning, 13 May, the whole complex movement started precisely on time. This time McPherson placed Crocker's DIV in the lead.[6] Almost immediately there was cavalry bickering, as Wirt Adams's horsemen tried to penetrate the Union cavalry screen and count noses. As the day wore on, it became hot and sultry, with the strange oppressiveness of an impending storm. As he marched through Clinton, McPherson incidentally achieved one of the interim objectives of the campaign by cutting the Southern Railroad of Mississippi.[7] Crocker passed through the town and camped a mile to the east, with Logan resting in the town itself.[8] The occupation of Clinton had two important advantages. First, breaking the railroad between Jackson and Edwards prevented supplies and reinforcements from reaching Pemberton's army. Second, and perhaps even more important, it severed the telegraph line connecting Pemberton with Jackson, thus forcing the Rebels to depend upon couriers for communication. They would need some twelve hours to send a dispatch and receive a reply. That would be far too long a time to permit adequate coordination of forces in a situation as fluid as this one.

Putting Tuttle's DIV in the lead, Sherman reached Raymond by noon. At this point, a powerful advance guard was pushed out well to the front, because Sherman feared that Gregg might be waiting in ambush. After all, McPherson had reported that Gregg had had two brigades at the Battle of Raymond, and he might have been reinforced from the troops reputedly at Jackson. Sure enough, four miles east of Raymond the advance guard was fired upon, but it turned out to be only a cavalry picket. Tuttle's DIV stopped for the night a half-mile east of Mississippi Springs, and Steele's DIV camped four miles east of Raymond.[9] To everyone's surprise, there was no contact with the Rebels after that one brief spat. Sherman, Grant, and their staffs spent the night in Raymond.

Sherman and McPherson knew well the deadly danger of being defeated in detail, so they almost instinctively sought a means of coordination. There was a good road connecting Mississippi Springs with Clinton, and, as soon as the two columns were in possession of the two ends of the road, couriers began to flow back and forth along it. One of McPherson's first messages to Sherman reported that there were indeed fortifications around Jackson and that Joseph E. Johnston had arrived.[10] How McPherson obtained this information so quickly is something of a mystery, but later events suggest that there was a well-organized Union spy ring in Jackson. In any event, the news was bad, because Joe Johnston's reputation was high in both Union and Confederate circles.

McClernand had a singularly difficult problem. His men not only had a long way to march, but also they had first to disengage from the Confederate roadblock on the Telegraph Road south of Edwards (2,500 yards north of Mt. Moriah). The problem became even more serious on the morning of 13 May, when McClernand's pickets reported that the roadblock had developed overnight into a long gray battle line.[11] They also confirmed that the line was commanded by John Bowen. This, too, was bad news.

McClernand formed Hovey's DIV into line of battle and moved it forward threateningly toward the Confederate position until it was less than a mile away. Fortunately, the configuration of the ground was such that the Mt. Moriah road junction could not be seen from the Confederate position. McClernand then moved Carr's and Osterhaus's DIVs across Whittaker's Ford to the Mt. Moriah road junction and marched rapidly away to the southeast, toward Raymond; forded Bakers Creek (the bridge had been washed out by freshet some weeks previously); and halted in a strong position to wait for Hovey.[12] Hovey moved his people out of the battle line a regiment at a time, covered by skirmishers, and got away across Bakers Creek without further difficulty. Just as they crossed the creek, the rear guard was attacked by a detachment of Confederate cavalry, but a few volleys from the rear guard drove them back, and there was no further trouble.[13] All three divisions camped for the night just west of Raymond.

Still farther west, A. J. Smith's DIV of McClernand's corps moved south and then east toward Auburn, without molestation of any kind. They had just settled into their camps at Auburn when MG Frank Blair's DIV of Sherman's corps came tramping down the road from Cayuga, escorting a 200-wagon train filled with ammunition and hardtack.[14]

Grant was more than satisfied on the evening of 13 May. He had disengaged cleanly from the Confederate forces to his front and already had four divisions within striking distance of Jackson, with five more only a day's march away.

Heavy rains began falling during the night. By the time the Federal army started forward on the morning of 14 May, the unsurfaced Mississippi roads already were turning into seemingly bottomless mud. Grant reconciled himself to the fact that the movements of the army necessarily would be slow and difficult. And so it proved.[15] Despite leaving their bivouacs a mile east of Clinton at 0500, it was 0900 before the van of McPherson's advance reached the point where the Clinton Road crosses the railroad. It had taken the troops four hours to advance four miles.

On the Raymond Road, Grant rode with Sherman on the dreary morning of 14 May. Tuttle's DIV marched in the van, screened by cavalry.[16] The cavalrymen could not believe their luck; there was not a Rebel to be seen. Tuttle regarded this with grave concern, because it looked like the makings of an ambush. To be on the safe side, he called in the cavalry and put one of his best infantry regiments out in front, supported by an artillery battery.[17]

Still no opposition. The advance guard reached the top of the gentle ridge overlooking Caney Creek, about six miles from Jackson, about 0900.

CONFEDERATE PERSPECTIVE

Late on the evening of 12 May, Pemberton heard the news that Gregg had been defeated in a battle just south of Raymond. When he learned that the Federal force had consisted of at least two divisions, he knew immediately that his previous analysis of Grant's intentions had been nonsense. He now realized that all three of the columns moving north toward the railroad were of corps strength, and he had no troops whatever other than a few cavalry between Jackson and Edwards. If the Yankees chose to cut the railroad, there was absolutely nothing he could do about it. They also might turn east toward Jackson.[18] If they did, and if they moved quickly, Jackson might well be lost, because the only troops available for its defense were Gregg's and Walker's brigades and a few advanced elements of Gist's BDE, which was coming from the East Coast, assuming that they arrived in time. To be sure, Maxey's BDE from Port Hudson was due to arrive at any moment, and there were a couple of odd regiments. In total, however, they would amount to only about twelve thousand men, even when fully assembled. Pemberton was only too aware that the fortifications around Jackson were incomplete, so if Grant struck with all his strength, the city likely would fall.

The first thing to do was to make Jackson as secure as possible, so Pemberton instructed Gregg not to try to attack the Federal forces again, but to retreat into the fortifications of the city. Pemberton also thought that something might be done if the force south of Edwards tried to disengage. If the movement could be detected in time, the Army of Vicksburg might be able to strike at the rear of the force moving toward Jackson or at least cut its supply line to Grand Gulf and thus dislocate the Federal movement. On the morning of 13 May, he sent Loring to take charge of the troops at Edwards, with instructions to send out strong patrols to determine the intentions of the Union forces to the south.[19] He also sent a message to GEN Joseph E. Johnston, who was somewhere west of Meridian en route to Jackson, informing him of his general dispositions, and telling him that Edwards was being threatened from the south by a Union corps.[20]

Pemberton had other things to distract him, as well. Forney, who had been left in command of Vicksburg, reported that a brigade of infantry from Memphis had landed at Young's Point and another brigade had moved into Bower's Landing, across the river from Warrenton.[21] This again raised the threat of a direct amphibious attack on Vicksburg and prevented Pemberton from stripping the city of infantry in order to strengthen his army of maneuver, which now was concentrated in the Big Black Bridge–Edwards area.

Loring arrived in Bowen's lines south of Edwards about midmorning, to find everything ominously quiet. As Pemberton had instructed, he sent out patrols, but the only thing they found was the tail of a Federal column just crossing Baker Creek on the Mt. Moriah–Raymond Road. The patrol tried to interfere, but the Yankees brushed them off and continued on their way to the east, toward Raymond.[22] Loring did not immediately report any of this to Pemberton; instead, he waited until late on the evening of 13 May to bring his chief up to date. Thus it was not until nearly midnight that Pemberton learned that a Union corps no longer was threatening Edwards, but instead was marching at full speed toward Jackson![23]

After the Battle of Raymond, on 12 May, Gregg's brigade had withdrawn on the Mississippi Springs Road and camped three miles east of Raymond. At this point, he was joined by Walker's small brigade (about a thousand men) and a regiment of mounted infantry.[24] The next morning, 13 May, Gregg, in response to Pemberton's order not to pick another fight, grudgingly withdrew to just east of Mississippi Springs. About noon, he learned that Clinton had been occupied by two Union divisions, and at almost the same moment his pickets out toward Raymond reported that two more Yankee divisions had moved into Raymond from the west. At this point, with Pemberton's instructions to retreat into Jackson in hand, Gregg rapidly withdrew his force into the fortifications of Jackson, reaching the city around dark.

GEN Joe Johnston, traveling by railroad, received Pemberton's message, which had been sent early on the afternoon of 13 May, while he was still fifty miles east of Jackson. Johnston arrived in Jackson late on the afternoon of 13 May. Shortly after nightfall, Gregg reported to him, telling him that Pemberton had concentrated his army at Edwards and that four divisions of Federal troops, under Sherman, were at Clinton. Gregg also told him that there were only six thousand troops in Jackson, a number clearly inadequate to defend the place.[25]

Johnston accepted at face value Gregg's statement that all the Federal troops threatening Jackson were concentrated at Clinton, and agreed with Gregg's assessment that there simply were not enough Confederate troops and not enough time to organize a defense. Furthermore, when he was shown a map, he realized that, even if Pemberton marched instantly from Edwards, he would be a long time coming. The telegraph no longer worked, so communication was entirely by courier, and it was a five- or six-hour ride on a fast horse from Jackson to Pemberton's headquarters at Bovina, even under the best of circumstances. In other words, Pemberton wouldn't get a message dispatched at 2100 on 13 May until perhaps 0300 on 14 May. By the time the troops were organized and marshaled for the march, most of 14 May would be gone. Then two more days would be required to make the march, assuming ideal marching conditions and no interference from anybody. The calculation indicated that Pemberton could not possibly be on the scene until late on the afternoon of 16 May. Sadly, he wired President Davis, in Richmond, VA: "I am too late."[26]

However, by this time he had learned that Gist's and Maxey's brigades were on their way. Gist was coming from the east over the Southern Railroad of Mississippi and was expected momentarily, but Maxey was coming up from Port Hudson on the New Orleans, Jackson & Great Northern Railroad, and Johnston knew that the railroad had been chewed to bits by Union cavalry raids, so there was no telling when he might arrive. That meant that he could expect a reinforcement of only about three thousand men within the next couple of days, with another three thousand at some indefinite time in the future.[27] Still, that would bring the Jackson force up to perhaps nine thousand men, most of whom were good combat troops, and that was the equivalent of almost two Union divisions. With such a force, he might be able to hold Jackson long enough for Pemberton to reach the neighborhood of Clinton with the Vicksburg army. Then, with luck, he might be able to catch Grant's forces from both front and rear. Perhaps with this in mind, Johnston sent Pemberton a message at 2100 on 13 May, informing him of the Federal force at Clinton and suggesting that Pemberton bring the Vicksburg army east to strike the four Federal divisions which were presumed to be at Clinton from the rear while they were engaged with the Jackson forces. So important was this message that he sent copies by three separate couriers.[28]

By the early morning hours of 14 May, Johnston was having second thoughts. He considered the weak fortifications, the fact that the units in Jackson never had worked together before, and that Sherman was (as he believed) at Clinton, less than ten miles away, with four divisions. Perhaps he also had reflected that Grant was unlikely to let McClernand's corps sit idle while Pemberton marched away. If the four Union divisions which

Gregg had reported at Clinton turned west instead of east, Pemberton's Vicksburg army might be attacked simultaneously from both front and rear, with entirely predictable results. Following these meditations, at 0300 on the morning of 14 May, he ordered the city of Jackson evacuated. He took this step despite the fact that no pressure of any kind had yet been exerted on the city.[29]

Johnston placed Gregg in command of the city and ordered him to hold off the Yankees as long as possible. He and his staff then left immediately for Canton, twenty-four miles to the northeast. It was raining heavily, and the unpaved streets quickly were turning to mud. Perhaps because of the mud, he did not continue on to Canton but instead stopped at Tougaloo, only seven miles to the north-northeast.

Gregg had two possible courses of action. He could put his men into the half-completed earthworks which ringed the city, or he could move his little army outside the city and fight a battle somewhere along the Clinton Road on a site of his choosing. After some thought, Gregg chose the second option. The major difficulty with the earthworks was that the segment defending the Clinton Road was poorly sited. It consisted of a sharp salient that projected 300 yards or so from the general trend of the works, and both the Clinton Road and the railroad entered the works nearly at the point. Gregg feared that, with four divisions, the Union commander simply would extend his line and assault both flanks, cave in the sides, and capture most or all of his force, which was barely large enough to man the riflepits in the salient angle. If that happened quickly, all the other troops in the city might well be lost. Better to buy time by fighting outside the city. He was grateful that the Yankees had made his task simpler by concentrating all their troops into a single force attacking along the Clinton Road.

With this in mind, Gregg began to move his taskforce out of the city shortly after 0300, 14 May, with COL Colquitt in tactical command. Colquitt's little 900-man brigade (it consisted of three small infantry regiments and a four-gun battery) led the way, followed by Walker's 1,000-man brigade. Gregg's own brigade, temporarily commanded by COL Farquharson, was kept inside the city as a last-ditch reserve.[30]

Colquitt chose a position about three miles from the center of the city, on a low ridge that ran transverse to the Clinton Road. Only Colquitt's BDE was deployed;[31] Walker's troops were kept in column on the Clinton Road, some distance to the rear. In specifying this disposition, Gregg's reasoning probably was that he could not realistically hope to stop the Union advance; after all, his total force in the city numbered less than five thousand, while the Federal force at Clinton consisted of four divisions, conservatively numbered at twenty thousand. Gregg's objective was to buy time, not to defeat the enemy. His disposition would force the Yankees to deploy and make a formal assault, and that would take time. When threatened by overwhelming force, he would retreat and repeat the process. Two or three such cycles and the whole day would be gone, and in that time everything useful would have been removed from the town.

Having started Colquitt and Walker on their way, Gregg turned his attention to doing what he could with the few State Troops in the city. Of course, they could not be expected to stand against the veteran Federal infantry, but they could man batteries and give the appearance of strength.[32] One head peering over a parapet looks very much like any other. The appearance alone would make the Yankees move slowly and cautiously.

COMMENTARY

Gregg's report to Johnston on the night of 13 May needs careful examination, because it undoubtedly led Johnston badly astray. It is clear that Gregg repeated the error that he and Pemberton previously had made, and which had led to the Battle of Raymond: assuming that Grant would not separate his forces in the face of the enemy. Gregg assumed that the Yankees would be concentrating their forces for a blow at Jackson and that, therefore, the two divisions at Raymond were marching to join the two already at Clinton. He assumed that the skirmishers who had banged away at his pickets while he was near Mississippi Springs were simply guarding the flank of that movement. It is interesting to note that Gregg gave Johnston his interpretation of the situation at Clinton as if it were fact. He had retreated into Jackson so confident of his analysis that he had made no effort to keep in contact with the Union force that had hit his picket lines west of Mississippi Springs. As a result, Johnston remained unaware of the existence of Sherman's two divisions marching up the Raymond Road, and focused his attention on the Clinton column.

It is also worthy of note that Gregg identified the four divisions at Clinton as being commanded by Sherman, which suggests that he still did not know whom he had been fighting at Raymond on 12 May.

Furthermore, while Gregg's estimate of the number of Confederate troops in Jackson was technically correct, it was by no means the whole truth. Later in the evening, when Johnston had a chance to check carefully, he discovered that, while there indeed were about 6,000 men in and about the city, another 6,000 were expected to arrive within twenty-four hours. Thus, if the city could be held for even one day, there was at least a chance that it might be held forever. Twelve thousand men behind fortifications, even not very good ones, could be expected to resist at least double, and possibly triple, their number.

Johnston's message to Pemberton, sent late on the night of 13 May, also requires close examination. It is twenty-six miles from Edwards to Jackson, a very long day's march. It is only ten miles from Clinton to the center of Jackson. It is clear that Johnston was assuming that his troops in Jackson would be able to resist long enough for the Vicksburg army to reach the vicinity of Jackson and attack. Conservatively, that meant that Johnston had to hold for at least two days. If he did not, then Pemberton might find himself attacking Union troops ensconced behind the Jackson fortifications.

Johnston seems to have ignored the fact that the Army of the Tennessee included far more than four divisions. He must have assumed that McClernand's corps would remain quietly in place south of Edwards while Pemberton slipped away and marched to Jackson. It is hard to understand why he would believe that Grant would permit his army to be separated into two wings so far apart that they could not supply mutual support.

23

Too Little and Too Late: Battle of Jackson 14 May 1863

Maps: 13. The Region between Edwards, Canton, and Jackson
14. The Battlefield of Jackson
45–47. The Battle of Jackson

METEOROLOGICAL AND GEOGRAPHICAL CONTEXT

The weather in Central Mississippi in the spring is generated primarily by strong frontal systems that move from west to east across the state, and their passage is characterized by violent thunderstorms. These fronts commonly pull warm, moist air up from the Gulf of Mexico, and it is not unusual for such a storm to deposit an inch or more of rain in less than an hour. The storms are accompanied by very strong and gusty winds and remarkably intense displays of lightning. A common pattern includes several clear, hot days, growing increasingly oppressive, terminated by a day of violent storm, followed again by clear weather. In extreme cases, such a day of storm can deposit as much as eight inches of rain, and two or three are not uncommon.

The soils of the region are mostly silty clays, with relatively low capacity to absorb water. As a result, there is little subsurface storage of water; a long rainless spell causes all of the minor streams to go dry, and even the larger creeks commonly are reduced to a trickle. However, a day of heavy rain is enough to fill the dry or nearly dry channels with deep, swift, unfordable torrents. The transition from dry channel to raging flood can occur within a few hours, but the condition rarely persists for more than a day or two.

Jackson is built on a gently rolling topographic surface, with no really prominent terrain features. In 1863, it was a city of less than four thousand people. It was, however, the political and economic center of the State of Mississippi. It was basically a commercial and agricultural center, with only the very modest industrial development common to Deep South cities at that time. Even so, it had grist mills, spinning mills, weaving mills, tanneries, harness shops, a foundry, railroad shops, and extensive food depots. It was a transportation center of major importance, because it lay at the junction of north-south and east-west railroads; thus it was an essential link in the system of internal communication of the Confederate Department of the West.

Two major roads entered the city from the west, one from Clinton, which ran roughly parallel to, but 500 yards south of, the Southern Railroad of Mississippi (SRRM); and another from Raymond, which entered the city from the southwest. A third road led off to the northeast toward Canton, a flourishing town some twenty-four miles away. The eastern edge of the city was bounded by the unfordable Pearl River. This river was crossed by a single railroad bridge, which carried the SRRM across the river nearly a mile south of the center of the city; and two wagon bridges, which crossed the river about 800 yards above the railroad bridge.

FEDERAL PERSPECTIVE

A few minutes after the skirmish line leading McPherson's advance toward Jackson along the Clinton Road crossed the railroad, it reached the crest of a low ridge where it almost immediately came under fire from a battery of artillery on a ridge about 1,700 yards to their front.[1] The fire was deadly accurate, considering the range and the weather. Crocker, in command of McPherson's lead division, deployed smoothly and began to move slowly forward. The Confederate artillery was very trying, despite the fact that Crocker brought up his own guns for counterbattery fire.[2] Crocker was puzzled; the rain made it hard to see, but the Confederate line seemed thin and short. It looked to be no more than 600 yards long, which meant that it could not exceed perhaps a thousand men. His division could eat a force of that size for breakfast. Still, the fact that they were standing there, obviously ready and waiting, made Crocker cautious.

By about 1000, Crocker's DIV had moved to within 500 yards of the

Confederate line, and Crocker noted that his line extended far beyond both flanks of the Rebel battle line. The Federal line was poised for the assault when the heavens opened and the rain fell in such torrents that the men dared not open their ammunition boxes. There was nothing for Crocker to do but wait.[3]

By this time, Logan's DIV had caught up, and McPherson, not knowing what else to do with them, put two of Logan's brigades out on the left flank, extending the Union battle line well out into the valley of Town Creek. One of the brigade commanders noticed that a large Confederate battle line suddenly appeared through the murk, but it was on the other side of Town Creek, and the creek was in flood. Since he couldn't get to it, nor it to him, McPherson simply ignored it.

Finally, about 1100, the rain abated. Crocker ordered his men to fix bayonets and launched them in a single wave toward the Confederate battle line.[4] Strangely enough, the Confederates stood firm, even though outnumbered five or six to one. The Union flanks wrapped around the ends of the Confederate lines, and, after a few terrible moments of savage hand-to-hand fighting, the Rebel line disintegrated and fled to the rear.[5]

As usual, the assault had disorganized the Union formations, so there was a halt to straighten things out.[6] Everyone was puzzled; why had the Rebels clung so tenaciously to their position, even in the face of such a disparity in numbers? Confusion makes for caution, so, when the advance was resumed, it was slow and careful. The rain had mostly stopped, and visibility was improving. As the advance passed the bridge across Town Creek, a patrol checked out the land north of the stream but found no trace of the Rebel force that had been there earlier. After a bit over a mile, the advance guard began to receive artillery fire from a line of earthworks about 800 yards ahead.[7] The road passed through the fortifications at a salient angle which seemed to project well out from the general line. It was about 1500.

Crocker had scarcely begun his deployment when he noticed that the Rebel artillery had fallen silent. A combat patrol that went forward to draw fire drew none, pressed on, and entered the works without opposition. The Confederates were gone, although four of their artillery pieces were still emplaced in the works.[8]

Meanwhile, out on the Raymond Road, Sherman's advance guard moved slowly and cautiously over the crest of a low ridge and began dropping down a gentle slope into the valley of Caney Creek, about six miles from Jackson. The creek was filled from the recent rains, and the bridge was scarcely more than wide enough for a single wagon. Suddenly there came the spiteful crack of cavalry carbines. It was about 0900.

No match for Tuttle's infantry, the Confederate cavalry fell back slowly. About 0930, the men of Tuttle's DIV began to hear the roar of artillery drifting down from the northwest, and they exchanged knowing glances. McPherson was in action on the Clinton Road, and there was going to be a fight for Jackson. A half-hour later, the advance guard started down the slope toward the bridge across Lynch Creek, only two miles southwest of the State Capitol building, and suddenly stopped, realizing that a Rebel battle line was deployed across the road on the far side of the creek.[9] The creek was a bank-full torrent and obviously unfordable, and again the bridge was scarcely wide enough for a wagon.

Sherman and Grant, riding forward for a look, recognized they had something of a problem. The only way across the flooded creek was the bridge. If the Rebel battle line stood fast, it could sweep the bridge with sheets of rifle fire. Sherman thought of Horatius at the bridge across the Tiber and decided that he had an answer for that. He brought Tuttle's two batteries of artillery forward and opened fire.[10] The Confederate infantry stood it for twenty interminable minutes, then pulled back into the woods in front of the fortifications, a mile to the northeast.[11]

Tuttle was across the bridge in an instant, and in a few more minutes his division had deployed and resumed the advance. The Confederates did not contest the advance, but quickly retreated into their fortifications.[12] Now the shoe was on the other foot, because, when the Union infantry began to approach the works, they came under fire by a ten-gun battery. Soon four more Rebel guns joined the chorus. Union counter-battery was completely ineffective; the Confederate guns were well protected by sturdy earthworks.[13]

Sherman deployed Tuttle's three brigades in front of the earthworks and settled down to think. The force that had contested the Union crossing of Lynch Creek had consisted of only two regiments. If that was all the Rebels had, they could not possibly man the enormous length of riflepits that he could see from where he stood. So he sent a regiment off to the right to test the theory. Sure enough, when the men eventually came to the place where the New Orleans, Jackson & Great Northern Railroad (NOJ&GNRR) entered the works, there was no sign of life.[14] The troops crept cautiously through the gap. Still nothing. They turned to the west and eventually found themselves behind the Confederate batteries that were holding Tuttle's DIV at bay. When it was over, the Federals had bagged ten guns and 150 prisoners.[15] More important, they had occupied Jackson without a serious fight.

Within a few minutes of entering the fortifications, Grant knew that the Confederate army had fled to the northeast, toward Canton. He didn't care about that. By the time it got reorganized enough to be a threat, he and his army would be long gone on the way to Vicksburg. His gamble had worked beyond all expectation.

CONFEDERATE PERSPECTIVE

About 0800, a mud-spattered and very excited courier found Gregg at his position on the Clinton Road and staggered him with the news that a powerful Yankee force was advancing up the Raymond Road and already was within a few miles of the city. There were no reports of strength; the Confederate cavalry had not been able to penetrate the screen of Union horsemen. Gregg still could not bring himself to believe that Grant actually had launched a converging attack. He assumed that the Raymond Road force consisted of perhaps a brigade detached from one of the four divisions on the Clinton Road. Nevertheless, it had to be blocked, or it would simply walk into the city.

It was a problem, because he had very little with which to block it. He hastily recalled an infantry battalion and a battery of artillery from Walker's brigade, added it to COL Thompson's regiment of mounted infantry, and sent them out to do what they could. COL Thompson took his little taskforce about two miles southwest of the city and placed them on the north bank of Lynch Creek. The creek was in flood from the all-night rain and clearly was unfordable. With luck, they might be able to burn the bridge.

Gregg was not very worried about the Yankee column on the Raymond Road. He still thought that the only real threat was the four-division force on the Clinton Road. After thinking about it for a while, he decided that he had the means further to delay the approach of the Clinton Road column. His own brigade had been held in Jackson for emergencies, under the command of COL Farquharson. He instructed the colonel to march out of Jackson via the Clinton Road to a point about two miles from the center of the city, where a road branches off to the north. Farquharson was to take his brigade out that road, cross Town Creek, and then turn left and deploy as if in preparation for an attack on the Union left flank. Gregg thought the threat of the nearly three thousand men in the brigade would persuade the Yankees to deploy a substantial part of their force in opposition, thus improving Colquitt's chances of delaying their advance along the Clinton Road.[16]

A little after 0900, a courier from Colquitt arrived with the news that the Federal van on the Clinton Road was in sight and had been engaged with artillery at long range. The Yankees did exactly what was expected of them: they deployed smoothly to left and right, brought up a battery of artillery, and obviously began to organize for an attack. So far, so good.

About 0930, it began to rain in torrents. The troops dared not open their cartridge boxes, but the rain did delay the Union deployments. However, the rain soon slackened, and about 1100 the inevitable assault began. By this time, Farquharson's brigade had completed its march and had deployed, in accord with Gregg's instructions, north of Town Creek and off the left flank of the Union battle line. After deploying, Farquharson realized the futility of the gesture, because Town Creek was a raging torrent, utterly impossible to cross, so his presence was no threat whatever to the Federals.

When the Union assault finally came, it was irresistible. It simply rolled across Colquitt's battle line, despite the bitter resistance of the Southerners.[17] In fact, they resisted too fiercely, so that when the line broke, it shattered and, in a near rout, fled down the Clinton Road. When the stream of fugitives passed Gregg, who had come out of the city with Farquharson and now was with Walker's brigade, he realized that they were so shattered that they would not be able to rally and form a new line, as he had planned. By this time, he also realized that there would not be time to withdraw Farquharson's brigade across the single narrow bridge across flooded Town Creek before the Yankees arrived, so he sent a courier to tell Farquharson to withdraw to the east and retreat up the railroad toward Tougaloo. Even worse, it was abundantly clear that Walker's two small regiments would not be able to delay the Yankees for more than a moment or two, and so he formed them into a rear guard and slowly withdrew into the half-completed fortifications, shepherding Colquitt's stragglers ahead of them.[18] By this time, it was a bit after 1400.

True to form, once the Southerners had been driven off their ridge, the Yankees stopped to reorganize, and it was not until about 1430 that they resumed their advance. When it came, it was slow but overwhelming.

As soon as Gregg arrived back inside the fortifications, he was informed that the army's supply trains had left Jackson en route for Canton. This was the news he had been waiting for. He regarded his mission as accomplished, and his only remaining task was to withdraw as many troops as possible. He was informed, too, that the Yankee force on the Raymond Road was very large, at least a division; but, while Thompson had been forced to fall back inside the fortifications, the Yankees were not forcing the issue. They seemed to be intimidated by a battery of artillery that was shelling them from the shelter of the earthworks.

That was perfect, as far as Gregg was concerned. He ordered Thompson to pull his infantry out and march as rapidly as possible for Canton. The guns which seemed to be holding the Raymond Road force at bay would continue to fire; they were manned by State Troops and local volunteers and could be sacrificed. Walker's and Colquitt's troops were then quietly withdrawn from the salient on the Clinton Road. By 1500, the last Confederate formation had left the city, en route toward Canton and safety.[19]

Jackson, the capital of the State of Mississippi, had fallen to the Army of the Tennessee, and a vital link in the communications network of the Confederacy was about to be destroyed.

24

Toward Vicksburg at Last: Countermarch 14 May–15 May 1863

Maps: 13. The Region between Edwards, Canton, and Jackson
14. The Battlefield of Jackson
48. Disposition of Forces in the Region between Edwards, Canton, and Jackson: 2200, 15 May 1863

FEDERAL PERSPECTIVE

Once the city of Jackson had fallen, Grant set his troops to work destroying all the military and public property in the place. The bridges across the Pearl River were burned, and the railroad tracks destroyed beyond hope of repair for several miles in all directions.[1] They would not be put back in operation until after the war.

Johnston had used the Bowman House, the most elegant hotel in Jackson, as his headquarters during his brief stay. Grant, Sherman, and McPherson met there about 1600 on 14 May to rest, exchange mutual congratulations, and lay plans for the next day.[2] At this point, McPherson handed Grant a dispatch. To Grant's complete amazement, it was a copy of a message that Rebel GEN Johnston had sent to Pemberton on the evening of 13 May, ordering Pemberton to Clinton to effect a junction with his Jackson army. One of the three couriers to whom the message had been entrusted was one of Stephen Hurlbut's agents, and he had been clever enough to realize that three couriers implied great importance, so he had ridden directly to the first Yankee he could find. Thus it was that, on the evening of 14 May, Grant had in his hand the strategic plan of the Confederate forces.

Nevertheless, the order was confusing in the extreme. At the time Johnston had written it (and it was dated 2100, 13 May), Johnston already knew that Clinton was occupied by Federal forces. Yet here was Johnston planning to move both his own and Pemberton's forces to Clinton! How was this to be done? Johnston's only possible route would be to march westward from somewhere north of Jackson, perhaps Calhoun, to Meridianville, and then south toward Clinton. It would take a day to get organized at Calhoun, and another two days to march the nearly thirty miles from Calhoun to Clinton, so he could not hope to arrive before 16 or 17 May. Much could happen in three days.

Perhaps even more puzzling, how was Pemberton supposed to get there? Pemberton almost certainly would not know that Jackson had fallen so quickly, and he very well might not even know that Clinton was still occupied by Federal forces. That being so, he likely would assume that Johnston was ordering him to strike at the rear of a Federal army engaged in an attack on Jackson. And that meant that he would march to Clinton by the shortest route from Edwards—namely, the road south of the railroad.

In principle, possession of the Confederate strategic plan gave the Federals a stunning advantage. However, exploiting it was not quite so straightforward as might be supposed. In the first place, it suggested that Johnston commanded a force large enough to be a threat, in the event that he was able to strike at the Federal flank or rear while they were engaged with Pemberton's Army of Vicksburg. The logical place to seek an engagement with Pemberton's army would be somewhere in the vicinity of Clinton, but that scenario held little appeal. The problem was that the Union supply route ran up the road from Grand Gulf through Rocky Springs, Auburn, Dillon's farm, Raymond, and Mississippi Springs to Jackson. If Pemberton's army moved eastward along the Jackson Road, it would be converging on that supply line and in fact would be only six miles from it when it reached the road junction south of Bolton. On the other hand, the Army of the Tennessee, moving westward from Jackson, would be two or three times as far away, and it was almost impossible to imagine that the Confederates would not sever the line at or near Raymond. That would be serious, and perhaps fatal, because a defeat or even a check might force the Unionists to withdraw to the east or north, away from their supply line. That would leave them stranded in the middle of Mississippi in a situation not unlike that faced by Xenophon and his Greeks in 401 B.C., after the defeat of Cyrus in Babylonia.[3]

One possible course of action was to send Sherman's corps toward Canton with all possible speed, thus forcing Johnston still farther away from Clinton, and meanwhile turn westward with McClernand's and McPherson's corps to deal with Pemberton. Such a force probably could hold Pemberton in check until Sherman dealt with Johnston and returned. But that course of action left the supply line vulnerable.

The second course of action would be to ignore Johnston's force, hoping that at least a couple of days would be required for them to get organized for an offensive. Meanwhile, Grant would turn westward with the all of the force he could muster, hoping to meet Pemberton's army somewhere west of Bolton. That had the dual advantage of protecting the supply line and keeping the army concentrated. Grant reflected with some satisfaction that the Army of the Tennessee was positioned almost ideally for the second course of action. By nightfall on 14 May, he had four divisions concentrated in and around Jackson. In addition, McClernand had three divisions strung out on the road between Forest Hill Church and Raymond, with another, along with one of Sherman's, at New Auburn.

The only possible snag was that Pemberton might march for Clinton via a detour to the north through Brownsville, but Grant believed he would try the direct route, chiefly because it would give Pemberton a better opportunity to strike Grant's rear while the Federals were trying to reduce Jackson. Grant had every reason to assume that Pemberton would be unaware of the speed with which the city had been taken and would believe that Johnston still held it.

Grant therefore made his plans on the assumption that Pemberton would march east from Edwards along the Jackson Road.[4] Of course, it was possible that he would take the Brownsville route, and, to guard against that, Grant sent strong cavalry patrols out into the region north and northwest of Clinton. Grant's initial plan was to concentrate around Bolton on the night of 15 May and meet Pemberton and his army just west of the village on the following day.[5] The Union couriers had a busy night getting the word to everyone.

Osterhaus marched at dawn on 15 May through Raymond and continued on up the road to Bolton. As usual, McClernand was marching with his favorite division commander, and together they reached the town about 0900. At Bolton they picked up information that Pemberton and the Army of Vicksburg were still at Edwards.[6] Welcome news, but surprising; on the basis of Johnston's order, the Rebel army should have been somewhere between Bolton and Edwards. However, since it was dilatory, there was no point in waiting for it. Osterhaus was ordered south again, to a road junction three miles south of the village. At this point, the Middle Road ran westward to Edwards. The division halted on the Middle Road, still early in the day, only a half-mile west of the Bolton–Raymond Road. Osterhaus deployed his men in line of battle facing westward and told them to keep their powder dry.[7]

Carr's DIV, which had been camped at Forest Hill Church, about six miles west of Jackson, came up and camped for the night around the road junction behind Osterhaus.[8] Hovey, who had been camped near Raymond, marched at dawn and reached Clinton, thinking he was headed for Jackson. At Clinton a new order reached him, and he marched westward to Bolton, reaching the village a bit after noon.[9] About 1600, McPherson's cavalry came swinging up the road. They passed through the village and camped in line of battle facing northwest.[10] This was, of course, a precaution against the possibility that Pemberton's army had marched via Brownsville and somehow had escaped detection by the patrols out in that direction. Logan's DIV stopped for the night just east the village, Boomer's and Sanborn's BDEs of Crocker's DIV camped three miles southeast of the town, and Holmes's BDE bivouacked in a field north of Clinton.[11] Blair, still nursing the huge supply train, which included the army's pontoon train, marched into Raymond late that afternoon and camped just west of town. A. J. Smith's DIV of McClernand's corps followed close behind Blair, but it passed on through and camped for the night about a mile west of the town, around the junction of the Bolton and Raymond roads.[12] Sherman's two divisions in Jackson stayed in the city to complete the destruction. Their orders were to march for Clinton next morning.

Grant reached Clinton, seven miles behind his front lines, at 1645 that afternoon. He had every reason to be satisfied; by nightfall, six of his divisions, about 27,000 men, would be concentrated along a seven-mile front stretching from Raymond to Bolton, and in such position that all of the roads leading directly eastward from Edwards would be blocked by a strong force. Another division, with an additional 5,000 men, would be in close supporting position.[13] Sherman, with two more divisions, was less than a day's march away, in Jackson. Since he had not met Pemberton's army at Bolton, as he more or less had expected, and the scouts operating northwest of Bolton had found nothing, the Rebel army might still be at Edwards. If so, so much the better, because the Union forces were perfectly positioned to use those same three roads into Edwards, and no one of them would have to support the movement of more than three divisions.

CONFEDERATE PERSPECTIVE

The courier from Loring who had arrived in Pemberton's headquarters at Bovina late on the evening of 13 May also had informed him that there were no longer any Union troops at either Montgomery's Bridge or Whittaker's Ford, the two crossings of Fourteenmile Creek south of Edwards. So there was no question about it; the Union army was marching to attack Jackson. Pemberton had no idea where Gregg and Walker were located or what might be happening to them, but it was obvious that the two Southern brigades would be unable to deal with the whole weight of the Army of the Tennessee.

Pemberton's immediate reaction was that this might present an opportunity for seizing the initiative. He had three possible courses of action open to him. First, he could assemble the Vicksburg field army and start in pursuit. However, the army could not possibly start moving until the next morning, 14 May, and by that time Grant would have an eighteen-hour head start and likely would be knocking on the gates of Jackson. Still, GEN Johnston was now in Jackson, and strong reinforcements were on the way. Perhaps he could hold the city for a day or two, long enough for Pemberton to arrive and attack Grant's rear. With luck, they might be able to crush him like a walnut. However, one troubling factor was that most of the Vicksburg army had been locked in defensive positions for a long time and were scarcely more than garrison troops. While Pemberton had every confidence in them as defenders, he was less confident that they could endure the fatigue of long marches followed by hard fighting. Furthermore, a converging attack would require close coordination, and Pemberton had no faith whatever that his communications with Johnston were good enough to cope with any sort of rapidly changing situation. With the Army of the Tennessee between himself and Johnston, it took a courier six to twelve hours to make the circuitous journey through Brownsville—far too long for effective coordination of a converging attack.

The second possible course of action was to do nothing but await events. To be sure, Jackson would fall, and the Confederacy could ill afford to lose the railroads and manufacturing industries of Jackson; but Johnston undoubtedly would escape toward Canton with all the military supplies and troops. As soon as Grant turned back to the west toward Vicksburg, Johnston could be depended upon to follow him closely. Grant would be forced to attack Pemberton in the fortified position already prepared at Big Black Bridge; perhaps, while Grant was attacking Pemberton, Johnston could fall on his rear and defeat and maybe even destroy the Union army. The trouble with this course of action was that it left the initiative entirely in Grant's hands, and there was no way of knowing what he might do. He might, for example, force a crossing of the Big Black River at Bridgeport and the crossings to the north, and thus put a major river barrier between his army and Johnston's, while at the same time outflanking Pemberton's position at the Big Black Bridge. Pemberton was reluctant to risk that.

The third possible course of action was to march south and east to find and obstruct Grant's supply line, which certainly must be following the main road from Grand Gulf through Rocky Springs to Reganton, and then on through Auburn and Dillon's farm to Raymond. Of course, it was possible, albeit highly unlikely, that it ran through Utica to Raymond. In either case, Pemberton would be able to find a good defensive position where his troops could fight to best advantage, and Grant would be forced to attack him to secure his line of communications. Furthermore, Johnston again would be following closely on Grant's rear, waiting to strike. The only potential flaw in this plan was that Grant might bypass Pemberton and lunge directly for Vicksburg, hoping to seize the city and reestablish contact with the Mississippi River before Pemberton could react. The obvious answer to this was to leave Forney's and Smith's DIVs in Vicksburg to man the defenses.

A few minutes after dawn on 14 May, while Pemberton was preparing to leave Bovina en route to Edwards to assume direct field command of the Army of Vicksburg, a dead-tired courier rode up and handed him a dispatch from GEN Joe Johnston. It was the message that Johnston had sent from Jackson at about 2100 on 13 May, directing Pemberton immediately to bring his field army to Clinton to effect a junction with Johnston and the Jackson army.

Pemberton read the message with a growing sense of astonishment and dismay. His mental map of the region was detailed and precise. If Johnston were forced to evacuate Jackson, then it was virtually certain that he would withdraw toward Canton, twenty-four miles northeast of Jackson. Clinton was eight miles west of Jackson, and if the Yankees were in occupation of Jackson, they would also be in occupation of Clinton. He was being asked to effect a junction in a town already held by the enemy! Pemberton could only interpret that as a plan for a converging attack on Grant; that is, it was a variant of Pemberton's own first option.

He immediately wrote to Johnston, telling him that he was moving at once with his whole available force from Edwards. It amounted to about twenty-three thousand men. He left Forney's and Smith's DIVs, plus the River Defense troops, totaling perhaps thirteen thousand men, behind[14] to secure Vicksburg against the threat of an amphibious assault from across the river.

By the time he arrived at Edwards, Pemberton had concluded that Johnston was asking the impossible. The terrible rains of the previous few hours had turned the roads into quagmires which would make movement extremely slow and laborious. If he took the direct road from Edwards to Clinton and the rain continued, it would take him two days of frightful effort, even though the distance was only sixteen miles. His army would be strung out along a single narrow road and terribly vulnerable to being cut in two by an attack from McClernand's corps, which he knew to be somewhere in the Raymond area. On the other hand, if he detoured to the north through Brownsville, it might take him as many as three days, and in that time anything could happen. Nevertheless, he hesitated to disobey a direct order without exploring all possibilities, so he called a council of war.[15]

At the council, Pemberton read Johnston's dispatch, reminded his officers that his first duty was to defend Vicksburg, and cited his reasons for believing that an attempt to join Johnston was a recipe for disaster.[16] Bowen and most of his officers believed that Johnston was a truly great general and urged that his orders be obeyed,[17] evidently on the grounds that he must have a plan, even though it was not apparent to them. Loring and Stevenson argued for an advance against Grant's supply line; that is, for Pemberton's third option. This plan seemed to have the merit of forcing the Yankees to march to the southern drum, a situation much to be desired, but it had the compensating disadvantage of opening a way for the Yankees to get to Vicksburg via the northern crossings of the Big Black. Pemberton himself wanted to fall back to the entrenchments at Big Black Bridge and fight a defensive battle, largely because the events of the last couple of days had amply demonstrated that his army of maneuver was not very maneuverable, simply because it had been in garrison too long.

In the end, Pemberton let himself be swayed by the opinions of his two senior division commanders, and opted for the advance against the Union supply line.[18] He choose Dillon's farm as his objective. At 1740 on 14 May, he started a courier on his way to Johnston to inform him of his decision[19] and then wrote orders specifying that his troops were to be on the road by 0800 the next morning, 15 May. They were to take the direct Edwards–

Raymond road as far as the Turkey Creek Road, and follow it south to Dillon's farm. The entire distance was only ten miles, and Pemberton thought they could do it easily in a single day, even though the roads were still muddy from the storm which had raged for nearly all of the previous twenty-four hours. However, the weather had cleared, and he knew that Mississippi roads dry fast, so he expected them to be in reasonably good condition by the next morning, assuming there was no more rain.

Pemberton might have chosen to march south to Mt. Moriah and followed the Mt. Moriah Road to Dillon's. The two routes are almost exactly the same distance. However, Pemberton knew that the bridge across Bakers Creek on the Mt. Moriah Road was gone, because Bowen's attack on the tail of McClernand's column had occurred there. Pemberton also knew that Mississippi creeks were subject to flash floods after heavy rains, so he was undoubtedly certain that the creek would be unfordable after the storm of the previous day.

The following morning, 15 May, it was discovered that the men had not been issued sufficient rations for a long march,[20] and by the time the rations could be brought up and distributed, it was 1300. The only good thing about the delay was that the roads had dried considerably, so marching conditions were much better. But when the advance guard of Loring's DIV reached the Lower Bakers Creek Bridge, the men discovered that the bridge had been washed out and that the creek was running bank full. It was unfordable even by cavalry.[21] For some reason, Wirt Adams, who commanded Pemberton's only effective scouting force, had failed either to notice or to report the status of the bridge, even though it was on one of the major east-west roads of the region.

After much confusion, Pemberton decided to detour northward to the Upper Bakers Creek Bridge, then along the Jackson Road to the Crossroad (the junction of the Jackson, Middle, and Ratliff roads, 700 yards south of Champion Hill), then south-southwest along the Ratliff Road to the Raymond Road near the Coker house.[22] It was perhaps 1500 by the time the head of the column started northward on a miserable farm track across the sodden Bakers Creek bottoms. By the time the head of Loring's DIV reached the Raymond Road near the Coker house, it was nearly dark. Here a scout reported that Wirt Adams's cavalry patrols had encountered a strong Yankee picket line five miles to the east. Pemberton had no idea whether the Yankee pickets were guarding the rear of McClernand's corps or the van of a Union army heading west, but in either event, caution was in order. He ordered Loring to stop where he was and put a strong picket out at the Jeff Davis house, about 500 yards east of the junction of the Turkey Creek Road and the Raymond Road.[23] Pemberton and Loring spent the night at the Ellison house, 800 yards east of Jackson Creek and only 600 yards west of the Turkey Creek Road.[24] Pemberton had no idea where Johnston was or what his plans were.

By 0100, 16 May, the Army of Vicksburg finally had settled down for the night. Loring's DIV, 6,500 strong, rested along the Raymond and Ratliff roads between the Ellison house and the Ratliff house. Bowen's 4,800 men were camped along the Ratliff Road immediately behind Loring's men, with the tail of the division about a mile south of the Cross-road.[25] Poor Carter Stevenson had not been able to leave Edwards until 1700 on 15 May because of the congestion caused by the detour forced by the washed-out bridge, so he did not catch up to Bowen until about midnight. His three lead brigades—Cumming's, Barton's, and Lee's, about 9,000 men—stretched out along the Ratliff Road from the tail of Bowen's column to the Crossroad. The army's train of more than two hundred wagons parked along the Jackson Road from the Crossroad to a point near the Austin house, and behind the wagons was Reynolds's BDE of Stevenson's division,[26] about another 2,700 men.

In the meantime, Johnston's force (it was too small to be termed an army) had retreated up the Canton Road after being expelled from Jackson on the afternoon of 14 May. Johnston left Tougaloo about 0800 on 15 May, en route to Canton, and was intercepted about 0830 by the courier whom Pemberton had sent from Edwards at 1740 on 14 May. That is, it had taken the man something like fifteen hours to cover the distance between Edwards and Tougaloo. This was the message informing Johnston that Pemberton was taking the Vicksburg army south to sever Grant's supply line to Grand Gulf.

When Johnston looked at the date, he assumed that it was the only reply Pemberton had made to his order written from Jackson at 0300 on 14 May. That had been thirty hours previously. The date told him that it had taken the courier almost fifteen hours to make the journey from Edwards, but Johnston assumed that was because the man had had trouble finding him. There would have been no such problem going the other way, so Johnston assumed that Pemberton had deliberated for eight hours or so before replying to his order. And Pemberton then had had the temerity to disobey what Johnston regarded as a reasonable and lawful order. In any event, he blew sky high. He instantly wrote to Pemberton in peremptory terms, telling him to move directly to Clinton, where Johnston would meet him with six thousand troops.[27]

Pemberton's courier carrying the message he had written on the morning of 14 May did not arrive at Johnston's headquarters until many hours later; when it did, Johnston simply ignored it.[28]

As Johnston penned his order to Pemberton, he had no certain knowledge of Pemberton's location, except that Pemberton's last message indicated that he would be somewhere between Raymond and Auburn, astride Grant's supply line to Grand Gulf. He knew for certain that a portion of the Army of the Tennessee had occupied Jackson, but he had no idea where the remainder of it was located. However, a glance at a map would disclose that, in order to reach Pemberton while avoiding bluecoats, a courier leaving from Tougaloo would have to ride via Brownsville to Edwards and then southeast to Dillon's farm, where Pemberton presumably was located. That is about forty-five long, muddy miles. Assuming ten hours to make the trip (an exceedingly optimistic estimate, considering that it had taken fifteen hours for the last courier to get from Edwards to Tougaloo), that would mean that Pemberton likely would get the order directing him to march immediately for Clinton not earlier than 1900 that night, 15 May. Pemberton's troops would be unable to march until the following morning, and, if he took the most direct route from his probable location, he would take the road through Raymond. It is fifteen miles, a day's march, from Dillon's farm via Raymond to Clinton, so Pemberton presumably would reach the vicinity of the town on the late afternoon of 16 May, at the very earliest.

To make the probability of Federal defeat as high as possible, Johnston would have to be in a position to attack Clinton at the same time that Pemberton's army arrived on the scene. Much of Johnston's force was in and around Tougaloo and Ridgeland on the early morning of 15 May. Thus, he was in a perfect position to move his troops westward to the bottoms along Bogue Chitto on 15 May, from which point he would have been in an excellent position to march southward to Clinton on the following day, the day Pemberton could be expected to be approaching Clinton from the south. With luck and good management, any Yankees in Clinton would be caught between hammer and anvil.

However, that is not what Johnston did. Having sent his peremptory order off to Pemberton, Johnston continued his leisurely withdrawal toward Canton, which meant that his troops were marching almost directly away from Clinton. That night, 15 May, he and his troops spent the night in Calhoun, after an easy march of only eight miles.[29] He had, however, sent a squadron of Wirt Adams's cavalry back toward Jackson to find out what the Yankees were up to. They discovered that the bluecoats were marching briskly away toward Clinton, but they had the satisfaction of arriving just in time to fire on and kill the last Yankee officer in the city.

Johnston evidently believed that the Army of the Tennessee would be exhausted by its long marches and several battles, and that, after completing the destruction of Jackson, Grant would take the opportunity to let his men rest for a day or two. He knew that they had evacuated Jackson, so the likely location for the rest period was Clinton. However, instead of moving in that direction on the following day, 16 May, the day Pemberton was to be expected to reach Clinton and attack the Yankee army, Johnston and his army rested quietly at Calhoun. There was no notable sense of urgency. No patrols were sent out to determine the locations of either Grant's or Pemberton's armies.

Meanwhile, far away in Richmond, Virginia, President Davis had been notified of the fall of Jackson and realized that the fate of the Mississippi Valley now hung in the balance. Davis was a westerner. He and his brother Joseph had neighboring plantations in a huge meander loop of the Mississippi River just north of Grand Gulf, and he knew in the marrow of his bones just how critical the great River was to the fortunes of the Confederacy. The River must be held at all costs. The critical need was manpower, and the only ready sources were Braxton Bragg's Army of Tennessee and Robert E. Lee's Army of Northern Virginia. Bragg was threatened by MG Rosecrans's Army of the Cumberland, in Middle Tennessee, but during the first four days of May, Lee's army had won a crushing victory over the Army of the Potomac at Chancellorsville. On the basis of past experience, the Army of the Potomac could be expected to require at least three or four months to reorganize and refit, so there was no immediate threat to Lee and his troops.

With this thought in mind, Davis had proposed, very shortly after Bowen's defeat at Port Gibson, that Lee detach some of his manpower to the West. Lee was not enthused. He cited all manner of difficulties: the distance was too great, the troops might become ill in the Deep South's climate, they might not be put to good use. Davis understood the implication; Lee was suggesting that neither Pemberton nor Johnston was smart enough to use his troops properly! Lee even suggested that it was all a tempest in a teapot, because the climate in Mississippi was so severe as to prevent Grant from taking Vicksburg! If there was a problem, Lee argued, the best way to solve it was for him to invade Pennsylvania, because the threat to Washington, Baltimore, and Philadelphia would "certainly draw their troops from the southern coasts, and give some respite in that quarter."[30] Finally Davis asked Lee to come to Richmond for a conference. Lee arrived on 14 May, and he, Seddon, and Davis spent the whole of that and the following day in private conference in Davis's office.[31] At the end of the day, long after dark, Lee had made his point: none of his troops would go west, and he would invade Pennsylvania with his Army of Northern Virginia. Davis felt that he needed the approval of his full cabinet for such a momentous decision, and the meeting was held on Friday, 16 May.[32] Lee argued that many advantages would accrue if his invasion plan were followed. First, his army would gar-ner desperately needed supplies for the Confederate forces from the rich agricultural regions north of the border. Second, the invasion would give the farmers of northern Virginia, especially those in the Shenandoah Valley, a chance to plant and harvest their crops free from interference. Third, the invasion would force the Federals to move the Army of the Potomac north-ward to protect Washington and Baltimore. Fourth and most important, the apparent threat would be so great that the panic-stricken Lincoln govern-ment would withdraw troops from Mississippi, thus saving Vicksburg.

Davis and Postmaster General John Reagan were not convinced, but Lee was persuasive. In the face of Lee's adamant refusal to consider a detachment from the Army of Northern Virginia, Davis at last yielded. Thus was launched the ill-fated Gettysburg Campaign, which reached its blood-soaked climax on 4 July. Even more important, perhaps, no troops from Virginia were sent westward to the succor of Vicksburg.

25

The Approach to Champion Hill 16 May 1863

Maps: 13. The Region between Edwards, Canton, and Jackson
15. The Battlefield of Champion Hill
49. The Battle of Champion Hill: First Contact: 0900, 16 May 1863

GEOGRAPHIC CONTEXT

While most of the interior plain of west-central Mississippi is a land of low relief and gently rolling hills, there are a few isolated erosion remnants that project high above the surrounding surface. One of these hill masses rises from the plain about five miles east of Edwards. Its summit is well over one hundred feet above the general level, and its northern face drops relatively steeply to the floodplain of Bakers Creek, but its southern slopes are open and gently rolling. The higher portions of the hill mass were uncultivated and grown up in scrub and second-growth timber. The broad, flat floodplain of Bakers Creek borders the hill mass on the north and west; to the south and east is only the gently undulating surface of the general landscape. Although most of the creek bottoms and the undulating plain were under cultivation, there were also scattered woodlots, some fairly extensive.

The main highway from Jackson to Vicksburg, the Jackson Road, passes through Bolton and then follows the Bakers Creek plain along the northern base of the hill until almost directly north of it. The road then makes a sharp turn southward and climbs over a subordinate shoulder of the main hill mass. This subordinate peak is Champion Hill, named after a family who lived in a plantation home near its northern base.

After passing over the crest of Champion Hill, the Jackson Road continues to the south along the crest of a ridge for 800 yards. There it turns abruptly to the northwest and follows along the crest of a gradually declining ridge for nearly 2,500 yards, where it again debouches onto the Bakers Creek plain. Here the road turns sharply west, crosses Bakers Creek on a sturdy wooden bridge, and continues on into Edwards.

At the place on the top of the hill where the road turns from south to northwest, a country road comes in from the east, having crossed over the highest crest of the hill mass. This is the Middle Road, which continues to the east until it intersects the Bolton–Raymond Road about three miles south of Bolton. Another road, the Ratliff Road, leads off to the southwest from the junction of the Middle Road and the Jackson Road. It meanders more or less along the top of a gentle ridge for nearly 4,000 yards until it intersects the Raymond Road, the main route between Edwards and Raymond.

To the east of the Ratliff Road is the broad, gentle valley of Jackson Creek, almost entirely under cultivation except for a fringe of trees along the creek itself. The creek is dry during most of the summer months, rarely containing water more than ankle deep. Low banks permitted easy fording everywhere along its length. The Raymond Road crosses Bakers Creek about 3,500 yards west of the junction of the Ratliff Road with the Raymond Road. The Raymond Road bridge across Bakers Creek had washed out during a storm in late April and had never been rebuilt. The banks were high and very steep, making fording with wheeled vehicles very difficult, even when the water was low. On the morning of 16 May it was not low, but instead was running bank full from the heavy rains two days earlier.

The soils comprising the hilltops in this region are relatively light and easily eroded. One consequence is that roads on hillsides and hilltops tended to become sunken roads after a few years. Each rain produced small gullies in the road surface, and the next time the road was graded, its elevation was reduced by an inch or so. As a result of this process, the Jackson Road, from the Crossroad to the foot of the hill just east of Bakers Creek, was a sunken road with nearly vertical banks from two to five feet high.

FEDERAL PERSPECTIVE

By the evening of 15 May, Grant already had issued orders to his divisions to start westward early the next morning. Blair and A. J. Smith, who were camped around the junction of the Raymond and Bolton roads, were ordered to start westward on the Raymond Road at 0500. Osterhaus and Carr, who were camped near the junction of the Middle and Bolton roads, had a shorter distance to go, so they were told to wait until 0600 before starting westward. Hovey, on the Jackson Road, was also ordered to start west at 0600, with Logan and Crocker falling in behind. A message also went to Sherman, in Jackson, to get his two divisions on the road as soon as possible, but Grant knew they would be so far behind that they could be regarded only as distant support. Grant went to bed that night in Clinton, satisfied that he had done all he could.

He was awakened about 0530 on the morning of 16 May and introduced to two railroad men who had just come through the lines from Edwards.[1] They told him that eighty Confederate regiments of infantry and ten batteries of artillery, perhaps twenty-five thousand men in all, were poised at Edwards and ready to move east. Edwards was not fortified, but there were riflepits on the east bank at Big Black Bridge and artillery covering the bridge itself.[2] Grant accepted the information at face value, although no one has ever explained why two railroad men should have had such a wonderful eye for military detail, or indeed why two Southern railroaders felt impelled to report to the commander of the Federal army.

The testimony of the two railroad men gave Grant two important pieces of information: it fixed the location of Pemberton's army as of 0200 15 May, and it provided a precise estimate of the size of the opposing force. Both were highly satisfying. First, they meant that the Union force of seven divisions which was already on the scene substantially outnumbered the Rebel force. Second, the location of Pemberton's force, coupled with the information in Johnston's captured dispatch, seemed to translate into a near certainty that Pemberton would march directly eastward from Edwards along the Jackson Road. That meant that Grant's three-division force on the Jackson Road would meet them head-on.

There were two potential problems with this scenario. In the first place, when the two columns met, the force applied to the enemy upon contact would consist of a single division, and hours might be expended in bringing the others up, along a single congested road. To be sure, both armies would suffer the same handicap, but Grant needed to wring some advantage out of the situation, if at all possible. The second difficulty was that the Union force on the Jackson Road would be greatly outnumbered by Pemberton's Confederates. The question was how to exploit the existing disposition of the other four divisions he had in the area.

Actually, the question almost answered itself, because Pemberton might march on any one, or any combination of, the three roads leading eastward from Edwards; Grant dared not leave those roads uncovered. Fortunately, the existing Union dispositions already covered all the possibilities, so Grant let stand his orders of the previous evening. If the entire Rebel army was on the Jackson Road, Grant would depend upon moving the two Union divisions on the Middle Road across country to the battle scene, and on getting Sherman's two divisions forward in time to be of service. The axiom that dictates concentrating forces in the face of the enemy thus would be conserved, albeit in a rather unconventional way. This did not cover the possibility that the Rebel army was en route to Brownsville, but the cavalry patrols in that direction had seen nothing, so Grant did not consider such an eventuality at all likely.

All three columns started westward exactly on time. There were cavalry screens well in advance of each column, and patrols combed the country between the roads to prevent infiltration by Rebel scouts. Grant had told his commanders to be careful. Do not, he said, bring on an engagement unless you are certain of success.[3] His goal in issuing such an instruction was to insure a coordinated attack; he did not want a piecemeal effort.

A. J. Smith moved westward on the Raymond Road with Burbridge's BDE in the advance, and Blair's DIV bringing up the rear. Near the Gillespie house, less than four miles west of the Bolton Road junction, the cavalry advance guard was fired upon, and the precision of the gray-clad horsemen identified them instantly as regulars, not State Troops.[4] Smith knew what that meant and deployed Burbridge's BDE in anticipation of serious trouble. The Rebels fell back slowly and stubbornly; and then, from a hilltop near the junction of Turkey Creek Road, an infantry force opened up with musketry. A. J. Smith brought up a battery, but the Rebels ignored the shells, and Burbridge's advance came to a stop. It was about 0900.

McClernand, riding with Osterhaus on the Middle Road, began after a time to wonder if the Confederates really were nearby. After nearly two hours, nothing whatever had disturbed the morning calm. Suddenly, about 0800, the thud of artillery fire drifted up from the south. Couriers were sent to inform the column on the Jackson Road that contact had been made.[5] Finally the road, now running along a narrow ridgecrest with deep ravines on both sides, turned sharply north. As the cavalry point started up a long slope toward the dominating and heavily wooded crest of a hill, it was greeted with carbine fire from Rebel cavalry. Osterhaus deployed a regiment of infantry and pushed ahead. When they were about 100 yards short of the crest of the hill, a sharp volley of rifle fire met them, and the advance abruptly stopped. It was about 0900.[6]

Hovey and Logan led their divisions out of Bolton at 0600 on the Jackson Road. Grant and McPherson marched with Logan. Behind Logan came the army's ammunition and supply train, which consisted of more than two hundred wagons. Marching well back behind the wagons came Crocker's DIV. The road ran through a pleasant agricultural landscape, and the march was dull and uneventful until a foraging party decided to raid a beehive near the road. It was a mistake; a whole regiment was routed by the tiny yellow warriors.[7] Then, about 0900, the troops reached a point about three miles west of Bolton, where the road turned abruptly south and began to climb steeply toward a dominating crest about a mile away. As the cavalry advance guard rode past an imposing white house set among trees to the left of the road, they were fired upon from a knoll 300 yards to the south.

CONFEDERATE PERSPECTIVE

Relations among the men of the Confederate high command of the Vicksburg army were strained. Loring thought Pemberton was a dunce or a traitor; after all, he had not accepted any of Loring's plans for dealing with the Yankees. Bowen blamed Pemberton for the defeat at Port Gibson and regarded him as incompetent or worse. Both Loring and Bowen wanted to see Pemberton removed from command, and Loring at one point had come perilously close to saying that he would be willing to see the Vicksburg army defeated if it resulted in Pemberton's dismissal.

As Bowen had gone into camp along the Ratliff Road ridge late the previous night, 15 May, he had seen the glow of what could only be an army's campfires reflected against the low-hanging clouds to the east,[8] but he had not bothered to pass this information on to Pemberton. As dawn broke on 16 May, both Pemberton and Loring knew that one of Wirt Adams's patrols had been fired on by Yankee pickets somewhere east of the junction of the Turkey Creek and Raymond roads, but they did not know whether it was the rear guard of McClernand's corps as it marched eastward toward Jackson, or the advance guard of Grant's army as it marched westward toward Edwards. Indeed, it was more likely nothing more than a roving Yankee cavalry patrol.

Pemberton was not in a hurry to start the army toward Dillon's farm, because he knew that Carter Stevenson's men had not bedded down until well after midnight, and he wanted the army to be fresh. By 0800, the division commanders had assembled at Mrs. Ellison's for the morning briefing when the rumble of artillery came in from the east. With the echoes came Wirt Adams, whose horsemen had picketed the Raymond Road out as far as the Gillespie house, about four miles west of the junction of the Bolton and Raymond roads.[9] He told the assembled generals that, at 0700, a Yankee cavalry force supported by infantry had hit his pickets at the Gillespie house and was forcing its way westward. The roar of artillery indicated that the Unionists now had brought up some cannon.[10] This must mean that the Army of the Tennessee had finished whatever business it had been conducting in the east and now was moving west in force.

At this moment, a courier arrived with the dispatch GEN Johnston had written on the morning of 15 May from north of Tougaloo. It had been almost twenty-four hours on the way. It told Pemberton of the fall of Jackson and included Johnston's peremptory order for Pemberton to meet him at Clinton. This time Pemberton decided to obey.[11] He had perfectly cogent reasons for changing his mind. In the first place, his movement toward Dillon's farm was based on the assumption that the Union army would be facing toward Jackson. Pemberton had hoped to be established in a good defensive position before that army could reverse itself, but the news of the fall of Jackson, plus the sound of artillery to the east, meant that the Army of the Tennessee already had turned back and was again moving west. Thus, instead of fighting a defensive battle on ground of his own choosing, Pemberton would be forced to fight a meeting engagement on unfamiliar ground against a numerically superior foe.

Second, Pemberton assumed that Johnston surely must know that Clinton was occupied by the Federal army, so the instruction to meet at Clinton could not be taken at face value. Trying to visualize Johnston's battle plan, Pemberton deduced that he planned to unite the two Confederate forces somewhere north of Clinton. With a united force approximately equal to the Yankees numerically, they then could strike the Army of the Tennessee from the flank and rear as it was attempting to force a crossing of the Big Black. While this plan was dangerous because it allowed the Union army to get between the Confederate field army and Vicksburg, it at least had the merit of offering a reasonable chance of beating the Yankees in the field.

Thus, about 0830 on 16 May, Pemberton sent a dispatch to his commander, via mounted courier, telling him of his current situation, stating that he was moving the Vicksburg army to Clinton, and giving as a proposed line of march the route to Edwards, Queen's Hill Church, Mt. Olive Church, and so into Clinton from the northwest. At the same time, he ordered the army to turn around and march back through Edwards and out the Brownsville Road.[12]

As Carter Stevenson rode back to his division, he began to worry about the Crossroad, where the Ratliff, Middle and Jackson roads merged. If the main body of the Federals was advancing up the Raymond Road, as seemed likely, they might well have cavalry forces out on both the Middle and Jackson roads. If they got in among the wagons parked around the Crossroad, there would be hell to pay. He ordered Reynolds, whose brigade guarded the train, to get the wagons turned around and headed back for Edwards with all possible dispatch. The wagoneers scarcely had had time to bed down before the new orders came, but they set to work with a will to turn the wagons around on the narrow, sunken, ridgetop road.

Pemberton had one other serious problem to deal with. He was certain that there would be substantial Federal forces coming up the Grand Gulf–Reganton–Dillon's road, if for no other reason than that Grant would have to guard his supply trains. When Pemberton marched his army off to the northeast toward Brownsville, Big Black Bridge would be uncovered, and it was guarded only by Vaughn's East Tennessee BDE. That might well not be enough, if the Yankees happened to have a division or so marching along their supply road in the vicinity of Auburn and were able to divert it to attack the Big Black Bridge. So, to MG Forney in Vicksburg went an order to send Baldwin's BDE to the bridge as soon as possible. Baldwin's and Vaughn's BDEs together, defending the prepared fortifications east of the bridge, should be able to beat off even a couple of divisions, if necessary.

As soon as the meeting at the Ellison house broke up, Loring, with Pemberton's concurrence, deployed his entire division in line of battle on a gentle rise about 400 yards west of the little bridge across Jackson Creek.[13] He had no idea what was east of him on the Raymond Road, except that there were both infantry and artillery. However, as soon as Carter Stevenson's and Bowen's DIVs got under way on their march back toward Edwards via the Jackson Road, Loring was to disengage and follow. In the meantime, Bowen advanced Green's brigade slightly to a position in the left rear of Loring's left-flank brigade, and Cockrell simply moved to the east to a favorable position on the crest of the ridge. It was a superb defensive position, because long, open slopes provided almost ideal fields of fire all the way to the channel of Jackson Creek.

While Reynolds and the train were getting turned around and clearing the Crossroad, Lee slipped his brigade to the left to provide security for the road junction. This was simple precaution, taken to secure the Crossroad until the order to march for Edwards came from Pemberton. The Middle Road was a worry, so Carter Stevenson sent a nine-company combat team from Cumming's BDE 600 yards eastward of the vital Crossroad to the thick woods at the crest of Bolls Hill, and a combat patrol was sent out a mile farther to the east as a precaution. As he reflected upon the situation, Lee realized that the road junction was absolutely vital, since it was the only connection between the bulk of the army and the Jackson Road bridge across rampaging Bakers Creek. He deployed in line of battle, with artillery support, facing east toward the Middle Road.[14]

At first Lee did not expect trouble from the north. The principle of concentration of force surely would prevent the Yankees from advancing on such a broad front; it was more than three miles from the Raymond Road at the Jackson Creek crossing to the Champion house on the Jackson Road. Still, the more he thought about it, the more uneasy he became about the road coming in from the north over Champion Hill, especially after a local farmer told him it was the main Jackson Road, and that it led directly to Bolton, Clinton, and Jackson. That is, it represented the most direct road connection between Jackson and Edwards.

Finally he sent a patrol out to the crest of Champion Hill, 700 yards to the north. The commander of the patrol was a bright lad, and one look convinced him that he couldn't see through the trees well enough to provide adequate warning, so he moved forward to a knoll just south of the Champion house, 700 yards north of the crest of the hill and near its northern base.[15] To this initiative may be ascribed the survival of the Vicksburg army.

Shortly before 0900, a powerful Union force struck Cumming's roadblock on the Middle Road. While there was a lot of noisy shooting, Cumming's Georgians had no trouble containing the attack.[16] On the Raymond Road, a very powerful Union battle line, complete with artillery support, struck the roadblock at the J. Davis house at the Turkey Creek Road junction, but the attack was not pressed, and the roadblock seemed in no danger.[17]

By 0900, Pemberton had left the Ellison house and set up shop in the Roberts house on the Ratliff Road ridge. The Roberts house was chosen because it seemed the best location from which to supervise the disengagement from the Yankee forces on the Middle and Raymond roads, where contacts on both roads indicated beyond reasonable doubt that the Army of the Tennessee already was marching westward. Pemberton was not unduly concerned, because the wagon train soon would be out of the way and the road would be clear for a march to Edwards, and the Yankees to the east certainly were not pressing their attack. It looked as if he would be able to disengage without difficulty. He then would march the army to the road junction 1,000 yards northeast of Edwards and then northeast along the road to Brownsville. Somewhere along the Brownsville Road, he confidently could expect to meet Johnston. The combined armies then would turn back to the west and, with good fortune, catch Grant's Army of the Tennessee trying to force a crossing of the Big Black River. It was even possible that they might be caught with one foot on each bank, in which case the outcome would be a foregone conclusion, and the threat to Vicksburg would be ended, perhaps forever.

This same morning, twenty-six miles away to the east-northeast, Johnston and his army rested quietly at Calhoun. There was no sense of urgency, nor were any patrols sent out, beyond those of a detachment of Wirt Adams's cavalry, which had reoccupied Jackson.

26

Battle of Champion Hill
16 April 1863

Maps: 49–55. Battle of Champion Hill, 16 May 1863

NAMES AND PLACES

In order to avoid confusion and long circumlocutions in the narrative that follows, names for several terrain features that figured prominently in the battle are listed here. These are not "real" names, in the sense that they were used at the time or are used now; rather, they are simply conveniences for the sake of clarity in this narrative. The critical features also are named on the map entitled "The Battlefield of Champion Hill."

Austin Creek is the stream in the first ravine north of the Jackson Road after it turns westward from the Crossroad.

Austin Ridge is the dominating ridge extending west-northwest from the Crossroad. The Jackson Road follows its crest all the way to the Bakers Creek bottoms.

Bolls Hill is the highest hill in the region; the Middle Road passes over its crest about 1,200 yards east of the Crossroad.

Coker Road joins the Ratliff Road 300 yards north of the Raymond Road, and joins the Lower Bridge Road about 1,500 yards nearly straight north.

Crossroad Ridge is the high ridge extending south from the crest of Champion Hill to the Crossroad; the Jackson Road runs north-south along its crest.

Lee's Ridge is the long ridge extending west-northwest from the crest of Champion Hill.

Ratliff Road is the road connecting the Crossroad with the Raymond
   Road near the Coker House. This road is not so named at present,
   but the name was used in 1863.
Roberts Creek is the stream draining the valley south of the Jackson
   Road after it turns westward at the Crossroad.
Upper Bakers Creek Bridge is the bridge that carries the Jackson Road
   across Bakers Creek.
Lower Bakers Creek Bridge is the bridge that carried the Raymond
   Road across Bakers Creek. It had been washed away in a storm
   several weeks prior to the Battle of Champion Hill.
Lower Bridge Road is a farm road that joins the Raymond Road at a
   point about 800 yards east of the Lower Bakers Creek Bridge and
   the Ratliff Road about 1,100 yards northeast of the Ratliff house.

Phase I: Confrontation 0900–1130, 16 May 1863

FEDERAL PERSPECTIVE

When the 1 IN CAV, covering the advance of the Union column moving west
on the Jackson Road, was fired upon from the knoll south of the Champion
house, BG McGinnis, who commanded the lead brigade of Hovey's DIV,
rode forward to look the situation over.[1] What he saw filled him with astonishment and joy: gray-clad regiments hastily filing into position on the crest
of the ridge a mile to the south! He instantly realized that the Union army
had achieved tactical surprise.[2] Scarcely pausing to think, he sent a courier
to Hovey and began to deploy without awaiting orders. Hovey promptly sent
a courier to his corps commander, McClernand, who was with Osterhaus
on the Middle Road, asking if he should attack.[3] About 0930, McClernand
wrote to Grant, mentioning Hovey's question, and then he in turn asked if
his force on the Middle Road should attack.[4] By this time Grant had reached
the Champion house, so he and McClernand were less than two miles airline apart. It should have taken McClernand's courier perhaps twenty minutes to make the trip, had he cut directly across country, as Hovey's messenger had done. Instead, McClernand's courier rode all the way back to the
Bolton Road, across to the Jackson Road, and so west to Grant, a total distance of more than eleven miles. As a result, Grant did not receive

McClernand's message until 1230, by which time it was no longer relevant.[5] The moment Grant got the message, he sent a reply telling McClernand that he should attack if the situation warranted. Unfortunately, he gave the paper to the same courier, who again rode around the loop, so McClernand did not get the reply until after 1400!

However, McClernand assumed (or at least said he assumed) that the absence of a reply from Grant indicated that Grant did not want an attack, and so the four powerful divisions under McClernand's command, two on the Middle Road and two on the Raymond Road, sat idle while they waited for word from their corps commander. At the same time, Grant was completely out of communication with his senior corps commander for the entire course of the battle.

Grant took one look at the situation as he could see it from the Champion house and ordered the wagons on the Jackson Road into the ditches so that the infantry and artillery could move forward quickly. The wagon train was extensive, and, until it had cleared the road, Crocker's DIV, which was marching well behind the wagons, could not move forward.

As the brigades of Hovey's and Logan's DIVs arrived, McPherson, who had tactical command of the column on the Jackson Road, ordered them deployed left and right into line of battle in preparation for an assault.[6] Deployment was slow and difficult to the left of the road, because the ground leading up to the east face of Champion Hill was cut with innumerable small but steep ravines and was so covered with scrub and brush that an assault necessarily would move slowly. To the right, the ground was open and clear, and McPherson deployed both Hovey's and Logan's DIVs primarily in that direction.[7]

Grant knew the Confederates had been taken by surprise, because he could see them hastily shifting commands along the ridgetop in an effort to conform to his own deployment. Furthermore, when he first arrived on the scene, there were only two guns in action from the Confederate lines. Later two more were added, but Grant thought it remarkable that the southerners were using only four guns to defend a line well over a mile in length. It could only mean that they were having trouble bringing them forward, and he smiled to himself in satisfaction. By 1100, both Logan's and Hovey's DIVs were fully deployed and ready to advance, and Crocker's DIV was fast approaching along the Jackson Road.[8]

Grant nodded to McPherson, the corps commander waved his men forward, and the line began to advance smoothly and steadily across the fields toward the base of the long ridge on which the Confederate line lay. The Rebels replied with sheets of rifle fire, but to little effect. Both Hovey's and Logan's artillery, thirty-eight guns in all, were in action, although Grant expected that they would not be very effective. The Rebel infantry on top of the hill made a very poor target; to do any damage, a shell had to be exactly right in both fuze setting and elevation.

Out on the right flank of the Union line, John Stevenson, whose brigade extended well beyond the left flank of the Johnnies on the crest of the ridge, noticed that the Rebels were trying frantically to extend their own line to match his. Stevenson's skirmishers had almost reached the crest of the ridge when suddenly they were hurled back by the arrival of a couple of new gray-clad regiments. To Stevenson's astonishment, those two regiments did not stop in an extension of the previous Rebel line; instead, they kept right on down the hill. As soon as they came out into the open, every regiment in the Federal line that was within range opened fire. The Union cannoneers instantly shifted target from the hard-to-hit line at the top of the ridge to the easy-to-hit troops in the open, bombarding the attacking gray line with shell. After no more than about 50 yards, the attack faltered, and the Rebels dropped back to form another line on the crest of the hill, leaving many gray-clad bodies littering the field below the belt of trees.

A few minutes later, yet another Confederate regiment emerged from the line of trees along the ridgetop and surged down the hill. The Federal commanders were dumbfounded. It looked to them as if that single regiment were assaulting two Union divisions! Again the Union artillery concentrated on that isolated line, and in a few minutes it, too, drew back, leaving crumpled bodies on the slope.[9]

By 1130, the Union infantry line had reached within about 200 yards of the Confederate position, well within final assault distance. Crocker's DIV was moving up, but it was still two or three miles back down the Jackson Road.

On the Middle Road, Osterhaus pushed slowly and carefully forward along a ridge that grew steadily narrower and steeper. He feared an ambush. Sure enough, just as his skirmish line was nearing the crest of Bolls Hill, it was greeted by a volley of musketry. That meant infantry, and Osterhaus became even more cautious. The hilltop and the ravines all about were covered with dense timber, which made it very difficult to evaluate the situation. Both McClernand and Osterhaus were so concerned about running into an ambush that every move was made with great deliberation. By 0900, Osterhaus had deployed all four regiments of Garrard's BDE and brought up a battery of artillery, but the Rebels in the woods ahead refused to budge. McClernand, without specific orders from Grant, refused to give the order to attack. And there the matter rested through the long morning.[10]

On the Raymond Road, A. J. Smith's DIV led the Union advance. Smith had been told not to bring on a general engagement unless he was certain of success, and Smith was taking no chances. When his skirmish line encountered a Rebel roadblock manned by infantry just east of the junction of the Davis and Raymond roads, his advance came to a stop. However, shortly after 0900, the Southerners in the roadblock suddenly withdrew, and A. J. Smith slowly resumed his advance.

When Burbridge's BDE, which led the advance, started down the gentle incline leading to Jackson Creek, it came under long-range fire from artillery emplaced on a commanding ridge 2,000 yards to the west. Smith halted, deployed Burbridge's BDE, and pushed slowly on. The bridge across Jackson Creek was afire, and, although the stream was readily fordable everywhere, Smith halted his advance until the bridge could be rebuilt.[11] That was easier said than done, because a battery of Rebel artillery on a ridge about 1,000 yards to the north made the work more than slightly hazardous. Smith brought up a battery of 10-pdr Parrott rifles, which soon silenced the Confederate guns. The bridge completed, Burbridge crossed and mounted the crest of a low ridge transverse to the Raymond Road and about 500 yards west of Jackson Creek. Here the advance again came to a stop, for a solid Confederate battle line extended all along the next ridge to the west, 800 yards away. It was about 1130.[12]

CONFEDERATE PERSPECTIVE

As of 0900, the Confederate plan was to disengage, march via the Jackson Road to the junction of the Jackson and Brownsville roads, 1,000 yards northeast of Edwards, and then head northeast out the Brownsville Road. This looked entirely practical to Loring, because he was under no pressure whatever from the Union force to his front. The roadblock at the Davis house, a few yards east of the junction of the Turkey Creek and Raymond roads, seemed to be holding easily. The Yankee infantry had not even moved forward into effective small-arms range.

Shortly after 0900, Loring realized that the Coker House ridge, about 800 yards to the west of his position, was somewhat higher and offered a stronger position. It still covered the Ratliff Road, which, so far as he knew at the time, afforded the only lateral communication behind Confederate lines. It was the road along which he was to withdraw as soon as Pemberton ordered him to do so. Without consulting Pemberton, Loring called in the roadblock at the Davis house and without molestation moved his men back to the Coker House ridge. Indeed, it took the Yankees a long time to close up to within extreme artillery range.[13] As the two roadblock regiments crossed Jackson Creek, they burned the bridge, even though the water was scarcely ankle deep.

Wirt Adams's cavalry also fell back and picketed the approach to the washed-out Lower Bakers Creek Bridge. Adams noted that the water level was falling rapidly and that the stream was now fordable, albeit with difficulty, but he did not notify Pemberton of this interesting fact. There was no reason why he should have done so; his presence there was purely precautionary, because Pemberton had no intention of using the Raymond Road at this time.

At dawn, Bowen's DIV lay along the Ratliff Road, waiting for Stevenson's DIV to begin its march back toward Edwards. At a little before 0900, when the news of the Federal infantry contact with Loring's roadblock at the Davis house reached him, he deployed his division along the Ratliff Ridge just east of the road, in effect forming an extension of Loring's left flank.[14] He could see no activity of any kind to his front, yet there was action on both the Middle and Raymond roads, so purely as a precaution he sent a strong combat patrol eastward across the headwaters of Jackson Creek to see what was out there. They penetrated for perhaps 1,000 yards without finding anything.[15]

Lee had started out the day with his left flank just covering the Crossroad and his right flank a bit south of the Roberts house. About 0915, a runner from Lee's picket on the knoll south of the Champion house arrived at Lee's headquarters at the Crossroad with the shattering news that, contrary to all expectation, a powerful Federal column was rapidly approaching on the Jackson Road. Lee was horrified. In his present disposition, an attack coming south along Crossroad Ridge would hit him in the flank and roll his line right up.[16] Federal control of the Crossroad would mean that the army's wagon train would be captured, and there would be no retreat for the rest of the army, because the Crossroad controlled the only road to the Upper Bakers Creek Bridge, which was the only way to get across flooded Bakers Creek. Here was potential for a real disaster. Lee sent a message to Carter Stevenson informing him of the situation,[17] and Stevenson immediately passed it on to Pemberton.

It was Pemberton's first real intimation that a battle might be shaping up. However, he was not unduly alarmed, even though by this time he knew that Grant was moving westward in anticipation of a fight. It seemed most unlikely that an experienced general like Grant would divide his forces into three widely separate columns on the eve of battle. That being the case, the force on the Jackson Road almost certainly was nothing more than a flank guard, because the strong forces pushing westward on both the Middle and Raymond roads must constitute the major part of Grant's troops. He decided to continue with the original plan, which still depended upon getting the wagon train safely turned around and on its way to Edwards. The wagoneers and Reynolds's men were working hard, but it was a difficult task and would take a bit more time.

Lee was unconvinced that the Yankee presence on the Jackson Road was only a patrol, because his men had reported infantry. If it was a real force, even if only a brigade, then Lee was in a dreadfully vulnerable position. The only thing he could do was to shift his command to the left and occupy the crest of Champion Hill. He felt reasonably comfortable in doing that, because the Yankee advance against the roadblock on the Middle Road was lethargic in the extreme. In fact, Lee feared that it was a feint, designed to cover a real attack coming up the Jackson Road. He notified Stevenson, his division commander, and Cumming, who commanded the brigade immediately to the south, of his intentions and the reasons for it, and moved quickly to the north up the Jackson Road to the crest of Champion Hill.[18]

What he found there was a configuration almost like the roof of an L-shaped house. From the high crest of the hill, a ridge (Lee's Ridge) ran westward, with open fields below the wooded crest extending to the north into the Bakers Creek bottoms. From the same hilltop, another rooflike ridge (Crossroad Ridge) ran southward to the Crossroad, although this ridge was mostly open and cultivated on the top. The Jackson Road came up to the crest of the hill from the east-northeast, following a lesser ridge, and then continued south along Crossroad Ridge to the Crossroad. It was not a good place, because Lee would have to deploy around a salient angle, always a tactically weak position. But he did the best he could, with most of his troops deployed along Lee's Ridge and facing north, but with a short right flank refused, facing east. There were places for only two guns, but fortunately they were on the very crest of the hill commanding the Jackson Road.

At this time, Lee's plan was to protect the Crossroad only until the remainder of the army had withdrawn toward Edwards, after which he would disengage and bring up the rear. However, as he looked north from the top of his hill, watching blue regiment after blue regiment pour down the Jackson Road and deploy smoothly and methodically across the fields near the Champion house, he realized with dismay that there was to be no disengagement; the battle would be fought on this hill. The Yankees brushed the little outpost on the knoll contemptuously aside, and skirmishers began advancing up the hill. As the minutes ticked away, the Union line extended farther and farther to the left until it extended far beyond Lee's left flank. An assault would simply wrap around his left, and his whole position would be carried away. Lee extended his line westward along the crest of Lee's Ridge until it was stretched into a single line of riflemen, but it was not enough.[19] In desperation, he shifted his entire brigade to the left, and Cumming sent three regiments to extend his line. These actions opened a gap 300 yards wide between Cumming's regiments on the crest of Champion Hill and his remaining two regiments at the Crossroad.[20]

About 1100, Carter Stevenson, thoroughly alarmed, sent a staff officer to Pemberton, both to inform him of the continuing shifts to the left and to argue that the immense marshaling of forces in the north meant that the primary thrust of the Union army was going to be along the Jackson Road.[21] He also told Pemberton what Pemberton had been waiting to hear: the wagon train at last was turned around and on its way back toward Edwards, with Reynolds's BDE as guard.

As long as that wagon train had blocked the road, Pemberton's hands had been tied; no infantry could move until the wagons were out of the way, and moving them had taken too long. Stevenson's message convinced him that there were indeed strong formations on the Jackson Road, as well as on the Middle and Raymond roads. Because of those damnable wagons, he was not going to be able to disengage, as he had planned. If Vicksburg was to avoid a siege, the decision was going to be made here, on the slopes of Champion Hill. Worse places could be imagined; Loring and Bowen occupied excellent defensive positions, with the long, smooth, open slopes in front of the their ridgetop positions providing excellent fields of fire for both infantry and artillery. Only Stevenson's position on the crest of Champion Hill was weak.

Despite the reports of large Union formations on the Jackson Road, Pemberton remained convinced that the main Union attack would develop on either the Raymond or Middle roads.[22] He thought the major effort probably would come on the Raymond Road, because McClernand's powerful corps, which had obviously reached Raymond, after disengaging from Bowen at Mt. Moriah, would surely use the Raymond Road on a march westward toward Edwards. It seemed likely that Grant would use those fresh troops—who had not been involved in either the long march to Jackson and back, or whatever fighting had taken place around Jackson—as his spearhead. Furthermore, troops on that road would be closer to the supply trains which Pemberton knew were moving up the main road from Grand Gulf. Finally, it was possible that at least several of Grant's divisions would be still engaged with Johnston's force north of Jackson. If so, the troops on the Raymond and Middle roads might well constitute all the troops Grant had available, and Pemberton might be offered a chance to defeat the Army of the Tennessee in detail. It was an exhilarating thought.

For that reason, Pemberton did nothing to alter the dispositions of Bowen and Loring, because they were well placed to receive an attack on that end of the line. He did not go to the crest of Champion Hill to see the situation on the north slopes of Champion Hill for himself. He was, of course, getting a steady flow of reports from all three of his division commanders, and Loring and Bowen were both reporting continuing pressure on their front. He did not go to check on the substance of those reports, either. That was not his style. He was the army commander, and he left tactical decisions to his division commanders.

Pemberton simply did not believe that Grant would so fragment his army as to put a strong column on each of the three roads leading east, because that would mean that Grant was advancing on a front of four miles by three routes separated by such difficult terrain that communication between the columns would be slow, if not impossible. To Pemberton's eye, this looked as if the Yankees were coming perilously close to violating the axiom that one should always concentrate in the face of the enemy. He had too much respect for Grant as a general to believe that the Federal commander would do anything so foolish. Therefore, the force in the north could only be a strong security guard for the right flank.

From his vantage point on the crest of Champion Hill, Carter Stevenson saw the situation quite differently. There were at least two, and possibly three, Yankee divisions deployed across the base of Champion Hill. Their line extended so far to the west that he assumed their plan was to turn Lee's left flank, which was dangling in air. Something had to be done, but the only force available was Barton's BDE, which was facing east, with its left flank near the Crossroad. If Barton were removed to support Lee, the result would be a huge hole in the Confederate line, and the only thing preventing a Union penetration at that point would be the roadblock out on the hilltop on the Middle Road, 1,200 yards to the east. Still, the Yankees were not exerting any significant pressure on that point, so Stevenson felt that pulling Barton out to stiffen and extend the line on Lee's Ridge was by far the lesser of two evils.

He ordered Barton out of position south of the Crossroad and put him in on the left of Lee, to further extend the Confederate line to the west.[23] There was no place to put artillery on the ridge where the infantry was deployed, so he sent a couple of batteries out along the Jackson Road to a point about 200 yards west of the Austin house, from which position they could bring the extreme right flank of the Union line under fire, albeit at long range.[24] He thought this might help to prevent Barton's left from being turned. The Jackson Road at last was free of wagons, so the artillery was able to move freely.

By 1100, the Union battle line, which could be identified as two full divisions, began to move steadily forward. Despite everything the Confederates could do, by 1130 it had reached within 200 yards of the Confederate line and clearly was getting set for an assault. When Barton's Georgians arrived on Lee's left, they were just in time to crush and hurl back a Yankee skirmish line that was trying to wrap around the flank. But Barton's Georgians thought they had won a major victory and, instead of stopping at the crest of the ridge in an extension of Lee's line, they kept on going. That was a mistake. They ran into sheets of fire from the solid blue infantry lines on the slopes below, as well as a storm of shell-fire from at least six batteries of Union artillery. Men began going down in increasing numbers. The blue Yankee uniforms were hard to see against the vivid green of the spring fields, while the Georgians were silhouetted against the sky. The Georgians grudgingly fell back to the crest of Lee's Ridge and tied into Lee's left flank.

On the Raymond Road, the Federal infantry, in about brigade strength, finally had crossed Jackson Creek, but it was staying well back from Loring's line along the ridge. The only activity was a little more or less harmless artillery dueling. The roadblock on the Middle Road was holding without difficulty, so the Crossroad was safe.

The two Confederate batteries which had been emplaced on the Austin Ridge 100 yards west of the Austin house opened up on the Yankee left flank regiments, but they had to shoot across the entire valley of Austin Creek, so at first the range was too long and the ground so complicated that the Rebel gunners had trouble finding a suitable target. The blue wave kept right on coming. Sure enough, it began to wrap around Barton's exposed left flank. In their wheel toward Barton's left flank, the Yankees carelessly permitted their own right-flank regiments to move out onto the south flank of the end of Lee's Ridge, a move that brought them out in the open and within 500 yards of the Confederate gunners on the

Austin Ridge, at which point the latter opened fire with canister. That stopped the attack on Barton's flank, all right; the blue regiments changed front, crossed Austin Creek, and began to work their way up the north face of Austin Ridge toward the unsupported artillery batteries.

The Union artillery, too, was in action. Stevenson and Lee counted at least six batteries emplaced on the low ridge that paralleled Lee's battle line about 1,000 yards to the north. Furthermore, their fire was deadly accurate, and too many men were going down. Lee thought that something might be done, because there was a largish gap between two of the attacking Union brigades. He sent a single regiment forward with the mission of spiking the guns, but the instant the southerners started down the hill, the Union artillery shifted target and ripped the attack to shreds.[25] It was not an auspicious beginning.

Phase II: Temporary Victory 1130–1300, 16 May 1863

FEDERAL PERSPECTIVE

Grant and McPherson, from their position near the road in front of the Champion house, had watched the Rebel forces on the crest of Champion Hill and Lee's Ridge struggle to extend their line to the west to match the Union deployment. Both were bewildered by the attack of what looked like a mere two regiments way out on the west flank, and then, a little later, by the attack of a single regiment from near the center of the southern line. It all looked so senseless, given the enormous strength of the Union battle line which extended across the northern face of Champion Hill. Furthermore, both attacks had been made without artillery support. That was interesting, as it suggested that, for some strange reason, the Confederates were unable to bring guns forward. If so, so much the better.

The only thing the two Union generals could think of was that these were spoiling attacks, designed to delay the Union assault while additional Rebel troops were brought up. Grant had assumed that, by this time, McClernand's troops on the Middle and Raymond roads would be in action and engaging the full attention of the balance of Pemberton's army. He could not see through the intervening hill masses, and the sound of battle on the slopes of Champion Hill to his front drowned out any sounds that might be generated from other engagements several miles away. However, if those attacks somehow had been delayed, then time might be more important than had initially been apparent.

Accordingly, when Hovey and Logan reported about 1130 that their men were in position for a final assault on the ridge to the south, Grant told them to go, even though his reserve division, Crocker's, was still a mile or two distant down the Jackson Road. In an instant, the entire Union line, five infantry brigades strong, surged forward. At the center, the resistance was very strong, and at first little progress was made. But on the left, where Hovey's two brigades attacked the two sides of the salient on the crest of Champion Hill, the attack rolled right up the hill and over the crest, capturing the guns there and sending the defending Rebels fleeing to the south.[26] The Union regiments at the right flank of the breakthrough in the salient turned rapidly westward to attack the Confederates still holding a segment of their original battle line on the crest of Lee's Ridge.[27]

Out on the right flank, John Stevenson's BDE had begun to wrap around the Confederate left flank when it began to receive artillery fire from a couple of batteries on a high ridge about 900 yards south of the Rebel battle line and separated from it by the deep ravine of Austin Creek. Stevenson's right flank regiments changed front and attacked the batteries, but it turned out to be tough going, because the hill was steep and scored with small ravines. When the Union attack reached within about 400 yards of the guns, it became clear that they were unsupported by infantry. To Stevenson, it looked like a golden opportunity to acquire some artillery.

By 1215, it was clear that the Confederate remnants trying to hold their original battle line were in an untenable position. Both ends of their line had been flanked, and in front the Union assault forces were less than 50 yards away. Sure enough, the Rebel line began to fray, and then suddenly it vanished, the men running without much order to the south, down into the Austin Creek ravine. By 1230, the original Rebel position along Lee's Ridge was entirely in Union hands. However, the tangle of little ravines on the sides of Champion Hill, plus the desperate Confederate resistance, had so disorganized the regiments that they had to stop to reform. They soon resumed the advance, but momentum was lost only a few yards south of the crest of the hill, and the attack stalled.[28]

Logan and Hovey worked hard, and by 1330 they were ready to resume, even though the men were very tired and ammunition was beginning to run short. Again the whole line went forward, and this time Hovey's troops on the Union left swept down Crossroad Ridge and over the Crossroad, to be finally brought to a stop by the sight of a new line of Rebel riflemen deployed across the Ratliff Road ridge about 100 yards south of the Roberts house.[29]

In the middle of the Union line, the terrain of Austin's Creek ravine, coupled with stubborn resistance from a Confederate line on the ridge to the south, brought the attack to a stop well short of the ridgetop. However, out on the right flank, John Stevenson's BDE finally found itself within striking distance of the eight guns which had been giving the Federals trouble all day. In one final surge, the men overran the guns and found themselves in command of the Jackson Road. Some of the Rebels to their front retreated to the west along the Jackson Road,[30] presumably toward Edwards, while others kept going to the south across Robert's Creek or east toward a portion of the Confederate line along the Austin Ridge which refused to be budged.

Stevenson was so far from McPherson and Grant that he was unable to communicate his success, so they were unaware that the Jackson Road had been cut. They did, however, know that the Crossroad had been occupied, and McPherson went forward to deal with the situation. At this juncture, Crocker's DIV began to arrive at the Champion house, led by Sanborn's BDE. As far as Grant knew, only the Confederate left was still resisting strongly, so he sent Sanborn's BDE out in that direction to add weight to the attack. When Boomer's BDE arrived a few minutes later, Grant held it at the Champion house as a reserve, pending the development of a need somewhere along the line. He had no idea what was transpiring on either the Raymond Road or the Middle Road.[31] It was as if McClernand and four divisions had vanished from the face of the earth.

CONFEDERATE PERSPECTIVE

Carter Stevenson and his three brigade commanders on the field— Barton, Lee, and Cumming—watched with increasing dismay as the Union line swung like a massive gate and inched forward, until at last it was only 250 yards or so from the Confederate line all across the north face of Champion Hill. Worse, it lapped around both ends of the line. The left flank, held by Barton's Georgians, was in the air, protected only by two batteries of artillery emplaced far back on the Austin Ridge near the Austin house.[32] Those guns were unsupported by infantry, and Barton was certain that they were too far away to be of any material help, but there was no way to get guns onto Lee's Ridge in time to be of use. The Union deployment made it obvious that the right flank, the salient angle at the top of Champion Hill, was going to be attacked on both the north and east faces.

By this time, Pemberton was all too aware that a major action was developing on the Jackson Road. At the same time, both Loring and Bowen also were reporting that they were under heavy attack. Pemberton had not expected to fight a battle at this locale, and it had developed so rapidly that he had not been able to make appropriate dispositions, including the formation of a reserve of any kind. Under such circumstances, Pemberton could do little but await events and hope that at least one of the Union attacks would stall, so that portions of one of his three divisions could be detached to use as a reserve to strengthen weak spots elsewhere.

Promptly at 1130, the whole blue line on the Jackson Road front surged forward like an irresistible tide. Barton's left-flank regiments were taken in flank and began to crumble. Lee's line held, as did the right of Barton's, but it was not enough. The Union wave hit Cumming's three regiments, which held the top of Champion Hill, from both north and east, sweeping over the top, capturing the guns, and forcing Cumming's Georgians, bitterly resisting, southward toward the Crossroad. Some of the Union regiments which had occupied the top of Champion Hill turned like lightning and began to press westward into Lee's now unprotected right flank.

In the lull following the initial breakthrough, while the Union regiments were trying desperately to reform in order to continue the attack, Cumming tried to rally his men in an effort to save the Crossroad.

From his position at the Roberts house, Pemberton could see not only the crest of Champion Hill but the whole reach of the Jackson Road west of the Crossroad. When he saw the blue wave come pouring across the crest of Champion Hill and down the Jackson Road toward the Crossroad, Pemberton understood that the crisis was at hand. Contrary to his earlier conviction, the main Federal effort was along the Jackson Road. Furthermore, one serious look at the tenuous Confederate line defending the Crossroad was enough to convince him that Stevenson's DIV could not stop the Yankees without help. With the Crossroad gone, the army would be cut in two, and defeat would be certain. That portion of the army west of the Crossroad presumably could retreat safely across the Upper Bakers Creek Bridge, but with the Lower Bakers Creek Bridge out, Bowen's and Loring's DIVs along the Ratliff Road might well be trapped and captured or destroyed.

The impending disaster might yet be averted if the vital Crossroad could be made secure, after which perhaps something might yet be done to salvage a victory from the present plight. During the lull following the initial Yankee breakthrough on the crest of Champion Hill, Pemberton realized that, despite the reports he had been receiving from Bowen and Loring, there were no sounds of battle rolling up from the south or east. Indeed, from his position near the Roberts house, Pemberton could see that there was no action at all in the direction of the Middle Road. The inescapable conclusion was that neither Loring nor Bowen was seriously engaged, and that meant that portions of their commands could be shifted to meet the attack on the Crossroad.

At 1300, Pemberton sent a staff officer to both Bowen and Loring, directing them to leave rear guards on the Raymond Road and come at once to the support of Stevenson. The staff officer returned twenty minutes later, red-faced and furious. Bowen had scarcely glanced at the dispatch and remarked that he would refuse to do so unless given a peremptory order, because "the enemy are in heavy force on my front." One of Loring's staff officers was present in Bowen's headquarters and had confirmed that Loring felt the same way.

Pemberton had no choice. He was so distraught that he had trouble mounting his horse, but nevertheless he rode to Cockrell's headquarters and personally ordered that gallant commander to take his brigade to the aid of Stevenson. Brave Cockrell and his men did not share their division commander's sentiments about Pemberton. He and his Missourians had listened all morning while the sounds of desperate battle had rolled down from the north, while they sat idle. Pemberton's arrival was like the elixir of youth; they were out of line and marching north to the sound of the guns almost before he had issued his order.

About 1300, Carter Stevenson realized that the breakthrough at the crest of Champion Hill had made the rest of his line on Lee's Ridge untenable, and he ordered his remaining regiments to retreat south across Austin Creek and reform on the Austin Ridge, thus protecting the Jackson Road withdrawal route. The line which quickly formed there was anchored at the Crossroad by four guns of Waddell's Battery, and at the Austin house[33] by more guns from the Cherokee and 1 MS batteries.[34] But the commands were horribly mixed, and many regiments existed only as fragments. Carter Stevenson thought he had a little while to get set, because he knew that the Yankees would be almost as badly disorganized by victory as he was by defeat.

But long before he could get his new line organized along the Jackson Road, a solid blue line all along his front surged forward once again. At the Crossroad, a blue flood poured out of the woods 200 yards to the north and swept across the road junction, capturing the artillery and sweeping Cumming's shaken regiments back to the south. Pemberton met the fleeing men at the Roberts house, 700 yards south of the Crossroad, and managed to rally many of them, so that a semblance of a battle line was established across the road 100 yards north of the house.[35] Just at this moment, Cockrell's Missourians arrived and deployed across the Ratliff Road ridge and westward along the farm road that ran along the crest of the ridge south of Roberts Creek.

Out on the west flank of the Confederate line, a powerful Union infantry attack stormed up the ridge, obviously directed against the eight-gun artillery concentration near the Austin house. In spite of everything the Confederate gunners could do, the Federals kept on coming.[36] Finally they swept over the guns and across the vital Jackson Road. Barton and his two left-flank regiments were pushed off to the west, and they fell back to take up a position on the west bank of Bakers Creek, hoping to hold the Upper Bakers Creek Bridge in the event that other Confederate units managed to retreat in that direction.[37] Barton's remaining regiments were shattered and dispersed to the south, but Lee managed to change front with his left-flank regiment and halt the thrust of the Yankees eastward along the Jackson Road.

By 1430, the Confederate line had stabilized, after a fashion.[38] Pemberton knew this development reflected not so much a strong line of resistance as the fact that the Union attackers had become so disorganized by success that they had been forced to stop to sort things out. The Confederate situation was critical. The Crossroad was occupied by Federal forces, as was a stretch of the Jackson Road out near the Austin house. Not only had the Confederate army been cut in two, but their only line of retreat had been cut off. Pemberton realized that the only chance for the survival of his army was to wrest control of the Crossroad from the Yankees and then smash down the Jackson Road to dislodge the Union forces around the Austin house. He ordered Cockrell to strike as hard as he could at the obviously disorganized Yankees at the Crossroad.[39]

COMMENTARY

Bowen's and Loring's reports to Pemberton early in the battle to the effect that they were under heavy pressure were entirely false. At this point, Loring was engaged in nothing more than some long-distance artillery dueling, and no blue uniforms were in sight from Bowen's position. But of course Pemberton did not know that and took the reports at face value.

Phase III: Counterattack
1400–1500, 16 May 1863

FEDERAL PERSPECTIVE

About 1345, McGinnis, at the crest of Champion Hill, saw what appeared to be a fresh Confederate division deploying across the Ratliff Road ridge south of the Crossroad. If that division attacked, as it seemed intent on doing, his tired and disorganized men certainly would not be able to resist it. He sent an urgent message to Hovey, telling him of the situation; but before a reply could reach him, the Confederate line rolled forward in the most abandoned assault McGinnis had ever seen.[40] The tired and disorganized troops occupying the Crossroad resisted only briefly and then gave way in rout. The Rebel left-flank brigade swept up the Jackson Road and over the top of Champion Hill with scarcely a pause.[41] However, the right-flank brigade ran into desperate Union resistance east of the Jackson Road, as well as very difficult terrain, so it was unable to move as rapidly.[42]

Of course, McGinnis's message to Hovey also found its way to Grant. Grant realized instantly that most of his reserves had been committed and that the counterattack coming over the crest of Champion Hill would be very difficult to stop without help. The obvious answer was to strike the flank of the counterattacking force. Grant was confused and troubled, because Hovey's men at the Crossroad had seen no sign whatever of McClernand's two-division force on the Middle Road. In fact, the Confederates had seemed entirely unconcerned about any threat from that direction. That seemed to mean that McClernand somehow had been delayed or that Grant's message to attack, which had been sent at 1235, had not reached him. He wrote a new order, telling McClernand to attack immediately, and sent it off by a courier who was instructed to get to the Middle Road by the shortest possible route. Grant, at the Champion house, was only about 2,500 yards as the crow flies from McClernand's position on the Middle Road, but a courier could not go that way because the Confederate force occupying Bolls Hill lay between. To stay clear of Rebels, the messenger had to go about a mile eastward on the Jackson Road and then cut south across very difficult country for another mile and a half before reaching the Middle Road and McClernand's headquarters. The total time required was on the order of thirty minutes or a bit more.

With his dispatches safely off, Grant turned his attention to the situation in his immediate front. It was not good. McGinnis's veterans had disintegrated and were streaming past the Champion house in rout.[43] Grant knew they would rally as soon as the pressure was off, but that would take time. In the meantime, his only immediate resource was Boomer's BDE of Crocker's DIV, which already was deployed across the Jackson Road north of the Champion house. Holmes's BDE was still in march column, well back down the Jackson Road, and would not be on the scene for another thirty minutes or more. Hovey had no infantry with which to help Boomer, but he was the acknowledged master of artillery in the Army of the Tennessee. He concentrated sixteen cannon off Boomer's left flank, and when the Confederates began to lap around, the guns loosed such a storm of shell that the attack not only stopped but fell back into the shelter of some small ravines on the east face of Champion Hill.[44]

Still the attack refused to die, and even stolid Grant was shaken. Behind Boomer's line was nothing but McGinnis's shattered brigade, which had not yet had time to rally and reform, and Holmes's BDE, still in march column.[45] Behind them was the wagon train of the army. If Boomer failed, the army would be cut in two and the train lost. Such a disaster might well prove irretrievable. In this crisis, Grant came very close to losing his nerve. He hastily sent to Sanborn, who was heading for the right flank to support John Stevenson but had not yet reached a position where he could deploy, to send aid as quickly as possible. Sanborn did the best he could; he couldn't bring his whole brigade, but he brought two regiments which, in a surprisingly short time, fell in on Boomer's right. Grant also asked McPherson to recall John Stevenson's BDE, which was far out on the right flank.[46] Grant did not know that Stevenson was sitting astride the Jackson Road, squarely across one of the Confederate escape routes. In fact, as far as Grant knew, Stevenson had not been seriously committed. What he knew of the battle actually were only those things which had occurred along the Jackson Road as far as the Crossroad and on Lee's Ridge. When Stevenson got the order, he was reluctant to obey. It is likely that he alone, of all the Union commanders, realized just how strategic his position was. But, like the good soldier that he was, he abandoned his position and started back toward the Champion house.

Once safely behind Boomer's solid line, Hovey's men rallied and quickly reformed. As soon as regimental units got large enough to recognize, Hovey managed to replenish their cartridge boxes and fed them back into the fight.[47] With this increment of strength, plus the telling effect of Hovey's concentration of artillery, the Union line not only held but began to inch slowly forward. The crisis was over.

Meanwhile, unbeknownst to the army commander, Leggett's BDE of Logan's DIV was mostly disposed near the bottom of the Austin Creek ravine, facing south. The terrain was very broken and heavily wooded, and the resistance from the Rebels at the top of the Austin Ridge had been fierce, so their attack had stalled. To try to get it moving again, they had, by Herculean efforts, managed to bring a battery of artillery forward. Just at that moment, the sounds of battle from the Crossroad Ridge, to the east, rose to a crescendo, and moments later a flood of routed bluecoats poured back down the ridge, with a Rebel battle line in pursuit. The whole circus passed right by Leggett's left flank, leaving it dangling in the air.

Leggett hastily changed the front of his left-flank regiment, expecting an attack into that open flank momentarily. It was not long in coming, but it was not very determined, and his men easily beat it off with the help of the battery of guns that so fortuitously had been brought up a few moments before. Both Leggett and Logan now realized that a powerful Confederate force was behind them, but, instead of abandoning their position, their thoughts turned to organizing a strike into the rear of the Rebels who had gone past their flank.

CONFEDERATE PERSPECTIVE

When Pemberton, in sheer desperation, had ridden to Cockrell to order him to go to the assistance of Carter Stevenson, he had sent a peremptory order to Bowen at the same time, instructing him to bring Green's brigade to the Roberts house as rapidly as possible. In the intervening period, Bowen had had time for second thoughts. Perhaps he realized that he had permitted petty spite to threaten the very life of the Confederacy, or perhaps he realized that, in many other armies, he probably would have been charged with treason and executed out of hand. In any event, he immediately pulled Green's BDE out of its position on the Ratliff Road ridge and started north. He arrived at the Roberts house at about the time that the Union attack at the Crossroad ran out of steam and just before Cockrell began an attack in an attempt to regain the vital position.[48]

With both of Bowen's brigades up, Pemberton took a few minutes to get properly set and then launched the whole Trans-Mississippi division at the blue line south of the Crossroad. Bowen expected but little resistance, because he knew the Union soldiery would be tired, disorganized, and critically short of ammunition, and because he knew his division to be the best fighting men in either army. Nevertheless, resist they did, for ten terrible minutes, before they began to give. The withdrawal almost instantly turned into a rout. The Confederate line swept across the Crossroad, up the Crossroad Ridge and over the crest of Champion Hill, while the panicked Federal soldiers fled before it.[49]

However, as Cockrell reached the crest of the hill, he was surprised to discover a fresh Union brigade deployed across the road near the base of the hill about 600 yards to the north. With his men disorganized by the pursuit, he decided to take a moment to reorganize before taking on this new threat. He sent runners back for more ammunition and deployed westward along the crest of Lee's Ridge, because Green's brigade was coming up on his right and needed room to deploy. The ammunition runners soon returned with word that Carter Stevenson had ordered his wagons off the field. Bowen never forgave Stevenson for what he regarded as a major error, even though he later discovered that his divisional wagons had been a part of the army's train, all of which had been ordered off the field early that morning, before the battle began.

In any event, there was no more ammunition; the battle would be fought with the bullets in the soldier's cartridge boxes. In a few minutes, Green's brigade came up on his right, and the two brigades then started down the hill, confident that they would be able to sweep away a single Union brigade, even if they had to do it with their bayonets alone.[50]

Bowen's terrible charge had swept away the entire left flank of the Yankee army on Champion Hill, leaving the left flank of the troops in the Austin Creek ravine in the air. Lee realized the situation almost at once and launched a couple of regiments at what he supposed was the end of the Union line, which rested in the bottom of the Austin's Creek ravine, about 300 yards northeast of the Cook house.[51] Somehow the Yankees had managed to get a battery of artillery into this unlikely location, and point-blank charges of canister halted the Confederate attack long before it made firm contact with the Union infantry.[52]

In the meantime, some of Cumming's men had rallied behind Bowen's DIV, and they now moved into position, facing west across the head of Austin's Creek, in an attempt to protect the flank of Bowen's breakthrough. It was not much of a battle line, since it consisted only of fragments of regiments, some no larger than the size of a normal company.

When Bowen's men resumed their advance down the north face of Champion Hill, they ran into solid sheets of musketry from the fresh Union brigade marshaled there. Tired, disorganized, short of ammunition, and without artillery support, not even the Trans-Mississippians could stand it. The attack stopped, and, for long minutes, the two sides slugged it out at point-blank range.[53] The worst was a concentration of Union artillery on their left flank, which drove Green's Trans-Mississippians back into the shelter of some small ravines.[54]

Bowen began to despair as yet another Union brigade began to deploy smoothly to the left of the Union line. As soon as they were in position, individual regiments began to click into the line, and Bowen realized that they were the units which his first assault had broken and routed. And, all the while, those terrible guns off the left flank of the Union line tore relentlessly at his helpless men, now virtually without ammunition. The cartridge boxes of the dead and wounded were gleaned, but it was not enough. The only hope was to hold on until Loring's powerful division came up in support.

Meanwhile, when Bowen left the Ratliff Road ridge with Green's BDE, Loring had shifted Buford's BDE to the left in an effort to close the huge gap in the Confederate line, which extended from the Ratliff house to the Roberts house. Featherston also was shifted left, to a position on the Coker house ridge southwest of the Ratliff house, and Tilghman's BDE was withdrawn west along the Raymond Road to a ridge 600 yards west of the Coker house. Pemberton had not ordered these moves. In fact, Pemberton had ordered Loring to leave nothing but a roadblock behind on the Raymond Road and to bring his entire division north to the battle for the Jackson Road. Like Bowen, Loring ignored the command.

Phase IV: Final Breakthrough
1400–1630, 16 May 1863

FEDERAL PERSPECTIVE

At 1430, when Bowen's powerful counterattack finally was stopped in front of Boomer's determined riflemen, the situation was frightfully confused. Grant had no idea how many men the Confederates would be able to throw into the fight. He was aware, however, that Hovey's troops had occupied the Crossroad for a time and that there had been no sign whatever of McClernand's column, which should have been attacking down the Middle Road. In fact, the Confederates at the Crossroad had showed no concern whatever about Union forces to the east. Grant must have concluded either that McClernand had been delayed far to the east or that the Confederates already had fought the two Middle Road divisions, defeated them, and pushed them back out of the way. Nor was there word of any kind about the situation on the Raymond Road. Four of his seven divisions seemingly had vanished as if they had never existed.

The troops who had been driven off Lee's Ridge and Champion Hill long since had been identified as three brigades of Carter Stevenson's DIV, which meant that the location of at least one brigade of that division remained unclear. The author of the terrible counterattack had been easy to identify as the old nemesis, John Bowen. That left Loring's DIV unaccounted for. For all Grant knew, Forney's DIV or M. L. Smith's DIV from the Vicksburg garrison also might have joined the field army during the last twenty-four hours. In other words, there was at least a possibility that Pemberton would be able to throw another ten or twelve thousand men into the fight on the north face of Champion Hill.

Grant had very few reserves with which to counter such a threat. The only infantry immediately available was Holmes's BDE of Crocker's DIV, which by this time had filed into place on Boomer's left. Hovey's troops were rallying, and in a few more minutes several of those regiments would be ready to be put back into the line. A message had gone to John Stevenson, way out on the western flank, to come at once with his brigade. Grant assumed that he had not been seriously engaged, and presumably he was on the way, but it was hard to say how long it would take him to march all the way around, across country, to reach the force in front of the Champion house. Sherman's two divisions, Steele's and Tuttle's, still were hours away.

The one resource Grant had in abundance was artillery, and now that the Confederates were out in the open where the guns could get at them, their effect would be telling. Indeed, Green's BDE, on the right flank of the Confederate attack, had been effectively stopped by Hovey's sixteen-gun concentration.

Grant had no idea what had happened to Logan's DIV, which had vanished over the crest of Lee's Ridge. Bowen's assault had been made on such a narrow front that Grant suspected that they had swept right on past Logan's left flank, leaving it dangling in air. However, if Logan's flank was in the air, then so was Bowen's; perhaps a determined thrust from the west would be able to get in behind them and cause a bit of trouble. Well, two regiments of Sanborn's BDE of Crocker's DIV were out there somewhere. They were fresh, and if they struck into the angle between Bowen and the remnants of Carter Stevenson's DIV on the Crossroad Ridge, Bowen might be forced to pull back.

As it happened, Sanborn had awakened to the possibility within a few minutes after Bowen's attack had gone past, and he had started his two regiments cautiously eastward up the tangled gullies forming the head of the Austin Creek ravine. In this very difficult terrain, they were opposed by small groups of determined Confederates, so the going was slow. The time was now about 1515.

At the Champion house, Grant, Crocker, and McPherson suddenly noticed that the rifle fire from Bowen's troops was dropping in volume and growing erratic. They could see up the hill along the Jackson Road and knew that no substantial numbers of Confederate ammunition bearers were coming forward. The conclusion was inescapable: Bowen's men were running out of ammunition. McPherson waved his men forward, and, slowly at first and then with increasing momentum, the blue line began to inch up the hill. The movement gained speed with every passing moment, and, in a surprisingly short time, Crocker's two brigades, now supported by Hovey's reformed and resupplied men, had regained the crest of the hill and begun to push south along the Jackson Road toward the Crossroad. By 1600, the stubbornly fighting Confederates had been pushed back to within a few yards of the Crossroad.

Grant now realized that he had victory in his grasp, and his thoughts began to turn to bagging as much of the Confederate army as he could. Stevenson's BDE had not yet arrived, and there was now clearly no need for it, so he sent a messenger ordering it to return to its former position and continue the attack on the Austin Ridge. At this time, he still did not know that it already had been across the ridge, but had withdrawn on his order!

Grant's letter to McClernand, sent from the Champion house at 1235, finally reached McClernand on the Middle Road about 1415. A few moments later, at about 1430, a courier from Grant arrived.[55] He had ridden cross-country, having left Grant only fifteen minutes earlier, almost the moment Grant had realized that Bowen's counterattack was going to be a serious threat. With responsibility for bringing on an engagement unequivocally in Grant's hands, McClernand at last ordered Osterhaus forward.[56] Not too surprisingly, his two brigades simply swamped the single Confederate regiment holding the roadblock. But when Osterhaus's battle line reached the crest of the hill which the Confederates had held for so long, they stopped.[57] Both Osterhaus and McClernand evidently felt that they had won the battle which Grant had ordered. They were still more than 1,200 yards from the Crossroad and in dense timber, so they could see nothing of what was transpiring in that direction. They did send a skirmish line cautiously to probe the land to the west, but the move was precautionary, not bellicose.

As soon as he had received Grant's order to attack, McClernand had passed the message on to A. J. Smith, who commanded the force on the Raymond Road.[58] A. J. Smith's force consisted of two divisions, his own and Blair's, of Sherman's XV Corps. Without direct orders from McClernand to bring on an engagement, A. J. Smith had felt that his hands were tied, and hence he had not pressed hard against the Confederates on his front. Communications between the Middle Road and the Raymond Road were excellent, because there was a good farm road connecting the J. Davis house on the Raymond Road with the Middle Road. Thus, the distance by road between McClernand and A. J. Smith was only about three and a half miles. A good courier could make the trip in twenty minutes. Smith should have received the order no later than 1530. Yet he made no move whatever to hasten his advance or to exert greater pressure on the Confederate force in his front.[59]

As a result of Osterhaus's pause at the top of the hill east of the Crossroad, Crocker's and Hovey's line, now moving smoothly southward along the Jackson Road toward the Crossroad against slackening resistance, passed right across the front of Osterhaus's division, only 1,200 yards to the east. While Osterhaus and McClernand could not see what was happening around the Crossroad, they must have been able to hear the roar of the battle moving across their front. Yet McClernand made no move whatever to help.

In contrast, McPherson's men now sensed victory and, exulting, drove southward toward the Crossroad. The Confederate line in front of them, formerly so tenacious, began to unravel; in a few moments it broke completely and streamed away to the south, scarcely more than a cloud of stragglers. As Crocker's men moved across the Crossroad, a fresh Confederate brigade suddenly made its appearance on a ridge transverse to the Ratliff Road about 600 yards to the south.[60] Hovey and Crocker realized that their men were tired and disorganized, so they stopped to rest and reorganize before taking on the new battle line to the south. But they rested in line of battle, solidly holding the vital Crossroad.[61]

A few minutes later, a blue-clad skirmish line came out of the trees 200 yards east of the Crossroad, and within moments Grant knew that now he had two more fresh divisions, Osterhaus's and Carr's, which could be thrown into the fray if needed.[62]

Out to the west, on the north face of the Austin Ridge, Logan's men had found the combination of terrain and stiff resistance too much to cope with, and their attack had stalled at about the time of Bowen's counterattack. The conflict along the ridge had settled down to a firefight, with neither side suffering much damage or gaining much advantage. When Stevenson's BDE withdrew from its position across the Austin Ridge in response to Grant's orders during Bowen's counterattack, J. E. Smith had extended a line of skirmishers out to the west along Austin Creek, but they had not advanced up the ridge, even though unopposed. Gradually the firing along Austin Ridge ceased, and an eerie silence fell over the field. Then, suddenly, about 1600, John Stevenson's BDE resumed its former position on J. E. Smith's right, but instead of stopping, it moved right on up the ridge and over the top, occupying almost the same position it had left some time before. Once in firm possession of the Jackson Road, Stevenson's men then turned and began to push slowly and cautiously eastward, only to find that the Confederates had evaporated. In a few moments, the entire ridgetop, from the Crossroad nearly to Bakers Creek, was firmly in Union hands.[63]

From the Cook house, Logan could look south and see a Confederate line of battle forming on the crest of the ridge beyond the valley of Roberts Creek, scarcely 600 yards away. Logan's men were tired and disorganized from their all-day effort, so Logan told them to rest where they were, but to do so in line of battle. He felt in his bones that the fight was over, but one never knew; and that line beyond Roberts Creek could not be ignored. A few moments later, a courier from Grant arrived to tell him that Osterhaus's and Carr's DIVs had arrived on the Middle Road within supporting distance of the Crossroad, and Logan knew that the battle had been won.

CONFEDERATE PERSPECTIVE

About 1415, as soon as Pemberton realized that Bowen's attack was successful beyond all expectation, he turned to Loring for the fresh troops he needed to exploit the breakthrough. Loring already had been ordered twice to bring his division north, and when precious minutes ticked away with no sign of him, Pemberton finally sent a staff officer to urge him to march immediately, regardless of what was on his front. Loring, all righteous indignation, asked if Pemberton knew that the enemy on the Raymond Road was in great force, implying that it was all he could do to hold his own. The staff officer replied that he didn't know what Pemberton knew, but that he, Loring, had been given an order, and the responsibility for obeying it was his. When this exchange was reported to Pemberton, the general again swallowed both anger and pride and sent an aide to explain the situation in detail. Thus persuaded, Loring agreed at last to put Buford's and Featherston's BDEs on the road toward Champion Hill.[64]

It was now 1500, and, back at the Roberts house, Pemberton learned that Bowen's counterattack had stalled just short of final success.[65] Still no Loring. Then the news came that the Federals again were attacking and were driving Bowen back.

Meanwhile, Bowen and his two brigadiers, Cockrell and Green, tried hard to keep their attack going. Despite all efforts, however, it could not be maintained with bayonets alone. They stripped every cartridge from the dead and wounded and sent runners back for more, but all in vain. Slowly they began to fall back, one grudging step at a time. Then another fresh Union brigade deployed on the left of the first brigade, and the pace of retreat accelerated. To make matters worse, it dawned on the Yankees on the west flank of Bowen's penetration that Bowen's flank was open, and they began to drive eastward up out of the Austin Creek bottom toward the Crossroad Ridge. To stop them, there were only the shattered remnants of Cumming's regiments, who were no match for the disciplined Yankees, made bold and brave by sensed victory.

By 1600, Pemberton was informed that Bowen's men, still bitterly resisting, had been pushed back over the crest of Champion Hill. And then came the final blow. The Yankee force on the Middle Road suddenly came alive, and the Confederate roadblock on the hilltop 700 yards east of the Crossroad abruptly collapsed. A few moments later word arrived that at least a brigade of Federal infantry had occupied the top of Bolls Hill, and evidently there were more men behind that brigade. Thus blue-clad infantry occupied both flanks as well as the front of Bowen's embattled division. And now Bowen, who had allowed Carter Stevenson's DIV to be destroyed while he pursued his personal vendetta against Pemberton, ignoring the latter's orders, now found himself in an identical position, waiting for Loring's DIV to arrive. He called for help, just as Stevenson before him had done.[66] It would have made a good title for a Victorian melodrama, had anyone had time to think about it: *The Betrayer Betrayed.*

In despair, Pemberton mounted his horse and rode south along the Ratliff Road to locate Loring and bring him north to support Bowen.[67] A half-mile southwest of the Roberts house, Pemberton met Buford, riding at the head of his hurrying brigade. It was now 1545, and the Union force pressing up Austin Ridge had almost reached the road. Bowen was trying desperately to hang onto the Crossroad. Pemberton told Buford to split his brigade, with half to support the people trying to hold Austin Ridge and the other half to help Bowen hold the Crossroad.[68] Just as Buford started two of his regiments across country toward the Cook house on the Austin Ridge, a haze of stragglers began to flow past from the direction of the Crossroad. Realizing that the Crossroad was the point most threatened, he ignored

Pemberton's order and took his brigade down the Ratliff Road to support Bowen. Bowen's line broke before Buford's men could deploy, so he formed across the road at the Roberts house and watched helplessly as the triumphant Federals occupied the Crossroad.[69] For some reason the Federals made no move to continue the attack, but rather contented themselves with deploying in overwhelming force in a line covering the Crossroad.

Meanwhile, Pemberton had ridden all the way to the Ratliff house without finding any trace of Loring. Here he was able to look down a long nose of ridge and see a Union division deployed across the Raymond Road, only 1,000 yards to the southwest. There were some Union cannon shooting sporadically at something still farther to the west, but there was no other sign of activity. Since the Yankees were shooting at something off to the west, and since he had seen no trace of Loring's DIV, Pemberton assumed that the Yankee gunners must be firing at Loring's people. That meant that Loring, presumably with both Featherston's and Tilghman's BDEs, had fallen back and uncovered the junction of the Ratliff and Raymond roads, opening a way directly onto the rear of Bowen's and Stevenson's DIVs around the Crossroad! In horror and despair, Pemberton spurred back down the Ratliff Road to the Roberts house, where Bowen sadly informed him that the Crossroad was lost and that there was no hope whatever of retaking it. The battle had been lost, and the retreat route to Edwards had been cut off. Bowen's and Stevenson's DIVs were in a trap.

In the face of such a disaster, Pemberton had to do what he could to save the troops. He ordered the remnants of his army south of the Crossroad and along the Austin Ridge to withdraw across country toward the Lower Bakers Creek Bridge. If the creek proved impassable, then he and his men would retreat across country to the south. They might well lose all their artillery and wagons, but at least the men might survive to fight another day.

Just as Pemberton's aides were leaving with withdrawal instructions, one of Loring's aides arrived and told him calmly that Featherston's BDE was falling in on Buford's left, extending the line to the west along the ridge south of Roberts Creek.[70] The aide explained that Featherston had taken the Coker Road, which led north from the Coker house, instead of the Ratliff Road. It made a long loop to the west and finally rejoined the Ratliff Road about 1,100 yards northeast of the Ratliff house, which explained why Pemberton had missed meeting them on his excursion.[71] Loring had not abandoned the army after all.

A few moments later, a courier from Lee arrived, informing Pemberton that Loring had ordered him to withdraw from his position on the Austin

Ridge and to put his brigade into line on Featherston's left flank on Roberts Ridge. Loring, he said, was preparing an attack on the Yankees who were now holding the Austin Ridge![72] Pemberton was stunned; Loring had the authority neither to command Lee nor to order a general attack. Further, he clearly had no conception of the actual situation; an attack by a single brigade on Austin Ridge would serve only to shed more blood uselessly. And it would be a single brigade; Lee's men were desperately tired and virtually out of ammunition and thus would be of little help. Even if such an attack succeeded in occupying the Jackson Road, the Federal concentration at the Crossroad would smash into the flank and sweep Featherston and Lee away. Pemberton quickly sent an order to Loring to deploy to cover the retreat of Lee's BDE and Bowen's shattered division, and to gather up any stragglers from Cumming's and Barton's BDEs that he might find.[73]

Now, like a benediction, came one of Wirt Adams's couriers, to inform Pemberton that a road branched off Loring's bypass road and led more or less directly to the Lower Bakers Creek Bridge. Even better, MAJ Lockett's engineers had rebuilt the bridge. Moreover, the water was down, and the stream now could be readily forded.[74] At this point, Loring also told Pemberton that Tilghman's BDE was holding the Union force on the Raymond Road at bay. Deployed on a ridge 1,000 yards east of the point where the newly discovered road joined the Raymond Road, the BDE thus was in a position to cover the withdrawal of the Confederate army. Positioning Tilghman may have been the only intelligent thing Loring had done all day.

Phase V: Victory and Defeat
1600–2300, 16 May 1863

FEDERAL PERSPECTIVE

By the time Grant reached the Crossroad about 1645, Crocker and Hovey were holding it in a grip of iron, and Logan occupied the entire length of the Austin Ridge. To the south, a Confederate battle line was forming on the ridge south of Roberts Creek, 700 yards away. Even though it did not look particularly substantial, Grant decided that the potential threat could not be ignored. McPherson hastily sorted out his commands, and in a short time Hovey and Crocker started slowly southward,[75] although the men hated every step that brought them closer to yet more battle. However, the gray battle line drew back slowly, even before the infantry came within small-arms range; as the advance continued, the pace of withdrawal quickened. Soon it was clear that the Confederates were not interested in fighting and only wanted to delay the Union advance. That told Grant unambiguously that he had won and that Pemberton was withdrawing from the field.

At last McClernand and his two divisions on the Middle Road came down off Bolls Hill, and Grant immediately halted Hovey's and Crocker's tired men and put McClernand in charge of exploiting what obviously was a decisive victory. McClernand took his time deciding what to do, but eventually he sent Carr and his division after the retreating Rebels.[76] By that time, the tail of the Confederate column had vanished to the southwest.

Out on the Austin Ridge, John Stevenson again had occupied a section of the Jackson Road west of the Austin house. He long since had identified the Rebel infantry which had been contesting his advance as Barton's BDE. He had noted that a regiment or more of the Georgians had withdrawn to the west down the Jackson Road toward the Upper Bakers Creek Bridge, while the remainder had been forced to the southeast. Stevenson could see dust clouds rising from beyond the ridge south of Roberts Creek, and he decided they were being raised by retreating Confederate formations. Exhilarated by what he now realized was a smashing victory, his thoughts turned to exploitation. He sent his 8 IL south across country, hoping they would be able to get astride the Rebel escape route, while he personally led the remainder of his brigade, plus a battery of artillery, down the Jackson Road to seize the Upper Bakers Creek Bridge.[77] He figured that Barton's men would try to hold it but would be so shattered by their defeat earlier in the day that they would not offer much resistance.

The 8 IL arrived on the Lower Bridge Road just after the tail of Loring's retreating column had passed and just in time to meet McClernand and Lawler, whose brigade formed the head of Carr's pursuing troops. McClernand sent Lawler on down the Lower Bridge Road toward the Lower Bakers Creek Bridge, just to keep the pressure on. Then he sent Benton's BDE, next in line, across country to assist John Stevenson in his attempt to seize the Upper Bakers Creek Bridge. Lawler marched on down the road for a time and gathered in some five hundred Rebel stragglers, but he stopped about 1,000 yards short of the Raymond Road. At this point, for some inexplicable reason, he decided that there was no point in continuing and returned to the Roberts house on the Ratliff Road.[78]

In contrast, John Stevenson reached the Upper Bakers Creek Bridge at about 1715, brushed away a couple of Confederate vedettes, and found the bridge undefended.[79] He was so astonished that he feared a trap and deployed his troops in battle array west of the bridge, ready for any eventuality. McClernand, accompanied by Benton's BDE, arrived about 1730. McClernand realized that he had been granted a golden opportunity; the main Rebel army was retreating toward Edwards via the Raymond Road, but McClernand held the Upper Bakers Creek Bridge, which was closer to Edwards than the Lower Bakers Creek Bridge. With luck, he might get to Edwards before the retreating Rebels. He couldn't quite figure out how it had all happened, but there it was. As always, it took McClernand a while to decide what to do, so it was about 1800 before he started Benton's BDE down a miserable country track leading south, hoping that he would be able to get across the Raymond Road east of Edwards before the entire Confederate army had passed. At almost the same time that Benton started out, a cavalry scout came in and reported that a strong Rebel force was approaching along a country road coming in from the north.[80] McClernand had planned on sending Stevenson's BDE into Edwards, but he dared not lose the Upper Bakers Creek Bridge, so he sent Stevenson to deal with the Rebel force to the north. It turned out that it was easily discouraged; a couple of rounds from Stevenson's artillery turned it back.[81]

Benton marched south on his farm track. When he was about 1,000 yards north of the Raymond Road, he crossed a low ridge to discover a gray column passing on the Raymond Road to the south. Instead of pressing on and blocking the road with his infantry, he stopped and tried to interdict it with his artillery. The time was about 1910. The long-range shell-fire did nothing except make the Confederates on the Raymond Road march faster. At dark, Benton decided that he could do no more, turned around, and went back to the Jackson Road and so on into Edwards, where he arrived about 2100, far too late to be of any use whatever. The last of the Confederates were long gone.

Late in the evening, Lawler's BDE and Osterhaus's DIV arrived at the Upper Bakers Creek Bridge, and McClernand sent them on to Edwards,[82] hoping to fragment the retreating Confederate army still further, but they did not arrive until nearly midnight, far too late to catch anybody except a few stragglers.

On the Raymond Road, A. J. Smith's and Blair's DIVs by 1500 had moved slowly forward to the Coker House ridge, following the earlier withdrawal of the Confederate force to a low ridge 600 yards farther west. Smith thought that the Southern force amounted to a brigade, possibly even a division, since it was liberally supplied with artillery. In any event, it refused to budge. A. J. Smith deployed his infantry and artillery but made no move to attack. Instead, he tried to dislodge the Rebels with artillery alone. He had twenty-four guns and the Rebels seemed to have sixteen, but the odds were not good enough, and the Southerners clung to their ridge like leeches.

Finally, about 1645, most of the Confederate infantry force in front of A. J. Smith suddenly vanished, leaving only an artillery battery and a single regiment behind. Still A. J. Smith refused to move forward. Finally, at a few minutes after 1900, the Rebel artillery limbered up and vanished beyond the crest of the ridge.[83] A. J. Smith waited a suitably long period for something to happen and then moved very slowly and cautiously forward. His glacier-slow advance down the Raymond Road actually had moved only about 500 yards west of the ridge, which the Confederates had held for most of the afternoon, when night fell. At this point, he called off the action and let his men bivouac along the road. He was still more than 600 yards short of the Lower Bakers Creek Bridge, but it didn't matter, because all the Confederates were long gone.

CONFEDERATE PERSPECTIVE

The news that there existed a direct road to the Lower Bakers Creek Bridge and that the bridge had been rebuilt[84] meant that the Confederate army had, against all expectation, an avenue of retreat that could be made secure against Federal interference and that would permit the withdrawal of artillery and ambulances as well. Pemberton sent Cumming's BDE first; it was scarcely more than an armed mob, so thoroughly had it been shattered. Next came the remnants of Barton's BDE; two whole regiments were missing, and nobody knew what had happened to them. Lee's BDE followed next, in good order, followed by Bowen's Trans-Mississippi division. Bowen's troops were so little shaken that they were willing to go back into the fight if they could refill their cartridge boxes.[85]

While Bowen's DIV and the fragments of Carter Stevenson's DIV marched rapidly away toward the Lower Bakers Creek Bridge, Loring kept Buford's and Featherston's BDEs in line of battle on the ridge south of Roberts Creek, thus sealing off the roads to the south and west. The Yankees were not idle, and within an hour a powerful blue battle line, amply supported by artillery, began to move slowly and ponderously southward from the Crossroad. Loring fell back slowly before this overwhelming force before it got within effective small-arms range.[86] The Yankee artillery was deadly accurate, and Buford's BDE, which was acting as rear guard, began to incur casualties. As the pressure increased, the rate of withdrawal also increased, and soon both Featherston's and Buford's BDEs were hurrying down the road toward the Lower Bakers Creek Bridge as fast as their legs would take them.

All this time, Tilghman and his brigade were fending off the powerful Union force on the Raymond Road. Tilghman had occupied a ridge about 1,100 yards east of the Lower Bakers Creek Bridge and had easily held against the Yankees, who, despite being in overwhelming force, showed no disposition to attack, contenting themselves with long-range artillery fire. Even that turned out to be dangerous; about 1720, a shell exploded at Tilghman's feet, killing him instantly. COL A. E. Reynolds assumed command, and about 1800 he was informed that the army had reached the Raymond Road and was crossing Bakers Creek. COL Reynolds immediately set about breaking contact and joining the withdrawal.[87] Fortunately he did it in slow motion, because the report was somewhat premature; only Carter Stevenson's and Bowen's troops actually had crossed by this time. Loring and his other two brigades were still marching down the Lower Bridge Road toward the bridge, but they were yet a half-hour away.

Cumming's BDE and Barton's two regiments crossed the Lower Bakers Creek Bridge first and headed for Edwards and the Big Black Bridge as rapidly as their exhaustion permitted. Lee, with his brigade still intact, crossed the bridge and deployed on the west bank to guard the crossing until Bowen's two brigades had crossed.

Pemberton had ridden with Bowen, and, as soon as they crossed Bakers Creek, at about 1800, he ordered Bowen to relieve Lee and hold the crossing until all of the army had crossed to safety.[88] Bowen placed his infantry in positions where they could sweep the eastern approaches to the bridge, unlimbered his artillery, and settled down to wait. Pemberton then rode for Big Black Bridge, assuming, with some reason, that Loring's troops, which had scarcely been in action all day, would be able easily to break contact and escape across the Lower Bakers Creek Bridge. Pemberton's concern at this point was to make certain that BG Vaughn, who commanded the troops in the fortified line east of the Big Black Bridge, was manning the defenses properly.[89]

Cumming's and Barton's men covered the distance between the Lower Bakers Creek Bridge and the Big Black Bridge without incident. Not so Lee. When his tired men marched for Edwards after being relieved by Bowen at the Lower Bakers Creek Bridge, all went well at first, but they were scarcely halfway to Edwards when a Federal battery about

1,000 yards north of the road opened up and shelled them as they hurried past. There were few casualties, but the implications were terrifying. Bowen heard the guns and panicked, believing they meant that the Federals were already in Edwards and thus across his retreat route to Big Black Bridge. He sent a message to Loring, telling him that he was abandoning the bridge, but he did not tell Loring the reason for the decision or any indication of his plans. He and his men then marched across country to the Telegraph Road, from which a country road bypassed Edwards on the south. He reached the fortified line at Big Black Bridge at midnight. Both he and his men were exhausted and dispirited.

About 1900, Loring's advance guard regiment reached the Lower Bakers Creek Bridge, crossed, and marched for Edwards. A mile beyond the bridge, the regiment received artillery fire from a battery 1,000 yards to the north[90] but pressed on toward Edwards. Then, suddenly, when it was less than a mile away, fires blossomed in the town. The regimental commander interpreted this as evidence that the Yankees were in possession and turned back. He met Loring at the Lower Bakers Creek Bridge about 1930. Unlike Bowen, Loring had no idea of the configuration of the roads south of Edwards. Because Bowen's message to him earlier had said only that he was evacuating the Lower Bakers Creek Bridge area, Loring assumed that Bowen had been pushed off somewhere to the south. If so, then it was possible that Bowen and his division were lost. Loring now had no idea what to do. A local planter told him that there was no road on the west bank of Bakers Creek that connected the Raymond Road with the Telegraph Road south of Edwards, but that there was a road along the east bank of the creek that eventually connected to the Mt. Moriah–Dillon's Farm road, from which a road did lead directly to Big Black Bridge.

Loring set off down a road that turned into a track, then into a muddy trail in dense timber, through which neither wagons nor artillery could be forced. He abandoned both[91] and eventually, sometime during the early morning hours of 17 May, emerged onto the Mt. Moriah–Dillon's Farm road, well southeast of Bakers Creek. Here he encountered yet another helpful local, who told him that, contrary to what he had been told earlier, there were no roads bypassing Edwards on the south, so Loring abandoned his efforts to rejoin the main army, marched southeast toward Auburn, and two days later reached the Jackson, New Orleans & Great Northern Railroad at Crystal Springs, well to the south of Jackson. He had no artillery or wagons, no baggage of any kind, and many of his men were even without their rifles.[92] His division had been destroyed as a fighting unit without ever engaging in anything more serious than a skirmish. At no time during his adventure did he see fit to send a courier to Pemberton, telling him of either his plight or plans. It would have been easy. An experienced man readily could have found his way across country to the Telegraph Road south of Fourteenmile Creek, then onto the Baldwin's Ferry–New Auburn Road, across Fourteenmile Creek at Montgomery's Bridge, and so into the Big Black Bridge area at Smith's farm. The total distance would have been something like thirteen miles, so Pemberton should have had word by midnight.

However, Loring did not send word, so Pemberton was completely ignorant of Loring's fate and instead believed that his division, which was fresh and undamaged by action at Champion Hill, was following along in Bowen's wake toward safety within the fortifications at Big Black Bridge.

Meanwhile, Barton and his pair of regiments, which had been pushed off to the west by the Yankee occupation of the Austin Ridge relatively early in the battle, had withdrawn to the Upper Bakers Creek Bridge and deployed on the west bank, determined to hold it at all costs.[93] Barton figured that Pemberton would make every effort to retake the Jackson Road, because it was the only escape route open to the army. He realized that his two defeated regiments, tired, dispirited, and short of ammunition, could not hold the bridge against a determined attack, so at 1430 he sent a courier to COL A. W. Reynolds, whose brigade guarded the army's wagon train somewhere north of Edwards on the Brownsville Road, to send help. Help unexpectedly arrived at 1530, much earlier than he had hoped, in the shape a large detachment of Wirt Adams's cavalry. Barton sent the horsemen across to the east bank as vedettes and settled down to await events.

Another of Adams's cavalrymen arrived from the south about 1700 with the news that the Army of Vicksburg had been defeated and was retreating across Bakers Creek via the Raymond Road. The news of the defeat was bad, but the word that there was an alternative escape route for the army was like a gift from heaven. Barton assumed that there was no point in holding the Jackson Road bridge any longer, so he called in his pickets and marched for Edwards.[94] Evidently it did not occur to him, or perhaps he did not know, that the Jackson Road route to Edwards was shorter than the Raymond Road route and that therefore he was opening an avenue by which the Yankees could reach Edwards and cut off the retreat of the main body of Pemberton's army. Furthermore, in his haste to leave, he forgot to notify A. W. Reynolds.

Barton's courier found A. W. Reynolds and the wagon train on the Brownsville Road about three and a half miles northeast of Edwards. Reynolds now was faced with a terrible dilemma; he dared not leave the train unguarded, but he had to go to Barton's aid. He compromised by dividing his forces. He left two of his regiments to guard the train and took the other two down a farm road that seemed to head in the direction of the Upper Bakers Creek Bridge.[95] Just as he and his men came down off the ridge onto the Bakers Creek flats, however, they encountered a solid blue infantry line supported by artillery.[96] The sight convinced Reynolds that he was too late to be of any help to Barton, and he immediately withdrew to the north.

COMMENTARY

The last act of the Battle of Champion Hill was over, and an extraordinary battle it had been. The casualty figures are revealing.

Table 1
Casualty Figures for the Battle of Champion Hill

	Total Casualties
Army of Vicksburg (Confederate)	
Loring's DIV	117
Bowen's DIV	868
Stevenson's DIV	3,761
Army of the Tennessee (Union)	
Raymond Road Force:	
A. J. Smith's DIV	25
Blair's DIV	0
Middle Road Force:	
Osterhaus' DIV	130
Carr's DIV	3
Jackson Road Force:	
Logan's DIV	407
Crocker's DIV	510
Hovey's DIV	1,202

NOTE: The casualty figures are more instructive if viewed according to the positions of the units on the field.

From these data, some obvious conclusions may be drawn.

1. Given that McPherson was in tactical command of the Jackson Road force and Grant normally left tactical conduct in the hands of

his corps commanders, it was McPherson who won the tactical battle of Champion Hill.

2. The three divisions comprising the Jackson Road force won the battle virtually alone.

3. The two divisions comprising the Raymond Road force never actually got into action at all. Of the Middle Road force, only one division was engaged, and that scarcely seriously.

4. Hovey's casualty rate exceeded 20 percent. His troops were responsible for the initial breakthrough which resulted in the first occupation of the Crossroad. This division was the one primarily struck by Bowen's counterattack, and it participated in the final offensive that recaptured the Crossroad and ended the battle.

5. In the Confederate forces, only Stevenson's and Bowen's DIVs were seriously engaged; Loring's DIV was engaged in nothing more serious than minor skirmishing.

27

Hegira of the Confederate Wagon Train 16 May 1863

Maps: 10. The Region between Vicksburg, Bruinsburg, and Raymond
      15. The Battlefield of Champion Hill

FEDERAL PERSPECTIVE

As Grant and his Army of the Tennessee moved westward toward Edwards from Bolton and Raymond, he was more than a little uneasy about his northern flank. Grant knew that GEN Joe Johnston's Jackson army had not been badly hurt by the brief engagement in front of Jackson on 14 May. In principle, there was no reason why Johnston should not march rapidly westward from somewhere northeast of Jackson and strike the rear or right flank of the Union army on its march toward Edwards. Grant was not seriously concerned about a blow at his rear, because Sherman's two divisions would serve as a rear guard to the main army. However, if Johnston started from a convenient place on the Mississippi Central Railroad north of Jackson—Midway, say— and marched via Brownsville, it was only 28 miles to Queen's Hill Church on the Brownsville Road north of Baker's Creek. It therefore was possible that by dint of hard marching, Johnston might arrive on his north flank with something like ten thousand men, and that would be a serious matter, especially if he arrived in the middle of a contest with Pemberton.

As a result, Grant had kept COL Clark Wright and his 6 MO CAV patrolling the region north of Bakers Creek. Of course, Wright's cavalrymen would not be able to stop Johnston's infantry, but at least they would give warning. All through 15 and 16 May, Wright's horsemen had probed the countryside north and northeast of the army's line of march and found absolutely nothing. It was a little hard to believe.

Then, late on the afternoon of 16 May, with victory at Champion Hill assured, Grant sent a courier to COL Wright, freeing him from his guard duties. Like mastiffs unleashed, Wright and his blue-clad horsemen rode westward looking for trouble. Just before dark, on the Bridgeport Road north of Edwards, they overtook a huge Confederate wagon train, which was moving rapidly westward toward the floating bridge across the Big Black River at Bridgeport. Wright and his cavalrymen drove right in, only to find that the wagon train was guarded by several squadrons of Rebel cavalry, as well as a brigade of very determined infantry, supported with artillery. The train also was traveling along a road through a landscape of sharp ridges and deep ravines, very much like that at Port Gibson. Of all possible landscapes, it was the one least suited to cavalry, because there was almost no flat ground on which a horse could readily maneuver. Despite the disadvantages, Wright tried again and again, but he never was able to break through to the wagons. During the early hours of the night, they managed to get away across the river. Worse, they destroyed the bridge behind them, despite the Yankee horse soldiers' best efforts.[1]

CONFEDERATE PERSPECTIVE

When the Army of Vicksburg left Edwards on the afternoon of 15 May, it was followed by a supply train consisting of more than two hundred wagons. They contained rations, ammunition, fodder for the animals, and all the other impedimenta of an army on the move. However, the confusion that resulted from the washed-out bridge across Bakers Creek on the Raymond Road so delayed the departure of the infantry and artillery that the wagon train was unable to leave Edwards until midnight. By the time the first wagon caught up with the tail of Carter Stevenson's column at the Crossroad, it was daybreak on 16 May.[2] COL A. W. Reynolds, whose brigade was responsible for train security, immediately put roadblocks out on both the Middle Road and on the top of Champion Hill. The rest of his men were so tired that they simply stopped where they were and sought slumber along the road.

They got precious little, because, shortly after 0800, a courier arrived from Pemberton, the army commander, with an order to turn the train around, return to Edwards, and then continue to the northeast along the Brownsville Road.[3] The Jackson Road was the main Vicksburg–Jackson highway, and it was well maintained, but it nevertheless was unsurfaced. Every time the rain-washed ruts in the surface were graded smooth, a little more of the road surface was removed. The result was that the Jackson Road along Austin Ridge, from the Crossroad to the Upper Bakers Creek Bridge, in fact was a sunken road, with nearly vertical banks on both sides anywhere from a few inches to several feet high. The road also was narrow, not everywhere wide enough for two wagons to pass.

Reynolds's first reaction to Pemberton's order was despair; how was he going to get two hundred wagons turned around on that narrow sunken road? But he set to work with a will, had his men cut openings in the banks, and by Herculean efforts managed to get the two hundred wagons facing westward by 1100. It was an incredible, if largely unsung, achievement. While the wagoneers were getting their wagons turned around, Yankees had shown up on both the Middle and Jackson roads. Reynolds had been able to call in his roadblocks, because Lee and Cumming had taken over the task of providing security on those sectors.[4] Thus, once the wagons were pointing in the right direction, Reynolds was able to get the convoy started promptly on its way to Edwards, with his infantry bringing up the rear.

As the train trundled back down the long hill to the Upper Bakers Creek Bridge, the drivers had no idea what was going on. The fact that they were retreating naturally started floods of rumors. One was that Union cavalry was nearby. Since about 1030, the drivers had heard the grumble of artillery off to the north and east, and that did not seem to bode well.

Reynolds knew that Lee's BDE had hurried off to the north, to the crest of Champion Hill, and that implied the presence of infantry and cavalry, along with the artillery which now could be heard plainly. He had disquieting visions of blue-clad cavalry getting in among the wagons, but nothing materialized, and by 1200 the train reached the junction with the Brownsville Road east of Edwards. The men could hear a terrible battle raging behind them and concluded that their compatriots were being defeated; else why would the wagon train be retreating? They were certain of only one thing: they were now all alone in the world.

To the surprise and dismay of the wagoneers, when they reached the Brownsville Road junction, they were directed to turn north into the Brownsville Road instead of continuing on the Jackson Road through Edwards as they had expected. Two and a half miles north of the village,

Reynolds ordered the train halted.[5] The tail of the wagon train was just north-east of the junction of the Bridgeport Road.

The Brownsville Road runs along the crest of a broad, high ridge which forms the north side of the Bakers Creek valley. From his position, Reynolds could look to the southeast across the valley and see the clouds of smoke and hear the roar of the battle raging on Champion Hill. Having no real idea of what to expect, he decided to sit tight and await events. He deployed his brigade in line of battle on the side of the hill facing Bakers Creek,[6] and there it stayed through the long afternoon, while the climactic battle for the Mississippi Valley thundered on to its fateful conclusion on the hill across the valley, only three miles away. By midafternoon, the battle evidently was over, for the sound of firing had died away to nearly nothing, and the only people Reynolds could see on the hillsides beyond Bakers Creek all wore blue uniforms. A little after 1500, a courier arrived from Carter Stevenson, carrying a dispatch confirming the disaster and an order for Reynolds to get the wagons across the Big Black River as quickly as possible. This made sense to Reynolds, because a Union victory meant that blue-clad horsemen soon would be prowling the countryside in all directions.

Before he could take action, however, a second courier came galloping up. This one came from Barton, carrying an urgent request for reinforcements to enable Barton to hold the Upper Bakers Creek Bridge against the expected Yankee pursuit. Responding to Carter Stevenson's order meant that the wagoneers had to turn their wagons around on a narrow road for the second time that day, and this time everyone was dead tired. However, it was at last done. By about 1730, the train had started on its way to Bridgeport, where a pontoon bridge made it possible to cross the Big Black River. But what to do about Barton's plea for help? Reynolds's solution was to divide his forces. He detached two regiments and a section of artillery to guard the train and started south along a country track toward the Upper Bakers Creek Bridge with his remaining two regiments and four guns.[7] He had less than three miles to go.

As Reynolds and his two regiments, at around 1900, reached the bottom of the hills about 1,000 yards northwest of the Upper Bakers Creek Bridge, they were brought up short by shell-fire from a battery supported by a long line of blue-clad infantry.[8] That force made it very clear to Reynolds that there were no longer any Confederates around the bridge to help, so he instantly turned around and retraced his path. His only thought now was to overtake the wagons, because, he reasoned, the presence of a Union force closer to Edwards than he was might well mean that the Bridgeport Road would be blocked. He caught up with the train about a mile and a half east of Bridgeport and was pleased to discover that a large detachment of Wirt Adams's cavalry had joined up, too.

It was well that the cavalry had appeared, because the train was in serious trouble. Union cavalry arrived while the head of the train was still a mile east of Bridgeport, and it drove in with abandon. In a swirling, confusing battle, Reynolds's steady infantry and Wirt Adams's cavalry beat off attack after attack, all through the remaining hour of daylight. Fortune was on the side of the Confederate defenders, however, for the very rough and wooded terrain was entirely unsuitable for cavalry but almost ideal for defending infantry. Finally, under cover of darkness, the wagons were taken across the river, followed by Wirt Adams's horsemen. The infantry brought up the rear and destroyed the bridge after crossing.[9] At last the men were safe on the west bank of an unfordable stream.

So it was that prompt and intelligent action saved perhaps 350 tons of vital supplies for the Confederate army in Vicksburg.

28
Pursuit and Retreat
17 May 1863

GEOGRAPHIC CONTEXT

The Big Black River and its floodplain are the dominant features of the terrain in the region between Edwards and Bovina. The river enters the region from the north, flowing in a sinuous course trending almost directly south until it reaches a point about one and a half miles west-northwest of Edwards. Here it makes an abrupt turn and flows west-northwest through an almost ruler-straight reach for four miles, at which point it makes a second sharp turn and flows away to the south in a series of looping meanders.

The floodplain is from three to four miles wide and consists mostly of extensive areas of swamp, wet for most of the year and filled with dense stands of tupelo, bald cypress, and willow. However, the floodplain is bordered in many places by a series of low terraces that usually are above the spring floods and accordingly are ideal for farming. The channel itself is rarely more than 40 yards wide, but the water is deep and swift. It was navigable for small steamboats as far upstream as Amsterdam, a hamlet right at the bend where the river turns from south to west.

Five river miles below Amsterdam, the Southern Railroad of Mississippi (SRRM) crossed the river on Big Black Bridge, a high wooden trestle with a short lift span. The Confederates had spiked the span shut and planked over the ties so that the bridge could be used for artillery and wagons, as well as trains. Below Big Black Bridge, all the crossings are ferries, but above the bridge some of the crossings are fords, although they can be used as such only during periods of low water. About 350 yards south (downstream) of Big Black Bridge, the Jackson Road crossed the river on a ferry. There had been attempts to maintain a highway bridge at that point, but it had a distressing tendency to wash away during periods of high water. Eight airline miles to the south was Baldwin's Ferry, on the road connecting Auburn and Vicksburg.

Upstream from Big Black Bridge, the next crossing was Hooker's Ferry, two and a half miles west of Edwards, on the east-west reach of the river. Coaker's Ferry was about two miles northwest of Edwards; and Bridgeport, which boasted a floating bridge, was another mile and a half upstream from Coaker's Ferry. Two miles above Bridgeport was Messenger's Ford (or Ferry; the terms were used interchangeably), where a bar above the mouth of Messenger's Creek formed a shoal that made a good crossing during low water. Another two miles upstream was Jones' Ford, and another three miles north of that was Birdsong's Ferry, on a road connecting Bolton and the hamlet of Oak Ridge. Oak Ridge was on the Benton Road, northeast of Vicksburg. Even at low water, the Big Black was a significant obstacle, because its banks were so high, steep, and slippery that they were difficult even for cavalry and infantry, and impassable by wheeled vehicles.

The SRRM leaves the village of Edwards and crosses the Big Black River floodplain in an almost perfectly straight line. It was raised on a low embankment almost all the way across the floodplain, but about 1,000 yards west of Smith's Station, the embankment grew steadily higher until, about 1,300 yards east of the river, the embankment ended. The tracks then continued on a wooden trestle that grew higher and higher, at last vaulting the river on the Big Black Bridge to meet the bluffs on the western bank. At this point, the bluffs were some sixty feet above the level of the floodplain across the channel, but the bridge connected with a ravine, so that the rails were only some twenty feet above the normal high-water point.

FEDERAL PERSPECTIVE

Resting on the porch of the Roberts house on the evening of the Battle of Champion Hill, Grant was reasonably content. He knew that Carter Stevenson's DIV, the largest formation in Pemberton's army, had been mauled very badly and that Bowen's Trans-Mississippi division had been hurt almost as much. He knew that Big Black Bridge was fortified, and he assumed that the Confederates would withdraw to the shelter of those lines while they rested and reorganized. Grant calculated that the next day, 17 May, the Rebels would withdraw to the west bank of the Big Black and perhaps attempt to hold the crossings until the movements of the Army of Vicksburg and the Jackson army could be coordinated.

As Grant saw it, his problem was to force a crossing of the Big Black River before the Rebels had regained their strength and will. If he did not, there was still a danger that the Army of the Tennessee might, despite its solid victory at Champion Hill, be trapped between the Big Black River and a resurgent Confederate army led by Joseph Johnston. Grant was not particularly worried about supplies for the immediate future, because the supply line through Grand Gulf was working so well that even the officers' baggage was beginning to catch up with them. Nevertheless, in the long run, he had to regain contact with the Navy and his river-borne supply line or risk eventual exhaustion and defeat, because that long wagon road back to Grand Gulf simply could not be defended. Johnston could sever it south of Edwards if he moved briskly, while Grant was preoccupied with Pemberton's Vicksburg army. Alternatively, Pemberton could sever it at Willows or Rocky Springs by sending a force across the Big Black at Hankinson's Ferry, if Grant delayed too long in forcing the line of the Big Black River somewhere in the vicinity of Edwards. So the first priorities were to get across the Big Black River and back into contact with the Mississippi, preferably somewhere north of Vicksburg. That would eliminate any need for long wagon hauls across the Louisiana swamps and would save manpower, horseflesh, and time.

By late on the night of 16 May, the Army of the Tennessee was well positioned to exploit its victory. Sherman, with Tuttle's and Steele's DIVs, was camped at Bolton; and two brigades of Blair's DIV were bivouacked along the Raymond Road near the Coker house. Blair's third brigade (Ewing's) was still a day's march away, back down the road to Grand Gulf. McPherson was with Grant at the Roberts house, with Logan's DIV camped along the Jackson Road west of the Crossroad and Crocker's DIV camped on the ridge west of the Roberts house. Even Ransom's BDE of McArthur's DIV, which had been escorting a 200-wagon supply train up from Grand Gulf, was on the scene, having arrived at the Crossroad about dark. McClernand was at Edwards with Osterhaus's DIV, A. J. Smith's DIV was camped along the Raymond Road about 1,000 yards east of the

Lower Bakers Creek Bridge, and Hovey was camped around the Crossroad. Carr's DIV, which McClernand had used in his pursuit of the withdrawing Confederates, was split; Benton's BDE was in Edwards, Lawler's
BDE was on the west bank of Bakers Creek at the Upper Bakers Creek
Bridge, and Stone's BDE was camped along the Lower Bridge Road west
of its junction with the Ratliff Road. Thus, Grant now had almost his
entire army of maneuver ready at hand. Furthermore, Wright's 6 MO
CAV already controlled the east bank at Bridgeport,[1] suggesting that a
crossing could be forced at that point without serious difficulty.

McClernand was ordered to move with Osterhaus's, Carr's, and A. J.
Late that evening, Grant wrote to Sherman, directing him to march
his two divisions directly to Bridgeport and force a crossing, thus flanking Pemberton out of his defenses at the Big Black Bridge.[2] Sherman got
this message during the night and had Tuttle's and Steele's DIVs on the
road at dawn. Blair, who had husbanded the army's pontoon train all the
way from Grand Gulf, got a message directing him to bring the pontoon
train directly to Bridgeport.[3] With luck, Blair would have the bridge already laid by the time Sherman got there with Tuttle and Steele. Sherman
could be depended upon to get across with a minimum of delay.

McClernand was ordered to move with Osterhaus's, Carr's, and A. J.
Smith's DIVs through Edwards in a thrust directly at the Big Black
Bridge. If Pemberton defended the fortifications on the east bank, so
much the better; Sherman would cross at Bridgeport, outflank them, and,
with luck, bag a few of them before they could get away. If they did not
defend the bridgehead, Sherman might get into position north of
Vicksburg early enough to prevent the Rebels from escaping to the north,
toward Yazoo City. Hovey's DIV, which had fought so valiantly at Champion Hill, would be left to police the battlefield and take a well-earned
rest. McPherson, with Logan's and Crocker's DIVs, would follow along
behind McClernand to provide support, should that become necessary.

During the night, it became increasingly apparent that McClernand
had botched the pursuit of the Rebels, despite the fact that he had had
four divisions which had scarcely participated in the battle and therefore
were fresh and in perfect order. The two divisions on the Raymond Road
had bivouacked before they ever got to the Lower Baker Creek Bridge
and so had not participated in the pursuit in any way. It was true that
Osterhaus's two brigades, plus Benton's BDE of Carr's DIV, had managed
to get into Edwards during the night, via the Jackson Road, but they were
far too late to interfere with the Confederate retreat. By late on the night
of 16 May, Grant realized that Pemberton's army had gotten away clean;

he assumed that, shortly after dawn, the Confederate troops all would be safely on the west bank of the formidable Big Black River. Under the circumstances, the best Grant could hope for during 17 May was to reach the Big Black and force a crossing at Bridgeport.

Blair's troops, with the pontoon train, were on the road by 0430 on 17 May and arrived at Bridgeport at 1000. There were Confederate riflemen on the far shore, but a few well-placed charges of canister from Blair's artillery discouraged them.[4] By the time Sherman arrived with Tuttle's and Steele's DIVs at 1400, the pontoon bridge was nearly finished. By dark, Blair's DIV was across and camped two miles west of the river on the Brooks plantation.[5]

McPherson's troops, tired from the desperate battle of the previous day, did not move out of their camps until about 1000 on 17 May. Logan's DIV, accompanied by Crocker's DIV (which now was commanded by BG Isaac Quinby), marched through Edwards and arrived at Amsterdam about noon.[6] Hovey's DIV, plus Holmes's BDE of Quinby's DIV, remained on Champion Hill, burying the dead, giving aid to the wounded, and policing up the battlefield.[7] Ransom's BDE of McArthur's DIV joined the general move to Amsterdam.

McClernand, possibly conscious that his men had failed miserably in their pursuit of the retreating Rebels on 16 May, had his men on the road by 0330 on the morning of 17 May. Benton's BDE of Carr's DIV led the way west out of Edwards in inky blackness.[8] Benton expected an ambush and moved at glacial speed. With full light, the march moved a bit faster, and about four miles west of Edwards, just west of the Robert Smith farm, the advance was fired upon by skirmishers. Benton's men pressed on and burst through a fringe of wood and out into a cornfield. Four hundred yards away they saw a long line of parapets with Rebel battle flags hanging limply above them in the still morning air.

CONFEDERATE PERSPECTIVE

When Pemberton reached his headquarters in Bovina about 2100 on the evening of 16 May,[9] he was faced with a series of agonizing decisions. The first and most immediate was how long to attempt to defend the fortified bridgehead on the east bank of the Big Black River at Big Black Bridge. He clearly had to defend it for a time, because he knew that the Army of Vicksburg was retreating westward from the field of Champion Hill, and the shattered units would need time to cross the river, as well as a period of quiet, once across, to rest and reorganize. With that in mind, as he passed through the *tête-de-pont* (fortified bridgehead) on the way to Bovina, he ordered BG Vaughn, whose East Tennessee brigade already was in the fortified bridgehead, to man the lines and to move all the wagons to the west bank, thus clearing the area for defense.[10] He also left word that Bowen was to assume command of the bridgehead as soon as he arrived on the scene.

Pemberton's second problem was whether to retreat immediately to the fortified lines at Vicksburg, or to attempt to hold the crossings of the Big Black River. To some degree, the decision rested on the condition of his troops. He knew that Barton's and Cumming's BDEs of Carter Stevenson's DIV had been so punished at Champion Hill that they would be essentially useless for at least several days. However, Lee's BDE of Stevenson's DIV, while very tired and battered, was still intact and would be ready for action after a brief rest. And Bowen's two brigades, even though roughly handled at Champion Hill, were still intact and probably could be depended upon. Loring's DIV of three brigades hardly had been touched, and Pemberton confidently expected it to move into the Big Black *tête-de-pont* in fighting trim during the early morning hours of 17 May. Vaughn's BDE already was deployed in the bridgehead. Furthermore, Baldwin's BDE of Forney's DIV had moved forward from Vicksburg to Bovina during 16 May, so it, too, was available for employment. He thus had eight infantry brigades fit for combat and in position to defend the river.

Champion Hill had been a salutary lesson, however, and Pemberton now realized that Grant had no hesitancy about dividing his army and advancing on multiple fronts. This almost certainly meant that he would attempt to force crossings simultaneously at several places. The practical implication of this was that powerful forces would have to be placed opposite all the viable crossings. There were a lot of them, including Baldwin's Ferry, the Big Black Bridge itself, Hooker's Ferry, Coaker's Ferry, and Bridgeport. In fact, it was even possible that Grant might strike at Messenger's Ford or Jones' Ford, still farther upstream from Bridgeport, because good roads connected them with Edwards. In effect, Pemberton had one brigade for each potential crossing site.

The difficulty, of course, was that Grant undoubtedly would concentrate on one or two or three of them. Pemberton no longer had any scouting forces on the eastern bank of the Big Black, so there was no way of knowing where the Yankee forces would assemble. One brigade never would be able to hold the river against a whole Union corps. Furthermore, he could not defend the crossings by establishing a large force at a central position and moving it laterally to any threatened point, because there were no roads paralleling the river on the west bank that were capable of supporting rapid movement. Thus, despite the obvious advantages of holding the river line as long as possible, Pemberton reluctantly decided that it was impractical for him to do so. He would hold the Big Black Bridge *tête-de-pont* until all the troops who had fought at Champion Hill were safely across, and then he would retreat into Vicksburg.

Even that decision was only the beginning. The larger issue was whether to hold Vicksburg itself. Once the Army of the Tennessee was across the Big Black River, nothing Pemberton could do would prevent it from reestablishing contact with the Federal navy, and that meant the certain investment of the city. If, for some unimaginable reason, Joe Johnston could not assemble a force to break the siege that would ensue, Vicksburg, the Vicksburg army, and the Mississippi River would be lost. Pemberton was quite aware that, in such a situation, military wisdom demanded that the army be saved. Furthermore, it could be done readily; he could abandon Vicksburg and retreat northward up the Mechanicsburg Corridor toward Yazoo City, without ever taking the main army into the city. There were a number of advantages, including the fact that most of his commissary supplies came from the Delta, so he actually would be shortening—and protecting—his supply line. In addition, the terrain in that direction was well suited for defense, which meant that Grant's forces could be held off until a junction could be effected with Johnston's army somewhere northeast of Vicksburg. In theory, the combined armies then could take the offensive, defeat the Army of the Tennessee, and retake Vicksburg.

Against these obvious advantages was the fact that Pemberton had received unequivocal orders from President Jefferson Davis to defend Vicksburg at all costs. In the face of such an order, Pemberton believed he had no choice but to withdraw inside the fortified lines and hold the place until he was relieved. Perhaps even more important was the fear that even the combined forces of the Jackson and Vicksburg armies would be unable to retake Vicksburg, once the Yankees were established within its fortified perimeter. After all, the Confederacy would not be able actually to besiege the place, because Porter's ironclads still would control the river, and the Federal transport fleet would be able to bring in unlimited supplies and reinforcements. On balance, the only practical decision was to hold Vicksburg at all costs and to depend upon Johnston and the Confederacy to break the inevitable siege.

Pemberton also had a purely personal problem with any proposal to abandon Vicksburg. Earlier in the war, while he had commanded the Department of South Carolina, Georgia and Florida, it had become increasingly obvious that the Yankees were getting set to lay siege to Charleston, SC. Pemberton had stated publicly that, in the event Charleston were besieged, the army should be evacuated to save the troops, even if that meant losing the city.[11] The public outcry at such heresy was intense. Pemberton was reluctant to subject himself to a replay of that scenario.

Lee's, Barton's, and Cumming's BDEs of Stevenson's DIV began to arrive in the fortified lines east of the Big Black Bridge about 2200 on the evening of 16 May. Pemberton ordered them to cross the river and march on to Mt. Alban, another five miles west of Big Black Bridge, but they were so exhausted and disorganized that they were forced to halt and camp in the fields around Bovina.[12] Bowen and his two Trans-Mississippi brigades arrived in the bridgehead about midnight, with their formations intact. Bowen immediately assumed command, as Pemberton had ordered.[13] Additional small groups trickled in during the remainder of the night, but even those dwindled to nothing by 0500 on the morning of 17 May. There was no sign of Loring. Pemberton was worried but not unduly so, because Loring had a habit of not reporting to his commanding general. Pemberton assumed that he was retreating slowly in the face of the enemy, preventing the latter from gobbling up the many Confederate stragglers. He had little choice, therefore, but to hold the bridgehead until Loring arrived.[14]

Pemberton was more concerned over the fate of the army's supply train. There had been no word of it since sending it off under the guard of A. W. Reynolds's brigade before the Battle of Champion Hill. As far as Pemberton knew, it had moved out the Brownsville Road from Edwards, and it might still be there. If so, it had been lost, and that would be a serious blow indeed. However, during the early morning of 17 May, word came in from Reynolds that the train had safely crossed the Big Black at Bridgeport and even now was en route to Vicksburg via the Bridgeport Road. Furthermore, after the wagons had crossed, Reynolds had been clever enough to destroy the floating bridge and leave a picket on the west bank to discourage the Yankees from attempting a crossing there. This meant not only that the wagons were safe, but also that another combat-ready infantry brigade, Reynolds's, was available for duty. It still was not enough to warrant an attempt to hold the line of the river, however, so Pemberton let Reynolds continue on toward Vicksburg, where his troops soon would be needed to man the defense lines.

29

Rout in the Bridgehead 17 May 1863

Maps: 16. The Battlefield of Big Black Bridge
       17. The Northeastern Approaches to Vicksburg
       57. The Battle of Big Black Bridge, 1030, 17 May 1863

GEOGRAPHIC CONTEXT

The floodplain east of the Big Black Bridge was mostly very flat, but several shallow bayous crossed it, running generally north and south. One of these originated about 200 yards south of the railroad and flowed north, passing under the railroad embankment about 1,700 yards east of Big Black Bridge. From this point, the bayou continued on to the north, to discharge at last into the river about 1,000 yards north of the railroad. North of the railroad, it was filled with waist-deep water, in which grew many of the bald cypress and tupelo trees ubiquitous in the floodplain swamps and bayous of Mississippi. South of the railroad, the bayou quickly faded into a broad, gentle swale, boggy but free of standing water, which at last terminated against a low natural levee bordering Gin Lake, 800 yards to the southwest. Pemberton's brilliant young chief engineer, MAJ Lockett, who had designed and constructed the fortifications guarding the eastern approaches to Big Black Bridge, had used this bayou and swale as a moat fronting a sturdy line of breastworks. The soil was so difficult to work that the breastworks were constructed mostly of cotton bales and large logs.

South of the railroad, the fields in front of the defensive line were open and under cultivation for well over a mile to the east. North of the railroad, however, the field was open for only about 400 yards in front of the works. Beyond that was a dense patch of timber. Lockett had assumed that any serious attack necessarily would be supported by artillery. Because the woods north of the railroad were so thick as to prevent its deployment, all serious assaults would come across the open fields south of the railroad. Accordingly, he had pierced the breastworks for cannon in this sector; but, north of the railroad, where he believed an artillery attack to be impractical, no provisions were made for guns. However, as an added defense against infantry assault, he had ordered all the trees in the bayou cut down to form an abatis.

At the extreme northern end of the line, near where it ended against the Big Black River, Lockett had constructed a detached line of breastworks on the east side of the fronting bayou, angled so that fire from the parapet would enfilade a line assaulting the main line behind the bayou. The detached work was barely large enough to hold a regiment.

Lockett was quite concerned about the fact that the narrow railroad bridge would be inadequate to support the crossing of large numbers of troops, wagons, and artillery. However, a small steamboat, *Dot,* had been trapped in the Big Black by the fall of Grand Gulf, and Lockett discovered that she was just about as long as the river was wide. He moored her across the stream at the Jackson Road ferry crossing, about 350 yards below the railroad bridge; ripped out her machinery; planked her decks; and converted her into a highly effective floating bridge.[1]

FEDERAL PERSPECTIVE

When Carr's advance guard was fired upon from the woods near the Smith house on the Jackson Road, Carr rode forward in the growing light of early morning to see if the opposition was serious. The Rebel pickets gave ground so readily under pressure from Carr's skirmishers that the advance scarcely slowed and in a few moments arrived at the western edge of the trees. Where it halted abruptly. Only 400 yards away, a strong line of breastworks blocked the path to the west, extending north and south as far as the eye could see. So the rumors were correct: Big Black Bridge indeed was fortified.

Carr immediately deployed Benton's BDE in a line just inside the woods north of the road and sent Lawler and his brigade to continue the line to the north. The movements were slow and halting, because the woods were so thick that even infantry passage was difficult, and artillery movement impossible. As a result, all the Federal batteries were deployed south of the road in the open fields.[2] Soon Osterhaus, McClernand, and Grant arrived on the scene. Osterhaus deployed his division in the open fields south of the railroad and moved forward to within about 300 yards of the Confederate lines, at which point the Rebel artillery began to take their toll, so Osterhaus ordered his men to lie down and wait for further orders.[3]

Grant was impressed by the strength of the works, but he thought that his men, emboldened by the victory at Champion Hill, would have little trouble taking them. He nonetheless felt it unwise to put all his eggs in one basket, so he sent a message to Sherman, ordering him to force a crossing at Bridgeport with all possible dispatch, even though he hoped that McClernand's troops could overrun the fortifications so quickly that they would be able to capture Big Black Bridge before it could be destroyed.[4]

The answer to the breastworks was artillery, and most of the guns of both Carr's and Osterhaus's DIVs, some twenty-two in all, soon were in action. Because of the dense woods north of the road, most of them had been forced to deploy south of the road in the open fields, and all their fire was directed at the Confederate breastworks opposite them. There was not room for all of them, and one enterprising commander of a section of 20-pdr Parrott rifles looked about for an alternative position. He soon discovered a little farm trail through the dense woods north of the railroad. With a little work, he could get his guns through it. Soon they were at work knocking holes in the cotton-bale-and-log breastworks beyond a narrow bayou only 400 yards away.[5]

BG Michael K. Lawler, who commanded the right-flank brigade of the Union deployment, looked across the 400-yard gap between the trees and the Rebel breastwork with considerable apprehension; it was going to be a bloody business to storm that line with only two pieces of artillery for support. Then, like the answer to a prayer, some of Lawler's scouts came in and said that there was a little depression in the floodplain scarcely a stone's throw from the Confederate works near the north end of the line; it offered a sheltered approach to the center of the Rebel line north of the railroad. Mountainous Lawler (he stood six feet, three inches tall and weighed 250 pounds) saw this as a golden opportunity and asked Carr, his division commander, for authority to assault. Carr told him to go ahead.

Lawler got his men all set just inside the tree line and then moved his entire brigade in a single quick rush across the open field in full sight of the Rebels and into the meander scar, where the men were sheltered and concealed. Here he took his time getting everything organized. To his gratification, the two 20-pdr Parrotts seemed to be right on target, chewing up the Rebel parapet in fine fashion. It was now approaching 0900.

Lawler was so close to the Confederate lines that he could see the regimental battle flags. He realized that he was only slightly north of the junction between Green's troops, who had been mauled at Champion Hill, and Vaughn's East Tennesseeans. East Tennessee was deeply pro-Union, and it was likely that many of the men in Vaughn's brigade had been drafted into the Rebel army against their will. Thus there was a chance that they would not fight very hard for the Confederacy. He could hardly have hoped for more.

Then, on signal, he launched his brigade in one massive column directly at the juncture between Green and Vaughn.[6] He was so close that the startled Southerners had time for only one volley, and then the bayonet-tipped blue wave had stormed across the waist-deep moat, over the parapets, and into the thin line of Confederates behind it. Many of the Rebels turned and ran for the bridges, but many others threw down their arms and surrendered.[7] Most of Lawler's men were so overwhelmed by the number of captives that they lost momentum and stopped after a few minutes. However, the right-flank regiments turned right, kept going, and eventually captured most of the people in the detached line of riflepits near the river.[8]

Grant, from his position on the Jackson Road, watched in complete fascination. The moment Lawler's incredible charge broke through the Confederate line, Benton's men came out of the tree line and charged across the 400 yards separating them from the Confederate works. Osterhaus's men, south of the railroad, saw their comrades north of the railroad dash forward, and they in turn sprang to their feet and drove forward. Thus it was that, within a minute or two of the initial breakthrough, the entire line of breastworks was in Union hands. Scarcely a shot had been fired at anybody except Lawler and his men.[9]

Like Lawler, Benton and Osterhaus were unprepared for the number of prisoners and the chaos they found inside the fortified lines. They halted to dress lines and sort out commands before starting westward in pursuit. In the interval, most of the Confederates who had escaped immediate capture fled to the west bank.[10] As the first Union regiments approached the east bank, the Big Black Bridge burst into flames and soon collapsed into the river. There were solid lines of butternut infantry on the top of the bluffs beyond the river, and a couple of big 24-pdr guns began to fire into the exposed Union formations.[11]

McClernand ordered his men back out of danger, and he and Grant watched sadly as both the railroad bridge and a little steamboat the Confederates had been using as an expedient bridge were consumed by flames. It was obvious to Grant that he was not going to cross at Big Black Bridge without a serious fight. He sighed and turned to other devices.[12]

CONFEDERATE PERSPECTIVE

As soon as Bowen entered the fortified bridgehead in the predawn dimness of 17 May, he was handed Pemberton's order to hold the position only until Loring had passed through the lines, after which he was free to evacuate as he saw fit.[13] Bowen was unhappy about being placed in command and displeased with what he found there. The fortifications seemed sturdy enough but were too long for the number of men he had. Pemberton had ordered him to use his own two brigades and also had given him Vaughn's BDE of East Tennesseeans, plus a regiment from Baldwin's BDE—a total of perhaps five thousand men. The line was nearly 1,800 yards long, which meant that he had something like one man for each foot of breastwork. Under ordinary circumstances, that was enough, but his men were tired and dispirited. Nor did he trust the men of Vaughn's brigade; they were essentially garrison troops, and many of them had been drafted in East Tennessee, which was widely known for its strong pro-Union political sentiments. Bowen was uncertain that they would fight hard for a political entity of which they well might disapprove.

Cockrell's BDE, which had been hurt less at Champion Hill than Green's BDE, was placed in the works south of the railroad, because that seemed the likeliest place for an attack. Bowen had eighteen guns available, and he emplaced them all south of the railroad, where they could sweep the approaches to the works out to their extreme ranges. Bowen placed Vaughn's BDE behind the breastworks extending for 500 yards north of the railroad. Green's BDE held the sector from Vaughn's left to the river. At the northern end of the line, a detached line of riflepits projected at an eccentric angle from the main works; it was separated from them by the fronting bayou. Bowen did not man these entrenchments, because he was trying to conserve manpower and because he thought that the dense woods opposite the lines north of the railroad would prevent any effective assault in that sector. Green's and Cockrell's men, tired to near exhaustion by their extraordinary exertions on Champion Hill and the long retreat into the bridgehead, lay down behind the breastworks to catch what sleep they could.

Pemberton, in Bovina, was up before dawn. He had such respect for the fighting ability of Bowen and his Trans-Mississippians that he had little fear for the safety of the fortifications east of the river. His chief immediate concern was that the Yankees would succeed in forcing a crossing either north or south of Big Black Bridge before Loring arrived. He had no hope of preventing a crossing, but he had arranged to have all of the crossings picketed, so that he would have ample warning. He also sent a dispatch off to Johnston, whose whereabouts Pemberton did not know, telling him of Champion Hill and his present situation, and asking for orders.[14]

At dawn, about 0530, the sound of artillery rolled in from the east, and Pemberton knew that the Yankees had arrived ahead of Loring. He had no idea where Loring was, but he thought it likely that he and his division had withdrawn to the south and perhaps would cross the Big Black River at Baldwin's Ferry or Hall's Ferry. There was thus reason to believe that he soon would rejoin; to that end, there was merit in defending the line of the Big Black as long as possible. His only hope now was that Bowen would beat off the initial attacks, after which the bridgehead could perhaps be evacuated without serious loss.

In the bridgehead, Bowen had sent pickets out into the predawn darkness to take positions well forward of the fortified line. Just before full light, a few minutes after 0500, he heard the crackle of rifle fire to the east and knew that the Yankees had arrived. Within an amazingly short time, bluecoated infantry in seemingly limitless numbers had deployed across the entire front. About 0530, the deadly Federal artillery, which Bowen had learned to respect at Champion Hill, unlimbered and went into action from near the railroad. To Bowen's surprise and dismay, the damned Yankees were deploying large forces in the woods north of the railroad. He had not expected that, because he, like Lockett, had thought that the only practical route for an assault was the open fields south of the railroad embankment. Not that the Yankees were ignoring those fields; by 0600, at least a division of Federal infantry was deployed there.

About this time, Lockett visited the fortified lines and was appalled by the poor morale of the troops behind the breastworks. He sent a courier to Pemberton, telling him that he feared the bridgehead could not be held and asking for permission to prepare both the railroad bridge and the makeshift floating bridge for destruction. When Pemberton's concurrence arrived, Lockett immediately loaded both bridge and poor little *Dot* with flammables, so that they could be burned on short notice.[15]

Soon more Union artillery came up, and the Federal infantry lines inched closer. Against all expectations, much of the activity was out on the north end of the line, next to the river. Somehow the Yankees even managed to get a couple of 20-pdr Parrott rifles through the "impassable" woods and promptly began to knock holes in the laboriously constructed parapets. Bowen hastily detached a regiment to occupy the outwork beyond the fronting bayou, hoping to discourage the attack that seemed to be building in that quarter. About 0800, what seemed to be a whole Yankee brigade suddenly burst out of the trees on the extreme northern end of the line. The regiment in the detached work opened fire but had time for only a round or two before the bluecoats vanished into a gentle swale between the lines. They did not emerge. It was uncanny.

For about an hour, nothing much happened. Then, suddenly, at 0900, the brigade of Union infantry that had hidden in the swale near the northern end of the line suddenly emerged in a solid column, aiming directly at the junction between Vaughn's and Green's brigades. There was time for only a single volley before the bayonet-tipped column smashed across the fronting bayou and over the breastworks.[16]

South of the railroad, Cockrell's attention had been distracted by some Union movements in front of his lines, but when he heard the sudden crescendo of noise from the north, he leaped to the top of the railroad embankment just in time to see the blue wave strike the junction between Green's Arkansans and Vaughn's East Tennesseeans. The Confederate line shattered like glass before a hammer blow. This was too much even for iron-souled Cockrell and his Missourians; as one man, they turned and sprinted for the bridges.[17] Green's men, north of the breakthrough, held for a moment, until the right-flank Federal regiments changed front and drove into their open flank. Then his men, too, headed for the bridges. The regiment in the line of detached breastworks was enveloped by the Union advance. Some men were captured, and many tried to swim the river to safety. Some few made it.[18]

When Pemberton received Lockett's message from the bridgehead, asking for permission to prepare the bridges for quick destruction, he tried to find some means of reinforcing his forces east of the river. Stevenson's three brigades had not yet left their camps at Bovina, but Pemberton knew that only Lee's BDE, which had fought so long and valiantly at Champion Hill, was in any shape to fight, so he told Lee to take his brigade to the bridgehead as quickly as he could get the men on the road.[19]

Lockett was so worried about the bridgehead that he watched the developing situation from the bluffs on the west bank and thus saw the Confederate army in the bridgehead dissolve into a fleeing mass of fugitives. For a moment, it looked as if the Yankees might sweep across on the heels of the rout. At that moment, however, Lee's BDE arrived on the bluffs, and Lockett realized that, together, Lee and Baldwin very likely would be able to hold the west bank. And so it developed. The rout flowed over the river to safety, and Lockett fired both bridge and steamboat after almost every straggler had passed.[20]

Somewhat to Lockett's surprise, the Yankees made no effort to force an immediate crossing. Pemberton arrived at the top of the bluff overlooking the flaming bridges and for a few moments toyed with the idea of holding the line of the Big Black River. However, reason prevailed. He could see Bowen's hitherto unshakable Trans-Mississippians flowing past in rout and concluded that not even they could be depended upon to fight again until they had been given time to rest and refit. That left him with Lee's and Baldwin's BDEs, and they were so few that he would have scarcely a regiment for each potential crossing site. It was only too obvious that a single regiment would not be able to hold for more than a few moments. Sadly, Pemberton ordered the remnants of the army back to Vicksburg, placing Carter Stevenson in command of the retreat.[21] Indeed, to call it a retreat dignified the movement; all who saw it characterized it as a rout.

30

Johnston after the Battle of Jackson 14 May–20 May 1863

Map: 13. The Region between Edwards, Canton, and Jackson

From just north of Tougaloo on 15 May, GEN Joseph Johnston peremptorily ordered Pemberton to meet him at Clinton. Having set that train in motion, his obvious responsibility was to render all possible aid to his subordinate. He had few resources. At the time of the fall of Jackson on 14 May, reinforcements were on their way to Johnston, albeit not very many. Gist's BDE, which at the time of the battle had reached Brandon, only fourteen road miles east of Jackson, hastily was withdrawn to Forest, forty-five miles east of Jackson.[1] Maxey's BDE, which was moving up the New Orleans, Jackson & Great Northern Railroad from Port Hudson, quickly was withdrawn to Brookhaven, fifty-five miles south of Jackson.[2] These forces totaled perhaps six thousand men.

The center of Jackson was a smoking ruin. The railroads had been destroyed for miles in all directions; the bridges across the Pearl River had been burned; the food stocks in the city had been either removed for use by Johnston's army, seized by Sherman's people for their own use, or destroyed; and the surplus food in the larders of the farms to the west had been stripped by Union foragers. In fact, the lack of food in the Jackson area was so severe that, during the ensuing weeks, Johnston's major source of commissary supplies was the fertile Delta west of the Yazoo River.

Because the reinforcements which were to have arrived within the next twenty-four hours had been forced away, there was no real hope of any effective additions to Johnston's manpower for at least several days. Accordingly, he would have to do the best he could with the six thousand men he had. He could have remained at Tougaloo on 14 and 15 May, because the Federals had lost interest in him, once he had been pushed out of Jackson; but instead, on 15 May, he retreated to Calhoun, another ten miles to the northeast.[3] Had he remained in Tougaloo until time to march for the rendezvous at Clinton, Gregg's men would have had an easy march of only twelve miles. The move to Calhoun, which added another ten miles, made the trip to Clinton a hard day's march, rather than an easy one.

It has been suggested that the reason for the removal to the north was the shortage of food in the Jackson area, and that the move was intended to shorten the distance to Johnston's only real source of commissary supplies, the Delta region west of Yazoo City. However, those supplies arrived in his camps by railroad from the north, and the railroad and telegraph were intact north of Tougaloo. It is difficult to believe that an additional ten miles of distance on the railroad would have made any significant difference.

Johnston and his army rested at Calhoun all day on 16 May.[4] There was no notable sense of urgency. Johnston knew by the evening of 15 May that the Army of the Tennessee had evacuated Jackson on that day, because Wirt Adams's cavalry patrols had skirmished with the rear guard as it was leaving the city.[5] Even had he chosen to avoid Jackson, he could have marched to Clinton via the direct Ridgeland–Clinton road on 16 May, a distance of about thirty road miles. That is a very long day's march for an army under even the best of circumstances.

By this time, Johnston surely must have known that it took at least twelve hours for a courier to reach Pemberton. So Johnston could have hypothesized a timeline something like this:

> 0900, 15 May. Johnston sends dispatch from Tougaloo.
> 2100, 15 May. Dispatch arrives in Pemberton's hands.
> 0500, 16 May. Pemberton begins march to Clinton.
> 1900, 16 May. Pemberton reaches Clinton, assuming perfect marching conditions and no trouble; if conditions were less than perfect, he might only be on the road somewhere north of Bolton.

In any event, to reach the rendezvous at roughly the same time as Pemberton, Johnston should have left Calhoun not later than 0500 on 16 May. Instead, he and his army spent the day quietly resting in the shade.

On the evening of 16 May, a courier from Pemberton rode in with a dispatch Pemberton had written at Mrs. Ellison's plantation, five miles east of Edwards on the Raymond Road, on the morning of 16 May.[6] It had taken the courier more than twelve hours to make the journey. The letter told Johnston where Pemberton was located, what the current situation was, and that the Army of Vicksburg was going to march immediately for Clinton, giving as a proposed line of march the route from Edwards to Queen's Hill Church to Mount Olive Church and so into Clinton from the northwest. The road distance is about twenty-six miles, or a bit more than a day of hard marching. In other words, had Pemberton started on time, he would have been expected to arrive in Clinton either very late on 16 May or, much more likely, around noon on 17 May. Johnston received Pemberton's message only a few hours earlier than Pemberton's earliest practical arrival time in Clinton; so, to keep the rendezvous, he should have had Gregg's men on the road within the hour, for an all-night forced march.

Johnston did not order Gregg to march until the following morning, 17 May. Even worse, for reasons known only to himself, he planned to march to Clinton via Livingston and Cheatham's plantation, a distance of thirty miles. Under ideal conditions, such a march could be expected to take well over a day, which means that he could not have hoped to arrive at Clinton until midmorning on 18 May, at the very earliest. Had Pemberton been able to follow his proposed plan, he would have been cooling his heels in Clinton for something like twenty-four hours before Johnston's force arrived! Had the Yankees been in Clinton, they would have been offered an ideal opportunity to defeat the Confederates in detail, even had Johnston's army already been en route. Which, of course, it was not.

Johnston did finally move as planned on 17 May, but once again there was no sense of urgency. The army got as far as Cheatham's plantation, only eighteen miles from Calhoun and twelve miles short of Clinton.[7] Late that evening, a courier from Pemberton arrived at Johnston's headquarters at Cheatham's plantation, with a letter which the Pennsylvanian had written that morning from Bovina, reporting the devastating defeat at Champion Hill. A little later, two local citizens came into camp with the news that the *tête-de-pont* at Big Black Bridge had been crushed and that the Vicksburg army had retreated in disorder toward Vicksburg.[8]

There now was not much Johnston could do. He knew that President Davis had ordered Pemberton to hold Vicksburg at any cost, but his own inclination was to let the city go and save the army. Because every moment would count if that were to be done, he hastily wrote to Pemberton, directing him to abandon the city and escape to the northeast with his army while there was yet time.[9] His stated intention was to cross the Big Black River at Kibbey's Ferry and meet Pemberton and the Vicksburg army at Mechanicsburg. The next morning, 18 May, Johnston ordered Gregg to move to Vernon, five miles north of Cheatham's plantation, as the first step of this plan. He, however, remained behind at Cheatham's. The owners were close personal friends.

Again, Johnston's lack of urgency seems strange. The order directing Pemberton to evacuate Vicksburg and march toward Mechanicsburg was sent during the early evening of 17 May and could not possibly have gotten to Pemberton in less than ten or twelve hours. Assuming that Pemberton received it on the morning of 18 May, he perhaps could have gotten his tired and dispirited men on the road by late that evening, but more likely it would have been the following morning, 19 May. It is more than thirty road miles from Vicksburg to Mechanicsburg, which means that the Vicksburg army could not possibly have arrived before the afternoon of 20 May. The twenty-two miles from Cheatham's plantation to Mechanicsburg via Kibbey's Ferry almost surely would have required an elapsed time of at least a day and a half, considering the delays that inevitably would have developed in getting his troops across the Big Black River on a ferry that was intended for farm wagons, not the transport of an army. In other words, had Johnston ordered Gregg to march for Mechanicsburg with all possible speed on the morning of 18 May, he perhaps could have arrived at the rendezvous on the afternoon of 19 May, something like twenty-four hours before Pemberton could be expected. That would have given him time to select, prepare, and occupy a position from which to beat off a Federal pursuit, should one be following Pemberton closely. Instead, Gregg and the army moved a bare five miles on 18 May.

On the afternoon of 18 May, another courier found Johnston at Cheatham's and gave him a message that Pemberton had written from inside Vicksburg on 17 May. From the context, Johnston realized that he had not yet received the order to evacuate. There was nothing he could do except hope that, when the message did arrive, Pemberton would heed it, and that the Yankees would be so dilatory in investing the city as to allow him to escape. Johnston then rode north to join Gregg at Vernon, but Johnston did not order Gregg to move across Kibbey's Ferry in the direction of Mechanicsburg. Instead, the troops spent a quiet day in camp. It is difficult to escape the conclusion that Johnston had no intention of trying to rendezvous with the Vicksburg army.

At Vernon, on the morning of 19 May, Johnston received still another message from Pemberton, this one written from inside Vicksburg, reporting that escape was impractical because the Union already had closed all roads to the north. Again, there was nothing Johnston could do except move his army to Canton and begin the task of assembling an Army of Relief. His troops reached Canton on the following day, 20 May. Perhaps it is worth noting that Johnston's troops marched faster when going away from an enemy than when moving toward it.

What seems so remarkable about this recital is that Johnston ordered Pemberton to follow courses of action which Johnston quite obviously had no intention of supporting. Why? To what end? What could the Confederacy possibly gain from such a course of action? What could Johnston hope to gain?

31

Across the Final Barrier
17 May–18 May 1863

Maps: 8. The Defenses of Vicksburg
     16. The Battlefield of Big Black Bridge
     17. The Northeastern Approaches to Vicksburg

GEOGRAPHIC CONTEXT

The Big Black River between Messenger's Ford and the Mississippi River flows in an alluvial valley. There is no rock at the surface or in the bed of the river. The sediments of the floodplain are mostly soft clays, silts, and very fine sand, so the bed and banks are quite unstable and relatively soft. The channel is only 40–70 yards wide; but at low-water stages, the banks are very steep and 20 or more feet high. The water level is subject to very rapid and, in 1863, unpredictable changes.

All of these factors made it very difficult to build a conventional trestle bridge—i.e., one made of wooden pilings for piers and wooden beams and stringers supporting the roadway. Such a bridge was even more difficult to maintain, because it tended to wash away during the first freshet. The normal seasonal change in water level was about 30 feet, so a low-level trestle bridge built at low-water stage had no chance whatever of surviving through the first flash flood. For this reason, most of the highway crossings were either ferries or floating bridges. The railroad, of course, required a permanent bridge, and it was constructed by sinking masonry foundations very deeply into the riverbed and raising the superstructure well above flood level.

FEDERAL PERSPECTIVE

As Grant watched the burning Big Black Bridge late on the morning of 17 May, he assumed that the Confederates would defend the crossing until forced out of it. The terrain was so favorable to the defense, with that big bluff on the west bank looming over the river, that Grant decided it was senseless to waste manpower trying to force a crossing at that point, as long as other alternatives were available. He had two ready at hand. Two divisions of the XVII Corps were at Amsterdam, and there were known to be ferry crossings in the vicinity, so he sent a message to McPherson to seek them out and build bridges as quickly as possible.[1] The second string on his bow was Sherman, who already had been ordered to Bridgeport. No doubt Sherman's man Blair was already there with the army's pontoon train. If the crossing were not seriously defended, Sherman could be counted on to get across without delay. Since the action was going to be in the Amsterdam-Bridgeport area, Grant decided to go there and watch the proceedings. But first he ordered McClernand to do his best to construct a bridge near the burned railroad bridge. Grant intended this exercise more as a diversion than as a serious attempt to cross the river.[2]

Late that afternoon, Grant left the captured bridgehead and rode back to join Sherman at Bridgeport. As he approached Amsterdam, he found Ransom's BDE busy at work building a bridge at Hooker's Ferry, 1.6 miles downstream from Amsterdam, and Sanborn's BDE equally busy on a bridge at Coaker's Ferry, only about a half-mile above the hamlet.[3] McPherson confidently expected both to be finished by nightfall, and he already had patrols on the far bank. The Big Black River was not going to be a serious barrier.

When he arrived at Bridgeport just before dark, Grant found his red-bearded friend Sherman contemplating a pontoon bridge already completed across the stream. To his complete satisfaction, Blair's DIV was already across and out of sight on the road to Vicksburg, and Steele's DIV was getting ready to cross.[4] As a precaution against getting beyond ready supporting distance, Sherman had told Blair to stop for the night two miles west of the river, at the farm of Mr. Brooks. Steele would camp for the night on the west bank, with Tuttle remaining on the east bank until morning.[5] As Grant and Sherman sat companionably on a log watching Steele's men cross the bridge by flaring torchlight, Grant reflected that, in another day or two at the most, he almost certainly would be back in touch with RADM Porter and the Mississippi River, the ultimate lifeline to his sources of supply in the North.

Next morning, 18 May, Grant crossed with Tuttle and started up the Bridgeport Road toward Vicksburg, trailing Blair's and Steele's DIVs.[6] Blair and Sherman were marching with Giles Smith's BDE, Blair's advance guard, at 1000 when the head of the column reached the junction of the Bridgeport and Benton roads. No one had seen a Rebel soldier.

At dawn on 18 May, McPherson's engineers told him that the bridges at both Hooker's and Coaker's ferries were ready for troops to cross. The Coaker's Ferry bridge was a wonder; it used cotton bales as floats. Ransom's BDE of McArthur's DIV, accompanied by McPherson, led the way across the river and northwestward up a miserable plantation road, scarcely more than a pair of wheel tracks. The XVII Corps followed Ransom up the road, except for Sanborn's BDE of Quinby's DIV (it had been Crocker's DIV until late the previous day), which was charged with guarding the bridges. Four miles from the river, Ransom and McPherson came to a road junction near the Flowers plantation, only to find the crossroad jammed with Sherman's troops. McPherson's men complained bitterly of the injustice of it all, grumbling that the XV Corps had trailed behind during the whole infernal campaign, and now they were going to have the honor of being first at Vicksburg! The men on the road turned out to be of Tuttle's DIV, and there was nothing to do but wait until they had passed. Not until late morning were McPherson and Ransom able to resume their march toward Vicksburg.[7]

The day was blindingly hot and chokingly dry. Sherman's infantry, artillery, and wagon train converted the Bridgeport Road into ankle-deep dust, which rose in suffocating clouds. Intervals opened between units in order to allow the dust to settle, and this delayed progress, so it was almost dark by the time the head of McPherson's column reached the junction of the Bridgeport and Jackson roads.[8] The soldiers had been listening to the rumble of artillery for more than an hour, so they knew that Vicksburg was close at hand and that Sherman's men indeed had been first.

Meanwhile, back at the Big Black Bridge, McClernand's engineers did not take kindly to the notion that they were building a bridge as a diversion. It reflected upon their honor. They figured that they could build one despite the presence on the west bank of a lot of pesky Johnnies with rifles. They found a suitable site about 150 yards above the ruined railroad bridge and started to work on a raft bridge. It was hard and dangerous work, and little was accomplished amid a continual rain of sniper fire. At last night fell, and work then progressed more rapidly, but the Rebel snipers remained a damned nuisance. Suddenly, about midnight, the galling fire stopped, and McClernand's engineers went to work in earnest. By dawn, 18 May, the bridge was finished, and Burbridge's BDE of A. J. Smith's DIV stormed across.[9] The men found not a soul. By 0900, A. J. Smith's DIV was well west of Bovina, with Osterhaus's DIV and Benton's BDE of Carr's DIV following close behind. Lawler, the hero of the Battle of the Bridgehead, was left behind to guard the bridge.[10]

CONFEDERATE PERSPECTIVE

After the debacle at the Big Black Bridge, Pemberton left Carter Stevenson in charge of the withdrawal into the Vicksburg defenses. Stevenson's first act was to order the three remaining regiments of Baldwin's BDE (the fourth had been sent across to reinforce Bowen earlier and had been caught in the debacle), which had remained on the west bank and therefore had been untouched by the catastrophe in the bridgehead, to hold the west bank at all costs, to give the shattered army time to reach the safety of the Vicksburg defenses.[11]

With the evidence of rout all around him,[12] Pemberton at first despaired of holding the city, but he nevertheless was determined to do what he could. When he arrived in Vicksburg early in the afternoon of 17 May, he went directly to Forney's headquarters, where his first action was to write to GEN Johnston, telling him dispassionately of the events at Big Black Bridge and informing him that the shattered army at that moment was fleeing toward Vicksburg.[13] His next act was to marshal what he had. As he reflected on the matter, he realized that he was not wholly without resources.[14] Of course, he would have to evacuate Warrenton and Snyder's Bluff; otherwise, they would be cut off and captured. In any event, the troops in the outlying fortifications would be required to augment the garrison of the city. They had been untouched by defeat and would be reliable.

To Hébert at Snyder's Bluff and Moore at Warrenton went orders to evacuate their positions, spike the big guns, and bring their brigades and everything edible from the countryside into Vicksburg.[15] Shoup's BDE already was in the city and needed only to be concentrated.[16] At about 1600, Waul and his 800-man TX Legion came in from Mt. Alban. Waul had not waited for orders; he had heard news of the disaster and knew that Pemberton would be concentrating every man to hold the city.[17]

Pemberton thought that the Federals would be following close upon the heels of his retreating troops. However, he knew that, once they were in front of the fortifications, it would take them some time to get set for an assault. He believed that, with Forney's and Martin L. Smith's four fresh brigades, he could fend off the first Federal thrusts at the city. That would give Bowen's and Stevenson's DIVs time enough to rest and recover their morale; thereafter, he felt confident that he could hold the city until the Confederate government could assemble an army to relieve it.

About 1830, Pemberton received word that Baldwin had disengaged and withdrawn from the river at Big Black Bridge. This was better news than Pemberton had hoped for, as it seemed to imply that Grant probably would not get any significant number of men across until the next morning. He would have to build a bridge, and that would take time. Even if he did not, it would not matter greatly, because Wirt Adams had reported that a powerful Yankee force was at Bridgeport. That force was unopposed, so it certainly would have a bridge completed by dawn the next day, 18 May.

Then, at dusk, the first of the routed troops began to trickle into the city. Pemberton was horrified at the spectacle, which was far worse than he had expected. This was not an army, but an armed mob. The officers were not even trying to restore order. The regiments had disintegrated, and the men simply poured down the roads into the city in a disorderly flood.[18] All Pemberton could do was establish rallying points for the various units and direct men to go to them. There they would be permitted to rest, since it clearly would be impossible to restore discipline and organization until the morning.[19] Reynolds's BDE of Stevenson's DIV, however, came in via the Bridgeport Road, still faithfully escorting the wagon train. These men had seen no action other than the skirmishing with Federal cavalry beyond the Big Black River, and, while they were tired, their organization and morale were intact. Finally, against all hope, at the tail of the wrack was one disciplined unit, Lee's sturdy Alabamans, who had fought so nobly at Champion Hill and who had guarded the Big Black Bridge with Baldwin while the rout crossed the river.

Lee confirmed the news that Baldwin had intended to hold the river line until 1800, after which he would withdraw slowly, acting as a rear guard. Much later, Baldwin and his regiments reached the city; but one of Lee's regiments, the 23 AL, turned up missing. Everybody assumed that somehow it had not gotten the word to evacuate and was still back along the river, if it hadn't been captured by the Yankees. As it turned out, the regiment had not gotten the word but was fine. COL Franklin E. Keck, the 23 AL's commander, had noticed the Federals trying to build a bridge 150 yards above the ruined railroad bridge and had done his best to discourage the efforts until midnight. Then he finally realized that the rest of the army was gone and decided to leave, too. Keck's men marched calmly and proudly into the city early the next morning, 18 May.[20]

With the arrival of Baldwin's BDE, Pemberton had six sound brigades with which to fend off the expected initial attacks the next morning. Forney's two BDEs, Hébert's and Moore's, had seen no action at all. Of Martin L. Smith's two BDEs (Shoup's and Baldwin's), only Baldwin's had seen any action, and that only the minor skirmishing after the battle at the Big Black Bridge. Reynolds's and Lee's BDEs, of Carter Stevenson's DIV, rounded out the six. Lee's men certainly had seen plenty of action, but they obviously were in good shape and completely dependable. In addition, Pemberton had Waul's TX Legion, which mustered only about 800 men but was thoroughly reliable.

The first Federal thrusts surely would come down the three roads leading into the city from the east: Baldwin's Ferry Road, the Jackson Road, and the Graveyard Road. If those points could be defended until Bowen's troops and two of Stevenson's BDEs recovered their spirit, the city certainly could be held. All Pemberton needed was a little time.

At 0030 on 19 May, Moore's BDE from Warrenton came into the lines, and Pemberton directed it immediately into the fortifications between the railroad cut and the Jackson Road. By 0500, Moore reported that he was ready for action.[21] At 0230, Hébert arrived from Snyder's Bluff and was sent to man the works from the Jackson Road to Graveyard Road. By 0830, he reported his men ready for anything.[22] Lee was sent to man the works from the railroad cut to Square Fort,[23] and Baldwin was put into the lines extending from Fort Hill westward, because Pemberton felt confident that one of Grant's first steps would be to strike for the Yazoo River, where he could reestablish communication with his supply line down the Mississippi. Thus an attack might come down the Valley Road from the north. Pemberton put his last remaining sound brigade, A. W. Reynolds's, into the lines guarding the Hall's Ferry Road. It was possible that an attack could come in from that direction, because there were roads which connected the Hall's Ferry and Jackson roads southeast of the city. Having been misled several times by Grant's tendency to use multiple columns in his advances, Pemberton was not about to make the same mistake again.

At no time during the retreat from the debacle of Big Black Bridge did Pemberton consider evacuating Vicksburg in order to save his army. In the first place, President Davis's order to defend Vicksburg had been unequivocal, and Pemberton believed he had no choice but to obey Davis's command. In the second place, his field army, which now consisted of Bowen's and Stevenson's DIVs, was so badly shattered that he believed it would disintegrate if forced to abandon Vicksburg, the city for which the men had suffered so much. Forney's and Martin Smith's DIVs had been in garrison so long that Pemberton doubted they could sustain the rigors and fatigues of a campaign of maneuver. In short, he feared that the Army of Vicksburg simply would evaporate through desertion and straggling if an attempt were made to escape. On the other hand, there was every likelihood that, resting behind the Vicksburg fortifications, even Stevenson's demoralized brigades would recover their élan, in which case Vicksburg could be held until Johnston raised an army of relief and came to the rescue.

32

Investment of Vicksburg
18 May–19 May 1863

Maps: 8. The Defenses of Vicksburg
     17. The Northeastern Approaches to Vicksburg
     18. The Vicinity of the Stockade Redan
     58. Disposition of Forces in the Northeastern Approaches to
         Vicksburg: 1600, 17 May 1863

FEDERAL PERSPECTIVE

Blair and Sherman were riding near the head of the column moving westward along the Bridgeport Road on the morning of 18 May. Blair's DIV was in the lead, with Steele's following close behind, but Tuttle's DIV was perhaps two hours away. Tuttle had left Mower's BDE behind to guard the Bridgeport pontoon bridge.[1] About 1000, a courier from the advance guard arrived with the news that it had reached the junction of the Benton and Bridgeport roads, only five miles from Vicksburg. Sherman knew that the Benton Road had connections with the defense complex at Snyder's and Drumgould's bluffs, and, fearing that a large body of Confederate troops might still be there, he decided to wait until all his men were up before proceeding.[2] He did not want an unexpected attack on his rear which might pin him against the Vicksburg defenses or cut his column in two, so, while he waited for Tuttle, he sent a powerful combat patrol out to the north on the Benton Road.

After Tuttle, with Buckland's and Matthies's BDEs, finally closed up about 1300, Blair continued cautiously down the Benton Road toward Vicksburg. Another mile brought the head of the column to the junction of the Jackson and Benton roads, but there was still no sign of Rebels.

Another thousand yards brought Blair's advance guard to the Graveyard Road junction. Still no sign of Confederates, although everybody knew the Yankees must be almost within shouting distance of Vicksburg. Giles Smith, whose BDE formed the van, was convinced that an ambush was in the offing and brought a battery of artillery forward to command the junction of the Jackson and Graveyard roads. Then he sent a regiment of infantry down each road to spring the trap.

About this time, Grant rode up to tell Sherman that, because McClernand's corps was going to advance along the Baldwin's Ferry Road, McPherson would use the Jackson Road, and Sherman was to use the Graveyard Road.[3] The patrol headed north on the Graveyard Road had gone less than 1,000 yards when at last it was fired upon by a Rebel skirmish line. Everybody breathed a sigh of relief. Sherman and Blair were astonished to discover that the earthworks forming the Vicksburg landward defenses were visible over the heads of the Rebel skirmishers. The Southerners gave ground readily enough; and, in a short while, the Union advance had reached within 800 yards of a formidable strongpoint that closed the Graveyard Road. Blair brought up a battery and put it on a knoll 900 yards from the fortifications. Thus his artillery had the honor of firing the first rounds against the landward defenses of the mighty fortress. It was about 1700.

With daylight waning, Blair moved his infantry forward and deployed Kilby Smith's BDE across the Graveyard Road, with the line extending from a point on the Long Spur about 250 yards south of the road to a point on the Northwest Spur about 100 yards northwest of the road. Giles Smith's BDE was moved forward to a position on Kilby Smith's right, so that his line extended the Federal battle line to the very end of the Northwest Spur. Ewing's BDE had moved out to the west along the North Ridge and at dawn on 19 May occupied a position that effectively extended Giles Smith's right flank still farther to the west; the deep ravine of Mint Spring Bayou, however, separated Ewing's left from Giles Smith's right.

While Blair was moving forward to envelop the Stockade Redan complex, one of Sherman's scouts reported that, at a point 900 yards northeast of the Stockade Redan, a country road led north from its intersection with Graveyard Road. This country road turned west after a short distance and seemed to head in the direction of the Yazoo River. Contact with the Yazoo and the Union navy was very high on Sherman's priority list, and he immediately ordered Steele and his division to investigate.[4] Sure enough, there was a road junction 800 yards north of the Graveyard Road, and one branch led off to the west. Another 700 yards down the west-trending road, Steele's point was fired upon by Rebels in a strong line of earthworks. Steele scratched his head; if this road led to the Yazoo, getting there might turn out to be a bit of a problem.

The ground was very broken, much like that at Port Gibson. Unlike the Port Gibson terrain, though, this ground was heavily wooded. Nevertheless, eventually Steele managed to deploy his infantry and even found a place for his artillery before sending skirmishers forward.[5] He gradually built up his skirmish line but made no attack. Sherman and Grant were attracted by the noise, but neither made any suggestions. With darkness, the firing stopped, and Steele's men slept in line of battle.[6]

Early the following morning, 19 May, Sherman's scouts told him that the road leading off from the junction 500 yards behind Steele's advance led north and then west. Sherman instantly realized that it must lead to the Rebel fortifications at Drumgould's and Snyder's bluffs, and probably to the Yazoo River. He ordered Matthies's BDE of Tuttle's DIV to explore the road to its end, just to make sure that no Confederate force pounced on his division's flank and rear while he was occupied with Vicksburg. Sherman also sent another cavalry patrol up the Benton Road, which he knew had connections with Snyder's Bluff.

A little cautious probing by Steele's skirmishers at daybreak on 19 May revealed that the earthworks to their front had been evacuated. Steele didn't know quite what to make of this, especially when he found evidence of a hasty departure, including a spiked 24-pdr siege gun. Grant and Sherman rode up while Steele was hesitating. Both urged Steele to resume the advance without delay, so that contact with the river and Admiral Porter could be established.

The cautious advance to the west was resumed, along a narrow road that was heavily wooded on both sides. Finally, about 0830, at a point about 700 yards west of the place where the road entered the earthworks, the advance guard suddenly turned a corner, and before them lay the immensity of the Mississippi Valley. Like Xenophon's Ten Thousand when they saw the Black Sea, the Yankees loosed a deep-toned roar of triumph. Back down the column ran the joyous news: "The River! The River!"[7] Grant and Sherman heard the swelling cheers and hastened forward, to stand at last on the edge of the mighty valley. Sherman turned to his commander and, in a voice rough with emotion, gave Grant his greatest tribute, an earnest admission that he had been wrong and Grant right: "Until this moment I was not certain that the campaign would succeed. But this is success, even if we never take Vicksburg!"[8]

Steele was still puzzled. Finding the Mississippi was all well and good, but where were the Confederates? For all he knew, a major portion of the Confederate forces might have withdrawn to the north, toward Yazoo City. The region in that direction had been the major source of Confederate commissary supplies, so it was all too likely that there was a large force up that way, just waiting to fall on his flank. To forestall any such event, he sent a strong combat patrol down a wagon trail leading westward, to find and block the Valley Road to Yazoo City.

He knew that the main Confederate defenses must lie somewhere to the south of him, but he had no idea how far away they were. Just to make sure that he wasn't falling into a trap, Steele detached Thayer's BDE, which had been bringing up the rear of his column, and sent it south across country to probe for the Confederate line. He then took his two remaining BDEs, Manter's and Woods's, and resumed advancing cautiously down the road to the southwest. After advancing about 1,000 yards, they found themselves on the north rim of the gorgelike valley of Mint Spring Bayou. All of the tributaries to Mint Spring Bayou enter from the north, so the northern line of bluffs is ragged and discontinuous. Not so the southern wall of the valley; Fort Hill Ridge forms an unbroken rampart more than 150 feet high along its entire length. Atop that natural wall, Steele could see a continuous line of riflepits, above which snapped the bright bunting of Rebel battle flags. The wall was only 800 yards away. Alert infantry occupied the riflepits, and cannon were poised in embrasures all along the line. Steele's advance came to an abrupt stop. He had found the main Rebel line.

In the meantime, the patrol Steele had sent out to block the Valley Road quickly discovered that the wagon trail joined the Valley Road about 2,500 yards north-northeast of Fort Hill. Not a Southerner was in sight, so the men pushed cautiously northward up the road for another 4,000 yards, where they found a road coming down out of the hills to the east. Assuming, quite properly, that this road must communicate with the Benton Road and thus offer a route into the rear of Sherman's corps, the patrol established its roadblock a few hundred yards to the north. Scouts also were sent out to the west, along the natural levee along the west side of Chickasaw Bayou, to make contact with RADM Porter and the navy.

During this time, Thayer's BDE was struggling southward in line of battle through the deep and contorted ravine of Second Branch. About noon, Grant's order for an assault on the Confederate lines at 1400 reached the men while they still were groping their way southward. Thayer was willing, but first he needed to find something to attack.

Finally, just before 1400, Thayer's scouts passed around the west end of North Ridge (it is not very high, but the crest is almost knifelike) and reached the end of the Second Branch ravine, only about 300 yards from the Confederate defense line. Unbeknownst to Thayer, Ewing's BDE of Blair's DIV was poised to assault the Stockade Redan and the 27 LA Lunette from the North Ridge, 600 yards to the east. Thayer's troops barely had time to dress their lines behind the crest of the ridge before the 1400 deadline. The soldiers looked at the escarpment across the valley with dismay; it was so steep that it could barely be climbed.

McPherson's corps had been forced to follow along behind Sherman's on the Bridgeport Road[9] and so had not reached the vicinity of Vicksburg until late afternoon on 18 May. McPherson was riding with Ransom, whose BDE led the way. Grant met the pair when they reached the junction of the Bridgeport and Jackson roads and told them that the XVII Corps was to advance the following day along the Jackson Road. In the meantime, they might as well camp where they were. Logan and Quinby camped around the road junction, but Ransom continued on down the Jackson Road until he was within 1,200 yards of the Confederate fortifications.[10] Scouts told him that there were two big earthworks guarding the Jackson Road and that riflepits went out of sight in both directions.

Meanwhile, McClernand's corps had continued its advance westward from Bovina along the Jackson Road on 18 May, with Burbridge's BDE of A. J. Smith's DIV in the lead. Shortly after 0900, Burbridge's men began to find discarded rifles, knapsacks, and other gear beside the road. Instantly they interpreted the flotsam as a sure sign of demoralization. Taking it as proof that there would be no serious opposition, Burbridge pressed on rapidly. At Mt. Alban, a courier from Grant met him with directions to follow the Baldwin's Ferry Road into the city, so the advance turned sharply south, away from the Jackson Road. Eventually, after another 2.5 miles, the men intercepted the Baldwin's Ferry Road a half-mile southeast of the Oates farm. Still no sign of Rebels. McClernand knew that he was very close to Vicksburg and, not wanting to start an engagement late in the day, halted at about 1530 in the valley of Hatcher Bayou, near the tiny community of Beechwood. Scouts followed the Baldwin's Ferry Road and shortly returned with word that, about 2.5 miles to the northwest, the way was barred by a line of fortifications stretching beyond visibility to both the north and the south.[11] The troops had reached Vicksburg but had not yet seen an enemy soldier.

Grant told Sherman that he was making no move to close the Hall's

Ferry and Warrenton roads. It was almost as if he were encouraging Pemberton to move his army out of the city to the south. In fact, it may be that Grant rather hoped this would occur; if it did, the Southern army would be trapped in a pocket formed by the Mississippi and Big Black rivers, with no realistic possibility of obtaining supplies of any kind. Pemberton then would have been forced to attack the Army of the Tennessee in an attempt to break out of the box. This would have been the reverse of Port Gibson; the Rebels would be attacking the Federals across the same kind of terrain. Grant did not expect Pemberton to swallow the bait.

CONFEDERATE PERSPECTIVE

There was no doubt in Pemberton's mind that the Federal army would move immediately to invest Vicksburg. Given the speed of the Yankees' movements over the last several days, he was certain that he had very little time. However, it seemed likely that it would take the Northern generals awhile to organize an assault, if they decided to make one, so there would be plenty of warning. Nevertheless, the first priority was to see that the fortifications were manned, however thinly. There was no point in establishing picket lines in front of the works, because any delay they could effect would be trivial. Since there was going to be a siege, every scrap of food would be important, so the second priority was to send out parties to strip the environs of the city of everything edible by either man or beast. Virtually everything in the immediate vicinity that could be eaten was brought into the city, including animals, and, by nightfall on 18 May, a large quantity of food and forage, as well as a sizable herd of cattle, had been assembled.

Late on the morning of 18 May, a food-gathering party northeast of the city was surprised by the advance guard of a Union column marching eastward along the Graveyard Road.[12] There was a bit of noisy but harmless gunfire, while the party hastily withdrew into the city at the Stockade Redan.

Baldwin, whose BDE held the outpost line north of Mint Spring Bayou, had felt from the beginning that his position was very weak. He could be supported only via the road along Indian Mound Ridge, which was a march of nearly two miles from the main Vicksburg defense line. A rapidly developing attack in force might well overrun him before aid could reach him. About 1400 on 18 May, his worst fears were realized, when a powerful Yankee force came down the road from the east.[13] He called for help, and within an hour Cockrell's Missouri BDE and four guns were on their way. They arrived in line about 1630, and that ended the immediate threat.[14]

Baldwin didn't know it, but people in high places also viewed his position as untenable. During the morning of 18 May, one of Pemberton's engineer officers toured the lines north of Mint Spring Bayou and realized that they were commanded in several places by ground that the Yankees shortly would occupy. He immediately sent a note to Pemberton recommending that Indian Mound Ridge be abandoned.[15] The note took Pemberton by surprise. He had supposed that M. L. Smith's DIV, which occupied the lines on the northern end of the defense system, occupied Lockett's line of works along Fort Hill Ridge. Now, when he discovered that Smith, without authority, had advanced his line north of Mint Spring Bayou, the Pennsylvanian immediately ordered him back to the Fort Hill Ridge line.

Pemberton was well aware that evacuation of the outer works would give the Yankees artillery positions only 600 yards from his main defense line, but he felt that the Fort Hill Ridge inherently was so strong that the Federal artillery would not pose a serious threat.[16] M. L. Smith moved stealthily out of the position north of Mint Spring Bayou at 0300 on 19 May and into the lines along Fort Hill Ridge. Shoup occupied the line from the Stockade Redan to a point about 800 yards to the west; Baldwin then filled the gap between Shoup's left and Vaughn's right, and Cockrell returned to the reserve in rear of Baldwin. Both Baldwin and Shoup found the earthworks in a ruinous state and spent the rest of the night and all the next morning frantically trying to improve them.[17]

33

First Assault on the Stockade Redan 19 May 1863

GEOGRAPHIC CONTEXT

The Graveyard Road approaches the Stockade Redan from the northeast, running atop the Graveyard Road Ridge. This ridge, almost as high as the little knoll upon which the frowning redan was built, forms the watershed between Mint Spring and Glass bayous. The Short Spur, trending south, branches off from the Graveyard Road Ridge at a point 180 yards northeast of the face of the Stockade Redan. Another ridge, the Long Spur, also trends to the south, but from a point on the Graveyard Road Ridge 350 yards from the redan. The junction of the Graveyard Road Ridge and the Long Spur is marked by a prominent knoll, from which the short Northwest Spur drops into the Mint Spring Bayou ravine. About 500 yards from the Stockade Redan, the Graveyard Road Ridge turns almost due north and continues for another 400 yards, to a point where the North Ridge, which forms the northern slope of Mint Spring Bayou, leads sinuously away to the west, at an elevation equal to that of Fort Hill Ridge. At the junction, the North Ridge also continues on to the east, with the Graveyard Road running along it for some 1,000 yards, at which point both ridge and road turn abruptly south to join the Jackson Road at a point 1,800 yards due east of the Stockade Redan. Between the redan and the road junction lies an incredible tangle of ravines, all forming the headwaters of Glass Bayou.

The ridgetops and many of the less precipitous side slopes were under cultivation and almost free of trees. Thus, there were unobstructed lines of sight across the ravine that fronted the Confederate defense line along almost its entire length. The ravine bottoms, being wet and boggy, mostly had not been cleared for cultivation, but the trees growing there all had been cut down and laced together with telegraph wire to form a dense abatis. Since the establishment of the Vicksburg National Military Park, nearly the entire area has been allowed to grow up into tall forest, so it takes an active imagination to picture the virtually bare landscape that existed in May 1863.[1]

FEDERAL PERSPECTIVE

On the afternoon of 18 May, Grant and his senior commanders were reasonably confident of being able to take Vicksburg by storm. Some of the Union officers felt that a strong show of force would be enough to induce the Rebels to throw down their arms and surrender. Grant was not so sanguine as that, but he nevertheless believed that the Southern soldiery "had been much demoralized" by the terrible defeat at Champion Hill and the debacle at Big Black Bridge, and he thought that a determined assault would simply roll right over the Rebels.

Grant was only too aware that the Southerners had a remarkable ability to recover quickly from a defeat, so he knew that time was on their side. If he waited until all his men were up, Pemberton's troops might well recover their morale and make the success of an assault at least problematical. Therefore, he determined to strike with all possible power as quickly as possible. He informed his corps commanders late on the evening of 18 May that he proposed to attack the very next day.

Shortly after daylight on 19 May, Grant had visited Sherman's position in front of the Stockade Redan complex. Thus he knew that those men were all in position, or so nearly so as to make little difference. He then moved back to Mount Ararat, on the Jackson Road about 1,000 yards southwest of the junction of the Graveyard and Jackson roads. The point was chosen not because it was the highest hill in the area, but because it was the only place from which he could see nearly the whole length of the Rebel line, from the Stockade Redan on the north to the Square Fort on the south. He could not, however, see the Union troops, since they were mostly sheltered in the valley bottoms; consequently, he had no clear idea as to where either McPherson's or McClernand's men were located. Having received no reports to the contrary, he assumed that the other two corps were, like Sherman's, in positions in close proximity to the Confederate works. On that basis, at 0900 of 19 May, he issued an order for a general attack on the Confederate works. It was to be launched at 1400 that same afternoon, and the signal would be three deliberate salvos from Sherman's artillery.[2]

All three corps spent the morning hours of 19 May moving into positions from which an assault could be launched. The terrain was terrible, very like that at Port Gibson. The ridgetops were so narrow there was little room to deploy, and deep and precipitous ravines made maneuvering very slow and difficult. Good positions for artillery were in especially short supply. McClernand and his XIII Corps had thought they were close to the Rebel lines when they stopped for the night near Beechwood on the Baldwin's Ferry Road on the night of 18 May, but in fact 3,000 very difficult yards separated them from the earthworks. Ever one for the flamboyant gesture, McClernand took his entire staff forward on the morning of 19 May for a personal reconnaissance. The group rode briskly up the long hill leading out of Hatcher Bayou bottom, to emerge at last on the crest of Durden Ridge, which rises between Hatcher Bayou and Durden Creek. From here they could see the Rebel works, but to McClernand's surprise and dismay, they were still over a mile away.[3]

McClernand could see a powerful earthwork (the 2 TX Lunette) just south of the place where the Baldwin's Ferry Road passed through the line of riflepits. A second earthwork (the Railroad Redoubt), if possible even stronger, projected from the line just south of where the railroad passed through the lines in a deep cut. Another 1,000 yards to the southwest was a third huge earthwork (Square Fort), perched upon a commanding knoll. Collectively, the three strongpoints commanded a front of about 1,400 yards, and they were connected by a continuous line of riflepits. Further, those riflepits went out of sight to both north and south.

McClernand began to move his divisions into position, albeit with no real sense of urgency, even though he had received Grant's orders for a general assault on the works that same afternoon. A. J. Smith's DIV was deployed just behind the crest of Durden Ridge, with his left flank on Baldwin's Ferry Road and his right flank on the railroad.[4] Next to arrive was Osterhaus, who deployed BG Albert Lee's BDE to extend A. J. Smith's line southward along

Durden Ridge, with his right flank on the Baldwin's Ferry Road and his left-flank regiment nearly opposite Square Fort.[5] Osterhaus kept Lindsey's BDE as a close-in reserve. Benton's BDE, of Carr's DIV, was left in march order well back along the Baldwin's Ferry Road, to act as a distant reserve. The rest of Carr's DIV was still back at Big Black Bridge, policing up the battle-field; and Hovey's DIV was on the road between Bolton and Beechwood. By the time all of McClernand's assault forces were neatly in line, it was 1000. The Rebel lines were still more than 2,000 yards away, far out of assault range. Even the artillery, which had been emplaced along Durden Ridge, was barely able to reach the Confederate lines. Nevertheless, at 1000 they opened fire. The Rebels did not deign to respond.

Osterhaus and A. J. Smith sent a skirmish line forward. After it had pushed a few Rebel snipers out of the way,[6] the infantry battle lines of the two divisions moved smoothly forward across the open valley and up the eastern face of Porter's Chapel Ridge. When they reached the crest, they were still 1,000 yards from the Confederate line, but the Rebel artillery promptly opened fire. When McClernand reached the top of the ridge, he was dismayed to discover that there was yet another ridge between his men and the enemy! While not as high as Porters Chapel Ridge, the eastern face of Two Mile Ridge was a nightmare of vicious little ravines.

At 1400, when the artillery boomed its three salvos to signal the assault, McClernand's battle line moved smoothly forward down the western side of Porters Chapel Ridge and across the creek. Instantly it broke up into tiny knots of blue-clad soldiery, each trying to find a way up through the maze of ravines on Two Mile Ridge. When the knots emerged on top, all sem-blance of a battle line had been lost. Furthermore, the line, if such it could be called, now was within easy range of the Confederate artillery, and men began to go down. The Union artillery, far away on Durden Ridge, could provide no effective counterbattery fire. There was no hope whatever of continuing the assault, and both Osterhaus and A. J. Smith withdrew their men behind the crest of Two Mile Ridge and dug in. Nightfall found them holding a line extending from about 600 yards southeast of Square Fort, across the valley of Two Mile Branch, then along Two Mile Ridge to a point about 600 yards east of the strongpoint controlling the Baldwin's Ferry Road.[7] The infantry had scarcely fired a shot; and, despite a thunderous three-hour cannonade, the artillery had yet to fire an effective round.

McPherson, with Logan's and Quinby's DIVs, had camped on the night of 18 May in the fields around the junction of the Jackson and Bridgeport roads, about 2,800 airline yards directly east of the Stockade

Redan. In response to Grant's directive to get into assault position as quickly as possible, during the morning of 19 May, Ransom's BDE of McArthur's DIV had pushed slowly westward along a huge, irregular ridge separating the North and South forks of Glass Bayou. The terrain was frightful—nothing but tangled canebrakes filling deep ravines that seemed to go nowhere.

At first light on 19 May, Blair's DIV of Sherman's XV Corps already was in close proximity to the Stockade Redan. Skirmishers moved forward, and, despite great difficulties with the treacherous ground and the abatis, soon worked their way to the base of the slopes leading up to the Rebel earthworks. They raked the parapets with sniper fire, mostly just to make the Johnnies keep their heads down. There was almost no Confederate response, which seemed a good sign.

Sherman looked at the Stockade Redan complex and did not like what he saw. The only avenue open to direct assault was straight down the Graveyard Road Ridge. Unfortunately, a force coming down that ridge would be faced not only with direct head-on fire from the parapets of the Stockade Redan, but also with flanking fire from the 27 LA and Green's lunettes. Of course, McPherson's men were supposed to take out Green's Lunette, so perhaps he did not have to worry about Rebel fire from that direction. The slopes of the hillsides leading down into the ravines both east and north of the Rebel positions were without cover of any kind. Even if resistance were only modest, the butcher's bill was going to be high.

When Sherman's order to attack arrived in Blair's headquarters a few minutes after 0900, he simply moved all his regiments forward to the crests of their respective ridges and got set. The Graveyard Road would be the axis of Kilby Smith's advance, with two regiments north of the road and three south of it. His objective was the east face of Stockade Redan. Giles Smith's five regiments were aimed at the north face of the redan. His chief difficulty was that there were only about 650 yards of ridgetop on which to deploy ten regiments, so both brigades had regiments stacked up behind each other, greatly reducing their effective volume of fire. Ewing's objective was the 27 LA Lunette. Batteries were emplaced on all three ridges during the night, the closest being only 500 yards from the exterior slope of the Stockade Redan.

At 0930, Blair's three batteries (sixteen guns) opened fire, concentrating on the scarp of the Stockade Redan. Blair hoped to collapse it into the ditch and thus form a ramp that his assaulting infantry could climb, but the guns were too small and too few to be effective. Now Blair began to worry seriously, because there had been no time to provide his men with scaling ladders or even picks and shovels.

A few minutes before 1400, Blair's artillery fell silent. Then, promptly at 1400, Blair's batteries fired three precisely timed salvos, and his infantry moved forward like a tidal wave. Instantly the parapets came alive, and a terrible storm of rifle fire began to tear at the Union soldiery. Nevertheless, Kilby Smith's left flank regiments passed through the first of two ravines separating them from the Stockade Redan without much difficulty. Then they came out on the crest of Short Spur, only 150 yards from the ditch in front of the Stockade Redan, and here a perfect storm of rifle fire swept them and forced them back to seek protection behind the ridge. Here the lines were dressed and the men encouraged to make one more valiant effort. The attack moved forward, and some few of the men actually reached and entered the ditch in front of the redan.[8]

North of the road there was no intervening ridge; instead, Kilby Smith's right-wing regiments had to advance along the side of a steep north-facing slope that dropped into the Mint Spring Bayou ravine. Here the abatis was much less dense, and the men were partly sheltered from the Rebels manning the parapets of the Stockade Redan. They were not sheltered from the fire coming from the 27 LA Lunette, however, and they found the enfilade fire very galling.[9] Nevertheless, the two regiments drove forward quickly all the way to the ditch in front of the Stockade Redan, where they were sheltered from the fire of both the redan and the lunette. Once in the ditch, they discovered that the exterior slope of the redan had been damaged only slightly by the artillery bombardment, and they were utterly unable to climb the steep slope. To go back would be suicidal, so there they stayed.

Giles Smith's objective was the north face of the Stockade Redan. He looked at the 300 yards of coverless slopes in front of him and realized that his only hope was to suppress the defensive fire until his men could reach the ditch in front of the redan. He deployed the 8 MO in a single line across the face of the ridge and ordered them to sweep the Rebel parapets with the highest possible volume of fire. Promptly at 1400, his four assault regiments moved over the crest of Northwest Spur and plunged headlong into the ravine in an all-out assault on the Stockade Redan. Despite the covering fire of the 8 MO, a dreadful hail of rifle fire thinned the ranks as they struggled and fought their way through the abatis and up the slope toward the north face of the redan.

The 1 BN of the U.S. 13 INF formed the left of Giles Smith's assault line. Despite sheets of Rebel fire, the men reached the ditch and managed to climb part of the way up the scarp before being forced back. Grim Sherman, accustomed to valor, called the performance "unparalleled in the Army." Since that day, the colors of the 13 U.S. INF flaunt the words: "First at Vicksburg." The price was dreadful; the battalion lost 43 percent of its men during that single brief afternoon.

But now the men in the ditch—Kilby Smith's on the east face, and 13 U.S. INF on the north face—were in a trap, unable to go either forward or back, while over them the storm raged on.[10]

Giles Smith's two right-flank regiments aimed their thrust at the wooden stockade connecting the Stockade Redan and the 27 LA Lunette, assuming that the artillery preparation would have battered holes through the rampart. These two regiments were not so subject to the frightful crossfire from redan and lunette as the left-wing regiments, and as a result they suffered far fewer casualties. Nevertheless, their assault carried only to within a few yards of the wooden palisade. Here they stopped, fought to a standstill by savage volleys from the 36 MS, which was firing through gaps in the upright timbers forming the stockade.[11]

Farther west, Ewing's BDE swept over the crest of North Ridge and plunged down into the Mint Spring Bayou ravine, cheering wildly. Two of the regiments struck an impenetrable section of the abatis in the valley bottom and abruptly were brought to a stop, but the other two regiments found an easy passage through the obstacles and swept up the eastern slope of Mint Spring Bayou to within a few yards of the parapet of the lunette. Here they finally were brought to a stop by a storm of musketry from the Southern defenders.[12]

Meanwhile, Ransom, of McArthur's DIV, had worked his way westward along his ridge until about 1300, when he came out on a commanding nose that overlooked the gorgelike valley of the North Fork of Glass Bayou. Only 400 yards away, on the far side of the abatis-choked ravine, he could see the Confederate earthworks.[13] He had only an hour before the time specified for the beginning of the assault. In that short period, poor Ransom had to reconnoiter the ground in front of him and make a tactical plan. In an attempt to save time, he immediately deployed his four regiments as best he could, and two of his regimental commanders mistook the deployment orders for a directive to launch their attack, so they jumped off seventeen minutes before 1400. One regiment never got through the abatis, but one of them found an easy passage and stormed the hill ahead of them, all alone in the world. The blue line actually got to within 100 yards of the Confederate riflepits before being brought to a stop.[14]

Out to the west, Thayer's regiments dressed his lines in the shelter of the tip of North Ridge, and promptly at 1400 they went surging forward. Two of the regiments went forward over the top of the tip of North Ridge, while the other two circled around the western end. The moment they reached the bottom of Mint Spring Bayou, they began receiving intense rifle fire from the Confederate lines. They crossed the bayou with a rush and took shelter in a small area of defilade at the base of the slope. Crossing even the few yards of exposed ground on the north side of Mint Spring Bayou already had cost them fifty casualties, and it seemed very clear that any attempt to climb the slope looming over their heads would result in many more. The best thing to do was to stay in the defiladed area, crowded as it was, until nightfall. After dark, Thayer quietly withdrew his men to shelter behind North Ridge.[15]

About 0930, when Steele first received the order to assault at 1400, he was on the crest of Indian Mound Ridge near the head of First Branch. He could look across the basin of First Branch and see the incredible escarpment that formed the south wall of Mint Spring Bayou, and the earthworks atop it. Sherman's assault order placed him on the horns of a dilemma. He had been ordered to find a way to the Yazoo River, and he had no idea what lay ahead of him along the ridge he was following. Moreover, now he also had to assault the line of fortifications to the south.

Steele's solution was to send Manter's BDE across country down the ravine of First Branch. Unlike much of the terrain in the environs of Vicksburg, the valley of First Branch is broad and gentle, lacking the deep and narrow ravines so common elsewhere; but it was filled with a jungle of second-growth timber and canebrakes, so movement was very slow. The best that Manter could do was to occupy the tips of several low spurs on the north side of Mint Spring Bayou by 1400, the time set for the launching of the general assault. There was no possibility whatever that Manter's BDE could launch an assault, though they took ten casualties, chiefly from long-range sniper fire.

Steele, with Woods's BDE, continued on westward along the ridge and in a short time discovered that the road he had been following continued on down the crest of the ridge, where it was completely exposed to the Confederate riflemen and artillery on the escarpment south of Mint Spring Bayou. To avoid needless casualties, he moved off the road and, sheltered behind the crest of Indian Mound Ridge, continued on to the southwest. By 1400, the time Grant had specified for the assault, he was still 800 yards northeast of Fort Hill. Furthermore, though he knew that the Valley Road must be ahead of him somewhere, he had not yet encountered it, so he was not yet in a position to strike for the Yazoo and Porter's ships. He was not going to be able to obey either of the two orders he had received from his corps commander.

Well, first things first. The first thing was to make his present position secure against a possible counterattack. Woods led his men forward and began the construction of a line of riflepits on the forward face of Indian Mound Ridge. It proved to be dangerous work; the Confederate works were so far above his position that the infantry was subjected to a galling plunging fire from the Rebel artillery.

The obvious solution was to suppress the Rebel fire with counterbattery, so Steele directed CPT Clemens Landgraeber and his six guns to help Woods out. Woods wanted the artillery down near the tip of the ridge, where it would be close enough to the Rebel artillery positions to be reasonably effective. Landgraeber and his six guns would have to traverse the whole length of the ridge, in full view of the Southerners. Landgraeber lined his guns up along the road in the last sheltered position; looked carefully at that long, dreadfully exposed ridgetop; took a deep breath; and dashed forward. The moment the battery came into view, the Southerners opened fire with everything that would shoot. By the time he got to Woods's post, Landgraeber had lost four horses and earned the title "The Flying Dutchman."[16]

The moment Landgraeber unlimbered his guns, he began receiving fire from Rebel sharpshooters concealed in a house about 300 yards to the southwest. Steele finally was forced to send a patrol to clean them out. When, after a bitter little skirmish, the Federals occupied the house and an Indian mound another 300 yards to the southwest,[17] they found themselves only 150 yards from the bank of the Mississippi, looking directly into the open flank of the Water Battery. The battery was less than 300 yards from the top of the Indian mound, but on the opposite side of the Mint Spring Bayou ravine. This was much too inviting a target to ignore, and within minutes Union sharpshooters had forced the evacuation of the battery. That night, the Confederates came out in force and threw up traverses covering the flank and rear; by daybreak of 20 May, the guns were back in operation.

Landgraeber's counterbattery fire was utterly ineffectual. It was very hard to hit those guns far away and far above him on the skyline; his shells tended to go whistling over the tops of the parapets, to explode harmlessly somewhere in the air high above Glass Bayou.

Occupation of the Indian mound had another important fringe benefit, though: it had resulted in cutting the Valley Road, which ran through a low saddle midway between the sniper house and the Indian mound. Steele exultantly realized that he had sealed the last road entering Vicksburg from the north. There would be no escape for the Rebel garrison in that direction. Furthermore, the way to the Yazoo River was now open; all he had to do was find it.

By late afternoon, both Sherman and Blair knew that the assault on the Stockade Redan had failed. However, Sherman had no way of knowing how the assaults on other segments of the line were faring. For all he knew, one or more of them might be on the brink of success. If a breakthrough were made elsewhere on the perimeter, resistance on his front might suddenly collapse. To prepare for that eventuality, should it occur, he brought his reserve, Buckland's BDE of Tuttle's DIV, forward on the Graveyard Road behind Kilby Smith.[18] But he did not commit it.

Despite the fact that the assault had failed, desultory fighting continued in front of the redan all through the long, hot afternoon. Soldiers are adaptable. Here and there, groups of Union riflemen formed themselves into fire teams. Whenever a Rebel head popped above the parapet to take aim, one of the fire teams would loose a volley. It was a bit wasteful of ammunition, perhaps, but it was notably successful in persuading the Johnnies to keep their heads down.

Blair's principal worry at this point was that the Confederates would launch a counterattack which his disorganized men would be unable to stop. Tuttle's DIV, which was lined up along the Graveyard Road just out of range, probably could be counted on to stop such an attack eventually, but it surely would allow the Confederates to reap a rich harvest of captured bluecoats. To counter the potential threat, Buckland's BDE of Tuttle's DIV was ordered to establish a strong line of outposts in the ravine bottoms, thus ensuring at least a measure of organized resistance.[19] Then, at dark, the men on the slopes and in the ditches were brought out, a few at a time, to safety. Against all expectations, the morale of the Confederate defenders had proven unshakable.

CONFEDERATE PERSPECTIVE

Pemberton was fully aware that salients are weak points in defense lines; he had recognized from the beginning that the Stockade Redan was a likely target for a Union assault. Further, there was no doubt in his mind

that Grant would attempt to take the city by storm. Because he was uncertain of the reliability of many of the troops involved in the debacles of
Champion Hill and Big Black Bridge, he placed Hébert's BDE of
Forney's DIV, which was fresh and, he hoped, unaffected by the events
of the last few days, in the Stockade Redan and Green's Lunette. Shoup's
LA BDE of Martin L. Smith's DIV, similarly untouched by the recent
disasters, held the 27 LA Lunette.[20]

Smith and his men watched carefully during the morning as the Yankees moved westward along Indian Mound Ridge. So confident were they
that, when an attack developed opposite the 26 LA Redoubt at 1400 on
19 May, Shoup's men beat it off almost casually and went back to their
work improving the riflepits. About 1430, the monotony was broken when
a Yankee battery suddenly appeared on the top of Indian Mound Ridge,
dashing madly down the nose of the ridge toward the Indian mound.
Everybody dropped his shovel and grabbed a musket. It was fun! Just like
a turkey shoot! The men blazed away with everything that would throw a
projectile, small arms and artillery alike.[21] It was all over in minutes, worse
luck. Then they went back to digging.

Elsewhere along the line, the men manning the parapets were not quite
so buoyant. As the day wore on, it began to be evident from the marshaling
of Union forces along the Graveyard Road that the attack on the Stockade
Redan was going to be in great force. Federal skirmishers appeared at dawn.
They worked their way through the abatis filling the valley bottoms in front
of the works and made damned nuisances of themselves by firing at every
head that peeped over the parapet. Forney reported that the troops belonged to Sherman's corps, and that was cause for alarm. About 0930, three
Federal batteries opened fire, with almost all the guns directed at the Stockade Redan. It was obvious that they were trying to knock out the lone gun
emplaced there and to collapse the parapet into the ditch as a prelude to an
infantry assault. Knowing what was coming, Pemberton called Cockrell's
BDE of Bowen's DIV up from the reserve to stiffen the troops manning the
Stockade Redan complex.[22] The Missourians had not been in place long
when, about 1340, a single regiment penetrated the abatis in the bottom of
Glass Bayou and came charging up the slope toward the riflepits just south
of Green's Lunette. A single regiment was not a credible threat, and the
Rebel defenders easily brought it to a stop while it was still 100 yards from
the parapets.[23]

During this brief engagement, however, about 1345, the Federal artillery suddenly and inexplicably fell silent. The explanation was not long in

coming. Exactly at 1400, the Union artillery fired three deliberate salvos, and long blue lines of infantry poured over the ridges east and northeast of the Stockade Redan and swept into the ravines, converging on the redan.

Another line swept down from the North Ridge. It was separated from the main attack by a large gap, and it soon became obvious that its objective was the 27 LA Lunette. That permitted the Confederate riflemen in Green's Lunette to concentrate their attention on the Federal infantry advancing against the Stockade Redan from the Long Spur.

Matters were not so simple around the Stockade Redan complex. The blue lines rolled forward despite an absolute storm of defensive rifle fire. To the defenders' surprise and gratification, none of the attackers carried scaling ladders. The morning's artillery bombardment had not seriously damaged the faces of the parapets, so the Yankees were going to have a bit of trouble climbing the exterior slopes, even if they got close enough. The force directed against the 27 LA Lunette finally lost momentum, and the blue soldiery sought shelter behind stumps and folds of ground. It continued to be dangerous to peek over the parapet, because the Yankees kept up a patter of rifle fire; but the attack was clearly stalled, albeit only a few yards from the face of the lunette.

But the converging attack on the Stockade Redan kept right on coming, despite everything the defenders could do. Finally a few of the Federal soldiers reached the ditch and tried frantically to climb the exterior slope. Here the attack finally stalled. Still, there would be no safety until those men in the ditch were eliminated. Yet eliminating them was not easy. One of the problems was that the Yankee infantry hugging the slopes beyond the ditch concentrated a volley at every Confederate head that showed above the works. Hand grenades tossed over the parapets tended to come sailing right back. Some 12-pdr spherical artillery shells rolled over the top of the parapet worked better, but still the Yankees refused to budge.

Gradually the storm died away, and after dark there were stealthy sounds of movement, clearly indicating that the Federals were withdrawing. Everybody breathed a sigh of relief. The Yankees were not, after all, unbeatable. Vicksburg would hold.

When all the reports were in, Pemberton realized that the Great Redoubt and 3 LA Redan, where the Jackson Road came through the lines, and the Railroad Redoubt and 2 TX Lunette, where the railroad came into the city, all had been the targets of attacks. The efforts had been so ineffectual, however, that the invaders had been stopped almost before the defending infantry fired a shot. After experiencing the speed and resolution of the Yankee offensives at Champion Hill and Big Black Bridge, Pemberton thought the attack seemed entirely out of character.

COMMENTARY

When Union infantry forced the evacuation of the Water Battery, it probably would have been possible for the force to cross Mint Spring Bayou and occupy the work. Almost certainly, the Yankees could not have kept it, but they might have held it long enough to spike the guns and blow up the magazine. Had they done so, the history of the following forty-seven days might have been very different.

Landgraeber and his battery were in less danger during their dash down Indian Mound Ridge than they appeared to be. Hitting a moving target with a muzzle-loading cannon is notoriously difficult. Higgins's River Defense artillerymen had discovered that it was not easy to hit even a target as big and slow-moving as one of the Federal ironclads. It must be remembered that, in order to aim the piece, the trail had to be moved, which was a time-consuming and inexact process. Elevation was controlled by a screw under the breech, and changing it also was slow and prone to error. Coordinating these two processes in order to hit a fast-moving target (and it must be remembered that the Flying Dutchman was driving down a steep hill along a road that converged on the Confederate works, so he was continuously changing range, elevation, and direction) bordered on the impossible. One suspects that the four horses were lost to rifle fire rather than cannon fire, because many of the Southern soldiers knew how to hunt. For them, shooting at a moving target would have been an everyday affair.

34

Second Assault
20 May–22 May 1863

Maps: 1. The Theater of Operations
        8. The Defenses of Vicksburg

FEDERAL PERSPECTIVE

After the stinging repulse of 19 May had demonstrated that the Confederate army in Vicksburg was far from being a demoralized mob, Grant was prepared to initiate siege operations. Many of his senior officers, however, felt that the repulse had resulted primarily from lack of preparation. They argued that, if the whole army were brought up and thrown into the contest, Vicksburg surely would fall. They pointed out that neither McClernand's nor McPherson's corps had been seriously engaged and that even Sherman's attack on the Stockade Redan complex had been organized hastily and conducted without adequate artillery support and without detailed planning. Many of the men in the ranks felt the same way, partly because they wanted all other alternatives exhausted before they were subjected to the indignity and drudgery of siege operations.

Grant reluctantly accepted the will of what seemed to be a majority and decided to make another attempt to take the city by storm. Other reasons were perhaps more compelling. Up in Tennessee, Confederate GEN Braxton Bragg's Army of Tennessee held a line along the Duck River, defending Chattanooga and Atlanta. A quick victory at Vicksburg would free troops in overwhelming strength to break that line and seize Chattanooga and perhaps even Atlanta as well. In addition, Port Hudson, downriver near Baton Rouge, surely would fall as soon as Vicksburg was in Union hands, and that would mean an early opening of the Mississippi. That was one of the primary objectives of the war in the West and would yield immeasurable political, as well as strategic, benefits. Finally, there was the threat of Johnston, who, it could be safely assumed, was collecting an army to relieve Vicksburg and crush the Army of the Tennessee in the process. A quick victory at Vicksburg would make it possible for the Federals to turn eastward and shatter Johnston's army before it became a serious threat.[1] If the city did not fall quickly, it would be necessary to build up a huge army in order both to contain Vicksburg and to fend off Johnston, and that could be achieved only by stripping other posts and armies of manpower. Grant found it easy to imagine an alert Confederate commander taking advantage of such a situation to inflict irreparable damage on the Union cause. On balance, an early victory at Vicksburg was worth a fairly high price.

Having made his decision, Grant determined that the second assault would be with every man and every gun that he could bring to bear. Thus, during the two days of 20 and 21 May, all of the available strength of the Army of the Tennessee moved forward into assault positions, and virtually every piece of artillery in the army was emplaced.

Grant had two basic options. First, he could concentrate his army and make the assault on a very narrow front, hoping to punch a hole through the Confederate line by sheer mass. McClernand had proposed that scheme,[2] but Grant had rejected the idea, chiefly because he knew that narrow-front penetrations require overwhelming speed, mass, and, above all, firepower at the point of contact. He recognized that Vicksburg's tangled and broken terrain made all three of these vital factors impossible to attain. There simply were no places where large bodies of men and large masses of artillery could be deployed without days, and perhaps weeks, of preparation, and the precipitous ravines and steep hills made rapid movement almost impossible.

The second possible approach was to attack on the broadest possible front, overwhelming the defenders by manpower and massed firepower. Such an attack would depend less on speed than on relentless pressure. Pressure applied all along the line would force the commitment of Confederate reserves, and a weakness at any point then could be exploited. Primarily because of the terrain, Grant chose the broad-front option and ordered each of his three corps to attack all along their assigned fronts.

CONFEDERATE PERSPECTIVE

Pemberton had been greatly relieved and vastly encouraged by the events of 19 May. His men had made it abundantly clear that the bitter depression engendered by Champion Hill and Big Black Bridge had passed. Pemberton now was confident that he could hold Vicksburg for a very long time. Eventually, of course, the Federals could bring so many men down the Mississippi that he would be overwhelmed, but it would take weeks for such a concentration to be assembled; in that time, surely GEN Johnston would have assembled a force adequate to relieve the city. Believing that everyone in the Confederacy understood that the loss of Vicksburg almost surely meant the ultimate defeat of the Confederacy itself, Pemberton was certain that the Confederacy would subordinate every other interest to the relief of the city. Given this assumption, he set his men to the task of making certain that the Yankees were held at bay. Working parties improved the fortifications, communications roads were built, camps were improved, and organizations were streamlined.

The men in the trenches reported on the morning of 20 May that the Yankees did not seem to be making preparations for siege warfare. Pemberton assumed that this meant that another attempt would be made to take the city by storm. In the Stockade Redan complex, Hébert's and Cockrell's infantrymen, having decisively defeated the attack on 19 May, were altogether confident that they could do it again.

Stockade Redan Complex
22 May 1863

Maps: 62–64. The Second Assault on the Stockade Redan: 22 May
           1863

FEDERAL PERSPECTIVE

It is clear, based on subsequent events, that Sherman did not fully understand the reasoning behind Grant's decision. He had thought long and hard about the reasons for his defeat in front of the Stockade Redan on 19 May and had concluded that there were two major causes. First, there had been a lack of artillery support. That could be remedied to some extent, and, during 20 and 21 May, he concentrated twenty guns along the Graveyard Road,[3] which was about as many as the terrain would hold. The second cause of failure, Sherman thought, had been the disorganization produced by the broad belts of abatis. This time, Sherman hoped to avoid the abatis by ramming an assault column right down the road. The hope was that a storming party could go in over the salient angle of the Stockade Redan, whereupon Blair's and Tuttle's DIVs would be fed into the gap. With luck and good management, this would be enough to crack the Rebel lines wide open. Thus, Sherman's tactical plan for the assault on the Stockade Redan complex was a penetration on a very narrow front. The necessary firepower at the point of contact would be achieved by deploying large numbers of sharpshooters on the Long Ridge, on the North Ridge, and in the ravines in front of the works, while the artillery could shell the works without fear of endangering friendly troops until the assault party almost reached the exterior slope. In short, Sherman's tactical plan was in direct opposition to Grant's strategic plan.

At dawn on 22 May, the sharpshooters were in position, and the storming party, 150 strong, had formed on the Graveyard Road about 500 yards from the parapet of the Stockade Redan. Blair's BDEs—Ewing's in the lead, followed by Giles Smith's and Kilby Smith's—were strung out in a column along Graveyard Road behind the storming party, ready to exploit any success the party might achieve. Tuttle's DIV, also in column, was massed along the road still farther back.[4]

At daybreak, Sherman's five batteries along the Graveyard Road opened up, concentrating on the Stockade Redan. By midmorning, the face of the redan was badly shattered and the gun embrasures pounded to ruin. Then, at 1000, just before the infantry assault was scheduled to begin, the Federal artillerymen shifted their fire to the riflepits on either side of the Stockade Redan, in an effort to suppress any fire support they might offer to the redan. This was the signal for the sharpshooters secretly advanced during the night to open fire on the parapet to make the Johnnies in the redan keep their heads down.

The sharpshooter fire did not work as well as expected, for a straightforward geometric reason. The riflemen in the ravine bottoms, among the abatis, were about 100 feet lower than the parapet of the redan and its companion works, and only about 300 feet away. The parapets were so thick that riflemen in the ravine could not actually see the heads of the defenders because they were masked by the forward edge of the parapet, although the defenders readily could see the Graveyard Road, which is at about the same elevation as the knoll on which the strongpoints rest. Thus, only the riflemen along the crests of the Short Spur, the Long Ridge, and the North Ridge were in positions to hit the Rebel defenders. For the most part, they were too far away to be effective.

At the same instant when the Union sharpshooters opened fire, the storming party of 150 volunteers raced from cover and started down the Graveyard Road, each man carrying a scaling ladder or plank. For one long moment, it seemed that the plan would work, but then a spatter of musketry came from the redan. It quickly grew in volume until it was a blaze of fire. The storming party began to melt away under the hail of bullets but kept on going, up and into the ditch and halfway up the exterior slope. Here it stalled, held for a moment, and then slid back into the shelter of the ditch.[5]

Close behind the storming party came the 30 OH, eight men abreast, arms at the trail, and cheering wildly. As the men reached the road cut 150 yards from the salient angle, the storming party ahead of them vanished into the ditch. The Rebel riflemen instantly switched their attention from the storming party, which they could no longer hit, to the 30 OH, which they could. The head of the column simply melted into the earth, as nearly the entire Confederate line concentrated against them. Bodies piled up in the road cut so thickly that the living could not advance without stepping on the dead and dying.[6] Some of the bolder souls kept going and joined the remnants of the storming party in the ditch, but most of the soldiers refused to pass the carpet of slain comrades and sought shelter behind the ridge to left and right of the road.[7] Here they cowered helplessly, as the next regiment charged forward.

But as the second regiment (the 37 OH) approached the zone of death, it simply stopped.[8] Some men huddled in frightened clusters. Others simply lay down in the road, as if already dead. A few sought shelter along the Short Spur. Nothing the officers could do could restore order. At last Blair, furious but helpless, ordered Ewing's two remaining regiments to deploy behind the ridge south of the blood-soaked road cut and charge the southeast face of the Stockade Redan.[9] The infantrymen had seen this tried on 19 May and refused to go farther than the crest of the ridge, along the same line where Kilby Smith's attack had stopped seventy-two hours before. Their effort was not altogether wasted, however. They blazed away with such fury that the Rebel fire slackened enough to enable Ewing to withdraw the uninjured and the walking wounded from the road cut.[10]

The attack up the Graveyard Road quite obviously was stalled after only twenty minutes of action, but Blair was not yet ready to admit complete failure. If the Stockade Redan itself could not be penetrated, perhaps one of its supporting works could be taken. Experience on 19 May had indicated that the 27th LA Lunette was a very tough nut, so this time he decided to strike at Green's Redan. He sent Giles Smith's and Kilby Smith's BDEs off into the ravines south of the Graveyard Road, but the going was so rough that it was well after noon before they reached a point 300 yards east-southeast of Green's Redan.

From here, Giles Smith could see that a nose of ridge ran directly toward the redan. He immediately deployed and began pushing up the nose. He had not gone far when he discovered, to his surprise, that another ridge off to his left also led toward the redan. And it was occupied by Ransom's BDE of McPherson's corps! Well, any help was welcome. Within about twenty minutes, Giles Smith's line had reached within about 100 yards of the face of the redan. By this time, all action elsewhere along the line had ceased, and Giles Smith had the undivided attention of the whole Confederate line. Unable to advance, his men settled down to a savage and prolonged firefight.[11] Kilby Smith, finding no place in which to deploy, simply waited for Giles Smith to move forward.[12]

While the firefight raged, Giles Smith and Ransom did a bit of coordination. About 1345, Giles Smith dispatched a courier to tell Sherman that he was ready to launch an all-out assault.[13] Approval came about 1415, and Giles Smith and Ransom immediately waved their waiting lines forward to the attack. The instant the blue lines surged forward, the Rebel entrenchments erupted in flame. Nevertheless, two of the regiments drove past the salient angle of Green's Redan and reached within 25 yards of the riflepits to the north of it, but there they ran out of steam. They held for a few moments, but the Rebel riflemen in Green's Redan were able to rake the whole line unmercifully, so Smith ordered them back. They gave only some 75 yards, then clung to their ridge and began to dig like moles. By nightfall, they had thrown up a formidable line of earthworks right across the front of Green's Redan, less than 100 yards away from it.[14]

On Giles Smith's left, Ransom's BDE fared no better. Within a few minutes, the attack began to waver. Like Giles Smith's men, they got within about 25 yards of the Rebel works and were forced to a standstill. At last, after a prolonged firefight, the assault regiments pulled back to safety, covered by steady volleys from the reserve regiments.[15] It was about 1600.

Sherman had had enough; he was going to waste no more precious lives to no purpose. Then came a message from Grant, ordering a resumption of the attack. McClernand had reported that his forces at the Railroad Redoubt were on the verge of a breakthrough, and he had requested that the assault be resumed all along the line in order to prevent the Rebels from sending reinforcements to his sector.[16] Both Grant and Sherman doubted McClernand's reports, but they were not on the scene and couldn't judge.

With grave doubts, Sherman directed Tuttle to bring his division forward into assault position. By 1500, Tuttle had marshaled Mower's BDE, followed by Matthies's BDE, in column along the road for an another attempt at the Stockade Redan.[17] Tuttle's third BDE, Buckland's, was sent out to man the North and Long ridges to provide covering fire. The artillery was already in action. Both Sherman and Tuttle could hear the roar of battle coming from the direction of Green's Redan, although the configuration of the ground prevented them from seeing very much. The sound was comforting, because it meant that no enfilade fire was going to come from that direction as the assault columns stormed down the Graveyard Road.

About 1530, Tuttle waved his men forward[18] and into a repeat of the morning. When the advance regiment reached the deadly road cut, Confederate rifle fire cut it to bits. The second regiment ran into the fragments and stopped. Sherman, watching from a knoll not far away, turned to Tuttle: "This is murder. Order those troops back."[19]

And that was the end. The second assault on the Stockade Redan, like the first, had ended in bloody failure.

CONFEDERATE PERSPECTIVE

At dawn on 22 May, the newly emplaced Federal artillery opened up, and the shelling turned out to be far more damaging than before. The lone gun in the redan was knocked out, the embrasures were knocked into ruins, and large masses of earth were blasted off the face of the exterior slope and dumped into the ditches. Everything inside the work was covered with dust and explosion-driven earth, and the dazed Missourians and Mississippians cowered in whatever shelter could be found. Then, at 1000, the men in the Stockade Redan suddenly awoke to the realization that the Union artillery had shifted its fire to the riflepits on either side. The Southerners rubbed the dust from their eyes and peered cautiously over the parapet just in time to see a small body of men, each clutching a plank or a scaling ladder, burst from concealment and race down the Graveyard Road toward the Stockade

Redan. At the same instant, the landscape in front of the redan sparkled with the muzzle flashes of Union sharpshooters.

For a moment, this storm of musketry cleared the parapets of Confederate defenders, but they rallied quickly and directed a steadily increasing hail of small-arms fire at the Union storming party as it passed through the road cut 100 yards east of the redan. More and more of Hébert's Mississippians and Cockrell's Missourians joined the battle, until a double rank of riflemen were pouring a deadly concentration at the Union storming party. Still it came on, until it reached the ditch, crossed it, and surged partway up the exterior slope. Here, at last, the wave broke. The Confederate officers caught their breaths in relief; it had come very close.

At first it seemed that the Yankees had had enough, but then, suddenly, about 1300, a powerful force of blue-clad infantry appeared in the ravine east of Green's Redan and started up the two ridges that radiated from that strongpoint. Up to that point, there had been no direct threat to the redan, so the Confederates had been free to concentrate on the troops attacking along the Graveyard Road. Now they switched targets with a will and brought the attack to a stop a comfortable 100 yards away from the ditch fronting the redoubt. But the Yankees, despite being halted, blazed away with every gun that would shoot, and the Confederates soon realized that more trouble lay in store.

Sure enough, at a little after 1400, the whole blue line opposite Green's Redan suddenly surged forward. One part of the line drove right past the salient angle of the redan and reached within 25 yards of the riflepits halfway between Green's Redan and the Stockade Redan. Another part of the line drove to within a few yards of the riflepits south of the strongpoint, but there the defending fire finally halted the advance. The Yankees were terribly persistent and clung like leeches to their positions most of the afternoon, even though the firefight gradually died away to a spatter of sniper fire.

Long before that happened, though, the men in the Stockade Redan realized that there was still one more act to play. About 1500, the Union artillery suddenly resumed firing, and infantry lines out along both Long Ridge and North Ridge suddenly began raking the parapets of the redan and the adjacent riflepits with fire. Tired as they were, the men prepared for one more bout. At 1530, a blue column suddenly raced from shelter and stormed down the Graveyard Road, in a repetition of the morning's attack. This time the defenders waited until the head of the Yankee col-

umn reached the road cut, 150 yards in front of the works, and then fired
in volley. The blue column frayed and staggered, but some of it came on
and reached the ditch to join the men from the morning's attack, who
were still there. Other blue-clad men were still racing forward, so plenty
of targets remained. The road cut filled with bodies, and then, after only
twenty minutes of action, the Federals stopped coming. Fire dwindled
toward silence as the last hours of the day ticked away.

The action was over, and again the Stockade Redan had held.
Pemberton's men had bought time, and now Vicksburg's fate was up to
Johnston and the rest of the Confederacy.

Railroad Redoubt
22 May 1863

Maps: 65. The Assault on the Railroad Redoubt: Initial Deployment:
              1000, 22 May 1863
          66–67. The Second Assault on the Railroad Redoubt: 22 May 1863

GEOGRAPHIC CONTEXT

The Railroad Redoubt guarded the place where the Southern Railroad
of Mississippi passed through the defense lines in a cut about 20 feet
deep. It was semienclosed, being open only at the rear, and the main body
projected far forward, well ahead of the remainder of the line. The interior was divided into three compartments by lateral traverses. About 400
yards to the northeast was the 2 TX Lunette, guarding Baldwin's Ferry
Road. The two works were within line of sight of each other, and fire from
their parapets could sweep the head of the ravine which lay to the east.
The bottom of the ravine was less than 100 yards from the ditch of the
Railroad Redoubt. It was filled with an abatis made by cutting down the
trees and binding them together with telegraph wire.

Beyond the ravine was Two Mile Ridge, nearly as high as the defense
line ridge. Its summit, which trended almost straight south from a point 300
yards southeast of the 2 TX Lunette, is about 300 yards from the ditch of
the Railroad Redoubt. To the east is yet another deep ravine, beyond which
is the ridge that carried the Porters Chapel Road. The junction of Baldwin's
Ferry and Porters Chapel roads was 700 yards east-southeast of the tip of

the Railroad Redoubt, but it could not be seen from the parapet because the intervening ridge was too high. The tops of the ridges all were under cultivation and free of trees and brush.

FEDERAL PERSPECTIVE

Perhaps sensitive concerning their failure to make an assault on 19 May, McClernand and his division commanders spent 20 and 21 May making intensive preparations for the assault which Grant had ordered for 22 May. By the morning of 22 May, the XIII Corps was within assaulting distance along a front of more than 2,000 yards, extending from the 2 TX Lunette on the north to Square Fort on the south.[20] As one consequence of having such a broad front, McClernand's troops were spread so thin that, for all practical purposes, only a single brigade remained in reserve. McClernand had wanted the entire three-corps assault to be made on a narrow front, but he had been overruled by Grant. Unlike Sherman, he then had tailored his tactical plan to conform to Grant's strategic one. In consequence, McClernand's plan for the assault on 22 May included simultaneous attacks on all three of the strongpoints opposite his corps: Square Fort, the Railroad Redoubt, and the 2 TX Lunette. However, he intended to aim his strongest blow at the Railroad Redoubt.

McClernand recalled Hovey's magnificent handling of artillery at Port Gibson and Champion Hill and, since his division had been relegated to a supporting role, McClernand made him a sort of ex-officio chief of artillery for the left flank. Hovey assembled a concentration of twenty-four guns in a position where they could bear on the projecting tip of the Railroad Redoubt. At daybreak on 22 May, they opened fire. By 1000, the time scheduled for the beginning of the infantry assault, the rampart at the tip of the redoubt had been breached and the ditch filled with earth.[21]

McClernand placed BG Eugene Carr in tactical command of the attacks on the Railroad Redoubt and the 2 TX Lunette. The two earthworks were so close together as to be mutually supporting, and Carr realized that he had to attack both simultaneously. For this task, he had his own division and A. J. Smith's. However, instead of assigning his own division to one of the two earthworks and A. J. Smith's to the other, Carr deployed his two divisions in double line, with his own division constituting the first line and A. J. Smith's forming the second. Lawler's BDE of Carr's DIV and Landram's BDE of A. J. Smith's were to attack the Railroad Redoubt, while Benton's BDE of Carr's DIV and Burbridge's

BDE of Smith's were to strike at the 2 TX Lunette.[22] In effect, this meant that each attack would be commanded half by Carr and half by Smith.

While the artillery preparation was going on, Carr deployed his division behind the ridge 400 yards east of the Rebel lines. Lawler's BDE of Carr's DIV was deployed south of the railroad and behind the crest of the ridge, 400 yards east of the Railroad Redoubt, with the redoubt as its objective. It was supported by Landram's BDE, initially deployed on the Porters Chapel Ridge, another 400 yards to the rear of Lawler. Benton's BDE of Carr's DIV was deployed north of the railroad, and its objective was the south face of the 2 TX Lunette and the line of riflepits connecting the Railroad Redoubt and the lunette. Burbridge's BDE of A. J. Smith's DIV was deployed in regimental columns behind a ridge some 500 yards from the 2 TX Lunette and north of Baldwin's Ferry Road.

At 1000, right on schedule, the guns fell silent and the infantry moved smoothly forward to the attack. As Lawler's men swept over the brow of the ridge to their front, they were met only by ragged rifle fire. There was no Rebel artillery. Lawler's two right-flank regiments drove straight for the obviously breached tip of the Railroad Redoubt, while the two left flank regiments bypassed the tip of the redoubt and struck for the riflepits to the southwest.[23] The left flank regiments crossed the long nose of ridge that projects south from the Railroad Redoubt, crossed the ravine beyond, and climbed up the far slope to within 25 yards of the Confederate riflepits before their momentum failed. They stuck grimly to their position and engaged the Rebels to their front in a savage firefight.

Lawler's men swept through the abatis in the ravine, up the slope, and into the ditch in front of the Railroad Redoubt. Some climbed the exterior slope, a feat made possible by the artillery preparation, and began firing over the parapet into the interior of the redoubt. About a dozen men climbed through the breach at the tip, and, in a brief but savage hand-to-hand melee, drove the defenders back across the first traverse. They could go no farther, because an absolute storm of rifle fire swept the top of the parapets and traverses from a line of riflepits behind the redoubt. And here the position stabilized for a time.[24]

Shortly, however, gray-clad infantrymen began climbing out of their entrenchments behind the redoubt and forming in the open, as if for a charge. The Union infantry, stalled in front of the riflepits southwest of the redoubt, gratefully switched targets from the Southerners in front of them in the riflepits, whom they could not hurt, to the Rebels in the open on the ridge behind the redoubt, whom they could. The Rebels in the

open stood the fire for only a few minutes, then withdrew to the shelter
of their entrenchments, their ranks much thinned.[25]

When it was clear that Lawler's attack had stalled, Landram's BDE
moved to his support. Although taking losses coming across the intervening ridge, Landram's men were unable to respond, because Lawler's
troops were directly in the line of fire. Two of the regiments reached the
ditch without much trouble, but they could go no farther. The other two
regiments, unable to find room in the ditch, lay down on the glacis.[26] They
were in a position such that no Rebel was visible. By this time, every man
of the assault forces had been committed.

Lawler soon noticed stirrings behind the Confederate lines and interpreted them as indicating the arrival of Confederate reserves. He ex-
horted his men to hold tight to what they had, and he sent a courier to
McClernand to ask for help.[27] While waiting for a reply, COL Stone and
LTC C. W. Dunlap of the 21 IA climbed to the parapet of the Railroad
Redoubt, hoping to find a way forward. Seconds later, they both tumbled
back into the ditch, one dead and the other seriously wounded.[28]

Over the next several hours, McClernand sent a series of messages
to Grant, informing him that his troops had gained control of sections of
the Confederate line but had been brought to a stand. He also said that
he would be able to force a penetration if strong diversions were made
elsewhere along the line and if he were given reinforcements. He had no
more reserves of his own.[29]

Grant had established his command post on Mount Ararat, on the Jackson Road 1,000 yards east of the 3 LA Redan, because it was the only place
from which all of the major points of attack could be seen, from the Railroad Redoubt (2,600 yards to the southwest) to the Stockade Redan (1,400
yards almost due north). From his aerie, he had watched the waves of attack strike against the Confederate works and break like surf against gran-
ite. He could see McClernand's battle flags on the wall of the Railroad Redoubt, but the clouds of battle smoke that continually welled up from it
indicated that no breakthrough had been achieved.[30] He therefore did not
believe McClernand's messages, but McClernand was the man on the spot,
and Grant had no choice but to take his messages at face value. He therefore authorized McClernand to use Quinby's DIV of McPherson's corps,[31]
which was not seriously engaged, and ordered both McPherson and
Sherman to renew their attacks.

As soon as Quinby's DIV arrived, Carr ordered Boomer to attack the
riflepits between the 2 TX Lunette and the railroad,[32] hoping that, even

if the attack did not penetrate, it would suppress the enfilading fire being placed across the northeastern approaches to the Railroad Redoubt. Boomer deployed in double line of battle behind the ridge north of the Two Mile Bridge and advanced to the attack.[33]

As Boomer's men came over the ridge, the riflepits 500 yards to their front blazed furiously at them, and the Texans in the lunette to their right front raked their flank. Only the Railroad Redoubt, 400 yards to the west, remained silent, and the men were mightily cheered to see the colors of Union regiments floating from the parapet. Boomer stopped in a ravine halfway to the riflepits to dress his lines and change his formation.[34] His men were sheltered from the riflepits to his front, but the ravine was open to the south and fully exposed to the Railroad Redoubt, only 250 yards from his left flank. Then, just as he was about to give the order to resume the advance, a burst of musketry erupted from the Railroad Redoubt, and Boomer fell, mortally wounded.

COL Holden Putnam of the 93 IL took command and sent an aide to tell BG Carr that the Railroad Redoubt again was in Rebel hands, and that an attack on the riflepits north of the railroad would be suicidal under the circumstances. Carr, who already had learned of the Rebel resurgence into the Railroad Redoubt, told Putnam to stay where he was until dark, after which he was free to pull out.[35]

The assault on the Railroad Redoubt, like those on the Stockade Redan, had ended in failure. Now no recourse remained but the shovel. The next day, preparations for the siege began in earnest.

CONFEDERATE PERSPECTIVE

After the Federal attack on 19 May had been repulsed so easily, most of the Confederates in the lines relaxed, thinking that the Yankees had learned their lesson. Not Pemberton. He knew the temper of the army in front of Vicksburg better than any of his men, and he was reasonably certain that the Yankees would try again. He was led to that conclusion when he reflected that only Sherman's corps had been seriously committed; it seemed beyond hope that Grant would fail to try again with his entire army. His view was strengthened during the quiet days of 20 and 21 May, as the Federals obviously were marshaling their forces. Because much of the activity seemed to be opposite the Railroad Redoubt and the 2 TX Lunette, on the afternoon of 21 May he alerted two of his reserve units, Green's BDE and Waul's TX Legion, to move into position to support that section of the line.

When the Federal artillery batteries opposite the 2 TX Lunette and the Railroad Redoubt suddenly opened a concentrated fire on the lunette, the redoubt, and the adjacent riflepits at dawn on 22 May, Pemberton was convinced that his intuition had been correct. His satisfaction was short-lived, however, for the Union artillery was effective almost beyond belief.[36] Within moments, the three Confederate guns in the Railroad Redoubt had been knocked out, and shells ate relentlessly at the tip of the earthwork, collapsing the exterior slope into the ditch and chewing the parapet to bits. Within the work, the men of the 30 AL cowered helplessly behind the parapets, appalled at the ferocity of the barrage. The parapet at the tip of the salient was breached, and men began to fall. LT J. M. Pearson asked for permission to withdraw his men to a safer place, but his request was refused.[37]

When the Union cannonade went on interminably, BG Stephen D. Lee, who commanded the defense line from the Baldwin's Ferry Road to Square Fort, and COL Waul of the TX Legion, who commanded the reserve, both knew that an assault was coming. When the guns abruptly fell silent at 1000, Waul moved his men forward and manned the line of riflepits that had been constructed across the base of the Railroad Redoubt as a second line of defense.[38] Within the Railroad Redoubt, LT Pearson leaped from shelter and peered over the parapet just in time to see solid lines of blue-clad infantry in the ravine to the east spring to their feet and drive forward toward the redoubt.[39]

The men of the 30 AL in the redoubt, as well as the men of the 46 AL in the riflepits north of the railroad, sprang to the firing step and began pouring increasing volumes of musketry into the advancing Federals. The Yankee line thinned at every step, but it kept on coming. Despite all that Pearson and his riflemen could do, it reached the ditch in front of the redoubt.

Perhaps a score of the Northerners climbed through the gap in the parapet that had been created by the artillery fire, and they ejected the Southern garrison in the first compartment of the redoubt after a brief hand-to-hand fight. Pearson and his men, behind the first traverse, dared not raise their heads because their compatriots in the trench behind the redoubt were sending a blizzard of musket fire that grazed the top of the traverse. They were shooting at some of the Yankees who had climbed the exterior wall and were trying to wriggle across the top of the parapet and so gain access to the interior of the second compartment of the fort. Unable to go further, the Yanks planted their flag on the exterior slope and contented themselves with blazing away at the riflepits behind the fort. The Federal squad in the tip of the fort rapidly was eroding under the continuous hail of fire, so after a few minutes it withdrew to the exterior slope of the redoubt.[40]

Not all of the Federal assault forces had been directed at the Railroad Redoubt. The attackers' battle line had extended far to the south, and they drove across the long nose of ridge that extended for 300 yards south of the tip of the redoubt, through the ravine west of it, and up the slope toward the riflepits south-southeast of the base of the redoubt. They got within 25 yards of the breastworks before being brought to a halt.

When the Federal attack penetrated into the Railroad Redoubt, Waul brought his TX Legion out of cover and deployed it in the open across the base of the redoubt. That was a mistake, because the position was exposed to fire from Federal troops who had attacked the riflepits south of the strongpoint. Unable to hurt the Alabamans in the riflepits to their front, they turned their guns upon the Texans, and the Texas ranks began to thin with appalling speed. Discretion soon overcame valor, and Waul again withdrew his men to the shelter of the riflepits.[41]

About 1300, COL Shelley of the 30 AL sent CPT H. P. Ogden and fifteen volunteers forward to clear the Yankees from the ditch in front of the redoubt. They stormed over the top of the first traverse and into a blizzard of musketry that killed CPT Ogden and sent the rest of the party fleeing in panic.

LT Pearson and twelve of his men remained behind, cowering in the second compartment. That, too, was a mistake. In the lull that followed the defeat of the Alabamans, the Yankees reentered the redoubt through the gap at the tip and captured LT Pearson and his twelve doughty companions. The Yanks dared not remain inside even the first compartment, so they again withdrew to the ditch, leaving the first compartment of the Railroad Redoubt empty. Through the afternoon, while the firing dwindled away to sporadic bursts, the Confederate officers tried desperately to think of a way to drive the Yankees out of the ditch without at the same time suffering casualties vastly disproportionate to the benefits gained.

About midafternoon, BG Lee saw a new battle line emerge from cover and drive toward the 2 TX Lunette and the riflepits north of the railroad. He knew that, without the support of the Railroad Redoubt's flanking fire, those riflepits were terribly vulnerable. In despair, Lee turned to COL Waul and asked if the Texans could retake the fort. Waul formed a party of thirty-five volunteers, and at 1730 the storming party leaped from the trenches and raced toward the open gorge of the Railroad Redoubt. The sudden onslaught rolled the whole length of the redoubt without pause.[42] The Yankees who had dug into the top of the parapet were swept away. With the Union attackers driven into the ditch, one party of Texans set to work sealing the breach in the salient angle, while another opened fire on the flank of the Yankee battle line that was attacking the riflepits 250 yards to the north.

The instant the success of the counterattack was assured, Waul ordered two more companies of the TX Legion into the redoubt, with orders to clear the Yankees from the ditch. The Federals clinging to the slope beyond the ditch then withdrew slowly and sullenly into the ravine to the east, and firing gradually died away.[43] The all-out assault on the Railroad Redoubt had failed.

Pemberton was content. He was confident that Grant would undertake no more assaults but instead would resort to formal siege operations. The Confederates had ammunition in plenty and food enough for six weeks or more, and in that time GEN Joe Johnston certainly would be able to marshal an army large enough to effect the relief of the fortress. In fact, with good fortune, it was possible that Pemberton and Johnston might be able to coordinate an attack on the siege lines that would result in a Federal defeat and at least temporary withdrawal of the Army of the Tennessee.

COMMENTARY

The practice of attacking multiple objectives with a double line of troops, each commanded by a different officer, such as the arrangement used by Carr in his attack on the 2 TX Lunette and the Railroad Redoubt, was not, as we now know, a sound arrangement. It was, however, a common practice during the Civil War.

35

Attacks on the Louisiana Posts
30 May–30 June 1863

Maps: 1. Theater of Operations
      4. Southern Sector
      9. Northeastern Louisiana
     23. Battlefield of Milliken's Bend

CONFEDERATE PERSPECTIVE

John Pemberton's letter to GEN Edmund Kirby Smith,[1] which arrived in Smith's headquarters north of Alexandria, LA, on 13 May 1863, had been written on 9 May, so it took only four days to reach him. Quite remarkable, considering the distance and the difficulties between them. One of these was the Mississippi River, which was haunted by a Federal naval squadron. In any event, the letter informed Kirby Smith that Grant was across the Mississippi and threatening Vicksburg, and that Grant's army was supported by a long, thin supply line through Louisiana. It ended with a plea that Kirby Smith attack that supply line, it being the duty of every Confederate to aid in the defense of Vicksburg. Smith was more or less forced to ignore this plea, if for no other reason than that he had no way to respond. At this time, Banks's Union army still occupied Alexandria, and the only two battle-worthy forces available were MG John G. Walker's TX DIV and MG Richard Taylor's small force, which was retreating up the Red River from Alexandria toward Natchitoches. Walker's DIV was at Monroe,[2] unable to move south by riverboat because of a Federal naval squadron in the Ouachita below Harrisonburg. In any event, Kirby Smith felt that freeing southern Louisiana of Yankees had a higher priority, so it was easy to decide to continue the movements he had already planned. These involved a juncture between Walker and Taylor somewhere in the Natchitoches area, after which the combined force would drive the Yankees back to Berwick Bay. Accordingly, on 14 May, he ordered Walker to march overland from Monroe, away from the Mississippi, to Natchitoches.[3]

MG Taylor's relationship with Kirby Smith was not particularly harmonious; Taylor thought Smith stupid and unimaginative. Nevertheless, Taylor held a position in the Department of the Trans-Mississippi analogous to that of a corps commander. This despite the fact that his total force consisted of less than 10,000 men, only very slightly more than a normal Confederate division. Even that was illusory, because more than half that strength was distributed in small detachments over much of Louisiana, so his actual force above Alexandria numbered only about 4,000 men. In comparison, Walker's Texas DIV was a battle-worthy force of approximately 5,000 men.

A few days earlier, Kirby Smith had concluded that the combined force of Walker and Taylor, which together amounted to perhaps 9,000 men, was inadequate to take the offensive against Banks, whose force was estimated at about 20,000. Consequently, on 10 May, Smith had directed LTG Theophilus Holmes, commander of the District of Arkansas, to send another brigade of infantry south as rapidly as possible. Holmes didn't much like the order, because he felt himself to be seriously threatened by blue-clad armies. North of him, most of southern Missouri was solidly held by the Federals, and there were large forces across the Mississippi River at Memphis, as well as a big garrison at Helena, AR. Even worse, naval control of the Mississippi gave the Unionists the power to assemble and land a large force almost anywhere they chose along his eastern frontier. In view of this, he resented being asked to give up any significant part of his combat power to deal with whatever problem Kirby Smith thought he had in southern Louisiana.

Nevertheless, Holmes had to give the appearance of respecting Kirby Smith's orders, so on 11 May he selected BG James C. Tappan's INF BDE for the move southward. This unit consisted of about 2,000 semitrained recruits, poorly equipped and lacking artillery. By the time the brigade was ready to leave Little Rock on 17 May for the long march south, a significant proportion of the men had deserted.

Then, on 15 May, everything changed. Kirby Smith learned that, for some completely inexplicable reason, the Yankees were withdrawing from Alexandria, even though they were under no pressure from Taylor's forces. However, instead of regarding this as a release, Smith became even more determined to drive the Yankees out of southern Louisiana as soon as possible. The only modification he made in his order to Walker was to march to Campti, a small community on the Red River a few miles above Natchitoches. There was nothing for Walker to do but obey, and on 16 May he began to move his entire command westward. By 22 May, both Walker and Taylor were camped on the shores of Black Lake, just north of Campti on the Red River.[4]

However, by 20 May, two things had become clear. First, the Yankee naval forces had withdrawn to the mouth of the Red River, so the Louisiana waterways once again could be used safely, at least as long as the confluence of the Black and the Red rivers was avoided. Second, Banks's blue-clad army was withdrawing to the southeast, apparently toward Berwick Bay. Thus freed from the need to expel the Yankees from that portion of southern Louisiana west of Berwick Bay, Kirby Smith's thoughts at last turned to Vicksburg. On that day he wrote to Taylor, emphasizing that Grant's threat to Vicksburg now took precedence over everything and that all else had to be sacrificed to meet that threat.[5] He went on to propose that Taylor take Walker's DIV up the Tensas River and seize the Bayou Vidal area, thus breaking Grant's supply line. At worst, that would check Grant; at best it would force him to withdraw.

Taylor was stunned by the proposal, which ran directly counter to all Kirby Smith's earlier actions. He argued vehemently that the Federal campaign against Vicksburg could not be affected significantly by direct action in Louisiana.[6] His counterproposal was to overrun Berwick Bay and threaten New Orleans. Banks would be forced to pull his forces out of Baton Rouge; that would free the Port Hudson garrison, which then could march north to assist the Confederate forces defending Vicksburg. Kirby Smith rejected Taylor's plan on the grounds that it was too subtle to be understood by the public. The Confederate government, said Kirby Smith, was "urgent for some effort on our part in behalf of Vicksburg, and that public opinion would condemn us if we do not try to do something."[7] In other words, as far as Kirby Smith was concerned, the real objective was not to rescue Vicksburg, but rather to polish his image before the general public and his masters in Richmond.

Taylor remained unconvinced, but, to satisfy Kirby Smith, he ordered Walker to take his Texas DIV to the Mississippi River in accord with Kirby Smith's plan, while his own little "army" remained facing the Yankees around Berwick Bay. It is worth noting that Taylor commanded the expedition, although he had no troops of his own in the force; the "army" consisted only of Walker's DIV. Friction between Taylor and Walker perhaps was inevitable.

In preparation for Walker's arrival in the theater of operations opposite Vicksburg, Kirby Smith sent a message to LTC Harrison, ordering him, with his 15 LA CAV BN, to meet Taylor and Walker at Buck's plantation on the Tensas River, five miles west of Bayou Vidal. Taylor had visited that area frequently in the years before the war and understood the geography. He knew that the Union base on the Mississippi shore was Grand Gulf, so his plan of campaign assumed that the Federals would use the high, dry area between Mrs. Perkins's plantation and Ione as a staging area and supply depot.

Federal gunboats remained in the lower Red River, so the plan was for Walker to march overland to Le Croix Ferry on the Little River.[8] There he would put his men aboard a transport fleet, follow the Little River to its junction with the Ouachita, continue down the Ouachita to the Tensas, and then move up the Tensas to Bucks plantation. The water in the backswamps now was so low that the road from Bucks plantation to Bayou Vidal should be passable.

Taylor and Walker left Campti on 26 May and pulled into the bank at Bucks' plantation at 2000 on 30 May.[9] There was no sign of Harrison and his horsemen. Because the garrison at Lake Providence had been actively and aggressively probing the surrounding region in some strength over the past couple of weeks, while there had been no activity of any kind from the posts of Milliken's Bend and Young's Point, Taylor reasoned that the greatest likelihood of Federal interference would come from the Union force at Lake Providence. Taylor thought that, if the Yankees came as far south as Delhi, they might be a serious embarrassment. Thus, as the fleet passed the Ouachita, he detached 13 TX DSMTD CAV with instructions to sail up the Ouachita to Monroe, go by rail to Delhi, and march to Floyd to reinforce COL F. A. Bartlett's 13 LA CAV BN, which was the only Confederate force currently opposing the Federals in the Lake Providence area.

Despite the lack of Harrison's troopers to guide them through the swamps, Taylor and McCulloch's BDE of Walker's DIV marched eastward from Bucks's plantation to Bayou Vidal (they had to wade for only a short distance, and the water was shallow) and then along the Yankee-built road to Mrs. Perkins's plantation. Instead of a bustling supply depot, they found an empty regimental camp; the Federal garrison had managed to escape aboard a transport under the cover of the big guns of one of RADM Porter's ironclads.[10]

Taylor's initial blow had landed in empty air, but at least it yielded some useful, if disturbing, intelligence. The local inhabitants told him,

first, that the Yankees no longer were using the supply roads below
Milliken's Bend, and that meant that they must have reestablished contact with the Mississippi River above Vicksburg. Second, Vicksburg was
already under siege. Third, Lake Providence was not important. Fourth,
the posts at Milliken's Bend and Young's Point were primarily supply
depots. They were, said the informants, enormous and stuffed with all
kinds of goodies badly needed by the Confederate army.

Taylor's mouth watered at the thought, and he decided immediately
to attack and loot the two depots. Doing so probably would not break the
siege, since the bluecoats could resupply their armies directly via the
River, but it certainly would inconvenience them. With luck, it might
persuade them to divert large forces from the siege lines; just possibly,
Johnston and Pemberton could take advantage of that.

He did not even consider marching up Roundaway Bayou for a direct attack on the two posts, because he assumed that the countryside
soon would be swarming with Yankees, now that they knew a Confederate force was in the area. If he took his division up the Roundaway Bayou
Road, the Union command of the Mississippi River made it all too likely
that the Yanks would land a large force behind him at New Carthage
while, at the same time, blocking the road south of Richmond. He would
be trapped on a single narrow road, unable to go either forward or back.
His best bet was to circle back through Delhi, so that he could launch his
attack from Richmond, which was the only suitable staging area in the
region. There was yet another overriding consideration; he was short of
food, and the rich farms along Bayou Macon were the best sources of
commissary supplies in the region.

Back at Bucks's plantation on the morning of 1 June, Taylor decided
to attack Lake Providence as well as Milliken's Bend and Young's Point,
in part as a diversion but also to destroy the surrounding plantations,
which were supplying cotton to the North.

He moved Walker's DIV by steamboat from Bucks' plantation to the
west bank of the Tensas River to the Indian Lake Road, then marched it
across the swamps to Flowers' plantation on Bayou Macon and then up
Bayou Macon to the railroad bridge just east of Delhi.[11] He put his engineers to work building a trestle bridge across Bayou Macon to replace
the burned railroad bridge. About this time, some of Harrison's 15 LA
CAV BN finally made an appearance, and the troopers assured Taylor
that there were no Yankees in residence in Richmond. Taylor nevertheless sent a combat patrol forward to Richmond, both to confirm the

cavalrymen's information and to scout out the local scene. The patrol reached the hamlet at dusk on 3 June and, to Taylor's delight, found that the Yankee-built bridge across Roundaway Bayou was still there. The long-absent Harrison was there, too.

By 1600 on 4 June, the bridge across Bayou Macon had been completed, which meant that supply wagons readily could reach Richmond from Delhi, where Paul Hébert, always reliable, had established a commissary depot. As soon as the bridge was finished, Taylor rode on with his staff to Richmond, arriving about 2000. Here he learned from Harrison that no Yankee supply roads now were operating in Louisiana and that the Union garrison at Lake Providence consisted of only a few companies of cavalry. Most important of all, Harrison reported that the garrison of Young's Point numbered less than 600, mostly convalescents and quartermaster troops. The most strongly defended post was Milliken's Bend, which was garrisoned by an infantry brigade composed of half-trained black troops. It seemed clear that Walker's 5,000 men could deal simultaneously with both Milliken's Bend and Young's Point.[12] Lake Providence could be destroyed by cavalry, there being a reinforced battalion under COL Frank A. Bartlett already in the area.

Meanwhile, far to the south in the Red River valley, Kirby Smith tried hard to think of additional ways of doing material harm to the Federal campaign against Vicksburg, while at the same time not disrupting his own plans for southern Louisiana. He had long been disturbed by the fact that the Federal government was using the rich agricultural region between Bayou Macon and the Mississippi River south of Lake Providence to grow cotton for the Union, and he longed to put a stop to the practice. Given the importance of the region to the Unionists, they might be goaded into sending large forces to defend it if it were threatened. Thus, on 4 June, an order went to Theophilus Holmes in Little Rock to send a cavalry brigade to operate against the Union garrison at Lake Providence, and to burn every plantation in the area that was growing cotton for the Union.[13] This order was sent in complete ignorance of Taylor's plan to occupy Lake Providence as part of his operation against the Yankee posts in Louisiana.

Holmes was reluctant to send one of his regular brigades, because he regarded the threat of the Union forces in Missouri and Tennessee as very real. Thus, on 5 June, he organized a provisional cavalry brigade under the command of COL William H Parsons. The component units were widely scattered, so they were told to rendezvous at Gaines' Landing, on the west bank of the Mississippi, twelve miles above Greenville, MS.

Taylor planned to begin the approach march on Milliken's Bend and

Young's Point from Richmond at 1900 on 6 June.[14] McCulloch's BDE was to attack Milliken's Bend, and Hawes's BDE was to occupy Young's Point. COL Bartlett's force, consisting of 13 LA CAV BN plus 13 TX CAV, which was at Floyd, would attack and seize Lake Providence. Walker, with Randal's BDE and the divisional artillery, would remain at Lums, LA, as a strategic reserve. It was true that Hawes's BDE would have much farther to march than McCulloch's, but, since the garrison of convalescents and quartermaster troops at Young's Point could not be expected to offer much resistance, it should not take Hawes's men long to occupy the post. In fact, Taylor did not expect much resistance even from the garrison of Milliken's Bend; he was so contemptuous of black troops that he expected them to throw down their arms and run at the first fire.

As soon as Young's Point had been taken, LT Stephen Routh, Signal Officer, was to establish communication with the Vicksburg garrison. What he would say to the people in Vicksburg was left to Routh's imagination. In any event, after both Young's Point and Milliken's Bend were overrun, McCulloch and Hawes were to rendezvous at Duckport, leaving small working parties to salvage war materiel from the camps. The Confederate forces were to bring no wagon trains with them; because the two posts were logistics bases, Taylor expected to seize large numbers of wagons and horses with which to carry away the captured booty.

Taylor was familiar with the road between Oak Grove and Lums, or at least he had been before the Federals modified and improved it. The road to Young's Point was another matter, and, about 0200 in the morning, 6 June, he sent Harrison and his 15 LA CAV BN to reconnoiter it, leaving a picket to guard the road junction north of Lums.

The first perturbation in Taylor's plans occurred about 0600, when the pickets at Lums came galloping in with the news that a strong Federal cavalry force had dislodged them an hour before. A short while later, another scout came in with a report that a Federal infantry force following behind the cavalry had reached Tallulah plantation and then inexplicably had withdrawn toward Milliken's Bend. Then, about 1100, Harrison came back from his excursion toward Young's Point. He had reconnoitered the approaches to Young's Point, found nothing of interest, and on the way back had managed to ambush a Federal cavalry force and take twenty-five prisoners. He then had encountered a Federal infantry force just north of Lums, but it had withdrawn toward Milliken's Bend after a brief skirmish.

Federal cavalry patrols in the area were not unexpected, but the presence of infantry seemed to indicate that the Unionists suspected that something was afoot and were probing for information. Nevertheless, because only Confederate cavalry had been involved, Taylor was not seriously concerned. He assumed that the Yankees would interpret the skirmishing as simple patrol activity and not the vanguard of a powerful infantry force. At about this same time, Walker's DIV tramped into Richmond. All the pieces were now assembled for the destruction of the Federal positions in Louisiana.

Walker's DIV left Richmond at 1900, right on time, for its approach march to Milliken's Bend and Young's Point. McCulloch's men, who were to attack Milliken's Bend, carried a black flag with a death's head signifying no quarter. This was done with Taylor's approval. It was widely recognized that he believed that any blacks found in arms against the Confederacy deserved only death.

Walker's DIV arrived at Lums at 1030, and here the column divided, with Hawes's BDE starting up the Walnut Bayou Road for Young's Point, while McCulloch's BDE marched north toward Milliken's Bend. Taylor ordered Walker, with Randal's BDE and the DIV ARTY, to remain in reserve at Lums. Thus Walker, the division commander, was left behind while Taylor marched off with two-thirds of Walker's men. Walker never forgave Taylor for the implied slight.

The night was very dark, but at 0300 on 7 June, McCulloch saw the top of a levee against the night sky, perhaps 2,000 yards away. He assumed that it represented the principal defense line of the camp. He halted his men and deployed them in total silence. There had been no sign that the Federals were aware of the presence of Confederates, and both Taylor and McCulloch were convinced that they had achieved a complete surprise.

The Confederate battle line, preceded by a small cavalry advance guard, moved silently along the road toward the levee. Suddenly, when the advance was still about 600 yards from the embankment, absolutely without warning a volley of rifle fire lanced out of the darkness and sent the cavalry reeling back.[15] The Confederate infantrymen pressed resolutely on, only to discover that the area between them and the levee was crossed by a series of drainage ditches grown up in brambles, cat's-claw, and brush; each successive line was bitterly defended by Yankee skirmishers.[16]

Despite the resistance, the Yankee skirmishers could not stop the steady advance of the Confederate battle line, and at last the gray-clad infantrymen found themselves less than 100 yards from the levee. The men now could see that it was about 10 feet high and crowned with a breastwork made of cotton bales. The regiments paused briefly to align their fronts, then charged. As they reached the base of the levee, a single terrible volley crashed out, and the Confederate charge faltered. Almost unbelievably, along most of the line there was no more firing, and, after a pause, the Southerners rallied and rushed forward in the eerie silence, up the levee and over the breastwork.[17]

The black regiments disintegrated and fled to the rear after a brief hand-to-hand melee. None of them fired a shot after that first crashing volley. Things went less well out on the right flank of the Confederate line; there the charging Confederates were met by steady volleys from what seemed to be a single regiment, and their charge split like a wave around a rock. With Confederates on both flanks, the men in blue calmly changed front and fought their way back to a second levee which ran close along the river bank. Nevertheless, McCulloch's men were left in possession of the camp.

However, it was now light enough to see clearly, and McCulloch was astonished to discover that, while his men held the camp and the line of breastworks, he had not achieved a decisive victory. There was another levee along the river bank some 400 yards behind the first, and the Yankees obviously were rallying behind it. Worse, from the top of the captured breastworks he could see a giant ironclad lying in the Mississippi River. As he watched, the ship's great guns boomed sullenly, and a pair of giant shells sailed over the river-bank levee and exploded in the camp, right among his men,[18] who were trying to get organized for an assault on the river-bank levee line.

McCulloch thought that perhaps he could dislodge the defenders of the river-bank levee by crossing the embankment beyond the defender's right flank and rolling them up. He put 19 TX to the task, but the instant the Texans appeared on the top of the levee, the ironclad shifted to grape and blasted them back. That done, the ironclad resumed dropping its shells among the Confederate troops in the space between the levees. Its accuracy was astonishing. McCulloch was sure that the gunners in the ship could not see over the levee; nevertheless the shells seemed to follow his men as if drawn by magnets. At last McCulloch could stand it no more and ordered his men back to safety behind the outer levee.

With his offensive stalled, McCulloch sent a courier speeding back to Walker, telling him that the attack was a failure unless strong reinforcements could be sent. It was now about 0900. A second gunboat arrived long before any response from Walker could be expected. McCulloch knew that it was hopeless to attempt to assault that second levee line in the face of the fire from the big naval guns, so he sadly ordered his men back toward Lums. He had lost 44 men killed, 131 wounded, and 10 missing. These casualties amounted to 12.3 percent of the attacking force.

The retreat met Walker hastening north with Randal's BDE about 1030. A brief conference was enough to convince Walker of the soundness of McCulloch's decision. Even the divisional artillery would make no difference; the huge guns of those damnable black ironclads would simply sweep them away. As the combined column returned to Richmond, it burned every building and seized every pound of food and forage and every head of livestock from the farms along Walnut Bayou.

Meanwhile, Hawes's BDE had encountered troubles of its own. Hawes had planned to use a bridge across Walnut Bayou at Mrs. Amis's plantation, four miles southeast of Lums, but he discovered that it had been destroyed some time earlier. Eventually another was found at Hoggett's plantation,[19] six miles farther east. By that time, it was growing light, and the hope of a surprise assault at dawn had gone glimmering.

It was not until 1030 that Hawes's advance guard made contact with Union pickets in the woods west of Young's Point. Hawes deployed and moved forward, expecting the woods to shelter his approach all the way to the edge of the camp. When he broke into the open, however, he discovered that the camp was still well over a mile away. Hawes advanced confidently into the open, assuming that the garrison of invalids and quartermaster troops would panic at the sight of his battle line. It didn't quite work out that way. Three blue-clad regiments marched out of the camp and deployed quickly and smoothly into a line of battle while the Southern battle line was still 1,000 yards away. One look was enough to reveal that these were no convalescents or stevedores; these were combat troops! Furthermore, three of those damned gunboats were lying off the post with their gunports open and guns run out. Sure enough, two of them opened fire, and, although the range was so great that the shells did no damage, Hawes well knew that the situation would change as the range diminished.

Realizing that Taylor's grand plan had failed,[20] Hawes ordered an immediate withdrawal. The brigade reached the bridge at Hoggett's plantation about 1530; the heat had been terrible, and, with the men so tired and dispirited, there had been many stragglers. Morale sank still farther when a courier arrived from McCulloch about 1800, giving the sad news of the repulse at Milliken's Bend. A few minutes later, a message from Walker arrived, ordering the troops back to Richmond.[21]

Far to the north, Bartlett's intent was to begin his attack on Lake

Providence from his camp at Floyd. In preparation, he built a bridge across Bayou Macon opposite the hamlet. Once across Bayou Macon, he would first capture Lake Providence, burn the Federal Camp of Instruction, and then range through the surrounding region burning the farms that were raising cotton for the U.S. Treasury Department.[22] He had one 6-pdr gun and about 900 men, more than enough to deal with the few companies of cavalry that comprised the Lake Providence garrison.

By the morning of 8 June, when all his preparations were complete, Bartlett had changed his mind. There was only a single poor and narrow road through the backswamps between Bayou Macon and the dry farmlands around Lake Providence, and he feared that even a few determined men might make a Thermopylae of it. Thus, instead of crossing at Floyd, he marched upstream to Caledonia and built another bridge across Bayou Macon. Here the ground between Bayou Macon and Lake Providence was higher, drier, and less densely wooded. The bridge was not completed until 1800, so Bartlett delayed his crossing until the next morning.

The next morning, 9 June, Bartlett crossed Bayou Macon and marched confidently toward Lake Providence. At Baxter Bayou, six miles northwest of Lake Providence, his advance encountered a Yankee cavalry picket. The Confederate advance continued, but going was slow against Yankees who fought with uncharacteristic determination. Then about 1000, all movement ceased; the bluecoats had burned the bridge across Tensas Bayou, and they bitterly opposed all efforts by Bartlett's men to build a new one. As the day wore on, more and more Yankees appeared on the far bank. Finally Bartlett realized that the opposition had as many men as he had. He could not even use his artillery effectively, because Yankee snipers began to pick off the gun crew. There was nothing for it but to withdraw.[23] However, instead of returning to Caledonia, he marched down the west bank of Tensas Bayou and crossed Bayou Macon on his new bridge at Floyd.

On the night of 7 June, long before Bartlett had even started his abortive attack on Lake Providence, Taylor realized that his offensive had failed miserably. Because he had been opposed to the effort from the beginning, he now felt justified in abandoning all further action in northern Louisiana; he ordered Walker to move his entire DIV to Monroe as quickly as possible, collect the necessary steamboats, and send the force by water to Alexandria.[24] Walker was not averse to leaving the scene of failure behind him, but his division most definitely was not in shape for a long march, so he stayed in Richmond to let them rest. Taylor, however, went on ahead to Monroe.

Taylor had been deeply shocked and disoriented by the failure of his offensive against the Federal posts in Louisiana. The orders issued to his subordinates while he waited in Monroe for a boat to take him south have an almost dreamlike quality. First, he ordered Hébert to send Tappan's BDE to Richmond as soon as it arrived. Next, he left orders for Tappan and Harrison to gain control of the west bank opposite Vicksburg and reopen communications with Pemberton, though how that was to be done he did not say. Third, he ordered Hébert to collect a herd of beef cattle and swim them across the Mississippi River to Vicksburg as soon as Tappan and Harrison had gained control of the west bank!

While en route down the Ouachita River from Monroe, Taylor reflected that GEN Johnston was very skillful and that the Confederacy east of the Mississippi River surely would strain every nerve to save Vicksburg. He concluded that Johnston probably would force the Union army to withdraw from Vicksburg and retreat to Memphis. Such a retreat inevitably would be accompanied by confusion, if not chaos, in the Federal army. During this time, he also learned of a new Union wagon road from Walnut Bayou to Bowers' Landing. With these thoughts in mind, he sent a message to Walker ordering him to stay at Richmond to be in position to take advantage of any opportunities offered. While there, Walker should break up the Bowers' Landing Road.[25]

Taylor also had time to write an account of the disastrous campaign to Kirby Smith, his commander. He told Kirby Smith that he himself was not to blame. He had been poorly served by everybody: "Had common vigor and judgment been displayed, the work would all have been completed by 8 A.M."[26] He went on to say that he intended to withdraw Walker's DIV to the Red River as soon as Tappan's BDE reached Richmond. (He evidently had forgotten his order to Walker to stay at Richmond to take advantage of the anticipated Union retreat from Vicksburg.)

Tappan's BDE arrived at Monroe on June 11; in accord with Taylor's orders, Hébert immediately sent it on by railroad to Delhi. At the same time, Hébert forwarded Taylor's last order to Walker, who was still resting at Richmond, telling him to sit tight. A few hours later, Walker received Taylor's order directing him to break up the Bower's Landing Road.

Walker was far from enchanted at the thought of again trying the issue with the Federal garrisons in Louisiana, and he decided to wait until Tappan's BDE arrived. His men were tired and dispirited; worse, malaria was beginning to break out in the ranks. In the meantime, because he feared a Union counteroffensive, he pushed a picket out to the critical road junction north of Lums; there the Confederates could watch for Federal activity.

Sure enough, early on the morning of 15 June, the picket at Lums came racing back to Richmond with the news that it had been evicted by 8,000 Yankees with three batteries of artillery.[27] That was two divisions, far more troops and artillery than Walker had in his ranks, afflicted as they were by disease and battle casualties. He instantly ordered his wagon train to withdraw toward Delhi. He sent LTC Culbertson and his 18 TX forward to take a position blocking the road one mile north of the Roundaway Bayou bridge, with instructions to hold long enough to allow the evacuation of Richmond.[28] McCulloch's and Hawes's BDEs were placed in line of battle south of the Roundaway Bayou bridge; Randal's BDE was in Delhi and unavailable.

Culbertson had fought at Milliken's Bend and vividly remembered the drainage ditches that had proven so troublesome during the early phases of the Confederate attack; he was delighted to discover a similar set immediately south of the railroad. With his men concealed in one of those ditches, he waited until the Union advance came across the railroad embankment before opening fire. The Yankees recoiled but then deployed a powerful infantry battle line and moved slowly and inexorably forward. Soon Culbertson's line was both outflanked and outgunned, and the Texans were forced back across the bridge.

Walker hated to lose the bridge; it would be useful in the future if the Yankees could be persuaded to withdraw. For a short while he thought that he might be able to hold it, but the Federals brought up overwhelming strength, and at last Walker ordered the bridge burned and instructed his men to withdraw toward Delhi along the south bank of Roundaway Bayou. By 1800 that night, 15 June, Walker, with McCulloch's and Hawes's BDEs, had crossed the Tensas River, four miles east of Delhi. When no Yankees had appeared on the east bank of the Tensas after a few hours, Walker sent Harrison to probe toward Richmond. Meanwhile, Randal's BDE had moved to Monroe.

Harrison returned next morning, 16 June, reporting that he had ridden as far as Lums without seeing any sign of bluecoats. Walker found this completely unbelievable; so certain was he that he was closely threatened that he burned the Tensas River bridge and withdrew his men toward Delhi. That same morning, Tappan's BDE arrived in Delhi, and the following day Randal's BDE also arrived,[29] giving Walker a combined force of about 6,000 men. Walker knew that it was not really a fighting force; many men were deserting, there was much illness in the ranks, and morale was desperately low. Rumors of Vicksburg's imminent fall ran through the ranks like an icy flood.

Under the circumstances, Walker believed that another attack on Milliken's Bend or Young's Point would only result in yet another defeat. Nevertheless, it was clear that something had to be done to help Pemberton or at least give the appearance of helping him. But whatever it was, it had to be an action that would avoid a major confrontation with the Federal army. Walker also was certain that, while the Federal garrison at Lake Providence was stronger than he originally had been led to believe, it nevertheless was not strong enough to seriously interfere if he took his entire force into the area. Furthermore, once the Southerners occupied the area around Transylvania, an artillery battery could be emplaced on Transylvania Bend and, with luck, disrupt the Federal supply line down the Mississippi River. It was even possible that such an incursion into Yankee-held territory would panic the Federal high command into diverting a division or two from the siege lines around Vicksburg. If that diversion were to occur at the moment when Johnston's Army of Relief struck, it might make a critical difference. There was no way to coordinate such an action with Johnston, of course, but who knew? Luck might be with the Southerners for a change.

Walker and his mini-army, which consisted of Walker's TX DIV (sadly depleted by battle casualties and disease), Tappan's INF BDE, and 13 and 15 LA CAV BNs, left Delhi on 22 June and that evening camped at Monticello, on the east bank of Bayou Macon. For the next five days, Confederate parties roamed the region between Bayou Macon and the Tensas River. Every building was burned. Blacks who worked the farms were herded into gangs and marched westward, to be returned to their original owners. Blacks found in arms were summarily executed, as were white landowners suspected of being disloyal to the Confederacy. Not even the Shenandoah Valley was scorched as thoroughly as this small region of Louisiana.

During this interval, on 25 June, Parsons's PROV CAV BDE finally assembled at Gaines' Landing and moved south in response to Holmes's order. On 28 June, the brigade arrived at Monticello, and Walker promptly added it to his command.[30]

On the same day Parsons arrived, Walker's pioneers completed a bridge across the Tensas River near Jackson's Ferry; on 29 June, the combined force crossed over and began the work of destroying the region between the Tensas and Mississippi rivers. Walker established his headquarters about 2,000 yards northwest of the hamlet of Transylvania. From there he sent an artillery battery to Transylvania Bend, about five miles above Goodrich's Landing, to interrupt Union shipping on the Mississippi River. Late that afternoon, 29 June, the battery fired on what the gunners thought was an unarmed transport. Instead of fleeing, the vessel turned toward their position on the bank and, to their complete dismay, opened a deadly accurate fire with 12-pdr guns. In a few brief minutes, three of the Confederates had been killed. The rest limbered up and fled.[31]

That same evening, a courier arrived at Walker's camp with an order from Taylor: march immediately for Berwick Bay. Walker was delighted. He had his men on the way back to Delhi at dawn the next morning, 30 June.

On 30 June, Kirby Smith's representative to Joe Johnston's council of war at Canton returned to Smith's headquarters and reported that Johnston considered Vicksburg's situation to be "almost hopeless."[32] This was distressing news indeed. If Johnston thought the case hopeless, then there was little that Kirby Smith could do. However, he was determined at least to give the appearance of activity. The only force he had that even remotely was in a position to do something constructive was Walker's force in Louisiana opposite Vicksburg. He sent a message to Walker, canceling Taylor's earlier order telling Walker to return to the Red River and ordering him to remain at Delhi until he, Kirby Smith, got there. It was a long trip, and Smith didn't get to the rendezvous until 5 July.[33] Walker, of course, immediately told Smith of his activities south of Lake Providence and of the failure of his artillery to interdict Federal shipping on the Mississippi River.

Neither Kirby Smith nor Walker could think of anything constructive that could be done, but at last they decided to make one more attempt to interfere with the Federal lifeline down the Mississippi. The scheme was to move Walker's force to Ashton, twenty river miles above Lake Providence, and try once again to close the river with field artillery. Ashton was chosen because the shipping channel at this point lay very close to the west bank of the river. Walker's force left Delhi on 7 July for the long march northward, only to learn, a few hours later, that Vicksburg already had fallen. Utterly despondent, the troops returned to Delhi.[34]

FEDERAL PERSPECTIVE

Grant never had felt comfortable about the outpost at Lake Providence. After McPherson's corps moved out in early April, its sole function was to guard the plantations in the surrounding region that were growing cotton for the U.S. Treasury Department, and Grant resented the diversion of military resources for such a purpose. As a result, he left the garrison pretty much to its own devices. However, the commander of the

Lake Providence garrison, BG Hugh Reid, took his duties very seriously. Thus, when news came in that a Rebel force had raided the plantations around Ashton on 2 May and carried off a number of blacks, he reacted sharply. The very next day, he rode north with a company of his 1 KS MTD INF to investigate.

Of course, the Rebels were long gone by the time he arrived, but he learned that the Southerners were concentrating cavalry at Caledonia with the avowed intent of raiding the U.S.-operated cotton plantations. He realized that he could not protect the area with a passive defense, because the raiders could strike anywhere and be gone before his reaction forces could arrive on the scene. The obvious answer was to push the raiders out of the area.

Thus, on 8 May, CPT Gustavus Zesch with 6 COs of 1 KS MTD INF rode forth to smash the Rebel concentration at Caledonia. Zesch found far more Rebels at Caledonia than he had bargained for and withdrew to Old River. Next day, 9 May, Reid sent MAJ William Roberts with nine companies of 1 KS MTD INF and a 100-man detachment of 16 WI INF to eradicate the nest at Caledonia. Roberts found Bayou Macon too deep to ford, so he paused to build a bridge.[35]

Next morning, he crossed Bayou Macon on his new bridge and ran into an ambush a mile west of town, but he pushed hard, and the Rebels fled west toward Pin Hook, leaving a couple of prisoners in his hands. The prisoners told him that COL Bartlett, who commanded the 13 LA CAV BN, was marching north from Delhi with 1,500 men. Undaunted, Roberts left his infantry to guard his bridge and moved west toward Pin Hook in two columns.[36] Both columns were ambushed and forced back,[37] so Roberts burned his brand-new bridge at Caledonia and returned to Lake Providence. The effort to suppress the Rebel raiding obviously had been a failure, but Roberts had learned one thing that Reid thought was important: Confederate MG Walker was at Monroe with his entire TX DIV.

Reid sent a message south by the first steamboat, and, by the morning of 11 May, BG Jeremiah C. Sullivan, who commanded the District of North East Louisiana from his headquarters at Young's Point, had the news. Later the same day, Grant had it, too.[38] Over the next several days, there was a persistent buzz of rumors that a Rebel attack on the Trans-Mississippi posts was impending.[39]

Grant was concerned, not because the loss of either Milliken's Bend or Young's Point, or both, would be critical from a purely military point of view, but because he feared that the public would regard their loss as a major defeat. The political fallout might well be difficult for Lincoln's government to deal with. With this in mind, Grant urged Sullivan to make every effort not only to find out what the Rebels in Louisiana were up to, but also to get his posts ready to resist. And preparing the garrisons to resist would entail extraordinary efforts, because the garrison at Milliken's Bend consisted mostly of newly recruited black troops who were so poorly trained that they could barely load their weapons. Grant's distress grew with the passing days, because Sullivan seemed to be wholly incapable of understanding the importance of Grant's requests.

Then, on the afternoon of 31 May, the field telegraph from Warrenton brought news that the little Union garrison at Mrs. Perkins's plantation had been forced to evacuate by a large Confederate infantry force—at least a brigade and maybe more. Grant had expected the Confederate blow to be aimed at Young's Point, because he had assumed that the Rebel high command would know that the overland supply line through Louisiana to Mrs. Perkins's had been abandoned and that the Union wagons now were using the road from Walnut Bayou to Bowers' Landing. The strike at Mrs. Perkins's told him that the Confederate leaders had not known that.

Well, they knew it now. The next blow certainly would fall on Milliken's Bend or Young's Point, or possibly both. There was some satisfaction in knowing that it would take them several days to shift their forces from Mrs. Perkins's to Delhi, the only practical jumping-off place for an attack on the Louisiana posts. Then, on 3 June, Grant received a message from Sullivan to the effect that there were rumors of an impending Rebel attack!

This was too much for Grant to stomach. The affair at Mrs. Perkins's clearly was more than a rumor, yet Sullivan not only had no plan to deal with an attack but was not even taking steps to find out where it was coming from, in what strength, or when. Grant promptly sent orders to BG Elias S. Dennis to go to Young's Point, relieve Sullivan, and take command of the District of Northeast Louisiana.

Dennis arrived at Young's Point on 4 June, to find the post buzzing with rumors that the Rebels were in Richmond. This seemed entirely reasonable to Dennis; a glance at a map showed him that Richmond was by far the best place from which to launch an attack on either Milliken's Bend or Young's Point. Dennis instantly sent patrols out to separate fact from fancy, and on 5 June they told him that, indeed, the Rebels were in Richmond, and in great strength. The next question was: when are they coming? He ordered COL Hermann Lieb, commander at Milliken's Bend, to send a reconnaissance in force toward Richmond to find out. He half-expected the reconnaissance force to meet the Rebel advance guard somewhere south of Oak Grove.

Next morning, 6 June, Lieb sent COL Christopher H. Anderson, with 10 IL CAV and 9 LA INF (AD), southward from Milliken's Bend to look for trouble. Anderson's advance dislodged a Rebel picket at Lums, which was not unexpected. The pickets fled toward Richmond, but the road gave indication of the passage of a large body toward Young's Point, so Anderson split his forces, his cavalry heading east and his infantry west. As Anderson led his untrained infantrymen toward Richmond, he reflected that any determined opposition almost surely would turn them into a fleeing mob. By the time his advance reached the railroad embankment north of the Roundaway Bayou bridge, it became clear that the road had been heavily used by cavalry. Because of the uncertain quality of his troops, he dared go no farther. He turned back, only to hear the sound of gunfire from down the Walnut Bayou Road as he reached the road junction north of Lums. He had just managed to get his infantry deployed and facing south, when his cavalrymen came racing up in a mob, looking back over their shoulders at an equivalent mob of pursuing Rebel horsemen. One smashing volley from the infantry was enough to send the Rebels reeling back.

Anderson knew that this was an ephemeral victory, because his raw black soldiers would need a long time to get ready to fire another volley. His response was to withdraw slowly toward Milliken's Bend, while trying to look as menacing as possible. Back at Milliken's Bend, the cavalry reported thirty-three men missing, presumably killed or captured by the Rebels. It was not an auspicious beginning. Nevertheless, the patrol had served its purpose, and Lieb notified Dennis that the Richmond area was swarming with very aggressive Rebels.

Dennis assumed that the Confederates would strike first at Milliken's Bend, because it would involve a much shorter approach march from their staging area at Richmond. He knew well the state of training of the four black regiments comprising the bulk of the garrison of Milliken's Bend, and he feared that they would not be able to resist an aggressive attack. However, there was always the chance that the Rebels would surprise him by striking at Young's Point, so he dared not strip the Point of troops in order to strengthen Lieb's garrison. He did the best he could; he sent his best combat regiment, 23 IA, by boat to Milliken's Bend on the afternoon of 6 June. He also sent a message across to the naval anchorage off the mouth of the Yazoo River and asked RADM Porter for naval support. That very evening, to Lieb's and Dennis's utter satisfaction, mighty *Choctaw* slid to anchor just offshore at Milliken's Bend. *Choctaw* mounted 100-pdr Parrott rifles and 9-in Dahlgrens. Lieb doubled his pickets, sent scouts forward, and prepared for a sleepless night.

At 0300 the next morning,[40] 7 June, Lieb deployed his infantry behind the cotton-bale breastworks on the outer levee, which formed the effective perimeter of Milliken's Bend. His only reliable regiment, 23 IA INF, was placed near the left of his line. The black soldiers of the other four regiments were so calm and determined that Lieb was reasonably certain that they would be able to fire one volley under control. After that, they would have only their bayonets, and their training with that instrument had been minimal. The 18 IL CAV was dismounted and sent forward as skirmishers, with orders to resist as strongly as possible. They were confident that they could make life uncomfortable for the butternuts, because the whole area fronting the outer levee, 600 yards wide, was a maze of drainage ditches grown up with briars, cat's-claw, and brush. The attackers would have difficulty maintaining effective battle alignment, so a determined line of skirmishers ought to be able to take a considerable toll.

The skirmishers were barely in place when a long battle line came into view in the darkness, moving slowly and quietly. The skirmishers nudged each other and grinned; the Rebels thought they were going to pull a surprise. Sure enough, the Rebel battle line disintegrated at the first volley from the concealed Union riflemen.[41] True, the butternuts quickly reorganized and came on, but so difficult was the combination of terrain[42] and tenacious resistance that it took an hour for the advance to reach open ground 100 yards from the base of the outer levee.

Here there was a pause while the Rebels aligned their regiments for an assault. All that while, scarcely a sound came from the Federal troops waiting tensely behind their flimsy breastworks. In the growing light of dawn, the black soldiers could see that some of the Rebel regiments carried black flags with a death's head, the traditional symbol meaning "no quarter." At last the charge came, like a single wave. It was met at the foot of the levee by a single crashing volley that sent the gray line back in shock. But that was all. Under the pressure of battle, very few of the black soldiers managed to reload their rifles.

The Rebels rallied in the almost surreal silence, paused, and then came forward up the levee, over the breastworks, and into the Federal line.[43] After a brief hand-to-hand melee, the blue formations disintegrated, their component atoms fleeing desperately to the inner levee that lined the Mississippi River shore, 400 yards away.

All, that is, except for the section of the line manned by the veteran 23 IA. Here the Southern charge was met by steady volleys of rifle fire, and the charging line split like the tide around a reef. When the black regiments on either side broke up, the Iowans changed front with parade-ground precision and blasted their way through the press back to the line of the inner levee, where they again changed front and spread along the levee to provide cover for those panic-stricken black soldiers who had managed to reach the river bank.

Out in the river, *Choctaw's* gun crews were standing by at battle stations, unable to fire because of Union troops masking the Rebel lines. But now the huge guns bellowed, lobbing their giant shells over the inner levee and into the camp area between the two levee lines, now filled with victorious Southerners. The naval gunners could not see over the levee, but on it was a party of alert soldiers who watched the fall of the shot, and directed the gunners with arm signals.[44] It worked like magic; the big shells fell wherever a group of Rebels gathered together.

Soon the ad hoc fire-control party noticed that a Confederate regiment was organizing to charge across the levee beyond the right flank of the makeshift defense line that had rallied along the inner levee, with the obvious intention of taking it in flank and rolling it up. When the charge topped the levee, *Choctaw* was ready, and the Rebels were shattered and swept back by a storm of grape and canister from the giant naval guns firing at nearly point-blank range.

By 0830, the Confederate troops between the two levee lines were withdrawn to relative safety behind the outer levee, leaving only small parties behind to loot the camp. At about the same time, the old timberclad gunboat *Lexington* arrived on the scene and added her fire to that of *Choctaw*. After a few minutes, even the looters withdrew beyond the outer levee, and soon it was clear that the Confederates were retreating toward Oak Grove. Milliken's Bend had been held, but only barely, and only with the help of the navy.

The butcher's bill was ghastly: 101 killed, 285 wounded, 266 missing—61 percent of the initial strength of 1,061 men. It was the highest casualty rate of the war for any post successfully defended.

Porter also had sent naval support to Young's Point, in the form of the tinclads *Petrel* and *Romeo*. They arrived off shore at 0400 on the morning of 7 June. Everybody expected that, if an attack came, it would come at dawn, and Dennis had his three Illinois regiments mustered and ready well before the first light crept into the sky. By full light, nothing had happened, and everybody was breathing easier.

About this time word, came down the river that Milliken's Bend was under such heavy attack that it was doubtful the post could be held. Dennis was in a quandary; if he sent troops to help Milliken's Bend and the Rebels attacked Young's Point, he might lose Young's Point. The Point was far more important than Milliken's Bend. On the other hand, if he retained his troops and there was no attack on Young's Point, he could expect sharp questions from Grant. He decided that Grant's displeasure was the lesser of two evils and kept his men where they were.

Then, quite unexpectedly, about 1030, the Federal outposts two miles west of the Young's Point perimeter saw a Rebel line coming forward through the woods and opened fire. Dennis breathed a sigh of relief; he had guessed right. He immediately marched his Illini out and deployed in front of the perimeter defenses at about the same time that a powerful Rebel battle line emerge from the woods 2,000 yards away. The butternut line came forward slowly and then stopped about 1,000 yards away, well outside effective rifle range. Out in the river, *Petrel* and *Romeo* opened fire, lobbing shells over the camp and the Union line, but the distance was so great that the shells fell short of the Rebels and did no damage.[45]

About 1145, the Rebels began to withdraw without firing a shot. The moment Dennis was certain the Confederates were withdrawing, he loaded 120 IL and 131 IL on transports and sent them to Milliken's Bend. There was no need; by the time they got there, the Rebels were gone.

Grant learned of the attack on Milliken's Bend about 1000 on 7 June. By that time, it was clear that the post had held, but he feared that the Rebels would try again. After all, the attack had been made only in brigade strength and without the benefit of artillery, and he knew that Walker's entire division was somewhere in the area. He had just the answer. BG Joseph A. Mower and his "Eagle Brigade" had just returned to Snyder's Bluff after Kimball's abortive expedition to Mechanicsburg, so Grant ordered Mower to proceed immediately to Young's Point. He also sent a message telling Dennis that Mower was on his way and suggesting that, with Mower's men, he would have force enough to drive the Rebels out of Richmond and occupy Monroe.[46] Grant also ordered Reid, at Lake Providence, to send 8 and 10 LA INF (AD) to Milliken's Bend; they could garrison the post, while Dennis's four Illinois regiments, plus Mower's BDE, took the offensive.

Up at Lake Providence, Reid also knew about the attack on Milliken's Bend by midafternoon on 7 June, and he reasoned that the Rebels were almost certain to direct something at him, if for no other reason than to keep him from detaching troops to help Milliken's Bend. He put his men on alert and strengthened his pickets. However, nothing whatever happened, which seemed very odd. There were persistent scouting reports that the Rebels were going to strike, but no information as to when or in what force.

It was at this juncture that Grant's order to send 8 and 10 LA INF (AD) to Milliken's Bend reached Reid. Obeying the order would mean reducing his garrison to a single regiment, and doing so almost certainly would mean the loss of his post if the rumors of an impending attack proved true. Reid decided to procrastinate a bit. Then, early on the morning of 9 June, just as he had about concluded that his area was being ignored, a strong butternut force of infantry and cavalry, supported by artillery, hit his outpost at Baxter Bayou, six miles north of Lake Providence, and began pushing strongly southward. Reid promptly marched out of Lake Providence with his garrison and took a position behind Tensas Bayou.[47] He burned the bridge as soon as the last of his pickets was across and settled down to prevent the Confederates from crossing.

For the next ten hours there was a lot of noisy rifle fire, mostly harmless. At 2000, the Rebels drew back and marched away down the west bank of Tensas Bayou. Reid followed them with scouts, and next day they crossed to the west bank of the Tensas River on a brand-new bridge at Jackson's Ferry. That evening, Reid, aglow with the conviction that he had outsmarted both the Rebels and his own army commander, put the two Louisiana regiments aboard transports and sent them off to Milliken's Bend as Grant had directed.

RADM Porter maintained a remarkably efficient intelligence service in Louisiana, and his spies had been reporting that the Confederate force at Richmond had not withdrawn to the west after the defeat at Milliken's Bend. That worried Porter, because it looked to him as if the Rebels were going to try again. His fleet used Young's Point as a naval depot, and he hated to be inconvenienced by a Rebel occupation of it, however brief. Porter was frustrated by the fact that his warships could influence events directly only within range of their guns, and Richmond was much too far inland. Furthermore, the only land force he controlled was Ellet's Marine Brigade, and it was needed to help defend the Snyder's Bluff complex.

Porter's opportunity came on 12 June, when Sooy Smith's DIV began arriving at Snyder's Bluff from Memphis. That meant that Ellet's Marines no longer were needed. With Porter's connivance, Ellet promptly reclaimed his boats from the shipping pool, loaded his men, and sailed across the Mississippi to Young's Point. Porter had suggested that Ellet talk to Mower in terms of doing something about the Rebel force at Richmond. Just as Porter had anticipated, Mower wanted to start for Richmond immediately, but cooler heads prevailed. The final plan involved marching Mower's BDE from Young's Point to Lums via the Walnut Bayou Road, while Ellet and his Marine BDE sailed to Milliken's Bend, from whence they would march overland to Lums. The combined force then would drive on Richmond.

Heavy rain delayed the operation for several days, but finally, on 14 June, Mower's men tramped out of Young's Point, aiming for a rendezvous with Ellet's Marine BDE at Lums at 0600 on 15 June. Ellet and his Marine BDE had a poor reputation for punctuality, but, almost miraculously, this time they and Mower's BDE arrived at Lums practically simultaneously, ejected a Rebel picket, and together headed for Richmond, with Ellet's CAV BN in the lead.[48]

The cavalrymen were fired upon as they crossed the railroad embankment north of Richmond, but Ellet and Mower deployed and moved forward, pushing the Rebel skirmishers before them. By 0930, the Federal line had reached Roundaway Bayou, only to discover a Confederate battle line supported by artillery on the south bank. Even though it looked like a division front, Mower was far from intimidated. He couldn't make a direct crossing in the face of the Confederate artillery fire, so he left Ellet to entertain the gunners while he took his brigade upstream to look for a crossing. He never found one, but, while he was looking, the Rebels burned the bridge and began to withdraw westward along the south bank of Roundaway Bayou.

Ellet's CAV followed them, and by evening the Rebels were safely across the Tensas River and had burned that bridge as well. Mower figured that there was no point whatever in attempting a crossing of the Tensas in the face of a Rebel force that he was certain outnumbered his own, so he and Ellet quietly withdrew to Young's Point and Milliken's Bend. Porter was enchanted, and even Grant was pleased. However, Grant told the admiral and Dennis, the commander of the Louisiana posts, that there still might be a need for Mower's BDE on the west bank of the river, because there were reports from reliable sources that Pemberton was building a fleet of small boats with the intent of ferrying his army across to Louisiana and escaping. Porter thought that was sheer nonsense, but he alerted his ironclads nonetheless. Grant ordered Mower to remain at Milliken's Bend, picket the river, and emplace his artillery to command the likely landing sites. In this manner, the deadly "Eagle Brigade," one of the best fighting brigades in the Army of the Tennessee, became a more or less permanent part of the District of Northeast Louisiana.

Dennis could not quite believe that his troubles were at an end. He was certain that the Rebels would try again and that the next time they would come in greater strength. That being so, he needed to improve the fighting efficiency of his forces. One of the steps he took, with Grant's approval, was organizing a new brigade under COL George W. Neeley at Young's Point. It was comprised of the three Illinois regiments of the Young's Point garrison, plus 63 IL from Mower's BDE. Another step was to send strong combat patrols to keep tabs on what was happening in the Richmond area. By 24 June, all reports having been negative, Dennis finally concluded that the threat was at an end.

Events proved him wrong, however. On 29 June, Reid's scouts reported that Confederate forces were burning plantations in the area between the upper Tensas River and the Mississippi. Reid immediately notified COL William Wood, commanding the Post of Goodrich's Landing, as well as Grant and Porter. Porter told Grant that he would take care of the matter and ordered Ellet and his Marine BDE to proceed immediately to Goodrich's Landing. Ellet arrived there about 1930 on 29 June, to discover that *John Raine,* the armed transport assigned to the Marine BDE's CAV BN, had received artillery fire from the bank about five miles above Goodrich's Landing. The Rebels apparently had thought she was an unarmed transport, and when *John Raine* had replied with her two 12-pdr howitzers, the Rebels hurriedly limbered up and left. A landing party had found three dead Rebels.[49] Scouts said that the area between Goodrich's Landing and Lake Providence was swarming with Rebels, who were burning plantations and carrying off blacks.

On 30 June, Reid sent 1 KS MTD INF south from Lake Providence to investigate, and five miles south of town they ran into a large Rebel cavalry force which drove them back for two miles. At about the same time, Ellet's Marines and Wood's two regiments from the Goodrich's Landing garrison moved cautiously toward Transylvania. They found no Southern troops, but the few local people who had survived the incursion reported that the Southerners were withdrawing rapidly to the southwest.[50] Ellet sent COL Hubbard and his "Horse Marines," plus the Marine Brigade's artillery battery, in pursuit, with Ellet and the Marine INF following as rapidly as possible. Woods meanwhile returned to Goodrich's Landing with his two regiments. Hubbard caught up with the Rebels at

Jackson's Ferry, just as the last of them were crossing the bridge across the Tensas River. The Confederates held it until Ellet and the infantry arrived, then burned it and withdrew toward Floyd.

Later, when Wood and Reid investigated, they found the entire region between Bayou Macon and the Mississippi a wasteland. Every building had been burned. All the freed slaves had been herded together and driven off to the west, back into slavery. Some of the blacks had been hanged or shot, as had some of the white landowners. Horses had been carried off, but all other animals had been slaughtered and left in the fields. It was the most thorough example of devastation that either of the officers had ever seen.

36

Siege: War by Shovel
24 May–3 July 1863

Map: 18. The Vicinity of the Stockade Redan

It is popularly assumed that, in a siege, the defending forces have over-whelming advantages. After all, the defenders are sheltered behind sturdy walls, while the besiegers are "out in the open." However, things are not quite so simple, and the siege of Vicksburg amply illustrates the realities.

The earthworks at Vicksburg were made according to a "standard" pattern. When the Confederacy organized its military services, it simply put new covers on the military manuals of the United States. Both sides worked from essentially the same textbooks. The manual on fortifications specified that the rampart of an earthwork should be 14 feet thick, fronted by a ditch 18 feet wide and 10 feet deep. Not all of Vicksburg's strongpoints met these precise specifications, but the variations seem to be have been caused by lack of time, rather than any questions about the validity of the instructions.

What neither side appreciated was that the standard rampart design did not take into account two major variables. First, not all soils have the same resistance to projectile penetration. The standard dimensions in U.S. field manuals had been derived from experience gained primarily on the southeastern coasts of the United States, and the soils of that region are predominantly sandy. We now know that sandy soils are far more resistant to penetration than soils composed of grains smaller in size. The soils at Vicksburg are loess, an almost pure silt, and such soils offer far less resistance to penetration than sands.

The second factor is that the manuals were old. They had been derived from experience with smoothbore artillery, not rifled guns. The high-aspect-ratio projectiles of rifled artillery have far greater penetrating power than spherical shot of equivalent weight, diameter, or velocity.

Of course, no one at the time fully understood these things, so the standard textbook design went unchallenged. The consequences were interesting. Blair's DIV included a battery of 20-pdr Parrott rifles, and when these rifles opened fire on the Stockade Redan on 18 May, their projectiles went right through the rampart, which was 14 feet thick, and exploded somewhere over Glass Bayou, far in the rear. The explosions did no damage, of course, but, as each shell came through the rampart, it spread loose earth pretty liberally over everything. The eruption of such a round through the rear of the rampart must have been terrifying to the defenders, not to mention downright dangerous.

The response of the Confederate engineer officers was to line the inside of the ramparts with cotton bales, cover them with about 2 feet of earth, and revet them with light wooden walls. This quick fix was successful, in that it stopped the rifle shells very efficiently. However, one small factor was overlooked: the rifle shells penetrated the cotton, stopped, exploded, and set the cotton on fire. It takes but little imagination to visualize the position of the Southern infantrymen, standing on the firing step of an earthwork in which the rampart is afire. Flames were not really the problem; the cotton simply smoldered and released huge clouds of stifling smoke.

The answer to that was to keep everything wet, but that is much easier to say than it was to do. It is very difficult to saturate a cotton bale; indeed, the bales were used from time to time as flotation elements in raft bridges. They could be in the water for days without becoming waterlogged and sinking. Add to the cotton bales' natural resistance to wetting the fact that the summer of 1863 was abnormally hot and dry, and one gets a sense of the dimensions of the problem facing the Confederate defenders.

It is normally assumed that a man behind an earthen rampart or breastwork is safer than one out in the open, and this is true if the person in the open is in the process of making an assault. However, it is not true during a siege operation. Consider the problem facing a Confederate defender. In order to spot a target, he must lift his head over the top of the parapet of his defending earthwork and search the terrain in front of him very carefully. His opponent is wearing a very dirty blue uniform which blends surprisingly well into the natural colors of the landscape, and he can be absolutely anywhere in the terrain beyond the ditch. In order to have any prospect of finding the blue-clad soldier in the ravine below, the Rebel had to keep his head over the parapet for a considerable length of time.

Now consider the attacker. He can sneak out during darkness and find himself a convenient hidey-hole behind a stump or log, or in a little fold of ground, or whatever. He can even dig a slit trench in the loose loess soil. His enemy has got to stick his head over the parapet, where it is silhouetted against the sky. The attacker doesn't really have to search at all; he need only wait for a head to pop up, and he already knows pretty much where it will appear. One result of this combination of circumstances is revealed by the casualty figures during the siege. The Confederates lost 3,176 men during the period 23 May to 3 July, while the Union lost only 600 during the same period. That is, for every Union loss, there were more than five Confederate casualties. Most of the Confederate casualties were due to head or upper body wounds.

A somewhat similar situation existed with respect to artillery. The Confederate artillery was distributed mostly in one- and two-gun emplacements all along the line. The interval between battery positions averaged about 250 yards. The result was that the guns generally were not mutually supporting. In contrast, the Union could move its guns about freely. The Yankees used that freedom to assemble concentrations at various places. Twenty Union guns against one, or even two or three, Confederate pieces was not much of a contest; by the end of the siege, the Union had achieved almost complete artillery domination.

The Confederates tried to hoard their guns, of course, for use against infantry during the assault they all assumed would come eventually, as well as for use against critical targets like sap-rollers. The normal procedure was to take the guns out of their emplacements and hide them in defilade behind the ridge. Every now and again, especially when a sap-roller or some other worthwhile target became especially tempting, a gun would be run forward quickly, to fire a round or two. This had very limited success, because the Federal gunners quickly tumbled to the procedure and initiated countermeasures. A Yankee battery would fire on the empty embrasure until virtually every round went through the opening. This caused little damage and no casualties, but that was not the point. They then would wait, sometimes for days, for the Rebel gun to appear. The moment it did, it would be greeted with a six- or twelve-gun salvo, most of the rounds of which went right through the embrasure. It was very hard on the Confederate guns and their crews. After a few such experiences, only the most extreme emergency could tempt the Confederate cannoneers to expose their precious guns.

Vicksburg's loess soil is almost ideal for mining operations because it is relatively soft and easy to excavate, while, at the same time, a tunnel or even a fair-sized room will stand indefinitely in undisturbed soil without supports or reveting. The civilian population of the city exploited this property by digging numerous "caves" in which people lived through the interminable shelling. The Union was equally quick to exploit the same property by driving mines toward and under almost every major Confederate strongpoint in the defense line. Of course, the Confederates heard the sounds of digging and in most cases immediately started digging their own mines. The Union miners naturally heard the sounds of the Confederate miners, and then it became a race. In the course of one of these contests, the Confederate engineers learned a trick. Even a small charge exploded deep underground so shattered the soil that it lost its ability to sustain tunnels or chambers without timbering and reveting. That effectively made mining impractical. By 4 July, several Confederate mining operations were under way, with the intent of treating the soil in front of their works so that it became unsuitable for tunneling.

The loess soil is completely free of stones and clay, which made the construction of saps surprisingly easy. The Union saps were entirely conventional, being about four feet deep, with the excavated soil thrown up into two parallel banks about two or two and a half feet high, one on each side of the trench. The banks brought the effective depth to more than six feet, enough to completely shelter the soldiers in the trench from rifle fire. They would not shelter the people inside from artillery fire, but the Confederate artillery was so thoroughly suppressed that it was not a consideration.

A sap approached the target strongpoint on a zigzag course, with the directions carefully plotted so that the Confederate defenders could not fire into the open end. However, when the end of the sap got close to the Confederate trenches, that became impossible; and at that point a sap-roller was placed across the open end, and rolled forward as the sap advanced. Most of the Union sap-rollers were made out of the local bamboo, which grew in immense profusion in all of the ravine bottoms. Even so, the Federal troops had harvested virtually every plant for many miles in all directions by the time the siege was over. The bamboo first was crushed by beating it with a heavy wooden mallet, and then it was formed into a large circular bundle and bound together with cord, at least at first. The Yankees soon ran out of cord and, as a substitute, used grapevines and the ubiquitous wirelike greenbrier that is the bane of Mississippi woodlands.

The sap-roller would stop a rifle shot but not an artillery shell, and every now and again the Confederate defenders would smuggle a gun into battery and put a shot through one. It was a habit very irritating to the men digging the sap. Moreover, the cane was highly flammable, and the Confederate defenders developed some very ingenious methods for setting the sap-rollers afire. One was a modern adaptation of the Amerindian fire arrow. A wooden shaft was formed to fit inside the bore of a musket, a wad of turpentine-soaked tow was affixed to the end and ignited, and the whole mass was fired into the tinder-dry cane comprising the sap-roller.[1] The musket must have kicked like the proverbial mule, but it worked.

Despite their tendency to catch fire, cotton bales were used for revetments. Wood, of course, was available in abundance. It was used for planking gun platforms, corduroying roads, revetting firing positions, and a multitude of other things, including fuel for cooking. When the siege was over, the local landscape had been nearly denuded of timber. The abatis, which the Confederate defenders had created in the ravines in front of their earthworks by felling all the trees in the boggy hollows, proved to be an excellent and convenient source of firewood for the Union soldiery, and most of it was gone by the time the siege ended.

By the siege's end, the Union earthworks were nearly as extensive as the Confederate ones, and in some ways they were even more elaborate. Unlike the Roman circumvallations, the Union siege line did not consist of a continuous line of entrenchments and earthworks around the city. Rather, it was a complex of strategically sited riflepits and artillery battery positions. Large gaps separated individual sections of riflepits, but it didn't matter, because each was positioned so as to command an avenue of approach with concentrated rifle and/or artillery fire. Many of the riflepit complexes were designed specifically to support artillery positions, to guard against the possibility of a Confederate sortie to destroy the guns.

37

Siege Operations 23 May–4 July 1863

Operations against Square Fort (Fort Garrott)

Maps: 8. The Defenses of Vicksburg
     20. The Vicinity of the Railroad Redoubt

COMMENTARY

The siege operations against Square Fort have been used to characterize siege operations at Vicksburg in general, primarily because the area around Square Fort still retains clear traces of approaches, parallels, saps, and the other appurtenances of formal siege operations. None of the other strongpoints retain these features. It must be remembered, however, that activities similar to those at Square Fort took place in front of every major strongpoint on the Confederate defense line.

GEOGRAPHIC CONTEXT

Square Fort commands a small plateau from which three spurs radiate. Long Spur trends first south-southwest for 250 yards, then turns south for another 800 yards. Middle Spur trends sinuously south-southeast from the plateau and ends after a distance of about 450 yards. Short Spur is less than 150 yards long and trends southeast from Square Fort. The head of the ravine to the east forms a half-bowl, concave side outward. The rim of the bowl was guarded by Confederate riflepits, terminating in an artillery position at a salient about 300 yards northeast of Square Fort. About 1,400 yards to the east, beyond the deep valley of Durden

Creek, the Porters Chapel Road provided easy north-south communication roughly parallel to the Confederate perimeter.

FEDERAL PERSPECTIVE

Following the repulse on 22 May, Osterhaus's infantrymen had thrown up an irregular line of riflepits opposite Square Fort. When Hovey's DIV relieved Osterhaus's DIV a few days later, these riflepits were strengthened and extended. They started at a point about 250 yards almost due south of the fort and continued in an irregular line more or less parallel to the Confederate earthworks to a point 350 yards east of the fort. Here the line turned sharply toward the southeast along a spur, until, 250 yards farther, it reached the bottom of a broad ravine tributary to Durden Creek. In the days that followed, the line of riflepits—dubbed Hovey's First Parallel—was extended another 100 yards to the north.

Hovey, whose bellicosity was legendary throughout the Army of the Tennessee, waited impatiently for MAJ William Tweeddale, engineer of XIII Corps, to give him plans for an approach. While he waited, he was far from idle. The riflepits were improved daily, and before long the sniper fire from them became so effective that Rebel targets were getting hard to find. At last, Hovey could stand the inactivity no longer. On the night of 14 June, Slack's BDE and Lindsey's BDE (of Osterhaus's DIV, the bulk of which was at Big Black Bridge) moved stealthily forward into no-man's-land and threw up a second line of riflepits that in some places was less than 100 yards from the Confederate lines. To Hovey's surprise, the Confederates made no effort to interfere. Soon the line of riflepits became known as Hovey's Second Parallel. It ran north for 100 yards along the spur 160 yards east of Square Fort, then turned northeast on a line roughly parallel to the Confederate earthworks, to terminate on the crest of a spur southeast of the small unnamed redan 480 yards northeast of Square Fort.

Tweeddale had been so busy with the approaches to the Railroad Redoubt and the 2d TX Lunette that it was not until mid-June that he felt able to devote any attention to Hovey's sector of the line. When he finally turned his attention to Square Fort, he decided on two parallel saps. One was to start from a sheltered spot in the ravine near the left flank of the second parallel, and the other from a small ravine between Short and Middle spurs.[1] They eventually would converge on the plateau 30 yards from the ditch of the fort. The two saps together were dubbed Hovey's Approach.

Both saps were started shortly after dark on the night of 23 June. The standard nightly truce was in effect in this sector of the lines, so work

progressed rapidly. That same night, on a ridge 400 yards south of Square
Fort, a third fatigue party threw up an artillery emplacement sited to
bring the east face of the fort under enfilade fire. Before dawn, the new
position, Battery No. 13, was occupied by two 20-pdr Parrott rifles. It
worked even better than expected; the Federal gunners discovered that
they could reach the entrance bridge of the fort.[2]

So effective was the unofficial nightly truce that the Federals did not
even bother to use sap-rollers. But there were moments of uncertainty. On
the night of 28 June, the Officer of the Day of 20 AL found the Union officer
who was directing the sappers and told him coldly that he had five minutes
to get his men back to the shelter of the Federal lines. The Union officer
scratched his head and remarked thoughtfully that that might not be wise,
considering that "there were over 300 pieces of artillery waiting for a hostile move." The threat was effective, and work continued as before.[3]

The two saps joined about 30 yards in front of Square Fort on the
night of 1 July, and a single sap then was aimed directly at the southeast
corner of the fort. This was so close that the men no longer dared depend
on the truce; from then on, a sap-roller guarded the head of the sap.
Progress now became agonizingly slow; by the morning of 3 July, the sap
still was 20 yards from the fort's counterscarp.[4]

While Hovey's Approach inched toward Square Fort, the men of
Slack's BDE became increasingly bored and dissatisfied with their part
in the siege. They held the middle of Hovey's line but were more or less
completely left out of the activities around Hovey's Approach. At last
Slack decided on an approach of his own. The Rebel riflepits 100 yards
north of Square Fort were neither strong nor particularly well sited. A
sap driven westward from the Second Parallel might well be able to break
through the lines at that point.

Both sides put pickets out into the debated area between the lines during the night, and they had long since established amicable relations, so there
was no difficulty arranging a conference. Extensive friendly chitchat with the
officers of 23 AL ended in assurances that the status quo would not be broken. Slack's men began work on Slack's Approach on the night of 30 June.
When they withdrew at dawn, the sap was within 80 yards of the Confederate riflepits. During the day, a second work party widened, deepened, and
strengthened the sap. That night, 1 July, COL Raynor of the 56 OH again
engaged the Rebels in pleasant conversation while his men dug furiously.
At daybreak, the head of the sap was only 50 yards from the Rebel trenches.
Among other things, Raynor had learned that the Alabama pickets did not
take up their positions in front of the works until well after dark. The next

night, Raynor sent his own pickets out early. They took up positions within 10 yards of the Rebel riflepits, well within the area previously held by the Alabamans. When the Rebels came out at the usual time, they protested furiously. Raynor, stalling for time, promised to carry the protest to Slack, but instead he urgently requested reinforcements. Slack sent the 28 IA, and Raynor, with the grim Hawkeyes at his back, told the Confederates that he intended to hold his position. The stunned Alabamans withdrew to their riflepits with all faith in Yankee honor shattered forever.

Even so, it took thirty minutes for the Confederates' wrath to boil over. When it did, a concentrated volley crashed out of their lines. The 28 IA replied in kind, and for two hours the Alabamans and Iowans blazed away at each other. Darkness prevented accuracy; the Iowans had two men wounded. Despite the firefight, work on the sap went on, and by dawn the Federals had constructed a parallel about 75 yards long, within 50 yards of the Alabama line.

That same morning, perhaps providentially for both sides, the guns fell silent in the pre-surrender truce.[5]

CONFEDERATE PERSPECTIVE

After the repulse of the Federal assault on 22 May, Lee and his Alabama BDE breathed a bit easier. Actually, despite the fact that the Railroad Redoubt had been a no-man's-land for several hours, there never had been any real danger of a Yankee breakthrough. The assault on Square Fort had been so easy to beat off that Lee was uneasy; his experience with Yankee assaults, gained at Champion Hill, suggested that it all had been much too facile. Thus, when morning dawned on 23 May, Lee was not too surprised to see that the Yankees had dug in all across the front of Square Fort. An almost continuous line of brand-new riflepits trended across the Middle Spur about 300 yards from Square Fort, and ran more or less parallel to the Confederate defense line to a knoll on a ridge 350 yards east of the fort.

As the days went on, powerful artillery positions were added to the Yankee earthworks, and this was particularly troubling, as Lee had only four field pieces to defend his entire front of 900 yards. Very soon, Federal counterbattery fire forced the Confederates to take their guns out of battery and conceal them in defilade behind the ridge, leaving the infantry unsupported.

Lee quickly identified the unit facing him as Hovey's DIV of McClernand's corps. The information was not encouraging. The relative inactivity of the Yankees on his front confused him, because Hovey had been aggressive beyond belief at Champion Hill. It seemed completely out of character. Then, suddenly, on the night of 15 June, the inactivity came to an end. At first light the next morning, the Confederates discovered that a new line of riflepits had been dug overnight. The pits started a mere 125 yards southeast of Square Fort and continued to the east at about that same distance from the Confederate works until they terminated only 75 yards from the Confederate line, about 500 yards northeast of Square Fort. The line was so strong that Lee made no effort to interfere with it. Furthermore, it became extremely dangerous to look over the parapets, because any head that showed against the skyline drew multiple blasts of sniper fire.

The Confederates stood the fire almost without reply for several days, but the strain of being fired upon without being able to reply effectively slowly built to an intolerable level. At last, on 17 June, COL Garrott of the 20 AL could stand it no longer; he seized a rifle from one of his men and jumped to the firing step of Square Fort to relieve his pent-up frustration. Before he could find a target, a Yankee sniper tumbled him back into the arms of his men, a bullet through his heart.[6] Thenceforth, the earthwork was called Fort Garrott in his honor.

On the morning of 23 June, there was a new and ominous development. Saps appeared on both the Middle and Long spurs and advanced slowly but steadily toward the ditch of Fort Garrott. Lee dared not use his artillery to destroy them; the moment a Southern gun was brought into battery, every Union gun within range opened fire on the position. It was impossible to keep a gun in action for more than a shot or two. In consequence, Lee was forced to watch helplessly as the heads of the saps moved inexorably closer and closer. Even worse was a new artillery emplacement which appeared on Long Spur, 400 yards south of Fort Garrott, on the morning of 23 June. It mounted two 20-pdr Parrott rifles and had been positioned so nicely that they enfiladed the east face of Fort Garrott, rendering it virtually untenable.

Boredom is the great enemy of both sides in a long siege. The participants lose sight of the objectives and instead turn to ways of making life more comfortable. Vicksburg was no exception. Before long, over extended sections of the lines, an unofficial understanding banned fighting or firing at night. Friendly relations between the pickets led to an exchange of news, as well as trading coffee for tobacco. The Rebels had an unlimited supply of the latter, while the Yankees had a monopoly on the former. Both sides thought they were getting the better end of the bargain.

When the heads of the saps began to get close enough to the ditch of Fort Garrott to constitute a realistic threat, however, Lee and his regimental commanders realized that the nightly truce was being used by the Yankees to their considerable advantage. They worked like beavers during the night and didn't even bother to use sap-rollers.

Finally, on 28 June, COL E. Pettus, commander of 20 AL, decided to put a stop to it. During the night, he made contact with the Union officer directing the sappers and told him firmly that he had five minutes to get his men back to the shelter of the Federal lines. The Federal officer considered the proposal for a moment, and then remarked thoughtfully that there was an awful lot of artillery in the Union lines just waiting for a hostile move. Pettus and Lee were less than enthralled by the prospect of repairing their earthworks after having them chewed to bits by the Union artillery. The truce held.

Dawn on 1 July revealed that the two saps finally had joined at a point 30 yards southeast of the southeast corner of the fort. The threat now was so imminent that Lee began the excavation of galleries for two mines which not only would destroy the heads of the saps, but also would make the soil unsuitable for mines, as well as more difficult for the Union sappers. While the Rebels dug their tunnels, the Yankees began pushing a sap up the ridge toward the southeast corner of the fort. Progress, however, was mercifully slow; on the morning of 3 July, the sap was still 20 yards from the counterscarp, too far away to be really dangerous.[7] Construction of the Confederate mines was equally slow. The head of the tunnel would not pass the perimeter of the fort for several more days at least.

Then, on the morning of 3 July, came word of a cease-fire. Vicksburg was going to be surrendered.

Artillery
23 May–4 July 1863

Maps: 8. The Defenses of Vicksburg
      19. The Vicinities of 3 LA Redan and the Great Redoubt
      21. The Vicinity of South Fort

When the Army of the Tennessee had arrived and closed around the city on 21 May, it brought with it approximately 180 pieces of field artillery, rang-

ing in size from 6-pdr smoothbores to 30-pdr Parrott rifles. The latter were
so heavy that they were not normally carried along with an army in the field;
the tube alone weighed 4,200 pounds. Under ordinary circumstances, the
largest guns considered to be field artillery were 20-pdr Parrott rifles, in
which the gun-tube weighed 1,750 pounds—about all that could be managed under field conditions. In contrast, a 6-pdr Wiard gun-tube weighed
only about 884 pounds,[8] making it one of the favorite guns of the cavalry,
because it could be hauled readily by a two-horse team.

A running controversy existed as to the merits of smoothbore versus
rifled guns. It must be remembered that the primary role of field artillery was direct support of the infantry. In this role, smoothbores had many
advantages, and many field artillerymen preferred them. They were easier
to load and therefore had a higher rate of fire. The shells had a larger
bursting charge per unit of weight, and, because fragments tended to be
both more numerous and of more uniform size, smoothbore shells were
more effective antipersonnel weapons than rifled shells. For equivalent
bore diameter, smoothbore shells were lighter, so more rounds could be
carried in the ammunition chests. When a smoothbore round hit the
ground, it tended to bounce and keep on going; a skilled gun crew often
deliberately fired short when in action against infantry, so that the projectile would ricochet into the enemy ranks. This was important, because
it made estimating the range far less critical. In contrast, rifled shells
tended to dig in and stay where they hit. Moreover, considering that the
dominant role of artillery was as an antipersonnel weapon, canister from
a smoothbore was somewhat more effective than from a rifle, because the
charge spread a good bit more. Perhaps equally important, the small balls
of the canister rounds tended to damage the grooves in a rifled gun, which
made the piece less accurate the next time shell was used.

The other side of the coin was that rifled guns were considerably
more accurate, especially at long ranges, and their higher muzzle velocity and heavier shells gave them a significantly longer range for equivalent calibers. Rifled guns could stand out of range and, with a little luck,
put a smoothbore battery of equivalent caliber out of action. The elon-
gated shells thrown by rifled guns had much greater penetrating power,
so, if the objective was to put a hole through something, the weapon of
choice was the rifled gun.

Strangely enough, smoothbores tended to be more effective against
earthworks, the standard fortification of the Civil War. Against earthworks,
a primary function of artillery was to batter the face of the parapet until it

could be climbed by the infantry. Smoothbore rounds did not penetrate very far, but their large bursting charge blew out a largish mass of earth, which fell back in front of the parapet. After a little while, a ramp of earth stood in front of the earthwork, serving as a highway for the attacking infantry. Rifled shells penetrated very deeply, and their comparatively small bursting charges often were inadequate to displace any significant quantity of earth.

If the enemy earthwork mounted artillery, one of the tasks of the attacking artillery was counterbattery—that is, to knock out the artillery pieces in the defending earthwork. For this role, there was no substitute for rifled guns. Their accuracy made it possible to put rounds through embrasures with considerable precision. If the parapet was not too thick, the projectiles could penetrate and explode in the gun compartment, killing crew members or defending infantry, or damaging guns, even if the embrasures could not be hit.

From all this, it is clear that a place existed for both kinds of guns, and the Army of the Tennessee was equipped with both, in a ratio of roughly two smoothbores for each rifle. The Confederate armies tended to have a ratio of smoothbores slightly higher than that.

As soon as the two sides settled down to siege operations, after the assault on 22 May had failed so decisively, the role of artillery changed drastically. Siege artillery at Vicksburg had two principle functions. First, Confederate artillery had to be suppressed. This was no small task when the target was a gun firing through a narrow embrasure and protected on both flanks by traverses. It was in this role that the Union rifled field artillery came into its own.

Second, the artillery had to breach the defensive parapets, or at least collapse the faces of the works so that they could be scaled by infantry. In this role, the field artillery was of limited utility, because the bursting charges were too small. The answer was big guns, and, before the siege was very old, the Federal forces had a number of large pieces emplaced. They ranged in size up to 9-in Dahlgren smoothbores. A gun-tube of that size weighed 9,080 pounds, so moving one of the monsters from a landing site on the Yazoo River into the siege lines was not to be undertaken lightly. However, it was worth the effort, because a few 9-in shells could convert an unscalable scarp into a slope easy for the infantry.

The Confederates were at something of a disadvantage from the very beginning, and things got worse as the siege progressed. For example, within a week or so, the Union began to push saps toward all of the major works. The field guns that the Confederates had emplaced in their works were relatively ineffective against these saps. The obvious counter would have been to move the big River Defense guns into the strongpoints and blow the heads of the approaching saps to kingdom come, but the Southerners dared not do so. That would have exposed the city to direct naval bombardment from Porter's ironclad squadrons and possibly even to the landing of infantry along the waterfront.

Furthermore, the Confederate field artillery was deployed in conformity to the conventions of the day. As a generalization, there was about one gun for every 250 yards of defense line. In most cases, the guns were individually emplaced. Two guns emplaced in a single battery position was uncommon, and only rarely were three guns emplaced in a single battery. This made the Confederates terribly vulnerable to Union counterbattery fire, because the Federal habit was to emplace at least a full battery of four to six guns in a single emplacement. The result was that battery-versus-battery duels tended to be pretty one-sided. Almost without exception, they ended with the lone Confederate gun being knocked out.

Sometimes the Union besiegers carried the doctrine of concentration to extremes. Or at least it must have looked so to the Confederates. On one occasion, the Yankees concentrated well over 100 guns against the 3 LA Redan, ranging in size from 3-in Ordnance rifles, which fired a projectile weighing 9.5 pounds, to some 42-pdr naval guns, which fired projectiles weighing 43 pounds. When this enormous concentration was directed against the 3 LA Redan, it rapidly reduced the walls to unsightly mounds of freshly turned earth. By the time the siege was over, similar concentrations, albeit somewhat smaller ones, could be directed at every major Confederate strongpoint.

The Confederates did have one piece at Vicksburg that proved appallingly effective. Higgins's River Defenses had a 10-in mortar mounted in South Fort. It was intended for use against warships, but the Confederates quickly learned that it was hopeless to try to hit a boat with it, so eventually they moved it into the landward defenses and used it against one of the Union approaches. A 10-in mortar fires an explosive projectile weighing 87.5 pounds; when those big shells began to land in the saps and parallels, the Union infantry tended to leave. Fortunately for the Union, the Confederates had only one, and it couldn't be everywhere, so the impact on the siege as a whole was minimal.

The mortar was so effective, however, that the Union copied it. They had no factory-made mortars suitable for use on land, so they fabricated some by boring out tree trunks and reinforcing them with iron bands. They could only fire a 12-pound shell about 150 yards, but that was enough to make life in several of the Confederate strongpoints extremely hazardous.[9]

By the time the siege ended, the Union had achieved nearly total artillery domination. The Confederate defenders were scarcely able to fire a gun. Many of those emplaced in the works at the beginning of the siege had been destroyed by direct hits, while others had been withdrawn to positions of safety, where they were kept handy for the day when the Union would launch another assault. Now and again, the defenders brought one forward into the lines for a special occasion, but the first round normally brought such a storm of counterbattery fire from the Union concentrations that keeping the gun in action was hopeless. It is of some interest to note that the Confederates did not, at any time during the siege, make an attempt to achieve a concentration of guns at any one point. They persisted in the penny-packet approach to the bitter end.

A sense of the growing and finally complete artillery domination perhaps can best be obtained by looking in some detail at four aspects of the situation.

3 LA REDAN

When Vicksburg was first invested, the 3 LA Redan mounted only a single gun, a 3-in rifle. Only two other pieces of artillery in the Confederate lines could bear on the Jackson Road, one in a battery north of the 3 LA Redan and another to the south, between the redan and the Great Redoubt. The three guns were used only to slam an occasional surprise round into the Federal lines. After each shot, they were hastily rolled back to safety behind the ridge line, to evade the savage counterbattery that invariably answered such sallies.

By 11 June, those three Confederate guns were opposed by four major Union batteries disposed in depth along the Jackson Road Ridge. Closest to the 3 LA Redan was *Battery Hickenlooper,* which crowned a knoll on the Jackson Road Ridge 150 yards to the east. It mounted two 24-pdr howitzers and a 6-pdr gun. It was so close to the Confederate lines that snipers were a serious problem, so the embrasures were fitted with strong wooden frames which supported heavy plank shutters. The *White House Battery* stood an a small rise 50 yards south of the Shirley house, after which it was named. *Battery McPherson* stood just to the south of the Jackson Road, some 620 yards east of the 3 LA Redan, in a position from which the guns could bear on both the 3 LA Redan and the Great Redoubt. Originally this battery mounted two 30-pdr Parrott rifles. *Battery Logan* stood on the ridge about 100 yards south of Battery McPherson and was sited so that its guns could bear on both the Great Redoubt and 3 LA Redan. In addition, a line of batteries containing more than 100 guns crowned the ridge 600 yards to the southeast of 3 LA Redan. This immense array of artillery was sited primarily to fire on the Great Redoubt, but it could also bear on the southeast face of 3 LA Redan.

The margin of Federal artillery superiority was increased still further on 11 June, when two giant 9-in Dahlgren smoothbores, borrowed from the navy, were emplaced in Battery McPherson. By mid-June, McPherson and Logan had become disenchanted with the effectiveness of the 24-pdr howitzers in Battery Hickenlooper. Thus, on 18 June, the two 30-pdr Parrott rifles emplaced in Battery McPherson were brought forward and installed in Battery Hickenlooper.

The Union artillerymen quickly developed a lethal one-two punch. First the high-velocity rifled Parrott shells, fired at virtually point-blank range, penetrated deep into the parapet of the 3 LA Redan, loosening the hard-packed earth and breaking up the revetting. This would be followed by one of the giant 9-in Dahlgren shells from Battery McPherson. The tremendous explosive power of the huge shells hurled vast quantities of soil out of the steadily eroding parapet. In a matter of hours, a breach had been blasted through the redan's parapet near the salient angle. That night the Louisianans swarmed over the work and managed to effect temporary repairs, but MAJ Lockett, Pemberton's chief engineer, realized full well that the Yankees could repeat the performance at any time and possibly even make the redan untenable. His solution was to throw up a strong line of riflepits across the base of the redan, in a position at least partially protected from the irresistible Union artillery.

SOUTH FORT

Only at South Fort did the landward defenses include big guns capable of reaching the Union investment lines. South Fort was a strongpoint on the extreme southern end of the Confederate defense line, and it had been designed both to serve as a part of the River Defenses and to guard the landward approach via the Warrenton Road. It mounted a 10-in columbiad, a 30-pdr Parrott rifle, and a 10-in mortar. Originally the gun platforms and embrasures had been configured such that the guns bore only on the Mississippi River. After the siege began, however, the Confederates hastily made modifications, so that, by 15 June, both the columbiad and the Parrott could fire down the ridge to the south. This, of course, was the direction from which any infantry attack would have to come.

When the Federal army invested Vicksburg, its troops eventually moved in close to South Fort and seized a position on the Warrenton Ridge 900 yards directly to the south. In 1863, the ridge on which the Warrenton Road runs was very sharp, with deep ravines running away to Stouts Bayou on the east and the Mississippi River on the west. The terrain configuration is not quite so apparent today, because a good deal of artificial smoothing, leveling, and filling has been done.

This extreme southern sector of the lines was relatively inactive until Federal BG Francis Herron's DIV arrived on the scene on 13 June. Herron took one look at the massive parapets of South Fort and realized that nothing could be done without artillery. All he had was field guns; nevertheless, on the night of 14 June, his artillerymen threw up a gun emplacement and mounted two 10-pdr Parrott rifles, the biggest pieces he had available.

At dawn the next morning, the Federal artillerymen opened fire, confident in the power of their weapons. The two shells screamed along the ridge and exploded deep inside the parapet of the Confederate earthwork. Almost like an echo, a gun replied from the fort with a deep-toned bellow. When its shell exploded in front of the field artillery emplacement, the roar shook the earth, and huge iron fragments went shrieking by on all sides. One came to rest in the Union emplacement, and the shocked artillerymen realized that it was from a 10-incher. The next round was closer and the next closer still. A hit from one of those shells could kill every man in a gun crew, so the Union artillerymen limbered up and got out before the bolt fell.

That night, the Union gunners strengthened their parapets and put the two Parrotts back into position. Next morning, as soon as there was light to see, the Rebel columbiad fired one round. It made a direct hit on one of the Parrotts and sent it flying away, a complete ruin. The Confederates had made their point: don't try to fight heavy artillery with field guns.

RADM Porter had a squadron of ironclads, led by mighty *Benton*, lying off Bowers' Landing, and that night Herron made contact with that ship. That afternoon, *Benton* slid into the Warrenton landing and offloaded four of her 32-pdr smoothbores.[10] Smoothbores, because by this time it was well understood that smoothbores were more effective against earthworks than rifles. *Benton* was the strongest vessel in the squadron below Vicksburg, the workhorse of the fleet. Here we see the Union navy partially disarming its major unit in order to provide artillery support for the army. It is a minor but thought-provoking example of the degree of cooperation achieved between the navy under David Porter and the army under Sam Grant.

A 32-pdr smoothbore gun tube weighs 7,200 pounds. These four were mounted on old-style naval gun carriages, which weighed about 1,000 pounds each. Moving guns and carriages up onto the bluffs, 150 feet overhead, was no trivial task. But the Union artillerymen set to work with a will, and, by 25 June, the four guns were in place and shooting. There were two emplacements on the ridge east of Stouts Bayou (which flows in the ravine to the east of Warrenton Ridge) and another on Warrenton Ridge, about 1,300 yards south of the parapet of South Fort. These guns helped materially, but a 32-pound shot still is no match for a 10-in columbiad, which throws a shot weighing 128 pounds.

So Herron went back to the navy, and this time Porter loaned him two of *Benton's* 42-pdr rifles. *Benton* normally carried fifteen guns, so, by this time, Herron had a substantial fraction of her armament. Porter wasn't sure that the army would know what to do with guns of such size, so he sent Acting Master J. Frank Reed along to supervise.[11] Reed directed the construction of a massive emplacement on a knoll 900 yards south of South Fort. On the night of 29 June, he announced that the guns were ready for action.

Meanwhile, the 10-in mortar, which had been mounted in South Fort, had proved useless against the Union ironclads and had been moved to a position in the siege lines, where it wreaked havoc in the Union trenches along the Jackson Road. The commander of South Fort, of course, noticed construction of a huge emplacement on Warrenton Ridge and realized that it was intended for big guns and called for the return of his mortar. It was back in position by about midnight on 29 June. Bright and early the next morning, Reed's 42-pdrs opened fire. From the very first shots, it was evident that the almost point-blank fire soon would breach the parapets. That gave Herron license to start planning an infantry assault. Then there was a dull report from inside the walls of South Fort, and a 10-in mortar round sailed overhead and burst just to the rear. The fourth round dropped squarely into Battery Benton, killing two men, wounding four, and silencing the guns.[12]

It took a couple of days to get the Union guns back in operation,[13] but now their fire was coordinated with that of the navy. The combined fire of

Battery Benton and the gunboats in the river kept the Rebel mortar opera-
tors so off-balance that they no longer could hit Battery Benton. The walls
of South Fort began to erode quickly under the combined fire. Herron
matured his plans for an assault, but all in vain. The next day, 4 July 1863,
the guns of both blue and gray fell silent in the presurrender truce.

Two points in this tale are worthy of note. First is the intimate and enthusiastic cooperation between the Federal army and navy. If one theme
characterizes the Vicksburg Campaign, surely this is it. Second, there is the
problem of fitting the weapon to the task. Light artillery—that is, field
guns—were fine against troops in the open, counterbattery against similar
guns, and even against hastily constructed field fortifications. But against
well-protected big guns, they were virtually impotent. Before they were able
to deal effectively with a single 10-in columbiad and a 10-in mortar, the
Federals had to marshal four 32-pdr smoothbores, two 42-pdr rifles, and
several batteries of field artillery. Plus, of course, the big guns mounted on
Porter's ironclads in the Mississippi River below.

WATERFRONT

Vicksburg had one iron foundry before the siege. It was located near the
railroad depot and was easily visible from the River. Fortunately, it was
well supplied with coal; and, as the siege wore on, people were encouraged to pick up shell fragments and bring them to the foundry, where they
were recast into shells. These were returned to the Yankees through the
bore of a cannon.[14] When the Federals heard about this, they were in-
censed. The first notion was to send an ironclad down to knock out the
foundry, but Porter took a dim view of that, since the ship would have to
stop right under the guns of the Wyman's Hill, Brooke, and Marine Hospital batteries. The admiral was unwilling to trade one of his ironclads for
a mere iron foundry. The mortar fleet tried to hit the foundry with its big
13-inch mortar shells, but the guns were too inaccurate, and the effort
was soon abandoned.

Porter now delegated the task to Ellet's Marine Brigade, which had
some 20-pdr Parrott rifles, which were ideal for the job. Ellet's men accepted the task with considerable enthusiasm, and on the night of 19
June, they started to build "Fort Adams" on DeSoto Point, right opposite the foundry. A strong casemated battery armored with railroad tracks,
it mounted a single 20-pdr Parrott rifle. It was finished by the morning
of 20 June, and, after a few ranging shots, the gunners began to score

hits.[15] The Confederates opened counterbattery fire from both the Wyman's Hill and Marine Hospital batteries, but the Union engineers had built strongly and well; even though the casemate was hit several times, the gun was uninjured. In a couple of days, the foundry was put out of operation,[16] and it did not resume until long after the end of the siege.

MORTAR FLEET

There are those who argue that the notion of total war originated during the Civil War, and one basis for the charge is the indiscriminate bombardment of Vicksburg by siege mortars. Early in the siege, the Union navy brought a fleet of six mortar boats down from the North, each of which mounted a single 13-in siege mortar. The boats were anchored behind DeSoto Point, and collectively they dropped an average of one 256-pound shell into the city every five minutes for the duration of the siege. One trouble was that the mortars were grossly inaccurate, so neither the Union gunners nor anyone else had any idea where the next shell would land; they fell indiscriminately all over the city. The civilian population tried to adapt to the rain of projectiles by digging caves in the loess hills and living in them. While this sounds distinctly uncomfortable, the caves actually were quite comfortable, being both cool and dry. Some were quite elaborate, consisting of several rooms.

The problem was that the fuses on the mortar shells were unreliable. It turned out to be almost impossible to make them explode at ground level, where they would achieve maximum effect. Instead, they tended to explode high in the air, scattering large chunks of shell casing far and wide. The shell fragments from air bursts were lethal enough, to be sure, but they were far less damaging than an explosion at ground level would have been.

As it turned out, those shells in which the fuses had been cut too long were even less effective. Vicksburg is built almost entirely on a stratum of loess which is up to 200 feet thick in places. As already has been noted, it is not very resistant to penetration. MAJ Lockett, the Confederate engineer, measured the depth of the hole made by a mortar shell when it hit the ground without exploding and found that it had stopped 37 feet below the surface. Even if the shell exploded, the result was scarcely more than a jet of smoke spurting from the hole, because the force of the explosion was insufficient to lift the mass of earth above it. Thus, with the exception of those few mortar shells which happened to make a direct hit on something vital, a high proportion of those which fell on the city during the siege literally vanished into the earth as if they had never been fired. In short, Vicksburg's peculiar soil materially reduced the effectiveness of the mortar bombardment. The reverse side of the coin is that, if one had made a direct hit on a cave dug by the civilian populace, the result would have been devastating. Fortunately, none of them ever were hit.

When the Federal forces entered the town after the siege, they were astonished at how little damage had been done by the incessant bombardment. They expected to find the town in ruins but instead found that a relatively small number of buildings had even been damaged by the mortar bombardment. As it turned out, the enormous effort required to keep the mortar battery operating was largely wasted; the bombardment had no significant effect on the conduct or conclusion of the siege.

Far more damaging were the shells from the artillery ringing the city. Inevitably, some of them went over the tops of the parapets and hit far inside the city. Those buildings which happened to be directly on an extension of a line between a Union battery and a Confederate strongpoint suffered greatly. McRaven, arguably the oldest house in the city, stood directly behind Fort Garrott and took several direct hits.

Battle in the Crater
25–26 June 1863

Maps: 8. The Defenses of Vicksburg
          19. The Vicinities of the 3 LA Redan and Great Redoubt

TACTICAL SITUATION

Two powerful Confederate earthworks guarded the point where the Jackson Road passed through the defense line. To the south of the road, crowning the highest hill on the defense line, was the Great Redoubt. The redoubt was difficult to approach from the Union siege lines, because it was fronted by long open slopes dropping into deep ravines. To the north of the Jackson Road, the 3 LA Redan crowned the ridge along which the Jackson Road ran, and thus it could be approached along a terrain feature not notably lower in elevation than the redan itself. Both the Great Redoubt and the 3 LA Redan were in the sector of responsibility of McPherson's XVII Corps.

By nightfall on 22 May, after the failure of the second Federal assault

on the Confederate lines, MG Logan's blue-suited infantry were left clinging to the Shirley House Ridge, which crossed the Jackson Road Ridge
400 yards east of 3 LA Redan. Union outposts were dug into a knoll on
Pemberton Ridge only 150 yards southeast of the parapet of Great Redoubt, but they constituted no more than a skirmish line; the main Union
position was another 300 yards to the southeast.

During the next three weeks, the Union engineers established powerful battery positions and strong lines of riflepits along the ridges, and
the army settled down to classical siege operations. McPherson's chief
engineer, CPT Hickenlooper, started the construction of Logan's Approach, a sap that angled back and forth across the Jackson Road Ridge,
aimed at the salient angle of 3 LA Redan. Things went well until 13 June,
when the head of the sap was only 40 yards from the parapet of the
redan. At this point, life in the sap suddenly became very dangerous,
because the Rebels began to drop huge 90-pound shells into the sap; they
came from a 10-in mortar newly emplaced southwest of the Great Redoubt. Nevertheless, progress continued, and by 16 June the head of the
sap was within 25 yards from the scarp of the redan. This brought it
within hand-grenade range of the Confederate lines, and life in the head
of the sap became even more hazardous. The Rebels had no purpose-
made hand grenades, so they used 6- and 12-pdr shells with five-second
fuses. Forward progress slowed dramatically. By 21 June, the head of the
sap was still 10 long yards from the parapet of 3 LA Redan. And here
progress stalled. The combination of grenades and 10-in mortar shells
simply made it impossible to work in the head of the sap.[17] Hickenlooper
tried to suppress some of the Rebel fire by extending two parallels to the
south of the head of the sap, so that the southeast face of 3 LA Redan
could be covered by close-range rifle fire, but this effort had little effect.

FEDERAL PERSPECTIVE

In this situation, Hickenlooper and Logan turned to alternate means of getting into the Rebel strongpoint. The obvious answer was a mine.[18] The loess
soil of Vicksburg was designed by the creator for mining, because tunnels
required no shoring or revetting. McPherson's corps included troops from
both the lead-mining districts of Missouri and the coal-mining districts of
Illinois and Ohio, so plenty of talent was available. Work began on 23 June,
and by 0900 on 25 June, a gallery 78 feet long had been carried under the
parapet of the Rebel strongpoint. Two side galleries, like the toes of a bird's

foot, also had been completed, and small chambers had been constructed at the tips of the three toes.[19] Meanwhile, Hickenlooper thoughtfully had "borrowed" 2,100 pounds of powder from the navy, as well as the necessary fusing. By 1300 on 25 June, Hickenlooper proudly reported to Logan and McPherson that his mine was ready to go.[20]

McPherson had kept Grant informed of the progress of Logan's Approach; on the morning of 25 June, the army commander rode over to the Jackson Road to see for himself how the mine was progressing. When he learned that it was ready to go, he set H-hour for 1500 and sent telegrams to his corps commanders, ordering them to have their forward works fully manned and ready for action when the mine exploded. Their function was to prevent the Rebels from reinforcing the Jackson Road sector. To this end, every artillery piece that could be brought to bear would blast the Rebel works for fifteen minutes as soon as the mine detonated. Then, if the Southerners showed any sign of shifting troops, the infantry would feint at the fortifications to pin the Rebels in place.[21]

McPherson's plan of attack was to drive right through the breach in the parapet of the redan while supporting fire from the infantry in the parallels kept the Rebels from concentrating on the flanks of the assault column. Leggett's BDE was the assaulting unit, perhaps because the "Lead Mine Regiment," 45 IL, came from the lead-mining district around Grant's home town, Galena, IL. The Lead Miners were given the dubious honor of being the spearhead of the attack. But at the very tip of the spear was a brave little party of ten pioneers, led by Hickenlooper and LT Tresilian; their task was to clear a way through the debris of the explosion for the assaulting infantrymen.

Everything was ready by a few minutes before 1500. The pioneers crouched in the head of the sap, barely 25 yards from the salient angle of the redan. To Hickenlooper fell the delicate task of lighting the ends of the fuses to the three charges at exactly the same moment, so that all the charges in the mine would detonate simultaneously. Behind the engineers, extending down the sap in a column of fours, bayonets fixed, were the Lead Miners, followed by the rest of Leggett's BDE. Behind Shirley House Ridge, three additional regiments were held in reserve. Thus eight veteran regiments stood ready for the breakthrough attempt.[22] The parallels were occupied by 100 picked sharpshooters, who were to cover the advance of the 45 IL by keeping the southern face of the redan under fire. Once the attack got rolling, they were to charge the works to their front, thus helping to bend back the shoulders of the breakthrough.

As 1500 neared, every soldier in the Army of the Tennessee tensed for the expected blast. The incessant rattle of musketry died away. The cannoneers loaded their pieces but held their fire, waiting to use their shells to sweep the Rebel parapets after the mine went off. The set time came and vanished into history, and still a deathlike stillness lay over the field. The men in the assaulting column began to shake under the strain, and, here and there along the close-packed approach trench, an infantryman, voice thin and high with tension, audibly wondered if the mine had misfired.[23]

The oppressive silence went on and on, ten minutes after the hour, twenty minutes, thirty minutes—and then the ground leaped and shuddered under a mighty shock. The parapet at the tip of the salient angle lifted smoothly into the air, then broke up gradually into fragments and disintegrated into an immense fountain of earth, shot through with ruddy flashes of fire and clouds of smoke. The whole vast spectacle seemed to occur in slow motion.

With the first shock, a deep-toned roar of triumph welled up from the throats of the Federal soldiers. At the same instant, every gunner convulsively yanked at the lanyard of his cannon. The combined noise was so great that the dull and prolonged roar of the mine itself was completely lost.[24]

Hickenlooper, Tresilian, and the ten pioneers leaped forward while clods of earth still rained down around them. They worked like madmen to clear away the shattered timbers and gabions at the head of the sap, then stood aside to let the Lead Miners pour through. The miners found themselves in a crater 30 feet wide and 12 feet deep, and shaped like an old-fashioned washbowl. The column stormed across the soft and still-smoking floor of the depression, climbed the western rim—and were hurled back into the crater by a savage blast of musketry, fired at point-blank range by an unshaken line of Rebels sheltered in a line of riflepits barely 15 yards away. This was the first intimation the Federals had that the defenders had constructed a second line of defense. The Illini rallied and tried again, and this time their charge carried them right up to the Rebel breastworks before they were beaten back by concentrated rifle fire. Within the first five minutes of the assault, the Union tide had reached its crest and ebbed.

COL Jasper Maltby, commander of 45 IL, realized that the fire of the Southern infantry would have to be suppressed if there was to be any reasonable hope of breaking through, so he sent men left and right to use the parapets of the redan as breastworks. By firing over the top, they could command the crater, as well as sweep the Confederate riflepits that now constituted the sole obstacle between himself and the city.

The men left in the crater were formed into three-man firing teams. One man fired from the rim of the crater, while the other two loaded rifles and passed them up. To the storm of musketry thus poured out was added a rain of hand grenades; the Rebel lines were within easy range.

Meanwhile, Hickenlooper, like Maltby, had realized that the contest had developed into a slugging match, so he hastily had some heavy cypress timbers loop-holed. These his pioneers brought forward and placed along the rim of the crater, while others dug away industriously to convert the western edge of the crater into a trench with a regular firing step. Still other men were busy with shovels, extending the head of the sap into the crater, so that Federal troops could move back and forth freely without being brought under fire. The loop-holed logs were barely in place when the muzzle of a 3-in rifle suddenly appeared over the Rebel parapet. Its first shell plowed into one of the logs, hurling it backward into the crater and sending a screaming shower of wooden splinters in all directions. One splinter badly wounded COL Maltby. A moment later, after CPT Leander Fisk was killed, BG Leggett was forced to assume personal command, because the Lead Miners had run out of officers. Leggett ordered the logs removed immediately, since it was obvious that, until the Rebel cannon could be put out of action, the timbers did more harm than good.[25]

Knocking out the Rebel gun proved unexpectedly difficult. The second line of riflepits was several feet lower than the parapet of the 3 LA Redan, so it could not be reached by Union artillery. All through the blazing afternoon, the deadly rifle now and then would poke its ugly snout forward and loose a blast of destruction toward the Union line.

The Rebels kept up a continual rain of hand-thrown shells. The Federal infantry fielded as many as they could and tossed them back into the Rebel lines. PVT William Lazarus of the 1 U.S. INF disposed of twenty in this way before he was killed. Leggett then organized a three-man team from the same unit to continue Lazarus's good work.

About 1800, Leggett pulled the battered Lead Mine Regiment out of the line and replaced it with 20 IL. All through the long afternoon, regiments were fed into the fight until their ammunition was exhausted, after which they were withdrawn, to be replaced by still another fresh regiment.[26]

During the afternoon, Hickenlooper and Leggett realized that somehow they had to get rid of that pesky 3-in rifle being used by the Rebels to such effect in the crater.[27] They also needed some firepower to breach the Rebel line of riflepits that was blocking the way into the city. With this in mind, Hickenlooper began constructing a two-gun emplacement in the crater. Tired though they were, Hickenlooper and his pioneers labored mightily through the night, while the battle thundered about them. By dawn, a heavily timbered casemate, deeply banked with earth, had been built in a position just far enough inside the crater to give its loopholes and embrasures command of the inside of the redan. It was connected to the approach by a trench secure against everything but mortar fire, and the flanks were tied to the original parapet of the redan by a strong line of riflepits.

Grant had watched the struggle for control of 3 LA Redan from Battery Hickenlooper. At dusk, he told McPherson that if Leggett still held the crater in the morning, the XVII Corps should try to seize control of the riflepits north of the redan.

All through the night the battle roared on. For some reason now unknown, the two guns which were to be emplaced in the "Crater Battery" never arrived. Without artillery to breach the Confederate parapet, the Union officers realized that a stalemate had developed. They allowed the firing gradually to die away.

When dawn finally came on 26 June, the Union was left in possession of most of the 3 LA Redan, but it had not opened a way into the city. Still, it held a position within 15 yards of the last Rebel defense line, which was an advantage, however tenuous. For that advantage, however, the Federals had paid a stiff price: 34 dead and 209 wounded.[28]

All through 26 and 27 June, McPherson and his men thought hard about how to break that last thin barrier that kept them out of Vicksburg. Finally they concluded that the mine had been a success; had it not been for that second line of trenches, they now would be in the city. Therefore, repeat the enterprise. Bright and early on the morning of 28 June, LT Russell and his coal miners filed into the casemate in the crater and began excavating a new mine. This time, the objective was the junction of the second Confederate line and the original parapet of the 3 LA Redan, some 50 yards to the northwest.[29] The work now went more smoothly than before; inexplicably, the Rebels had taken the 10-in mortar away. Scouts on the line to the south reported that its place had been taken by what looked like a 9-in Dahlgren smoothbore.

Very soon after starting the tunnel for the second mine, the Union miners heard the unmistakable sounds of Confederate counterminers. By 1 July, the sounds had become so loud that Hickenlooper asked McPherson for permission to charge and spring the mine before it was too late, despite the fact that it was still several yards short of its objective. McPherson asked Grant, and Grant told him to go ahead. Russell's miners, working with speed born of both skill and desperation, charged the gallery with 1,800 pounds of powder.

McPherson ordered Logan's men under arms, in the unlikely event that the Confederates tried a sortie,[30] but there was to be no infantry attack. Instead, the artillery would concentrate on 3 LA Redan and chew it to bits, if that were possible.

This time there was no delay; the mine went off at 1500, right on schedule. As before, it hurled a huge gout of pulverized earth into the air. Mingled with the clods of earth raining down into the Union approach, however, was a black man, so frightened he could barely talk but otherwise uninjured. The Union soldiers picked him up, dusted him off, and asked him how high he had gone. He said he wasn't sure but thought about three miles.[31]

Scarcely had the shock wave of the blast died away when every gun on the XVII Corps front opened a savage and prolonged fire on the Rebel works flanking the Jackson Road. Every gun which could be brought to bear poured a terrible hail of shells into the badly damaged parapet of the Confederate defense lines on either side of the 3 LA Redan. The Confederates made frantic efforts to repair their rapidly eroding parapets, but it was clear to the Union commanders that they could breach the works with their artillery alone any time they chose. After a few more moments, McPherson's guns fell silent, awaiting the day and hour when Grant would order the final assault.

The Confederates had lost most of the 3 LA Redan, but the Union failed to make a decisive penetration of the Confederate lines. However, the XVII Corps had gained a slight strategic advantage, in that there remained only a single thin line of riflepits between the Yankees and the city. When Grant was told of the results of the Federal cannonade on 3 LA Redan, he nodded in satisfaction. It was clear that the Union artillery could breach the Confederate defenses more or less at will, in which case an assault all along the line was virtually guaranteed success.

CONFEDERATE PERSPECTIVE

The Confederates in 3 LA Redan were well content with their defense of the work. The combination of 6- and 12-pdr shells, used as hand grenades, and the 90-pound mortar shells from the 10-in mortar mounted southwest of the 3 LA Redan clearly had brought work on the Yankee sap to a stop. Their satisfaction ended abruptly on 23 June, when they heard the unmistakable sounds of men working underground. MAJ Lockett, the chief engineer, fully understood that the Vicksburg soil was peculiarly amenable to mining. Instantly grasping what the Yankees were about, he ordered that a countermine be dug to intercept the Federal tunnel before charges could be placed.

His men were still working madly on the early afternoon of 25 June, when suddenly the sound of Union activity in the mine ceased, and an unnatural hush fell over the Federal lines. Lockett was not quite sure what that meant and kept his men hard at work on the countermine. Unlike Lockett, the soldiers in the redan thought they knew what it portended, and each breathed a sigh of relief when Hébert quietly passed the word to withdraw into the newly constructed line of riflepits across the base of the redan. The Appeal Artillery's 3-in rifle also was removed and placed on a new firing platform behind the riflepits, from which point it commanded the interior of the redan. Left behind were six brave men of 43 MS, who continued to dig furiously in an attempt to find the gallery of the Yankee mine.[32] Hébert, made uneasy by the unearthly silence, notified Pemberton that he was certain there was going to be an assault on his lines. It sounded so reasonable to Pemberton that he immediately ordered Cockrell to be ready to move a regiment of his MO BDE toward the 3 LA Redan at an instant's notice.

All doubt ended at 1530, when the ground leaped convulsively and the whole salient angle of 3 LA Redan lifted majestically into the air, leaving a huge gap in the parapet. Almost before the last of the debris had fallen back to earth, a column of Yankee infantry stormed through the gap, into the crater, and over the western lip. The men of 3 LA, sheltered from the blast by their newly constructed breastworks, were entirely unshaken by the explosion and instantly opened fire on the advancing Federal column. It came right up to the breastwork of the line of riflepits before breaking and falling back into the relative protection of the crater. From their positions barely 15 yards apart, blue and gray traded savage volleys of musketry.

When Cockrell saw the black explosion cloud rise over the Confederate lines, he ordered COL Eugene Erwin to hurry his 6 MO from its camp near the headwaters of Stouts Bayou to the aid of 3 LA. The sturdy Missourians reached the redan only a few minutes after the collapse of the initial Yankee surge. Unlike his renowned grandfather, Henry Clay, Erwin was a fire-eater. Appalled by the Yankee penetration of the redan, he leaped to the parapet, waved his sword in a sweeping gesture, and shouted, "Forward, boys, don't let the Louisianans go farther than you do!" Then he collapsed in death, with two Minié balls through his body. Erwin's second-in-command, MAJ Stephen Cooper, having no intention of wasting lives on a romantic gesture, countermanded Erwin's order and instead placed his men in the riflepits beside the Louisianans.[33]

Before long, the Confederates noticed that the bluecoats were bringing up heavy timbers with loop-holes cut in them to provide better protection to their riflemen on the rim of the crater. There was an answer to that. The cannoneers of the Arkansas Appeal Artillery loaded their 3-in rifle and in one quick operation rolled it into place, aimed the tube at one of the heavy logs, fired, and rolled the gun back out of danger. The result was completely satisfactory. The heavy timber was blasted backward into the crater, and, even in the Confederate riflepits and above the roar of musketry, the screams of men injured by the deadly spray of wooden splinters could be heard.[34] This tactic worked so well that the gunners were kept busy all afternoon.

The parapet of the new line of riflepits behind 3 LA Redan was slightly lower than the parapet of the redan, so the Union artillery could not reach it. However, the Federal infantrymen converted the parapet of the redan, as well as the western rim of the crater, into impromptu riflepits, from which they kept up a storm of musketry. They also began constructing in the crater what clearly was intended as an artillery battery.

The musketry went on and on, without abating, all afternoon. Nevertheless, the Confederates were so well protected from the Yankee fire that they suffered remarkably few casualties. In fact, when COL McCowan arrived with 5 MO about dark, Hébert told him that things were so thoroughly under control that he might as well bivouac. Cockrell arrived and overruled this, however, putting 5 MO into the line alongside 6 MO and thus relieving three companies of 3 LA for a well-earned rest.[35]

The firefight went on far into the night, finally dwindling away near daylight, 26 June. Here the situation stabilized, with the Yankees in firm possession of the interior of 3 LA Redan but the Confederates holding an unassailable line of riflepits across the base of the redan. The Confederates had lost twenty-one killed and seventy-three wounded, but they had retained the integrity of their line.

There matters rested until shortly after dawn on 28 June, when the

Confederate defenders once again heard the sound of miners working underground. The damned Yankees were going to try the same scheme again! This was serious indeed. If a second mine blew a hole in the line of new riflepits, there was no third line to which the defenders could fall back. If that line were breached, the city well might fall.

Lockett figured that the Federals would start their mine from the shelter of the newly constructed battery position in the crater. He liked to experiment and rigged up a barrel containing 125 pounds of powder with a fifteen-second fuze and rolled it over the parapet. It lodged against the face of the battery and exploded with a roar. When the smoke had cleared away, however, there was no detectable damage to the casemate, and the sounds of mining continued without pause. Lockett shrugged and ordered a countermine. This time, however, the working party consisted of eight blacks and a white supervisor; no soldiers were going to be buried this time.

About 1430 on 1 July, MAJ Lockett decided to make an inspection of the countermine and emerged a few minutes before 1500, reporting that all was going well. The countermine party was still feverishly at work at 1500 when the whole north face of the redan disintegrated in a spectacular explosion. Everybody working in the tunnel was killed. Falling debris buried alive some of the infantrymen in the new riflepits; others were hurled into the ravine to the west. When the casualties were counted up, 3 LA had 1 dead and 212 injured, the Appeal Artillery had 4 men injured, and 6 MO had 2 officers and several enlisted men killed, with many more injured. The survivors scrambled hastily back to their places, expecting another Federal attack, but it never came.[36]

When Lockett examined the position of the new crater, he realized that the objective had been the place where the new line of riflepits tied into the left-flank parapet of the 3 LA Redan, but that the Federal engineers had detonated the mine too soon. While the explosion had destroyed the north face of the redan, the new riflepits, as well as the line of old riflepits north of the redan, survived essentially intact. He congratulated himself, because it was clear that the Yankees had detonated their mine prematurely because of his own countermining operations. However, by removing the parapet of the redan, the mine had exposed the new riflepits to Union artillery, and that fact quickly became deadly serious.

Within minutes of the explosion of the mine, the Federal artillery opened up in the most concentrated bombardment Lockett had ever seen. The shells quickly cut their way through the parapet of the riflepits behind the second crater. Lockett and Cockrell put the infantry to work heaving dirt into the breach, but it was futile; for every shovelful added, a Yankee shell removed two. To stop the deadly erosion, Lockett, in a final act of desperation, had masses of earth rolled up in tent flies and wagon covers and rolled into the gap. It worked. The infantrymen shoveled frantically to reinforce the temporary barrier; within a few minutes, they had effectively, albeit crudely, sealed off the breach. At this point, the battered and demoralized 3 LA was withdrawn for a rest, with 6 MO extending its line to cover the whole front.

The power of the Union artillery amazed and depressed Lockett. There was no longer any question in his mind that the Yankee artillery could breach the Vicksburg defenses at any time the Union army officers chose to make the effort, and he so reported to Pemberton. To Pemberton, it meant that the next Union assault, when it came, would be irresistible; after the artillery preparation, there would be no fortifications left in which to take shelter.

Communications and Supply

GEOGRAPHIC CONTEXT

Because the Mississippi River approaches the bluffs at Vicksburg almost directly from the west, north of the city the vast floodplain spreads out for many miles. However, this plain is crossed by the navigable Yazoo River, which flows down from the north in a course that hugs the valley wall until it reaches the mouth of Virginia Bayou, about eleven miles north of Vicksburg. From this point, the Yazoo turns away to the southwest, eventually to discharge into the Mississippi nearly opposite Young's Point. In the triangle bounded by the Yazoo River on the north, the Mississippi on the south, and the valley wall on the east, much of the land is somewhat higher and therefore drier than most of the Mississippi Delta. A substantial natural levee borders the southern bank of the Yazoo, and a series of old natural levees, inherited from previous courses of the Mississippi, connect the Yazoo natural levee with the bluffs to the east.

South of Vicksburg, the Mississippi begins to trend westward, away from the line of the bluffs and out into the broad reaches of the flood-plain. At Warrenton, the river is already more than a half-mile away from the bluffs, and below that point the distance increases rapidly. At Warrenton, however, there was an almost imperceptible ridge of dry ground which was inundated only in extreme floods and which extended all the way from the bluffs to the river bank.

FEDERAL PERSPECTIVE

When the Army of the Tennessee closed around the northern end of the city on 18 May, two of Grant's highest priorities were to reestablish contact with RADM Porter's naval forces and to create a system which would provide the food and war materiel so badly needed by his army. In effect, this meant establishing places on the eastern shore of the Yazoo River where steamboats could discharge cargo easily, where there were large enough areas of dry ground to hold large supply depots, and from which roads could be built leading into the rear of the forces in the investment lines.

Both Grant and Sherman were familiar with the land north of the city. After all, Sherman had fought a battle at Chickasaw Bayou on 28–29 December 1862, and Grant personally had reconnoitered up the Yazoo as far as Snyder's Bluff on several occasions. Hence, the Federal commanders knew that the land south of the Yazoo met all the criteria for supply depots capable of sustaining the army. Accordingly, on the morning of 19 May, shortly after issuing orders for the assault that afternoon, Grant called in CPT Jenney, chief engineer of Sherman's corps, and asked him to find and develop a route from the Yazoo to the rear of the army. As it happened, Jenney had understood the need for an efficient supply system; and the previous day, while the army was moving into position north and east of the Vicksburg perimeter, he had reconnoitered the area between the Valley Road and the Yazoo River north of Vicksburg. He thus was able to tell Grant of a route that led from the base of the bluff at a point about one-half mile north of Mint Spring Bayou; along a series of natural levees bordering McNutt Lake and Long Lake; and finally reaching the Yazoo River at Mrs. Johnson's plantation, where there was a good landing and lots of dry, solid ground. A road would be only about five miles long and would require only the removal of some fallen trees and the bridging of several small streams. Even more important, he had found, to his astonishment, that transports shepherded by the navy already had dumped mountains of supplies at Mrs. Johnson's, along with wagons and teams to haul them! Porter had become aware of the

arrival of a defeated Rebel army in Vicksburg on the afternoon of 17 May;
with his usual intuition, he had anticipated that the Army of the Tennessee
would be in urgent need of supplies when it arrived on the scene. He had
sent a convoy of transports, covered by tinclads, up the Yazoo on 18 May, so
the supply depot that Grant needed already existed.[37] Grant was pleased.

After the assault of 19 May had failed, Grant no longer was optimistic about taking the city by storm and turned his attention to organizing
a proper supply system, in the all-too-likely event that his army would
have to settle down to a siege. It was likely to be a long one. Union scouts
had reported that the countryside had been stripped of food, so it was
abundantly clear to Grant that Pemberton had made extensive preparations to sustain a siege. That meant that the investment lines probably
would have to be extended to include the southern approaches, which up
to this time had been left open.

In the meantime, the engineers had picked up the pontoon bridge
used by Sherman's corps to cross the Big Black River at Bridgeport, and
they trundled it into the lines at Vicksburg on the afternoon of 19 May.[38]
So there it was, ready and waiting for its next assignment. Grant was busy
with other things on that day and the next, but on the morning of 21 May,
he ordered Jenney to take CO I, 35 MO and the pontoon train and open
the road to the supply depots on the Yazoo that Jenney had reconnoitered.
He also told MAJ Tweeddale, of Bissell's Engineer Regiment of the West,
to cooperate. Tweeddale took three companies of engineers and set to
work building the requisite smaller bridges and clearing fallen trees away,
while Jenney laid his pontoon bridges across the larger gaps. The road
was finished and wagons were rolling by 22 May.[39]

After thinking briefly about the problem, Grant decided that one road
was apt to be insufficient, especially if the siege became extended, so CPT
Hermann Klosterman was sent to find an alternate route. The good captain soon discovered two of them. One started from the base of the bluffs
about 3.5 miles north of Mint Spring Bayou and led along a natural levee
on the eastern shore of Thompson Lake. By this route, it was only a bit
over 2 miles from the base of the bluffs to the Yazoo, and building a road
would require a minimum of labor. Blair gave him the 83 IN, and the
Hoosiers must have worked like madmen, because the road was ready for
traffic by 1100 on the morning of 21 May.[40]

The third route was almost as good. It led from a point 2.5 miles north
of Mint Spring Bayou, along the natural levee bordering Chickasaw
Bayou on the west, and reached the Yazoo River after a distance of 2.5

miles. Chickasaw Bayou would have to be bridged, as well as several smaller streams, but the route was high and dry most of the way.

The wagons began to roll inland immediately. By late afternoon on 21 May, the first trains began to arrive in the rear of Sherman's corps. That was fortunate. On the afternoon of 19 May, before the first wagons reached the bluffs, a sullen private muttered "Hardtack!" as Grant rode along the line. Not until that moment had Grant realized how tired his troops were of corn meal. The general stopped, held up his hand for silence, and earnestly explained that every effort was being made to open communication with the river. Within a few hours, he said, the first commissary wagons would arrive. Complaints changed into a wave of exultant cheering. True to the general's promise, full rations, including hardtack and coffee, were issued that night.[41] The soldiers' faith was restored.

While hardtack and coffee were necessary, so was fresh food of all kinds. That was troublesome, because it would take at least several days to move such things down the Mississippi from the depots at Memphis and Cairo. In an effort to tide the army over, Grant had sent the 15 IL CAV to patrol the roads leading north and east from Snyder's Bluff, chiefly to watch out for Rebel movements in that direction but also to sweep up everything edible.[42] The men found very little.

Grant's concern with the possible presence of Confederates to the north, toward Mechanicsburg, was fueled by reports from his cavalry scouts on 20 May. They reported that the countryside was awash with rumors to the effect that Joe Johnston was heading toward Snyder's Bluff with his small army. Grant dared not lose Snyder's Bluff. It was the shield guarding the supply dumps that were rapidly developing along the Yazoo River. The only force of any size available was Pugh's BDE of Lauman's DIV, which had landed at Snyder's that morning. Grant told Lauman to reoccupy and improve the abandoned Rebel fortifications at Snyder's and to defend the supply depots to the death.[43]

The depots along the Yazoo took care of the needs of Sherman's and McPherson's corps, who were in position north and northeast of the city, but the roads from the Yazoo dumps to the rear of McClernand's corps were long and circuitous. Furthermore, the southern approaches to the city would be invested as soon as possible, and carrying supplies by wagon completely around the northern and western sides of Vicksburg, by existing roads a distance of almost twenty-five miles, would be too difficult and time-consuming. Some kind of supply arrangement for the south end of the investment lines clearly was in order. Fortunately, a solution was already in hand. The road which had been built earlier across the swamps, from Hecla Place on Walnut Bayou to Bowers' Landing, on the Louisiana shore just below Warrenton, was fully operational. The need for a supply depot at Grand Gulf had ceased to exist the moment the Army of the Tennessee had reestablished contact with the Mississippi, so nothing could be easier than simply to abandon Grand Gulf and make Warrenton the terminus of a network to supply the troops south of Vicksburg. Good roads already existed from Warrenton to the southern and southeastern approaches, and the wagons and teams from the abandoned supply line from Grand Gulf to Dillon's plantation were readily available, so this line began to function almost immediately.

Thus, by 22 May, Grant had a secure and efficient supply line all the way back to the factories of St. Louis and Pittsburgh. Supplies of all kinds came by water either directly to the Yazoo River landings or to Young's Point. From the Yazoo River landings, the wagon hauls to the rear of McPherson's corps were only about ten miles long. The supplies put ashore at Young's Point went by wagon first for three miles to the road along Walnut Bayou and then for an additional eight miles on the new road across the base of DeSoto Point to Bowers' landing. There transports ferried them across the river to Warrenton landing. The road distance to the rear of McClernand's corps from Warrenton landing again was only about ten miles.

When Herron's DIV arrived in mid-June, his men sealed in the southern and southeastern approaches to the city by establishing a line only a few hundred yards from the Confederate works and extending from the river to a point southeast of Fort Garrott. There they tied into the left flank of McClernand's corps. These troops were supplied via a military wagon road that began at the Warrenton Road bridge across Hatcher Bayou and followed the Hatcher Bayou and Durden Creek bottoms to the vicinity of Fort Garrott. This route proved so efficient that even the left-flank division of McClernand's corps was supplied primarily by it. The Army of the Tennessee never again suffered for lack of supplies.

Water was another matter altogether. Most of the inhabitants, both rural and urban, depended upon rainwater stored in cisterns for their water supply. Ground water is too deep to be reached by dug wells, and there are virtually no springs in the area. All the minor creeks go dry during the summer and autumn months, and even the major creeks are reduced to the merest trickle. To compound the problem, the weather during the entire period of the siege was abnormally hot and dry, which raised the demand for water to unusual levels.

Even crude figures for the amount of water required by the Union army are awesome. A man can get by (barely!) on a gallon of water per day for cooking and drinking—with none for washing or bathing. (A story—possibly apocryphal—explained why there were notably few mosquitoes that summer; even *they* couldn't stand the smell of so many unwashed bodies!)

At the time of the investment, the Army of the Tennessee numbered about 42,000, so the absolute minimum water requirement for the men in the army was 42,000 gallons per day.

Each horse requires about 4 gallons per day. There were twenty-six batteries of artillery, each with a complement of about 160 horses, so the artillery horses' water requirement was about 16,640 gallons per day.

There were nine regiments of cavalry, each with perhaps 350 horses, so the cavalry horses' requirement amounted to 12,600 gallons per day.

Each division had its complement of wagons, such as ambulances, and each officer was mounted. The total was perhaps 250 horses per division, and there were ten divisions, so the division horses would have required about 10,000 gallons per day.

These totals sum to about 81,240 gallons per day, as an absolute minimum.

Now consider the impact of such a force on the resources of the countryside. A normal farm cistern, full to the brim, held about 675 gallons. Thus, each day, the army that invested Vicksburg on 18 May would have had to empty about 120 full cisterns!

For all practical purposes, the only water readily available was in the Mississippi and Yazoo rivers and the major bayous. As a result, a good-sized fraction of the logistical effort of the Union army was spent in hauling water from those streams to the various regiments and batteries strung around the city.

Water weighs about 8.4 pounds per gallon. A 30-gallon wooden barrel weighs about 50 pounds, so a "water unit" (a barrel filled with water) weighs about 300 pounds. In theory, a standard army wagon could carry 6,000 pounds, but in practice the loads rarely exceeded 2,000 pounds, because horses or mules could not pull a heavier load under any but ideal conditions. If the roads were muddy or the hills steep, the sustainable load was even less. If we assume, generously, that the water-wagons at Vicksburg carried eight 300-pound barrels, each containing 30 gallons of water, then each wagon carried 240 gallons of water. To obtain 81,240 gallons each day, more than 338 wagons had to be devoted to the sole task of carrying water for the troops and their horses!

And this amount supplied only the 42,000-man army of investment! Imagine what it must have been like at the end of the siege, when the Union army in the vicinity of Vicksburg numbered nearly 77,000. In light of such numbers, the magnitude of the logistical effort required to maintain the investment of Vicksburg can be grasped at least dimly.

Grant established his headquarters on a ridgetop about 1,300 yards north of the Stockade Redan. Communication with the navy was no problem; a signal station, manned by naval personnel, was established on the Indian mound, from which point messages could be relayed quickly by semaphore to a ship in the river west of DeSoto Point, and from there to *Black Hawk*, anchored off the mouth of the Yazoo River. However, it was more than eleven long road miles from Grant's headquarters to the south end of the city, so it would take a courier something like two hours to make the trip, even on a good, fresh horse. Grant was all too aware that the Rebels, using their interior lines, could concentrate secretly anywhere along the defense perimeter. That meant that a breakout offensive down the Halls Ferry Road, for example, might be in progress ninety minutes or more before the army commander would hear of it. Coordination with such a time handicap would be impossible.Within two weeks of the investment, every corps headquarters was tied to the army's headquarters with telegraph lines. This meant that no place on the siege lines was more than a few minutes away from Grant's headquarters.

CONFEDERATE PERSPECTIVE

Vicksburg had been a major depot long before the city was invested. Arms, ammunition, and other military impedimenta had flowed into the city along the Southern Railroad of Mississippi, but a large proportion of the commissary supplies had come down from the rich agricultural regions of the Delta and by steamboat from the Red River country. The Red River traffic had been largely cut off after RADM Farragut, with *Hartford* and *Albatross,* took up a position at the mouth of the Red River on 16 March 1863, having run the Port Hudson batteries two days earlier. Thus, by the beginning of the Vicksburg Campaign, most of the food and forage used by the Vicksburg garrison came by water down the Yazoo as far as Snyder's Bluff, where it was put on wagons and carried along the Valley Road into the city. However, much also came from farms and plantations of the Loess Hills in the vicinity of Vicksburg.

As soon as the city was threatened with investment, Pemberton had ordered that every pound of food available in the surrounding countryside be brought into the city. The farms were stripped bare of everything edible, including livestock. Since facilities for refrigeration or salting meat were lacking, meat had to be kept on the hoof. The big problem was pasturage. At first, the cattle herds were kept in Stout's Bottom, near the south end of the city. That was a quiet sector of the lines for the first several weeks of the siege, and at first all went well. Then the Yankees somehow learned of the location of the herds and sent one of their big ironclads to a place in the river from which her big guns could reach Stout's Bottom.[44] Of course, when the big shells began to drop among the cattle, the Confederates had no choice but to move them. The herd was broken up into small groups and pastured wherever there was grass, including the City Cemetery.

Toward the end, food grew very short indeed, although the city still was far from starvation. At the time of the surrender, the commissary magazines still held at least another week's food supply.[45] Even so, shortages gave rise to all sorts of legends, some of which actually were true. Mule meat was eaten, but what has been forgotten is that, even before the war, the flesh of mules and horses was not really rare as a dietary component. It is said that one restaurant owner served rabbit-and-mule stew. He insisted, when queried about the proportions, that the proportions were equal: one rabbit for one mule. Of course, inevitably, tales were told about eating rats, but even such stories must be taken in context. At the time, a Louisiana Creole commented in a letter—still extant—that the rats of Vicksburg were almost as good as those they normally trapped in the swamps at home. Was he writing with tongue in cheek? Who knows?

Water was a major problem for the defenders, as for the besiegers. Most civilian dwellings depended upon cisterns fed by rainwater collected from the roofs of the buildings. Of course, those cisterns were designed for a population of about 5,000, and the soldiers raised the city's population to something like 35,000—far too many for the cisterns to accommodate.

To be sure, there was an unlimited supply of water in the Mississippi River, but getting it from that source was both dangerous and inconvenient. There always was the chance that a person getting water that way would be fired on by a sniper on DeSoto Point. Then, of course, such water had to be carried back to the dwelling, and that tended to be a trial.

For all practical purposes, all draft animals had been requisitioned long ago by the military, so most water had to be carried by hand. Carrying a couple of buckets of water for a mile or so was a chore soon dreaded by everyone. Bathing became even rarer than it had been before the siege. Carrying and heating water for anything other than cooking simply entailed too much effort.

Even fuel for cooking soon was in short supply. Nearly all cooking was done with wood, and there had been very little timber around the city to begin with. Before long, everything that could be burned had been burned, and civilians especially had to spend long hours scavenging for cooking fuel. Virtually all the picket fences and abandoned buildings in the city were fed to the cooking fires by the time the siege ended.

Pemberton never seriously contemplated a breakout attempt, even though he would have been able to concentrate a major part of his forces at any part of the lines in near-total secrecy. Tempting as the thought might have been, there was literally no place to go. A breakout to the south or east would place his army in a cul-de-sac formed by the unfordable Mississippi and Big Black rivers, and a breakout to the northeast would have led him into the impossible terrain of the Mechanicsburg Corridor, which he knew to be heavily fortified. Furthermore, Pemberton was aware that the Yankees had established a telegraph system, so an attempted breakout would have very little lead time before the Federals reacted.

Pemberton took a certain bleak satisfaction in knowing that there was a weak link in the Federal communications network. His signals people had noticed the semaphore system that connected the Indian mound with Porter's ships in the Mississippi River and rather quickly broke the code. Before long, Pemberton was reading all of Grant's mail to his naval colleague, as well as many of the messages that passed between the vessels of Porter's squadron.

Until mid-June, Pemberton had little trouble getting messages to GEN Johnston, although transmission took a bit of time. The Federal lines were very porous on the western shore of the River, and it was relatively easy for a courier to cross the River at Vicksburg, slip between the pickets on De Soto Point, re-cross the River below Vicksburg, ride around the investment lines, and so reach Jackson and Canton. In fact, a shipment of firing caps for small arms, which were in relatively short supply in the city, was delivered by this route only about two weeks before the surrender. Bulky things, like food, of course, were impossible to smuggle in.

38

Frustration in the Mechanicsburg Corridor 22 April–25 June 1863

Maps: 4. Southern Sector
      17. The Northeastern Approaches to Vicksburg
      22. The Mechanicsburg Corridor

GEOGRAPHY

The trapezoidal region lying between the Big Black and the Yazoo rivers and extending from Vicksburg northeast to Mechanicsburg is commonly called the Mechanicsburg Corridor. It is a continuation of the Loess Hills and consists primarily of a single ridge seven to ten miles wide, trending northeast-southwest. The area is characterized by the same wild tangle of knifelike ridges and deep ravines in which John Bowen and Grant had fought the Battle of Port Gibson. Along the sinuous watershed of the ridge runs the Benton Road, connecting Vicksburg with Mechanicsburg and Benton, the latter about fifty-five road miles away. For most of the distance between Vicksburg and Yazoo City, the watershed ridge is very narrow, with very steep sides; but, about five miles northeast of Vicksburg, the ridgetop broadens to form a rolling plateau some two miles wide and four miles long. Lying as it does at the headwaters of Muddy Creek, it sometimes is called the "Muddy Creek flat."

    The Yazoo River flows in a broadly meandering course along the eastern edge of the Mississippi River floodplain. Between the Yazoo River and the base of the bluffs runs the Valley Road, connecting Vicksburg with

Yazoo City, forty-five miles to the northeast. On the Yazoo River, thirty miles northeast of Vicksburg, stands the hamlet of Satartia. It has a good steamboat landing, and from it a good road runs four miles southeast to Mechanicsburg, where it crosses the Benton Road. The road continues to the east for another nine miles, to arrive at Pritchard's Crossroad. From there, good country roads run east-northeast to Vaughan, twenty-three miles away. Vaughan is connected to Yazoo City by a good wagon road via Benton. Vaughan is on the Mississippi Central Railroad, which connects Jackson with Grenada, MS, and Grand Junction, TN, and taps the rich agricultural districts of the northern Delta. South of Vaughan, the railroad crosses the swampy floodplain of the Big Black River on a long wooden trestle at Way's Bluff, ten miles north of Canton.

After flowing under the trestle at Way's Bluff, the Big Black flows tortuously southwest through a swampy, three-mile-wide floodplain for thirty-eight airline miles, then turns more or less directly south for another ten miles as the crow flies, to reach the village of Bridgeport, where a good road connecting Edwards and Vicksburg crosses the river.

There had been a floating bridge at Bridgeport, but it was destroyed immediately following the Battle of Champion Hill. Throughout its course, the river flows through a swampy floodplain from two to five miles wide. It is unfordable during periods of normal high water, but during extreme low-water periods, which sometimes occur in middle and late summer, the stream can be forded readily at a number of places. However, because the banks are high, steep, and treacherous, the river, except at prepared crossings, is a major military obstacle. There are a number of such prepared crossings north of Bridgeport:

Table 2
Big Black River Crossings North of Bridgeport

	Airline Miles above Bridgeport
Messenger's Ferry (often called Messenger's Ford)	2.0
Jones Ford	3.5
Birdsong's Ferry	5.5
Bush's Ford	8.0
Cox's Ferry	16.0
Kibbey's Ferry, on the Yazoo City–Jackson Turnpike	25.0
Moore's Ferry, on the direct Canton-Benton Road	43.0

There was a rickety little bridge, barely safe for a farm wagon, at Moore's Ferry. Four miles farther upstream was the Way's Bluff railroad trestle.

The water in the Yazoo River is so deep during periods of high water that even the big Union ironclads readily could ply between Vicksburg and Yazoo City. Indeed, given high water, they could go all the way to the Mississippi via the Yazoo Pass just below Helena, AR. However, there is a ledge of rock, Satartia Bar, across the channel just below Satartia; during periods of low water, only boats of very shallow draft could cross it. The little Union tinclad, *Cricket,* which drew only eighteen inches of water, readily could have made it, but even the larger tinclads, such as *Black Hawk,* were excluded.

FEDERAL PERSPECTIVE

After the Army of the Tennessee had failed to take Vicksburg by storm on 22 May, the prospect of a long siege changed the strategic equation. The time required to assemble a force to press the siege also would give the Confederates time to assemble a force with which to attack the besiegers. The Federal army around Vicksburg would have to be large enough to both contain Pemberton's men inside the city and protect itself from interference by GEN Joseph E. Johnston, who undoubtedly was raising an army somewhere in the vicinity of Jackson for the relief of Vicksburg . As a result, Grant immediately set to work to move adequate forces down the Mississippi River, drawing men from Hurlbut's forces in West Tennessee and even from the Army of the Ohio and the Department of the Missouri.

Of course, it would take time for those reinforcements to arrive on the scene, and Grant was all too aware that the Confederacy's interior lines of communication might make it possible for it to assemble troops in western Mississippi more rapidly than the Union could. That made it imperative that everything possible be done to interfere with Johnston's activities while Union troop strength grew to the level of safety. In fact, there was little that Grant could do. He dared not split his army and attack Johnston with a force of maneuver while he held Vicksburg with a siege force, because the failed assaults of 19 and 22 May had demonstrated clearly that the Confederate Army of Vicksburg remained a potent fighting force. If he made the maneuver force large enough to guarantee success against Johnston, there was at least a reasonable possibility that Pemberton would manage to break the siege and march his army away more or less intact. To be sure, that would leave the Mississippi River under Union control, which was the ultimate objective of the whole campaign; but the escape of Pemberton's army, once it had been locked up in Vicksburg, would be very hard to explain to the public in the North.

During the last days of May, Grant had little fear that Johnston would strike directly at Vicksburg, because the water in the Big Black River was still so high that Grant believed Johnston would not risk a crossing. However, there was nothing whatever to prevent him from shifting his army to the north bank of the river and concentrating at Mechanicsburg. From there he could drive down the Benton and Valley roads into the rear of the investment lines. Grant did not seriously fear that the Army of the Tennessee would be destroyed by such an offensive, but Johnston might manage to occupy Snyder's Bluff and cut the Yankee army off from its vital supply depots along the Yazoo. If those depots were occupied for any length of time, or, even worse, if the depots were destroyed, both Sherman's and McPherson's corps soon would be in desperate straits. They might even be forced to raise the siege and allow Pemberton's army to escape.

As the high-command triumvirate of Grant, Sherman, and Porter reflected on such matters, they realized that there were compelling reasons why a Confederate strike down the Mechanicsburg Corridor might appeal to Johnston. In the first place, the Federal command knew that a substantial part of the commissary supplies which supported Johnston's army in the Canton–Jackson area came from the Delta and the regions north of Jackson. There was good reason to suspect that a large proportion of those supplies flowed out of the Delta through Yazoo City. That meant that a Confederate drive down the Mechanicsburg Corridor readily could be supplied with food and fodder by a short and easy supply line from Yazoo City. On the other hand, if the drive were made from Jackson across the Big Black, those supplies would have to move by wagon train to Vaughan, then by rail across the long Way's Bluff trestle to Canton and Tougaloo. The railroad was destroyed south of that point, so supplies would have to proceed by wagon to the Big Black River east of Vicksburg. Grant had been saddled with a supply line rather like that during the campaign east of Vicksburg, and he suspected that Johnston would not tolerate such a situation if it could be avoided.

The second consideration was that Johnston could not realistically expect to destroy the Federal armies in front of Vicksburg; the best that he could hope for was to punch a hole through the Federal investment long enough to permit Pemberton's Vicksburg army to escape. An escape to the south or southwest simply would place the Confederates in a pocket formed by the Mississippi and the unfordable Big Black River. It was true that the Big Black could be bridged, but that would take time; and even more time would be required to effect the crossing. In those intervals, the Confederates would expect to be hard pressed by the Army of the Tennessee. Further, if the water in the Big Black stayed high, RADM Porter's tinclads could be expected to be there to play havoc with the bridges. The Vicksburg batteries were not a serious consideration; it had been demonstrated that unarmed and unarmored transports could be run past them, so the fast tinclads should have no problem. On balance, the only feasible escape route would be up the Mechanicsburg Corridor to Yazoo City and Benton.

The question in the collective mind of the Union triumvirate was: what could be done to interfere with Johnston's arrangements? Inevitably, the three focused on that long wooden railroad trestle at Way's Bluff. If that bridge could be destroyed, life would grow significantly more difficult for Johnston's Army of Relief. Destroying the bridge might even limit the number of troops which Johnston could keep supplied with food and forage.

Furthermore, there seemed to be an easy route to Way's Bluff. By this time, Grant had been told the story of Grierson's Raid, which seemed to indicate that a large cavalry force could move through the interior of Mississippi almost at will. He would assemble such a force, send it up the Benton Road to Mechanicsburg and Pritchard's Crossroad, then along country roads north of the Big Black River to Way's Bluff. The right flank of such a force would be protected, at least partially, by the unfordable Big Black River, across which there were no longer any bridges other than the flimsy span at Moore's Ferry. In principle, the north flank would be threatened by the Rebel garrison at Yazoo City; but Grant had pretty reliable information that the Yazoo City garrison was quite small, so it would be unlikely to come out looking for a fight if the Federal raiding force were sufficiently powerful.

On 23 May, the day following the abortive assaults on Vicksburg, Grant ordered all the cavalry units in the XV and XVII corps to concentrate at Snyder's Bluff in preparation for a raid on Way's Bluff. By nightfall on 23 May, about a thousand horse-soldiers had reached the rendezvous. Grant gave command of the raiding force to COL Amory Johnson, of whom he had good reports, and told him that he wanted the bridge at Way's Bluff burned and all food and forage destroyed in the area between the Big Black and the Yazoo rivers, as far north as Mechanicsburg.[1] If the earth in this area were thoroughly scorched, the Rebels would find it very difficult to operate even light cavalry forces in the region.

Johnson left Snyder's Bluff at dawn on 24 May and rode confidently up the Benton Road toward Mechanicsburg. He saw not a sign of Johnnies until about noon, when his van was within 1,000 yards of the town. Then, suddenly, musketry crackled from all around the head of his column. Johnson was completely nonplused; this was not going according to the script. He made no attempt to deploy and fight his way through the Rebel forces; instead, without the slightest hesitation, he hurriedly broke contact and headed back toward Snyder's Bluff, where he arrived the following morning.

Once safely back inside Union lines, he reported to Grant that "reliable sources" (carefully unspecified) had told him that the Rebels had between 6,000 and 8,000 men in and around Mechanicsburg.[2] Grant found this hard to believe; but, if it were true, then it looked very much like the kind of concentration that would precede a Rebel offensive down the Mechanicsburg Corridor. And that was a potentially serious problem. The best way to deal with it would be to send a force large enough to break it up before it grew to really dangerous size. Grant's response was to try to kill two birds with one stone; he would send a powerful infantry force to Mechanicsburg to break up the Rebel concentration, while the cavalry slipped past the battle and on to Way's Bluff.

On 26 May, the Federal commander organized an expeditionary force under the leadership of MG Frank Blair, reputedly one of Sherman's better division commanders. The expeditionary force would be a sort of pocket army, consisting of two provisional infantry divisions (about 11,000 men), a contingent of artillery, and Johnson's provisional cavalry force. The provisional divisions were commanded by BG Mower and MG McArthur, both very good men.[3]

That same night, Blair's expeditionary force moved out of the Snyder's Bluff defense perimeter, and, by nightfall of 28 May, it had reached the Hart farm, seven miles southwest of Claibornesville. The column had moved very slowly and deliberately, seizing and/or destroying food and forage as it went. At Hart's farm, Amory Johnson came in, radiating excitement, to report that a local planter, Richard Barkley, had stated that Confederate GEN A. P. Hill had just arrived with his corps from the Army of Northern Virginia, and that GEN Johnston now had 45,000 men at Canton and Jackson.[4] If true, this was chilling news indeed. A. P. Hill was one of Robert E. Lee's invincibles; and 45,000 men were more than Grant had in his army besieging Vicksburg.

Blair sent a courier racing back down the Benton Road to give the news to Grant,[5] and, early the next morning, moving slowly and cautiously, he continued his march toward Mechanicsburg. The expeditionary force passed through Mechanicsburg about 1300 and turned east on the road to Pritchard's Crossroad. About two miles east of Mechanicsburg, the advance guard, the 4 IA CAV, was ambushed by a Rebel cavalry force supported by artillery. Blair deployed and withdrew slowly to Mechanicsburg;[6] cavalry were not usually so bellicose, and the presence of artillery support suggested that the Rebels were the advance elements of a large infantry force. Maybe, thought Blair, it was in fact the advance guard of A. P. Hill's veterans from the Army of Northern Virginia. He sent another courier racing off to Grant.

Blair's message arrived at Grant's headquarters almost at the same time as a dispatch from BG Peter J. Osterhaus, whose division held the Big Black Bridge and guarded the eastern approaches to Vicksburg. Osterhaus reported lots of Rebel activity across the Big Black.[7] It took Grant only an instant to realize that the two reports contained the potential for disaster. If Johnston did in fact now have a large army east of the Big Black River (and Osterhaus's reports seemed to confirm that he did), then he could force a crossing somewhere north of Amsterdam, perhaps at Cox's Ferry, and get across the Benton and Valley roads. Blair would then be cut off and quite possibly lost. Grant immediately sent a courier back up the Benton Road to Blair, ordering him to get out as quickly as possible.[8] He also sent a message to his naval friend, Porter, asking that a gunboat be sent up the Yazoo to keep that stream open and provide gunnery support for Blair, if needed.

The courier reached Blair at Mechanicsburg in the wee small hours of 30 May. Blair could see the potential danger as well as Grant, and he knew that safety lay in the shelter of the naval force which he was certain would be in the Yazoo as soon as Porter's warships could steam up that far. As a result, Blair's withdrawal was first to Satartia on the Yazoo, and then down the Valley Road to Snyder's Bluff, which he reached late on the afternoon of 31 May. Despite the rapidity of the withdrawal, he did not forget to scorch the countryside as he passed through, so he was able to report to Grant that any Rebels trying to follow would have very slim pickings.[9]

Additional Union troops were arriving at Vicksburg almost every day, and the blue siege lines around the city were drawing tighter and tighter. Nevertheless, Grant still did not have enough men to organize an army designed specifically to oppose Johnston's Army of Relief, which Grant assumed was gathering like a thundercloud east of the Big Black River. The implication was that, sometime in the near future, Johnston would march westward in an attempt to relieve Pemberton and his trapped Army of Vicksburg. Grant was realistic enough to suspect that Pemberton and Johnston were in communication and that they would coordinate their actions. Because the unfordable Big Black River would prevent a ready escape to the south, Grant believed that Pemberton's only practical escape route was northeast toward Mechanicsburg. If this were true, then that was by far the most likely avenue of attack by Johnston's Army of Relief. Johnston would hit the Union investment line from the outside at the same moment that Pemberton would hit it from within the city. The combined attack might very well break through. This direction seemed even more likely, when the matter of commissary supplies was considered. Because the bulk of the Rebel food and fodder came from the Delta and northern areas, an attack down the Mechanicsburg Corridor meant short supply lines for Johnston's army and ready resupply for Pemberton's army if it broke into the clear.

Taken together, the intelligence that Johnston had perhaps as many as 45,000 men in the Canton-Jackson area; the intensified activity east of the Big Black reported by Osterhaus; and word from Blair that there were large Confederate forces in the Mechanicsburg area made Grant exceedingly uneasy. It was a combination he feared greatly, because it was precisely the disposition that would allow Johnston and the main army to cross the Big Black at some place like Cox's Ferry and join the force at Mechanicsburg, thus achieving a concentration in the proper position to launch an offensive against the siege lines around Vicksburg before the Federals could detect it.

Frank Blair was a very thoughtful man and shared Grant's unease. Something would have to be done to defuse the situation in the Mechanicsburg Corridor. He submitted a new plan to Grant on 2 June. The Federals should move an infantry brigade to Satartia by water, thus avoiding the fatigue of a long march, as well as observation by the Confederate scouts whom Blair assumed haunted the Mechanicsburg Corridor. From Satartia, the infantry would occupy Mechanicsburg, there forming a junction with Amory Johnson's cavalry, who would move up the Benton Road from Snyder's Bluff. This would force any Rebel cavalry in the Mechanicsburg Corridor to withdraw across the Big Black River or move northward toward Yazoo City, and would permit Union reconnaissance of the river crossings. Then, with the infantry holding Mechanicsburg or Pritchard's Crossroad, the cavalry would be free to strike at Way's Bluff.[10] If the operation were done quickly, it might not only destroy the Way's Bluff railroad bridge, but also dislocate any offensive plans Johnston might have.

When Grant asked Porter for naval support for Blair's scheme, Porter told CDR Walker, one of his ablest subordinates, to provide every possible assistance.[11] To Blair's surprise and chagrin, Grant gave command of the new expedition to BG Kimball, who had just arrived in the Yazoo area from Memphis.[12] He also made some changes in Blair's basic plan. If there really were large Confederate forces at Mechanicsburg, a brigade of infantry and another of cavalry might well be inadequate, so he told Kimball to use the two brigades of his own division that already had arrived in the Yazoo area, plus Mower's BDE and a battery of artillery.

Kimball's expeditionary force, consisting of Engelmann's and Montgomery's BDEs of Kimball's DIV, plus Mower's BDE, started up the Yazoo River in a transport fleet, escorted by several of CDR Walker's tinclads, late on the night of 3 June. Amory Johnson's PROV CAV BDE, now consisting of 1,200 men, started up the Benton Road at 0500 the next morning, 4 June. The infantrymen landed at Satartia without incident and, led by Mower's BDE, marched on Mechanicsburg; but, about a mile west of the hamlet, they were fired upon by a strong skirmish line. Mower and his veteran "Eagle Brigade," far from being intimidated, quickly deployed, brought up artillery, and pressed on. Suddenly all opposition vanished, and the Yankee force moved on to occupy the village. A few minutes later, Johnson's cavalry rode into sight. The horsemen had seen not a single Rebel.

Rather than stay with the troops bivouacked around Mechanicsburg, Kimball rode back to Satartia to spend a comfortable night aboard ship. There a message from Grant reached him, indicating that Rebel deserters had reported a strong force of infantry from Johnston's Army of Relief at Yazoo City. Grant strongly "suggested" that Kimball keep his infantry at Mechanicsburg until the situation could be assessed more carefully. Do not, said Grant, allow yourself to be defeated or encircled.[13]

This message did little for Kimball's peace of mind. The next day, he sent out a patrol to Cox's Ferry, where it burned the ferryboat. Another patrol investigated Pritchard's Crossroad, which it found defended by belligerent butternuts in entrenchments. Still another patrol rode to the outskirts of Yazoo City, close enough to see an estimated 20,000 infantrymen and twenty-five guns, all alert and ensconced in earthworks. These reports increased Kimball's disquiet, because they seemed to confirm the information from Grant's deserters. At this point, CDR Walker appeared and told Kimball that the water in the Yazoo River was dropping so rapidly that the tinclads would have to pull out within twenty-four hours or be trapped above Satartia Bar. At this, Kimball's nerves snapped. He ordered the immediate withdrawal of his expeditionary force to Snyder's Bluff,[14] reaching there on 7 June. The days had been blindingly hot, and there were many stragglers and even some dead from heat exhaustion.[15]

In the meantime, none of Grant's intelligence sources had confirmed any significant troop arrivals from the east, so he was fairly certain that Johnston's Army of Relief was growing only slowly, if at all. Accordingly, he simply did not believe Kimball's story of huge numbers of Rebels around Mechanicsburg. Grant reasoned that Johnston long since would have gone on the offensive if he actually had 20,000 Southerners at Yazoo City and another 45,000 at Canton and Jackson. Still, he could not be sure; to resolve the question, he desperately needed reliable information. As a last resort, he sent his old friend Charles Dana, the newspaper man, up the Mechanicsburg Corridor with a small cavalry escort.

Dana returned the next day, having ridden all the way to Mechanicsburg. Not only were there no Rebels to be seen, he said, but also there was no evidence that they were even interested in the area.[16] Grant couldn't quite believe that, either. In any case, it was clear that, since offensive operations had done nothing except tie up large bodies of men to no purpose, something different would have to be done. He called in MG Cadwallader Washburn, who had just arrived from Memphis, and told him to take command at Snyder's Bluff and fortify the area against attack from the northeast.

Amory Johnson and his PROV CAV BDE had proven useless, so Grant broke the unit up; 2 IL CAV went to Osterhaus at Big Black Bridge, 5 IL CAV and 4 IA CAV went to Washburn at Snyder's Bluff, and Johnson himself was exiled to serve as commander of the garrison at Grand Gulf, which no longer served a useful purpose and was held by scarcely more than a corporal's guard.

Troop-ship convoys continued to arrive from the North, and the arrival of Sooy Smith's DIV from Memphis on 11 June at last brought the Army of the Tennessee up to a strength which Grant deemed sufficient both to maintain the siege of Vicksburg and to fend off Johnston at the same time. On 22 June, he told Sherman, the only one of his corps commanders whom he fully trusted with an independent command, to form an Army of Maneuver. Grant gave him two brigades from the XV Corps, three from the XVII Corps, Parke's IX Corps, and Sooy Smith's DIV of

Washburn's XVI Corps, along with appropriate artillery and cavalry. All in all, there were about 25,000 men, nearly as many as had fought and won the Battle of Champion Hill.

To Grant's delight, Washburn turned out to be an active commander. He sent reconnaissance patrols fanning out into the Mechanicsburg Corridor, and in due course they came back with the news that Mechanicsburg had been reoccupied by Rebels and that the garrison at Yazoo City showed signs of movement. Washburn was convinced that the butternuts were getting set to hit him, but it seemed to him that the terrain in the Mechanicsburg Corridor was scarcely conducive to large-scale operations. Knowing that Johnston was a wily old fox, Washburn looked about for another route by which the Rebels might come. And he found one. Deer Creek flows down from the interior of the Delta and joins the Yazoo just above Haynes' Bluff, and Deer Creek was lined by productive plantations connected by a good road. If the butternuts somehow could get across the swamps between Yazoo City and the Rolling Fork, they could march down that road and appear on his doorstep with nearly complete surprise. Furthermore, they could move very fast, and they would not need a large commissary train, because the farms of Deer Creek would provide them with food and fodder.

Then, to make matters worse, on 12 June, one of Washburn's patrols scouting the Big Black River crossings ran into trouble on the approaches to Birdsong's Ferry. There was a brisk skirmish, and the 6 MO CAV came away with two prisoners who tattled that Nathan Bedford Forrest was at Mechanicsburg with 4,000 men. Forrest! If Forrest was on the scene, Washburn was convinced that the storm would not be long in coming. He could visualize a scenario in which Forrest and his horsemen would sweep down the Benton and Valley roads, the infantry force at Yazoo City would drive down the Deer Creek Road, and Johnston and the main body of the Army of Relief would storm across the crossings of the Big Black.

The Big Black front was Sherman's problem, but Washburn could do something about Deer Creek and Mechanicsburg. On 14 June, he sent a strong combat patrol up Deer Creek, and scouts out toward Mechanicsburg. The Mechanicsburg patrol returned on 15 June with the startling news that there were three Confederate divisions in the vicinity of the hamlet!

Sherman was inspecting Washburn's fortifications around Snyder's Bluff when this news came in, and he listened carefully to Washburn's argument that the Rebel force reported at Mechanicsburg was the beginning of an attack on the Snyder's Bluff lines, and that a Confederate march down the Lower Benton Road as far as Youngton would outflank the defenses.

Sherman had doubts about the reliability of the scout reports, but he agreed that the defense line was inadequate and ordered fortifications built to cover the Marshall house and the junction of the Bridgeport and Benton roads.

Grant, like Sherman, seriously doubted the validity of Washburn's scouting reports, but he dared not ignore them. Instead, he ordered Parke's IX Corps, newly arrived at Young's Point from Kentucky, to Snyder's Bluff to beef up the defenses.[17] Parke's troops arrived at Snyder's Bluff on 17 June and immediately were sent to occupy the defensive earthworks built by Sooy Smith's and Kimball's DIVs under Washburn's direction. The line ran from above Snyder's Bluff to a bit south of Templeton's farm, which lay about 3.5 miles north of the intersection of the Jackson and Benton roads.[18]

Washburn's Deer Creek patrol returned on 18 June without having seen anything more threatening than a few stray Rebel commissary officers. But they did bring back a hoard of food and forage from the Deer Creek plantations. Meanwhile, Grant's own intelligence system was providing far more reliable information. His spies told him that MG W. H. T. Walker was still at Yazoo City, that Loring was at Benton, and that Jackson's Rebel cavalry was dispersed in a screen guarding the infantry. For a heady moment, Grant was sorely tempted to launch Sherman's Army of Maneuver through Mechanicsburg and along the north bank of the Big Black River, driving a wedge between Johnston's force at Canton and Jackson, and Walker's and Loring's force at Yazoo City and Benton. Sherman then could wheel north and destroy or disperse the Rebels north of the Big Black, after which he could turn south, cross the Big Black River, and disperse Johnston's army. After a moment of euphoria, Grant decided that preparations would take several days, the secret could not be kept, and Johnston would be able to concentrate his entire army before Sherman could arrive on the scene.

The alternative was to fortify the Mechanicsburg Corridor even more heavily. Sherman inspected the improved works on 20 June and declared them impregnable, even stronger than the fortifications of Vicksburg itself. On the same day, a Federal scout operating deep inside the Confederate lines discovered that Johnston had concentrated his army and that it was located at Vernon. Osterhaus reported that the water in the Big Black River now was so low that it could be forded almost anywhere north of Amsterdam. That meant that Johnston's Army of Relief could come storming across the Big Black anywhere between Cox's Ferry and Amsterdam. Yet Johnston made no move whatever, and Grant and his alter ego, Sherman, were deeply puzzled.

Then, on the morning of 22 June, it looked for a time as if the puzzle had been solved. That morning, MAJ Alonzo Parkell led a strong patrol of 4 IA CAV to check on the fords of the Big Black. At the Hill plantation, he ran into a strong and aggressive Rebel force[19] that eventually broke Parkell's men and dispersed them after a savage skirmish. Grant leaped to the conclusion that the Rebel force represented the advance guard of Johnston's Army of Relief, which must be crossing at Birdsong's Ferry. That being so, Johnston's first objective unquestionably would be the plateau at the head of Muddy Creek, simply because that was the only area in the entire region where there was enough open and flat ground to deploy an army.

The answer to the threat was to order Sherman to take his Army of Maneuver and meet Johnston in the hills east of the Benton Road. Grant felt a certain satisfaction in the thought that, for the first time, he was going to have the terrain on his side. Nor was that a trivial advantage, for the countryside between the Benton Road and the Big Black River looked very much like the terrain in which the Battle of Port Gibson had been fought. Since Johnston would have nothing like the numerical superiority that Grant had enjoyed at Port Gibson, he expected Sherman to defeat Johnston with little difficulty.

Sherman was ready, and by noon of 23 June, he, with Tuttle's and McArthur's DIVs, was in the vicinity of the Strauss and Tribble farms, in position to interdict the roads from Birdsong's Ferry or Jones' Ford, or the Bridgeport Road at Tiffentown.[20] Parke's corps was busy fortifying a line running from Oak Ridge to one mile south of Neely's farm, with a powerful cavalry outpost well out on the Benton Road. Not content, Sherman sent the 72 OH and a section of artillery out to build a fortified roadblock at the Markham plantation, where it commanded the roads leading to Birdsong's Ferry and Jones' Ford. The 13 IA he delegated to Parson Fox's farm to build a similar fortified roadblock on the Messenger's Ford Road.[21]

Grant was certain that Johnston's attack would materialize within the next forty-eight hours and warned his corps commanders to be ready. To make certain that all the forces opposed to Johnston were coordinated, he put Osterhaus's DIV at Big Black Bridge under Sherman's control. This brought the Army of Maneuver to 34,000 men and seventy-two guns. Nor was that all. Grant gave Sherman authority to assume command of Herron's DIV and A. J. Smith's DIV, if need be.[22] That added another 10,000 men and twenty-four guns to the total.

Always active, Sherman probed the line of the Big Black River with cavalry. They picked up an occasional straggler, one of whom insisted that

Johnston was at Brownsville but that Breckinridge's DIV was still in Jackson.[23] On the other hand, on 25 June, Osterhaus captured a deserter from 6 TX CAV who insisted that Johnston was at Vernon with his whole army of about 35,000. Sherman and Grant were delighted; it looked like Johnston was going to try to cross the Big Black River along the reach between Messenger's Ford and Birdsong's Ferry, and the Army of Maneuver was perfectly disposed to meet him on that front.[24] Sherman leaned toward an attempt to cross at Messenger's Ford, so he sent Chamber's BDE and 10 OH BTRY to beef up the roadblock at Parson Fox's farm. In that terrain, a brigade could hold until the main army arrived on the scene. Meanwhile, Federal probing along the Big Black encountered nothing except an occasional Rebel cavalry patrol.

Upon reflection, Sherman began to feel that it was all a little too pat. Maybe the Confederate patrol activity along the Big Black River between Messenger's and Birdsong's was only a smokescreen, while the main body of the Army of Relief crossed the Big Black at Kibbey's Ferry and marched through Pritchard's Crossroad, Mechanicsburg, and down the Benton Road onto the flank of Sherman's army. Doubt grew until 28 June, when he sent COL Bussey with 800 cavalry to probe up the Benton Road, just to be sure. Bussey came back that same night, having ridden all the way to Mechanicsburg without seeing a single Rebel.[25]

That settled it; Johnston was coming directly west from Vernon and Brownsville. On 29 June, Sherman moved McArthur's PROV DIV to Tiffentown and began fortifying a line that ran from south of Parson Fox's house to Bryant's plantation, about 1.5 miles north of the parson's house. He also brought most of the troops still at Snyder's Bluff, mostly IX Corps people, forward to fortify a line from the Bryant plantation to Mrs. Neely's house,[26] and Sooy Smith's DIV was put to work extending the fortifications from Neely's to Oak Ridge. Osterhaus remained at Big Black Bridge, Tuttle's DIV was held in reserve at Tribble's farm, and Kimball's DIV guarded Snyder's Bluff. No matter what route Johnston used, he would be faced with a powerful line of earthworks manned by determined blue-clad infantry.

Sherman's guard on the Big Black at Messenger's Ford reported a good deal of Rebel activity on the east bank all through 28 and 29 June. On 30 June, he sent COL Chambers forward to build a small lunette on a hilltop 500 yards west of the ford,[27] just to make Johnston work for the privilege of crossing. There was little more that Sherman could do except improve his positions, while he waited for Johnston's next move.

CONFEDERATE PERSPECTIVE

COL Wirt Adams and his MS CAV had withdrawn to Jackson with Gregg's BDE after the Battle of Raymond, and to Canton after the Battle of Jackson, and so had escaped the debacles of Champion Hill and Big Black Bridge without damage. Once Vicksburg was encircled by the Yankee army, Johnston ordered Adams to move to the Mechanicsburg area to screen the vital supply line between Yazoo City and Vaughan, and to keep watch over the Federal forces around the northern end of Vicksburg. Because Johnston had no illusions about the ability of cavalry alone to offer effective resistance if the Yankees came in strength, he also gave Adams a detachment of 20 MS MTD INF to beef up his effectiveness. Adams took his duties seriously, and on 23 May his scouts reported that a large Union cavalry force was assembling at Snyder's Bluff.

There was only one possible objective for such a force: the railroad bridge at Way's Bluff. The Yankees would have to come up the Benton Road, and the best place for an ambush along that road was at the hamlet of Mechanicsburg. Sure enough, about noon on 24 May, right on schedule, the Yankee cavalry came swinging confidently up the Benton Road and into Adams's trap. To Adams's considerable surprise, the Yankees made no effort whatever to press an attack. Instead, they quietly withdrew after only a volley or two had been fired.[28] Butternut scouts followed them all the way back to Snyder's Bluff. Adams was confused; he could imagine no rational reason for the Yankee behavior.

When Wirt Adams informed BG States Rights Gist, commander of the Right Wing of Johnston's Army of Relief, of the Federal cavalry concentration at Snyder's Bluff on 24 May, Gist assumed that it was aimed at the Way's Bluff bridge or possibly Yazoo City. He also assumed that Wirt Adams's cavalry would be unable to stop the Yankees, so he ordered BG W. H. T. Walker to take his brigade of GA infantry from Canton to Deasonville, on the north side of the Big Black River and on the direct road from Yazoo City to Vaughan. This put Walker in position to move quickly toward Yazoo City if necessary, as well as to interdict the roads that a Yankee thrust at Way's Bluff would have to follow.

Meanwhile, back in Canton, Johnston on 25 May gave the recently promoted MG W. H. T. Walker command of the right wing of the Army of Relief. As part of the same shuffling of commands, COL Claudius Wilson assumed command of the GA BDE, and Gist resumed command his own BDE.

Johnston, who actively had opposed more cavalry for Pemberton, had made absolutely certain that his own cavalry forces were adequate, once he assumed direct command in Mississippi. As a result, cavalry reinforcements were arriving daily, so on 27 May he created a new CAV BDE under the command of BG John Adams, whose headquarters would be at Vernon. In addition to almost all Johnston's cavalry units, Adams was given the crack Brookhaven ARTY. His mission was to screen the line of the Big Black River from Big Black Bridge to Cox's Ferry, and to guard the approaches to Yazoo City and Way's Bluff.

John Adams hardly had settled into his chair when a courier from Wirt Adams arrived in his headquarters at Vernon, telling him that a big Yankee cavalry force was coming up the Benton Road toward Mechanicsburg. John Adams, confident in the power of his new command, decided he could handle the matter himself and did not notify Johnston. Next morning he crossed the Big Black River at Kibbey's Ferry with his entire command and marched on Mechanicsburg. About 1400, his advance guard topped a hill about two miles west of Mechanicsburg and encountered Yankee cavalrymen coming up the hill. The Confederates charged briskly, and the Yankee horsemen fell back. Then, suddenly, about a mile east of Mechanicsburg, the blue-clad horsemen evaporated. In their place was left a long blue infantry battle line.

John Adams was horrified. No one had warned him that the Yankee force included infantry, and he knew full well that his cavalrymen could not stand for a moment against Federal infantry. He hastily disengaged and retreated toward Pritchard's Crossroad, covering his withdrawal with the Brookhaven ARTY. So demoralized was he by the unexpected encounter that, on 29 May, he abandoned Pritchard's Crossroad and retreated across the Big Black at Kibbey's Ferry. Wirt Adams and his MS CAV stayed behind; they were old hands at this game of cat and mouse, and they remained in contact with the Federal forces.

Safely in his camp at Vernon, John Adams regained his composure. On the morning of 30 May, he sent a message to Johnston describing the event. This was Johnston's first inkling of the Yankee probe through Mechanicsburg! Johnston was understandably alarmed, because he knew that Wirt Adams's cavalry would not be able to stop a determined infantry probe to Way's Bluff. That same day, a courier from Wirt Adams arrived in John Adams's camp, telling him that the Yankees were withdrawing toward Satartia. This completely baffled John Adams, since there was nothing between the Yankee force and Way's Bluff except Wirt Adams's cavalrymen, and they would constitute no obstacle at all to a resolute infantry force. Nevertheless, he was gratified. He assembled his command, recrossed the Big Black, and marched on Mechanicsburg, reoccupying the town about noon. Once again, he neglected to inform Johnston of either his plans or the situation.

Meanwhile, in Canton, and entirely unaware of John Adams's move to join Wirt Adams, Johnston had decided that the only way to stop the Federal force at Mechanicsburg was to oppose it with infantry. He ordered Loring, at Jackson with 5,500 men, to move to Canton; and ordered Walker, at Canton, to march via Moore's Ferry to Benton, where he was to rendezvous with John Adams. Johnston had chosen Benton, instead of Pritchard's Crossroad, because the only reliable source of water north of the Big Black were the springs at the head of Cypress Creek, near Benton.

The weather was unseasonably hot and dry, and Walker's march turned into a bitter struggle, with many stragglers. There was no sign of John Adams when he arrived at Benton early on 31 May. Johnston had sent a message to John Adams at the same time he sent his orders to Loring and Walker; but, by the time the courier arrived at Vernon, John Adams had left for Mechanicsburg, so the message never reached him.

Walker now was deep in the fog of war. For all he knew, the Yankee column might be over the next hill. However, since it had not yet arrived, it must be somewhere between Benton and Mechanicsburg. Between himself and the Yankees, there would be, at the very least, Wirt Adams's MS CAV. He sent his aide toward Mechanicsburg to make contact.[29]

Benton was so far north of the most direct road between Mechanicsburg and Way's Bluff, however, that it was possible that the Federal force was somewhere south or southwest of Benton, so Walker sent an infantry patrol (he had no cavalry) out toward Myrtleville and Pritchard's Crossroad. The men found nothing whatever.

Meanwhile, Walker's aide rode hard and reached Mechanicsburg about 1100, and there he found John Adams.[30] He also found out that the Yankee force was long gone and that Walker's march to Benton therefore had been in vain. He wearily headed back to rejoin Walker at Benton. About the time he walked into Walker's tent, COL Ferguson and his combat team from the Delta marched into camp. Ferguson had been a dreadful thorn in the flesh of the Federals, who were trying to maintain a supply line down the Mississippi; but Johnston needed every man he could find and had pulled him out to add to his cavalry manpower.

The question in Johnston's mind was: why did the Federals not press their advance beyond Mechanicsville? No ready answer presented itself, but it was clear that the Union interest in the area had to be restrained, if for no other reason than that the long supply road from Yazoo City to Vaughan had to be protected. Back to Walker on 1 June went an order to move his force from Benton to Yazoo City, where he would be able to protect that vital transfer point from Yankee raids coming up the Yazoo.[31] As soon as he arrived, Walker immediately set his men to work improving the somewhat skeletal fortifications around the town.

On the same day, 1 June, MG John C. Breckinridge's DIV, with 5,600 men, arrived in Jackson, MS, from Middle Tennessee. With this addition, Johnston's Army of Relief numbered nearly 30,000.

Matters now settled into a routine, until the early morning of 4 June, when one of John Adams's scouts reported that a powerful naval squadron, including transports and tinclads, was on its way up the Yazoo. The scouts watched with great interest as a large infantry force disembarked at Satartia, but they did not interfere. However, with plenty of warning, John Adams deployed his force in a commanding position just west of Mechanicsburg and settled down to wait. In the meantime, he sent a courier dashing off to Walker, with the suggestion that Walker and his infantry come at once.

When the Yankee infantry began to deploy in front of his roadblock, John Adams's heart sank as he recognized the battle flags of the famed "Eagle Brigade," renowned as one of the best combat outfits in the Army of the Tennessee. Nevertheless, he resolved to hold as long as possible, in the hope that Walker soon would be down from Yazoo City to support him. The Union infantry had just begun to advance, supported by artillery, when an excited scout came galloping up with the news that a second powerful Yankee force was approaching up the Benton Road and was only minutes away. John Adams had no choice; it was hold on and be trapped, or retreat and escape. He chose the latter and withdrew to Pritchard's Crossroad, where he began to throw up entrenchments.[32] He need not have bothered; the Yankees occupied Mechanicsburg and then stopped.

There was a telegraph line from Yazoo City to Canton via Benton and Vaughan, and when John Adams's courier arrived at Walker's headquarters early on the afternoon of 4 June, Walker immediately notified Johnston of the situation. He also sent Ferguson's combat team to Pritchard's Crossroads to give John Adams some additional strength. Johnston reacted instantly to protect the Way's Bluff bridge and the supply road between Yazoo City and Vaughan by starting Loring's INF DIV and BG William H. Jackson's CAV DIV, which had just arrived from

Bragg's Army of Tennessee, from Canton toward Benton.[33] However, the day was so hot and dry that they barely reached a point three miles north of Moore's Ferry before they were forced to halt. Even so, there were many stragglers and some deaths from heat exhaustion.

Early on the morning of 6 June, a cautious probe westward from Pritchard's Crossroad revealed that the Yankees again had withdrawn from Mechanicsburg, so John Adams reoccupied the hamlet at 0630. He sent a courier to Walker at Yazoo City, who telegraphed the news to Johnston in Canton. Johnston was completely confused. Why send such a powerful force to Mechanicsburg unless the intent was to attack the Confederate supply system somewhere between Yazoo City and Way's Bluff? Unable to penetrate the Union design, Johnston sent Jackson's CAV DIV to Pritchard's Crossroad, where it would block the direct road between Mechanicsburg and Way's Bluff; and Loring's INF DIV to Benton, where it would be available to protect the supply line, wherever the blow eventually fell.

Jackson was equally confused and thought the whole thing might be some kind of elaborate ruse. Just to be sure, he sent Ross's CAV BDE to Satartia to keep a watch on the bluecoats. Ross followed the retreating Federals to within eight miles of Haynes' Bluff before concluding that the Yankees indeed were withdrawing inside their defenses.[34]

Johnston had no idea what the Federals were up to, but he realized that there were some advantages to Loring's and Walker's positions. For one thing, they were close to the Delta, the main source of supply for food and forage, and this made it much easier to subsist them than would have been the case if they were held south of the Big Black River. In addition, one of the chief options as to a route for the proposed attempt to relieve Vicksburg was the Mechanicsburg Corridor. If that route eventually were chosen, then Walker and Loring would be ideally disposed. So to Walker and Loring went directives to stay where they were and dig in.[35]

Now that Jackson's CAV DIV was in hand, Johnston decided that he no longer needed John Adams's PROV CAV BDE and broke it up and sent its units back to their parent organizations.[36] All except Wirt Adams's MS CAV; it had no parent organization, so it was permitted to remain at Mechanicsburg to prowl the Mechanicsburg Corridor.

By 11 June, Johnston's Army of Relief had grown strong enough so that Johnston began seriously to consider ways by which Vicksburg might be approached. He had two basic options. The first was to strike westward across the Big Black River on the front between Amsterdam and Bush's Ford. The second was to attack down the Mechanicsburg Corridor. The former course had one major advantage; the Army of Relief could be concentrated behind the Big Black River, where it would be safe from prying Yankee eyes. On the other hand, supplying the army with rations and fodder from its sources in the Delta and the north would involve a much longer and more difficult supply line, and the Big Black River remained a problem. Johnston was told that, while the water in the Big Black was so low that it could be forded in many places, it nevertheless remained a serious military obstacle because the banks along most of its length were high and steep. If Grant chose to defend the river line, it would be difficult to force a crossing; on the other hand, if Grant chose to fight somewhere west of the river, the Army of Relief would have the stream at its back, which would be awkward in the event of a defeat.

The Mechanicsburg Corridor route had the obvious advantages of short supply lines for food and forage and no large streams to cross. Its disadvantages were that the Army of Relief would be forced to concentrate in the vicinity of Mechanicsburg, an area which was wide open to Federal reconnaissance patrols. Moreover, the lines of the Big Black and the Yazoo rivers would restrict maneuverability. There would be no choice but to drive straight ahead down the narrow corridor between the two streams. At this point, Johnston had no information on the nature of the terrain in the corridor, even though Confederate forces had been prowling the area for weeks.

Johnston had had enough experience with the unreliable Confederate communications system to conclude that coordinating simultaneous movements in places as widely separated as Yazoo City and Jackson would be well-nigh impossible, so he directed Walker and Loring to move their divisions to Vernon.[37] That would concentrate his army in the area of Jackson, Canton, and Vernon. If he chose to attack down the Mechanicsburg Corridor, the army could cross the Big Black at Kibbey's Ferry or Cox's Ferry, or both; but if he chose to strike westward, the troops would be positioned to approach the river with a minimum of delay.

In either case, it was imperative that Johnston's movements be concealed from prying Yankee eyes to the fullest extent possible. To this end, he directed Jackson to detach Cosby's CAV BDE to Mechanicsburg, with a directive to guard the exits from the Mechanicsburg Corridor most diligently and to patrol aggressively in the direction of Vicksburg. Ross's TX CAV BDE was to move to Bolton, where it would be in position to guard the crossings of the Big Black River from Cox's Ferry to Baldwin's Ferry.

There was one major flaw in this disposition, and that was the possibility of another Federal incursion via the Yazoo River. Porter's ironclads were not the problem, because the water was so low that the bar at Satartia would not permit their passage. Some of those damnable tinclads could float on a heavy dew, though, and the Federals well might be tempted to send a squadron of them upstream. As a counter, Johnston asked CDR Isaac Brown, the commander of the Confederate naval installation at Yazoo City, to mine the river as far downstream from Yazoo City as practicable. At the same time, he ordered the big guns at Fort Pemberton to be brought to Yazoo City and emplaced.[38] Those guns had turned back Porter's ironclads and could be expected to make short work of a mere tinclad or two.

By the evening of 15 June, both Walker and Loring were safely in their camps at Vernon.[39] There had been patrol bickering all along the line of the Big Black south of Cox's Ferry, a clear indication that the Yankees were alert to the threat of a crossing in that area. Johnston still could not make up his mind as to a course of action, and precious days went by with no activity more serious than minor reorganizations of the Army of Relief.[40] French's DIV was organized on 21 June, consisting of McNair's, Maxey's, and Evans's BDEs, a total of eighteen regiments.

One of Johnston's complaints was that he knew virtually nothing about what Grant was doing, because the Yankee guard on the Big Black was almost airtight. An end run seemed in order, so, on 20 June, a large cavalry patrol from Cosby's CAV BDE, plus a detachment of Wirt Adams's ubiquitous Mississippi horsemen, headed south on the Benton Road. The patrol was commanded by LTC Robert Woods, a bold and resourceful man.

Two days later, Woods's patrol was riding south on the Lower Benton Road when it ran smack into a detachment of Yankees moving north near the Hill farm. Woods drove the bluecoats back across Bear Creek in a series of sharp little battles, before the Yankees finally broke and scattered near the Markham farm. Woods, while elated by his victory, was realistic enough to know that the Yankees would not take the loss lightly; they would send out infantry. He turned back and arrived at Mechanicsburg the next day, 23 June.[41] Johnston learned of the affair on 24 June. It told him in no uncertain terms that the Federals were very sensitive to activity along the Big Black. He would have to be careful.

39

Offense and Defense
20 May–4 July 1863

Maps: 5. The Core Region
17. The Northeastern Approaches to Vicksburg
22. The Mechanicsburg Corridor

Johnston and the Army of Relief

All through the final days of May and the month of June, while the Federal army pressed tighter and tighter around the Vicksburg perimeter, GEN Joseph E. Johnston remained at Canton attempting to gather enough force to defeat the Army of the Tennessee and relieve Vicksburg. As early as 18 May, he had realized that Vicksburg was going to be invested, with Pemberton's army trapped inside. He understood full well that the Union had a far larger pool of manpower from which to draw reinforcements than did the Confederacy, and he knew that Yankee control of the Mississippi gave the Union forces a secure supply corridor down which men and supplies could flow. Still, their manpower was widely dispersed, and it would take time for large forces to be assembled at Vicksburg. On the other hand, while Confederate resources were smaller and equally widely dispersed, they had the advantage of interior lines.

In principle, it seemed possible for the Confederacy to assemble an Army of Relief more rapidly than the Federals would be able to build up their army besieging Vicksburg. However, speed was of the essence, and Johnston cast about for a pool of manpower that could be assembled quickly. It soon became clear that the only such pool of trained and organized manpower in the Department of Mississippi and East Louisiana was the garrison of Port Hudson. Thus, on 19 May, he sent a message to Gardner, ordering him to evacuate the fortress and bring all his troops to Jackson as rapidly as possible.[1]

Like Pemberton, Gardner was under a direct presidential order to hold Port Hudson at all costs. Furthermore, Johnston's order made no sense. As long as Vicksburg and Port Hudson could be maintained, the Confederacy retained an avenue by which men and materiel could flow from the Trans-Mississippi to the Confederacy east of the Mississippi River. On the other hand, the moment Port Hudson was abandoned, the Union fleet in New Orleans would have free access all the way to the guns of Vicksburg. For all practical purposes, the river would become a wall dividing the Confederacy into two unequal halves. Trying to hold Vicksburg as an isolated fortress under such conditions would be not only useless but impossible.

Torn by these considerations, Gardner hesitated. Whom should he obey—his president and commander-in-chief, or his theater commander? Before he could make up his mind, blue-clad divisions led by Union MG Nathaniel Banks closed around his perimeter, and he was well and truly trapped, even as Pemberton was trapped in Vicksburg.[2]

The only other immediate source of manpower was Bragg's Army of Tennessee, northwest of Chattanooga. Despite the fact that, a few days previously, he had refused to send Pemberton assistance from that source, Johnston now appealed to President Davis for troops from that army. After all, Union MG Rosecrans, whose Army of the Cumberland lay about Murfreesborough, showed no signs of activity; so Bragg was under no direct threat. He had been under no greater threat earlier, but matters looked differently to Johnston now that the shoes were on his own feet. Under orders from both Davis and Johnston, Bragg ordered MG John Breckinridge's DIV from Tennessee to Jackson, MS, where it arrived on 1 June. This brought Johnston's Army of Relief up to about 30,000 men. The right wing was commanded by MG W. H. T. Walker and consisted of about 13,500 men, divided into five infantry brigades and one cavalry brigade. Walker's headquarters were at Yazoo City, his mission was to guard the Mechanicsburg Corridor and the supply line from the Delta.

The left wing was commanded by MG William Loring, whose headquarters were at Canton. After the debacle following Champion Hill, his division had been reequipped and joined by additional infantry, cavalry, and artillery forces, so that his wing totaled about 11,000 men of all arms.

Breckinridge's DIV, plus Maxey's BDE, constituted a separate force stationed in and around Jackson.

While this disposition seemed to scatter Johnston's forces widely, it in fact was well disposed for launching an attack down the Mechanicsburg Corridor. Each of the three forces could reach Mechanicsburg along converging roads, and by routes that were beyond the surveillance envelope of the Federal forces. Had he felt it necessary to do so, Johnston very likely could have achieved a concentration of 30,000 men at the northern end of the Mechanicsburg Corridor, without detection by the Union. His only serious problem would have been that old bugaboo of Confederate armies in the West: control. Coordinating the movements of three such widely separated columns, so that they arrived more or less simultaneously at Mechanicsburg, certainly would have taxed Confederate communications facilities to the limit, and Johnston well understood that.

As June wore on, President Davis and Secretary of War Seddon became increasingly concerned. They well knew that the Confederacy could reinforce much more rapidly at first than the Union, because of its internal communications. But they also knew that the Union had far greater reserves of manpower and that, given time, it would be able to marshal far more men at Vicksburg than the Confederacy. Thus, if Johnston were to attempt the relief of Vicksburg at all, it should be soon. On 4 June, Seddon wired Johnston, urging him to attack Grant immediately and offering to take full responsibility for whatever happened. By this time, Johnston's Army of Relief had grown to about 32,000 men. With the men in Vicksburg, this gave the Confederacy a total of about 62,000 men in the Vicksburg-Jackson region.

Johnston was full of reasons why he dared not attack. His cavalry was inadequate. He had too little artillery. The Big Black River was too much of a barrier. Seddon asked if he should withdraw more troops from Bragg in Tennessee. Johnston told him that it was a choice of losing either Tennessee or Mississippi, and if Seddon chose to lose Tennessee, that was his responsibility.

Nevertheless, Johnston at last was badgered into making moves preliminary to an offensive. His concern over the always unpredictable Confederate communications system was such that, instead of ordering a combined movement of the three parts of his army, he instead chose to assemble his entire force close to his headquarters at Canton by bringing Walker and Loring to Vernon, while leaving Breckinridge in Jackson. And there the army stayed as the critical days of June passed.

The continued presence of Union outposts east of the Big Black River at Big Black Bridge worried Johnston, because it suggested that the Northerners were holding a bridgehead for their own offensive purposes. There were a number of savage little fights in that area through the first two weeks of June, as the Confederate cavalry tried to push the Federals back across the stream.[3] Johnston could have done it easily, simply by sending an infantry brigade to do the job, but he hesitated to take such a step out of fear of precipitating a major confrontation for which he was not yet prepared. Rather, his thoughts focused primarily on the defensive, although he did not neglect making provision for a rapid retreat, should that become necessary. He was reasonably sure it would be. Instead of planning an offensive to seize control of the whole east bank of the Big Black, he contented himself with setting up a cavalry cordon that extended from Cox's Ferry on the Big Black through Bolton to Baldwin's Ferry, eight miles airline south of Big Black Bridge, thus leaving the region between Edwards and Big Black Bridge firmly in Union control.

On 15 June, Seddon wired Johnston the news that the IX Corps had been detached from the Union Army of the Ohio and sent to Grant. This disturbing news put an end to any intention Johnston might have had of attacking the force besieging Vicksburg. He wired Seddon, saying that he was convinced that Vicksburg could not be relieved, and he wrote to Pemberton even more succinctly: "I am too weak to save Vicksburg."[4] Seddon was horrified and wired back an order to attack.

Johnston was not to be moved. It was impolitic, however, simply to ignore the Secretary of War, so, in late June, Johnston assembled a council of war at Canton, the agenda being to discuss ways to relieve Vicksburg. Even Kirby Smith had a representative there. Johnston told the assembled group that he regarded Vicksburg's plight as "almost hopeless," so it perhaps is not surprising that the conferees were unable to make any substantive suggestions.[5] Of course, Johnston made certain that Secretary Seddon was informed promptly of the opinion of the council.

In Vicksburg, Pemberton's attention had been focused on the hope of breaking the siege and saving Vicksburg. However, with Johnston's message, Pemberton's mind turned at last to the possibility that the army at least might be saved. This freed his mind from preoccupation with the Mechanicsburg Corridor, and at last he realized that the water in the Big Black River was so low that Porter would be unable to get gunboats of any kind into it. Grand Gulf had been evacuated by the Yankees, so there would be no interference from a Yankee force south of the Big Black. On

21 June, Pemberton wrote to Johnston, suggesting that he attack north of the railroad while he, Pemberton, cut his way out to the south and escaped across the Big Black at Hankinson's Ferry.[6]

However, by this time Johnston had made up his mind not to let himself be drawn into a fight under any circumstances. He countered with a proposal that would avoid any necessity for action on his part, suggesting that Pemberton build a fleet of small boats and escape with his men across the Mississippi.[7] Pemberton knew that this was patent nonsense, and there is little question that Johnston knew it, too. Porter and his ironclads would have been among the small boats like sharks among minnows. When Pemberton received this message, it is possible that he reflected on the fact that, while Johnston deemed the Big Black too big an obstacle for himself, he saw the Mississippi as a minor hurdle for Pemberton.

Even had such an escape miraculously succeeded, it would have meant the effective loss of the Army of Vicksburg. That army would have been on the west side of the Mississippi, a river which from that day forward would have been completely under Union control. Pemberton realized, as Johnston evidently did not, that, once the Mississippi fell into Union hands, nothing that happened in the Trans-Mississippi would materially affect the outcome of the war.

Nevertheless, Pemberton's letter did awaken Johnston to the possibility that Vicksburg might be approached from the southeast, thus perhaps avoiding the need to make a frontal assault on the Big Black River front north of Amsterdam. Furthermore, because Pemberton had raised the issue, Johnston felt impelled at least to give the appearance of checking on the practicality of the scheme. Thus, on 25 June, he sent Wirt Adams and his cavalry to examine the river crossings below Big Black Bridge, and especially Hankinson's Ferry.[8] Early on the morning of 1 July, a detachment of the patrol heading toward Hankinson's Ferry from Rocky Springs suddenly was attacked by a small Federal infantry force. Wirt Adams immediately concentrated his scattered detachments and drove the Yankees back to the north bank of the Big Black.[9] Late the next day, 2 July, a Union infantry brigade appeared at Hankinson's Ferry and crossed to the south bank.[10] Wirt Adams's horsemen could not cope with that and quietly withdrew.

The conclusion Johnston drew from this was that the crossings south of Big Black Bridge were heavily guarded and that crossing in that quarter was likely to be as difficult as anywhere else. In addition, moving the Army of Relief another twenty-five or thirty miles to the south would place an intolerable strain on his already stressed supply system. Johnston put the idea out of his mind, making sure at the same time that Richmond was fully informed of the impracticality of an offensive in that region.

At last the pressure from Richmond to do something—anything—became irresistible. On the morning of 1 July, the Army of Relief began to move slowly toward the Big Black River. If Johnston had a plan for a campaign to relieve Vicksburg, he never communicated it to anyone. The movement was a disaster. Breckinridge's DIV moved out of Jackson and camped at Clinton, a distance of less than ten miles. At Clinton, some units reported that half their men were stragglers.[11] The month of inactivity had taken its toll. French's DIV marched to Brownsville, about twelve miles from its previous camp, losing stragglers in droves. Loring and Walker did not move so far and fared a bit better.[12]

The next day, the Army of Relief inched closer to the Big Black crossings, but the day after that it rested while Johnston held another council of war. The meeting lasted nine hours, most of it spent in a futile attempt to get accurate information from local citizens about the terrain, roads, and streams of the countryside between Vicksburg and the Big Black River. MG French wrote in his diary: "Nine hours were spent in vainly attempting to get accurate information from the citizens respecting the roads and streams. *Relatively little could be learned of the country on either side of the Big Black*" (author's emphasis).[13]

The conference convinced Johnston that an attempt to cross the Big Black River north of the railroad could only end in disaster, because the few fragments of information he had accumulated suggested not only that the terrain between the Big Black River and Vicksburg was very difficult, but also that the Federal forces were concentrated north and northeast of the city. This interpretation seemed to be confirmed by the fact that the Unionists were aggressively patrolling the fords and roads north of Big Black Bridge. That same evening, Johnston began to realize that his actions might be seen as less than laudatory; he had at least to give the appearance of activity. His options were not numerous. He dared not move north into the Mechanicsburg Corridor, because the Federals might lunge across the Big Black and cut him off from Jackson and Canton. He dared not simply fall back east, because Richmond might take a dim view of that.

During the day, Jackson's cavalry scouts reported that, despite the flurry of Union activity at Hankinson's Ferry the previous day, the crossings of the Big Black River south of Big Black Bridge now were all unguarded.[14] Further, Jackson had been informed that the Union works south of Vicksburg were less strong than elsewhere. On the basis of such bits of information, Johnston decided to move south through Edwards, with a view to crossing the Big Black River at Hankinson's Ferry and striking the Federal besieging army from the south. And so orders went out to begin the movement of the army to the south early the next morning, 4 July.

However, that same afternoon, 3 July, the roar of guns from the direction of Vicksburg suddenly stilled.[15] MG French thought he knew what that portended but kept silent in the interests of morale. French was not the only one who had noticed that the grumble of guns from the west had ceased, however, and by midmorning the camp was seething with rumors that Vicksburg had fallen. At dawn came confirmation: Pemberton had surrendered the city.

Sherman's Army of Maneuver 2 June–5 July 1863

Map: 68. Disposition of Forces in the Northeastern Approaches to Vicksburg: Sherman's Defense Line: 22 June 1863

At the time of its formation on 22 June, Sherman's Army of Maneuver consisted of two brigades of Tuttle's DIV from Sherman's own XV Corps, three brigades from McPherson's XVII Corps, all of Parke's IX Corps, Sooy Smith's DIV of Washburn's XVI Corps, and Osterhaus's DIV of McClernand's XIII Corps. By the afternoon of 23 June, the Army of Maneuver had occupied and fortified positions well forward on all of the roads leading westward from the crossings of the Big Black. Osterhaus's DIV, of course, remained in position guarding the Big Black Bridge, with cavalry scouts well out on the east bank. Kimball's DIV of Washburn's corps was to remain in reserve at Snyder's Bluff. The Army of Maneuver totaled about 34,000 men and seventy-two guns, a force as large as, or larger than, Johnston's Army of Relief. Furthermore, if Johnston finally did come across the Big Black, he would be fighting on ground of Sherman's choosing, in terrain not unlike that the Union had encountered at Port Gibson. Furthermore, Sherman and his men had scouted the countryside thoroughly and so knew every nook and cranny, whereas Johnston at best would know it only indirectly, through the eyes of his cavalry scouts. Neither Sherman nor Grant had any doubts whatever about the outcome.

The only thing that made Sherman unhappy was that he did not know exactly where Johnston was. Driven by his demands for information, cavalry patrols fanned out on all roads leading east and northeast. Collectively, the patrols established beyond doubt that Johnston was still east of the river, and one of them picked up a Rebel straggler near Birdsong's Ferry who insisted that Johnston was at Brownsville. Sherman assumed that Johnston's information on the geography of the area between the Mississippi River floodplain and the Big Black River was detailed and reliable. After all, at least until mid-June, his cavalry had been free to wander at will through the entire area. Furthermore, it was basically Rebel countryside, and local informants could be expected to fill in any gaps. Thus, Sherman's plans were based on the belief that his counterpart, Joe Johnston, had a clear picture of the general nature of the road network, the terrain, and, probably to a lesser degree, Sherman's dispositions.

Sherman figured that Johnston would attempt to force a crossing at Messenger's Ford, because a good road led from that point to Tiffentown, where it met the Bridgeport Road. The red-beard visualized a powerful Confederate force seizing the Tiffentown junction, then turning south to smash Osterhaus at Big Black Bridge. This would open the way for a second Rebel column to cross the Big Black River at that point. The Confederates then would turn west in two columns, one each on the Bridgeport and Jackson roads, and so proceed into the rear of the Federal investment force. This route would avoid all of Sherman's laboriously constructed fortifications.

However, Sherman was too pragmatic to assume that the enemy would think in the same way he did, so his response was to cover every conceivable contingency. His first move was to strengthen the existing roadblocks on all the roads leading west from the Big Black crossings and then seal the crossings so that no word of the Federal dispositions reached Johnston's ears. At the same time, he sent an 800-man cavalry force up the Benton Road to make sure that the Mechanicsburg Corridor held no surprises.

Grant could not believe that Johnston would make no effort to relieve Vicksburg, so he interpreted Johnston's apparent inaction as concealing some dark and devious plan. Unable to imagine what it was, Grant, like Sherman, was reduced to covering every contingency. On 29 June, he gave McArthur's DIV to Sherman, who moved it to Tiffentown, where it would be positioned to oppose the scenario that Sherman had envisioned earlier. That done, the next step was to move forward and fortify a line extending from Oak Ridge south to Mrs. Neely's plantation, then southeast past the Strauss and Tribble farms to Bryant's farm, and then south to Parson Fox's. This line placed fortifications across every road running west from the crossings of the Big Black except the Bridgeport Road. Finally, a lunette was built overlooking Messenger's Ford, which was regarded as the most likely crossing place.

Having fortified against every contingency he could think of, Sherman began pushing cavalry-infantry-artillery patrols across to the east bank of the Big Black River, hoping to find out exactly where Johnston and the Army of Relief were located and what their intentions were. For a change, Confederate security was airtight, and nothing of substance was learned until 1 July, when a Union patrol crossed the Big Black at Halls Ferry and reached Cayuga. Here the friendly natives told them that a Confederate cavalry force, 1,500 strong, had passed through en route to Rocky Springs. The next day, a Union patrol south of Hankinson's Ferry ran into a lot of Southern cavalry and was forced back across the Big Black River. Because Sherman insisted that Johnston was still north of the railroad, this made no sense whatever to Grant. However, it had to be checked out, and Grant sent Lawler's BDE of Carr's DIV. It found nothing except a few very belligerent Confederate cavalrymen.

On 2 July, there was a little spate of patrol activity opposite Sherman's front,[15] but the next day the Rebels seemed to have vanished. To Sherman, the very silence seemed ominous, but he could learn nothing. On 3 July, Grant, who was expecting the city to surrender at any moment, asked Sherman to make arrangements to launch his Army of Maneuver across the Big Black at a moment's notice.[16] Sherman's arrangements already had been made; he intended "to move light and rapid to interpose between Johnston's scattered forces."[17] Still, he asked Grant to send him the remainders of the XIII and XV corps as soon as the city surrendered. That would bring the Army of Maneuver up to thirteen divisions, which he regarded as more than enough to trounce Johnston, wherever he might be hiding.[18] Sherman intended to cross simultaneously at Big Black Bridge, Messenger's Ford, and Birdsong's Ferry; seek Johnston out; and destroy him.[19]

40

Forlorn Hope: Battle of Helena
4 July 1863

Maps: 1. The Theater of Operations
     2. Northern Sector
   24. The Battlefield of Helena

GEOGRAPHY

Memphis was the great Union depot through which manpower and supplies flowed southward to Grant's Army of the Tennessee in its trenches ringing Vicksburg. Between the two cities, the Mississippi River flows between low and unstable banks through a vast floodplain which is subject to flooding nearly every spring. The only exception is Helena, AR, fifty-five airline miles southwest of Memphis, where there is an area of high, dry ground. Here the west bank of the Mississippi impinges upon the southern tip of Crowley's Ridge, a remnant of an ancient landscape that rises like an island for 100 feet or more out of the vast, level floodplain. The high ground made it possible to build a town that, while safe from the annual flood, still was on the river and available to the steamboats carrying the commerce of the central plains. A network of good roads radiated into the interior of Arkansas, making Helena the most strategic location on the west bank of the Mississippi between Memphis and Vicksburg.

As such, the town did not long escape the attention of the Federal strategists, and it was occupied on 13 July 1862. Because it was scarcely more than a small enclave on the edge of territory largely held by the Confederacy, Helena was fortified almost immediately. The works were not particularly extensive, chiefly because the Federal engineers preferred small, compact fortifications that could be defended with a minimum of manpower. The design of the works at Helena was experimental, a deliberate attempt to use the excellent Union artillery as a substitute for manpower. The terrain lent itself to the concept. The town stood on a terrace forming a narrow shelf only about 600 yards wide, beyond which rose the hills of Crowley's Ridge. Just behind the town was a low ridge that dominated the town and the narrow creek-valley just to the west. Beyond that valley, three ravines radiated into Crowley's Ridge like the spokes of a wheel, and between each pair of ravines rose a sharp, steep ridge.

The close-in defense consisted of Fort Curtis, resting on the low ridge 200 yards west of the town. It mounted three 30-pdr Parrott rifles, with an effective range of 2,000 yards. The guns were mounted in such a way that they readily could be aimed in any direction, so they could command the town as well as the creek valley to the west and the hills beyond.

The perimeter defenses consisted of four strongpoints, each supported by one or more lines of riflepits. Each strongpoint mounted two field guns, arranged so that they, like the guns of Fort Curtis, could fire in any direction. Battery A stood on Rightor Hill, about 1,400 yards almost due north of Fort Curtis. Battery B stood on a nose of ridge beside the Upper St. Francis Road, about 1,300 yards northwest of Fort Curtis. Battery C was placed on a nose of Graveyard Hill, at a distance of about 900 yards southwest of Fort Curtis. Battery D crowned a similar nose of Hindman Hill, about 1,300 yards south-southwest of Fort Curtis. Batteries A and B were only about 700 yards apart, while batteries C and D were only about 600 yards apart. However, batteries B and C were about 1,200 yards apart and separated by a wide ravine. That ravine, however, was commanded for 2,000 yards, nearly to its head, by the heavy rifled guns in Fort Curtis, as well as by the guns of batteries B and C. Furthermore, the guns of Fort Curtis could fire directly into the rear and onto the flanks of all four of the perimeter batteries, and each of the perimeter batteries could fire into or onto the approaches to every other battery. The supporting riflepits were designed to halt or at least slow an attacking force, while the mutually supporting artillery of the four perimeter batteries and Fort Curtis decimated it. It was, in fact, a tightly integrated artillery trap.

The hills of Crowley's Ridge were mostly too steep to cultivate and so were grown up in forest. The defenders took advantage of that fact by fronting the works out to a distance of 1,000 yards or more with dense fields of abatis created by felling the forest trees outward and tying them together with telegraph wire. Where the roads ran through the woods, trees were carefully selected and marked so that, in an emergency, they quickly could be felled to block the roads.

Batteries A and D also commanded the narrow floodplain above and below the town, respectively. Below the town, at a distance of about 1,800 yards from Fort Curtis, a line of riflepits connected the levee and the base of Hindman Hill south of Battery D. No such provision was made north of town; here the floodplain was open and unimpeded except for the town levee, which bent back and connected to the Rightor Hill about 1,900 yards north of Battery A.

CONFEDERATE PERSPECTIVE

By 20 May 1863, it was clear, even to the Confederate government in Richmond, that Pemberton and his army were trapped in Vicksburg and that, unless something was done, the army ultimately would be forced to surrender. There was no doubt in Secretary of War Seddon's mind that the Union's capacity for bringing large numbers of men and supplies down the Mississippi was greater than the Confederacy's capacity to provide supplies and reinforcements by railroad, even if such supplies and reinforcements had been available. Unfortunately, they were not.

Seddon's mind therefore turned to the possibility of breaking the Federal supply line. That meant blocking the Mississippi River. On 23 May, he sent a telegram to GEN Joseph E. Johnston, then in Canton, MS, suggesting that the Department of the Trans-Mississippi attack and occupy Helena, fortify it, fit it with heavy guns, and from it interdict the Union supply line. Seddon thought this was such an obvious and workable idea that he had no doubt that Johnston would take immediate action.[1]

Johnston, however, seems to have had reservations. Not until 31 May did he forward Seddon's message on to Kirby Smith. With the Mississippi River under Union control, it was not easy to get a message to Shreveport, so Kirby Smith didn't receive the communication until 10 June.[2] This long delay was perhaps less critical than it might seem, because Kirby Smith independently had come to the same conclusion. On 4 June, six days before receiving Seddon's message, he wrote to Thomas C. Reynolds, Confederate governor of Missouri, that Helena was "the strategic point" and that it should be seized and fortified as an alternative to Vicksburg.[3] Other Confederate minds, including that of LTG Theophilus Holmes, who commanded Confederate forces in Arkansas, also had grasped the strategic implications; on his own initiative, he had left Little Rock on 8 June to confer with his principal field commander, MG Sterling Price, at Jacksonport, concerning the "propriety" of attacking and holding Helena. Unfortunately, Holmes's ambulance broke down en route (he always traveled by ambulance, being unable to ride a horse for more than a mile or two), so he was forced to return to Little Rock, but he sent a message to Price, telling him of his notion.[4]

Price instantly replied with unqualified enthusiasm; after all, he said, Marmaduke's scouts reported that there were only 4,000 men in the Helena garrison.[5] Holmes got Price's reply on 10 June, the same day Kirby Smith received Seddon's message. Kirby Smith finally forwarded Seddon's message to Holmes on 13 June, with the comment that, since he was too far from the scene of action to judge the practicality of the scheme, Holmes therefore was free to exercise his own judgment.

Now that responsibility for action rested with Holmes, he was troubled by Price's comment that there were "only" 4,000 men in the Helena garrison. The Confederate field forces in Arkansas numbered at best only about 8,000 effectives. It was widely held that a margin of three to one was required to attack a fortified place successfully. Holmes replied to Price's message by suggesting that maybe they ought to reconsider attacking Helena. As a counterproposal, he suggested the emplacement of a battery and a strong supporting force somewhere on the Mississippi south of Memphis. The artillery would interdict the river and force the Union to divert a large number of troops to eliminate it. Both actions would help Vicksburg.

Matters came to a head the next day, when a copy of Seddon's message to Johnston arrived at Little Rock. At the same time, information was flowing in from Marmaduke's scouts to the effect that the Yankees had stripped the Helena garrison of troops in order to reinforce the Army of the Tennessee in front of Vicksburg.[6] That was enough for Holmes; the next day, 15 June, he ordered Price to prepare his army for an offensive against Helena, and the following day he left for Jacksonport to assume field command.[7]

Holmes, Price, and Marmaduke sat down at Jacksonport on 18 June to plan their offensive. One problem was that most of those troops who could be concentrated into a field army were disposed primarily to guard against a Union thrust westward from Memphis. Marmaduke had Greene's CAV BDE at Wittsburg, guarding the crossings of the St. Francis River; while Shelby's CAV BDE was at Jacksonport in support of Price's infantry. Walker's CAV BDE was picketing the approaches to Helena.[8] Price's infantry were equally scattered; Parsons's and McRae's BDEs were at Jacksonport, but Fagan's BDE was at Little Rock.

It was ninety long miles from Jacksonport to Helena—five days of hard marching, if all went well. The final plan specified that the army would concentrate at Clarendon, on the White River, sixty-five miles south of Jacksonport, where it would make final preparations for the assault on Helena. Plans complete, Holmes returned to Little Rock. He had no intention of subjecting himself to the rigors of a march with the troops.

Right on schedule on 22 June, Parsons, McRae, and Shelby left Jacksonport and Greene left Wittsburg. All went well until the morning of 24 June. Then the heavens opened, and for four days it rained heavily and continuously. The unpaved roads of the Grand Prairie became a bottomless mire of black mud. The normally placid streams went over their banks. Bridges were swept away. Campgrounds flooded. Price had no pontoon train and no experienced engineer troops. Movement of any kind became one long, frustrating, exhausting battle. In an effort to save time, Clarendon was omitted as a staging area, and the army marched directly toward Helena. At last, Price's desperately tired and discouraged infantry reached Moro on 1 July. The cavalry had fared better; Shelby's CAV BDE had reached La Grange and had pickets within ten miles of Helena, while Greene's CAV BDE had reached Lexa and picketed the crossings of Lick Creek. The bridge at Lexa had been burned, evidently some time earlier, by the Yankees. Fagan's INF BDE had an easy time of it, because it went from Little Rock to DeVall's Bluff on the White River by rail and then by steamboat to Clarendon. Holmes traveled the same way and thus had no conception of the trials faced by the two infantry brigades with Price. He wrote to Price, complaining that the "terrible delays will thwart all my efforts."[9] Price may have wondered what efforts his commander had expended.

On 2 July, Parsons's and McRae's infantry moved forward to Lexa, on Lick Creek, ten miles west-northwest of Helena; while Fagan's INF BDE marched to Lick Creek on the Little Rock Road, twelve miles west of Helena.[10] Meanwhile, Shelby and Walker did their best to make their picket line around Helena airtight, so that no word of the planned attack would reach the Yankees.

Next day, 3 July, the army inched forward to within six miles of Helena; and Holmes, Price, Marmaduke, Walker, and Fagan met at the Allen Polk house, six miles from Helena on the Little Rock Road, to plan the final phase of the offensive. Holmes had been told by Marmaduke's scouts that the defenses were more formidable than had been believed, but the precise details were uncertain. Still, the outlines were clear: four small batteries in hilltop positions guarding the major roads into the town, with each supported by a modest array of riflepits. Surprisingly, the riflepits were not continuous, so there seemed to be no integrated defense perimeter. There was also an inner defense consisting of a slightly larger fort dominating the town from a low ridge to the west of it.[11] All in all, the defenses did not seem terribly formidable.

The plan upon which Holmes settled envisioned overwhelming the entire line by a single concerted attack all along the front. Price, with McRae's and Parsons's INF BDEs would drive down the Spring Creek Road and capture the battery on Graveyard Hill; Fagan's INF BDE would attack down the Hill Road and capture the battery on Hindman Hill; and Marmaduke would strike down the Old St. Francis Road and carry the crest of Rightor Hill, which was higher than the Federal battery on the extended nose of that hill. Once there, Marmaduke would emplace his artillery and blast the Yankees out of both the Rightor Hill battery and the battery guarding the Upper St. Francis Road. As soon as those two batteries were suppressed, Walker's CAV BDE would thrust down the Sterling Road into the city and take the fort on the hill west of town from the rear.[12] The assault would begin at daylight; despite the fact that all the officers carried watches, no specific time was set. As it turned out, "daylight" meant different things to different people! It must be said in the officers' defense that, in 1863, all times were set by local consensus; unified regional time zones were not introduced until after the transcontinental railroads had established a need for such. Thus, in the absence of an adequate time standard, Holmes fell back on astronomical time. His error was in his choice of words; he perhaps should have said *sunrise* instead of *daylight*.

The final approach marches began shortly after nightfall on the night of 3 July, when Walker's CAV BDE left the Bouie farm, near the junction of the Upper and Lower Little Rock roads, for his long march around the city to Porter's farm, four miles north of town on the Sterling Road.[13] Marmaduke, with Shelby's and Greene's CAV BDEs, left their camps at La Grange shortly before midnight; and the three infantry brigades of Price's DIV began their marches shortly after midnight. The complex plans began to unravel almost immediately. Marmaduke ran into almost impenetrable abatis and blocked roads while still two miles from the Federal defense perimeter; in an effort to find a way around them, he got lost in a maze of ravines. Eventually he decided to wait for daylight, when he would be able at least to see where he was going.

Fagan's INF BDE reached the junction of the Hill and Little Rock roads about 0200 on 4 July and sent COL Brooks and his 34 AR INF, plus

Etter's BTRY, to make a demonstration on the Little Rock Road while he proceeded via the Hill Road to his assault on the Federal lines on Hindman Hill. Price, with Parsons's and McRae's INF BDEs, turned off on a narrow track that led up a ravine toward Graveyard Hill. His advance was led by local guides who claimed to know the country well.

At about 0300, Brooks's advance was fired upon by a Yankee outpost at Beach Grove Plantation, still 1.5 miles from the Federal riflepits guarding the southern approaches to the city. Surprise now gone, Brooks pushed on until he began receiving fire from a line of riflepits to his front. He deployed his regiment near the Clements house, which stood near the base of a long nose projecting southward from Hindman Hill. It was now light enough to see. Evidently the Yankees could see, too, because a two-gun battery of 10-pdr Parrott rifles opened up from behind a levee about 1,000 yards to the northeast. The shells were on target, but they did little damage because Brooks's men dispersed their ranks a bit to minimize casualties. However, Brooks watched with some concern as a big paddlewheel steamer dropped down from an anchorage in front of the town and turned her bow upstream opposite Brooks's line. A moment later, three huge 8-in smoothbore shells crashed among his men.[14] The results were devastating. Brooks's men broke and took cover in the ravines west of the Clements house. Brooks tried to fight back with a pair of Etter's 10-pdr Parrott rifles, but it was no contest. The Confederate thrust along the Little Rock Road was over.

Meanwhile, Fagan's infantrymen had marched up the Hill Road, but, when they were still about a mile from the Federal works, they found the road obstructed and a dense field of abatis extending in both directions. None of the scouts had reported the obstacles, so there was not an ax in the whole brigade. There was nothing for it but to leave the wagons and artillery behind. Fagan's men filtered through the abatis with some difficulty, taking with them the crew of the artillery battery in hopes that they would be able to use the Yankee guns after the works to their front had been taken.

When Fagan's men reformed on the far side of the abatis, they discovered that they were still 600 yards from the battery position on Hindman Hill. Moreover, a line of riflepits ran across the ridge less than 100 yards to their front. Fagan had interpreted Holmes's use of "daybreak" to mean first light, so he waved his men forward as soon as he could see clearly. There was no surprise. As soon as Fagan's line emerged into the open, the riflepits to his front came alive, as did the two guns in the Federal battery. A brisk charge evicted the Federals, but there was a second line behind that, and behind that a third, and a fourth, and a fifth. All this time, the advancing troops were shelled unmercifully by the guns in the Hindman Hill battery, as well as the guns in the battery on Graveyard Hill. Toward the end, a battery far out in the floodplain to the west added its shells to the fire falling on the Confederate troops on the south side of Hindman Hill. The artillery fire from the battery on Graveyard Hill was particularly galling, because Price, with Parsons's and McRae's BDEs, was supposed to assault that battery at the same time that Fagan struck at the Hindman Hill battery, yet not a sound of firing came from that direction. By 0700, Fagan's advance had run out of steam, and it ground to a halt 150 yards short of its objective. There still was no sign of an attack on the Graveyard Hill battery.[15]

At first light, Price, with Parsons's and McRae's BDEs, was still 1.5 miles from the Federal defense line. The track he initially had followed had faded out well back; like Fagan, he had been forced to leave his artillery behind. About 0330, Price stopped to let his men rest, even though they had not yet reached their jump-off position. Just as the sky began to gray with approaching dawn, Price and his men heard the terrible sound of battle well up from the direction of Hindman Hill, but Price made no move to advance because he had interpreted Holmes's directive to attack at "daylight" to mean at sunrise.[16] Holmes rode up while it was still a few minutes shy of full light, realized what had happened, and urged Price to attack immediately, even though the sun was not yet up.[17] It was now about 0530, by which time Fagan's assault already had been brought to a halt. When Price finally got started, at about 0715, he drove hard, even though his men were being shelled by the guns to his front as well as by the battery on Hindman Hill to the south, and the battery beside the Upper St. Francis Road to the north.[18] Parsons's and McRae's men charged with complete abandon, and by 0800 both brigades reached the Federal battery on Graveyard Hill and overran it.

Utter confusion now reigned in the Confederate force on Graveyard Hill. Regiments were so mixed that commanders could not find their men. All this time, shells from the batteries to north and south continued to fall, and now huge 8-in shells began to impact on the hilltop. They were being fired from a Union gunboat in the river opposite the town.[19] After a few more minutes, three 30-pdr Parrott rifles in the fort at the edge of town began playing on the confused mass of soldiery, and a battery of rifled artillery far out in the floodplain to the southwest joined the action.

Price could find neither Parsons nor McRae. Finally, in desperation, he told a couple of the regimental commanders to organize an assault on the fort at the edge of town, 900 yards to the northeast.[20] The battle line that formed and began to move down the hill was made up of a random mixture of men from many different regiments. The guns from the fort and the batteries to north and south ripped and tore at their ranks as they moved down slope, and, by the time they reached the little creek bottom 400 yards southwest of the fort, they could stand the shelling no more. The line disintegrated, and men in small groups faded into the ravines to the west to escape the deadly rain of artillery shells.

Meanwhile, out on the north flank, Marmaduke had found his way back to the Old St. Francis Road shortly after daylight and resumed his advance on the Rightor Hill battery. The abatis still blocked his way, but, unlike Fagan and Price, he disassembled two of his guns and manhandled them through.[21] By 0500, he had reached a point 600 yards from the Rightor Hill battery, but here his dismounted cavalry were brought to a stop. He brought up his two guns and emplaced them on a knoll on the west flank of Rightor Hill, intending to blast a hole through the Federal riflepits on the west slope of the hill and flank the battery. The first rounds, however, awakened a Federal battery out in the floodplain to the east, and the Confederate gunners soon were forced to abandon their pieces. Then the Federal infantry boiled out of the entrenchments and captured the precious guns. Marmaduke's men rallied, and, after a confused struggle, were able to retake the two guns and drag them out of danger. Still, it was quite clear that the men could go no farther without help.[22]

Walker, who was supposed to sweep down the Sterling Road while Marmaduke kept the Rightor Hill battery occupied, never got through the abatis. The best he was able to do was build up a skirmish line south of the barrier, but it was not strong enough to make the slightest difference.[23]

It was now 0900. Price's men on Graveyard Hill and Fagan's men on Hindman Hill still were being shelled ceaselessly by Federal guns. Even the battery far away on Rightor Hill had joined in, despite the fact that Graveyard Hill was near the extreme limit of its range. The huge 8-in shells of the gunboat in the river continued to fall, like bolts of doom, into the confused and disheartened Confederate ranks.[24] Men drifted away to seek shelter in the ravines flanking Hindman and Graveyard hills, but even here the terrible fire followed them.[25]

Then, shortly after 0900, solid blue-clad battle lines suddenly formed at the foot of the hills and began to push rapidly westward into the wide valley down which the Spring Creek Road entered the city, as well as into the ravine between Graveyard and Hindman hills. At the same moment, the Federal artillery shifted its fire and began to concentrate on the bare ridgetops west of the battery positions, as well as on the heads of the ravines leading westward.[26] Other blue regiments began to converge on the Graveyard Hill battery, and another column thrust southwest from the riflepits supporting the battery on the Upper St. Francis Road. All the while, a terrible rain of iron from Union guns fell on the Confederate troops. Many men taking shelter in the Spring Creek Road ravine were cut off and captured. Others braved the storm of explosions sweeping the ridgetops and fled to the west.

Shortly after 1000, the Federal tide swept back over the Hindman Hill battery, forcing Holmes, Price, and the shattered remnants of McRae's and Parsons's BDEs to withdraw into the ravines to the west. At last, about 1030, Holmes realized that all was lost and ordered the remnants of his men to withdraw,[27] specifying the Allen Polk farm near Lick Creek as the rendezvous point. All through the afternoon and night, small groups straggled in. At dawn on 5 July, what remained of the army marched away to the northwest and safety. Holmes eventually reported sadly to Kirby Smith that his offensive had been a complete failure.[28] He reported 169 dead, 662 wounded, and 723 missing; that amounted to more than 20 percent of his total pre-battle force of 7,646.

FEDERAL PERSPECTIVE

MG Benjamin M. Prentiss commanded the District of Eastern Arkansas for the Union from the fortified enclave of Helena. He was not on good terms with MG Grant, having been involved in a controversy with him over precedence in rank early in the war; but his relations with MG Stephen Hurlbut, commander of XVI Corps of the Army of the Tennessee and of the depot city of Memphis, were correct if not cordial. In the summer of 1863, the job of commanding the fortified enclave of Helena was dull and uneventful, chiefly because the Confederate armies to the west seemed singularly inert. This began to change about 20 June, when Prentiss started hearing rumors that the Confederates in Arkansas were planning an attack. He was inclined to disbelieve the tales, although it was true that Union scouts were finding it more difficult than formerly to penetrate the Confederate picket line on the approaches to Helena.[29]

Unknown to Prentiss, RADM Porter maintained an extensive intelligence network in the Trans-Mississippi; and, on about 21 June, he received word from one of his agents in Arkansas that Rebel MG Sterling Price was moving toward the Mississippi in three columns from his base at Jacksonport.[30] The objective was unknown, but the obvious strategic goal of such a movement would be to interdict the Federal supply line down the Mississippi River. That would require one, or preferably several, batteries of heavy guns. Since Helena was the only place on the west bank of the Mississippi where the ground was high enough to be above the annual spring floodwaters, as well as the only place with a road network into the interior good enough to support the movement of heavy guns and their ammunition and supplies, Helena was the obvious choice.

Porter's immediate response was to order LCDR S. Ledyard Phelps, the naval officer responsible for the security of convoys between Island No. 10 and the mouth of the White River, to support the Helena garrison by every means within his power. Phelps took the threat as seriously as his commander; and, on 22 June, the timberclad gunboat *Tyler*, accompanied by tinclad *Hastings* and armed ram *General Bragg*, hove to off the town. When the ship captains reported that they were there to support Helena against the coming Rebel assault, Prentiss began to take the rumors a bit more seriously. His cavalry began to probe to the north and west, only to discover that the Rebel pickets resisted so strongly that the patrols could not penetrate.[31]

This looked much like the prelude to an attack, but Prentiss could not be certain; it might mean only that Price and Holmes were guarding their flank while they shifted troops to the south, either to counter Banks's siege of Port Hudson or to mount an attack on the Union posts across the Mississippi from Vicksburg. Then, on 24 June, a dispatch boat from Memphis delivered a letter from Hurlbut, warning that the Rebels were about to launch an attack on either New Madrid or Helena.[32] New Madrid made no sense; it was too far upriver. So it had to be Helena. Despite the nearly airtight Confederate blockade, bits and pieces of information came in over the next several days. By 28 June, Prentiss was convinced that his town was going to be attacked. He accelerated work to strengthen the defenses and ordered his men to be under arms by 0230 every morning until further notice.[33] He was *not* going to be surprised, as he had been at Shiloh.

At this juncture, *General Bragg* developed engine trouble, and her commander, LT Joshua Bishop, requested that he be permitted to take her to Memphis, the only place where she could be repaired. Prentiss told him to go ahead;[34] he didn't need the navy to help him defend Helena. He was about to receive a salutary lesson on the value of combined arms.

There were rumors that Confederate guerrillas were trying to establish a battery on the Mississippi above Helena near Island No. 10; and, on 29 June, *Hastings* went up to check the story out. This left only the venerable *Tyler* at Helena. Even though she was unarmored, she was a force to be reckoned with, for she mounted 8-in Dahlgren smoothbores and 30-pdr Parrott rifles, both with ranges long enough to permit them to fire completely across the town and register on the approaches to the four battery positions that comprised the principal defenses of the fortress.

As a part of his efforts to acquire advance warning of an attack, Prentiss urged his scouts to greater efforts. He was rewarded on 1 July, when they reported that there was a large Rebel force on the Spring Creek Road, obviously aimed at the city. Prentiss now put BG Frederick Salomon in tactical command of Helena's defenses. Salomon was a careful, thorough man who believed that the power of artillery was undervalued in the Union army. He advanced a line of pickets as far out from the main defense line as he dared, put his men on maximum alert, sent out pioneers to obstruct the roads by felling carefully preselected trees across them, and closed the last gaps in the deep fields of abatis that guarded the western approaches to the town.[35]

Salomon was especially concerned about the defenses guarding the southern and southwestern approaches to the city, because he considered the lines in that quarter to be much more vulnerable than those to the north and northwest. Many of the citizens of Helena were known to be strongly sympathetic to the Southern cause, and on that basis Salomon and Prentiss assumed that the Confederate high command would have detailed knowledge of the defenses. That being so, Salomon was certain that the major attack would be directed against batteries C and D, probably supported by a strong push from the south across the floodplain.

But forewarned was forearmed; at 0230 on the fateful morning of 4 July, Salomon's infantry filed silently into the riflepits and batteries, including Fort Curtis with its three big 30-pdr Parrott rifles. Skirmishers were pushed forward into the inner edge of the abatis, with an injunction to fire as soon as they saw a Rebel soldier. There was one exception; the advanced pickets on the Hill Road were to withdraw silently but maintain contact. In addition, the line of riflepits that ran between Hindman Hill and the levee was manned. Two of the 1 MO ARTY's 10-pdr Parrott rifles were placed behind the levee on the left flank of the line, while four of 3 IA ARTY's guns went on the right of the infantry line. The artillerymen in batteries A, B, C, and D had been warned that they might be overrun and told that under no circumstances were they to resist once the Rebel infantry had reached their parapets. Instead, they were to remove the primers and caps, so that the guns could not be fired, and withdraw to safety. The batteries had no traverses across their rears, so, if the Rebels occupied them, they would be in a box subjected to the direct fire of the 30-pdr Parrotts of Fort Curtis. Salomon and Prentiss were as ready as they ever would be and now simply waited, guns loaded, for the blow to fall.

The pickets on the Hill Road were barely in position early on the morning of 4 July, when a powerful Rebel force, marching with every attempt at secrecy, came up the road and hit the obstructions across the road and the abatis. Salomon was not at all surprised; it was exactly what he had expected.[36] The pickets, who had been cautioned not to resist, fell back silently and secretly before the Confederate advance. At the east edge of the abatis, just as they had been instructed, the skirmishers fired briskly into the obviously surprised and confused Rebel vanguard and then pulled back into the riflepits 600 yards in advance of Battery D. Salomon thought it odd that there seemed to be no action on the Spring Creek Road or the roads north of the city.

The eastern sky was scarcely turning gray with impending dawn when the butternuts filtered through the abatis. Although obviously disorganized by the obstacle, they launched a devastating attack on the multiple lines of riflepits on the south face of Hindman Hill. A few minutes later, another Rebel line came out of the abatis on the north flank of the hill. Within twenty minutes, the Federal infantry had been forced out of the complex of riflepits in advance of Battery D. But there the attack stalled. Now, with clear fields of fire, the guns of both batteries C and D opened fire on the exposed Southern soldiery on Hindman Hill.

As the attack on Battery D developed, within moments a Rebel force came up the Little Rock Road and hit the riflepits south of the city. *Tyler* heard the firing and dropped down to help as soon as there was light to see. Her giant 8-in shells smashed into a Rebel infantry line that was forming near the Clements house, shattered it, and drove it back into the ravines on the south face of Hindman Hill. The Federal infantry scarcely got to fire a shot.

Salomon and Prentiss were both puzzled; they had expected simultaneous strong attacks on both batteries C and D, because the two were mutually supporting. An attack on only one meant that the guns of the other would be free to attack the attacker. Finally, shortly after sunup, the question was resolved when a powerful Rebel infantry line penetrated the abatis on Graveyard Hill and attacked Battery C. By this time, the assault on Battery D had been brought to a halt, so the guns of that battery opened fire on the Rebel line driving toward Battery C along the southern flank of

Graveyard Hill. Even batteries B and A joined in, although the ranges were so great that their effectiveness was greatly reduced.

Despite the rain of shells, the Confederate assault was pressed with élan, and by 0700 Battery C had been overrun. The Federal cannoneers did exactly as they had been instructed; they removed the priming tubes and caps and ran to safety. Utterly disorganized by the victory, gray-clad troops swarmed in confusion over the hilltop in and around Battery C, while into the packed mass of humanity poured the massed fires of batteries A, B, and D, as well as fire from the three 30-pdr Parrott rifles in Fort Curtis. Far out in the floodplain to the south, the two Parrott rifles of 1 MO ARTY joined the barrage, firing over the heads of friendly troops in complete contradiction of conventional doctrine.[37] And now, out in the river, the 8-in Dahlgrens aboard *Tyler* joined the chorus, dropping their huge shells with mathematical precision onto the swarming hilltop.[38]

It seemed to the awed Union commanders that nothing could survive the hurricane of artillery fire that swept the crest of Graveyard Hill; but shortly, to their surprise, a battle line miraculously formed amid the blizzard and came resolutely down the hill toward Fort Curtis. The gunners of Fort Curtis switched fire, as did those of batteries B and D; and *Tyler* dropped downstream until her guns could play up the shallow valley between Fort Curtis and Battery C. The Rebel line frayed at every step and eventually came to a stop just west of the little creek that fronted the ridge on which Fort Curtis stood. The butternuts endured the rain of fire for only a moment, and then the line broke and fled into the ravines to the west, between batteries B and C.

Somehow a second battle line, this one of less than regimental size, formed on Graveyard Hill and started toward Battery D, but the combined fire of *Tyler* and Battery D broke it up before it even reached the bottom of Graveyard Hill.[39]

Meanwhile, shortly after 0600, a strong Rebel infantry force filtered through the abatis on Rightor Hill and moved toward Battery A. Unlike the forces assaulting batteries C and D, this column had artillery. They emplaced two guns on the east flank of Rightor Hill, with the obvious intention of attacking the riflepits protecting the right flank of Battery A. They had scarcely managed to get off a salvo, however, when the Union battery out in the floodplain opened counterfire. At the same moment, 29 IA INF, which held the riflepits on the east face of Rightor Hill, surged forward and captured the two Rebel guns.

The Confederates counterattacked, and for thirty minutes or so there was a seesaw battle for possession of the two pieces. At last the Rebels held them long enough to haul them away, and the battle settled down to nothing more than a smattering of skirmisher fire. There was no assault on Battery A, so its two guns were free to join the fight for Graveyard Hill.

It was now about 0900, and Salomon realized that the Rebel assaults had been broken. It was time to counterattack. Up to this point, he had not committed a single man of his infantry reserve, so he had abundant manpower which had not yet seen action. He now marshaled the men on the ridge south of Fort Curtis. Shortly after 0930, one column thrust into the valley between batteries B and C, while another pushed hard at the ravine between batteries C and D, as well as at the west face of Graveyard Hill. With the beginning of the infantry counterattack, the artillery, including the 30-pdr Parrott rifles of *Tyler*, switched targets and began to play on the open tops and sides of both Graveyard and Hindman hills. The shattered Confederate forces taking cover in the ravines on the hillsides would have to cross those ridges in order to escape to the west. There was little organized resistance.[40]

Many Rebels surrendered rather than face crossing those hilltops.[41] Others, braver or more foolhardy, made the attempt, and many died on the iron-swept slopes. Prentiss ended the pursuit about 1300 because he feared a Confederate counterattack. His first act was to send a fast boat to Memphis with a letter asking Hurlbut for reinforcements, and one to RADM Porter requesting additional gunboat support.[42] He had become a firm believer in the efficacy of naval gunfire.

The response was not long in coming. Tinclad *Covington* arrived that same night, and the next day the military transport *General Anderson* arrived with 117 IL. Both Porter and Hurlbut knew that the support was unnecessary, but neither was willing to quibble with the man who had ended the last threat to the Federal supply line down the Mississippi River.

Only later did Prentiss come to appreciate how total his victory had been. He counted 427 Confederate dead left on the field of battle, 327 wounded and captured, and 774 captured but without wounds, for a total of 1,528 men. Eventually he learned that the Confederates had entered the fight with about 7,700 men.[43] Only then did he realize that his defense had killed or captured nearly one out of every five of the attacking force. The Federal reliance on artillery as a substitute for manpower, coupled with naval artillery support, had succeeded beyond all expectation.

To be sure, the Federal losses were not light: 57 killed, 146 wounded, and 36 missing. Even so, that was less than 6 percent of a total garrison of about 4,000.[44] The butcher's bill was high, but the Union supply line to Vicksburg was safe.

41

Fall of the Fortress
4 July 1863

Maps: 8. The Defenses of Vicksburg
     19. The Vicinities of 3 LA Redan and the Great Redoubt
     20. The Vicinity of the Railroad Redoubt

Last Days

FEDERAL PERSPECTIVE

By the end of June, the formation of Sherman's Army of Maneuver relieved Grant of any anxiety concerning the possibility of interference from Johnston's Army of Relief. Johnston had had his best chance early in the game, when numbers were approximately equal; since he had done nothing then, it was unlikely that he would attempt anything now, when the odds so clearly were stacked against him. In the siege lines, Union artillery had achieved total domination, and the events of the previous few days had indicated beyond doubt that the Federal guns could breach the Rebel line almost at will. Saps and parallels had been driven close to all the major Confederate strongpoints, and many of those works were the targets of mines, which experience had demonstrated were capable of blowing holes in the parapets. Grant and his senior officers were convinced that a carefully planned assault would penetrate the defenses in a number of places. Grant told his corps commanders to prepare for an all-out final assault to be launched on 6 July.[1]

While there was little doubt of the success of an assault, Grant had no wish to pay a price such as the frightful losses incurred during the assaults on 19 and 22 May, even for victory. He needed a way to encourage Pemberton to surrender. And he thought he had such a device.

Pickets between the lines gossiped to pass the lonely hours, and on the night of 20 June a Confederate picket had confided that the Rebels in the riflepits had been stunned by the Union artillery bombardment that morning. They all knew beyond reasonable doubt, said the picket, that the Union artillery could breach the fortifications almost at will, and therefore there was little hope that a determined assault could be beaten off. The picket went on to say that the troops had been polled to find out if they were willing to try to cut their way out, and the result had been discouraging. Most had refused, and some even had threatened to mutiny if it were attempted.[2]

Even though the picket's tale probably was fabulous (no other record of such a canvass exists), the Union officers who recorded the story were predisposed to regard it as truth. They were quite certain that life in the Rebel trenches was becoming grimmer by the hour. The casualty list was growing, and food in the city was getting low. There was certainly reason to believe that morale was ebbing. In any event, the story was evidence of a mental condition that Grant thought he could exploit. He called some of his pickets in and told them to be sure to let their Rebel counterparts know that a grand assault was scheduled for 6 July. Giving the precise date was not revealing a secret, because there would be no way to conceal the necessary preparations; one way or another, the Rebels would have at least a few hours of warning. Grant assumed that the word would find its way quickly to Pemberton, and that Pemberton would realize, as Grant did, that, under the present conditions, the city could not hope to hold against a storm.

CONFEDERATE PERSPECTIVE

As the days of June wore away, morale within the besieged city sank ever lower. Yet the reasons for the decline were not the obvious ones of starvation or lack of ammunition or manpower. It is true that the garrison was on reduced rations, but there was food in the city for several more weeks. Nor was there any real shortage of ammunition. Strangely enough, despite the steady dribble of casualties, by 20 June there actually were in excess of 23,000 men fit for duty,[3] more than ever before. Many of the men wounded at

Champion Hill, Big Black Bridge, and the two assaults had been returned to duty. With only 5,700 in hospitals and convalescing, the rate of illness was high but not excessive for the time and place. Thus there were men enough to both fully man the works and constitute a mobile reserve to boot.

The collapse of morale, then, was not due to a lack of obvious physical resources. Some if it can be ascribed to sheer physical exhaustion. Pemberton had been forced to keep every able-bodied man in the trenches almost continuously, and long exposure to the relentless Mississippi elements was slowly debilitating the troops. Far worse, however, was the growing awareness that the Confederate position was hopeless. The men could look out over the great valley to the west and see a never-ending parade of smoke plumes from the Union transports pouring men and supplies into the Yankee armies, while their own supplies inevitably dwindled. The Southerners could peer cautiously over their parapets and see the Union siege works slowly push closer and closer. There was the growing suspicion that their countrymen had given them up for lost. To many, there seemed no escape but surrender.[4] After 23 June, Pemberton received no more letters from Johnston, and he interpreted that to mean that the siege lines now were so tight that communication with the outside was no longer possible. Without communication, there was no hope of a coordinated effort of any kind, and this in turn virtually certified that a breakout attempt would fail.

Then, on 28 June, a curious letter came into Pemberton's hands.[5] It purported to be from "many soldiers." It cited the authors' suffering and urged Pemberton to surrender them. Whether he accepted this remarkable document at face value is unknown. Yet the fact that he preserved it perhaps indicates that he regarded it as a mirror of his men's sentiments, even if the authorship was in question. Still, Pemberton waited another three days. By this time, the Confederate pickets had transferred Grant's message, so he knew that the Union was planning a final assault for 6 July, and he knew that his tired, hungry, and dispirited men could not hope to stop it. He was convinced that his adopted country had abandoned him and that no hope of help from the outside remained.

Yet he could not bring himself simply to give up. On 1 July, he sent a circular letter to his four division commanders, asking them if they thought a breakout was possible.[6] All four promptly passed the buck to their brigade commanders. Of all the division and brigade commanders, only Carter Stevenson and indomitable Stephen D. Lee[7] thought their men equal to the task. M. L. Smith and Forney argued that the physical condition of their men precluded such an attempt.[8] John Bowen, normally so sanguine, even suggested surrender.[9] At this juncture, Pemberton called a council of war. In the meeting, even Stevenson advised that the city be surrendered. Pemberton's own inclination was to make one final attempt to break out, but as usual he yielded to the opinions of his subordinates.[10]

The heartbroken general composed a letter to Grant, proposing that three commissioners be appointed by either side to arrange terms of capitulation. On the morning of 3 July, he asked John Bowen to deliver the letter to Grant.

Surrender

As so often happens, the soldiers knew that the end was in sight before the officers, and the Union pickets had become more than a little careless. About 1000 on 3 July, one of them on the Baldwin's Ferry Road glanced casually toward the 2 Texas Lunette and was momentarily stunned to see two Rebel officers, mounted and in full uniform, riding slowly toward him along the road. In reflex, he jerked his rifle to his shoulder and snapped off a shot in the general direction of the horsemen. The sudden shot aroused other riflemen, and in seconds a small fusillade was being aimed at the two figures. The Rebels stopped, made hasty movements about the flagstaff one of them carried. Seconds later, a white flag blossomed. Almost instantly, a hush fell over the lines.

The Confederate officers were MG John Bowen and LTC Louis M. Montgomery, the latter a member of Pemberton's staff. The pair was treated with meticulous courtesy, and Bowen asked to be taken to General Grant. The officer who carried both Bowen's request and Pemberton's letter to Grant came back nonplused; Grant had refused to see the Confederates. Bowen apparently was not surprised by this, for, without a sign of rancor, he suggested that Grant consider a meeting with Pemberton.[11] This time there was a longer delay, but at last a staff officer returned with a letter from Grant to Pemberton, as well as word that Grant had agreed to a meeting.

Satisfied, Bowen specified that a white flag would be raised where the Jackson Road passed through the Confederate lines, and that Grant could expect it to appear at 1500 in the event that Pemberton agreed to confer with the Union leader.[12] Bowen rode immediately to Pemberton's headquarters with Grant's letter, but he did not report the precise course of his conversation with the Union officers. Pemberton paled as he read Grant's message. The Federal commander refused to appoint commissioners. His only terms were unconditional surrender. However, he assured Pemberton that the Confederate troops would be treated with all the respect due prisoners of war.[13] Pemberton raised his eyes to Bowen and insisted in a shaking voice that he would never surrender the city unconditionally.

Bowen's action at this point is curious. He told Pemberton that Grant wanted an interview with him and would meet him between the lines at 1500 that afternoon if Pemberton approved. He stated this proposal in such terms that Pemberton was led to assume that it was Grant who had made the request. The fact that the idea had originated with Bowen was carefully concealed. The conclusion is inescapable: Bowen wanted the city to surrender and apparently believed that, once Pemberton and Grant could be brought face to face, this objective could be achieved. He was, it seems, willing to resort to a subterfuge to achieve his design. Never suspecting that Bowen was the author of the suggested meeting, Pemberton agreed.[14]

Shortly before 1500, the Union commanders began to assemble in the shade of a stunted oak behind their lines south of the Jackson Road.[15] The group included Grant, McPherson, Ord, Logan, A. J. Smith, and a goodly number of officers from their staffs. Promptly at 1500, a white flag showed above the Rebel works; moments later, Pemberton, Bowen, and Montgomery, all in full dress uniform, issued from the defenses. The Confederates dismounted and walked slowly forward to the shade of the oak. Bowen, aware that this was an historic moment, formally introduced all the officers present to each other. Grant and Pemberton needed no introduction; both had served in MG William J. Worth's DIV during the Mexican War.

Pemberton, under the impression that Grant had requested the meeting, waited for Grant to introduce the question of surrender. Grant, who undoubtedly believed that Pemberton had authorized Bowen to request a meeting, waited for Pemberton to broach the painful subject. It took Pemberton's keenly analytical mind only a moment to realize that there was a misunderstanding involved. With careful precision, he stated that it was his understanding that Grant had asked for the meeting.[16] Grant, startled, said that this was not the case. With sudden comprehension in his eyes, Pemberton turned coldly to Bowen,[17] but the exposure of his little intrigue mattered not a whit to Bowen at this stage, since apparently his purpose had been to bring the two leaders face to face. He calmly explained the actual situation to Pemberton; and Pemberton, aware that nothing could be gained by anger, turned back to Grant: "In your letter this morning you state that you have no other terms than an unconditional surrender."

"I have no other," agreed Grant.

"Then, sir, we will go to fighting again at once. I can assure you, sir, you will bury many more of your men before you will enter Vicksburg."[18]

Unmoved, Grant waited without word or change of expression. Nevertheless, he knew that, while the assault scheduled for 6 July almost certainly would take the city, the cost would be high. Unwilling to waste lives if it could be avoided, eventually he suggested that McPherson, Ord, Bowen, and Montgomery be permitted to converse in private, in the hope of reaching an agreement. Pemberton instantly agreed once more, since this looked as if Grant indirectly was accepting Pemberton's original proposal of commissioners, and that therefore Grant was trying to withdraw from his original position of unconditional surrender.[19]

Bowen's proposal was that the Confederate army march out with the honors of war, the men carrying their small arms and taking their field artillery. The occupying Federal troops would take the heavy artillery, the small arms not in the hands of troops, and all public property. Of course, Bowen knew that Grant would not accept such terms, but he also knew that he was forcing Grant into making a counterproposal. Grant was trapped in a dilemma. He needed a way to obtain all the benefits of unconditional surrender and at the same time allow the Confederates to obtain terms better than that. Badly needing time to think, Grant told Pemberton that he would propose new terms by 2200 that night.[20]

The moment the Confederates vanished into their works, Grant ordered his troops to cease firing. Porter was informed, via the semaphore station on the Walnut Hills, that an armistice was in effect while terms of surrender were being arranged. The admiral was delighted, especially in view of the fact that his intelligence service had predicted the surrender almost to the hour. That evening, for the first time in forty-six days, only the chirping of birds, the perpetual buzzing of insects, and the murmur of tens of thousands of soldiers discussing the prospects of peace broke the summer silence.

The moment Grant returned to his headquarters, he assembled his corps and division commanders and asked for suggestions. His men did their best to moderate his inflexible position, pointing out that paroling the Rebel troops would save steamboats, manpower, and supplies, and that these advantages would more than outweigh any gained by holding them as prisoners of war. Grant admitted the force of the argument, and the letter he drafted to Pemberton contained the offer of parole.[21] The rank and file would take nothing but clothing, and the officers would take only clothing, sidearms, and one horse. The Confederates could take any desired amount of food from their own stores, but they would be allowed only thirty wagons to carry it.[22]

Staying firmly in character, Pemberton called a council of war to assess the terms and yielded to the overwhelming majority opinion that the terms should be accepted; only Baldwin and S. D. Lee objected.[23] There was concern that the surrender would be on July 4, but Pemberton told the officers that an announcement of surrender on that day would gratify the Union's national vanity, and that it would yield more on that day than on any other.[24]

Grant's only concern at this point was that Pemberton might attempt a last-minute breakout. To MG Herron, guarding the southern exits of the city, went a terse warning to be on the lookout for trouble.[25] It is perhaps remarkable that Herron was singled out for this attention. The special warning may indicate the presence of a rather efficient espionage service operating within the beleaguered city, because it was in this direction that Pemberton had proposed making the attempt. However, it is equally likely that Grant realized, as did Pemberton, that it was the only direction that offered the slightest possibility of success.

Shortly after midnight, Confederate MG M. L. Smith appeared in front of the Union lines and promptly was escorted to Grant. Pemberton had accepted in principle but proposed that the garrison should march out with colors flying and under arms at ten o'clock that morning, before the Union troops entered the city.[26] Grant immediately agreed, and at dawn a Rebel courier crossed the lines and presented Grant with Pemberton's acceptance.

At 1000, exactly on schedule, white flags suddenly blossomed all along the Confederate line. Almost immediately, the long Rebel columns began issuing in parade formation from the city. Not a sound rose from the Union ranks. The gray-clad troops halted. The commands sounded subdued but crisp and clear.[27] Unit by unit, the Confederates stepped forward; stacked their arms; placed their knapsacks, belts, cartridge-boxes, and percussion-cap pouches in neat lines on the ground; and, proudly but sadly, laid their colors across the stacked arms. Then, looking neither to right nor left, they marched back into the city they had so valiantly defended. Along the Jackson Road, where Grant watched, the Union lines were entirely silent, but elsewhere the Federals broke into cheers as the Rebels marched back into their lines. For an instant, the gray ranks stiffened in fury, and then they realized that the cheers were not in exultation at victory but rather expressed a heart-felt tribute to the gallant defenders of Vicksburg.[28]

The long trial was over. On the horizon, many could see the bright promise of a land reunited, even though many yet would die before the promise could be realized.

42

Occupation
4 July–23 July 1863

Maps: 5. The Core Region
      8. The Defenses of Vicksburg

Out on the Mississippi River, in the predawn darkness of 4 July 1863, RADM Porter impatiently paced the deck of giant *Black Hawk*, awaiting word from Grant. Shortly after dawn, the arms of the semaphore station atop the Walnut Hills began to move, and moments later flags blossomed all through the fleet. The surrender had been signed.

At 1100, there was a flurry of activity around the courthouse, and Porter watched with immense satisfaction as the blue-and-white Rebel banner came down, to be replaced with the red, white, and blue of the United States. Flags flying and bands playing, *Black Hawk* led a parade of the squadrons to the city waterfront and dropped her gangplank at the foot of Jackson Street. A few minutes later, Grant and his staff came clattering down the hill. Admiral and general met at the head of the gangplank and grasped hands in mutual congratulation. Porter led the way into the saloon and called for wine in celebration of the greatest victory of the war. He curled his lip in disgust when his steward brought a bottle of Catawba—the sole content of the wine chest.[1] But the lowly Catawba was spiced with victory; and the officers, both army and navy, drank the toast with right good will.

Moments later, CPT William H. Dunn of Grant's staff stepped aboard *V. F. Wilson*, the fastest steamer available, clutching a dispatch destined for MG Halleck at the War Department in Washington.[2] *Wilson's* crew cast off instantly; already aboard was a navy courier with a dispatch for Secretary of the Navy Welles, from Porter's hand. The vessel stopped at Memphis on 6

July long enough to put Dunn ashore. He had assumed that the city would have telegraphic connections with the North. It did not, however, and by the time Dunn found this out and returned to the waterfront, *V. F. Wilson* already was out of sight around the bend, en route to Cairo.

A little before noon on 7 July, Mr. Welles walked into the office of Mr. Lincoln. The president was explaining some of the movements of the Army of the Tennessee to Secretary of the Treasury Salmon P. Chase and two or three others. Lincoln, brows raised at the interruption, accepted the sheet of paper silently proffered by Welles and read: "Sir: I have the honor to inform you that Vicksburg has surrendered to the U.S. forces on this 4th of July."[3] The president rose, forgetful of his audience, and started for the door: "I myself will telegraph this news to General Meade." At the door he suddenly stopped, remembering his forgotten conference. He turned to Welles with his gaunt face exultant, threw his arm around Welles's shoulder, and cried: "What can we do for the Secretary of the Navy for this glorious intelligence? He is always giving us good news. I cannot, in words, tell you my joy over this result. It is great, Mr. Welles, it is great!"[4]

Back at Memphis, the discomfited Dunn had to wait until 7 July to find a steamer, *Niagara,* that could take him to Cairo. Thus it was that the capital city already was celebrating the great triumph when Grant's message arrived. There was no question in Halleck's mind, however, as to who was the author of the victory. He already had recommended that Grant be promoted to the rank of permanent major general in the United States Army, the commission to date from July 4, 1863.[5]

In Vicksburg, amenities observed, the admiral and general and their staffs went ashore to inspect the captured city. The naval officers stared about them in disbelief. They totaled up the ammunition expended by the navy during the long bombardment—7,000 13-in mortar shells; 4,500 shells of various sizes fired from gunboats; and over 6,000 more shells from naval guns ashore. Stunned, they realized that, even with this prodigious expenditure, only a few buildings had been totally destroyed and only a few others heavily damaged. To be sure, virtually every pane of glass in the city was gone; the concussion of the mortar shells had accomplished that, if little else. Almost as stunning as the lack of damage was the civilian casualty list: only three persons killed and twelve wounded.[6] The reason soon was discovered. The people had honeycombed the hills with caves cut into the loess soil and had lived virtually as troglodytes through the bombardments.

Meanwhile, Logan was struggling to keep order in the fallen city. He assigned the 45 IL to duty as provost guards and sent the rest of his division back to the siege lines to occupy the now-abandoned Rebel fortifications. Logan's efforts to prevent looting and disorder initially were something less than successful. The wilder spirits in the Union army escaped supervision and found their way into the defenseless city. The safe in G. C. Kress's dry goods store was broken open and looted of twenty thousand dollars; W. H. Stephens's store was stripped of its contents, and many homes were plundered by unruly bands. When chided, the soldiers enunciated the immemorial philosophy of the conqueror: "We have fought hard enough to capture Vicksburg, and now we have got it, we intend to plunder every house in the d——d rebel city."[7] Logan had a different view, and glittering bayonets in the hands of 45 IL ended the looting abruptly.

Grant and his officers expected to find destruction, despair, and evidence of malnutrition on every hand. To their astonishment, the destruction was moderate, and there was no trace whatever of starvation. The Southerners, civilian and military, looked at least as healthy as the Yankees. Clothing was various but apparently adequate. The enlisted men wore unbleached or butternut cotton of all cuts and patterns, but the officers wore a more or less uniform dress of light blue jean. Almost all the officers carried swords, although in this regard there was no uniformity.

The Union ordnance officers found themselves with an immense harvest of weaponry on their hands. All told, there were 50 smoothbore field guns, 31 rifled field guns, 22 howitzers, 46 smoothbore siege guns, 21 rifled siege guns, 1 siege howitzer, and a 10-in mortar, for a total of 172 artillery pieces of all types. In addition, there were 38,000 artillery projectiles; 58,000 pounds of powder; and 4,800 artillery cartridges. Small arms were taken in proportion: 50,000 pieces, mostly excellent caliber .577 Enfield rifles, along with 600,000 rounds of ammunition and 350,000 percussion caps.[8]

Food was less abundant, but still extensive. The dumps contained 38,668 pounds of bacon; 5,000 bushels of peas; 51,241 pounds of rice; 92,234 pounds of sugar; 721 rations of flour; and 428,000 pounds of salt. There was enough for at least another week, and longer, if carefully husbanded.[9]

Pemberton, heartsick at the fate of his city, held himself aloof. If he retained any curiosity as to what had happened to Johnston, he gave no evidence of it. Once the decision to surrender the city had been made, his sole objective was to preserve the army so that it would be an effective fighting unit after the men had been exchanged.

Grant gave McPherson the job of paroling the Southern prisoners on 5 July, and his first act was to requisition every printing press in the city and set them all to work printing the necessary parole forms.[10] That was the easy part. Getting signatures on the forms turned out to be a far more difficult problem. A phrase in the articles of capitulation specified that officers were to retain their private property. The Confederates interpreted this to mean that they could take their slaves with them, since the slaves clearly were private property. The Union authorities insisted, of course, that human beings were not property and that therefore the blacks could not be removed.[11]

The argument got too hot for McPherson, so he passed the buck to Grant. Grant ruled that blacks were not property and could not be forced to accompany their former masters. If any of them chose to do so, however, even after being informed that they were free, they should be permitted to go. This sounded fine in theory, but it didn't work in practice. Logan reported heatedly that the Southerners were intimidating their servants even in the presence of Union parole officers.[12]

Grant and McPherson together wrote new regulations, this time specifying that blacks could accompany their "owners" only "in cases of families and sick and disabled officers." Pemberton objected, but it did no good; all the blacks in the departing columns of parolees were turned back except those attending sick or wounded officers.[13]

To almost everyone's considerable surprise, not all the Southerners were willing to sign paroles. The worst offenders were about 1,500 men from Louisiana and Tennessee who served in the River Defenses. Grant told them bluntly that they had a simple choice: sign paroles or be shipped north to prison camps. Meanwhile, they would be confined aboard boats and treated as prisoners of war, instead of being allowed virtual run of the city, like the rest of the captured Confederates. About half yielded to such pressure, but in the end Grant had to ship 709 of them north.[14]

Some of the Union officers thought that the Tennesseans, and perhaps some of the Louisianans as well, so resented being inducted into the Confederate army that they viewed a stay in Union prison camp as the lesser of two evils; if they were paroled, the Confederate authorities would try very hard to put them back into service. Such conjectures gained a measure of credibility on 8 July, when McPherson learned with wry amusement and some satisfaction that Pemberton also was having his troubles. It seems that substantial numbers of the 27 LA were escaping across the Mississippi in skiffs.[15] McPherson, like Pemberton, knew that most of the men who escaped across the river were gone forever, as far as the Confederacy was concerned. He solemnly assured Pemberton that he would ask the provost guard to double its vigilance to prevent such escapes. Remarkably enough, the flow continued.

By the evening of 10 July, the monumental task had been completed. McPherson had counted 29,491 men, of whom all but the recalcitrant 709 River Defense men had signed paroles. Pemberton informed McPherson that the army would leave the next day, except for 3,600 who were too ill or too badly wounded to march. M. L. Smith would stay behind and grant furloughs to these men as they recuperated enough to be capable of travel.[16]

Then, at the last moment, the Confederate nurses and hospital attendants began deserting their charges and joining the troops, in hopes of accompanying the army as it left the city. McPherson took a dim view of this, because it would leave the Federals with the task of caring for the Rebel sick, a chore hardly to be envied. Curiously, in this matter, Pemberton and McPherson were of one mind. Pemberton made sure that the Confederate hospital attendants stayed on the job, because he wanted to insure that the hospitalized men eventually would rejoin the army. It was clear to him that Union hospital attendants would result in something approaching 100 percent desertion, since they hardly could be expected to urge duty to the Cause upon the Rebels in their charge.[17]

All of these events freed Pemberton of any illusion that he would be able to keep the army together. He wrote President Davis on 10 July that many men already had deserted and that many more undoubtedly would do so as soon as the march began. There was almost nothing that could be done to prevent it, as his own provost guards were unarmed.

At 0400 on the morning of 11 July, Bowen's, Forney's, and M. L. Smith's DIVs marched out of the fallen citadel via the Jackson and Baldwin's Ferry roads. There were few vehicles, because parsimonious Grant had allowed them only one wagon for each division and brigade headquarters, one for the chief quartermaster, two for Pemberton's headquarters, and one for each regiment.[18] The melancholy columns met at Mt. Alban, crossed the river at Big Black Bridge (on the floating bridge constructed by McClernand's men after the Battle of the Big Black Bridge), and bivouacked for the night of 12 July at Raymond. Carter Stevenson's DIV left Vicksburg on 12 July and overtook the main body near Raymond the next day.

The columns dwindled perceptibly with each passing hour, as men simply stepped out of the unguarded formations and headed for home. The army swung south to avoid Jackson, crossed the Pearl River at Byram, and marched away into oblivion, leaving forever the valley of the great river they had fought so hard, so long, and so gallantly to defend.[19]

43

Cleaning Up Loose Ends
3 July–16 July 1863

Maps: 4. Southern Sector
     5. The Core Region

Johnston instantly canceled his plans for a move to the south on the early morning of 4 July, when confirmation of the surrender of Vicksburg arrived. He allowed Loring's, Walker's, and French's DIVs to rest quietly in camp while he perfected his plans for a withdrawal to Jackson. Breckinridge's DIV had started early from Bolton and did not receive word of either the fall of the city or the canceled march until it reached its evening bivouac near the Baker Creek Bridge on the Jackson Road. The next day, 6 July, Johnston began his withdrawal into the defenses of Jackson. He was not yet under any pressure whatever from the Yankees, although he was sure it would not be long in coming. His only objective now was to preserve his army.

The moment the surrender of the city had been confirmed, Grant sent a two-word message to Sherman over the field telegraph that connected all the corps headquarters of the Army of the Tennessee: "Go in." The red-beard was ready and waiting for such a message. Immediately he began pulling his widely scattered divisions out of their defensive positions covering the northeastern approaches to Vicksburg, and assembling them into a configuration suitable for an offensive toward the east.[1]

Bright and early on the morning of 6 July, three powerful Federal columns struck across the Big Black—one at Birdsong's Ferry, another at Messenger's Ferry, and a third at Big Black Bridge. No opposition of any kind developed until the army closed around the western approaches to the city of Jackson. Sherman had no intention of attempting to carry the city by storm; he knew what Rebel soldiers could do when sheltered by earthworks.

Instead, he spent the next several days extending his lines, intending to besiege the town.[2] If Johnston were foolish enough to remain in the city and allow himself to be invested, then eventually yet another Rebel army would fall into the Union net.

Johnston was not so foolish. He evacuated the city and moved his army to the east long before the investment was complete. On 17 July, Sherman's Army of Maneuver occupied the former capital of Mississippi once again.[3] This time the destruction was total. When the Union army evacuated the city on 23 July, nothing useful to the Confederacy remained. Johnston was not pursued. Neither Grant nor Sherman thought it worth the effort.

The final collapse of resistance at Vicksburg was almost, but not quite, the last act involved in splitting the Confederacy into two halves and opening the Mississippi River to northern commerce. Downstream 240 river miles, MG Frank Gardner and some 7,300 Confederates held out in their fortifications at Port Hudson. Outside their lines lay MG Banks's Union army of nearly 30,000 men. Just as at Vicksburg, the Federals had tried two major assaults and had been beaten off both times with heavy losses. Unable to take the fortress by storm, Banks had settled down to a regular siege and, by 7 July, had pushed his approaches up to the ditches fronting the works in many places.[4]

On that day, three days after the fall of Vicksburg, a letter arrived in Banks's headquarters from MG Grant announcing the fall of mighty Vicksburg.[5] The news ran like wildfire through the Union lines, evoking a storm of cheering. Union pickets quickly passed the word to their Confederate counterparts within the besieged town, and that same afternoon Gardner asked Banks for confirmation. Gardner was ready to surrender and only needed an excuse. His rations were entirely gone; unlike the garrison at Vicksburg, his men were on the ragged edge of starvation.[6]

That night Banks sent a copy of Grant's letter in for Gardner's perusal. Gardner replied by proposing three commissioners to arrange terms of surrender. The commissioners met at 0900 on 8 July, quickly agreed on terms, and the next morning the Rebel flag came down from the last Confederate outpost on the Mississippi. Banks found himself the proud possessor of about 6,340 prisoners, 7,500 small arms, and 51 pieces of artillery.[7] The fight for the great Mississippi Valley was over.

On 16 July, the packet *Imperial*, out of St. Louis, tied up at New Orleans after an uneventful voyage. In Washington City, Abraham Lincoln, in near exaltation, wrote to a friend: "The Father of Waters goes again unvexed to the sea."[8]

44

Mysteries, Questions, and Conjectures

Maps: 1. The Theater of Operations
5. The Core Region

No chronicler ever sees the totality of a complex series of events, because only bits and pieces are available for scrutiny. Further, each writer tells only the story that he or she wants told. It therefore is not at all strange that the accounts of contemporary commentators writing of the Vicksburg Campaign should vary so greatly, or that some very mysterious gaps and ambiguities should exist in those accounts. The authors of the time wrote little or nothing about some aspects of the campaign, so, as with every complex military effort, many minor (and some not-so-minor) mysteries remain.

A particularly intriguing one is this: who, or what, were the "intelligent contrabands" who almost magically appeared from time to time to aid the Unionists? The most notable example occurred late on the night of 29 April 1863, when such an individual evidently persuaded Grant to land at Bruinsburg rather than Rodney. It is not the only example. Another of these remarkable people appeared in Sherman's headquarters on 14 May and told him that there were no Confederate troops in the Jackson fortifications. Other examples are recorded throughout the campaign, and it is worth noting that somehow, on every occasion, these men managed to talk their way into the presence of the commanding officer, and the commanding officer paid very close attention to what they said.

The term *contraband* was more than a little elastic, but generally it referred to an escaped slave. Over most of the South, it was illegal to educate slaves. Such laws sometimes were ignored, but we nevertheless are left with the image of an ignorant, illiterate, ragged black person hiding out in the hills, having somehow escaped from his master and remained at liberty long enough to appear in a Federal camp. We now are expected to believe that men like Grant and his senior officers instantly changed their plans of campaign, which inevitably included placing major portions of the Army of the Tennessee in jeopardy, on the basis of the unsupported testimony of an escaped slave. It seems unlikely.

What, then, are we to make of these tales? It is difficult to escape the conclusion that the "contrabands" were both intelligent and intelligence agents, and that they formed part of an elaborate and highly efficient service operated by the Union command. There is abundant indirect evidence that such a system existed. The first wave of Union troops ashore at Bruinsburg "captured" a farmer who seemed too confused to flee. He turned out to be well known to Grant and eventually was identified as one of his agents.

Just after the Battle of Jackson, one of the three couriers entrusted by GEN Joseph Johnston with the crucial order directing Pemberton to meet him at Clinton, rode instead directly to the nearest Yankee force, which happened to be one of MG McPherson's DIVs. Some time earlier, that same man had been expelled from Memphis with much ceremony by MG Hurlbut, on the grounds that his notorious Southern sympathies were too obnoxious to tolerate.

On the evening before the Battle of Champion Hill, two railroad men came into Grant's headquarters at Bolton (it would be nice to know if they also brought an engine and cars) and gave him precise data on the size, location, and composition of Pemberton's army, which at that time was in the vicinity of Edwards. The information included, among other things, an almost perfect count of the number of artillery pieces and regiments available to the Rebels. It seems more than a little odd that two casual Southern railroad men would be so knowledgeable about military affairs.

MG Stephen Hurlbut, in his headquarters at Memphis, knew that COL Benjamin Grierson and his cavalry were safe a mere thirty hours after their arrival in Baton Rouge, after their epic raid the whole length of Mississippi. It took Grant's dispatches some sixty hours to make the trip from Young's Point to Memphis, roughly half the distance. The simplest explanation is a hypothetical intelligence network operating inside the Confederate telegraph system. Such a system would have made it possible to get a courier from Baton Rouge to a Confederate telegraph station somewhere in the vicinity, such as Burlington, LA. A telegraph message then could go to Coldwater, twenty-five miles south of Memphis, on the Mississippi & Tennessee Railroad. It could then be taken by courier to the Union lines below Memphis. But how could the message jump the gaps Grierson had created in the telegraph line along the New Orleans, Jackson & Great Northern Railroad below Jackson?

We are left with a shadowy impression of an astonishingly efficient and comprehensive Union spy network operating deep within the Confederacy. It is perhaps of interest to note that a substantial proportion of the agents seem to have been black. The odd thing about this is that few contemporary commentators even speculated on the possibility of such a system. A possible—but not very convincing—explanation is that spying was considered neither gentlemanly nor honorable at that time, and few people were willing to acknowledge publicly that such unseemly behavior might be widespread.

Intelligence agents are fish which swim best in a friendly sea. The notion that Central Mississippi was territory friendly to the Union forces runs counter to every intuition. Yet the facts are odd. The Army of the Tennessee, supposedly alien to the region between Bruinsburg and Rocky Springs, nevertheless moved unerringly through the network of crooked and confusing roads. At the same time, Confederate BG A. E. Reynolds's BDE, marching to support Bowen's force after the Battle of Port Gibson, lost its way between Big Bayou Pierre and Big Black River, and stayed lost for six to eight hours. It seems passing strange, because the road network was skeletal at best. There simply were not very many places where it was possible to take a false turn. Yet somehow the Johnnies did, with unfortunate consequences.

Consider these events. When the Union army was moving northward from Cayuga, Mrs. Jane Fisher Smith provided it with useful information, and her neighbors obviously approved. A local planter clearly misdirected Loring's DIV during the retreat from Champion Hill, so thoroughly that Loring lost everything with wheels. During Grierson's remarkable raid down the length of Mississippi, he and his horse soldiers actively were protected by the people of Summit. Two divisions of McPherson's Corps marched up the road from Utica to Raymond over a three-day period prior to the Battle of Raymond, without the Confederate authorities ever discovering either the size or composition of the force, because the country people kept all that a secret, even from the Southern cavalry.

Occam's Razor (the rule that we should first seek the simple solution) would suggest that most of the farmers of the region were pro-Union or at least not pro-Confederate. This may well explain why both Pemberton and Gregg believed that the Yankee force heading toward Raymond was only a small flank guard. Perhaps they believed that the local inhabitants were loyal and so could be counted upon to report any large movements of Yankee troops. When the reports did not materialize, the two commanders assumed that there were no large movements.

This interpretation goes far to explain what seems to be a singular ineptitude on the part of the Confederate intelligence services. Because nobody was giving out any information that would be helpful to the Confederacy, the Confederate intelligence officers, believing the countryside to be friendly, quite naturally may have assumed that there was no information. Yet we have seen that, when conditions were auspicious, as at Summit during Grierson's Raid, the locals enthusiastically indulged in more than a little downright lying to further the Union cause. As the British would say, it is "hard to take on board" the notion that a substantial proportion, and perhaps even a majority, of the populace was basically pro-Union; but how else may these singular events be explained?

Another mystery, much less sweeping but nonetheless intriguing, is this: why did the Confederates have such faith in the efficacy of the Vicksburg batteries? After all, Farragut had run the batteries twice with unarmored ships, once going upstream and once coming down. Ironclad *Essex* easily had survived a passage during the *Arkansas* episode on 22 July 1862. Even *Queen of the West*, an unarmored ram, had managed to slip past. To be sure, the batteries had been improved a great deal since those actions; but, even so, the faith of the Confederates seems inexplicable.

Those on the other side of the Mississippi River were much more realistic. There is no doubt of Porter's confidence that his ironclads could run the batteries at any time, at least going downstream. However, even he was not willing to put his ships to the test of running the gauntlet going upstream. He specifically warned Grant that taking the vessels below Vicksburg was a one-way trip. As it turned out, the batteries proved to be far more bark than bite.

Among the remarkable things about the campaign is the Confederate reaction during the few days following the Battle of Port Gibson and the evacuation of Grand Gulf. During that brief but crucial period, the Southerners seem to have made virtually no effort to keep in contact with the Federal forces. Had they done so, they might not have missed a great opportunity.

On 3 May, with the arrival of Taylor's and Barton's BDEs, Loring had an army of nearly seventeen thousand men in the vicinity of Hankinson's Ferry. The rapidly advancing Union XVII Corps, only eleven thousand strong, was widely separated. One division was being held by Cockrell's MO BDE on the Willows road; another was strung out in march order along the Ingleside Road; and the rest were beyond the Bayou Pierre, entirely out of the picture because the intervening single road from Port Gibson to Willows was crowded and obstructed by the motley trains of the two leading divisions.

Here was the potential for a Union disaster. Loring could have given Cockrell another brigade to hold the line of Kenison Creek against Crocker's DIV and launched his entire army against Logan's tired and attenuated column. Only a miracle would have prevented Logan from being pushed off at a tangent toward Grand Gulf. With that taken care of, Loring could have marched down the Ingleside–Rocky Springs Road and pounced on the wagon trains of the XVII Corps, cut off Crocker's line of retreat, and possibly gobbled up his entire division. Of course, Crocker would have tried to disengage from Cockrell and fall back toward Grindstone Ford; but, even had he succeeded, he would have been falling back along a single crowded road toward an unfordable stream spanned by a single narrow bridge. He almost certainly would have been badly cut up if Loring had pressed in boldly.

With two of his best divisions ruined, Grant's offensive surely would have sputtered, if not stopped entirely. It is possible that the damage would have earned enough time for Pemberton to assemble the Vicksburg army and lock Grant south of the Big Black River and west of Rocky Springs for a long time. It would not have won the campaign, but it would have made life immeasurably more difficult for the Yankees.

Another major mystery of the campaign is GEN Joseph Johnston's behavior during and immediately after the Battle of Jackson. His first message to President Davis ("I am too late") was sent from Jackson within hours of his arrival, long before he had any reasonable chance of making a detailed assessment of the situation. Later, while Vicksburg was under siege, he assembled a council of war, ostensibly to explore measures to relieve the city. GEN Kirby Smith's representative returned from the meeting to report that Johnston regarded the situation as hopeless, a position which cannot have improved the morale of his subordinates.

Consider the fact that, for all practical purposes, the last Union soldier left the east bank of the Big Black River north of Big Black Bridge on about 20 May. To be sure, the Union strongly held Big Black Bridge, and there were Union patrols operating on the east bank in the immediate vicinity of the bridge. Elsewhere, however, the land was free of blue-clad soldiery. Yet it was not until 2 July, near Brownsville, that Johnston at last assembled his senior commanders to plan a campaign for the relief of Vicksburg. The clear implication is that no planning had been done during the forty-seven days between 15 May and 2 July.

Furthermore, according to MG French, one of Johnston's senior division commanders, the primary problem which prevented the formulation of such a plan on 2 July was the lack of information on the terrain of the Mechanicsburg Corridor. Incredible as it seems, Johnston had been in Mississippi for more than six weeks, and in all that time he had made no effort whatever to determine the geography of the region in which he presumably would have to operate in order to relieve the city. He easily could have done so, because, until mid-June, Confederate patrols were free to roam at will almost anywhere in the region between the Big Black and the Yazoo rivers and north of the Bridgeport Road (i.e., in the Mechanicsburg Corridor). Moreover, Confederate forces controlled the east bank of the Big Black River north of Amsterdam. Johnston was an experienced officer and therefore certainly knew the crucial importance of terrain intelligence. It is difficult to escape the conclusion that he deliberately failed to gather terrain information, with the intent of using the lack thereof as a final justification for not taking his army into battle.

Overall, it is difficult to avoid the conclusion that Johnston deliberately sent Pemberton to his doom, while making only those moves which would give him the means to protect himself from inevitable criticism. From the fall of Jackson to the fall of Vicksburg, all Johnston's activities strongly support the same interpretation. But why?

Two major reasons may be conjectured. First, it may be that Johnston wanted Pemberton to fail and that he wanted that so badly that he was quite willing to see Vicksburg fall in order to achieve his personal goal. It is tempting to suspect that Johnston was a member of the Loring-Bowen cabal and simply was playing his part. Loring and Bowen so wanted Pemberton removed from command that both of them coldly and deliberately disobeyed direct orders at Champion Hill, apparently hoping that, as a result, the battle would be lost. Bowen, somewhat to his credit, eventually came to his senses and did his best to undo the damage already done, but Loring never did. Had these three people been operating in medieval Europe, they soon would have been escorted to the headsman's block.

A second possible reason stems from Johnston's early experience during the Civil War. Only once, prior to Vicksburg, had he actually launched an offensive. It was at Seven Pines, during the Peninsular Campaign in Virginia in May 1862. The effort not only failed, but also resulted in Johnston's being wounded twice, with near-fatal results. He remained on sick leave for many months. It is possible that Johnston had developed a deep-seated, but possibly subconscious, fear of battle, and especially offensive battle. As a result, he simply may have been taking extraordinary care to avoid being forced into battle.

Loring's behavior after Champion Hill is doubly mysterious. First, of course, is the matter of his "failure" to find a road around Edwards, considering that Bowen readily had managed to find such a route, only an hour or so before. Second, there is no indication that Loring tried to send a courier to Pemberton to inform him of his difficulties. Any reasonably diligent courier could have found his way to Bovina, since at this time the Confederates controlled all the crossings of the Big Black River south of Big Black Bridge. The unavoidable conclusion is that Loring sent no courier; it is at least reasonable to conclude that he never had any intention of rejoining Pemberton. It seems probable that Loring would expect Pemberton to try to hold the bridgehead at Big Black Bridge until he arrived with his division, so a decision not to go there, and not to tell Pemberton of his intentions, was tantamount to setting Pemberton up for yet another disaster.

Such behavior could have been expected to elicit strong criticism (at the very least) from Loring's superiors, but in fact nothing of the sort happened. When Loring, with his shattered division, finally joined Johnston at Jackson, there were no recriminations. Instead, Johnston accepted Loring as one of his senior commanders and rewarded him by placing him in command of the right wing of the Army of Relief. Remarkable treatment for a man who had lost his division under highly suspicious circumstances.

One of the more persistent mysteries of all is why John Pemberton has been so consistently maligned by historians of both Federal and Confederate persuasions. This question cannot be pursued in the depth it deserves, but a number of events and situations suggest that perhaps the tarnish is largely unjustified. Pemberton has been widely criticized because he stayed in Jackson while the storm was brewing opposite Vicksburg. His critics argue that he should have gone to Vicksburg, which obviously was the critical point. The problem with this argument is that Vicksburg is critical only in hindsight. It is well to keep in mind that Pemberton was commander of a department (the modern reader might substitute "theater"), not just commander of the Vicksburg defenses. Jackson was the communications hub of his department; it was the major railroad center, as well as a nexus for the telegraph system. Only from Jackson could Pemberton readily communicate with the Tallahatchie River defenses in the north, Port Hudson in the south, Yazoo City in the northwest, and Vicksburg and its various dependencies, including Grand Gulf and Snyder's Bluff, in the west. He was where a department commander should have been.

Was there a threat in the north? Certainly. It must not be forgotten that the Union controlled the Mississippi River. That reality almost certainly weighed heavily on Pemberton's mind, as is witnessed by the fact that he tried hard to monitor traffic on the river. He was all too aware that Grant might load four or five divisions on steamboats and be ashore at Memphis in two days. A force of that size, launched down the railroad toward Grenada and supported by a couple of Stephen Hurlbut's DIVs, would collapse the Tallahatchie defense line like a pricked balloon.

Was there a threat from the south? Certainly. Many Union strategists, including Halleck and perhaps Lincoln, wanted Grant to shift the maneuver forces of the Army of the Tennessee southward to join Banks in an assault on Port Hudson. Many of Pemberton's senior officers, including Carter Stevenson, thought that might be the reason for all the Federal activity opposite Vicksburg. To be sure, Stevenson vacillated; sometimes he thought the activity indicated preparations for an amphibious assault on the Vicksburg waterfront, and sometimes he worried about Port Hudson. The ironclads and transports which ran the Vicksburg batteries in mid-April just as well might have been intended to transport troops to Port Hudson as to support a crossing in a move against Vicksburg.

To us, with the benefit of 135 years of scholarly hindsight, it seems obvious that the disposition of Federal forces could be interpreted only as a movement to outflank Vicksburg, but that certainly was far from clear in 1863. Indeed, it was far from clear even to the Federal high command! Not until Grant was at Hankinson's Ferry did he at last make an unequivocal decision to proceed against Vicksburg rather than detach a corps or more to Port Hudson in support of Banks. Pemberton had to guard against any and all eventualities, and he could do that best by remaining at his center of communications—Jackson.

A second popular criticism of Pemberton's actions involves the series of events leading up to Champion Hill. It will be remembered that Pemberton's field army took up defensive positions south of Edwards on 12 May, in anticipation of a Union attack on Edwards and Big Black Bridge. Why, the critics ask, did he not assemble his army and launch an offensive to the south to strike into the flank of Grant's army, which was moving toward Raymond and Clinton along the Cayuga–Dillon's Farm Road?

This question, curiously enough, probably is an artifact of the way in which the campaign traditionally has been diagrammed. The blue symbols marking the route followed by the Army of the Tennessee invariably consist of two nice, smooth lines, one connecting Rocky Springs and Cayuga with Dillon's farm and Raymond, and the other connecting Rocky Springs with Utica, Raymond, and Jackson. The clear implication is that the early phases of the campaign were planned as an attack on Jackson.

The reality was quite different. Pemberton faced a real threat from the south, just as he thought. On 12 May, Grant's intention was to strike at Edwards with McClernand's four-division XIII corps, while Sherman's XV Corps struck northward from Dillon's and McPherson's XVII Corps struck through Raymond to cut the Southern Railroad of Mississippi at Bolton. The only mistake Pemberton made was his failure to realize the presence of Sherman and McPherson so far out on the right flank of the Union army.

It should be remembered that the failure of the Confederate intelligence system was responsible for that error. Given the information available to him, Pemberton had every reason to believe that the bulk of the maneuver forces of the Yankee army was poised just south of Edwards. And in fact, it was! Four out of the eight Union divisions present at that time just south of Fourteenmile Creek were getting ready for an offensive against Edwards. Instead of striking into a flank, an offensive to the south would have developed into a frontal attack on McClernand's XIII Corps.

Pemberton was wise not to risk such a venture. Many of his men had spent months in garrison, and Pemberton feared that they were not physically capable of the exertions required by offensive operations. He thought it better to wait and receive the Yankee attack in prepared positions, where the traditional advantages of the defense over the offense would multiply the effectiveness of his troops.

Still another point of criticism involves Pemberton's actions on the two days prior to Champion Hill. He first chose to disobey Johnston's order to join him at Clinton, in favor of Loring's and Stevenson's plan to march southeast from Edwards and take up a position at Dillon's farm, where he would be astride Grant's communication line to Grand Gulf. This had the merit of seizing the initiative, while at the same time forcing the Union army to attack him in a prepared position. In other words, it was an offensive which nevertheless exploited the advantages of the defense! Then, on the morning of 16 May, after Johnston's peremptory order reached him, he decided to abandon the Loring-Stevenson plan and obey Johnston's orders. On the face of it, this looks like indecisiveness of the worst possible sort.

Yet close examination of the circumstances makes Pemberton's case clear. On the night of 14 May, Pemberton knew only that the Yankee army was somewhere to the east of him. He did not know exactly where. His only eyes and ears were Wirt Adams's cavalry, and not even those magnificent horsemen could be everywhere. For all Pemberton knew, the Yankee army might have been concentrated in the vicinity of Raymond. If it was, then a march directly toward Clinton, the point selected by Johnston for the rendezvous, would put the Army of the Tennessee on his flank. Even worse, the Yankees might strike back to the west, overwhelm the guard on the Big Black Bridge, and seize Vicksburg before Pemberton could get his army turned around and into a blocking position. The Loring-Stevenson response to this situation was lifted straight out of conventional military wisdom: get across your enemy's supply line and force him to attack you in a position of your selection. The decision might well have been reinforced by the reflection that Johnston's order could have been written in haste; after all, he was new on the scene and would not yet have had a chance thoroughly to understand all its facets.

By the time Johnston's peremptory order reached Pemberton at the Ellison house, the situation had changed drastically. Pemberton now knew where Grant was, or at least he knew where he had been at the time Johnston had written his order. The logical thing for Grant to do was move westward down the Jackson Road and the Southern Railroad of Mississippi toward Vicksburg. If Pemberton had continued with his original plan, he actually would have been moving his army out of its blocking position between Grant and Vicksburg! The obvious countermove was at least to begin to obey Johnston's order, because that would shift the Vicksburg army back to Edwards, where it could more effectively cover the various crossings of the Big Black River, especially Big Black Bridge and Bridgeport. Once in that position, there would be time to decide whether to proceed to Clinton, as per Johnston's order. Viewed in this light, and knowing only those things that Pemberton knew at the time, his decisions make perfect sense.

The Battle of Champion Hill often is cited as an example of almost unbelievably bad management on the part of Pemberton; indeed, if one looks only at the movements of the Confederate troops, it seems so. To be sure, Pemberton did make a significant error in not recognizing early in the day that the primary Federal effort was developing on the Jackson Road front. But again, it is well to recall that he had only a single regiment of cavalry—not even enough to cover all the roads leading east from Edwards. That error was caused largely by his lack of eyes and ears. Even so, he recognized that the Jackson Road was the site of the primary threat early enough to design a counter, which consisted of moving Bowen's unopposed DIV, plus a portion of Loring's DIV, to the support of Carter Stevenson's hard-pressed forces on Champion Hill. That countermove failed not because of Pemberton, but rather because both Bowen and Loring deliberately disobeyed Pemberton's order. By the time Bowen came to his senses, it was too late.

Thus a long and one-sided feud between the Loring-Bowen faction and Pemberton came to its fatal conclusion. Loring had stated long before that he would be willing for Pemberton to lose a battle if it resulted in Pemberton's replacement. Bowen had concurred, and here was the golden opportunity. So, in the midst of a great battle, the two division commanders, evidently acting from motives no higher than personal spite, deliberately disobeyed orders from their commanding general.

To justify their behavior, both Bowen and Loring simply lied. Both claimed to be under heavy pressure. In fact, there was no enemy whatever on Bowen's front; the roadblock on the Middle Road was a combat team from Stevenson's DIV. Loring did have a Union brigade deployed on his front, but it had done nothing all day except exchange long-range artillery fire. There was certainly no pressure.

Finally, perhaps the severest criticism directed at Pemberton has concerned the decision which led to his being penned up in Vicksburg. Why, the critics ask, did he not simply retreat through Vicksburg and continue a withdrawal toward Mechanicsburg, thus saving his army? The reason usually cited in Pemberton's defense is that he had received a direct order from President Davis to defend Vicksburg at all costs. That order alone might have been sufficient, since it seemed to allow but small latitude for independent action. However, there were other reasons.

Earlier in the war, Pemberton had been in command of the defenses at Charleston, SC. Threatened with a siege, Pemberton had proposed abandoning the city in order to preserve the defending army. That proposal raised a firestorm of protest. Interestingly enough, foremost among the protesters was one Robert E. Lee, who argued that the city should be held, even if it meant fighting the Yankees in the streets, building by building. Now Pemberton was faced with another siege, and it is perhaps understandable that he decided to hold. After all, he probably was pretty certain that he understood the temper and the desires of the Southern body politic.

While both those reasons are cogent, the best answer may be obtained by looking at a map of the region (see map 5: The Core Region). When the army fell back into the city after the debacle of Big Black Bridge, it no longer was a dependable fighting force. For all practical purposes, the only troops who could be relied upon were M. L. Smith's and Forney's DIVs and Edward Higgins's River Defense forces; the rest of the army was so thoroughly shattered as to be useless. Countless numbers would have been lost during a forced march to Mechanicsburg, simply because they would drop out of the columns from sheer exhaustion or sheer discouragement. Furthermore, certainly by midnight of 17 May, Pemberton knew that the Yankees were across the Big Black River in force at Bridgeport. Good roads led from Bridgeport to Oak Ridge, Haynes' Bluff, and Snyder's Bluff, so it was all too likely that fast-marching blue-clad regiments would be astride the Benton and Valley roads within twenty-four hours. If they did not get there before the van of the retreating Confederates, they certainly would arrive in time to strike into the flank of the marching column. The result would be the certain loss of Vicksburg, plus the near-certain loss of a major portion of the Vicksburg army.

Given the situation, Pemberton's decision to hold the city seems entirely reasonable. After all, Pemberton knew that the Confederacy's second-best general (Johnston) was on the scene, and he could safely assume that relief was only a matter of time. That would save both city and army, as opposed to the high probability of losing both if an attempt were made to withdraw to the northeast.

If we keep firmly in mind the situation as Pemberton was able to see it, his decisions seem appropriate, almost without exception. Why, then, was Vicksburg lost? It is difficult to avoid concluding that two major factors were responsible.

First, Confederate intelligence was appallingly bad. As we have seen, some of the failure may be attributed to the widespread assumption that the local populace was uniformly and firmly pro-Confederacy. That is a proposition now very much in doubt. In contrast, the Union intelligence system seems to have been uniformly able.

Second, Pemberton was served poorly by both his subordinates and his immediate superior. There is little doubt that both Bowen and Loring actively sought his removal from command. So determined were they, and apparently so blinded by spite, that they were willing to lose a campaign in order to achieve their ends. Further, it is not unlikely that Johnston deliberately entered into the spirit of the game, even if he did not directly collude with Bowen and Loring.

In effect, Pemberton was a blind puppet, and his bitter enemies were managing the strings. It is amazing that he did as well as he did. In a mere forty-eight hours, once Pemberton and his army were trapped in Vicksburg (Loring was gone, and it is permissible to suspect that Bowen had been humbled by the realization of what he had done), Pemberton somehow was able to revitalize his troops so thoroughly that they managed to beat off two determined assaults by Sherman's veterans and another by McClernand's. Somehow that does not fit the stereotype of incompetence that shadows Pemberton's image.

I have come to see Pemberton as the leading actor in a classic tragedy, a man whom the gods, for their own inscrutable reasons, saw fit to destroy.

Like the Confederacy, the Union had its own internal problems. Grant and McClernand were not on amicable terms, and that circumstance very nearly led to a Union defeat at Champion Hill. Why did not McClernand, who commanded the columns on the Raymond and Middle roads, press hard against the forces opposed to him as soon as he heard the roar of battle develop on the Jackson Road? His explanation after the battle was that Grant's pre-battle order, which stated that he was not to bring on an engagement unless certain of success, prevented independent action. There is some justice in McClernand's contention; after all, he could not be certain of success. One may suspect deeper and darker motivations, however. McClernand knew that he was on Grant's blacklist, and his letter-of-the-law interpretation of Grant's order may have been intended to prevent Grant from charging him with having disobeyed an order. It has even been suggested that McClernand, like Bowen and Loring, wanted his commander to fail, in the conviction that command of the army then would devolve upon him. This argument is difficult to sustain, considering that McClernand was a highly intelligent man who surely must have realized that command of a defeated army deep in enemy territory is not a particularly enviable position.

In any event, one of the supreme ironies of Champion Hill is that Grant's order ("Do not bring on an engagement unless certain of success"), which was intended to prevent a piecemeal commitment of forces, actually resulted in the very situation it was designed to avoid: a piecemeal effort.

What are we to make of Sam Grant? He seems somehow to have

acquired the image of a stolid, unimaginative little plodder who won his battles and his war by sheer tenacity and superiority of numbers and resources. Shiloh often is cited as an example of his lack of "generalship," and certainly Shiloh was a near thing and no credit to any quality other than tenacity.

But the ninety-eight days before the fall of Vicksburg tell quite another story. When Grant made the decision on 29 March to pour his army south through Louisiana, he actually had no plan of campaign. To be sure, he had an objective—to take Vicksburg—but he had no real plan other than to try to land his troops at Warrenton. On the basis of what he found upon his arrival at Pointe Clear, he changed his mind. He would land at Grand Gulf. When Bowen beat off Porter's attack on the forts at Grand Gulf, Grant changed his mind yet again, this time deciding to land at Rodney. At Disharoon's plantation, he again changed his mind, on the basis of the "intelligent contraband's" report of conditions at Bruinsburg. At Hankinson's Ferry, on 3 May, Grant once more changed his mind, this time on the basis of McPherson's report of the terrain south of Vicksburg, plus the presence of a prepared defensive line at Redbone Church. On the night of 12 May, while Grant was at Dillon's farm with Sherman, the news of the Battle of Raymond once again caused him to change his immediate plan, this time from attacking Edwards and cutting the railroad, to an attack on Jackson. And so on.

The picture that emerges is of a man alert to every opportunity; mentally flexible enough to exploit circumstances without the slightest delay; in short, analytical, imaginative, opportunistic. There is little trace of the conventional stereotype.

Finally, the struggle for Vicksburg conventionally is portrayed as an army affair, one in which the navy played a relatively minor and peripheral role. One reason, perhaps, is that few historians have paid much attention to the logistics of the campaign. An old saw circulates in command and staff colleges: "Amateurs study tactics; professionals study logistics." There is enough truth in the adage to make it hard to refute. In the case of Vicksburg, it must never be forgotten that it was RADM Porter and his fleets of ironclads and tinclads which kept open that long supply line down the Mississippi River from Cairo to Vicksburg. There were only about twenty-five tinclads in service by the summer of 1863, covering nearly a thousand miles of main-stem river. Even at best, they were spread very thin indeed. Yet those weather-beaten, scurrying little boats were responsible for the safety of the hundreds of transports moving up and down that waterway, keeping the Army of the Tennessee supplied with everything from bread for the men to fodder for the horses and powder for the guns. Furthermore, those same ships probed the waterways of the Delta, one of the primary sources of Confederate food and forage during the summer of 1863, causing the southern commissary agents no end of problems. The tinclads provided security for the Union logistics system and devastation for the Confederate one.

Moreover, the presence of the ironclad fleet opposite Vicksburg all through the months of April, May, and June kept large numbers of troops locked in the Vicksburg defenses, when they would have served their cause better by joining the army of maneuver to the east of the city. The ironclads did it by providing a continual and credible threat to the River Defenses. At no time could Carter Stevenson ignore the possibility that those ironclads might appear in front of the city at any moment, escorting a vast fleet of transports and barges carrying blue-clad troops.

Nor must it be forgotten that it was 8-in shells from *Tyler* which helped break up the Confederate attack on Helena, and that it was the huge 9-in and 100-pdr shells from *Choctaw* which persuaded Confederate MG Walker not to continue his attack at Milliken's Bend. Indeed, Walker and his Texans were so late getting to the scene of action in large part because of RADM Porter's probe up the Red and Ouachita rivers in early May, following the Battle of Port Gibson.

There is little doubt that the threat posed by the huge guns of the ironclads was the factor that persuaded John Bowen at Grand Gulf not seriously to contest the advance of the Army of the Tennessee southward through Louisiana. He simply dared not leave his men on the western shore, once those grim black gunboats appeared on the scene. It is well to recall, too, that the first troops ashore at Bruinsburg poured over the bows of *Benton*. Her huge guns were not needed, as it turned out, but there is no doubt that the sight of those muzzles poking through the gunports gave everyone involved an enormous sense of security.

Even small things helped. Can we truly appreciate the thoughts of the army scouts who reached Johnson's plantation on the Yazoo River on 18 May, looking for a place to establish a supply depot, only to find one already there, courtesy of the navy? In these and countless other ways, the navy was there to lend a helping hand.

Without the navy, there would have been no campaign.

PART II

MAPS

About the Maps

All the maps in this book were compiled because of the author's general disenchantment with the maps typically used to illustrate the Civil War. Most such maps fall into three general categories.

The first and possibly most common is a more or less direct reproduction of a Civil War–era map. Such a map has the merit of authenticity, in the sense that it provides a flavor of the time, though very commonly at the expense of accuracy. Very little of the area of the United States west of the Appalachians was covered by planimetrically accurate maps by the 1860s, so the cartographic products of the period tend to be little more than sketch maps. There are, to be sure, a few maps of remarkable quality, such as those of portions of the Mississippi River, produced by the United States Coast Survey, under the direction of A. D. Bache, in 1864, for use by Admiral Porter and the Mississippi Squadron, U.S. Navy. Even such exceptional productions as these, however, used hachures to define topography, rather than the more accurate and readily interpretable contour lines, which had been known to the cartographic world since the concept's invention (by the Germans, of course!) in 1816.

Those maps covering large areas (a county or more, say) which were available to the military often were wildly inaccurate. Most of them, for example, tended to show roads between towns as straight lines, no matter what the true path was. In Mississippi and Louisiana, no straight road existed in 1863! Detailed topographic maps of battlefield-sized areas were largely nonexistent, so the armies were forced to construct their own as they went along. It is not difficult to imagine the problem. General Bluecoat, having no idea whatever as to the nature of the terrain in front of him, turns to his cavalry aide and says: "Captain, have a topographic map of the four square miles in front of me at my tent by one o'clock tomorrow morning!" The aide, like all the rest of the cavalry command, has been in the saddle for the last eighteen hours, but, like a good soldier, he salutes and says, "Yes, Sir!" During the remaining hours of daylight (if any) and the early hours of the night, his horse soldiers prowl through the countryside, trying to figure out the lay of the land, while at the same time keeping a wary eye out for Rebels, who are apt to shoot with very little provocation. Promptly at one o'clock, a map is delivered to General Bluecoat—and he fights his battle on the basis of that map! Of course, General Graycoat is in the same boat, so it all more or less evens out. However, the problem, from the historian's point of view, is that those sketch maps tended to find their way into the *Official Records* and memoirs, so they are preserved as true and accurate representations of the ground upon which the engagement was fought. But of course they are not and never were, and today it is often impossible to fit such a map into the actual terrain. As a result, military historians argue endlessly over exactly where General Bluecoat or General Graycoat placed his battle line.

The second general type of map employed in Civil War histories is the modern topographic map, which has the undoubted virtue of planimetric and (within limits) topographic accuracy. It is true that, in most instances, the gross shape of the topography is basically unchanged from 1863. Certainly, though, road and agricultural patterns change, rivers change their course, towns come and go. In 1863, for example, the range of hills upon which Vicksburg stands was under intensive cultivation, while today it is nearly all tall forest. Many of the nineteenth-century roads are no longer used, and their alignments are often buried in the dense vegetation of nearly one hundred years of uncontrolled forest growth. The world we see today and what the soldiers of 1863 saw are, more often than not, very different indeed. Plotting a Civil War scenario based on such maps leads to interpretive problems that sometimes seem insurmountable.

The third general class of maps is the schematic, or diagrammatic, form. Reality is largely stripped away, leaving a painted "billiard table" battlefield, utterly divorced from the realities of the actual terrain. These maps foster the concept of battle as a chess game, with armies moving as neat little blocks on a flat and featureless board. A model war on a model world.

The maps in this volume represent an attempt at a different kind of solution. The procedure was to start with the best available modern topographic maps, so that at least the topography and planimetry would be as correct as possible. Then modern cultural features were stripped away. On the pristine surface thus created was placed as much of the

Civil War–period cultural landscape as could be reconstructed. If nothing more, this procedure means that at least the towns are in the proper relative positions, and at least most of the roads follow an approximation of their nineteenth-century alignments.

Reconstruction of the 1863 road network presented special problems, because today's system often bears little resemblance to that of 135 years ago. Not surprisingly, an understanding of the way in which humans adapt to their environment proved very useful. Mississippi rivers and creeks are subject to frequent flash floods, and the creek "bottoms" tended to be boggy and swampy and unsuitable for agriculture, so people mostly stayed out of them. Hence roads tended to follow the ridgetops, descending into the difficult valley bottoms only when absolutely necessary. In 1863, the highway between Vicksburg and Port Gibson crossed only four stream channels in the entire distance—namely, Hatcher Bayou, Big Black River, Big Bayou Pierre, and Little Bayou Pierre. The small streams were avoided by sticking rigorously to the ridgetops. The road was as crooked as sin, but it was dry!

Along the Lower Mississippi River, both the cultural and physical landscapes change. The River, which is notorious for the rapidity with which it changes course, was a special problem. Such maps as those published in the official military atlas of the Civil War (George B. Davis, Leslie J. Perry, and Joseph W. Kirkley's *Atlas to Accompany the Official Records of the Union and Confederate Armies,* put out by the Government Printing Office in 1891–95) were excellent initial sources for the course of the river in 1863, but the details are often wrong. In this regard, it is useful to compare the remarkable United States Coast Survey maps produced for Admiral Porter, mentioned above, with the maps presented in *Atlas to Accompany the Official Records.* It is clear that the Coast Survey information sometimes failed to find its way into the files of the compilers of the *Official Records* atlas.

A major source for defining the course of the Mississippi River in 1863 was Harold N. Fiske's unique *Geological Investigation of the Alluvial Valley of the Lower Mississippi River* (1945).

The Mississippi River floodplain has not seen a significant inundation since 1927. Modern flood-control procedures, including the vast levee system, have altered the landscape almost beyond recognition. Today there are few significant obstacles to movement in any direction, because the plain is a dry, topographically featureless surface covered with endless agricultural fields. This is not the landscape which General Grant saw in the spring of

1863. At that time, the annual flood covered a vast majority of the plain with water every spring, and humans inhabited a landscape neither wholly water nor wholly land. Reconstructing the extent of those floods was a task that proved impossible in detail, even though the general picture presented in this book probably is not too far off the mark. Much of the evidence is anecdotal: family stories, diaries, traveler's tales, engineering reports, geological and botanical evidence, and so on. One would think that a water surface could readily be projected, so that the shape of the terrain itself would indicate where the waters went, but that is not so. The reasons are too complex to discuss here; suffice it to say that the surface of a Mississippi flood was far from flat.

The locations of farms and plantations are much easier to establish. There is an abundant, although scattered, literature. Furthermore, even though the buildings are long gone and forest covers the landscape around Vicksburg, the old cisterns often remain in place, marking the precise site of a farmstead or plantation.

In summary, the base maps included in this study are a fusion of modern geodesy and the cultural attributes of 1863. Not surprisingly, when the Civil War events were "played" on this reconstructed game board, many of the decisions made by the two contending sides, which previously had seemed so opaque, suddenly became astonishingly transparent.

A special word about the maps showing the dispositions of forces. Those which illustrate the positions of the contending forces in the intervals between battles primarily show units of division or brigade size. As a general rule, the "maneuver unit" of the Federal armies was the division, so the dispositions of the Union forces are shown in terms of units of that size. However, the maneuver unit of the Confederate forces tended to be the brigade, and the positions of the Confederate forces in most cases are shown as brigade units. However, some Confederate operations did maintain the integrity of the divisions, and in those instances they are displayed accordingly. Occasionally much smaller units are shown, but that occurs only when such a unit, normally a regiment or combat team of some kind, was operating as an independent agency and had some specific and relatively important significance to the campaign.

Each battle map is something of a special case. In general, the identification of units is carried only to the level required for reasonable clarity. Thus, for example, the general character of the Battle of Port Gibson can be elucidated by carrying unit designations only to the brigade level on both sides. However, the special conditions at Raymond made it impossible for the commanders to control their large formations, so both blue and gray fought the battle largely in regimental units, necessitating depiction at that level.

One thing should be kept firmly in mind: maneuvers are shown only in the degree of detail necessary to convey a reasonably realistic sense of the course of the action. I have tried to simplify and generalize the actual complexity, without sacrificing the essential character of the engagement.

All the maps are my own. Consequently, any errors (and I am certain there are many) are my own, as well.

List of Maps

BASE MAPS

1. The Theater of Operations
2. Northern Sector
3. The Region between Abbeville and Tupelo
4. Southern Sector
5. The Core Region
6. Physiographic Regions Significant to the Vicksburg Campaign
7. Typical Cross-sections of Physiographic Types in the Core Region
8. The Defenses of Vicksburg
9. Northeastern Louisiana
10. The Region between Vicksburg, Bruinsburg, and Raymond
11. The Battlefield of Port Gibson
12. The Vicinity of Raymond
13. The Region between Edwards, Canton, and Jackson
14. The Battlefield of Jackson
15. The Battlefield of Champion Hill
16. The Battlefield of Big Black Bridge
17. The Northeastern Approaches to Vicksburg
18. The Vicinity of the Stockade Redan
19. The Vicinity of 3 LA Redan and the Great Redoubt
20. The Vicinity of the Railroad Redoubt
21. The Vicinity of South Fort
22. The Mechanicsburg Corridor
23. The Battlefield of Milliken's Bend
24. The Battlefield of Helena

DISPOSITION OF FORCES MAPS

25. Disposition of Forces in the Theater of Operations: 29 March 1863
26. Disposition of Forces in Northeastern Louisiana: 17 April 1863

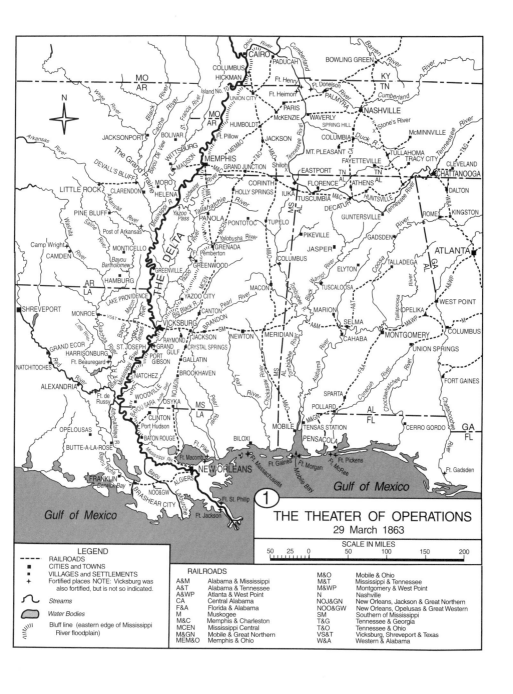

THE THEATER OF OPERATIONS
29 March 1863

SCALE IN MILES
50   25   0   50   100   150   200

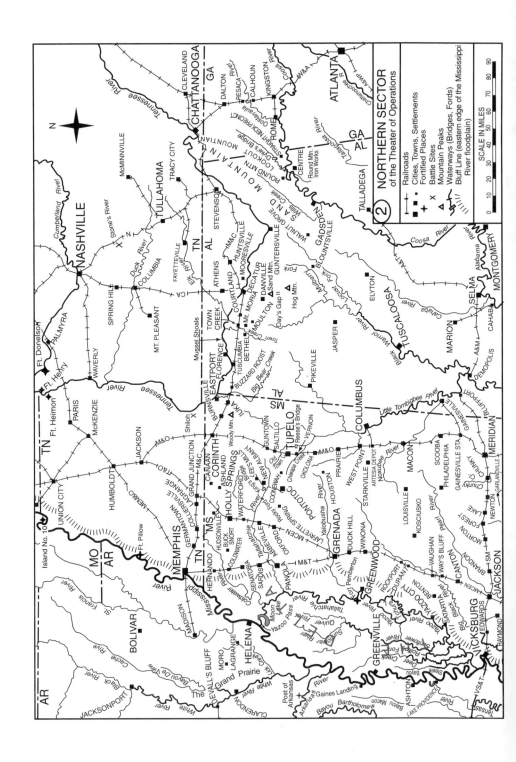

NORTHERN SECTOR
of the Theater of Operations

Railroads
Cities, Towns, Settlements
Fortified Places
Battle Sites
Mountain Peaks
Waterways (Bridges, Fords)
Bluff Line (eastern edge of the Mississippi River floodplain)

SCALE IN MILES
0 10 20 30 40 50 60 70 80 90

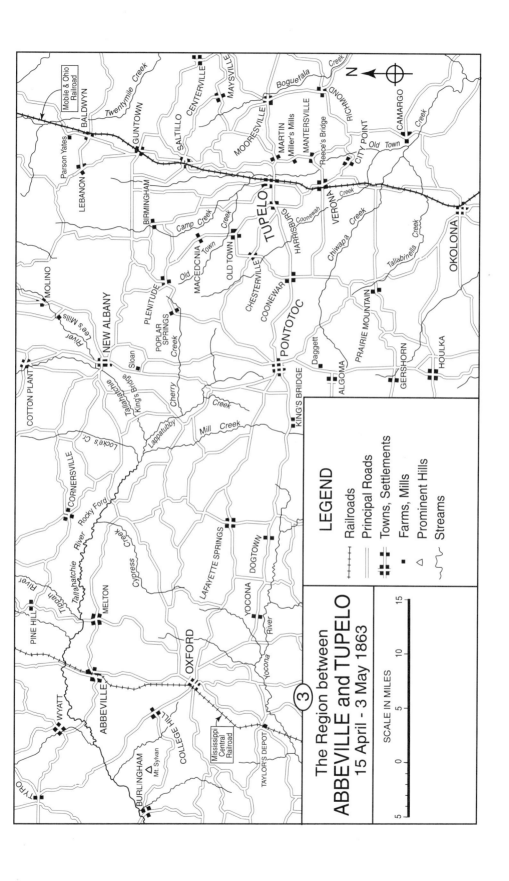

The Region between
ABBEVILLE and TUPELO
15 April - 3 May 1863

③

LEGEND

┼┼┼┼	Railroads
══	Principal Roads
■	Towns, Settlements
∙	Farms, Mills
△	Prominent Hills
∿	Streams

SCALE IN MILES

5   0   5   10   15

N

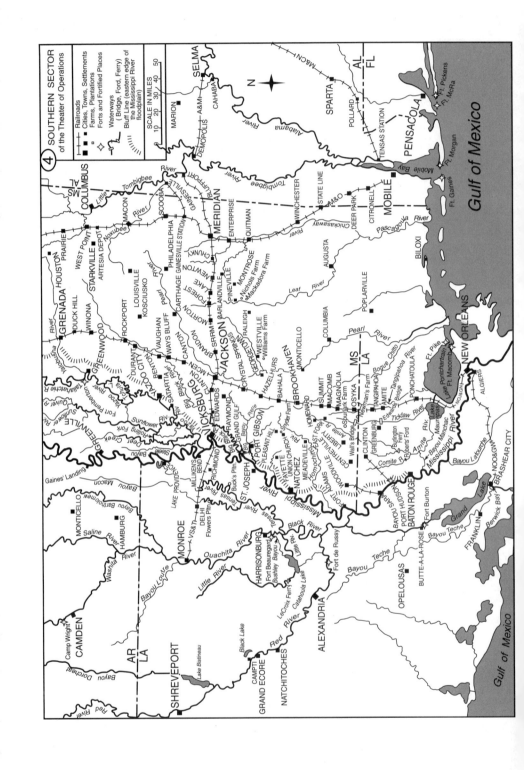

N

Gulf of Mexico

Gulf of Mexico

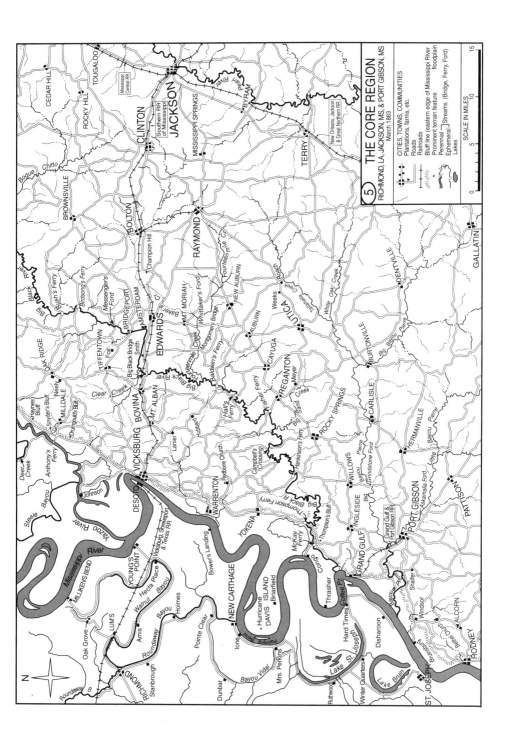

5 THE CORE REGION
RICHMOND, LA, JACKSON, MS, & PORT GIBSON, MS
March 1863

CITIES, TOWNS, COMMUNITIES
Plantations, farms, etc.
Roads
Railroads
Bluff line (eastern edge of Mississippi River floodplain)
Prominent terrain feature
Perennial / Ephemeral Streams (Bridge, Ferry, Ford)
Lakes

SCALE IN MILES
0   5   10   15

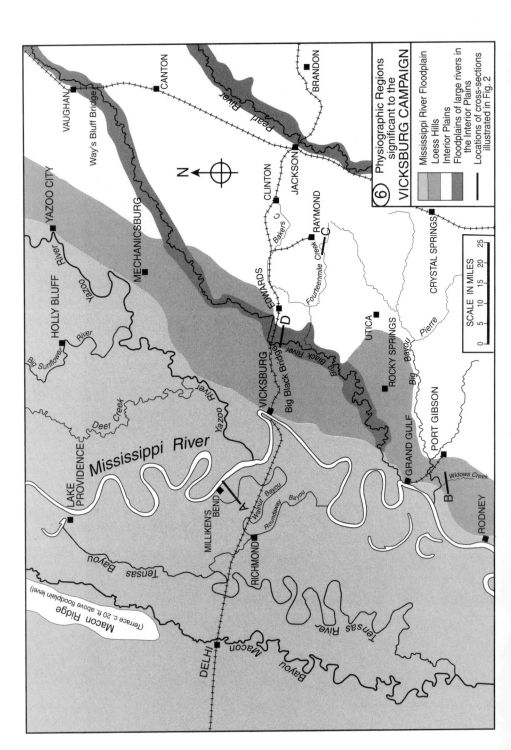

6 Physiographic Regions significant to the **VICKSBURG CAMPAIGN**

Mississippi River Floodplain
Loess Hills
Interior Plains
Floodplains of large rivers in the Interior Plains
Locations of cross-sections illustrated in Fig. 2

SCALE IN MILES
0 5 10 15 20 25

N

VAUGHAN
CANTON
Way's Bluff Bridge
Pearl River
BRANDON
YAZOO CITY
MECHANICSBURG
HOLLY BLUFF
Yazoo River
CLINTON
JACKSON
RAYMOND
Bakers C
Fourteenmile Creek
C
Big Sunflower River
EDWARDS
D
VICKSBURG
Big Black River
Big Black Bridge
UTICA
CRYSTAL SPRINGS
Deer Creek
LAKE PROVIDENCE
Mississippi River
Yazoo River
ROCKY SPRINGS
Big Bayou Pierre
MILLIKEN'S BEND
A
Walnut Bayou
Roundaway Bayou
GRAND GULF
PORT GIBSON
Widows Creek
B
RODNEY
RICHMOND
Tensas Bayou
DELHI
Bayou Macon
Tensas River
Macon Ridge
(terrace c. 20 ft. above floodplain level)

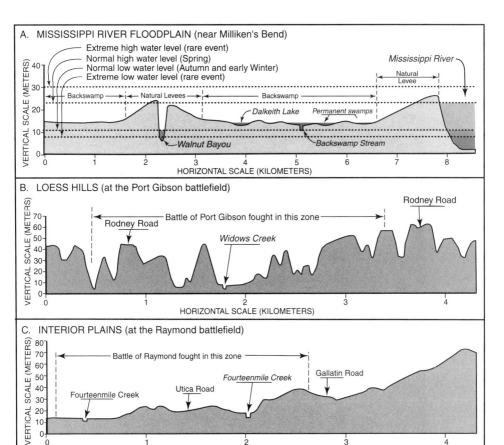

A. MISSISSIPPI RIVER FLOODPLAIN (near Milliken's Bend)

- Extreme high water level (rare event)
- Normal high water level (Spring)
- Normal low water level (Autumn and early Winter)
- Extreme low water level (rare event)

Mississippi River

Natural Levee

Backswamp ← → ← Natural Levees → ← Backswamp →

Dalkeith Lake

Permanent swamps

Walnut Bayou

Backswamp Stream

HORIZONTAL SCALE (KILOMETERS)

VERTICAL SCALE (METERS)

B. LOESS HILLS (at the Port Gibson battlefield)

Rodney Road

Rodney Road ← Battle of Port Gibson fought in this zone →

Widows Creek

HORIZONTAL SCALE (KILOMETERS)

VERTICAL SCALE (METERS)

C. INTERIOR PLAINS (at the Raymond battlefield)

← Battle of Raymond fought in this zone →

Fourteenmile Creek

Gallatin Road

Fourteenmile Creek

Utica Road

HORIZONTAL SCALE (KILOMETERS)

VERTICAL SCALE (METERS)

D. BIG BLACK RIVER FLOODPLAIN (near Big Black Bridge)

Interior Plains

Loess Hills

Natural Terrace

Backswamp

← Natural Levee Complex → ← Backswamp →

Big Black River

Ox-bow Lake

Backswamp Streams

HORIZONTAL SCALE (KILOMETERS)

VERTICAL SCALE (METERS)

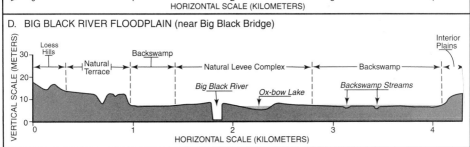

(7) Typical cross-sections of physiographic types in the Core Region of the Vicksburg Campaign, 19 March - 4 July 1863.

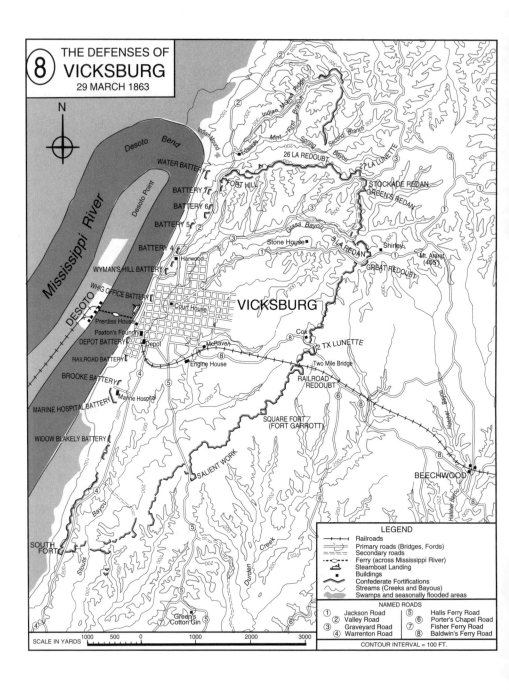

THE DEFENSES OF VICKSBURG
⑧
29 MARCH 1863

N

Desoto Bend

Indian Mound

WATER BATTERY

FORT HILL

26 LA REDOUBT

2 LA LUNETTE

STOCKADE REDAN

GREEN'S REDAN

BATTERY 7

BATTERY 6

BATTERY 5

Glass Bayou

3 LA REDAN

Stone House

Shirley

Mt. Ararat (405)

BATTERY 4

GREAT REDOUBT

Harwood

WYMAN'S HILL BATTERY

WHIG OFFICE BATTERY

DESOTO

VICKSBURG

Desoto Point

Mississippi River

Prentiss House

Court House

Paxton's Foundry

Cox

2 TX LUNETTE

DEPOT BATTERY

Depot

McRaven

RAILROAD BATTERY

Engine House

Two Mile Bridge

RAILROAD REDOUBT

BROOKE BATTERY

Marine Hospital

MARINE HOSPITAL BATTERY

SQUARE FORT (FORT GARROTT)

WIDOW BLAKELY BATTERY

Hatcher Bayou

BEECHWOOD

SALIENT WORK

Halbert Bayou

Stouts Bayou

Creek

Durden Creek

SOUTH FORT

Green's Cotton Gin

LEGEND

	Railroads
	Primary roads (Bridges, Fords)
	Secondary roads
	Ferry (across Mississippi River)
	Steamboat Landing
	Buildings
	Confederate Fortifications
	Streams (Creeks and Bayous)
	Swamps and seasonally flooded areas

NAMED ROADS

①	Jackson Road	⑤	Halls Ferry Road
②	Valley Road	⑥	Porter's Chapel Road
③	Graveyard Road	⑦	Fisher Ferry Road
④	Warrenton Road	⑧	Baldwin's Ferry Road

CONTOUR INTERVAL = 100 FT.

SCALE IN YARDS

1000 500 0 1000 2000 3000

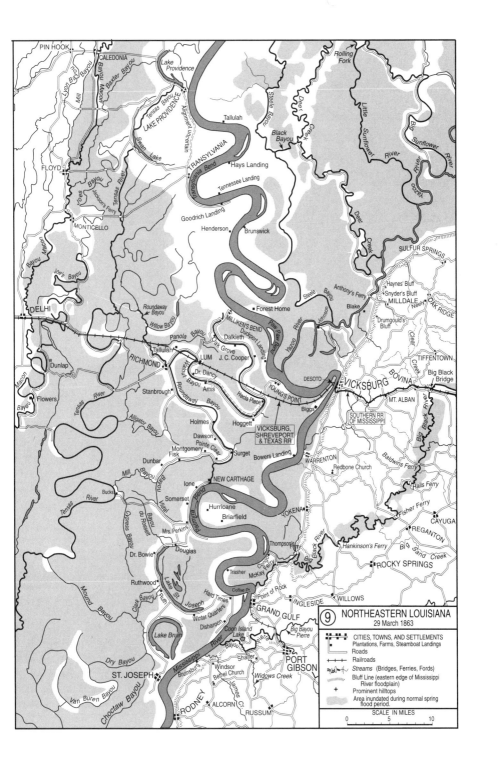

9 NORTHEASTERN LOUISIANA
29 March 1863

CITIES, TOWNS, AND SETTLEMENTS
Plantations, Farms, Steamboat Landings
Roads
Railroads
Streams (Bridges, Ferries, Fords)
Bluff Line (eastern edge of Mississippi River floodplain)
Prominent hilltops
Area inundated during normal spring flood period.

SCALE IN MILES
0   5   10

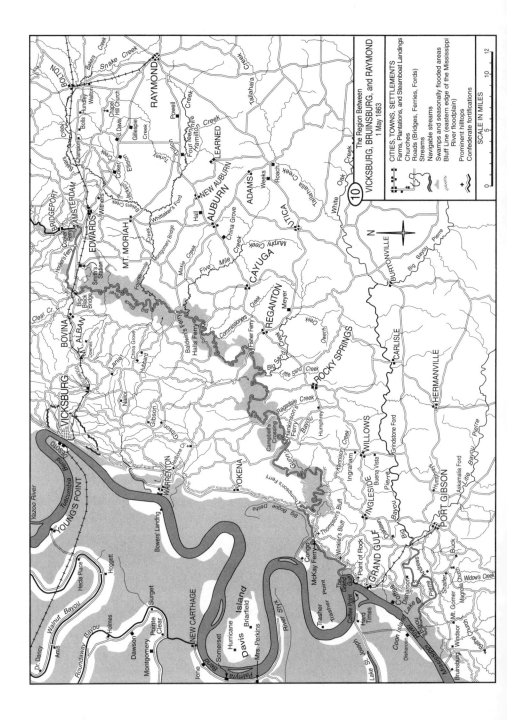

CITIES, TOWNS, SETTLEMENTS
Farms, Plantations, and Steamboat Landings
Churches
Roads (Bridges, Ferries, Fords)
Streams
Navigable streams
Swamps and seasonally flooded areas
Bluff Line (eastern edge of the Mississippi
River floodplain)
Prominent hilltops
Confederate fortifications

The Region Between
VICKSBURG, BRUINSBURG, and RAYMOND
1 May 1863

⑩

SCALE IN MILES
0   5   10   12

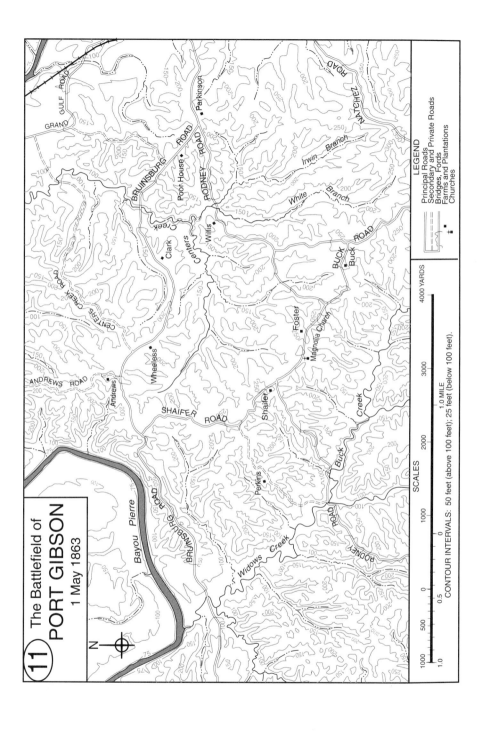

11 The Battlefield of
PORT GIBSON
1 May 1863

N

LEGEND
Principal Roads
Secondary and Private Roads
Bridges, Fords
Farms and Plantations
Churches

SCALES

1000   500   0   1000   2000   3000   4000 YARDS

1.0   0.5   0   1.0 MILE

CONTOUR INTERVALS: 50 feet (above 100 feet); 25 feet (below 100 feet).

GULF ROAD
GRAND
BRUNSBURG ROAD
RODNEY ROAD
Poor House
Parkinson
NATCHEZ ROAD
Irwin Branch
White Branch
Creek
Clark
Centers
Willis
BUCK ROAD
Buck
CENTERS CREEK ROAD
Foster
Magnolia Church
ANDREWS ROAD
Wheeless
Andrews
SHAIFER ROAD
Shaifer
Buck Creek
Bayou Pierre
BRUNSBURG ROAD
Perkins
RODNEY ROAD
Widows Creek

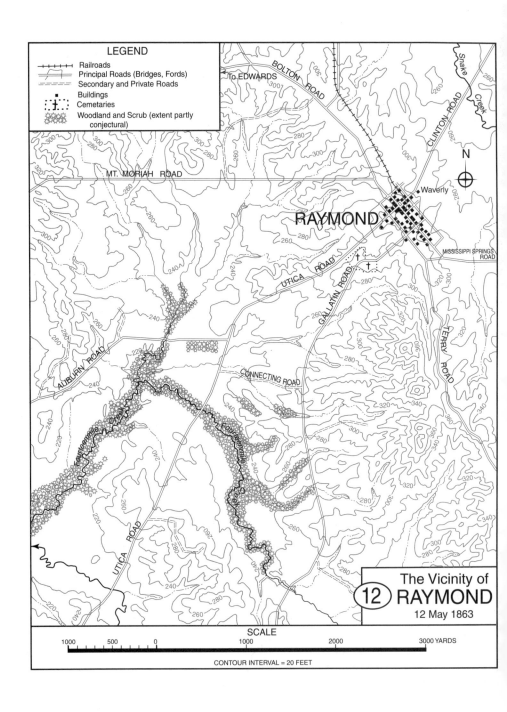

LEGEND

+-+-+-+-+	Railroads
	Principal Roads (Bridges, Fords)
- - - -	Secondary and Private Roads
■	Buildings
⚰	Cemeteries
	Woodland and Scrub (extent partly conjectural)

To EDWARDS
BOLTON ROAD
CLINTON ROAD
Snake Creek
N

MT. MORIAH ROAD

RAYMOND
• Waverly

MISSISSIPPI SPRINGS ROAD

UTICA ROAD
GALLATIN ROAD

AUBURN ROAD

CONNECTING ROAD

Fourteenmile Creek

Fourteenmile Creek

UTICA ROAD

TERRY ROAD

The Vicinity of
⑫ RAYMOND
12 May 1863

SCALE

1000 500 0 1000 2000 3000 YARDS

CONTOUR INTERVAL = 20 FEET

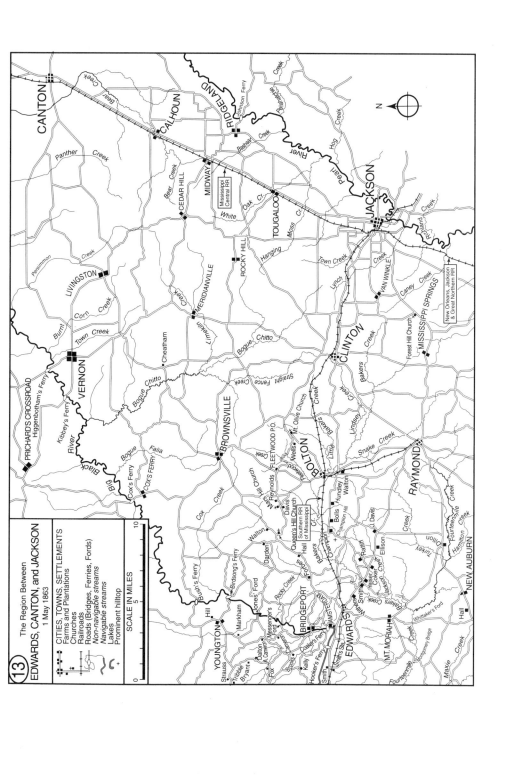

13

The Region Between
EDWARDS, CANTON, and JACKSON
1 May 1863

CITIES, TOWNS, SETTLEMENTS
Farms and Plantations
Churches
Railroads
Roads (Bridges, Ferries, Fords)
Non-navigable streams
Navigable streams
Lakes
Prominent hilltop

SCALE IN MILES

0   5   10

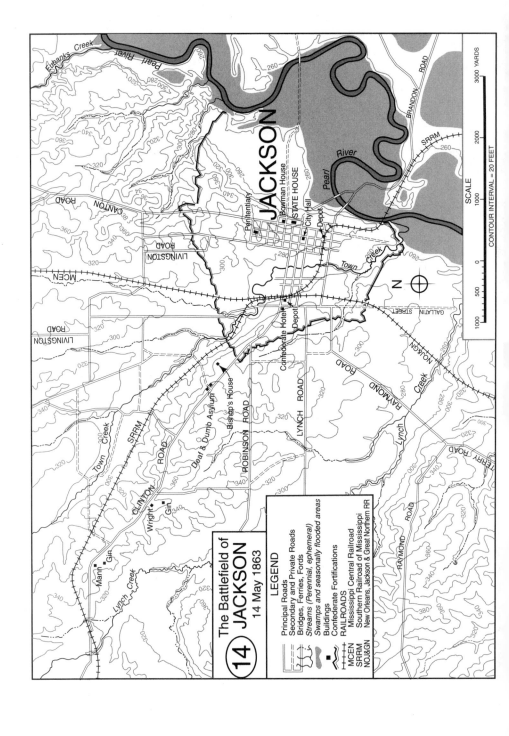

The Battlefield of
JACKSON
14 May 1863

14

LEGEND

Principal Roads
Secondary and Private Roads
Bridges, Ferries, Fords
Streams (Perennial, ephemeral)
Swamps and seasonally flooded areas
Buildings
Confederate Fortifications

RAILROADS
MCEN   Mississippi Central Railroad
SRRM   Southern Railroad of Mississippi
NOJ&GN New Orleans, Jackson & Great Northern RR

SCALE
CONTOUR INTERVAL = 20 FEET
3000 YARDS

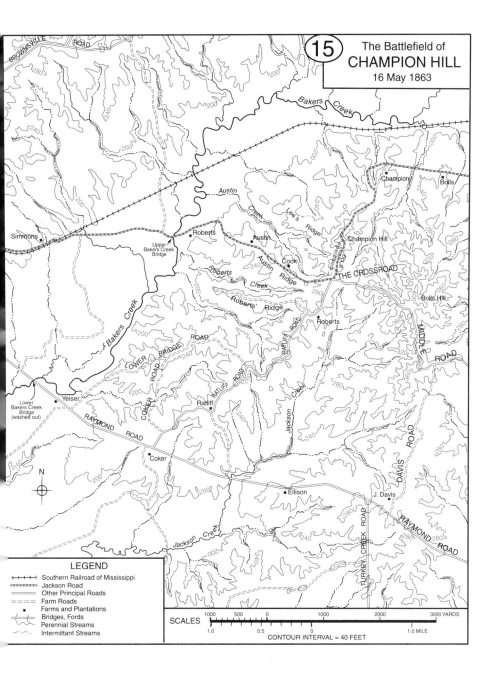

15 The Battlefield of
CHAMPION HILL
16 May 1863

BROWNSVILLE ROAD

Bakers Creek

Champion
Bolls

Austin
Lee's Ridge

Simmons
Roberts
Austin
Champion Hill

Upper Bakers Creek Bridge
Cook
THE CROSSROAD

Roberts
Austin Ridge
Bolls Hill

Roberts Creek
Roberts' Ridge
Roberts

LOWER
Bakers Creek
ROAD
BRIDGE
RATLIFF ROAD

Yeiser
HATLIFF ROAD
MIDDLE ROAD

Lower Bakers Creek Bridge (washed out)
Ratliff
Jackson Creek

RAYMOND ROAD

Coker

N
Ellison
J. Davis
DAVIS ROAD

Jackson Creek
RAYMOND ROAD

TURKEY CREEK ROAD

LEGEND
+++++ Southern Railroad of Mississippi
xxxxx Jackson Road
==== Other Principal Roads
==== Farm Roads
▪ Farms and Plantations
Bridges, Fords
Perennial Streams
Intermittant Streams

SCALES
1000 500 0   1000   2000   3000 YARDS
1.0   0.5   0   1.0 MILE
CONTOUR INTERVAL = 40 FEET

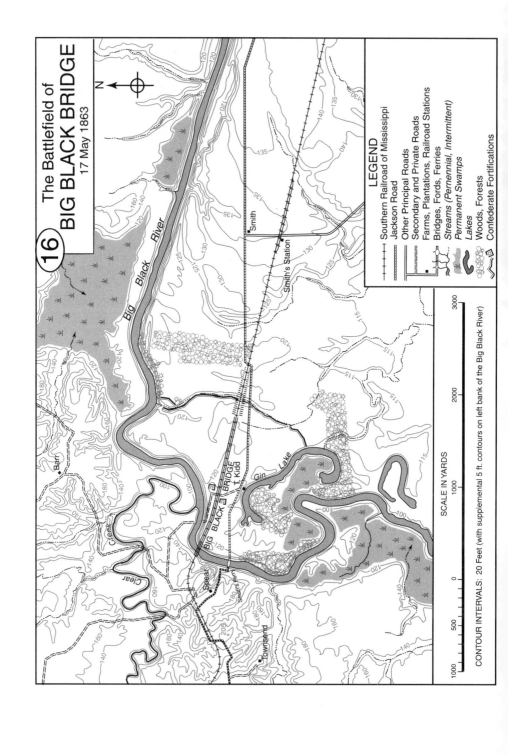

16

The Battlefield of
BIG BLACK BRIDGE
17 May 1863

N

LEGEND

Southern Railroad of Mississippi
Jackson Road
Other Principal Roads
Secondary and Private Roads
Farms, Plantations, Railroad Stations
Bridges, Fords, Ferries
Streams (Perennial, Intermittent)
Permanent Swamps
Lakes
Woods, Forests
Confederate Fortifications

Big Black River

Smith

Smith's Station

Barr

Gin Lake

BIG BLACK BRIDGE
Kidd

Clear Creek

Speat

Smith's Fan

Townsend

SCALE IN YARDS

0   500   1000   1000   2000   3000

CONTOUR INTERVALS: 20 Feet (with supplemental 5 ft. contours on left bank of the Big Black River)

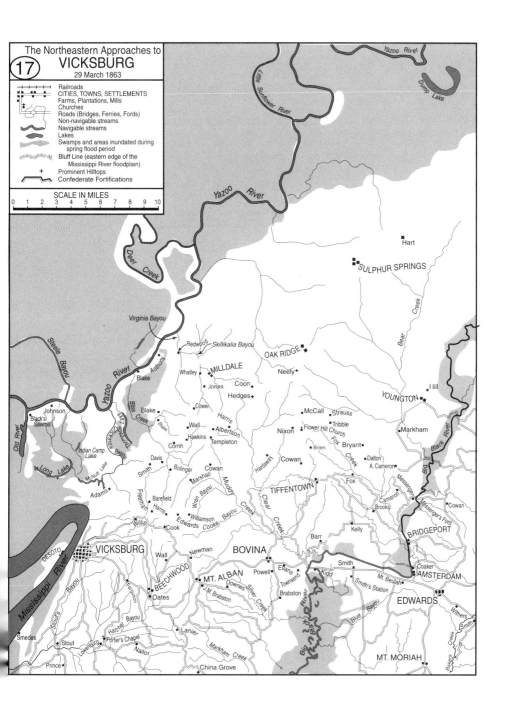

The Northeastern Approaches to
VICKSBURG
17
29 March 1863

Railroads
CITIES, TOWNS, SETTLEMENTS
Farms, Plantations, Mills
Churches
Roads (Bridges, Ferries, Fords)
Non-navigable streams
Navigable streams
Lakes
Swamps and areas inundated during
spring flood period
Bluff Line (eastern edge of the
Mississippi River floodplain)
Prominent Hilltops
Confederate Fortifications

SCALE IN MILES
0 1 2 3 4 5 6 7 8 9 10

Yazoo River
Little Sunflower River
Dump Lake
Deer Creek
Yazoo River
Virginia Bayou
Redwood
Skillikalia Bayou
Anthony
Whatley
Blake
MILLDALE
Jones
Coon
Hedges
Cower
Blake
Harris
Wall
Albertson
Hawkins
Templeton
Cornh
Davis
Smith
Bolinger
Cowan
Marshall
Barefield
Freeman
Harris
Williamson
Cooke
Edwards Cooke
Willis
Cook
Johnson
Black's Sawmill
Indian Camp Lake
Long Lake
Adams
Steele Bayou
Old River
Bliss Creek
Brake
McNutt Lake
Mississippi River Canal
DESOTO
Mississippi River
VICKSBURG
Wall
Newman
BOVINA
BEECHWOOD
MT. ALBAN
Powell
J.M. Brabston
Downes
Oates
Ferguson
Bayou
Harper Bayou
Smedes
Stout
Lowenburg
Porter's Chapel
Nailor
Prince
Lanier
Markham Creek
China Grove
OAK RIDGE
Neely
McCall
Strauss
Tribble
Nixon
Flower Hill Church
Bryant
Fox Creek
Brien
Cowan
Hardaway
Cowan
TIFFENTOWN
Fox
Wren Bayou
Muddy Creek
Clear Creek
Barr
Kelly
Evans
Smith
Kidd
Townsend
Brabston
Smith's Station
Mt. Beulah
Silver Creek
Blue Bayou
Black River
Hart
SULPHUR SPRINGS
Bear Creek
Hill
YOUNGTON
Markham
Dalton
A. Cameron
Cameron
Brooks
Cowan
BRIDGEPORT
Messenger's Ford
Messenger
Big Black River
Coaker
AMSTERDAM
EDWARDS
Withers
Smith
Bakers Creek
MT. MORIAH

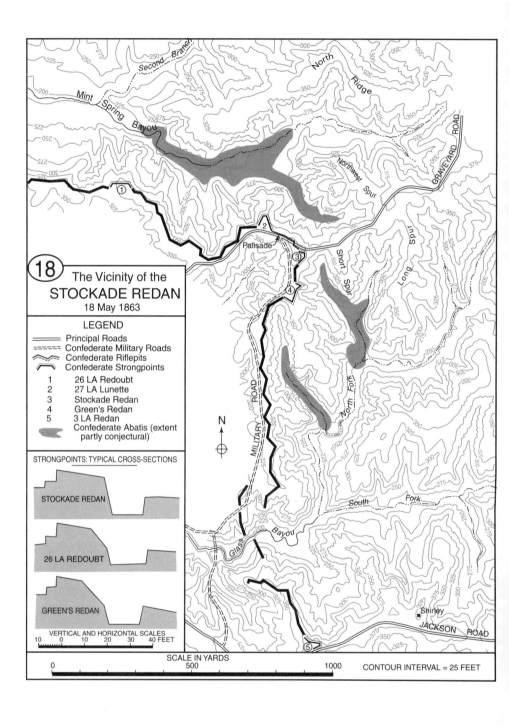

18 The Vicinity of the
STOCKADE REDAN
18 May 1863

LEGEND
═══ Principal Roads
╌╌╌ Confederate Military Roads
〰〰 Confederate Riflepits
⌒⌒ Confederate Strongpoints
1   26 LA Redoubt
2   27 LA Lunette
3   Stockade Redan
4   Green's Redan
5   3 LA Redan
▬ Confederate Abatis (extent
    partly conjectural)

STRONGPOINTS: TYPICAL CROSS-SECTIONS

STOCKADE REDAN

26 LA REDOUBT

GREEN'S REDAN

VERTICAL AND HORIZONTAL SCALES
10 0 10 20 30 40 FEET

N

SCALE IN YARDS
0   500   1000

CONTOUR INTERVAL = 25 FEET

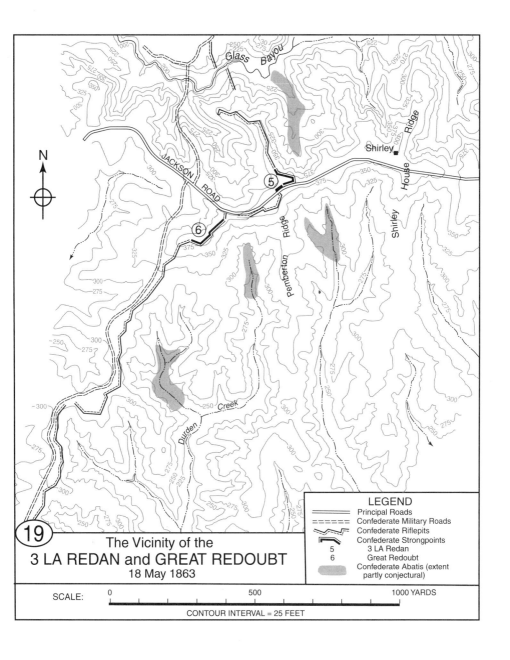

N

LEGEND
— Principal Roads
===== Confederate Military Roads
Confederate Riflepits
Confederate Strongpoints
5 3 LA Redan
6 Great Redoubt
Confederate Abatis (extent partly conjectural)

19 The Vicinity of the
3 LA REDAN and GREAT REDOUBT
18 May 1863

SCALE: 0 500 1000 YARDS

CONTOUR INTERVAL = 25 FEET

Glass Bayou

JACKSON ROAD

Shirley

Pemberton Ridge

Shirley House Ridge

Durden Creek

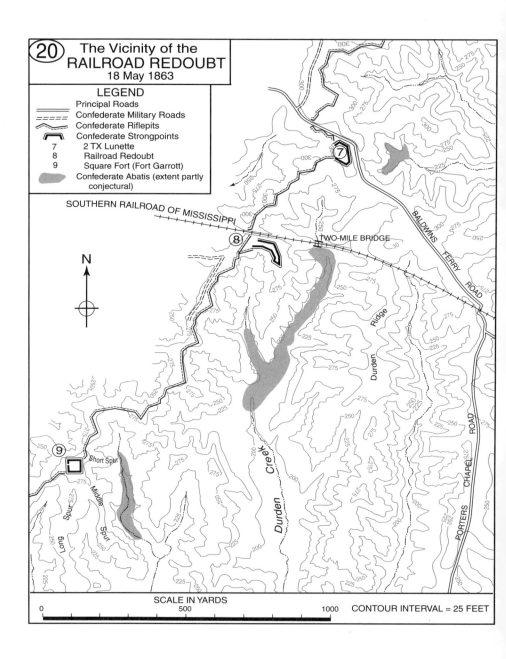

(20) The Vicinity of the
RAILROAD REDOUBT
18 May 1863

LEGEND
— Principal Roads
===== Confederate Military Roads
Confederate Riflepits
Confederate Strongpoints
7   2 TX Lunette
8   Railroad Redoubt
9   Square Fort (Fort Garrott)
Confederate Abatis (extent partly
     conjectural)

SOUTHERN RAILROAD OF MISSISSIPPI

N

TWO-MILE BRIDGE

BALDWINS FERRY ROAD

Durden Ridge

Durden Creek

Short Spur

Middle Spur

Long Spur

PORTERS CHAPEL ROAD

SCALE IN YARDS
0   500   1000   CONTOUR INTERVAL = 25 FEET

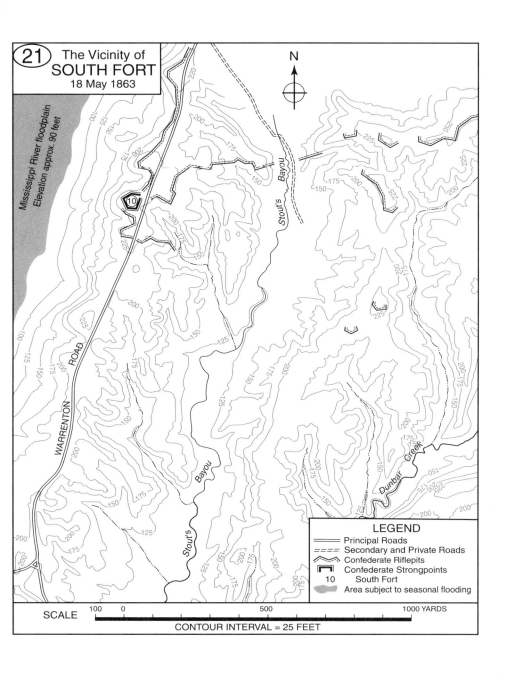

21 The Vicinity of
SOUTH FORT
18 May 1863

N

Mississippi River floodplain
Elevation approx. 90 feet

Stout's Bayou

Stout's Bayou

Dunbar Creek

WARRENTON ROAD

LEGEND
Principal Roads
Secondary and Private Roads
Confederate Riflepits
Confederate Strongpoints
10   South Fort
Area subject to seasonal flooding

SCALE   100   0   500   1000 YARDS

CONTOUR INTERVAL = 25 FEET

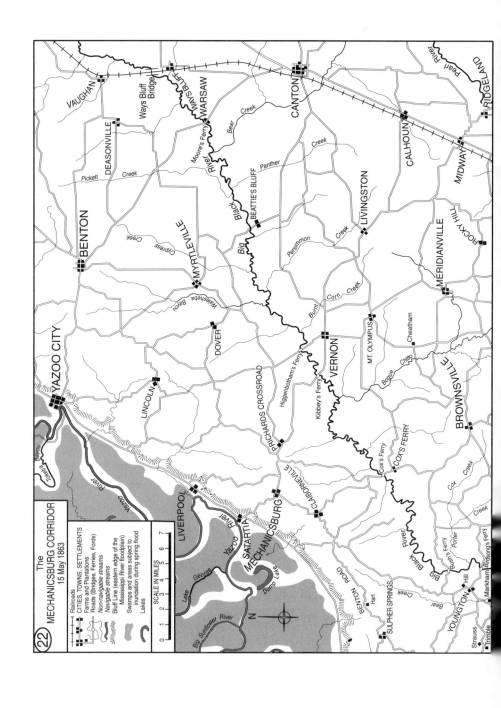

22 The
MECHANICSBURG CORRIDOR
15 May 1863

Railroads
CITIES, TOWNS, SETTLEMENTS
Farms and Plantations
Roads (Bridges, Ferries, Fords)
Non-navigable streams
Navigable streams
Bluff Line (eastern edge of the Mississippi River floodplain)
Swamps and areas subject to inundation during spring flood
Lakes

SCALE IN MILES
0 1 2 3 4 5 6 7

VAUGHAN
Ways Bluff Bridge
DEASONVILLE
Pickett Creek
BENTON
Moore's Ferry
WAYS BLUFF
WARSAW
Bear Creek
Bear Creek
CANTON
Creek
Panther Creek
BEATTIE'S BLUFF
Black River
Big
CALHOUN
LIVINGSTON
MIDWAY
RIDGELAND
Pearl River
ROCKY HILL
MERIDIANVILLE
Creek
Cypress
MYRTLEVILLE
Creek
Persimmon
Corn Creek
Cheatham
Wahsheeba Bayou
DOVER
Burnt
BROWNSVILLE
MT. OLYMPUS
Bogue Chitto
YAZOO CITY
LINCOLN
PRICHARDS CROSSROAD
Higgenbotham's Ferry
Kibbey's Ferry
VERNON
Cox's Ferry
COX'S FERRY
Bayou
River
Yazoo
LIVERPOOL
CLAIBORNEVILLE
SATARTIA
MECHANICSBURG
Dump Lake
Lake George
Yazoo River
Big Sunflower River
N
BENTON ROAD
Hart
SULPHER SPRINGS
Bear Creek
Big Black River
Bush's Ferry
Porter
Cox Creek
Creek
Markham
Bridson's Ferry
YOUNGTON
Hill
Strauss
Trimble

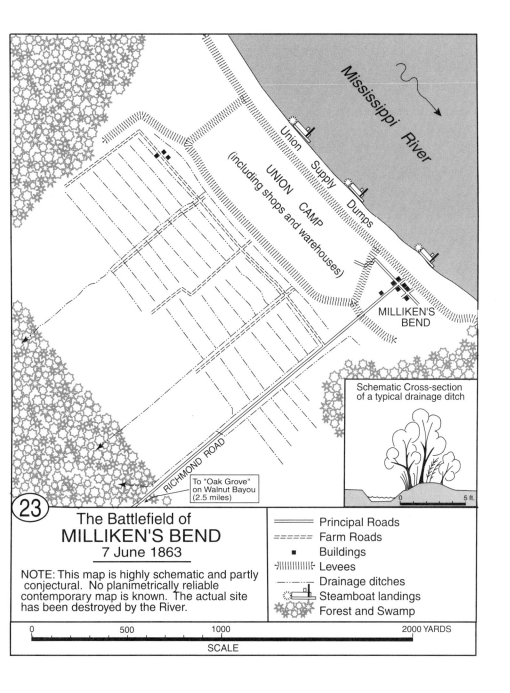

Mississippi River

Union Supply Dumps

UNION CAMP
(including shops and warehouses)

MILLIKEN'S
BEND

RICHMOND ROAD

To "Oak Grove"
on Walnut Bayou
(2.5 miles)

Schematic Cross-section
of a typical drainage ditch

0   5 ft.

23

The Battlefield of
MILLIKEN'S BEND
7 June 1863

NOTE: This map is highly schematic and partly
  conjectural. No planimetrically reliable
contemporary map is known. The actual site
has been destroyed by the River.

════════	Principal Roads
══════	Farm Roads
■	Buildings
⊣⁞⁞⁞⁞⁞⁞⁞⊢	Levees
·—·—·—·	Drainage ditches
	Steamboat landings
✳✳✳	Forest and Swamp

0   500   1000   2000 YARDS

SCALE

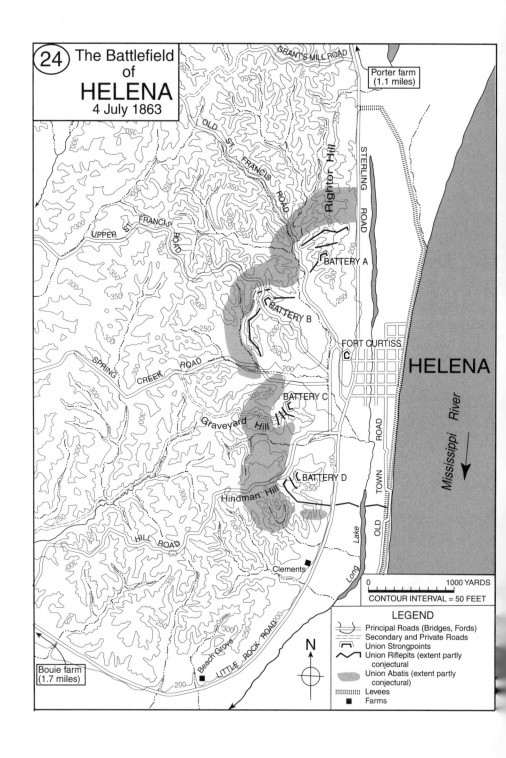

Porter farm
(1.1 miles)

GRANT'S MILL ROAD

OLD ST. FRANCIS ROAD

STERLING ROAD

Righter Hill

UPPER ST. FRANCIS ROAD

BATTERY A

BATTERY B

FORT CURTISS

HELENA

SPRING CREEK ROAD

BATTERY C

Graveyard Hill

Mississippi River

BATTERY D

Hindman Hill

OLD TOWN ROAD

Long Lake

HILL ROAD

Clements

0   1000 YARDS

CONTOUR INTERVAL = 50 FEET

Bouie farm
(1.7 miles)

Beach Grove

LITTLE ROCK ROAD

N

LEGEND

Principal Roads (Bridges, Fords)
Secondary and Private Roads
Union Strongpoints
Union Riflepits (extent partly
   conjectural
Union Abatis (extent partly
   conjectural)
Levees
Farms

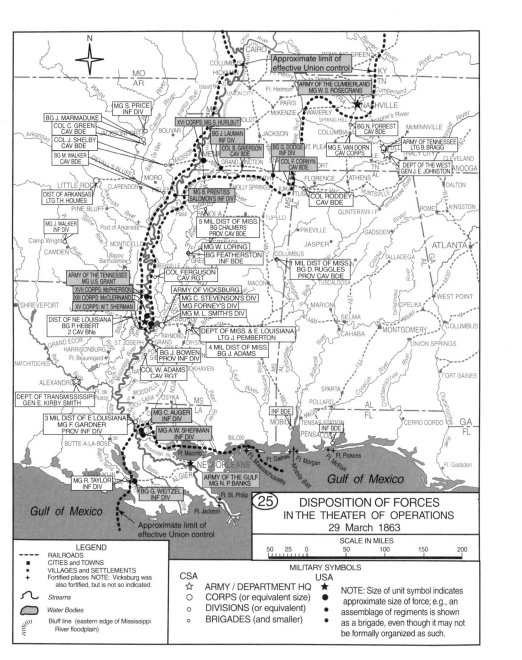

DISPOSITION OF FORCES
IN THE THEATER OF OPERATIONS
29 March 1863

25

SCALE IN MILES
50 25 0   50   100   150   200

LEGEND

- - - RAILROAD
■ CITIES AND TOWNS
▪ VILLAGES and SETTLEMENTS
+ Fortified places NOTE: Vicksburg was also fortified, but is not so indicated.

⌇ Streams

▱ Water Bodies

⦚⦚ Bluff line (eastern edge of Mississippi River floodplain)

MILITARY SYMBOLS

CSA
☆ ARMY / DEPARTMENT HQ
O CORPS (or equivalent size)
o DIVISIONS (or equivalent)
o BRIGADES (and smaller)

USA
★ ARMY / DEPARTMENT HQ
● CORPS (or equivalent size)
● DIVISIONS (or equivalent)
● BRIGADES (and smaller)

NOTE: Size of unit symbol indicates approximate size of force; e.g., an assemblage of regiments is shown as a brigade, even though it may not be formally organized as such.

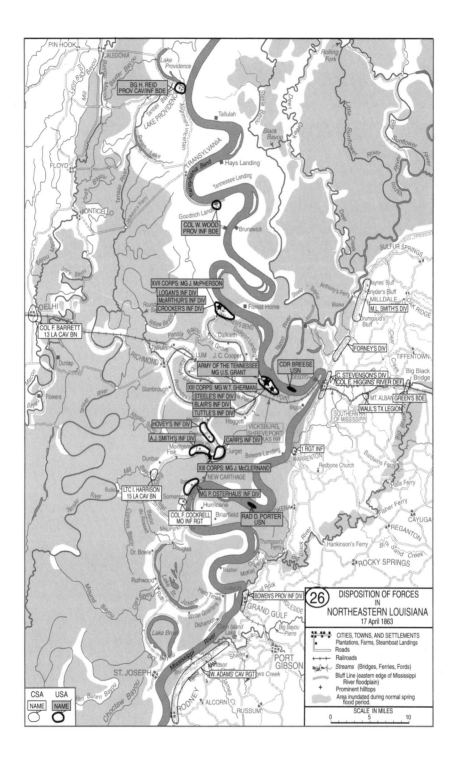

DISPOSITION OF FORCES
IN
NORTHEASTERN LOUISIANA
17 April 1863

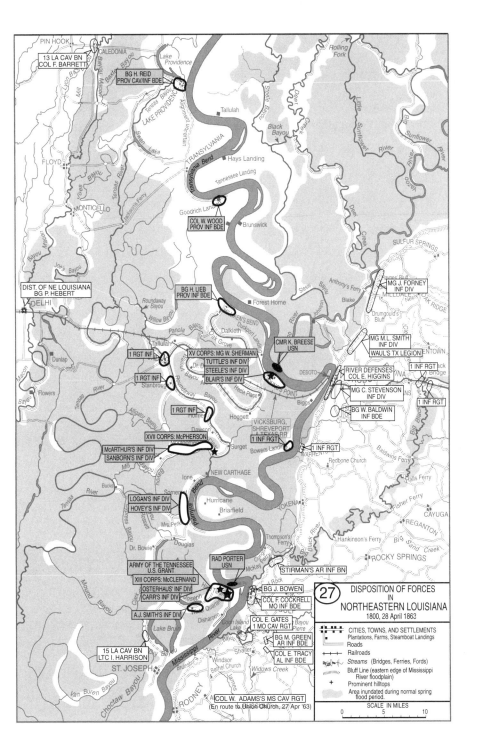

PIN HOOK

13 LA CAV BN
COL F. BARRETT
CALEDONIA

Lake
Providence

BG H. REID
PROV CAV/INF BDE

LAKE PROVIDENCE

Rolling
Fork

Tallulah

Black
Bayou

FLOYD

TRANSYLVANIA

Transylvania Bend

Hays Landing

Tennessee Landing

MONTICELLO

Goodrich Landing

Dr. D

COL W. WOOD
PROV INF BDE

Brunswick

SULFUR SPRINGS

DIST. OF NE LOUISIANA
BG P. HEBERT

DELHI

Roundaway
Bayou

Willow Bayou

BG H. LIEB
PROV INF BDE

Forest Home

Anthony's Ferry

MG J. FORNEY
INF DIV

MILLDALE

OAK RIDGE

Drumgould's
Bluff

Dunlap

Tallulah

1 RGT INF

XV CORPS: MG W. SHERMAN
TUTTLE'S INF DIV
STEELE'S INF DIV
BLAIR'S INF DIV

Dalkieth

CMR K. BREESE
USN

DESOTO

MG M.L. SMITH
INF DIV
WAUL'S TX LEGION

RIVER DEFENSES
COL E. HIGGINS

1 INF RGT

Flowers

Stanbrough

1 RGT INF

Hecla Place

MG C. STEVENSON
INF DIV

1 INF RGT

Bayou

1 RGT INF

Hoggett

Biggs

BG W. BALDWIN
INF BDE

Dawson

VICKSBURG,
SHREVEPORT
RR

1 INF RGT

XVII CORPS: McPherson

Surget

Bowers Landing

1 INF RGT

WARREN

McARTHUR'S INF DIV
SANBORN'S INF DIV

Ione

NEW CARTHAGE

Redbone Church

Halls Ferry

Baldwins Ferry

LOGAN'S INF DIV
HOVEY'S INF DIV

Hurricane

Briarfield

Mrs. Perk

TOKENA

Fisher Ferry

REGANTON

CAYUGA

Dr. Bowie

Douglas

Thompson's
Ferry

Black River

Hankinson's Ferry

Big
Sand
River

ROCKY SPRINGS

RAD PORTER
USN

McKay

STIRMAN'S AR INF BN

ARMY OF THE TENNESSEE
U.S. GRANT

XIII CORPS: McCLERNAND

OSTERHAUS' INF DIV
CARR'S INF DIV

BG J. BOWEN

COL F. COCKRELL
MO INF BDE

A.J. SMITH'S INF DIV

COL E. GATES
1 MO CAV RGT

15 LA CAV BN
LTC I. HARRISON

Lake Bruin

Bayou
Pierre

BG M. GREEN
AR INF BDE

COL E. TRACY
AL INF BDE

ST. JOSEPH

Windsor

Bethel Church

Widows Creek

RODNEY

COL W. ADAMS'S MS CAV RGT
(En route to Bhoe Church, 27 Apr '63)

Van Buren Bayou

Choctaw Bayou

DISPOSITION OF FORCES IN NORTHEASTERN LOUISIANA

27

1800, 28 April 1863

CITIES, TOWNS, AND SETTLEMENTS
Plantations, Farms, Steamboat Landings
Roads
Railroads
Streams (Bridges, Ferries, Fords)
Bluff Line (eastern edge of Mississippi River floodplain)
Prominent hilltops
Area inundated during normal spring flood period.

SCALE IN MILES
0   5   10

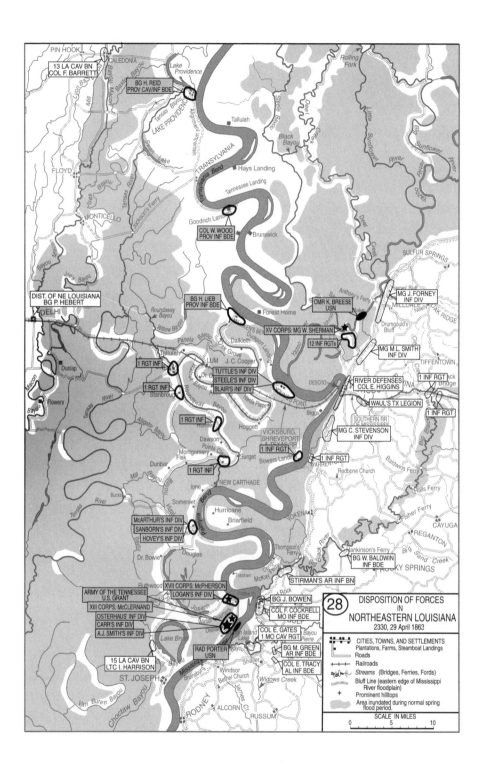

PIN HOOK

13 LA CAV BN
COL F. BARRETT

CALEDONIA

Lake
Providence

BG H. REID
PROV CAV/INF BDE

Rolling
Fork

Tallulah

Black
Bayou

SULFUR SPRINGS

FLOYD

TRANSYLVANIA

Hays Landing

Tennessee Landing

MONTICELLO

Goodrich Land.

COL W. WOOD
PROV INF BDE

Brunswick

DIST. OF NE LOUISIANA
BG P. HEBERT

DELHI

BG H. LIEB
PROV INF BDE

Forest Home

CMR K. BREESE
USN

MG J. FORNEY
INF DIV

MILLDALE

OAK RIDGE

XV CORPS: MG W. SHERMAN

Dalkieth

12 INF RGTs

MG M.L. SMITH
INF DIV

TIFFENTOWN

Dunlap

Tallulah

LUM   J. C. Cooper

1 RGT INF

Dr.

1 RGT INF

Stanbrough

TUTTLE'S INF DIV

STEELE'S INF DIV

BLAIR'S INF DIV

DESOTO

RIVER DEFENSES
COL E. HIGGINS

WAUL'S TX LEGION

1 INF RGT

1 INF RGT

Flowers

1 RGT INF

Home

Hoggett

VICKSBURG,
SHREVEPORT
& TEXAS RR

SOUTHERN RR
OF MISSISSIPPI

MG C. STEVENSON
INF DIV

Dawson

Montgomery   Fisk

Pointe Clear

Dunbar

1 RGT INF

Surget

1 INF RGT

Bowers Landing

WARRENTON

1 INF RGT

Redbone Church

Mill

NEW CARTHAGE

Ione

Somerset

Hurricane

Briafield

TOKENA

Halls Ferry

CAYUGA

McARTHUR'S INF DIV

SANBORN'S INF DIV

HOVEY'S INF DIV

Dr. Bowie

Douglas

Thompson's
Ferry

Hankinson's Ferry

BG W. BALDWIN
INF BDE

REGANTON

ROCKY SPRINGS

Trasher

STIRMAN'S AR INF BN

XVII CORPS: McPHERSON

ARMY OF THE TENNESSEE
U.S. GRANT

LOGAN'S INF DIV

BG J. BOWEN

XIII CORPS: McCLERNAND

COL F. COCKRELL
MO INF BDE

OSTERHAUS' INF DIV

CARR'S INF DIV

A.J. SMITH'S INF DIV

COL E. GATES
1 MO CAV RGT

Bayou
Pierre

RAD PORTER
USN

BG M. GREEN
AR INF BDE

15 LA CAV BN
LTC I. HARRISON

COL E. TRACY
AL INF BDE

Windsor

Bethel Church

Widows Creek

ST. JOSEPH

RODNEY   ALCORN C.

RUSSUM

28 DISPOSITION OF FORCES
IN
NORTHEASTERN LOUISIANA
2330, 29 April 1863

CITIES, TOWNS, AND SETTLEMENTS
Plantations, Farms, Steamboat Landings
Roads
Railroads
Streams (Bridges, Ferries, Fords)
Bluff Line (eastern edge of Mississippi
River floodplain)
Prominent hilltops
Area inundated during normal spring
flood period.

SCALE IN MILES
0   5   10

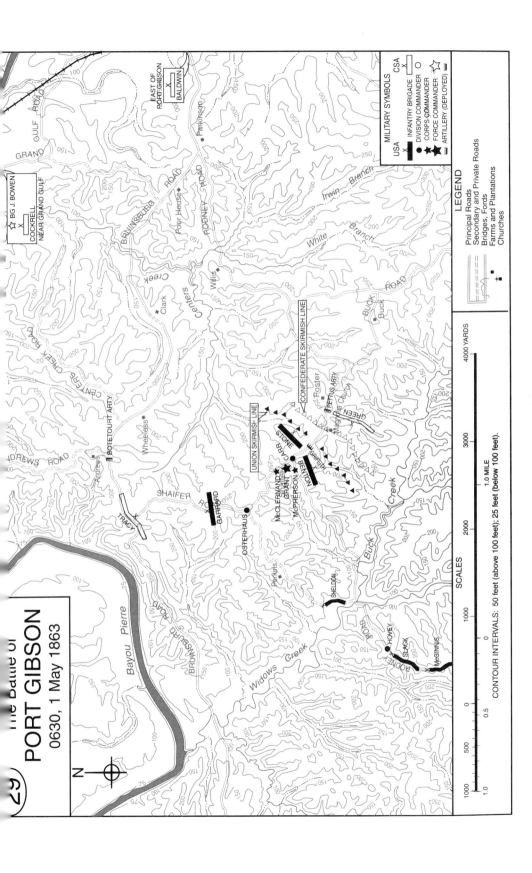

The Battle of
PORT GIBSON
0630, 1 May 1863

29

N

EAST OF
PORT GIBSON
BALDWIN

BG J. BOWEN
COCKRELL
NEAR GRAND GULF

GULF ROAD
GRAND GULF ROAD
BRUINSBURG ROAD
RODNEY ROAD
Parkinson
Poor Horse
Willis
Centers Creek
Clark
Irwin Branch
White Branch
BUCK ROAD
Buck
Foster
GREEN ARTY
Magnolia Church
DETTUS ARTY
CONFEDERATE SKIRMISH LINE
UNION SKIRMISH LINE
STONE
BALDWIN
GARRARD
GRIFFITH
TILGHMAN
McCLERNAND
GRANT
McPHERSON
Buck Creek
Wheeless
BOTETOURT ARTY
ANDREWS ROAD
Andrews
SHAIFER
SHAIFER ROAD
TRACY
OSTERHAUS
CENTERS CREEK ROAD
Perkins
SHELDON
RODNEY ROAD
HOVEY
STACK
McGINNIS
Widows Creek
Bayou Pierre
BRUINSBURG ROAD

LEGEND
MILITARY SYMBOLS
USA   CSA
INFANTRY BRIGADE
DIVISION COMMANDER
CORPS COMMANDER
FORCE COMMANDER
ARTILLERY (DEPLOYED)

Principal Roads
Secondary and Private Roads
Bridges, Fords
Farms and Plantations
Churches

SCALES
0   1000   2000   3000   4000 YARDS
0   1.0 MILE
1.0   0.5   0

CONTOUR INTERVALS: 50 feet (above 100 feet); 25 feet (below 100 feet).

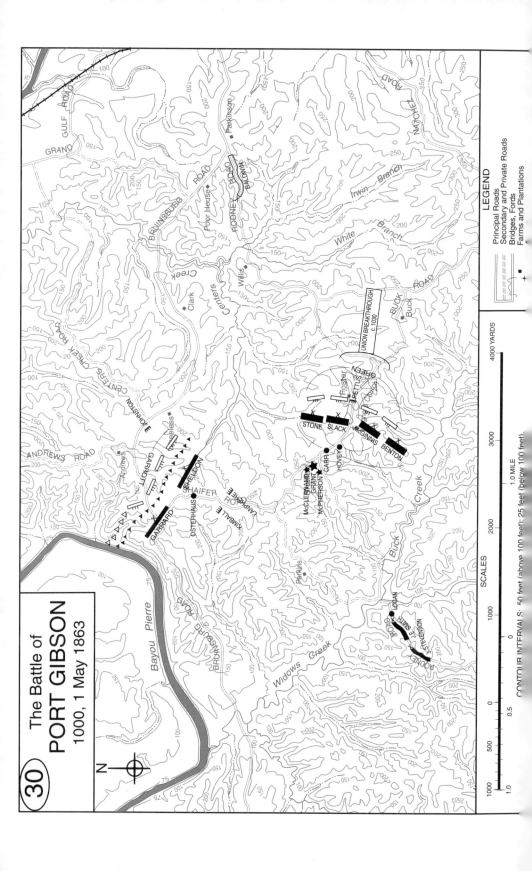

30

The Battle of
PORT GIBSON
1000, 1 May 1863

N

SCALES

1.0   0.5   0   1000

1.0 MILE
0   500   1000

0   1000   2000   3000   4000 YARDS

CONTOUR INTERVALS: 50 feet (above 100 feet); 25 feet (below 100 feet)

LEGEND

Principal Roads
Secondary and Private Roads
Bridges, Fords
Farms and Plantations

UNION BREAKTHROUGH
c. 1030

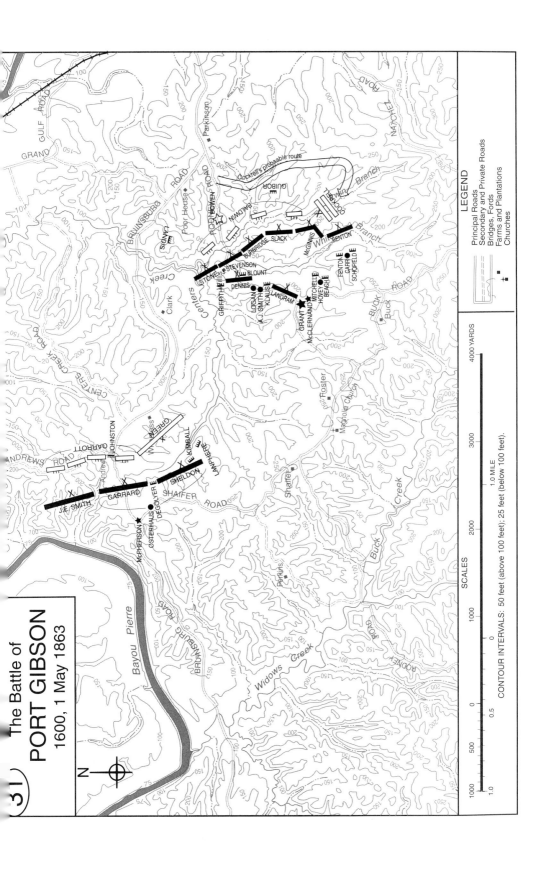

The Battle of
PORT GIBSON
1600, 1 May 1863

31

N

LEGEND
Principal Roads
Secondary and Private Roads
Bridges, Fords
Farms and Plantations
Churches

SCALES

1000   500   0   1000   2000   3000   4000 YARDS
1.0   0.5   0   1.0 MILE

CONTOUR INTERVALS: 50 feet (above 100 feet); 25 feet (below 100 feet).

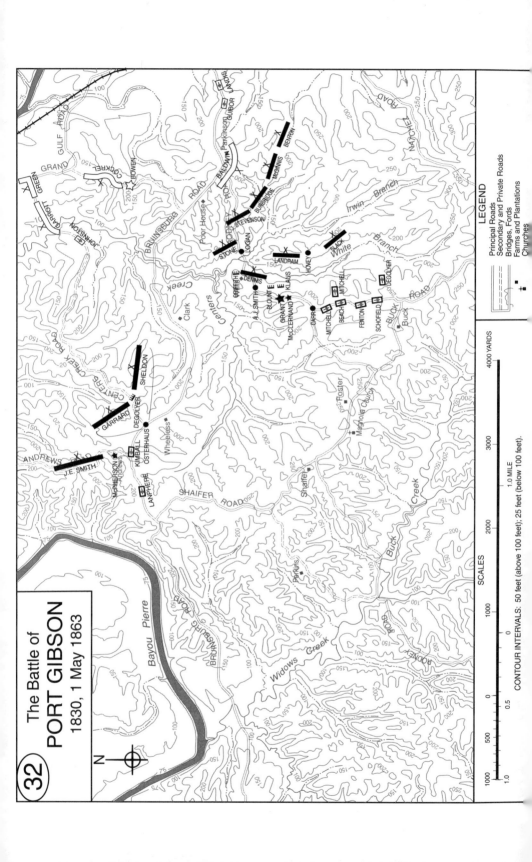

The Battle of
PORT GIBSON
1830, 1 May 1863

32

N

LEGEND

Principal Roads
Secondary and Private Roads
Bridges, Fords
Farms and Plantations
Churches

SCALES

1000   500   0   1000   2000   3000   4000 YARDS

1.0   0.5   0   1.0 MILE

CONTOUR INTERVALS: 50 feet (above 100 feet); 25 feet (below 100 feet).

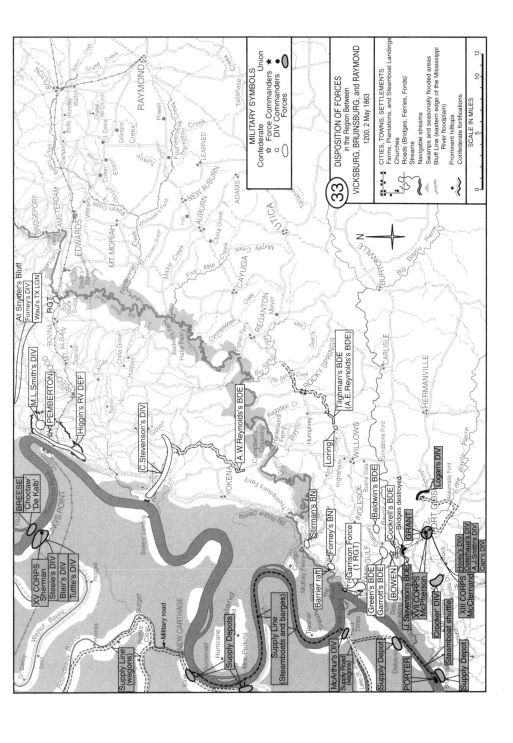

MILITARY SYMBOLS

	Confederate	Union
Force Commanders	☆	★
DIV Commanders	○	●
Forces	⬭	⬤

33 DISPOSITION OF FORCES
in the Region Between
VICKSBURG, BRUINSBURG, and RAYMOND
1200, 2 May 1863

CITIES, TOWNS, SETTLEMENTS
Farms, Plantations, and Steamboat Landings
Churches
Roads (Bridges, Ferries, Fords)
Streams
Navigable streams
Swamps and seasonally flooded areas
Bluff Line (eastern edge of the Mississippi River floodplain)
Prominent hilltops
Confederate fortifications

SCALE IN MILES
0   5   10   12

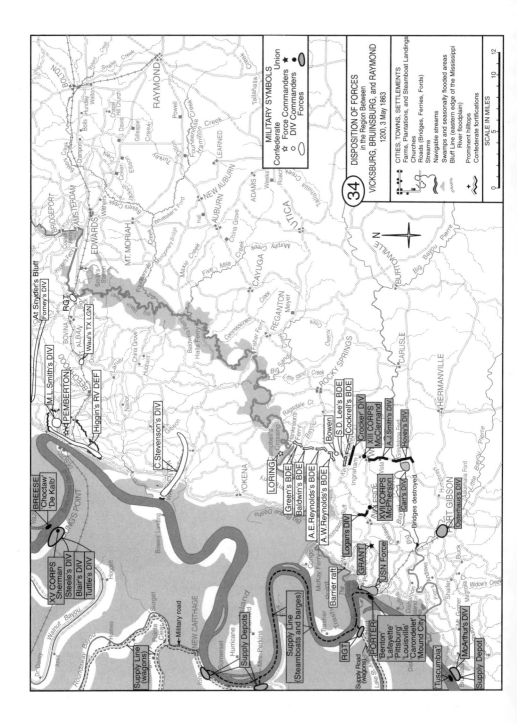

MILITARY SYMBOLS

	Confederate	Union
Force Commanders	☆	★
DIV Commanders	○	●
Forces	⬭	⬭

34 DISPOSITION OF FORCES
in the Region Between
VICKSBURG, BRUINSBURG, and RAYMOND
1200, 3 May 1863

CITIES, TOWNS, SETTLEMENTS
Farms, Plantations, and Steamboat Landings
Churches
Roads (Bridges, Ferries, Fords)
Streams
Navigable streams
Swamps and seasonally flooded areas
Bluff Line (eastern edge of the Mississippi
River floodplain)
Prominent hilltops
Confederate fortifications

SCALE IN MILES

0   5   10   12

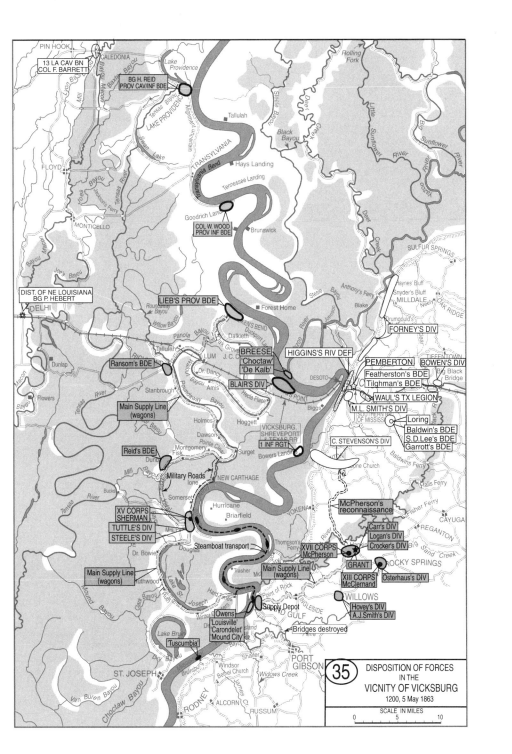

PIN HOOK
CALEDONIA
13 LA CAV BN
COL F. BARRETT
Lake Providence
BG H. REID
PROV CAV/INF BDE
LAKE PROVIDENCE
Tallulah
Rolling Fork
Black Bayou
FLOYD
TRANSYLVANIA
Hays Landing
Transylvania Bend
Tennessee Landing
MONTICELLO
Goodrich Landing
COL W. WOOD
PROV INF BDE
Brunswick
SULFUR SPRINGS
DIST. OF NE LOUISIANA
BG P. HEBERT
DELHI
LIEB'S PROV BDE
Forest Home
Anthony's Ferry
Haynes' Bluff
Snyder's Bluff
MILLDALE
OAK RIDGE
Drumgould's
FORNEY'S DIV
Dunlap
Ransom's BDE
BREESE
'Choctaw'
'De Kalb'
BLAIR'S DIV
HIGGINS'S RIV DEF
PEMBERTON
Featherston's BDE
Tilghman's BDE
WAUL'S TX LEGION
BOWEN'S DIV
Big Black Bridge
TIEFFENTOWN
Flowers
Stanbrough
VICKSBURG,
SHREVEPORT
& TEXAS RR
1 INF RGT
C. STEVENSON'S DIV
M.L. SMITH'S DIV
SOUTHERN
OF MISSISSI
Loring
Baldwin's BDE
S.D.Lee's BDE
Garrott's BDE
Reid's BDE
Bowers Landing
Stone Church
Baldwins Ferry
Halls Ferry
Military Roads
NEW CARTHAGE
Somerset
Hurricane
Briarfield
YOKENA
McPherson's
reconnaissance
Fisher Ferry
CAYUGA
REGANTON
XV CORPS
SHERMAN
TUTTLE'S DIV
STEELE'S DIV
Steamboat transport
Thompson's Ferry
XVII CORPS
McPherson
Carr's DIV
Logan's DIV
Crocker's DIV
ROCKY SPRINGS
Main Supply Line
(wagons)
GRANT
Main Supply Line
(wagons)
XIII CORPS
McClernand
Osterhaus's DIV
WILLOWS
Hovey's DIV
A.J. Smith's DIV
Supply Depot
Owens
'Louisville'
'Carondelet'
'Mound City'
GRAND GULF
Bridges destroyed
'Tuscumbia'
Lake Bruin
ST. JOSEPH
Windsor
Bethel Church
Widows Creek
PORT
GIBSON
RODNEY
ALCORN
RUSSUM
DISPOSITION OF FORCES
IN THE
VICINITY OF VICKSBURG
1200, 5 May 1863

35

SCALE IN MILES
0   5   10

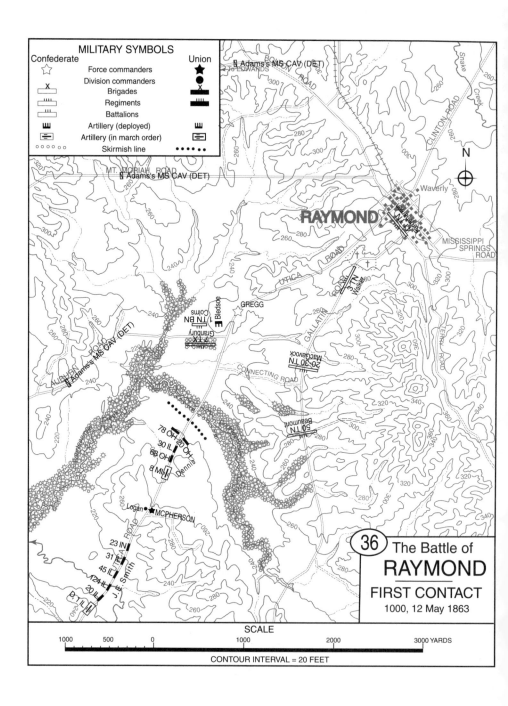

MILITARY SYMBOLS

Confederate   Union

☆ / ★   Force commanders

Division commanders

Brigades

Regiments

Battalions

Artillery (deployed)

Artillery (in march order)

○○○○○○ / ●●●●●●   Skirmish line

RAYMOND

Waverly

MISSISSIPPI SPRINGS ROAD

GREGG

Bledsoe

1 TN BN   Colms

7 TX   Granbury

3 TN   Walker

20-30 TN   MacDavock

50 TN   Beaumont

Adams's MS CAV (DET)

CONNECTING ROAD

78 OH / 20 OH

30 IL

68 OH   Dennis

8 MI

Logan ● MCPHERSON

23 IN

31 IL

45 IL

124 IL   J. E. Smith

20 IL

81 IL

36 The Battle of
RAYMOND
FIRST CONTACT
1000, 12 May 1863

SCALE

1000   500   0   1000   2000   3000 YARDS

CONTOUR INTERVAL = 20 FEET

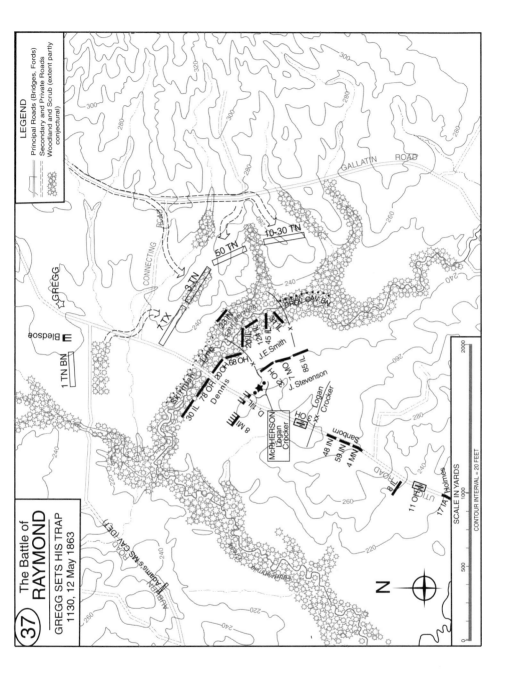

The Battle of RAYMOND

(37)

GREGG SETS HIS TRAP
1130, 12 May 1863

LEGEND

Principal Roads (Bridges, Fords)
Secondary and Private Roads
Woodland and Scrub (extent partly conjectural)

GALLATIN ROAD

CONNECTING ROAD

GREGG

Bledsoe

1 TN BN

3 TN

1 TX

50 TN

10-30 TN

25 TN

20 TN

41 TN

45 TN

BRD'N CAV BN

J.E. Smith

68 OH

20 OH

78 OH

30 IL

Skirmish line

Dennis

8 MI

D

7 MO

56 OH

J. Stevenson

McPHERSON
Logan
Crocker

HO
XX
Logan
Crocker

48 IN

59 IN

4 MN

Sanborn

11 OH

17 IA

Holmes

UTICA ROAD

ROAD

AUBURN & MS CAV (DET.)

N

SCALE IN YARDS

0   500   1000   2000

CONTOUR INTERVAL = 20 FEET

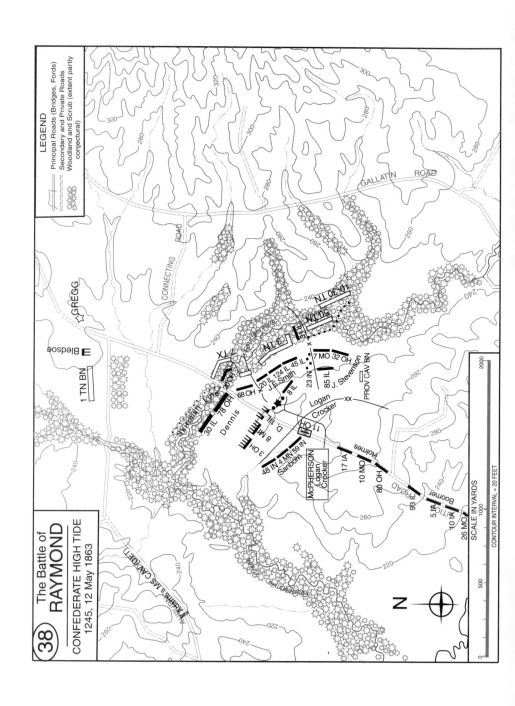

The Battle of
RAYMOND

38

CONFEDERATE HIGH TIDE
1245, 12 May 1863

LEGEND

Principal Roads (Bridges, Fords)

Secondary and Private Roads

Woodland and Scrub (extent partly conjectural)

GREGG

Bledsoe

1 TN BN

CONNECTING ROAD

GALLATIN ROAD

10 30 TN

3 TN

2 TX

Virginia's Line

30 IL   78 OH

Dennis

3 OH

8 MM

D 1

68 OH

20 IL 124 IL 45 IL

J.E. Smith

8 IL

23 IN

7 MO   32 OH

85 IL

J. Stevenson

PROV CAV BN

Logan
Crocker

11 OH

48 IN 4 MN 59 IN

Sanborn

McPHERSON
Logan
Crocker

17 IA

Holmes

10 MO

80 OH

Boomer

93 IL

5 IA

10 IA

26 MO

N

SCALE IN YARDS

0   500   1000   2000

CONTOUR INTERVAL = 20 FEET

ADAMS'S MIS CAVALRY(?)

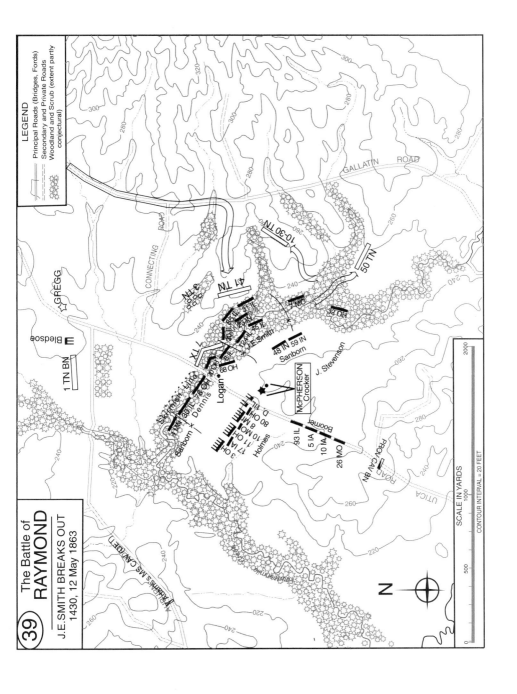

The Battle of
RAYMOND

J.E. SMITH BREAKS OUT
1430, 12 May 1863

LEGEND

Principal Roads (Bridges, Fords)
Secondary and Private Roads
Woodland and Scrub (extent partly conjectural)

GALLATIN ROAD

CONNECTING ROAD

10-30 TN

50 TN

41 TN

7 TN

XIX

J.E. Smith

MO

7 TN

Sanborn

Bledsoe

GREGG

1 TN BN

Logan

Skirmish Line

Sanborn

Dennis

48 IN

59 IN

Crocker

McPHERSON

J. Stevenson

3 OH

17 IA

10 MO

8 MO

80 OH

D

Holmes

Boomer

93 IL

5 IA

10 IA

26 MO

PROV CAV BN

UTICA ROAD

RABURN'S MIS CAV (DET)

FLEMINGVILLE

N

SCALE IN YARDS

500   1000   2000

CONTOUR INTERVAL = 20 FEET

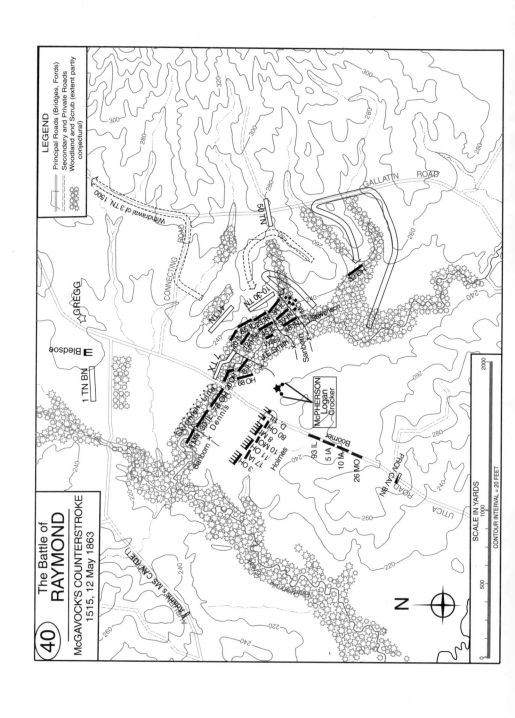

40 The Battle of RAYMOND

McGAVOCK'S COUNTERSTROKE
1515, 12 May 1863

LEGEND

Principal Roads (Bridges, Fords)
Secondary and Private Roads
Woodland and Scrub (extent partly conjectural)

GALLATIN ROAD

Withdrawal of 3 TN, 1500

CONNECTING ROAD

50 TN

10-30 TN

3 OH

1 TN

7 TX

Wiles

J. E. Smith

Sanborn

Stevenson

GREGG

Bledsoe

1 TN BN

Sanborn X Dennis

68 OH

Skirmish Line

7 MO
20 OH
23 IN
20 IL

McPHERSON
Logan
Crocker

3 OH
17 IA
11 MO
10 OH
8 MO
80 OH
D O OH

Holmes

93 IL
5 IA
10 IA
26 MO

Boomer

PROV CAV BN

UTICA ROAD

N

SCALE IN YARDS
0   500   1000   2000

CONTOUR INTERVAL = 20 FEET

Whitaker's MS CAV (DET)

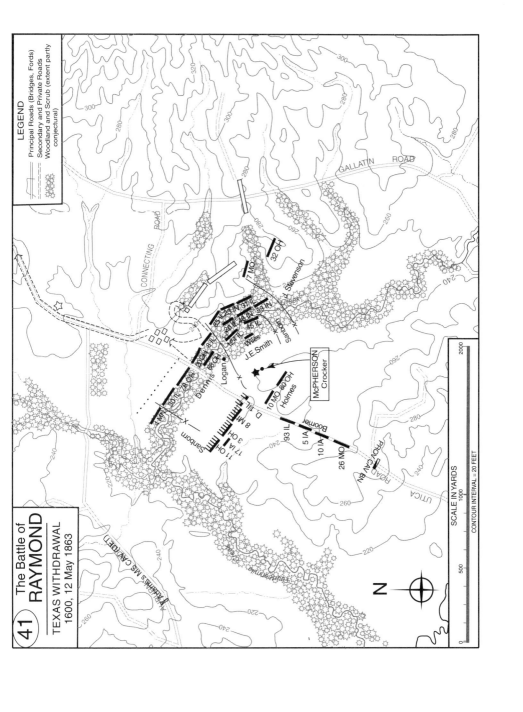

LEGEND
Principal Roads (Bridges, Fords)
Secondary and Private Roads
Woodland and Scrub (extent partly conjectural)

41 The Battle of
RAYMOND
TEXAS WITHDRAWAL
1600, 12 May 1863

SCALE IN YARDS
0   500   1000   2000
CONTOUR INTERVAL = 20 FEET

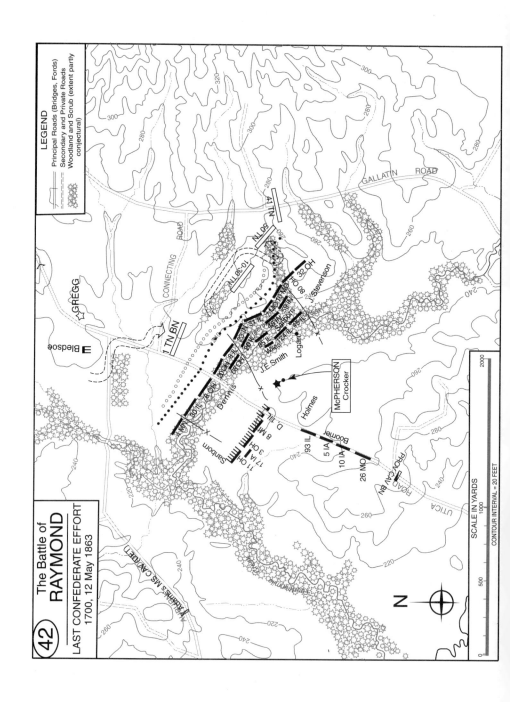

42

The Battle of
RAYMOND

LAST CONFEDERATE EFFORT
1700, 12 May 1863

LEGEND

Principal Roads (Bridges, Fords)
Secondary and Private Roads
Woodland and Scrub (extent partly
conjectural)

SCALE IN YARDS

0   500   1000   2000

CONTOUR INTERVAL = 20 FEET

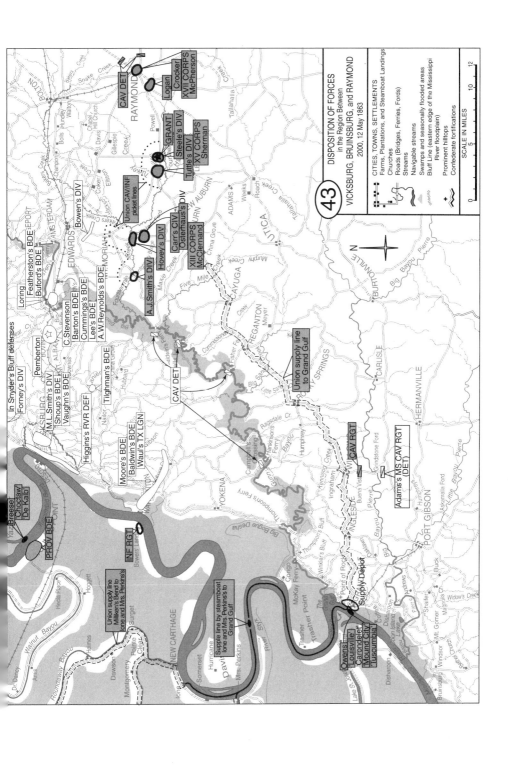

43

DISPOSITION OF FORCES
in the Region Between
VICKSBURG, BRUINSBURG, and RAYMOND
2000, 12 May 1863

CITIES, TOWNS, SETTLEMENTS
Farms, Plantations, and Steamboat Landings
Churches
Roads (Bridges, Ferries, Fords)
Streams
Navigable streams
Swamps and seasonally flooded areas
Bluff Line (eastern edge of the Mississippi
    River floodplain)
Prominent hilltops
Confederate fortifications

SCALE IN MILES
0   5   10   12

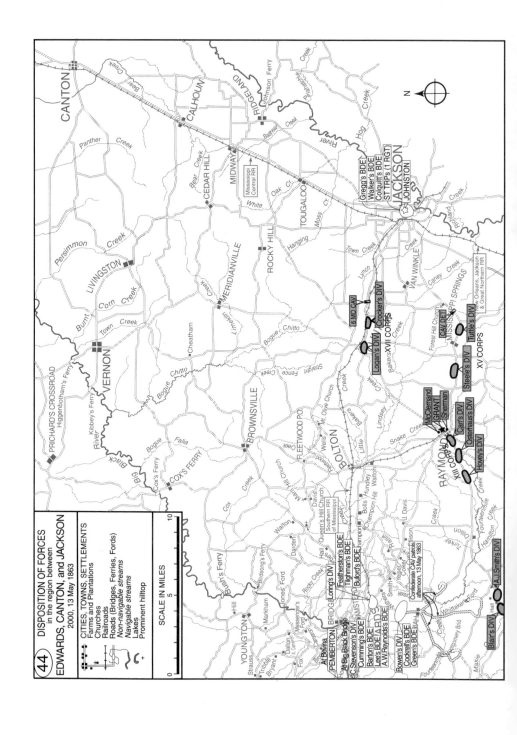

44 DISPOSITION OF FORCES
in the region between
EDWARDS, CANTON, and JACKSON
2000, 13 May 1863

CITIES, TOWNS, SETTLEMENTS
Farms and Plantations
Churches
Railroads
Roads (Bridges, Ferries, Fords)
Non-navigable streams
Navigable streams
Lakes
Prominent hilltop

SCALE IN MILES

0   5   10

CANTON

CALHOUN

RIDGELAND

Panther   Creek

Bear   Creek

CEDAR HILL

MIDWAY

Mississippi
Central RR

Persimmon   Creek

LIVINGSTON

Corn   Creek

Burnt   Creek

Town   Creek

VERNON

Cheatham

MERIDIANVILLE

ROCKY HILL

TOUGALOO

White

Oak   Ct.

Moss   Ct.

Hanging   Creek

Bogue   Chitto

Lamakin   Creek

Straight   Fence   Creek

Bogue   Chitto

PRICHARD'S CROSSROAD

Higgenbotham's Ferry

Kibbey's Ferry

Cox's Ferry

Big   Black   River

COX'S FERRY

Falia

Bogue   Creek

BROWNSVILLE

FLEETWOOD P.O.

Mt. Olive Church

Bakers   Creek

Lindsey   Creek

Snake   Creek

Little   Creek

Walton   Creek

Fleetwood   Creek

Mass Hill Church

BOLTON

Bolls   Hundley

Champion Hill

J. Davis

Queen's Hill Church

Southern RR
of Mississippi

Hall   Champion   Creek

Hampton

Reed

Smith   Creek

J. Davis

Confederate CAV patrols
afternoon, 13 May 1863

Turkey   Creek

Dillon

Fourteenmile   Creek

Hamilton   Creek

Whittaker   Ford

Montgomery Bird

Fourteenmile   Ford

Maxie

Hall

JACKSON

JOHNSTON

Gregg's BDE
Walker's BDE
Colquitt's BDE
ST TRPS (1 RGT)

6 MO CAV
X
Crocker's DIV

Logan's DIV   Crocker's   XVII CORPS

Bakers   Creek

VAN WINKLE

Caney   Creek

Forest Hill Church

Orleans, Jackson
& Great Northern RR

MISSISSIPPI SPRINGS

CAV DET
X

Tuttle's DIV

Steele's DIV

XV CORPS

Pinartown   Creek

Hog   Creek

Pearl   River

Town   Creek

Lynch   Creek

McClernand
GRANT
Sherman

Carr's DIV
Osterhaus's DIV

RAYMOND

Hovey's DIV

XIII CORPS

YOUNGTON

Strauss

Markham

Messenger's Ford

Birdsong's Ferry

Bush's Ferry

Jones Ford

Rocky   Creek

Dalton

Tribble   Fox

Bryant

Messenger's Ford

PEMBERTON   BRIDGE
At Bovina

At Big Black Bridge
S.C. Stevenson's DIV
Cumming's BDE

Barton's BDE
Lee's BDE
A.W.Reynolds BDE

Loring's DIV
Featherston's BDE
Tilghman's BDE
Buford's BDE

Bowen's DIV
Cockrell's BDE
Green's BDE

A.J. Smith's DIV

Blair's DIV

Darden

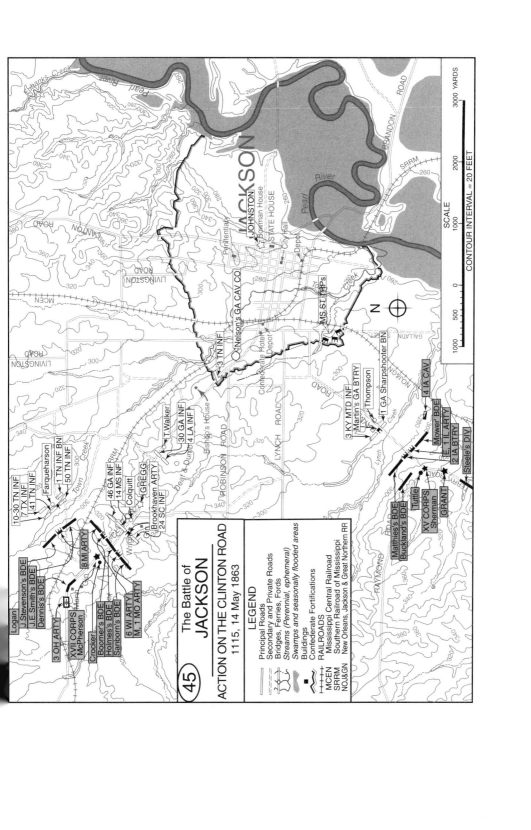

The Battle of
JACKSON
ACTION ON THE CLINTON ROAD
1115, 14 May 1863

45

LEGEND

Principal Roads
Secondary and Private Roads
Bridges, Ferries, Fords
Streams (Perennial, ephemeral)
Swamps and seasonally flooded areas
Buildings
Confederate Fortifications
RAILROADS
MCEN   Mississippi Central Railroad
SRRM   Southern Railroad of Mississippi
NOJ&GN New Orleans, Jackson & Great Northern RR

SCALE

0   500   1000   2000   3000 YARDS

CONTOUR INTERVAL = 20 FEET

JACKSON

Pearl River

E. Banks Creek

Pearl River

JOHNSTON
Bowman House
STATE HOUSE
City Hall
Penitentiary
Depot
Confederate Depot
MS. ST. TRP's

CLINTON ROAD
LIVINGSTON ROAD
LIVINGSTON ROAD

Town Creek

Logan
J. Stevenson's BDE
J.E. Smith's BDE
Dennis's BDE
3 OH ARTY
XVII CORPS
McPherson
Crocker
Boomer's BDE
Holmes's BDE
Sanborn's BDE
6 WI ARTY
M. 1 MO ARTY
8 MI ARTY

10-30 TN INF
7 TX INF
141 TN INF
Farqueharson
1 TN INF BN
50 TN INF

Wright
46 GA INF
14 MS INF
Colquitt
GREGG
Brookhaven ARTY
24 SC INF
RRM

T. Walker
30 GA INF
4 LA INF
Bishop's House
Dept & Dumb

3 TN INF
Nelson's GA CAV CO.
Confederate Hotel

ROBINSON ROAD

LYNCH ROAD

3 KY MTD INF
Martin's GA BTRY
Thompson
1 GA Sharpshooter BN
1 GA Sharpshooter BN

Lynch Creek

NOJ&GN

GALLATIN ROAD

N

Matthies's BDE
Buckland's BDE
Tuttle
KV CORPS
Sherman
GRANT

Mower' BDE
4 IA CAV
E. 1 IL ARTY
2 IA BTRY
Steele's DIV

RAYMOND ROAD

BRANDON ROAD

SRRM

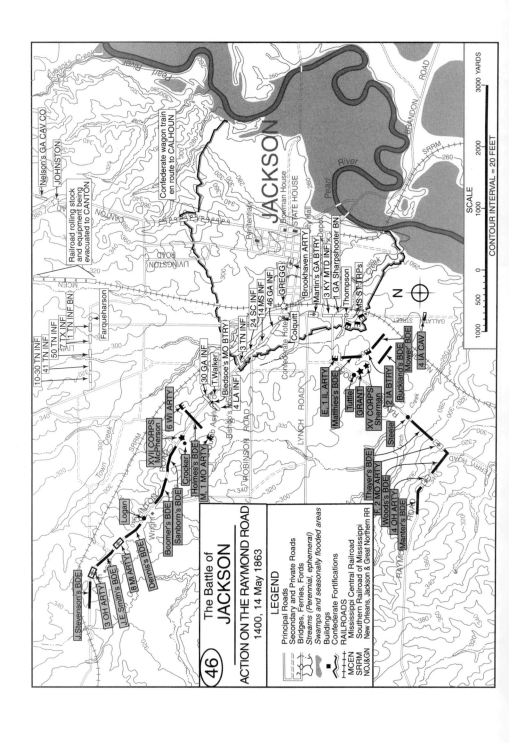

46

The Battle of JACKSON

ACTION ON THE RAYMOND ROAD
1400, 14 May 1863

LEGEND

	Principal Roads
	Secondary and Private Roads
	Bridges, Ferries, Fords
	Streams (Perennial, ephemeral)
	Swamps and seasonally flooded areas
	Buildings
	Confederate Fortifications
	RAILROADS
MCEN	Mississippi Central Railroad
SRRM	Southern Railroad of Mississippi
NOJ&GN	New Orleans, Jackson & Great Northern RR

SCALE

CONTOUR INTERVAL = 20 FEET

3000 YARDS

Confederate wagon train en route to CALHOUN

Railroad rolling stock and equipment being evacuated to CANTON

JACKSON

Nelson's GA CAV CO

JOHNSTON

Farquerharson

10-30 TN INF
41 TN INF
50 TN INF
47 TX INF
11 TN INF BN

State House
Bowman House
Penitentiary
City Hall
Depot

GREGG

Brookhaven ARTY
Martin's GA BTRY
3 KY MTD INF
1 GA Sharpshooter BN
Thompson
1 MS ST TRPs

46 GA INF
14 MS INF
24 SC INF
3 TN INF
Colquitt
Confederate Hotel

30 GA INF
T.Walker
Bledsoe's MO BTRY
4 LA INF

XVII CORPS
McPherson

6 WI ARTY

Crocker
Holmes's BDE
M. 1 MO ARTY
Boomer's BDE
Sanborn's BDE

Logan
Wright

J.Stevenson's BDE
3 OH ARTY
J.E.Smith's BDE
8 WI ARTY
Dennis's BDE

E. 1 IL ARTY
Matthies's BDE
Tuttle
GRANT
XV CORPS
Sherman
2 IA BTRY
Buckland's BDE
Mower's BDE
4 IA CAV

Steele
Thayer's BDE
F. 2 MO ARTY
Woods's BDE
4 OH ARTY
RAYMO
Manter's BDE
ROAD

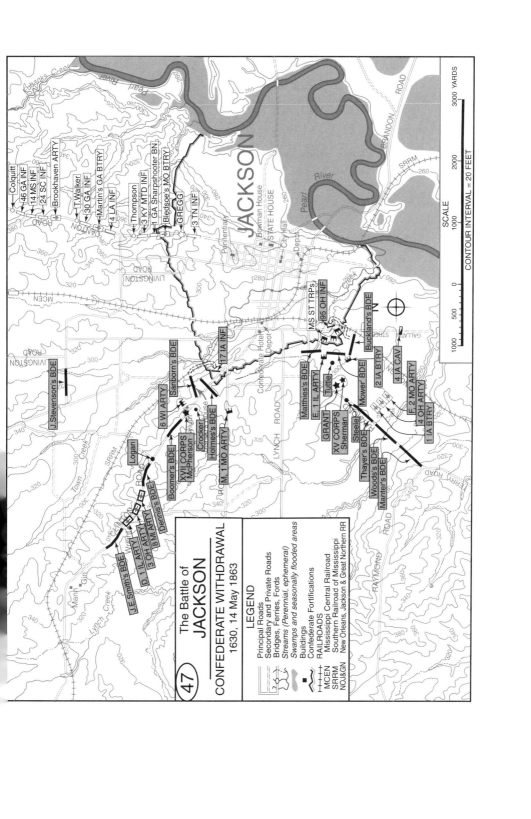

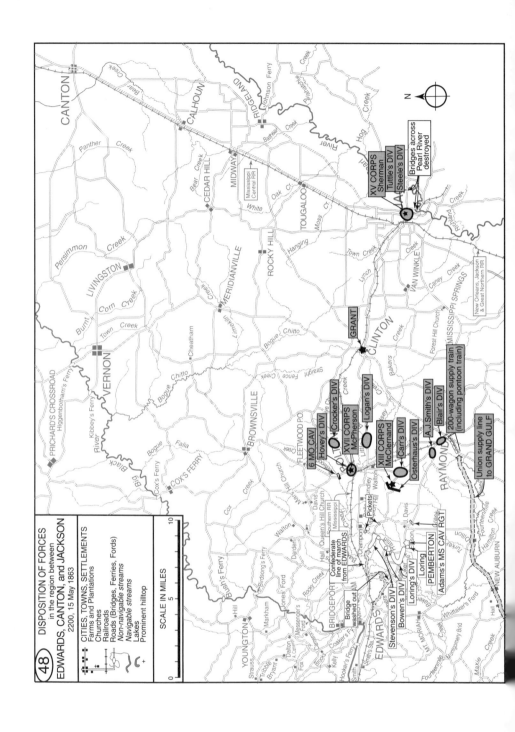

48 DISPOSITION OF FORCES
in the region between
EDWARDS, CANTON, and JACKSON
2200, 15 May 1863

CITIES, TOWNS, SETTLEMENTS
Farms and Plantations
Churches
Railroads
Roads (Bridges, Ferries, Fords)
Non-navigable streams
Navigable streams
Lakes
Prominent hilltop

SCALE IN MILES

0   5   10

CANTON

CALHOUN

RIDGELAND

Johnson Ferry

Bear Creek

Panther Creek

CEDAR HILL

MIDWAY

Mississippi Central RR

White

Oak Ct.

TOUGALOO

Moss Cr.

Hanging Creek

ROCKY HILL

VAN WINKLE

Town Creek

XV CORPS Sherman
Tuttle's DIV
Steele's DIV

Bridges across Pearl River destroyed

New Orleans, Jackson & Great Northern RR

MISSISSIPPI SPRINGS

Persimmon Creek

LIVINGSTON

Corn Creek

Burnt Cr.

Town Creek

Cheatham

MERIDIANVILLE

Lynch Creek

Caney Creek

Forest Hill Church

GRANT

CLINTON

Bakers Creek

VERNON

PRICHARD'S CROSSROAD

Higgenbotham's Ferry

Kibbey's Ferry

BROWNSVILLE

Straight Fence Creek

Bogue Chitto

Bogue Chitto

Falla Creek

FLEETWOOD P.O.

6 MO CAV
Hovey's DIV

XVII CORPS McPherson
Crocker's DIV
Logan's DIV

Mary Hill Church

Queen's Hill Church

XIII CORPS McClernand
Carr's DIV
Osterhaus's DIV

A.J.Smith's DIV
Blair's DIV

RAYMOND

200-wagon supply train (including pontoon train)

Union supply line to GRAND GULF

Big Black River

Cox's Ferry

COX'S FERRY

Cox Creek

Mary Hill Church

Pickets

Bush's Ferry

Birdsong's Ferry

Dardent

Walton Creek

Davis

Mississippi

Southern RR

PEMBERTON
Loring
Loring's DIV

Adams's MS CAV RGT

Hamilton Creek

Turner

Fourteenmile

NEW AUBURN

Maxie Creek

YOUNGTOWN

Hill

Markham

Jones's Ford

Dalton

Leach

Fox

Kelly

Bryant

Strauss

Trible

Smith

Shell's Sta.

Hooker's Fry.

Coakor's Fly.

Messenger's Ford

BRIDGEPORT

Bridge washed out

EDWARDS

Confederate line of march from EDWARDS

Stevenson's DIV

Bowen's DIV

Loring's DIV

MT. MORIAH

Davis

Baldwin

Rocky Bu.

Whittaker's Ford

Hall

Montgomery Bird

Fourteenmile Creek

N

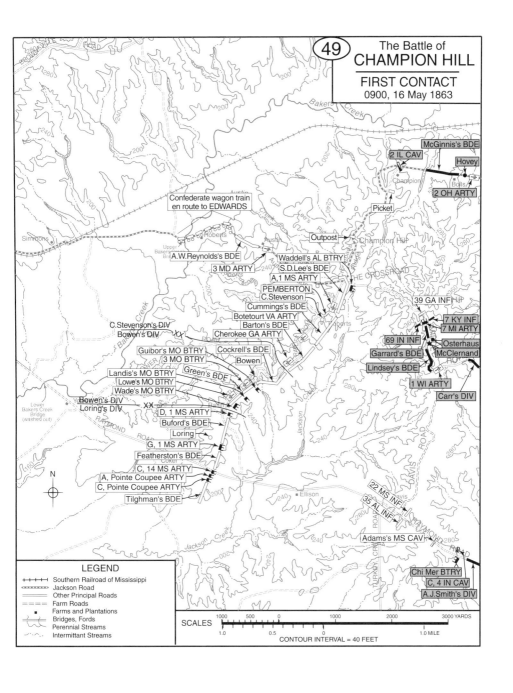

The Battle of **CHAMPION HILL**

49

FIRST CONTACT
0900, 16 May 1863

Confederate wagon train en route to EDWARDS

2 IL CAV

McGinnis's BDE

Hovey

2 OH ARTY

Picket

Outpost

A.W.Reynolds's BDE

3 MD ARTY

Waddell's AL BTRY

S.D.Lee's BDE

A,1 MS ARTY

PEMBERTON

C.Stevenson

Cummings's BDE

39 GA INF

Botetourt VA ARTY

Barton's BDE

C.Stevenson's DIV

Bowen's DIV

Cherokee GA ARTY

7 KY INF

7 MI ARTY

Guibor's MO BTRY

3 MO BTRY

Cockrell's BDE

Bowen

69 IN INF

Osterhaus

McClernand

Garrard's BDE

Landis's MO BTRY

Lowe's MO BTRY

Wade's MO BTRY

Green's BDE

Lindsey's BDE

1 WI ARTY

Bowen's DIV

Loring's DIV

D, 1 MS ARTY

Carr's DIV

Buford's BDE

Loring

G, 1 MS ARTY

Featherston's BDE

C, 14 MS ARTY

A, Pointe Coupee ARTY

C, Pointe Coupee ARTY

Tilghman's BDE

22 MS INF

35 AL INF

Ellison

Adams's MS CAV

N

Chi Mer BTRY

C, 4 IN CAV

A.J.Smith's DIV

LEGEND

+++++ Southern Railroad of Mississippi
======= Jackson Road
——— Other Principal Roads
==== Farm Roads
▪ Farms and Plantations
Bridges, Fords
Perennial Streams
Intermittant Streams

SCALES

1000 500 0 1000 2000 3000 YARDS

1.0 0.5 0 1.0 MILE

CONTOUR INTERVAL = 40 FEET

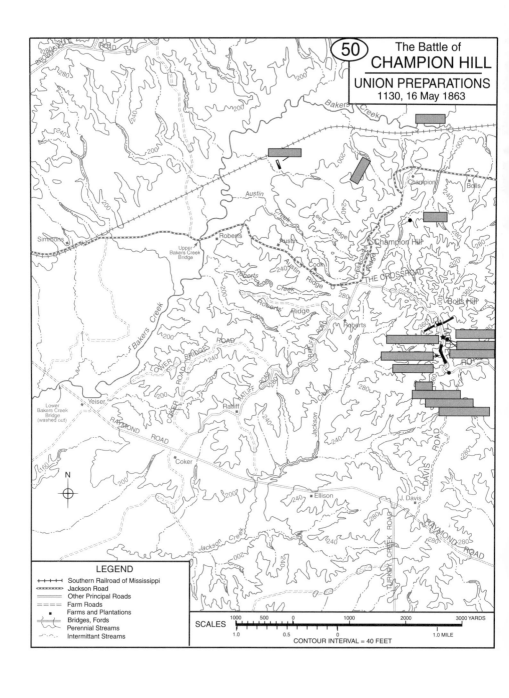

The Battle of
CHAMPION HILL
UNION PREPARATIONS
1130, 16 May 1863

50

LEGEND

+++++ Southern Railroad of Mississippi
Jackson Road
Other Principal Roads
==== Farm Roads
■ Farms and Plantations
Bridges, Fords
Perennial Streams
Intermittant Streams

SCALES

1000 500 0 1000 2000 3000 YARDS

1.0 0.5 0 1.0 MILE

CONTOUR INTERVAL = 40 FEET

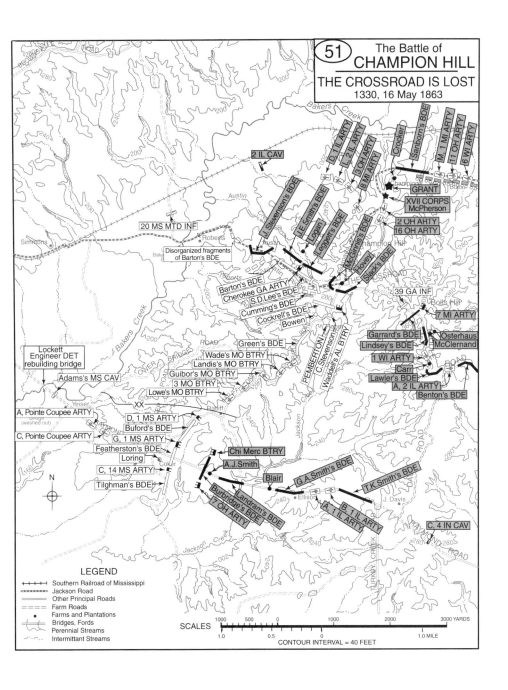

51 The Battle of
CHAMPION HILL

THE CROSSROAD IS LOST
1330, 16 May 1863

2 IL CAV

Crocker's BDE
Sanborn's BDE
M, 1 MI ARTY
11 OH ARTY
6 WI ARTY

D, 1 IL ARTY
L, 2 IL ARTY
3 OH ARTY
8 MI ARTY

GRANT

XVII CORPS
McPherson

2 OH ARTY
16 OH ARTY

20 MS MTD INF

J. Stevenson's BDE
I.E. Smith's BDE
Logan
Leggett's BDE
McGinnis's BDE
Hovey
Slack's BDE

Disorganized fragments
of Barton's BDE

39 GA INF

7 MI ARTY

Barton's BDE
Cherokee GA ARTY
S.D. Lee's BDE
Cumming's BDE
Cockrell's BDE
Bowen

Garrard's BDE
Lindsey's BDE
Osterhaus
McClernand
1 WI ARTY
Carr
A, 2 IL ARTY
Benton's BDE

Green's BDE

Lockett
Engineer DET
rebuilding bridge

Wade's MO BTRY
Landis's MO BTRY
Guibor's MO BTRY
3 MO BTRY
Lowe's MO BTRY

Adams's MS CAV

PEMBERTON
C. Stevenson
Waddell's AL BTRY

Lawler's BDE

Yeiser
XX
Ratliff

A, Pointe Coupee ARTY
(washed out)

C, Pointe Coupee ARTY

D, 1 MS ARTY
Buford's BDE
G, 1 MS ARTY

Chi Merc BTRY

Featherston's BDE
Loring
C, 14 MS ARTY

A.J. Smith

G.A. Smith's BDE
T.K. Smith's BDE

Blair

Tilghman's BDE

Burbridge's BDE
7 OH ARTY
Landram's BDE

Ellison

J. Davis

A, 1 IL ARTY
B, 1 IL ARTY

C, 4 IN CAV

N

LEGEND
Southern Railroad of Mississippi
Jackson Road
Other Principal Roads
Farm Roads
Farms and Plantations
Bridges, Fords
Perennial Streams
Intermittant Streams

SCALES

1000 500 0   1000   2000   3000 YARDS
1.0   0.5   0   1.0 MILE
CONTOUR INTERVAL = 40 FEET

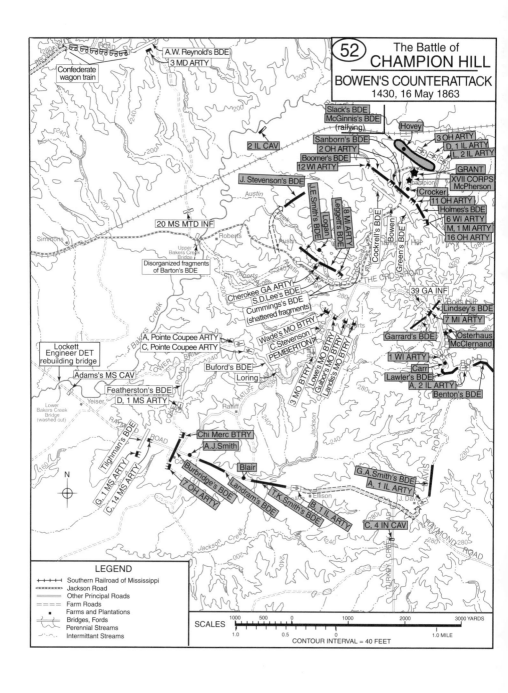

The Battle of
CHAMPION HILL
BOWEN'S COUNTERATTACK
1430, 16 May 1863

Confederate wagon train

A.W. Reynold's BDE
3 MD ARTY

Slack's BDE
McGinnis's BDE (rallying)
Hovey

2 IL CAV

Sanborn's BDE
2 OH ARTY
3 OH ARTY
D, 1 IL ARTY
L, 2 IL ARTY

Boomer's BDE
12 WI ARTY

J. Stevenson's BDE

Austin

GRANT
XVII CORPS
McPherson
Crocker

20 MS MTD INF

Roberts

J.E. Smith's BDE
Leggett's BDE
8 MI ARTY
Logan

11 OH ARTY
Holmes's BDE
6 WI ARTY
M, 1 MI ARTY
16 OH ARTY

Upper Bakers Creek Bridge

Cockrell's BDE
Bowen
Green's BDE

Disorganized fragments of Barton's BDE

THE CROSSROAD

39 GA INF

Cherokee GA ARTY
S.D.Lee's BDE
Cummings's BDE (shattered fragments)

Bolts Hill
Lindsey's BDE
7 MI ARTY

Lockett Engineer DET rebuilding bridge

A, Pointe Coupee ARTY
C, Pointe Coupee ARTY

Wade's MO BTRY
C.Stevenson
PEMBERTON

Garrard's BDE
Osterhaus
McClernand

3 MO BTRY
Lowe's MO BTRY
Guibor's MO BTRY
Landis's MO BTRY

1 WI ARTY
Carr
Lawler's BDE
A, 2 IL ARTY
Benton's BDE

Adams's MS CAV

Buford's BDE
Loring

Featherston's BDE
D, 1 MS ARTY

Lower Bakers Creek Bridge (washed out)

Yeiser

Ratliff

Chi Merc BTRY
A.J.Smith

Tilghman's BDE
G, 1 MS ARTY
C, 14 MS ARTY

Burbridge's BDE
7 OH ARTY
Landram's BDE
Blair
T.K. Smith's BDE
B, 1 IL ARTY

G.A. Smith's BDE
A, 1 IL ARTY

N

Ellison
J. Davis

C, 4 IN CAV

Jackson Creek

RAYMOND ROAD

LEGEND
|‖‖‖| Southern Railroad of Mississippi
Jackson Road
Other Principal Roads
Farm Roads
• Farms and Plantations
Bridges, Fords
Perennial Streams
Intermittant Streams

SCALES

1000   500   0   1000   2000   3000 YARDS

1.0   0.5   0   1.0 MILE

CONTOUR INTERVAL = 40 FEET

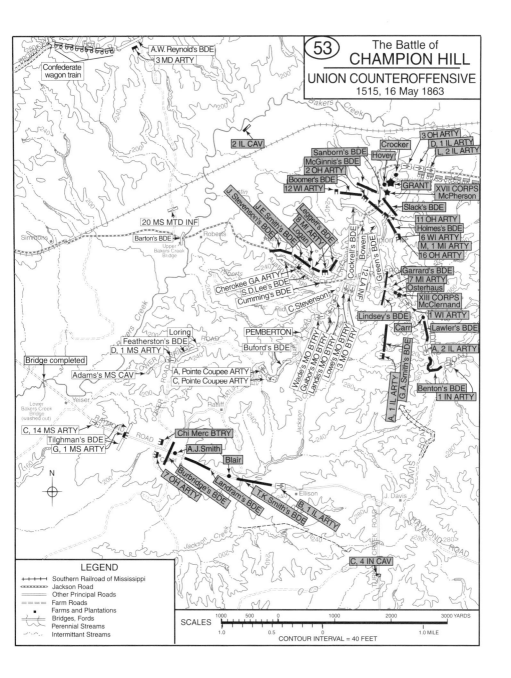

Confederate wagon train

A.W. Reynold's BDE
3 MD ARTY

54 The Battle of
CHAMPION HILL
UNION COUNTEROFFENSIVE
1515, 16 May 1863

2 IL CAV

3 OH ARTY
D, 1 IL ARTY
L, 2 IL ARTY

Crocker
Hovey

Sanborn's BDE
McGinnis's BDE
2 OH ARTY
Boomer's BDE
12 WI ARTY

GRANT
XVII CORPS
McPherson

Slack's BDE

11 OH ARTY
Holmes's BDE
6 WI ARTY
M, 1 MI ARTY
16 OH ARTY

20 MS MTD INF

J. Stevenson's BDE

J.E. Smith's BDE

Leggett's BDE
8 MI ARTY
Logan

Barton's BDE

Upper
Bakers Creek
Bridge

Simmons

Roberts

Cockrell's BDE

Bowen

Green's BDE

Garrard's BDE
7 MI ARTY
Osterhaus

Cherokee GA ARTY
S.D.Lee's BDE
Cumming's BDE

C. Stevenson

XIII CORPS
McClernand

1 WI ARTY

Lindsey's BDE

Carr

Lawler's BDE

Loring
Featherston's BDE
D, 1 MS ARTY

PEMBERTON

Buford's BDE

Wade's MO BTRY
Guibor's MO BTRY
Landis's MO BTRY
Lowe's MO BTRY
3 MO BTRY

A, 2 IL ARTY

Bridge completed

Adams's MS CAV

A, Pointe Coupee ARTY
C, Pointe Coupee ARTY

Yeiser

Ratliff

Benton's BDE
1 IN ARTY

Lower
Bakers Creek
Bridge
(washed out)

C, 14 MS ARTY
Tilghman's BDE
G, 1 MS ARTY

Chi Merc BTRY

A.J.Smith

Blair

Ellison

J. Davis

C, 4 IN CAV

Burbridge's BDE

Landram's BDE

T.K. Smith's BDE

B, 1 IL ARTY

Jackson Creek

7 OH ARTY

N

LEGEND
Southern Railroad of Mississippi
Jackson Road
Other Principal Roads
Farm Roads
Farms and Plantations
Bridges, Fords
Perennial Streams
Intermittant Streams

SCALES

1000   500   0   1000   2000   3000 YARDS
1.0   0.5   0   1.0 MILE
CONTOUR INTERVAL = 40 FEET

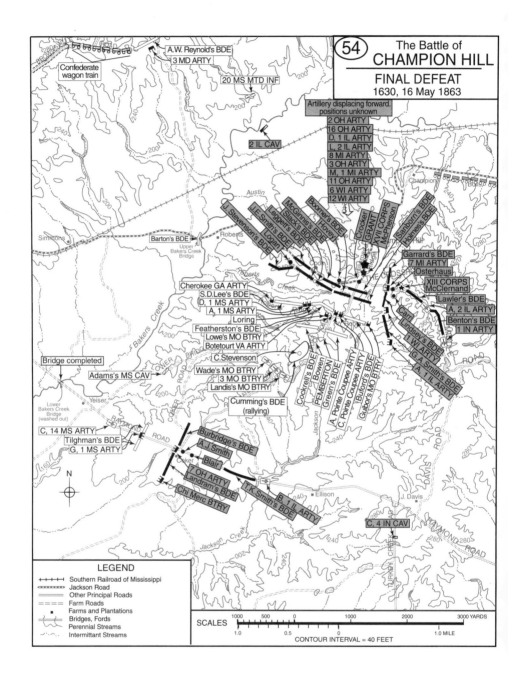

The Battle of
CHAMPION HILL
FINAL DEFEAT
1630, 16 May 1863

A.W. Reynold's BDE
3 MD ARTY
Confederate wagon train
20 MS MTD INF
2 IL CAV

Artillery displacing forward, positions unknown
2 OH ARTY
16 OH ARTY
D, 1 IL ARTY
L, 2 IL ARTY
8 MI ARTY
3 OH ARTY
M, 1 MI ARTY
11 OH ARTY
6 WI ARTY
12 WI ARTY

Austin

Barton's BDE
Upper Bakers Creek Bridge
Simmons
Roberts

J. Stevenson's BDE
J.E. Smith's BDE
Leggett's BDE
Slack's BDE
Logan
McGinnis's BDE
Boomer's BDE
Hovey
Crocker
GRANT
XVII CORPS
McPherson
Sanborn's BDE
Holmes's BDE

Garrard's BDE
7 MI ARTY
Osterhaus
XIII CORPS
McClernand

Cherokee GA ARTY
S.D.Lee's BDE
D, 1 MS ARTY
A, 1 MS ARTY
Loring
Featherston's BDE
Lowe's MO BTRY
Botetourt VA ARTY

Lawler's BDE
A, 2 IL ARTY
Benton's BDE
1 IN ARTY

Carr
Lindsey's BDE
1 W ARTY
G,A.Smith's BDE
A, 1 IL ARTY

C.Stevenson
Wade's MO BTRY
3 MO BTRY
Landis's MO BTRY

Cockrell's BDE
Bowen
Green's BDE
A. Pointe Coupee ARTY
C, Pointe Coupee ARTY
Buford's BDE
Guibor's MO BTRY
PEMBERTON

Adams's MS CAV
Bridge completed
LOWER Bridge
COKER ROAD

Cumming's BDE
(rallying)

Lower Bakers Creek Bridge (washed out)
Yeiser

C, 14 MS ARTY
Tilghman's BDE
G, 1 MS ARTY
RAYMOND ROAD

Burbridge's BDE
A.J. Smith
Blair
7 OH ARTY
Landram's BDE
Chi Merc BTRY
T.K. Smith's BDE
B, 1 IL ARTY

Ellison
J. Davis
C, 4 IN CAV
RAYMOND ROAD

N

Jackson Creek

LEGEND
Southern Railroad of Mississippi
Jackson Road
Other Principal Roads
Farm Roads
Farms and Plantations
Bridges, Fords
Perennial Streams
Intermittant Streams

SCALES
1000   500   0   1000   2000   3000 YARDS
1.0   0.5   0   1.0 MILE
CONTOUR INTERVAL = 40 FEET

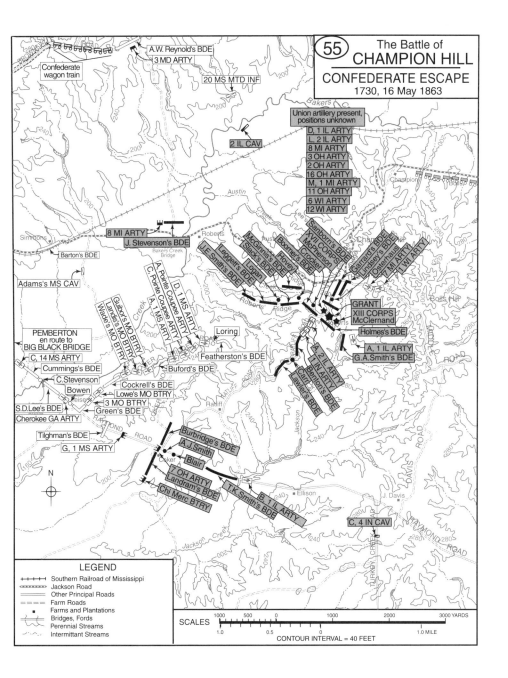

The Battle of **CHAMPION HILL**
CONFEDERATE ESCAPE
1730, 16 May 1863

55

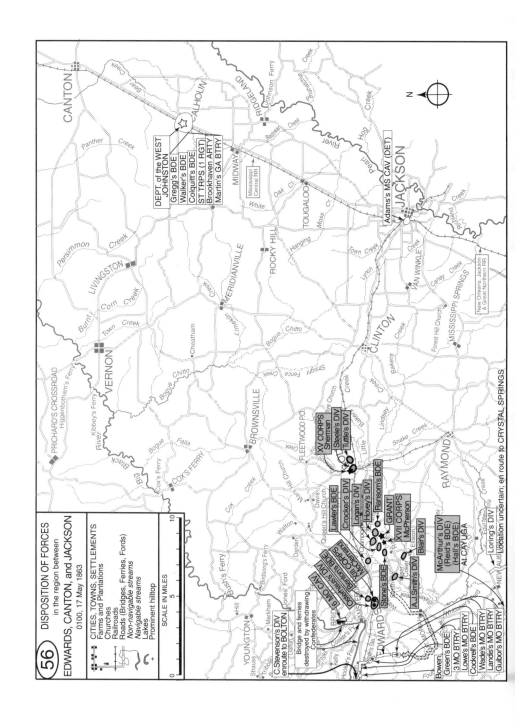

56 DISPOSITION OF FORCES
in the region between
EDWARDS, CANTON, and JACKSON
0100, 17 May 1863

CITIES, TOWNS, SETTLEMENTS
Farms and Plantations
Churches
Railroads
Roads (Bridges, Ferries, Fords)
Non-navigable streams
Navigable streams
Lakes
Prominent hilltop

SCALE IN MILES
0   5   10

CANTON

Bear Creek

Panther Creek

CALHOUN

RIDGELAND

Johnson Ferry

DEPT. of the WEST
JOHNSTON
Gregg's BDE
Walker's BDE
Colquitt's BDE
ST TRPS (1 RGT)
Brookhaven ARTY
Martin's GA BTRY

MIDWAY

Basnet Creek

Mississippi
Central RR

Oak Cr.

White

Pearl River

Hog Creek

Persimmon Creek

LIVINGSTON

Corn Creek

Burnt Cr.

Town Creek

VERNON

Kibbey's Ferry

Higginbotham's Ferry
PRICHARD'S CROSSROAD

Big Black River

Cheatham

Bogue Chitto

BROWNSVILLE

Bogue Falia

Cox's Ferry

COX'S FERRY

Cox Creek

Marsh Hill Church

MERIDIANVILLE

ROCKY HILL

Hanging Creek

Lynn

Town Creek

Moss. Cr.

TOUGALOO

JACKSON

Adams's MS CAV (DET)

VAN WINKLE

Caney Creek

Richland Creek

New Orleans, Jackson
& Great Northern RR

MISSISSIPPI SPRINGS

Forest Hill Church

CLINTON

Bakers Creek

Lindsey Creek

Straight Fence Creek

Queen's Hill Church

Baker's Creek

Little Creek

FLEETWOOD P.O.

XV CORPS
Sherman
Steele's DIV
Tuttle's DIV

Ransom's BDE

Lawler's BDE
Crocker's DIV
Logan's DIV
Hovey's DIV

GRANT
XVII CORPS
McPHERSON

Blair's DIV

RAYMOND

Snake Creek

Davis

Walton

Cox Creek

Queen's Hill Church

McArthur's DIV
(Reid's BDE)
(Hall's BDE)
At CAYUGA

Ellison

Stocket

Coker

Smith

Carter's

Baker's Ck.

Eauffidle Creek

Loring's DIV
NEW AUB (location uncertain; en route to CRYSTAL SPRINGS

III CORPS
McClernand
Osterhaus's DIV

Bolton

Walnut

Stone's BDE

A.J.Smith's DIV

6 MO CAV

BRIDGES

C.Stevenson's DIV
enroute to BOLTON

Bridge and ferries
destroyed by withdrawing
Confederates

Jones's Ford

Darden

Kelly

Coateau's Ferry

Hooker's Ferry

EDWARDS

Bowen
Green's BDE
3 MO BTRY
Lowe's MO BTRY
Wade's MO BTRY
Landis's MO BTRY
Guibor's MO BTRY

Cockrell's BDE

YOUNGSTON

Strauss

Markham

Bush's Ferry

Birdsong's Ferry

Hill

N

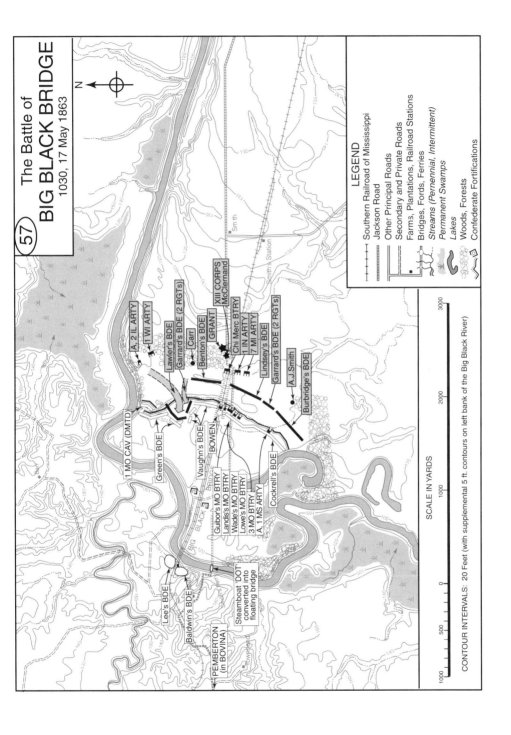

57 The Battle of
BIG BLACK BRIDGE
1030, 17 May 1863

LEGEND

Southern Railroad of Mississippi
Jackson Road
Other Principal Roads
Secondary and Private Roads
Farms, Plantations, Railroad Stations
Bridges, Fords, Ferries
Streams (Perennial, Intermittent)
Permanent Swamps
Lakes
Woods, Forests
Confederate Fortifications

SCALE IN YARDS

1000   500   0   1000   2000   3000

CONTOUR INTERVALS: 20 Feet (with supplemental 5 ft. contours on left bank of the Big Black River)

A, 2 IL ARTY
1 WI ARTY
Lawler's BDE
Garrard's BDE (2 RGTs)
Carr
Benton's BDE
GRANT
XIII CORPS
McClernand
Chi Merc BTRY
1 IN ARTY
7 MI ARTY
Lindsey's BDE
Garrard's BDE (2 RGTs)
A.J.Smith
Burbridge's BDE

1 MO CAV (DMTD)
Green's BDE
Vaughn's BDE
BOWEN
Guibor's MO BTRY
Landis's MO BTRY
Wade's MO BTRY
Lowe's MO BTRY
3 MO BTRY
A, 1 MS ARTY
Cockrell's BDE

Lee's BDE
Baldwin's BDE
PEMBERTON
(in BOVINA)
Steamboat "DOT"
converted into
floating bridge

Smth
Smith's Station

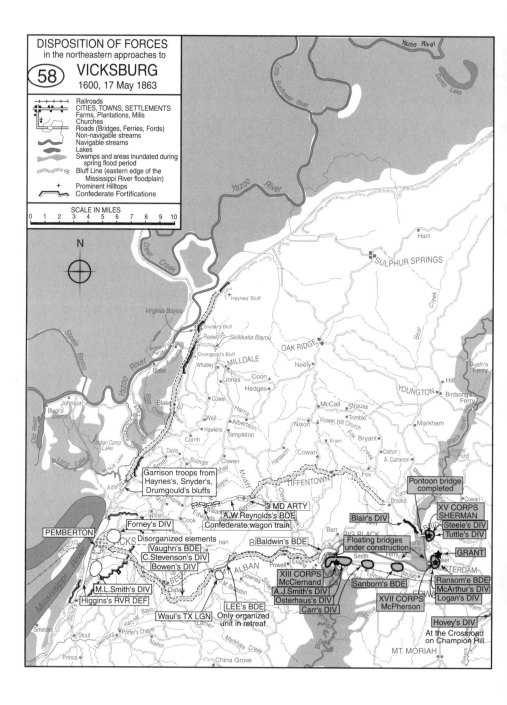

DISPOSITION OF FORCES
in the northeastern approaches to

(58) VICKSBURG
1600, 17 May 1863

Railroads
CITIES, TOWNS, SETTLEMENTS
Farms, Plantations, Mills
Churches
Roads (Bridges, Ferries, Fords)
Non-navigable streams
Navigable streams
Lakes
Swamps and areas inundated during
   spring flood period
Bluff Line (eastern edge of the
   Mississippi River floodplain)
Prominent Hilltops
Confederate Fortifications

SCALE IN MILES
0 1 2 3 4 5 6 7 8 9 10

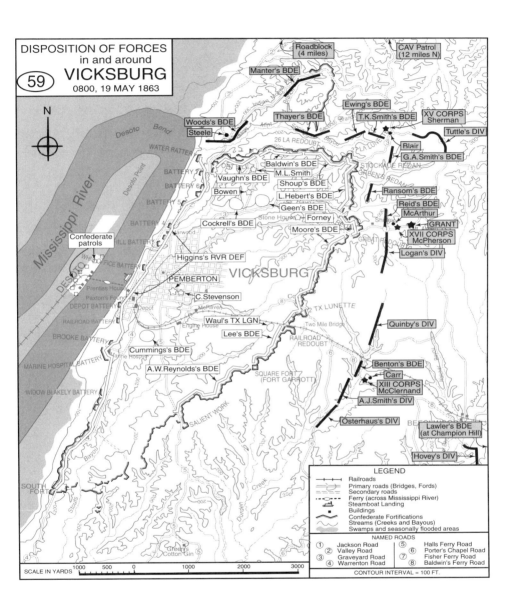

DISPOSITION OF FORCES
in and around
(59) VICKSBURG
0800, 19 MAY 1863

N

Roadblock (4 miles)
CAV Patrol (12 miles N)
Manter's BDE
Ewing's BDE
Thayer's BDE
T.K.Smith's BDE
XV CORPS Sherman
Tuttle's DIV
Woods's BDE
Steele
26 LA REDOUBT
Blair
G.A.Smith's BDE
STOCKADE REDAN
Baldwin's BDE
M.L.Smith
GREEN'S REDAN
Vaughn's BDE
Shoup's BDE
Ransom's BDE
Bowen
L.Hebert's BDE
Reid's BDE
Geen's BDE
McArthur
Cockrell's BDE
Stone House
Forney
GRANT
Moore's BDE
XVII CORPS McPherson
Confederate patrols
Logan's DIV
Higgins's RVR DEF
VICKSBURG
PEMBERTON
C.Stevenson
McRaven
Waul's TX LGN
Quinby's DIV
Engine House
Lee's BDE
RAILROAD REDOUBT
Cummings's BDE
Benton's BDE
A.W.Reynolds's BDE
Carr
SQUARE FORT (FORT GARROTT)
XIII CORPS McClernand
A.J.Smith's DIV
SALIENT WORK
Osterhaus's DIV
Lawler's BDE (at Champion Hill)
Hovey's DIV

Mississippi River
Desoto Bend
WATER BATTERY
BATTERY 7
BATTERY 6
Desoto Point
BATTERY 5
BATTERY 4
HILL BATTERY
OFFICE BATTERY
DESOTO
Prentiss House
Paxton's Pound
DEPOT BATTERY
Depot
RAILROAD BATTERY
BROOKE BATTERY
MARINE HOSPITAL BATTERY
Marine Hospital
WIDOW BLAKELY BATTERY
SOUTH FORT
Green's Cotton Gin

2 TX LUNETTE
Two Mile Bridge
GREAT REDOUBT

LEGEND
Railroads
Primary roads (Bridges, Fords)
Secondary roads
Ferry (across Mississippi River)
Steamboat Landing
Buildings
Confederate Fortifications
Streams (Creeks and Bayous)
Swamps and seasonally flooded areas

NAMED ROADS
① Jackson Road   ⑤ Halls Ferry Road
② Valley Road   ⑥ Porter's Chapel Road
③ Graveyard Road   ⑦ Fisher Ferry Road
④ Warrenton Road   ⑧ Baldwin's Ferry Road

SCALE IN YARDS 1000 500 0 1000 2000 3000
CONTOUR INTERVAL = 100 FT.

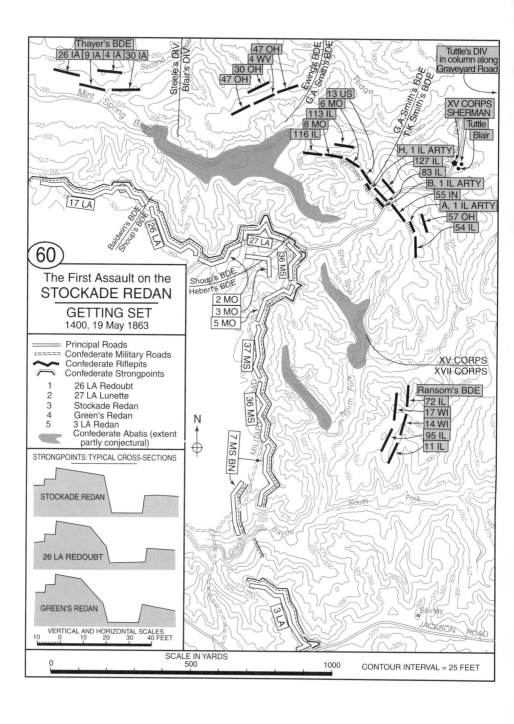

Thayer's BDE
26 IA | 9 IA | 4 IA | 30 IA

47 OH
4 WV
30 OH
47 OH

Tuttle's DIV
in column along
Graveyard Road

13 US
6 MO
113 IL
8 MO
116 IL

XV CORPS
SHERMAN
Tuttle
Blair

H, 1 IL ARTY
127 IL
83 IL
B, 1 IL ARTY
55 IN
A, 1 IL ARTY
57 OH
54 IL

17 LA

26 LA

27 LA

36 MS

Shoup's BDE
Hebert's BDE

2 MO
3 MO
5 MO

37 MS

36 MS

XV CORPS
XVII CORPS

Ransom's BDE
72 IL
17 WI
14 WI
95 IL
11 IL

7 MS BN

3 LA

60

The First Assault on the
STOCKADE REDAN
GETTING SET
1400, 19 May 1863

	Principal Roads
	Confederate Military Roads
	Confederate Riflepits
	Confederate Strongpoints
1	26 LA Redoubt
2	27 LA Lunette
3	Stockade Redan
4	Green's Redan
5	3 LA Redan
	Confederate Abatis (extent partly conjectural)

STRONGPOINTS: TYPICAL CROSS-SECTIONS

STOCKADE REDAN

26 LA REDOUBT

GREEN'S REDAN

VERTICAL AND HORIZONTAL SCALES
10   0   10   20   30   40 FEET

N

SCALE IN YARDS
0   500   1000   CONTOUR INTERVAL = 25 FEET

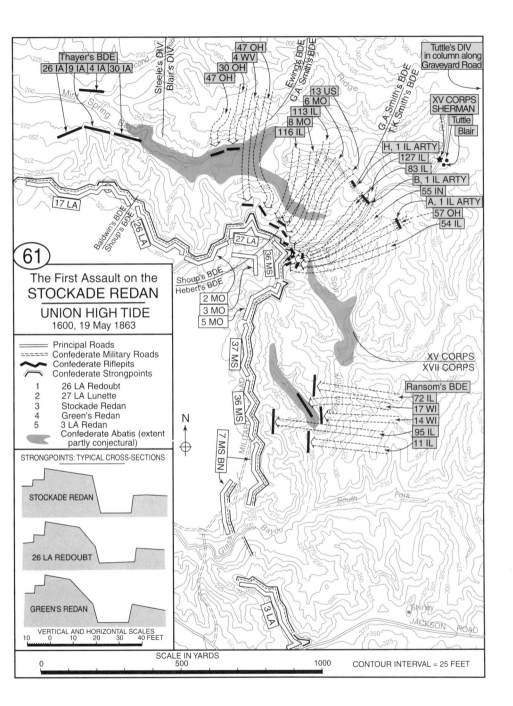

The First Assault on the
STOCKADE REDAN

UNION HIGH TIDE

1600, 19 May 1863

Principal Roads
Confederate Military Roads
Confederate Riflepits
Confederate Strongpoints

1 26 LA Redoubt
2 27 LA Lunette
3 Stockade Redan
4 Green's Redan
5 3 LA Redan
   Confederate Abatis (extent partly conjectural)

STRONGPOINTS: TYPICAL CROSS-SECTIONS

STOCKADE REDAN

26 LA REDOUBT

GREEN'S REDAN

VERTICAL AND HORIZONTAL SCALES
10   0   10   20   30   40 FEET

N

SCALE IN YARDS
0   500   1000

CONTOUR INTERVAL = 25 FEET

Thayer's BDE
26 IA 9 IA 4 IA 30 IA

Steele's DIV

Blair's DIV

47 OH
4 WV
30 OH
47 OH

Ewing's BDE
G.A. Smith's BDE

Ridge

Tuttle's DIV in column along Graveyard Road

13 US
6 MO
113 IL
8 MO
116 IL

G.A. Smith's BDE
T.K. Smith's BDE

XV CORPS
SHERMAN
Tuttle
Blair

H, 1 IL ARTY
127 IL
83 IL
B, 1 IL ARTY
55 IN
A, 1 IL ARTY
57 OH
54 IL

Mint
Spring
Bayou

17 LA

Baldwin's BDE
Shoup's BDE

26 LA

27 LA

36 MS

Shoup's BDE
Hebert's BDE

2 MO
3 MO
5 MO

37 MS

36 MS

7 MS BN

Spur

XV CORPS
XVII CORPS

Ransom's BDE
72 IL
17 WI
14 WI
95 IL
11 IL

South   Fork

Glass   Bayou

3 LA

Skiney

JACKSON   ROAD

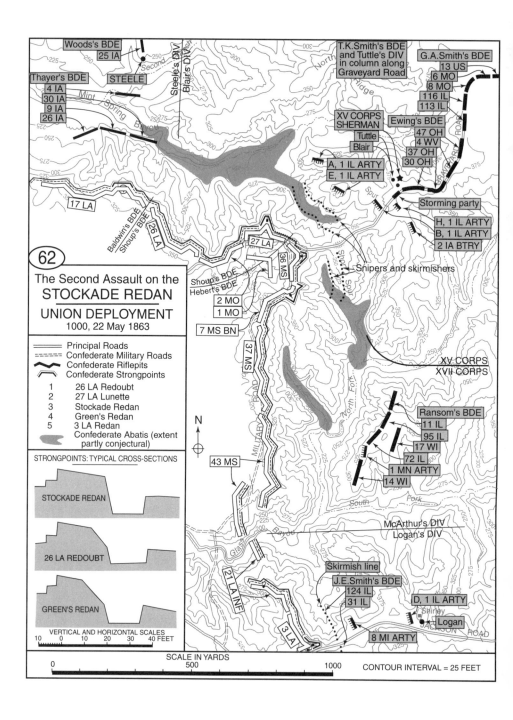

Woods's BDE
25 IA

Thayer's BDE
4 IA
30 IA
9 IA
26 IA

STEELE

T.K.Smith's BDE
and Tuttle's DIV
in column along
Graveyard Road

G.A.Smith's BDE
13 US
6 MO
8 MO
116 IL
113 IL

XV CORPS
SHERMAN
Tuttle
Blair

Ewing's BDE
47 OH
4 WV
37 OH
30 OH

A, 1 IL ARTY
E, 1 IL ARTY

Storming party

H, 1 IL ARTY
B, 1 IL ARTY
2 IA BTRY

17 LA

Baldwin's BDE
Shoup's BDE
26 LA

27 LA

36 MS

Snipers and skirmishers

Shoup's BDE
Hebert's BDE

2 MO
1 MO

7 MS BN

37 MS

XV CORPS
XVII CORPS

Ransom's BDE
11 IL
95 IL
17 WI
72 IL
1 MN ARTY
14 WI

43 MS

McArthur's DIV
Logan's DIV

Skirmish line
J.E.Smith's BDE
124 IL
31 IL

D, 1 IL ARTY

Logan

21 LA INF

3 LA

8 MI ARTY

62

The Second Assault on the
STOCKADE REDAN
UNION DEPLOYMENT
1000, 22 May 1863

=== Principal Roads
------ Confederate Military Roads
〰 Confederate Riflepits
⌒ Confederate Strongpoints
1   26 LA Redoubt
2   27 LA Lunette
3   Stockade Redan
4   Green's Redan
5   3 LA Redan
     Confederate Abatis (extent
     partly conjectural)

STRONGPOINTS: TYPICAL CROSS-SECTIONS

STOCKADE REDAN

26 LA REDOUBT

GREEN'S REDAN

VERTICAL AND HORIZONTAL SCALES
10   0   10   20   30   40 FEET

N

SCALE IN YARDS
0   500   1000

CONTOUR INTERVAL = 25 FEET

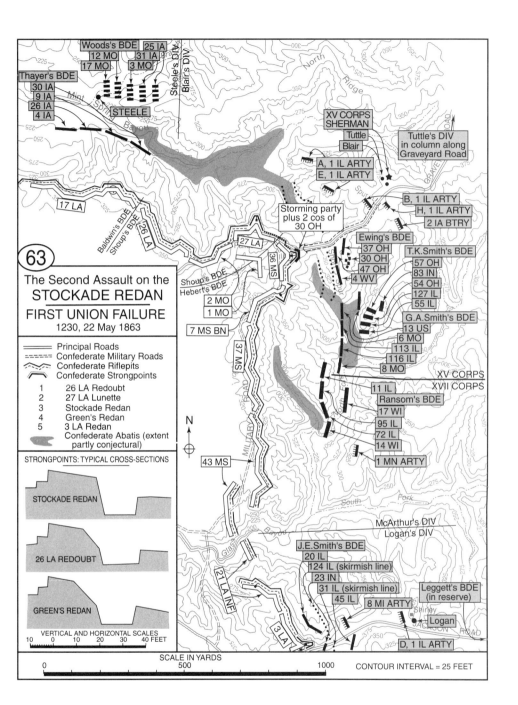

Woods's BDE — 25 IA / 12 MO / 31 IA / 17 MO / 3 MO

Thayer's BDE — 30 IA / 9 IA / 26 IA / 4 IA

Mint Spring Bayou

STEELE

Steele's DIV

Blair's DIV

North Ridge

XV CORPS
SHERMAN
Tuttle
Blair

Tuttle's DIV
in column along
Graveyard Road

GRAVEYARD ROAD

A, 1 IL ARTY
E, 1 IL ARTY

B, 1 IL ARTY
H, 1 IL ARTY
2 IA BTRY

17 LA

Baldwin's BDE

Shoup's BDE

26 LA

27 LA

36 MS

Storming party
plus 2 cos of
30 OH

Ewing's BDE
37 OH / 30 OH / 47 OH / 4 WV

T.K.Smith's BDE
57 OH / 83 IN / 54 OH / 127 IL / 55 IL

Shoup's BDE
Hebert's BDE

2 MO
1 MO

7 MS BN

37 MS

G.A.Smith's BDE
13 US / 6 MO / 113 IL / 116 IL
8 MO

XV CORPS
XVII CORPS

11 IL
Ransom's BDE
17 WI
95 IL
72 IL
14 WI

1 MN ARTY

43 MS

MILITARY ROAD

South Fork

McArthur's DIV
Logan's DIV

21 LA INF

Glass Bayou

J.E.Smith's BDE
20 IL
124 IL (skirmish line)
23 IN
31 IL (skirmish line)
45 IL   8 MI ARTY

Leggett's BDE
(in reserve)

Shirley

Logan

JACKSON ROAD

3 LA

D, 1 IL ARTY

63

The Second Assault on the
STOCKADE REDAN
FIRST UNION FAILURE
1230, 22 May 1863

═══ Principal Roads
----- Confederate Military Roads
⌇⌇⌇ Confederate Riflepits
⌄⌄⌄ Confederate Strongpoints

1   26 LA Redoubt
2   27 LA Lunette
3   Stockade Redan
4   Green's Redan
5   3 LA Redan
▨   Confederate Abatis (extent
     partly conjectural)

STRONGPOINTS: TYPICAL CROSS-SECTIONS

STOCKADE REDAN

26 LA REDOUBT

GREEN'S REDAN

VERTICAL AND HORIZONTAL SCALES
10   0   10   20   30   40 FEET

N

SCALE IN YARDS
0   500   1000

CONTOUR INTERVAL = 25 FEET

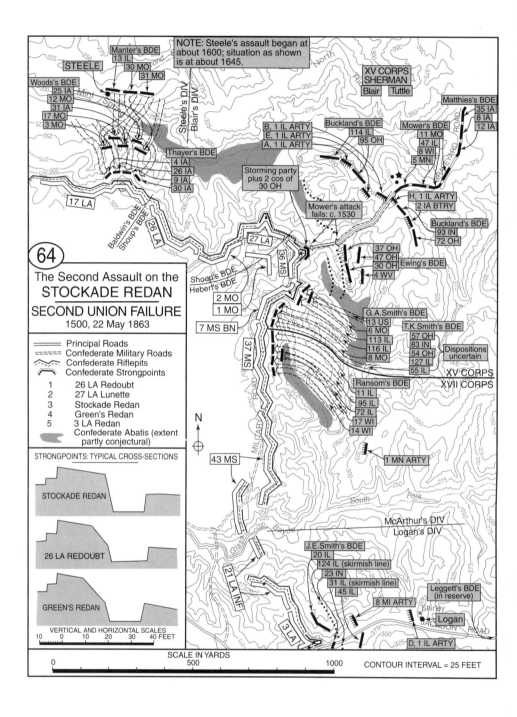

NOTE: Steele's assault began at about 1600; situation as shown is at about 1645.

STEELE

Manter's BDE
13 IL
30 MO
31 MO

Woods's BDE
25 IA
12 MO
31 IA
17 MO
3 MO

Steele's DIV
Blair's DIV

XV CORPS
SHERMAN
Blair   Tuttle

Matthies's BDE
35 IA
8 IA
12 IA

Thayer's BDE
4 IA
26 IA
9 IA
30 IA

17 LA

Buckland's BDE
114 IL
95 OH

Mower's BDE
11 MO
47 IL
8 WI
5 MN

B, 1 IL ARTY
E, 1 IL ARTY
A, 1 IL ARTY

Storming party
plus 2 cos of
30 OH

Mower's attack
fails: c. 1530

H, 1 IL ARTY
2 IA BTRY

Buckland's BDE
93 IN
72 OH

Baldwin's BDE
Shoup's BDE

26 LA

27 LA

36 MS

37 OH
47 OH
30 OH
4 WV

Ewing's BDE

64

The Second Assault on the
STOCKADE REDAN
SECOND UNION FAILURE
1500, 22 May 1863

Shoup's BDE
Hebert's BDE

2 MO
1 MO

7 MS BN

37 MS

G.A.Smith's BDE
13 US
6 MO
113 IL
116 IL
8 MO

T.K.Smith's BDE
57 OH
83 IN
54 OH
127 IL
55 IL

Dispositions
uncertain

XV CORPS
XVII CORPS

Principal Roads
Confederate Military Roads
Confederate Riflepits
Confederate Strongpoints
1   26 LA Redoubt
2   27 LA Lunette
3   Stockade Redan
4   Green's Redan
5   3 LA Redan
    Confederate Abatis (extent
    partly conjectural)

Ransom's BDE
11 IL
95 IL
72 IL
17 WI
14 WI

STRONGPOINTS: TYPICAL CROSS-SECTIONS

STOCKADE REDAN

26 LA REDOUBT

GREEN'S REDAN

VERTICAL AND HORIZONTAL SCALES
10   0   10   20   30   40 FEET

1 MN ARTY

N

43 MS

McArthur's DIV
Logan's DIV

J.E.Smith's BDE
20 IL
124 IL (skirmish line)
23 IN
31 IL (skirmish line)
45 IL

8 MI ARTY

Leggett's BDE
(in reserve)

Logan

21 LA INF

3 LA

D, 1 IL ARTY

SCALE IN YARDS
0   500   1000

CONTOUR INTERVAL = 25 FEET

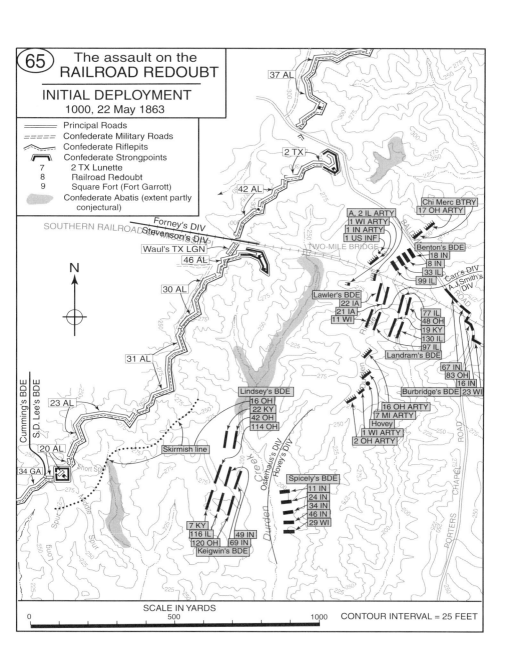

65 The assault on the
RAILROAD REDOUBT
INITIAL DEPLOYMENT
1000, 22 May 1863

Principal Roads
Confederate Military Roads
Confederate Riflepits
Confederate Strongpoints
7   2 TX Lunette
8   Railroad Redoubt
9   Square Fort (Fort Garrott)
Confederate Abatis (extent partly
   conjectural)

N

SCALE IN YARDS
0   500   1000   CONTOUR INTERVAL = 25 FEET

37 AL
2 TX
42 AL
Chi Merc BTRY
17 OH ARTY
A, 2 IL ARTY
1 WI ARTY
1 IN ARTY
1 US INF
Benton's BDE
18 IN
8 IN
33 IL
99 IL
Carr's DIV
A.J.Smith's DIV
Lawler's BDE
22 IA
21 IA
11 WI
77 IL
48 OH
19 KY
130 IL
97 IL
Landram's BDE
67 IN
83 OH
16 IN
Burbridge's BDE 23 WI
16 OH ARTY
7 MI ARTY
Hovey
1 WI ARTY
2 OH ARTY
Lindsey's BDE
16 OH
22 KY
42 OH
114 OH
Spicely's BDE
11 IN
24 IN
34 IN
46 IN
29 WI
Skirmish line
7 KY
116 IL
120 OH
49 IN
69 IN
Keigwin's BDE
Osterhaus's DIV
Hovey's DIV
Creek
Durden
SOUTHERN RAILROAD
Forney's DIV
Stevenson's DIV
Waul's TX LGN
46 AL
30 AL
31 AL
23 AL
20 AL
34 GA
Cumming's BDE
S.D. Lee's BDE
Short Spur
Middle Spur
Long Spur
TWO-MILE BRIDGE

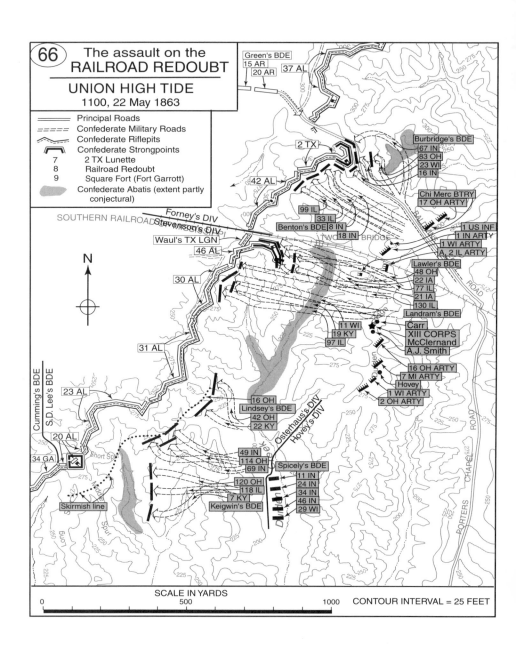

66 **The assault on the**
RAILROAD REDOUBT

UNION HIGH TIDE
1100, 22 May 1863

════	Principal Roads
═ ═ ═	Confederate Military Roads
∿∿∿	Confederate Riflepits
⌐¬	Confederate Strongpoints
7	2 TX Lunette
8	Railroad Redoubt
9	Square Fort (Fort Garrott)
▓	Confederate Abatis (extent partly conjectural)

Green's BDE
15 AR
20 AR
37 AL

2 TX

42 AL

Burbridge's BDE
67 IN
83 OH
23 WI
16 IN

Chi Merc BTRY
17 OH ARTY

Forney's DIV
SOUTHERN RAILROAD
Stevenson's DIV
Waul's TX LGN
46 AL

99 IL
33 IL
Benton's BDE 8 IN
18 IN

1 US INF
1 IN ARTY
1 WI ARTY
A, 2 IL ARTY

30 AL

Lawler's BDE
48 OH
22 IA
77 IL
21 IA
130 IL
Landram's BDE

31 AL

11 WI
19 KY
97 IL

Carr
XIII CORPS
McClernand
A.J. Smith

16 OH ARTY
7 MI ARTY
Hovey
1 WI ARTY
2 OH ARTY

23 AL

16 OH
Lindsey's BDE
42 OH
22 OH

Osterhaus's DIV
Hovey's DIV

Cumming's BDE
S.D. Lee's BDE
20 AL
34 GA
Short Spur

49 IN
114 OH
69 IN

Spicely's BDE
11 IN
24 IN
34 IN
46 IN
29 WI

120 OH
118 IL
7 KY
Keigwin's BDE

Skirmish line

N

SCALE IN YARDS

0   500   1000   CONTOUR INTERVAL = 25 FEET

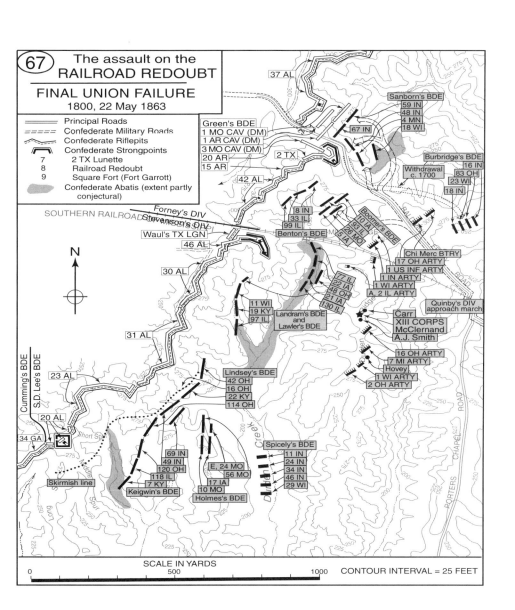

67 The assault on the
RAILROAD REDOUBT

FINAL UNION FAILURE
1800, 22 May 1863

Principal Roads
Confederate Military Roads
Confederate Riflepits
Confederate Strongpoints
7   2 TX Lunette
8   Railroad Redoubt
9   Square Fort (Fort Garrott)
Confederate Abatis (extent partly
    conjectural)

37 AL

Sanborn's BDE
59 IN
48 IN
4 MN
18 WI

Green's BDE
1 MO CAV (DM)
1 AR CAV (DM)
3 MO CAV (DM)
20 AR
15 AR

67 IN

2 TX

Burbridge's BDE
16 IN
83 OH
23 WI
18 IN

Withdrawal
c. 1700

42 AL

Forney's DIV
SOUTHERN RAILROAD   Stevenson's DIV

Waul's TX LGN

46 AL

30 AL

Benton's BDE

8 IN
33 IL
99 IL

Boomer's BDE
10 IA
93 IL
26 MO
5 IA

Chi Merc BTRY
17 OH ARTY
1 US INF ARTY
1 IN ARTY
1 WI ARTY
A, 2 IL ARTY

77 IL
22 IA
48 OH
21 IA
130 IL

N

11 WI
19 KY
97 IL

Landram's BDE
and
Lawler's BDE

Quinby's DIV
approach march

Carr
XIII CORPS
McClernand
A.J. Smith

31 AL

16 OH ARTY
7 MI ARTY
Hovey
1 WI ARTY
2 OH ARTY

Cumming's BDE
S.D. Lee's BDE

23 AL

Lindsey's BDE
42 OH
16 OH
22 KY
114 OH

20 AL

34 GA

Short Sp.

Skirmish line

Spicely's BDE
11 IN
24 IN
34 IN
46 IN
29 WI

69 IN
49 IN
120 OH
118 IL
7 KY

E, 24 MO
56 MO

17 IA
10 MO

Keigwin's BDE

Holmes's BDE

SCALE IN YARDS

0   500   1000   CONTOUR INTERVAL = 25 FEET

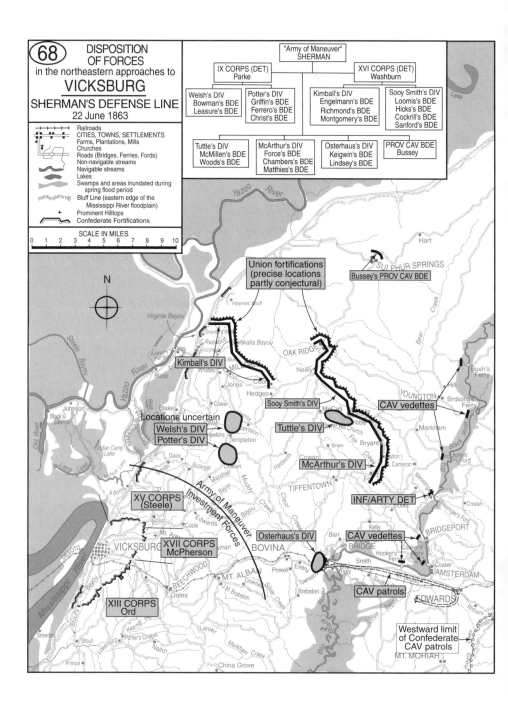

68 DISPOSITION OF FORCES in the northeastern approaches to **VICKSBURG**
SHERMAN'S DEFENSE LINE
22 June 1863

Railroads
CITIES, TOWNS, SETTLEMENTS
Farms, Plantations, Mills
Churches
Roads (Bridges, Ferries, Fords)
Non-navigable streams
Navigable streams
Lakes
Swamps and areas inundated during spring flood period
Bluff Line (eastern edge of the Mississippi River floodplain)
Prominent Hilltops
Confederate Fortifications

SCALE IN MILES
0 1 2 3 4 5 6 7 8 9 10

"Army of Maneuver" SHERMAN

IX CORPS (DET) Parke

XVI CORPS (DET) Washburn

Welsh's DIV
Bowman's BDE
Leasure's BDE

Potter's DIV
Griffin's BDE
Ferrero's BDE
Christ's BDE

Kimball's DIV
Engelmann's BDE
Richmond's BDE
Montgomery's BDE

Sooy Smith's DIV
Loomis's BDE
Hicks's BDE
Cockrill's BDE
Sanford's BDE

Tuttle's DIV
McMillen's BDE
Woods's BDE

McArthur's DIV
Force's BDE
Chambers's BDE
Matthies's BDE

Osterhaus's DIV
Keigwin's BDE
Lindsey's BDE

PROV CAV BDE
Bussey

N

Appendix
Command Structures of the Federal and Confederate Forces

High Command Structures of the Civil War, 1863

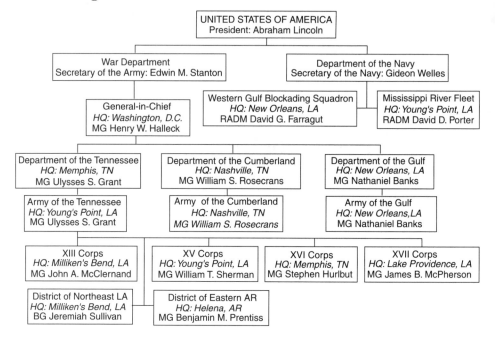

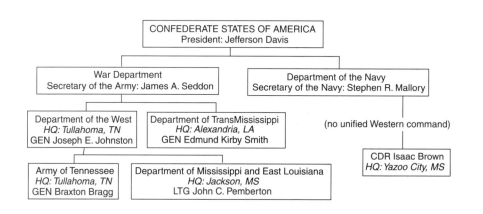

Command Structures of the Confederate Armies in the Lower Mississippi Valley, 19 March 1863

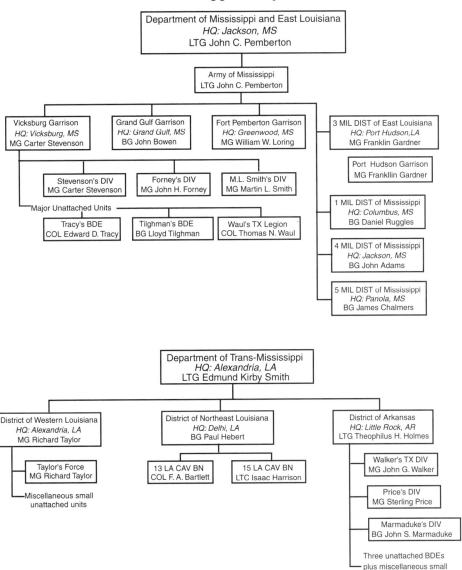

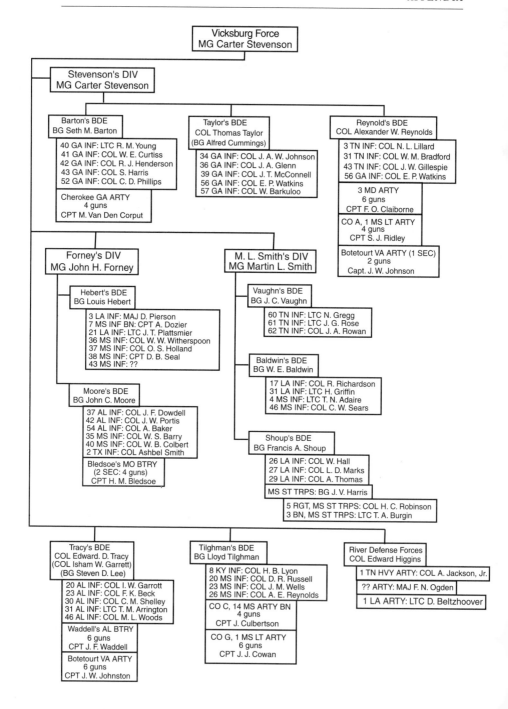

Vicksburg Force
MG Carter Stevenson

Stevenson's DIV
MG Carter Stevenson

Barton's BDE
BG Seth M. Barton

40 GA INF: LTC R. M. Young
41 GA INF: COL W. E. Curtiss
42 GA INF: COL R. J. Henderson
43 GA INF: COL S. Harris
52 GA INF: COL C. D. Phillips

Cherokee GA ARTY
4 guns
CPT M. Van Den Corput

Taylor's BDE
COL Thomas Taylor
(BG Alfred Cummings)

34 GA INF: COL J. A. W. Johnson
36 GA INF: COL J. A. Glenn
39 GA INF: COL J. T. McConnell
56 GA INF: COL E. P. Watkins
57 GA INF: COL W. Barkuloo

Reynold's BDE
COL Alexander W. Reynolds

3 TN INF: COL N. L. Lillard
31 TN INF: COL W. M. Bradford
43 TN INF: COL J. W. Gillespie
56 GA INF: COL E. P. Watkins

3 MD ARTY
6 guns
CPT F. O. Claiborne

CO A, 1 MS LT ARTY
4 guns
CPT S. J. Ridley

Botetourt VA ARTY (1 SEC)
2 guns
Capt. J. W. Johnson

Forney's DIV
MG John H. Forney

Hebert's BDE
BG Louis Hebert

3 LA INF: MAJ D. Pierson
7 MS INF BN: CPT A. Dozier
21 LA INF: LTC J. T. Plattsmier
36 MS INF: COL W. W. Witherspoon
37 MS INF: COL O. S. Holland
38 MS INF: CPT D. B. Seal
43 MS INF: ??

Moore's BDE
BG John C. Moore

37 AL INF: COL J. F. Dowdell
42 AL INF: COL J. W. Portis
54 AL INF: COL A. Baker
35 MS INF: COL W. S. Barry
40 MS INF: COL W. B. Colbert
2 TX INF: COL Ashbel Smith

Bledsoe's MO BTRY
(2 SEC: 4 guns)
CPT H. M. Bledsoe

M. L. Smith's DIV
MG Martin L. Smith

Vaughn's BDE
BG J. C. Vaughn

60 TN INF: LTC N. Gregg
61 TN INF: LTC J. G. Rose
62 TN INF: COL J. A. Rowan

Baldwin's BDE
BG W. E. Baldwin

17 LA INF: COL R. Richardson
31 LA INF: LTC H. Griffin
4 MS INF: LTC T. N. Adaire
46 MS INF: COL C. W. Sears

Shoup's BDE
BG Francis A. Shoup

26 LA INF: COL W. Hall
27 LA INF: COL L. D. Marks
29 LA INF: COL A. Thomas

MS ST TRPS: BG J. V. Harris

5 RGT, MS ST TRPS: COL H. C. Robinson
3 BN, MS ST TRPS: LTC T. A. Burgin

Tracy's BDE
COL Edward. D. Tracy
(COL Isham W. Garrett)
(BG Steven D. Lee)

20 AL INF: COL I. W. Garrott
23 AL INF: COL F. K. Beck
30 AL INF: COL C. M. Shelley
31 AL INF: LTC T. M. Arrington
46 AL INF: COL M. L. Woods

Waddell's AL BTRY
6 guns
CPT J. F. Waddell

Botetourt VA ARTY
6 guns
CPT J. W. Johnston

Tilghman's BDE
BG Lloyd Tilghman

8 KY INF: COL H. B. Lyon
20 MS INF: COL D. R. Russell
23 MS INF: COL J. M. Wells
26 MS INF: COL A. E. Reynolds

CO C, 14 MS ARTY BN
4 guns
CPT J. Culbertson

CO G, 1 MS LT ARTY
6 guns
CPT J. J. Cowan

River Defense Forces
COL Edward Higgins

1 TN HVY ARTY: COL A. Jackson, Jr.

?? ARTY: MAJ F. N. Ogden

1 LA ARTY: LTC D. Beltzhoover

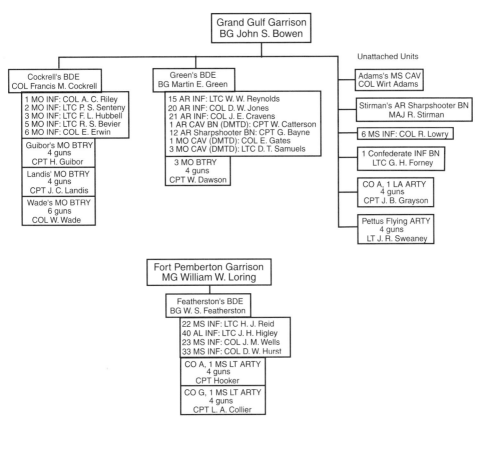

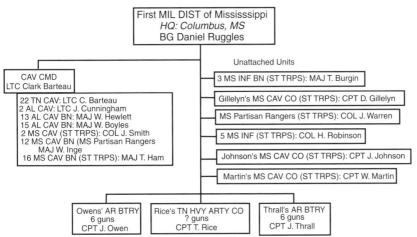

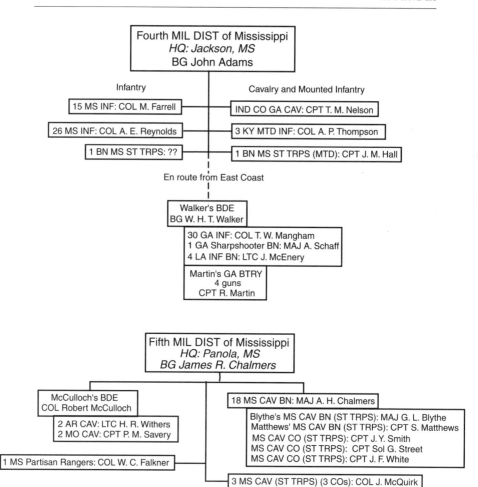

Fourth MIL DIST of Mississippi
HQ: Jackson, MS
BG John Adams

Infantry

Cavalry and Mounted Infantry

15 MS INF: COL M. Farrell

IND CO GA CAV: CPT T. M. Nelson

26 MS INF: COL A. E. Reynolds

3 KY MTD INF: COL A. P. Thompson

1 BN MS ST TRPS: ??

1 BN MS ST TRPS (MTD): CPT J. M. Hall

En route from East Coast

Walker's BDE
BG W. H. T. Walker

30 GA INF: COL T. W. Mangham
1 GA Sharpshooter BN: MAJ A. Schaff
4 LA INF BN: LTC J. McEnery

Martin's GA BTRY
4 guns
CPT R. Martin

Fifth MIL DIST of Mississippi
HQ: Panola, MS
BG James R. Chalmers

McCulloch's BDE
COL Robert McCulloch

18 MS CAV BN: MAJ A. H. Chalmers

2 AR CAV: LTC H. R. Withers
2 MO CAV: CPT P. M. Savery

Blythe's MS CAV BN (ST TRPS): MAJ G. L. Blythe
Matthews' MS CAV BN (ST TRPS): CPT S. Matthews
MS CAV CO (ST TRPS): CPT J. Y. Smith
MS CAV CO (ST TRPS): CPT Sol G. Street
MS CAV CO (ST TRPS): CPT J. F. White

1 MS Partisan Rangers: COL W. C. Falkner

3 MS CAV (ST TRPS) (3 COs): COL J. McQuirk

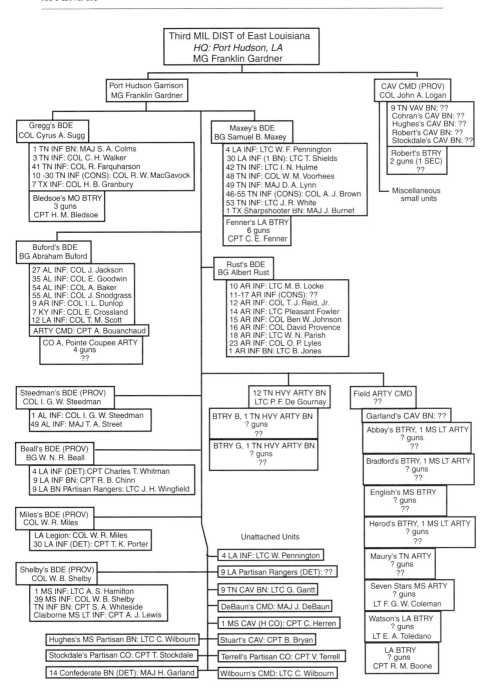

Third MIL DIST of East Louisiana
HQ: Port Hudson, LA
MG Franklin Gardner

Port Hudson Garrison
MG Franklin Gardner

CAV CMD (PROV)
COL John A. Logan

9 TN VAV BN: ??
Cohran's CAV BN: ??
Hughes's CAV BN: ??
Robert's CAV BN: ??
Stockdale's CAV BN: ??

Robert's BTRY
2 guns (1 SEC)
??

Miscellaneous
small units

Gregg's BDE
COL Cyrus A. Sugg

1 TN INF BN: MAJ S. A. Colms
3 TN INF: COL C. H. Walker
41 TN INF: COL R. Farquharson
10 -30 TN INF (CONS): COL R. W. MacGavock
7 TX INF: COL H. B. Granbury

Bledsoe's MO BTRY
3 guns
CPT H. M. Bledsoe

Maxey's BDE
BG Samuel B. Maxey

4 LA INF: LTC W. F. Pennington
30 LA INF (1 BN): LTC T. Shields
42 TN INF: LTC I. N. Hulme
48 TN INF: COL W. M. Voorhees
49 TN INF: MAJ D. A. Lynn
46-55 TN INF (CONS): COL A. J. Brown
53 TN INF: LTC J. R. White
1 TX Sharpshooter BN: MAJ J. Burnet

Fenner's LA BTRY
6 guns
CPT C. E. Fenner

Buford's BDE
BG Abraham Buford

27 AL INF: COL J. Jackson
35 AL INF: COL E. Goodwin
54 AL INF: COL A. Baker
55 AL INF: COL J. Snodgrass
9 AR INF: COL I. L. Dunlop
7 KY INF: COL E. Crossland
12 LA INF: COL T. M. Scott

ARTY CMD: CPT A. Bouanchaud

CO A, Pointe Coupee ARTY
4 guns
??

Rust's BDE
BG Albert Rust

10 AR INF: LTC M. B. Locke
11-17 AR INF (CONS): ??
12 AR INF: COL T. J. Reid, Jr.
14 AR INF: LTC Pleasant Fowler
15 AR INF: COL Ben W. Johnson
16 AR INF: COL David Provence
18 AR INF: LTC W. N. Parish
23 AR INF: COL O. P. Lyles
1 AR INF BN: LTC B. Jones

Steedman's BDE (PROV)
COL I. G. W. Steedman

1 AL INF: COL I. G. W. Steedman
49 AL INF: MAJ T. A. Street

Beall's BDE (PROV)
BG W. N. R. Beall

4 LA INF (DET):CPT Charles T. Whitman
9 LA INF BN: CPT R. B. Chinn
9 LA BN PArtisan Rangers: LTC J. H. Wingfield

Miles's BDE (PROV)
COL W. R. Miles

LA Legion: COL W. R. Miles
30 LA INF (DET): CPT T. K. Porter

Shelby's BDE (PROV)
COL W. B. Shelby

1 MS INF: LTC A. S. Hamilton
39 MS INF: COL W. B. Shelby
TN INF BN: CPT S. A. Whiteside
Claiborne MS LT INF: CPT A. J. Lewis

Hughes's MS Partisan BN: LTC C. Wilbourn

Stockdale's Partisan CO: CPT T. Stockdale

14 Confederate BN (DET): MAJ H. Garland

12 TN HVY ARTY BN
LTC P. F. De Gournay

BTRY B, 1 TN HVY ARTY BN
? guns
??

BTRY G, 1 TN HVY ARTY BN
? guns
??

Field ARTY CMD
??

Garland's CAV BN: ??

Abbay's BTRY, 1 MS LT ARTY
? guns
??

Bradford's BTRY, 1 MS LT ARTY
? guns
??

English's MS BTRY
? guns
??

Herod's BTRY, 1 MS LT ARTY
? guns
??

Maury's TN ARTY
? guns
??

Seven Stars MS ARTY
? guns
LT F. G. W. Coleman

Watson's LA BTRY
? guns
LT E. A. Toledano

LA BTRY
? guns
CPT R. M. Boone

Unattached Units

4 LA INF: LTC W. Pennington

9 LA Partisan Rangers (DET): ??

9 TN CAV BN: LTC G. Gantt

DeBaun's CMD: MAJ J. DeBaun

1 MS CAV (H CO): CPT C. Herren

Stuart's CAV: CPT B. Bryan

Terrell's Partisan CO: CPT V. Terrell

Wilbourn's CMD: LTC C. Wilbourn

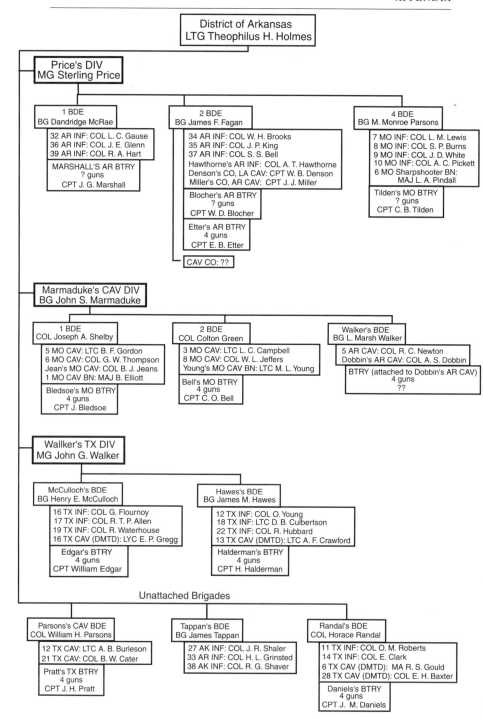

District of Arkansas
LTG Theophilus H. Holmes

Price's DIV
MG Sterling Price

1 BDE
BG Dandridge McRae

32 AR INF: COL L. C. Gause
36 AR INF: COL J. E. Glenn
39 AR INF: COL R. A. Hart

MARSHALL'S AR BTRY
? guns
CPT J. G. Marshall

2 BDE
BG James F. Fagan

34 AR INF: COL W. H. Brooks
35 AR INF: COL J. P. King
37 AR INF: COL S. S. Bell
Hawthorne's AR INF: COL A. T. Hawthorne
Denson's CO, LA CAV: CPT W. B. Denson
Miller's CO, AR CAV: CPT J. J. Miller

Blocher's AR BTRY
? guns
CPT W. D. Blocher

Etter's AR BTRY
4 guns
CPT E. B. Etter

CAV CO: ??

4 BDE
BG M. Monroe Parsons

7 MO INF: COL L. M. Lewis
8 MO INF: COL S. P. Burns
9 MO INF: COL J. D. White
10 MO INF: COL A. C. Pickett
6 MO Sharpshooter BN:
MAJ L. A. Pindall

Tilden's MO BTRY
? guns
CPT C. B. Tilden

Marmaduke's CAV DIV
BG John S. Marmaduke

1 BDE
COL Joseph A. Shelby

5 MO CAV: LTC B. F. Gordon
6 MO CAV: COL G. W. Thompson
Jean's MO CAV: COL B. J. Jeans
1 MO CAV BN: MAJ B. Elliott

Bledsoe's MO BTRY
4 guns
CPT J. Bledsoe

2 BDE
COL Colton Green

3 MO CAV: LTC L. C. Campbell
8 MO CAV: COL W. L. Jeffers
Young's MO CAV BN: LTC M. L. Young

Bell's MO BTRY
4 guns
CPT C. O. Bell

Walker's BDE
BG L. Marsh Walker

5 AR CAV: COL R. C. Newton
Dobbin's AR CAV: COL A. S. Dobbin

BTRY (attached to Dobbin's AR CAV)
4 guns
??

Wallker's TX DIV
MG John G. Walker

McCulloch's BDE
BG Henry E. McCulloch

16 TX INF: COL G. Flournoy
17 TX INF: COL R. T. P. Allen
19 TX INF: COL R. Waterhouse
16 TX CAV (DMTD): LYC E. P. Gregg

Edgar's BTRY
4 guns
CPT William Edgar

Hawes's BDE
BG James M. Hawes

12 TX INF: COL O. Young
18 TX INF: LTC D. B. Culbertson
22 TX INF: COL R. Hubbard
13 TX CAV (DMTD): LTC A. F. Crawford

Halderman's BTRY
4 guns
CPT H. Halderman

Unattached Brigades

Parsons's CAV BDE
COL William H. Parsons

12 TX CAV: LTC A. B. Burleson
21 TX CAV: COL B. W. Cater

Pratt's TX BTRY
4 guns
CPT J. H. Pratt

Tappan's BDE
BG James Tappan

27 AK INF: COL J. R. Shaler
33 AR INF: COL H. L. Grinsted
38 AK INF: COL R. G. Shaver

Randal's BDE
COL Horace Randal

11 TX INF: COL O. M. Roberts
14 TX INF: COL E. Clark
6 TX CAV (DMTD): MA R. S. Gould
28 TX CAV (DMTD): COL E. H. Baxter

Daniels's BTRY
4 guns
CPT J. M. Daniels

Command Structures of Components of the Army of the Tennessee, 29 March 1863

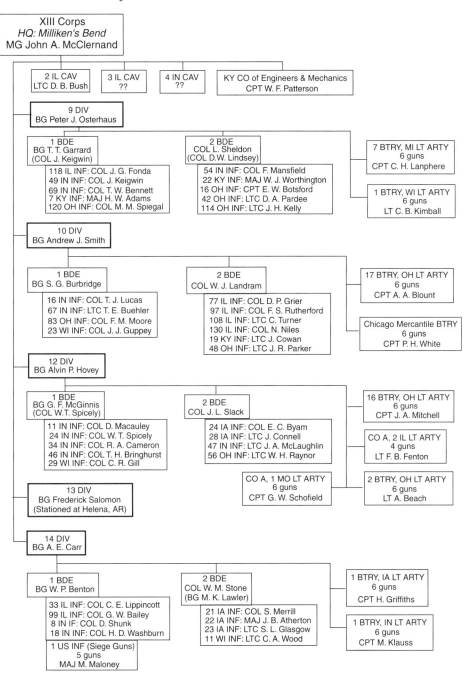

XIII Corps
HQ: Milliken's Bend
MG John A. McClernand

2 IL CAV
LTC D. B. Bush

3 IL CAV
??

4 IN CAV
??

KY CO of Engineers & Mechanics
CPT W. F. Patterson

9 DIV
BG Peter J. Osterhaus

1 BDE
BG T. T. Garrard
(COL J. Keigwin)

118 IL INF: COL J. G. Fonda
49 IN INF: COL J. Keigwin
69 IN INF: COL T. W. Bennett
7 KY INF: MAJ H. W. Adams
120 OH INF: COL M. M. Spiegal

2 BDE
COL L. Sheldon
(COL D.W. Lindsey)

54 IN INF: COL F. Mansfield
22 KY INF: MAJ W. J. Worthington
16 OH INF: CPT E. W. Botsford
42 OH INF: LTC D. A. Pardee
114 OH INF: LTC J. H. Kelly

7 BTRY, MI LT ARTY
6 guns
CPT C. H. Lanphere

1 BTRY, WI LT ARTY
6 guns
LT C. B. Kimball

10 DIV
BG Andrew J. Smith

1 BDE
BG S. G. Burbridge

16 IN INF: COL T. J. Lucas
67 IN INF: LTC T. E. Buehler
83 OH INF: COL F. M. Moore
23 WI INF: COL J. J. Guppey

2 BDE
COL W. J. Landram

77 IL INF: COL D. P. Grier
97 IL INF: COL F. S. Rutherford
108 IL INF: LTC C. Turner
130 IL INF: COL N. Niles
19 KY INF: LTC J. Cowan
48 OH INF: LTC J. R. Parker

17 BTRY, OH LT ARTY
6 guns
CPT A. A. Blount

Chicago Mercantile BTRY
6 guns
CPT P. H. White

12 DIV
BG Alvin P. Hovey

1 BDE
BG G. F. McGinnis
(COL W.T. Spicely)

11 IN INF: COL D. Macauley
24 IN INF: COL W. T. Spicely
34 IN INF: COL R. A. Cameron
46 IN INF: COL T. H. Bringhurst
29 WI INF: COL C. R. Gill

2 BDE
COL J. L. Slack

24 IA INF: COL E. C. Byam
28 IA INF: LTC J. Connell
47 IN INF: LTC J. A. McLaughlin
56 OH INF: LTC W. H. Raynor

CO A, 1 MO LT ARTY
6 guns
CPT G. W. Schofield

16 BTRY, OH LT ARTY
6 guns
CPT J. A. Mitchell

CO A, 2 IL LT ARTY
4 guns
LT F. B. Fenton

2 BTRY, OH LT ARTY
6 guns
LT A. Beach

13 DIV
BG Frederick Salomon
(Stationed at Helena, AR)

14 DIV
BG A. E. Carr

1 BDE
BG W. P. Benton

33 IL INF: COL C. E. Lippincott
99 IL INF: COL G. W. Bailey
8 IN IF: COL D. Shunk
18 IN INF: COL H. D. Washburn

1 US INF (Siege Guns)
5 guns
MAJ M. Maloney

2 BDE
COL W. M. Stone
(BG M. K. Lawler)

21 IA INF: COL S. Merrill
22 IA INF: MAJ J. B. Atherton
23 IA INF: LTC S. L. Glasgow
11 WI INF: LTC C. A. Wood

1 BTRY, IA LT ARTY
6 guns
CPT H. Griffiths

1 BTRY, IN LT ARTY
6 guns
CPT M. Klauss

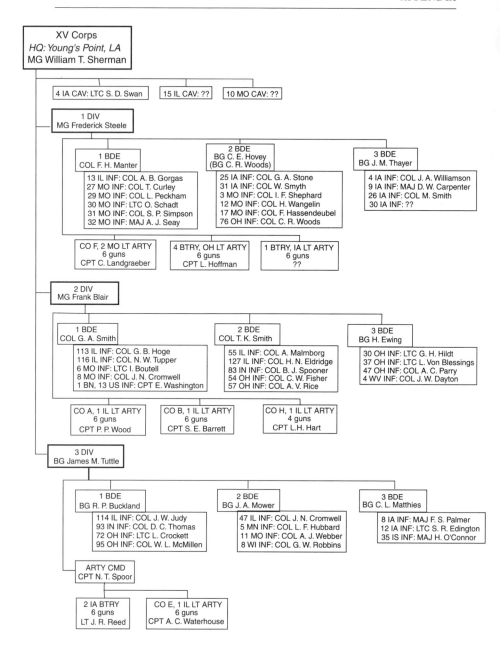

XV Corps
HQ: Young's Point, LA
MG William T. Sherman

4 IA CAV: LTC S. D. Swan   15 IL CAV: ??   10 MO CAV: ??

1 DIV
MG Frederick Steele

1 BDE
COL F. H. Manter

13 IL INF: COL A. B. Gorgas
27 MO INF: COL T. Curley
29 MO INF: COL L. Peckham
30 MO INF: LTC O. Schadt
31 MO INF: COL S. P. Simpson
32 MO INF: MAJ A. J. Seay

2 BDE
BG C. E. Hovey
(BG C. R. Woods)

25 IA INF: COL G. A. Stone
31 IA INF: COL W. Smyth
3 MO INF: COL I. F. Shephard
12 MO INF: COL H. Wangelin
17 MO INF: COL F. Hassendeubel
76 OH INF: COL C. R. Woods

3 BDE
BG J. M. Thayer

4 IA INF: COL J. A. Williamson
9 IA INF: MAJ D. W. Carpenter
26 IA INF: COL M. Smith
30 IA INF: ??

CO F, 2 MO LT ARTY
6 guns
CPT C. Landgraeber

4 BTRY, OH LT ARTY
6 guns
CPT L. Hoffman

1 BTRY, IA LT ARTY
6 guns
??

2 DIV
MG Frank Blair

1 BDE
COL G. A. Smith

113 IL INF: COL G. B. Hoge
116 IL INF: COL N. W. Tupper
6 MO INF: LTC I. Boutell
8 MO INF: COL J. N. Cromwell
1 BN, 13 US INF: CPT E. Washington

2 BDE
COL T. K. Smith

55 IL INF: COL A. Malmborg
127 IL INF: COL H. N. Eldridge
83 IN INF: COL B. J. Spooner
54 OH INF: COL C. W. Fisher
57 OH INF: COL A. V. Rice

3 BDE
BG H. Ewing

30 OH INF: LTC G. H. Hildt
37 OH INF: LTC L. Von Blessings
47 OH INF: COL A. C. Parry
4 WV INF: COL J. W. Dayton

CO A, 1 IL LT ARTY
6 guns
CPT P. P. Wood

CO B, 1 IL LT ARTY
6 guns
CPT S. E. Barrett

CO H, 1 IL LT ARTY
4 guns
CPT L.H. Hart

3 DIV
BG James M. Tuttle

1 BDE
BG R. P. Buckland

114 IL INF: COL J. W. Judy
93 IN INF: COL D. C. Thomas
72 OH INF: LTC L. Crockett
95 OH INF: COL W. L. McMillen

2 BDE
BG J. A. Mower

47 IL INF: COL J. N. Cromwell
5 MN INF: COL L. F. Hubbard
11 MO INF: COL A. J. Webber
8 WI INF: COL G. W. Robbins

3 BDE
BG C. L. Matthies

8 IA INF: MAJ F. S. Palmer
12 IA INF: LTC S. R. Edington
35 IS INF: MAJ H. O'Connor

ARTY CMD
CPT N. T. Spoor

2 IA BTRY
6 guns
LT J. R. Reed

CO E, 1 IL LT ARTY
6 guns
CPT A. C. Waterhouse

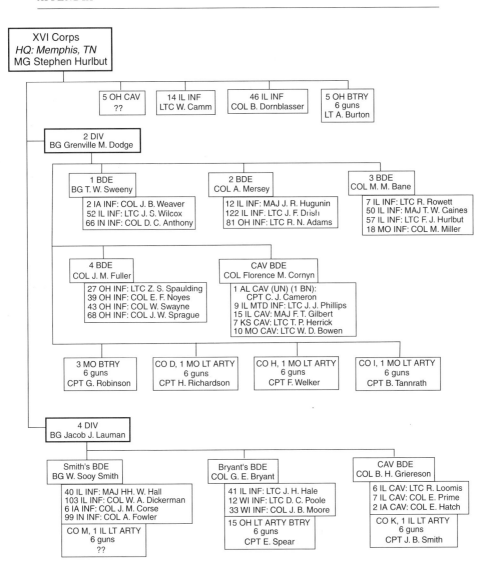

XVI Corps
HQ: Memphis, TN
MG Stephen Hurlbut

5 OH CAV
??

14 IL INF
LTC W. Camm

46 IL INF
COL B. Dornblasser

5 OH BTRY
6 guns
LT A. Burton

2 DIV
BG Grenville M. Dodge

1 BDE
BG T. W. Sweeny

2 IA INF: COL J. B. Weaver
52 IL INF: LTC J. S. Wilcox
66 IN INF: COL D. C. Anthony

2 BDE
COL A. Mersey

12 IL INF: MAJ J. R. Hugunin
122 IL INF: LTC J. F. Drish
81 OH INF: LTC R. N. Adams

3 BDE
COL M. M. Bane

7 IL INF: LTC R. Rowett
50 IL INF: MAJ T. W. Gaines
57 IL INF: LTC F. J. Hurlbut
18 MO INF: COL M. Miller

4 BDE
COL J. M. Fuller

27 OH INF: LTC Z. S. Spaulding
39 OH INF: COL E. F. Noyes
43 OH INF: COL W. Swayne
68 OH INF: COL J. W. Sprague

CAV BDE
COL Florence M. Cornyn

1 AL CAV (UN) (1 BN):
CPT C. J. Cameron
9 IL MTD INF: LTC J. J. Phillips
15 IL CAV: MAJ F. T. Gilbert
7 KS CAV: LTC T. P. Herrick
10 MO CAV: LTC W. D. Bowen

3 MO BTRY
6 guns
CPT G. Robinson

CO D, 1 MO LT ARTY
6 guns
CPT H. Richardson

CO H, 1 MO LT ARTY
6 guns
CPT F. Welker

CO I, 1 MO LT ARTY
6 guns
CPT B. Tannrath

4 DIV
BG Jacob J. Lauman

Smith's BDE
BG W. Sooy Smith

40 IL INF: MAJ HH. W. Hall
103 IL INF: COL W. A. Dickerman
6 IA INF: COL J. M. Corse
99 IN INF: COL A. Fowler

CO M, 1 IL LT ARTY
6 guns
??

Bryant's BDE
COL G. E. Bryant

41 IL INF: LTC J. H. Hale
12 WI INF: LTC D. C. Poole
33 WI INF: COL J. B. Moore

15 OH LT ARTY BTRY
6 guns
CPT E. Spear

CAV BDE
COL B. H. Grierson

6 IL CAV: LTC R. Loomis
7 IL CAV: COL E. Prime
2 IA CAV: COL E. Hatch

CO K, 1 IL LT ARTY
6 guns
CPT J. B. Smith

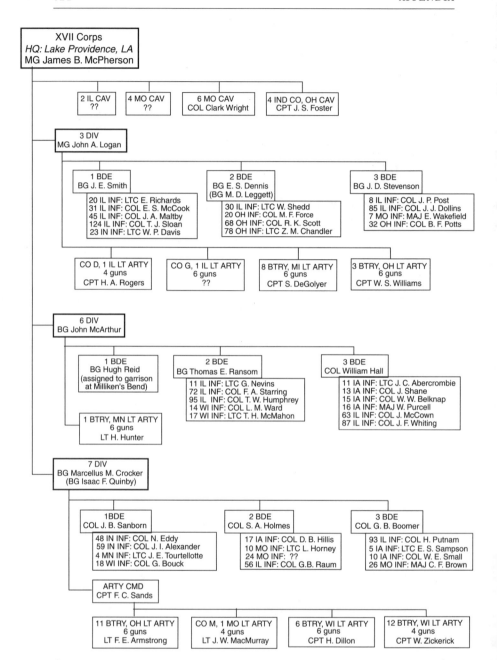

XVII Corps
HQ: Lake Providence, LA
MG James B. McPherson

2 IL CAV
??

4 MO CAV
??

6 MO CAV
COL Clark Wright

4 IND CO, OH CAV
CPT J. S. Foster

3 DIV
MG John A. Logan

1 BDE
BG J. E. Smith

20 IL INF: LTC E. Richards
31 IL INF: COL E. S. McCook
45 IL INF: COL J. A. Maltby
124 IL INF: COL T. J. Sloan
23 IN INF: LTC W. P. Davis

2 BDE
BG E. S. Dennis
(BG M. D. Leggett)

30 IL INF: LTC W. Shedd
20 OH INF: COL M. F. Force
68 OH INF: COL R. K. Scott
78 OH INF: LTC Z. M. Chandler

3 BDE
BG J. D. Stevenson

8 IL INF: COL J. P. Post
85 IL INF: COL J. J. Dollins
7 MO INF: MAJ E. Wakefield
32 OH INF: COL B. F. Potts

CO D, 1 IL LT ARTY
4 guns
CPT H. A. Rogers

CO G, 1 IL LT ARTY
6 guns
??

8 BTRY, MI LT ARTY
6 guns
CPT S. DeGolyer

3 BTRY, OH LT ARTY
6 guns
CPT W. S. Williams

6 DIV
BG John McArthur

1 BDE
BG Hugh Reid
(assigned to garrison
at Milliken's Bend)

1 BTRY, MN LT ARTY
6 guns
LT H. Hunter

2 BDE
BG Thomas E. Ransom

11 IL INF: LTC G. Nevins
72 IL INF: COL F. A. Starring
95 IL INF: COL T. W. Humphrey
14 WI INF: COL L. M. Ward
17 WI INF: LTC T. H. McMahon

3 BDE
COL William Hall

11 IA INF: LTC J. C. Abercrombie
13 IA INF: COL J. Shane
15 IA INF: COL W. W. Belknap
16 IA INF: MAJ W. Purcell
63 IL INF: COL J. McCown
87 IL INF: COL J. F. Whiting

7 DIV
BG Marcellus M. Crocker
(BG Isaac F. Quinby)

1 BDE
COL J. B. Sanborn

48 IN INF: COL N. Eddy
59 IN INF: COL J. I. Alexander
4 MN INF: LTC J. E. Tourtellotte
18 WI INF: COL G. Bouck

2 BDE
COL S. A. Holmes

17 IA INF: COL D. B. Hillis
10 MO INF: LTC L. Horney
24 MO INF: ??
56 IL INF: COL G.B. Raum

3 BDE
COL G. B. Boomer

93 IL INF: COL H. Putnam
5 IA INF: LTC E. S. Sampson
10 IA INF: COL W. E. Small
26 MO INF: MAJ C. F. Brown

ARTY CMD
CPT F. C. Sands

11 BTRY, OH LT ARTY
6 guns
LT F. E. Armstrong

CO M, 1 MO LT ARTY
4 guns
LT J. W. MacMurray

6 BTRY, WI LT ARTY
6 guns
CPT H. Dillon

12 BTRY, WI LT ARTY
4 guns
CPT W. Zickerick

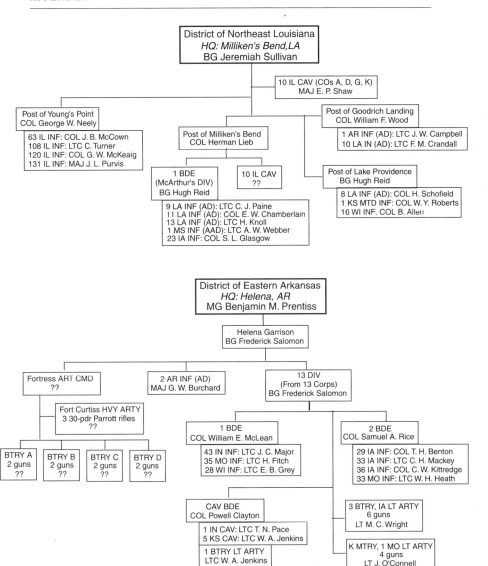

District of Northeast Louisiana
HQ: Milliken's Bend, LA
BG Jeremiah Sullivan

10 IL CAV (COs A, D, G, K)
MAJ E. P. Shaw

Post of Young's Point
COL George W. Neely

63 IL INF: COL J. B. McCown
108 IL INF: LTC C. Turner
120 IL INF: COL G. W. McKeaig
131 IL INF: MAJ J. L. Purvis

Post of Milliken's Bend
COL Herman Lieb

Post of Goodrich Landing
COL William F. Wood

1 AR INF (AD): LTC J. W. Campbell
10 LA IN (AD): LTC F. M. Crandall

1 BDE
(McArthur's DIV)
BG Hugh Reid

10 IL CAV
??

Post of Lake Providence
BG Hugh Reid

8 LA INF (AD): COL H. Schofield
1 KS MTD INF: COL W. Y. Roberts
16 WI INF. COL B. Allen

9 LA INF (AD): LTC C. J. Paine
11 LA INF (AD): COL E. W. Chamberlain
13 LA INF (AD): LTC H. Knoll
1 MS INF (AAD): LTC A. W. Webber
23 IA INF: COL S. L. Glasgow

District of Eastern Arkansas
HQ: Helena, AR
MG Benjamin M. Prentiss

Helena Garrison
BG Frederick Salomon

Fortress ART CMD
??

2 AR INF (AD)
MAJ G. W. Burchard

13 DIV
(From 13 Corps)
BG Frederick Salomon

Fort Curtiss HVY ARTY
3 30-pdr Parrott rifles
??

1 BDE
COL William E. McLean

2 BDE
COL Samuel A. Rice

BTRY A
2 guns
??

BTRY B
2 guns
??

BTRY C
2 guns
??

BTRY D
2 guns
??

43 IN INF: LTC J. C. Major
35 MO INF: LTC H. Fitch
28 WI INF: LTC E. B. Grey

29 IA INF: COL T. H. Benton
33 IA INF: LTC C. H. Mackey
36 IA INF: COL C. W. Kittredge
33 MO INF: LTC W. H. Heath

CAV BDE
COL Powell Clayton

3 BTRY, IA LT ARTY
6 guns
LT M. C. Wright

1 IN CAV: LTC T. N. Pace
5 KS CAV: LTC W. A. Jenkins

1 BTRY LT ARTY
LTC W. A. Jenkins

K MTRY, 1 MO LT ARTY
4 guns
LT J. O'Connell

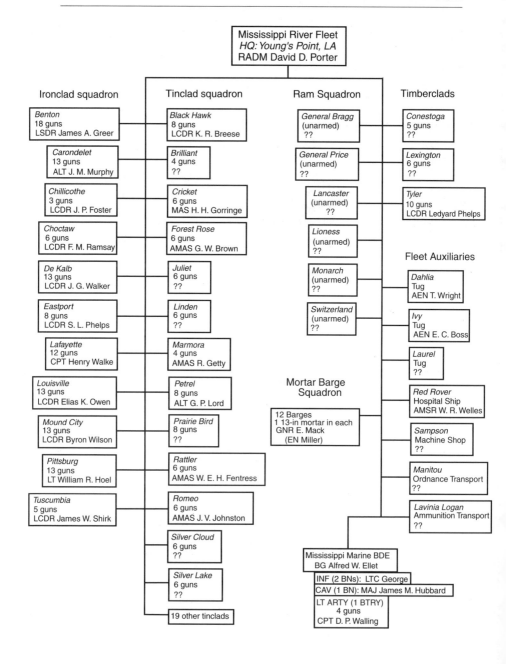

Mississippi River Fleet
HQ: Young's Point, LA
RADM David D. Porter

Ironclad squadron

Benton
18 guns
LSDR James A. Greer

Carondelet
13 guns
ALT J. M. Murphy

Chillicothe
3 guns
LCDR J. P. Foster

Choctaw
6 guns
LCDR F. M. Ramsay

De Kalb
13 guns
LCDR J. G. Walker

Eastport
8 guns
LCDR S. L. Phelps

Lafayette
12 guns
CPT Henry Walke

Louisville
13 guns
LCDR Elias K. Owen

Mound City
13 guns
LCDR Byron Wilson

Pittsburg
13 guns
LT William R. Hoel

Tuscumbia
5 guns
LCDR James W. Shirk

Tinclad squadron

Black Hawk
8 guns
LCDR K. R. Breese

Brilliant
4 guns
??

Cricket
6 guns
MAS H. H. Gorringe

Forest Rose
6 guns
AMAS G. W. Brown

Juliet
6 guns
??

Linden
6 guns
??

Marmora
4 guns
AMAS R. Getty

Petrel
8 guns
ALT G. P. Lord

Prairie Bird
8 guns
??

Rattler
6 guns
AMAS W. E. H. Fentress

Romeo
6 guns
AMAS J. V. Johnston

Silver Cloud
6 guns
??

Silver Lake
6 guns
??

19 other tinclads

Ram Squadron

General Bragg
(unarmed)
??

General Price
(unarmed)
??

Lancaster
(unarmed)
??

Lioness
(unarmed)
??

Monarch
(unarmed)
??

Switzerland
(unarmed)
??

Mortar Barge Squadron

12 Barges
1 13-in mortar in each
GNR E. Mack
(EN Miller)

Timberclads

Conestoga
5 guns
??

Lexington
6 guns
??

Tyler
10 guns
LCDR Ledyard Phelps

Fleet Auxiliaries

Dahlia
Tug
AEN T. Wright

Ivy
Tug
AEN E. C. Boss

Laurel
Tug
??

Red Rover
Hospital Ship
AMSR W. R. Welles

Sampson
Machine Shop
??

Manitou
Ordnance Transport
??

Lavinia Logan
Ammunition Transport
??

Mississippi Marine BDE
BG Alfred W. Ellet

INF (2 BNs): LTC George

CAV (1 BN): MAJ James M. Hubbard

LT ARTY (1 BTRY)
4 guns
CPT D. P. Walling

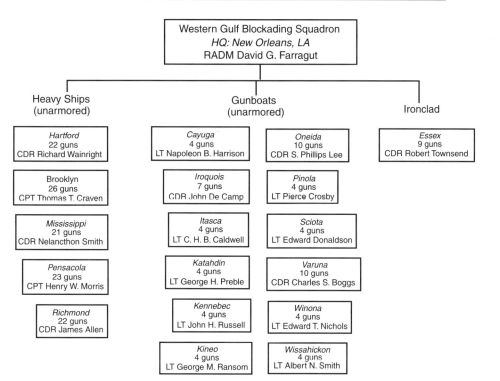

Western Gulf Blockading Squadron
HQ: New Orleans, LA
RADM David G. Farragut

Heavy Ships
(unarmored)

Gunboats
(unarmored)

Ironclad

Hartford
22 guns
CDR Richard Wainright

Cayuga
4 guns
LT Napoleon B. Harrison

Oneida
10 guns
CDR S. Phillips Lee

Essex
9 guns
CDR Robert Townsend

Brooklyn
26 guns
CPT Thomas T. Craven

Iroquois
7 guns
CDR John De Camp

Pinola
4 guns
LT Pierce Crosby

Mississippi
21 guns
CDR Nelancthon Smith

Itasca
4 guns
LT C. H. B. Caldwell

Sciota
4 guns
LT Edward Donaldson

Pensacola
23 guns
CPT Henry W. Morris

Katahdin
4 guns
LT George H. Preble

Varuna
10 guns
CDR Charles S. Boggs

Richmond
22 guns
CDR James Allen

Kennebec
4 guns
LT John H. Russell

Winona
4 guns
LT Edward T. Nichols

Kineo
4 guns
LT George M. Ransom

Wissahickon
4 guns
LT Albert N. Smith

Notes

ABBREVIATIONS

OR   *The War of the Rebellion: A Compilation of the Official Records of the Union and Confederate Armies.* 73 volumes, 128 parts. Washington, DC, 1880–1901.

ORN   *Official Records of the Union and Confederate Navies in the War of the Rebellion.* 31 volumes. Washington, DC, 1895–1926.

OR Atlas   Maj. George B. Davis, Leslie J. Perry, and Joseph W. Kirkley, *Atlas to Accompany the Official Records of the Union and Confederate Armies.* Washington, DC: Government Printing Office, 1891–95.

VNMP   Vicksburg National Military Park, Vicksburg, MS

1. PROLOGUE

1. "The Army of the Tennessee," *Harper's Weekly* 7 (337), 13 June 1865, 369; "General John A. Logan," *Harper's Weekly* 7 (408), 22 Oct. 1864, 675.
2. A. T. Mahan, "The Gulf and Inland Waters," *Campaigns of the Civil War* (New York: Charles Scribner's Sons, 1883), 47–49.
3. Ibid., 70–71.
4. George W. Morgan, "The Assault on Chickasaw Bluffs," in *Battles and Leaders of the Civil War* (New York: Castle Books, 1956), 3:462–71.
5. Edwin Cole Bearss, *The Campaign for Vicksburg* (Dayton, OH: Morningside, 1985), 1:509–30.
6. Francis V. Greene, "The Mississippi," in *Campaigns of the Civil War* (New York: Charles Scribner's Sons, 1883), 104–6.
7. S. H. Lockett, "The Defense of Vicksburg," in *Battles and Leaders of the Civil War* (New York: Castle Books, 1956), 3:482–83.
8. Michael B. Ballard, *Pemberton: A Biography* (Jackson: Univ. Press of Mississippi, 1991), 114–15.

2. THE GEOGRAPHIC SETTING

1. For additional information on the character of the floodplain, see Darwin Spearing, *Roadside Geology of Louisiana* (Missoula, MT: Mountain Press, 1995).
2. A. P. Adamson, *Brief History of the Thirtieth Georgia Regiment* (Griffin, GA: Mills Printing Co., 1912), 30.

3. LOGISTICS AND COMMUNICATIONS

1. State of Illinois, *Report of the Adjutant General*, 8 vols. (Springfield, OH, Office of the Adjutant General) 1900–1902; 6:367–68.
2. OR, ser. I, vol. 24, pt. 3, p. 284.

4. DEFENSES OF VICKSBURG

1. Maj. F. E. Prime, *Map of the Siege of Vicksburg by the U.S. Forces*, 1863.
2. OR, ser. I, vol. 24, pt. 2, pp. 336–37; OR, ser. I, vol. 24, pt. 3, p. 668; W. T. Rigby, ed., "Catalog of Affidavits for the Establishment of the Vicksburg National Military Park" (Files of VNMP); Edwin Bearss, "The Vicksburg River Defenses and the Enigma of Whistling Dick," *Journal of Mississippi History* 19 (Jan. 1957): 21–30
3. J. T. Whitehead to VNMP Commission, 7 July 1903, in VNMP; H. T. Norman to W. T. Rigby, 5 May 1904, VNMP.
4. J. W. Gaines, Affidavit, VNMP; W. C. Ellis, Affidavit, VNMP; A. L. Slack, Affidavit, VNMP; A. L. Slack to W. T. Rigby, 9 Sept. 1903, VNMP.
5. G. E. Hart, ed., *Photographic History of the Civil War*, 6 vols. (Secaucus, NJ: Blue and Grey Press, 1987), 3:205.
6. W. C. Capers to Starr, 7 Apr. 1863, VNMP; ORN, ser. I, vol. 24, p. 664; OR, ser. I, vol. 24, pt. 1, p. 480.
7. OR, ser. I, vol. 24, pt. 1, p. 480.
8. Mahan, "Gulf and Inland Waters," 103.
9. Prime, *Map of the Siege of Vicksburg*.
10. Ibid.
11. Ibid.
12. Ibid.
13. Ibid.

5. DECISION

1. Benjamin P. Thomas, *Abraham Lincoln* (New York: Knopf, 1952).
2. OR, ser. I, vol. 24, pt. 1, pp. 14, 70; OR, ser. I, vol. 24, pt. 3, pp. 33–34;

Ulysses S. Grant, *Personal Memoirs of U. S. Grant* (New York: Webster & Co., 1885), 1:457.

3. OR, ser. I, vol. 24, pt. 3, p. 152.

4. OR, ser. I, vol. 24, pt. 1, p. 25.

5. Ibid., p. 46.

6. Lockett, "Defense of Vicksburg," 3:485.

7. OR, ser. I, vol. 24, pt. 3, pp. 711–12, 719–20.

8. Lockett, "Defense of Vicksburg," 3:485.

9. OR, ser. I, vol. 24, pt. 3, p. 665.

10. Ibid.

6. FROM MILLIKEN'S BEND TO IONE

1. OR, ser. I, vol. 24, pt. 1, p. 46.

2. OR, ser. I, vol. 24, pt. 3, pp. 151–52.

3. Ibid.

4. OR, ser. I, vol. 24, pt. 1, p. 70; OR, ser. I, vol. 24, pt. 3, pp. 151–52.

5. OR, ser. I, vol. 24, pt. 1, p. 495.

6. Ibid.; Phillip N. Thienel, "Bridges in the Vicksburg Campaign," *Military Engineer* 47 (Nov.–Dec. 1955); Oran Perry, "Perry Tells Story of Siege of Vicksburg," *Vicksburg Evening Post*, 6 June 1926, clipping in VNMP.

7. OR, ser. I, vol. 24, pt. 1, p. 491; Oran Perry, "Perry Tells Story."

8. OR, ser. I, vol. 24, pt. 3, p. 158.

9. Capt. John N. Bell, Diary, in VNMP (hereafter cited as Bell Diary); OR, ser. I, vol. 24, pt. 3, p. 173.

10. OR, ser. I, vol. 24, pt. 1, p. 502; Bell Diary.

11. OR, ser. I, vol. 24, pt. 3, p. 168; OR, ser. I, vol. 24, pt. 1, p. 26.

12. OR, ser. I, vol. 24, pt. 3, p. 168; OR, ser. I, vol. 24, pt. 1, pp. 26, 491; Thienel, "Bridges."

13. OR, ser. I, vol. 24, pt. 1, pp. 491–92.

14. Ibid.

15. OR, ser. I, vol. 24, pt. 1, p. 171.

16. Oran Perry, "Perry Tells Story"; OR, ser. I, vol. 24, pt. 1, pp. 490–92.

17. Oran Perry, "Perry Tells Story"; OR, ser. I, vol. 24, pt. 1, pp. 47, 420–22.

18. OR, ser. I, vol. 24, pt. 1, p. 493; Sgt. Elias Moore, Company A, 114th Regiment, Ohio Volunteer Infantry, Diary, in VNMP (hereafter cited as Elias Moore Diary).

19. OR, ser. I, vol. 24, pt. 1, p. 124; OR, ser. I, vol. 24, pt. 3, p. 186; Lt. Ira W. Hunt, Company K, 11th Wisconsin, Diary, in VNMP (hereafter cited as Hunt Diary).

20. Hunt Diary; George Crooke, *The 21st Regiment of Iowa Volunteer Infantry* (Milwaukee, 1891), 50.

21. OR, ser. I, vol. 24, pt. 1, pp. 140, 494, 496, 497.

22. Oran Perry, "Perry Tells Story"; Col. W. H. Raynor, Diary, in VNMP (hereafter cited as Raynor Diary).

23. OR, ser. I, vol. 24, pt. 1, p. 491; Oran Perry, "Perry Tells Story"; OR, ser. I, vol. 24, pt. 3, p. 168.

24. OR, ser. I, vol. 24, pt. 3, pp. 713, 714.

25. Ibid., p. 720.

26. Ibid., p. 724.

27. Ibid.

28. Ibid., p. 733.

29. Ibid., p. 744.

30. Ibid., p. 745.

31. Ibid., p. 744.

32. OR, ser. I, vol. 24, pt. 1, pp. 140, 494, 496, 497.

33. OR, ser. I, vol. 24, pt. 3, pp. 751, 752.

7. RUNNING THE BATTERIES

1. ORN, ser. I, vol. 24, pp. 184, 552.

2. Grant, *Personal Memoirs*, 1:384.

3. ORN, ser. I, vol. 24, p. 555; Mahan, "Gulf and Inland Waters," 154–55; David D. Porter, *Incidents and Anecdotes of the Civil War* (New York: Appleton, 1885), 175.

4. Robert S. Henry, *The Story of the Confederacy* (New York: Bobbs-Merrill, 1931), 253; David D. Porter, *The Naval History of the Civil War* (New York: Sherman, 1886), 310.

5. ORN, ser. I, vol. 24, p. 556; Porter, *Incidents and Anecdotes*, 176.

6. Mahan, "Gulf and Inland Waters," 156.

7. *History of the Forty-sixth Regiment Indiana Volunteer Infantry, September 1861–September 1865*, compiled by committee (Logansport, IN, 1888), 54; OR, ser. I, vol. 24, pt. 1, p. 601.

8. Porter, *Incidents and Anecdotes*, 175; Porter, *Naval History*, 310.

9. OR, ser. I, vol. 24, pt. 3, p. 740.

10. Henry, *Story of the Confederacy*, 253.

11. J. H. Yates to W. T. Rigby, 22 June 1903, VNMP.

12. D. M. Upton to W. T. Rigby, 30 July 1903, VNMP; Simeon R. Martin, "Facts about Company I, 46th Mississippi Infantry," in VNMP.

8. FROM IONE PLANTATION TO HARD TIMES

1. OR, ser. I, vol. 24, pt. 3, pp. 204, 205.

2. Ibid.

3. OR, ser. I, vol. 24, pt. 1, pp. 77, 124, 125.

4. Ibid., p. 601.

5. OR, ser. I, vol. 24, pt. 3, p. 211.

6. Ibid.; ORN, ser. I, vol. 24, p. 704.

7. OR, ser. I, vol. 24, pt. 3, pp. 126, 127; Thienel, "Bridges"; Raynor Diary.

8. OR, ser. I, vol. 24, pt. 3, pp. 225, 226; ORN, ser. I, vol. 24, pp. 682, 683, 690, 705.

9. OR, ser. I, vol. 24, pt. 3, p. 222.

10. Ibid., pp. 221, 222, 228.

11. OR, ser. I, vol. 24, pt. 3, pp. 225, 226, 228; Elias Moore Diary.

12. OR, ser. I, vol. 24, pt. 3, p. 228; Capt. James B. Taylor, Company H, 120th Ohio Infantry Regiment, Diary, in VNMP (hereafter cited as James B. Taylor Diary).

13. OR, ser. I, vol. 24, pt. 1, p. 79.

14. Ibid., p. 80; OR, ser. I, vol. 24, pt. 3, p. 231.

15. OR, ser. I, vol. 24, pt. 1, p. 80.

16. Ibid., p. 187.

17. Ibid., pp. 634, 642, 725, 726, 774; OR, ser. I, vol. 24, pt. 3, p. 234; Brig. Gen. Joseph Stockton, Diary, in VNMP (hereafter cited as Stockton Diary); George Pomutz, History of the 15th Iowa Volunteer Infantry (Keokuk, IA, 1887), 255.

18. OR, ser. I, vol. 24, pt. 2, p. 231; OR, ser. I, vol. 24, pt. 1, pp. 751, 752.

19. OR, ser. I, vol. 24, pt. 1, pp. 127, 128.

20. Ibid., p. 81; Hunt Diary.

21. OR, ser. I, vol. 24, pt. 1, p. 634.

22. Ibid., p. 572.

23. Ibid., p. 81.

24. Ibid., p. 634.

25. OR, ser. I, vol. 24, pt. 3, p. 249.

26. William T. Sherman, Memoirs of Gen. William T. Sherman, 2 vols. (New York: Appleton, 1875), 1:347.

27. OR, ser. I, vol. 24, pt. 2, p. 296; Pomutz, History of the 15th Iowa, 225.

28. OR, ser. I, vol. 24, pt. 3, pp. 757, 748.

29. Ibid., pp. 756, 757.

30. Ibid., p. 757.

31. ORN, ser. I, vol. 24, p. 648; OR, ser. I, vol. 24, pt. 3, p. 776; OR, ser. I, vol. 24, pt. 1, pp. 792–93.

32. OR, ser. I, vol. 24, pt. 3, pp. 753, 755.

33. Ibid., p. 761.

34. Ibid.

35. Ibid., p. 771.

36. Ibid., p. 772.

37. Ibid., p. 775.

38. Ibid.

39. Ibid.

40. OR, ser. I, vol. 24, pt. 1, p. 552.

41. OR, ser. I, vol. 24, pt. 3, pp. 776, 777.

42. Ibid., pp. 779, 780.

43. ORN, ser. I, vol. 24, p. 648; OR, ser. I, vol. 24, pt. 3, p. 776.
44. OR, ser. I, vol. 24, pt. 3, p. 778.
45. Ibid., p. 779.
46. Ibid., p. 783.
47. Ibid.
48. D. Alexander Brown, *Grierson's Raid* (Urbana: Univ. of Illinois Press, 1954), 113.
49. OR, ser. I, vol. 24, pt. 1, p. 663.
50. OR, ser. I, vol. 24, pt. 3, p. 792.
51. Ibid., pp. 792–93.
52. Ibid., p. 797.
53. Ibid.
54. OR, ser. I, vol. 24, pt. 1, p. 257.
55. OR, ser. I, vol. 24, pt. 3, p. 800.
56. OR, ser. I, vol. 24, pt. 1, p. 678.

9. STRATEGY IN NORTH MISSISSIPPI

1. OR, ser. I, vol. 24, pt. 3, pp. 155, 156.
2. OR, ser. I, vol. 24, pt. 2, p. 207.
3. Ibid., p. 205.
4. Ibid.
5. OR, ser. I, vol. 24, pt. 3, pp. 702, 706, 733.
6. Ibid., pp. 702, 713.
7. OR, ser. I, vol. 24, pt. 2, p. 872; Thomas Jordan and J. P. Pryor, *The Campaigns of Lieutenant-General Forrest, and of Forrest's Cavalry* (New Orleans, LA, 1868), 251.

10. RAIDS FROM THE NORTH

1. OR, ser. I, vol. 24, pt. 2, p. 207.
2. OR, ser. I, vol. 24, pt. 1, pp. 281, 282, 285.
3. Ibid., p. 286.
4. Ibid.; ORN, ser. I, vol. 24, p. 529; OR, ser. I, vol. 23, pt. 1, p. 286.
5. OR, ser. I, vol. 23, pt. 2, pp. 245, 246.
6. OR, ser. I, vol. 23, pt. 1, pp. 247, 248, 255, 260.
7. Ibid., p. 287.
8. Jordan and Pryor, *Campaigns of Forrest*, 253; OR, ser. I, vol. 23, pt. 1, p. 260.
9. OR, ser. I, vol. 23, pt. 1, p. 287.
10. Jordan and Pryor, *Campaigns of Forrest*, 256, 257.
11. Ibid., 257, 258, 259; OR, ser. I, vol. 23, pt. 1, pp. 288, 289.
12. OR, ser. I, vol. 23, pt. 1, p. 292; A. C. Roach, *The Prisoner of War and How Treated,* ed. Robert S. Henry (Jackson, MS, 1956), 234–35.
13. OR, ser. I, vol. 23, pt. 1, p. 292; Roach, *Prisoner of War,* 235–36.

14. OR, ser. I, vol. 23, pt. 2, p. 788.
15. Jordan and Pryor, *Campaigns of Forrest*, 249, 250; OR, ser. I, vol. 23, pt. 1, p. 248.
16. OR, ser. I, vol. 23, pt. 1, p. 248.
17. Jordan and Pryor, *Campaigns of Forrest*, 253.
18. Ibid., 254, 255.
19. Ibid.
20. OR, ser. I, vol. 23, pt. 1, pp. 288, 289; Jordan and Pryor, *Campaigns of Forrest*, 258.
21. Jordan and Pryor, *Campaigns of Forrest*, 260, 261; Roach, *Prisoner of War*, 227–28; OR, ser. I, vol. 23, pt. 1, p. 289.
22. OR, ser. I, vol. 23, pt. 1, p. 292; Jordan and Pryor, *Campaigns of Forrest*, 272.
23. Jordan and Pryor, *Campaigns of Forrest*, 273.
24. OR, ser. I, vol. 23, pt. 1, p. 292; Roach, *Prisoner of War*, 235–36.
25. OR, ser. I, vol. 24, pt. 3, pp. 196, 203, 765; OR, ser. I, vol. 24, pt. 1, p. 562.
26. OR, ser. I, vol. 24, pt. 1, pp. 555, 563; OR, ser. I, vol. 24, pt. 3, p. 772.
27. OR, ser. I, vol. 24, pt. 1, pp. 556, 557, 558, 562.
28. OR, ser. I, vol. 24, pt. 1, p. 772.
29. Ibid., pp. 219, 220
30. OR, ser. I, vol. 24, pt. 1, pp. 554, 555.
31. OR, ser. I, vol. 24, pt. 3, pp. 217, 218.
32. OR, ser. I, vol. 24, pt. 1, p. 558.
33. Ibid., pp. 555, 558, 563.
34. Ibid., pp. 555, 563, 564.
35. OR, ser. I, vol. 24, pt. 3, p. 767.
36. OR, ser. I, vol. 24, pt. 1, pp. 556, 557, 562.
37. Ibid., pp. 556, 557, 558, 562.
38. Ibid., p. 558.
39. Ibid., pp. 563, 564.
40. OR, ser. I, vol. 24, pt. 3, p. 207.
41. OR, ser. I, vol. 24, pt. 1, p. 522.
42. Brown, *Grierson's Raid*, 23, 32, 53; OR, ser. I, vol. 24, pt. 1, p. 522.
43. OR, ser. I, vol. 24, pt. 1, p. 523.
44. Ibid., p. 522; Brown, *Grierson's Raid*, 43, 44.
45. OR, ser. I, vol. 24, pt. 1, p. 523; Brown, *Grierson's Raid*, 76–78.
46. OR, ser. I, vol. 24, pt. 1, p. 524; Brown, *Grierson's Raid*, 111.
47. OR, ser. I, vol. 24, pt. 1, pp. 524–25.
48. Ibid., p. 716.
49. Ibid., p. 531.
50. Ibid., p. 525.
51. Ibid., p. 526.
52. Ibid.
53. Ibid., pp. 526, 533.
54. Ibid., pp. 526–27.

55. Ibid., p. 527.
56. Ibid.
57. Ibid.
58. Brown, *Grierson's Raid,* 194–201; OR, ser. I, vol. 24, pt. 1, pp. 527, 539, 540.
59. Brown, *Grierson's Raid,* 203, 204; OR, ser. I, vol. 24, pt. 1, pp. 527, 543.
60. Brown, *Grierson's Raid,* 214; OR, ser. I, vol. 24, pt. 1, pp. 537, 538.
61. OR, ser. I, vol. 24, pt. 1, p. 528.
62. Brown, *Grierson's Raid,* 23; OR, ser. I, vol. 24, pt. 3, p. 767.
63. OR, ser. I, vol. 24, pt. 1, pp. 550–51, 560.
64. Ibid., p. 534; Brown, *Grierson's Raid,* 53.
65. OR, ser. I, vol. 24, pt. 1, p. 534.
66. OR, ser. I, vol. 24, pt. 3, p. 770.
67. Ibid., p. 769.
68. Ibid., p. 773.
69. Ibid., p. 535; Brown, *Grierson's Raid,* 90.
70. OR, ser. I, vol. 24, pt. 3, pp. 531, 536.
71. Ibid., pp. 532, 776.
72. Ibid., pp. 776, 777.
73. Brown, *Grierson's Raid,* 113.
74. OR, ser. I, vol. 24, pt. 3, p. 781.
75. OR, ser. I, vol. 24, pt. 1, p. 254; OR, ser. I, vol. 24, pt. 3, p. 782.
76. OR, ser. I, vol. 24, pt. 1, p. 544.
77. OR, ser. I, vol. 24, pt. 3, p. 792.
78. Ibid., p. 794.
79. Ibid., p. 792.
80. Ibid., p. 793; OR, ser. I, vol. 24, pt. 1, p. 545.
81. OR, ser. I, vol. 24, pt. 3, p. 799.
82. OR, ser. I, vol. 24, pt. 1, p. 545; OR, ser. I, vol. 24, pt. 3, p. 805.
83. OR, ser. I, vol. 24, pt. 3, pp. 801, 802.
84. Ibid., p. 814.
85. OR, ser. I, vol. 24, pt. 1, p. 521.
86. OR, ser. I, vol. 24, pt. 3, p. 247.
87. OR, ser. I, vol. 24, pt. 1, p. 579.
88. Ibid.
89. OR, ser. I, vol. 24, pt. 3, p. 813.
90. OR, ser. I, vol. 24, pt. 1, p. 579.
91. OR, ser. I, vol. 24, pt. 1, p. 579; OR, ser. I, vol. 24, pt. 3, pp. 820, 842.
92. OR, ser. I, vol. 24, pt. 1, p. 257.
93. Ibid., p. 693.
94. Ibid., pp. 257, 258, 690, 691, 692, 693.
95. Ibid., p. 258.
96. Ibid., p. 579.
97. OR, ser. I, vol. 24, pt. 3, p. 813.

98. Ibid., p. 805.

99. Ibid., p. 808.

100. OR, ser. I, vol. 24, pt. 1, p. 580.

101. OR, ser. I, vol. 24, pt. 3, pp. 807, 808, 814.

102. OR, ser. I, vol. 24, pt. 1, p. 580.

103. Ibid.

104. Ibid., p. 693.

105. Ibid.

106. OR, ser. I, vol. 23, pt. 1, p. 257.

107. Ibid., pp. 691, 692, 693.

108. Ibid., pp. 690, 691, 692, 693.

109. Ibid., pp. 257. 258, 690, 692, 693.

11. DEMONSTRATION AT DRUMGOULD'S BLUFF

1. OR, ser. I, vol. 24, pt. 3, p. 249.

2. Ibid., p. 245; C. E. Affeld, Diary, in VNMP (hereafter cited as Affeld Diary); ORN, ser. I, vol. 24, p. 589.

3. ORN, ser. I, vol. 24, p. 587; Affeld Diary.

4. ORN, ser. I, vol. 24, p. 589.

5. Ibid., pp. 591, 593, 595.

6. Ibid., pp. 592, 595.

7. ORN, ser. I, vol. 24, pp. 590, 592; William H. Tunnard, *A Southern Record; The History of the Third Regiment Louisiana Infantry*, ed. Edwin C. Bearss (Dayton, OH: 1970), 228; OR, ser. I, vol. 24, pt. 1, pp. 576–78.

8. ORN, ser. I, vol. 24, p. 590; Affeld Diary.

9. OR, ser. I, vol. 24, pt. 3, pp. 260–61.

10. ORN, ser. I, vol. 24, pp. 590, 592; Tunnard, *History of the Third Regiment Louisiana*, 228.

11. ORN, ser. I, vol. 24, p. 595; Affeld Diary.

12. OR, ser. I, vol. 24, pt. 2, p. 384; Tunnard, *History of the Third Regiment Louisiana*, 227.

13. OR, ser. I, vol. 24, pt. 2, p. 384.

14. OR, ser. I, vol. 24, pt. 1, pp. 577–78; Tunnard, *History of Third Regiment Louisiana*, 228.

15. OR, ser. I, vol. 24, pt. 1, p. 577.

16. ORN, ser. I, vol. 24, pp. 590, 592; Tunnard, *History of the Third Regiment Louisiana*, 228.

17. ORN, ser. I, vol. 24, p. 578.

18. OR, ser. I, vol. 24, pt. 3, p. 806.

19. ORN, ser. I, vol. 24, p. 590; Affeld Diary.

20. ORN, ser. I, vol. 24, pp. 590, 592; Tunnard, *History of the Third Regiment Louisiana*, 228.

12. BATTLE OF GRAND GULF

1. ORN, ser. I, vol. 24, p. 627.
2. Ibid., pp. 610–28; Mahan, "Gulf and Inland Waters," 160.
3. ORN, ser. I, vol. 24, pp. 607–28; Mahan, "Gulf and Inland Waters," 160.
4. ORN, ser. I, vol. 24, pp. 613, 620, 622.
5. Grant, *Personal Memoirs*, 1:396, 1:497; ORN, ser. I, vol. 24, p. 610; OR, ser. I, vol. 24, pt. 2, p. 142.
6. ORN, ser. I, vol. 24, pp. 610–28; OR, ser. I, vol. 24, pt. 1, p. 574.
7. *Pine Bluff (AR) Commercial,* 17 Dec. 1904, clipping in VNMP; ORN, ser. I, vol. 24, pp. 611, 620.
8. Grant, *Personal Memoirs*, 1:397; Charles A. Dana, *Recollections of the Civil War* (New York, 1902), 43; Greene, "The Mississippi," 124, 125.
9. ORN, ser. I, vol. 24, p. 623.
10. Ibid., pp. 608–28.
11. OR, ser. I, vol. 24, pt. 1, pp. 663–64; ORN, ser. I, vol. 24, pp. 626–28; Mahan, "Gulf and Inland Waters," 158–59; *Pine Bluff (AR) Commercial,* 17 Dec. 1904; Personal site examination by author, 1958–99.
12. *Pine Bluff (AR) Commercial,* 17 Dec. 1904.
13. OR, ser. I, vol. 24, pt. 1, pp. 574–75, 678.
14. Mahan, "Gulf and Inland Waters," 161.
15. ORN, ser. I, vol. 24, p. 623.
16. OR, ser. I, vol. 24, pt. 1, p. 576.
17. OR, ser. I, vol. 24, pt. 3, p. 804.
18. ORN, ser. I, vol. 24, pp. 628–29.

13. LANDING AT BRUINSBURG

1. ORN, ser. I, vol. 24, pp. 615–26; Mahan, "Gulf and Inland Waters," 162; Payne to W. T. Rigby, 16 Dec. 1910, in VNMP.
2. OR, ser. I, vol. 24, pt. 9, p. 48; Grant, *Personal Memoirs*, 1:398; Greene, "The Mississippi," 125.
3. OR, ser. I, vol. 24, pt. 3, pp. 246, 260–61.
4. OR, ser. I, vol. 24, pt. 1, pp. 48, 142, 601, 615; *History of the 46th Regiment Indiana Volunteer Infantry, Sept. 1861–Sept. 1865,* compiled by committee (Logansport, IN, 1888), 46.
5. *History of the 46th Regiment Indiana* (1888), 46.
6. Ibid., 56, 57.
7. Personal examination by author, 1958–99.
8. Greene, "The Mississippi," 125.
9. OR, ser. I, vol. 24, pt. 1, pp. 601, 615.
10. *History of the 46th Regiment Indiana* (1888), 55; Charles A. Hobbs, Diary, in VNMP.
11. Maj. Frank Swigart, *Washington (DC) National Tribune,* 23 Dec. 1886.

12. OR, ser. I, vol. 24, pt. 1, p. 143.

13. Ibid., pp. 628, 631; Personal examination by author, 1966–99.

14. Crooke, *21st Regiment of Iowa*, 54.

15. OR, ser. I, vol. 24, pt. 1, pp. 634, 642, 643, 651.

16. Ibid., p. 643; ORN, ser. I, vol. 25, pp. 46–48.

17. Ibid., pp. 634, 642.

18. Crooke, *21st Regiment of Iowa*, 61.

19. Grant, *Personal Memoirs*, 1:407, 1:408.

20. OR, ser. I, vol. 24, pt. 1, p. 663.

21. Ibid., p. 672.

22. Ibid.

23. Ibid., pp. 663, 678.

24. Ibid., p. 658.

25. Ibid., p. 672.

26. Ibid., pp. 672, 678.

27. Ibid., p. 672; *Pine Bluff (AR) Commercial*, 17 Dec. 1904, clipping in VNMP.

28. OR, ser. I, vol. 24, pt. 1, p. 658.

29. Ibid., p. 663.

30. OR, ser. I, vol. 24, pt. 3, pp. 804, 805.

31. Greene, "The Mississippi," 127.

32. OR, ser. I, vol. 24, pt. 1, p. 675.

33. OR, ser. I, vol. 24, pt. 3, p. 804; Greene, "The Mississippi," 126.

14. BATTLE OF PORT GIBSON

1. OR, ser. I, vol. 24, pt. 1, pp. 628, 631.

2. *Pine Bluff (AR) Commercial*, 17 Dec. 1904.

3. OR, ser. I, vol. 24, pt. 1, pp. 628, 629.

4. Ibid., pp. 615, 625, 629, 672; Crooke, *21st Regiment of Iowa*, 54, 55; Hunt Diary.

5. OR, ser. I, vol. 24, pt. 1, p. 143.

6. Ibid., pp. 615, 675.

7. Ibid., p. 625.

8. Ibid., pp. 143, 585, 586, 588, 591.

9. Ibid., pp. 615–16, 620, 621, 625; Crooke, *21st Regiment of Iowa*, 57; Isaac H. Elliott, *History of the 33rd Regiment Illinois Veteran Volunteer Infantry in the Civil War, 22 Aug. 1861 to 7 Dec. 1865* (Gibson City, IL, 1902), 30.

10. OR, ser. I, vol. 24, pt. 1, pp. 626, 664.

11. Ibid., pp. 144, 145, 593, 599, 602, 603, 606, 607, 609–11, 613, 626; A. K. Shaifer, Map, *The Battle of Port Gibson*, in VNMP.

12. OR, ser. I, vol. 24, pt. 1, pp. 603, 607, 622.

13. Ibid., p. 145.

14. Ibid., p. 627.

15. Ibid., pp. 611, 629, 630.

16. Ibid., pp. 603–4.
17. Ibid., p. 604.
18. Ibid., pp. 604, 607, 611, 613, 627, 668–69.
19. Ibid., p. 676.
20. Ibid., pp. 653, 666, 676.
21. Ibid.
22. Ibid., p. 679.
23. Ibid., p. 690.
24. Ibid., p. 680.
25. Ibid., pp. 143, 635, 643, 681.
26. Ibid., p. 49.
27. Ibid., pp. 588, 643, 681.
28. Ibid., p. 681.
29. Ibid., p. 672.
30. Ibid.; *Pine Bluff (AR) Commercial,* 17 Dec. 1904.
31. John Hubbard, interview by Warren E. Grabau. Port Gibson, MS, 1958. The bullet hole in the west wall of the Shaifer house has been carefully preserved.
32. *Pine Bluff (AR) Commercial,* 17 Dec. 1904.
33. OR, ser. I, vol. 24, pt. 1, p. 678; OR Atlas, pl. 31, fig. 6; Francis G. Obenchain, Map, *Part of the Battlefield of Port Gibson, Mississippi, May 1, 1863,* in VNMP.
34. OR, ser. I, vol. 24, pt. 1, p. 678.
35. Ibid., pp. 586, 591.
36. Ibid., p. 664.
37. Ibid., pp. 615, 675.
38. Ibid., p. 679.
39. Ibid., p. 668.
40. Ibid., p. 625; Crooke, *21st Regiment of Iowa,* 57; Elliott, *History of the 33rd Illinois,* 38.
41. OR, ser. I, vol. 24, pt. 1, pp. 626, 664, 672, 673.
42. Ibid., pp. 626, 664.
43. Ibid., pp. 607, 622.
44. Ibid., p. 673.
45. Ibid., pp. 664, 676.
46. Ibid., pp. 675, 676.
47. Ibid., p. 664.
48. Ibid.
49. Ibid., p. 668.
50. Ibid., p. 604.
51. Ibid.
52. Ibid., p. 676.
53 Ibid.
54. Ibid., p. 666.

55. Ibid., pp. 588, 643, 681.
56. Ibid., pp. 673, 681.
57. Ibid., p. 643.

15. ADVANCE TO THE BIG BLACK RIVER

1. OR, ser. I, vol. 24, pt. 1, pp. 726, 727, 774.
2. Ibid., p. 677.
3. Ibid., pp. 594, 595.
4. Ibid., pp. 128, 635; Thienel, "Bridges."
5. OR, ser. I, vol. 24, pt. 3, p. 262.
6. OR, ser. I, vol. 24, pt. 1, pp. 635, 706.
7. Ibid., p. 603.
8. Ibid., pp. 653, 654.
9. Thomas B. Marshall, *History of the 83rd Ohio Volunteer Infantry: The Grey-hound Regiment* (Cincinnati, OH, 1912), 76.
10. OR, ser. I, vol. 24, pt. 1, p. 635.
11. Ibid., p. 129; Thienel, "Bridges."
12. OR, ser. I, vol. 24, pt. 1, p. 635; Thienel, "Bridges."
13. OR, ser. I, vol. 24, pt. 1., pp. 656, 707.
14. Ibid., pp. 636, 645, 707.
15. Ibid., pp. 49, 735; Grant, *Personal Memoirs,* 1:409.
16. ORN, ser. I, vol. 24, pp. 627, 645.
17. OR, ser. I, vol. 24, pt. 1, pp. 722, 727, 781.
18. Ibid., pp. 722, 723, 727.
19. Ibid., pp. 638, 669, 722, 723, 774.
20. Ibid., pp. 636, 645; Osborn H. Oldroyd, *A Soldier's Story of the Siege of Vicksburg* (Springfield,OH, 1885), 2.
21. OR, ser. I, vol. 24, pt. 1, p. 50.
22. Ibid., p. 669.
23. Ibid., p. 660.
24. Ibid., p. 666.
25. Ibid., pp. 655–57.
26. Ibid.
27. Ibid., pp. 666, 677.
28. Ibid., pp. 655–57, 666.
29. Ibid., pp. 666, 677.
30. Ibid., p. 656.
31. Ibid., pp. 656–57.
32. Ibid., pp. 656, 666.
33. Ibid., pp. 655–57.
34. Ibid., pp. 656, 666.
35. Ibid., pp. 635, 707.

36. Ibid., p. 669.

37. OR, ser. I, vol. 24, pt. 3, p. 823.

38. OR, ser. I, vol. 24, pt. 1, pp. 656, 707.

39. Ibid., pp. 722, 727, 781.

40. Ibid., pp. 636, 669, 683, 722, 723, 727, 774.

41. Ibid., pp. 636, 645; Oldroyd, *Soldier's Story*, 2.

16. LOGISTICS, COMMUNICATIONS, AND REINFORCEMENTS

1. OR, ser. I, vol. 24, pt. 1, pp. 32, 33.

2. OR, ser. I, vol. 24, pt. 3, pp. 246, 260–61.

3. ORN, ser. I, vol. 24, pp. 590, 595.

4. E. Paul Reichelm, "The Taking of Vicksburg," *Bayonne (NJ) Herald*, 11 Jan. 1902; OR, ser. I, vol. 24, pt. 1, p. 758; OR, ser. I, vol. 24, pt. 3, p. 271.

5. Reichelm, "Taking of Vicksburg"; OR, ser. I, vol. 24, pt. 1, p. 758.

6. Reichelm, "Taking of Vicksburg"; OR, ser. I, vol. 24, pt. 2, p. 250; OR, ser. I, vol. 24, pt. 1, p. 759.

7. OR, ser. I, vol. 24, pt. 1, p. 759; Reichelm, "Taking of Vicksburg."

8. OR, ser. I, vol. 24, pt. 1, p. 759; Reichelm, "Taking of Vicksburg."

9. OR, ser. I, vol. 24, pt. 3, p. 268.

10. OR, ser. I, vol. 24, pt. 2, pp. 187, 281.

11. ORN, ser. I, vol. 24, pp. 663, 664, 703.

12. OR, ser. I, vol. 24, pt. 2, pp. 187, 281.

13. OR, ser. I, vol. 24, pt. 3, pp. 273, 274, 275.

14. Stockton Diary.

15. OR, ser. I, vol. 24, pt. 3, p. 287; OR, ser. I, vol. 24, pt. 2, p. 297; Stockton Diary; Pomutz, *History of the 15th Iowa*.

16. OR, ser. I, vol. 24, pt. 3, p. 810.

17. Ibid., pp. 839, 840, 849, 851; OR, ser. I, vol. 24, pt. 1, p. 736.

17. MAKING TROUBLE IN THE TRANS-MISSISSIPPI

1. ORN, ser. I, vol. 24, pp. 627, 645.

2. Ibid., pp. 684, 706.

3. Ibid., pp. 626, 699.

4. Ibid., pp. 627, 645; Mahan, "Gulf and Inland Waters," 166.

5. Mahan, "Gulf and Inland Waters," 166.

6. Ibid.

7. Ibid.

8. Ibid.

9. ORN, ser. I, vol. 24, pp. 645, 646, 685; Mahan, "Gulf and Inland Waters," 166.

10. OR, ser. I, vol. 24, pt. 1, p. 700; *Natchez (MS) Daily Courier*, 19 May 1863.

11. OR, ser. I, vol. 24, pt. 1, p. 700; Mahan, "Gulf and Inland Waters," 166.

12. Mahan, "Gulf and Inland Waters," 167.

13. Ibid.

14. Ibid., 168.

15. Ibid., 164.

16. Ibid., 164–65.

17. OR, ser. I, vol. 15, p. 1041.

18. Joseph P. Blessington, *The Campaigns of Walker's Texas Division* (New York: Lang, Little & Co., 1875), 78.

19. Ibid.; OR, ser. I, vol. 22, pt. 2, p. 840; OR, ser. I, vol. 15, pp. 1057, 1058.

20. Mahan, "Gulf and Inland Waters," 165.

21. ORN, ser. I, vol. 24, p. 645; Mahan, "Gulf and Inland Waters," 166.

22. Blessington, *Texas Division*, 81, 82; OR, ser. I, vol. 15, pp. 1081–83.

23. OR, ser. I, vol. 24, pt. 3, p. 846.

24. OR, ser. I, vol. 24, pt. 2, p. 5.

18. TOWARD EDWARDS AND THE RAILROAD

1. OR, ser. I, vol. 24, pt. 1, p. 50.

2. OR, ser. I, vol. 24, pt. 2, p. 12; James B. Taylor Diary; Elias Moore Diary.

3. OR, ser. I, vol. 24, pt. 3, p. 836; OR, ser. I, vol. 24, pt. 2, p. 314.

4. OR, ser. I, vol. 24, pt. 3, p. 277.

5. Ibid., p. 133; Hunt Diary.

6. OR, ser. I, vol. 24, pt. 3, p. 283.

7. OR, ser. I, vol. 24, pt. 1, pp. 822, 823, 824.

8. Ibid., pp. 656, 828–31.

9. Ibid., pp. 822, 823.

10. OR, ser. I, vol. 24, pt. 2, p. 12.

11. OR, ser. I, vol. 24, pt. 1, pp. 822, 823.

12. Ibid., p. 823.

13. Ibid., pp. 828, 829.

14. Ibid., pp. 656, 828–31.

15. Ibid., p. 822.

16. OR, ser. I, vol. 24, pt. 3, p. 834.

17. Ibid., p. 133; Col. Charles E. Hooker, "Mississippi," in *Confederate Military History; a Library of Confederate States History*, 11 vols., ed. Gen. Clement A. Evans (Atlanta, GA: Confederate Publishing House, 1899), 7:137.

18. OR, ser. I, vol. 24, pt. 3; Hooker, "Mississippi."

19. Greene, "The Mississippi," 162.

20. OR, ser. I, vol. 24, pt. 3, p. 279.

21. Ibid., p. 834; OR, ser. I, vol. 24, pt. 2, pp. 40, 118.

22. OR, ser. I, vol. 24, pt. 2, p. 399.

23. OR, ser. I, vol. 24, pt. 3, pp. 835, 836, 839, 840.

24. Ibid., pp. 834, 835, 841, 842.

25. Ibid., p. 842; OR, ser. I, vol. 24, pt. 1, p. 259.
26. OR, ser. I, vol. 24, pt. 3, p. 845.

19. AIMING FOR THE RAILROAD

1. OR, ser. I, vol. 24, pt. 3, p. 279.
2. Ibid., pp. 279–80.
3. Ibid., pp. 283, 287.
4 Grant, *Personal Memoirs,* 1:412; OR, ser. I, vol. 24, pt. 1, p. 84.
5. OR, ser. I, vol. 24, pt. 3, p. 282; Marshall, *History of 83rd Ohio,* 77.
6. *History of the 46th Regiment Indiana* (1888), 59.
7. OR, ser. I, vol. 24, pt. 3, p. 284.
8. Ibid., p. 285.
9. Ibid., p. 636; Oldroyd, *Soldier's Story,* 6; OR, ser. I, vol. 24, pt. 1, p. 636.
10. OR, ser. I, vol. 24, pt. 3, pp. 292, 293; OR, ser. I, vol. 24, pt. 2, p. 12.
11. OR, ser. I, vol. 24, pt. 2, p. 250; Reichelm, "Taking of Vicksburg."
12. OR, ser. I, vol. 24, pt. 3, pp. 292, 293; OR, ser. I, vol. 24, pt. 2, p. 12.
13. OR, ser. I, vol. 24, pt. 3, p. 296; W. B. Halsey, Diary, in VNMP (hereafter cited as Halsey Diary).
14. OR, ser. I, vol. 24, pt. 3, p. 296; OR, ser. I, vol. 24, pt. 1, p. 762.
15. F. L. Yates, personal conversations with Warren E. Grabau, Cayuga, MS, 1958.
16. OR, ser. I, vol. 24, pt. 1, p. 639.
17. Ibid., p. 735.
18. OR, ser. I, vol. 24, pt. 2, p. 31.
19. Ibid., pp. 4, 31, 40, 118, 167; *History of the 46th Regiment Indiana* (1888), 59; OR, ser. I, vol. 24, pt. 1, p. 147; Raynor Diary; OR, ser. I, vol. 24, pt. 3, pp. 146, 147.
20. OR, ser. I, vol. 24, pt. 1, p. 753.
21. Ibid., pp. 753, 759, 769; Reichelm, "Taking of Vicksburg"; OR, ser. I, vol. 24, pt. 2, p. 250; OR, ser. I, vol. 24, pt. 3, p. 299.
22. OR, ser. I, vol. 24, pt. 3, p. 845.
23. Ibid.
24. Ibid., pp. 849, 851; OR, ser. I, vol. 24, pt. 1, p. 736.
25. OR, ser. I, vol. 24, pt. 3, p. 849.
26. Ibid., p. 851.
27. Ibid.
28. Ibid., pp. 863, 865; OR, ser. I, vol. 24, pt. 2, p. 399.
29. OR, ser. I, vol. 24, pt. 3, p. 851.
30. OR, ser. I, vol. 24, pt. 1, p. 736.
31. OR, ser. I, vol. 24, pt. 3, p. 855.
32. OR, ser. I, vol. 24, pt. 2, pp. 856, 857, 858.
33. Ibid., pp. 861, 862.
34. Ibid., p. 863.
35. OR, ser. I, vol. 24, pt. 1, p. 261.

20. MCPHERSON'S APPROACH MARCH TO RAYMOND

1. OR, ser. I, vol. 24, pt. 1, p. 714.
2. Ibid., pp. 637, 714.
3. Ibid., p. 736.
4. OR, ser. I, vol. 24, pt. 3, pp. 851, 853.
5. OR, ser. I, vol. 24, pt. 1, p. 737.
6. Ibid.
7. Ibid.
8. Ibid., pp. 739, 741, 743, 747.

21. CONFUSION COMPOUNDED

Note: This account is an extreme abridgement of a very detailed reconstruction of the Battle of Raymond by Edwin C. Bearss and Warren E. Grabau,
published in the *Jackson (MS) Clarion Ledger* in 1958: "The Battle of
Raymond," 5 Jan.; "Battle of Raymond Had False Reports," 12 Jan.; "Rebels
Surprise Yanks in Jungle-like Warfare," 19 Jan.; "Yanks Begin Victory Move,"
26 Jan.; "Tide of Conflict Begins to Turn," 2 Feb.; Yanks Win Battle of
Raymond," 9 Feb.

1. OR, ser. I, vol. 24, pt. 1, p. 645.
2. Ibid., pp. 637, 645.
3. Ibid., p. 645.
4. Oldroyd, *Soldier's Story,* 7, 8.
5. OR, ser. I, vol. 24, pt. 1, pp. 645, 646, 716.
6. Ibid., p. 646.
7. Ibid., pp. 716, 717, 721, 742, 743, 745, 782.
8. Ibid., pp. 737, 741, 743, 747, 739.
9. Ibid., pp. 737, 739, 743.
10. Ibid., p. 747.
11. Ibid., pp. 708, 740.
12. Ibid., p. 740.
13. Ibid., pp. 715, 718, 748; Oldroyd, *Soldier's Story,* 7, 8.
14. John B. Lindsey, *Military Annals of Tennessee. Confederate* (Nashville, TN,
    1886), 323–32; OR, ser. I, vol. 24, pt. 1, pp. 716, 717, 741.
15. OR, ser. I, vol. 24, pt. 1, p. 746.

22. THE APPROACH TO JACKSON

1. OR, ser. I, vol. 24, pt. 3, p. 300; Grant, *Personal Memoirs,* 1:417.
2. OR, ser. I, vol. 24, pt. 1, p. 50.
3. Greene, "The Mississippi," 143; Grant, *Personal Memoirs,* 1:417; Matthew
    Forney Steele, *American Campaigns,* 2 vols. (N.p.: Adams, 1909), 1:408.

4. OR, ser. I, vol. 24, pt. 3, p. 330.

5. Ibid.

6. OR, ser. I, vol. 24, pt. 1, pp. 638, 735.

7. Ibid., p. 638; OR, ser. I, vol. 24, pt. 2, pp. 198–99.

8. OR, ser. I, vol. 24, pt. 1, p. 729.

9. Ibid., pp. 753, 759, 767; OR, ser. I, vol. 24, pt. 2, p. 250.

10. OR, ser. I, vol. 24, pt. 3, p. 309; OR, ser. I, vol. 24, pt. 1, p. 753.

11. OR, ser. I, vol. 24, pt. 2, pp. 116, 118; Raynor Diary.

12. OR, ser. I, vol. 24, pt. 1, p. 147.

13. OR, ser. I, vol. 24, pt. 2, p. 41.

14. OR, ser. I, vol. 24, pt. 1, p. 147; OR, ser. I, vol. 24, pt. 2, pp. 36, 41.

15. Oldroyd, *Soldier's Story*, 8, 9.

16. OR, ser. I, vol. 24, pt. 1, p. 775.

17. OR, ser. I, vol. 24, pt. 3, p. 308.

18. Ibid., p. 309; OR, ser. I, vol. 24, pt. 1, p. 753.

19. OR, ser. I, vol. 24, pt. 3, pp. 873, 874; OR, ser. I, vol. 24, pt. 2, p. 69.

20. OR, ser. I, vol. 24, pt. 1, pp. 239, 260; Joseph E. Johnston, *Narrative of Military Operations, Directed, During the Late War Between the States* (New York: Appleton, 1874), 174–75.

21. OR, ser. I, vol. 24, pt. 1, pp. 871, 872.

22. OR, ser. I, vol. 24, pt. 2, pp. 41, 118.

23. OR, ser. I, vol. 24, pt. 3, p. 875.

24. OR, ser. I, vol. 24, pt. 1, p. 739.

25. Ibid., p. 239; Grant, *Personal Memoirs*, 1:423.

26. OR, ser. I, vol. 24, pt. 1, p. 215; Greene, "The Mississippi," 146.

27. OR, ser. I, vol. 24, pt. 1, p. 239; Johnston, *Narrative*, 175–76.

28. OR, ser. I, vol. 24, pt. 1, p. 239; Gilbert E. Govan and James W. Livingood, *The Story of Gen. Joseph E. Johnston, C.S.A.: A Different Valor* (Indianapolis, IN: Bobbs-Merrill, 1956), 198–99.

29. OR, ser. I, vol. 24, pt. 1, p. 785.

30. Ibid., pp. 785, 786.

31. W. B. Capers, *The Soldier-Bishop: Ellison Capers* (New York: Neale Publ. Co., 1912), 61–62; OR, ser. I, vol. 24, pt. 1, pp. 775, 782, 787.

32. OR, ser. I, vol. 24, pt. 1, p. 786; Dunbar Rowland, *The Official and Statistical Record of the State of Mississippi* (Nashville, TN, 1908), 893, 894; Oldroyd, *Soldier's Story*, 8, 9.

23. TOO LITTLE AND TOO LATE

1. OR, ser. I, vol. 24, pt. 1, pp. 775, 782.

2. Ibid.

3. Ibid., p. 638.

4. Ibid., pp. 638, 729; Capers, *Soldier-Bishop*, 61.

5. OR, ser. I, vol. 24, pt. 1, pp. 729, 775, 777, 782, 786.
6. H. S. Keene, Diary, in VNMP.
7. OR, ser. I, vol. 24, pt. 1, p. 639.
8. Ibid., pp. 775, 780, 783.
9. Ibid., pp. 753, 767.
10. Ibid., pp. 753, 759, 762, 770.
11. OR, ser. I, vol. 24, pt. 2, p. 284; OR, ser. I, vol. 24, pt. 1, p. 753.
12. OR, ser. I, vol. 24, pt. 1, p. 786; Jefferson Brumbach to wife, 20 May 1863, VNMP.
13. OR, ser. I, vol. 24, pt. 1, pp. 762, 765, 766; Brumbach to wife; Byron C. Bryner, *Bugle Echoes: The Story of the Illinois 47th* (Springfield, IL.: Phillips, 1902), 79.
14. OR, ser. I, vol. 24, pt. 1, p. 770.
15. Ibid., pp. 759, 766, 768, 770; Brumbach to wife.
16. OR, ser. I, vol. 24, pt. 1, p. 786.
17. Ibid., pp. 729, 755, 777, 782, 786; Capers, *Soldier-Bishop*, 61.
18. OR, ser. I, vol. 24, pt. 1, pp. 729, 775, 777, 782.
19. Ibid., p. 786.

24. TOWARD VICKSBURG AT LAST

1. OR, ser. I, vol. 24, pt. 1, p. 754; OR, ser. I, vol. 24, pt. 3, p. 312.
2. OR, ser. I, vol. 24, pt. 1, p. 639; Grant, *Personal Memoirs*, 1:423.
3. Xenophon, "The Anabasis of Cyrus," trans. Henry G. Dakyns, in *The Greek Historians*, 2 vols. (New York: Random House, 1942), 2:222–365.
4. Grant, *Personal Memoirs*, 1:425; OR, ser. I, vol. 24, pt. 3, p. 310.
5. Grant, *Personal Memoirs*, 1:425; OR, ser. I, vol. 24, pt. 3, p. 310.
6. OR, ser. I, vol. 24, pt. 2, pp. 12, 13; Raynor Diary.
7. OR, ser. I, vol. 24, pt. 2, pp. 12, 13; Elias Moore Diary.
8. OR, ser. I, vol. 24, pt. 1, p. 616; Hunt Diary.
9. OR, ser. I, vol. 24, pt. 2, p. 41; Raynor Diary; *History of the 46th Regiment Indiana* (1888), 60.
10. OR, ser. I, vol. 24, pt. 1, pp. 639, 646, 647, 730, 776.
11. Ibid.
12. OR, ser. I, vol. 24, pt. 2, pp. 31, 255; Hunt Diary.
13. Stephen D. Lee, "Campaign for Vicksburg," *Publications of the Mississippi Historical Society* 3 (1900): 35.
14. OR, ser. I, vol. 24, pt. 3, p. 877.
15. OR, ser. I, vol. 24, pt. 1, p. 261.
16. OR, ser. I, vol. 24, pt. 2, p. 125.
17. OR, ser. I, vol. 24, pt. 1, p. 261.
18. OR, ser. I, vol. 24, pt. 1; OR, ser. I, vol. 24, pt. 2, p. 125; Lockett, "Defense of Vicksburg," 3:487; Johnston, *Narrative*, 181.
19. OR, ser. I, vol. 24, pt. 3, p. 876.

20. John C. Pemberton III, *Pemberton: Defender of Vicksburg* (Chapel Hill, NC: Univ. of North Carolina Press, 1942), 150.

21. OR, ser. I, vol. 24, pt. 1, p. 74.

22. OR, ser. I, vol. 24, pt. 2, p. 125.

23. Ibid., p. 75; OR, ser. I, vol. 24, pt. 1, p. 262.

24. OR, ser. I, vol. 24, pt. 2, p. 75; OR, ser. I, vol. 24, pt. 1, p. 262.

25. OR, ser. I, vol. 24, pt. 2, pp. 110–14.

26. Ibid., pp. 93, 107.

27. OR, ser. I, vol. 24, pt. 3, p. 882; Johnston, *Narrative,* 179–80.

28. Johnston, *Narrative,* 179–80.

29. OR, ser. I, vol. 24, pt. 3, p. 884.

30. Steven E. Woodworth, *Davis and Lee at War* (Lawrence: Univ. Press of Kansas, 1995), 229.

31. John B. Jones, *Rebel War Clerk's Diary* (New York: Sagamore Press, 1958), 209–10.

32. Ibid., 210–14.

25. THE APPROACH TO CHAMPION HILL

1. James H. Wilson, "Staff Officer's Journal of the Vicksburg Campaign, April 30 to July 4, 1863," *Journal of the Military Service Institute of the United States* 43 (155, 157) (July–Aug. 1908): 107.

2. Ibid.; OR, ser. I, vol. 24, pt. 1, pp. 51–52.

3. OR, ser. I, vol. 24, pt. 3, p. 319; Grant, *Personal Memoirs,* 1:428.

4. OR, ser. I, vol. 24, pt. 2, p. 87.

5. OR, ser. I, vol. 24, pt. 3, p. 316.

6. OR, ser. I, vol. 24, pt. 2, pp. 14–29.

7. John H. Raynor, "Vicksburg Revisited," *Toledo (OH) Daily Blade,* 15 Nov. 1902.

8. OR, ser. I, vol. 24, pt. 2, pp. 110–14.

9. Ibid., pp. 75, 93, 94; OR, ser. I, vol. 24, pt. 1, p. 163.

10. OR, ser. I, vol. 24, pt. 2, pp. 32, 88; OR, ser. I, vol. 24, pt. 1, p. 263.

11. Greene, "The Mississippi," 152.

12. OR, ser. I, vol. 24, pt. 2, p. 94; OR, ser. I, vol. 24, pt. 3, p. 884.

13. OR, ser. I, vol. 24, pt. 2, pp. 75, 83, 91.

14. Ibid., pp. 94, 108.

15. Stephen D. Lee, "Campaign for Vicksburg," 36.

16. OR, ser. I, vol. 24, pt. 2, pp. 14–29, 134.

17. Ibid., pp. 32, 38, 88.

26. BATTLE OF CHAMPION HILL

1. OR, ser. I, vol. 24, pt. 2, pp. 41, 49, 53.

2. OR, ser. I, vol. 24, pt. 1, p. 52.

3. Ibid., p. 149.

4. OR, ser. I, vol. 24, pt. 3, pp. 316, 317.

5. Ibid., p. 319.

6. OR, ser. I, vol. 24, pt. 2, pp. 52, 57, 58.

7. OR, ser. I, vol. 24, pt. 1, p. 717.

8. Ibid., pp. 633, 647, 709; OR, ser. I, vol. 24, pt. 2, p. 42.

9. OR, ser. I, vol. 24, pt. 1, pp. 640, 709; OR, ser. I, vol. 24, pt. 2, pp. 101–102.

10. OR, ser. I, vol. 24, pt. 2, p. 225.

11. Ibid., p. 32.

12. Ibid., pp. 32, 37, 38, 110.

13. Ibid., p. 32.

14. Ibid., pp. 110, 116.

15. Ibid., p. 110.

16. Stephen D. Lee, "Campaign for Vicksburg," 37.

17. OR, ser. I, vol. 24, pt. 2, p. 101.

18. Stephen D. Lee, "Campaign for Vicksburg," 40.

19. Ibid., 41–42; OR, ser. I, vol. 24, pt. 2, p. 101.

20. Stephen D. Lee, "Campaign for Vicksburg," 41–42.

21. Ibid., 38; OR, ser. I, vol. 24, pt. 2, pp. 94, 101, 104.

22. OR, ser. I, vol. 24, pt. 2, pp. 94, 101, 104.

23. Ibid., pp. 101, 104.

24. Oldroyd, *Soldier's Story*, 11; OR, ser. I, vol. 24, pt. 1, pp. 717, 718; Frank Anderson to Capt. W. T. Rigby, 10 Nov. 1903, VNMP.

25. OR, ser. I, vol. 24, pt. 1, pp. 640, 709; OR, ser. I, vol. 24, pt. 2, pp. 101–2.

26. Oldroyd, *Soldier's Story*, 12; OR, ser. I, vol. 24, pt. 2, pp. 40–49, 105.

27. OR, ser. I, vol. 24, pt. 2, pp. 49, 55, 105.

28. Ibid., p. 100.

29. Ibid., pp. 20, 55; Greene, "Mississippi," 157.

30. OR, ser. I, vol. 24, pt. 1, p. 718; OR, ser. I, vol. 24, pt. 2, pp. 95, 100; William T. Moore, "The Battle of Baker's Creek—A Thrilling Experience," *Vicksburg (MS) Daily Herald*, 5 Oct. 1902.

31. OR, ser. I, vol. 24, pt. 3, p. 318.

32. Oldroyd, *Soldier's Story*, 11.

33. OR, ser. I, vol. 24, pt. 2, pp. 40–49; Oldroyd, *Soldier's Story*, 12.

34. Stephen D. Lee, "Campaign for Vicksburg," 45; OR, ser. I, vol. 24, pt. 2, p. 105.

35. Stephen D. Lee, "Campaign for Vicksburg," 157; OR, ser. I, vol. 24, pt. 2, pp. 55, 120.

36. OR, ser. I, vol. 24, pt. 1, pp. 717, 718; Frank Anderson to Capt. T. W. Rigby, 10 Nov. 1903, VNMP.

37. OR, ser. I, vol. 24, pt. 1, p. 718; OR, ser. I, vol. 24, pt. 2, pp. 95, 100; William T. Moore, "Battle of Baker's Creek."

38. OR, ser. I, vol. 24, pt. 2, pp. 110, 111.

39. Ibid., p. 116.

40. Ibid., pp. 49, 50, 55, 56.

41. Ibid., pp. 49, 50, 111.

42. Ibid., pp. 111, 116, 118–19.

43. Ibid., pp. 65, 66, 314.

44. Ibid., p. 44.

45. OR, ser. I, vol. 24, pt. 1, pp. 776, 779, 783.

46. Ibid.

47. OR, ser. I, vol. 24, pt. 2, pp. 44, 50, 56.

48. Ibid., p. 116.

49. Ibid., pp. 55, 56, 111, 116, 118–19.

50. Ibid., pp. 111, 116.

51. Ibid., p. 102.

52. Oldroyd, *Soldier's Story*, 11.

53. OR, ser. I, vol. 24, pt. 2, pp. 66, 314.

54. Ibid., p. 44.

55. Ibid., p. 44; OR, ser. I, vol. 24, pt. 1, p. 149.

56. OR, ser. I, vol. 24, pt. 2, p. 44.

57. Ibid., p. 15.

58. OR, ser. I, vol. 24, pt. 3, p. 318.

59. OR, ser. I, vol. 24, pt. 2, pp. 76, 79, 80, 83, 91.

60. Ibid., p. 84.

61. Ibid., pp. 15, 44, 50, 56, 63, 111, 117.

62. Ibid., pp. 83–84.

63. OR, ser. I, vol. 24, pt. 1, p. 718.

64. OR, ser. I, vol. 24, pt. 2, p. 126.

65. OR, ser. I, vol. 24, pt. 1, p. 264.

66. Stephen D. Lee, "Campaign for Vicksburg," 48.

67. OR, ser. I, vol. 24, pt. 1, p. 264.

68. OR, ser. I, vol. 24, pt. 2, pp. 83–84.

69. Ibid., p. 84.

70. OR, ser. I, vol. 24, pt. 1, p. 265.

71. OR, ser. I, vol. 24, pt. 2, pp. 76, 93.

72. Ibid.

73. Ibid.; OR, ser. I, vol. 24, pt. 1, p. 265.

74. OR, ser. I, vol. 24, pt. 2, p. 77.

75. OR, ser. I, vol. 24, pt. 1, p. 718; OR, ser. I, vol. 24, pt. 2, pp. 84, 135.

76. OR, ser. I, vol. 24, pt. 1, pp. 53, 616.

77. Ibid., p. 718.

78. Ibid., pp. 135, 718.

79. OR, ser. I, vol. 24, pt. 2, p. 100.

80. Ibid., p. 108.

81. OR, ser. I, vol. 24, pt. 1, p. 151.

82. Ibid., pp. 16, 24, 108, 143.

83. Ibid., pp. 77, 78, 80, 81.
84. Ibid., pp. 76, 77, 92; OR, ser. I, vol. 24, pt. 1, p. 265.
85. OR, ser. I, vol. 24, pt. 1, pp. 102, 106, 112.
86. OR, ser. I, vol. 24, pt. 2, pp. 84, 135; OR, ser. I, vol. 24, pt. 1, p. 718.
87. OR, ser. I, vol. 24, pt. 2, pp. 77, 78, 81.
88. Ibid., pp. 112, 117.
89. OR, ser. I, vol. 24, pt. 1, p. 265.
90. OR, ser. I, vol. 24, pt. 2, pp. 77, 89, 90.
91. Grant, *Personal Memoirs*, 1:436.
92. OR, ser. I, vol. 24, pt. 2, pp. 78, 81, 256.
93. OR, ser. I, vol. 24, pt. 1, p. 718; OR, ser. I, vol. 24, pt. 2, pp. 95, 100; William T. Moore, "Battle of Baker's Creek."
94. OR, ser. I, vol. 24, pt. 2, p. 100.
95. Ibid., p. 108.
96. OR, ser. I, vol. 24, pt. 2, p. 108; OR, ser. I, vol. 24, pt. 1, p. 151.

27. HEGIRA OF THE CONFEDERATE WAGON TRAIN

1. OR, ser. I, vol. 24, pt. 2, pp. 16, 24, 108, 143; OR, ser. I, vol. 24, pt. 1, p. 151.
2. OR, ser. I, vol. 24, pt. 2, p. 108.
3. Ibid., p. 94; OR, ser. I, vol. 24, pt. 3, p. 884.
4. OR, ser. I, vol. 24, pt. 2, p. 94; OR, ser. I, vol. 24, pt. 3, p. 884.
5. OR, ser. I, vol. 24, pt. 2, p. 108.
6. Ibid.
7. Ibid.
8. Ibid.; OR, ser. I, vol. 24, pt. 1, p. 151.
9. OR, ser. I, vol. 24, pt. 2, pp. 16, 24, 108, 143; OR, ser. I, vol. 24, pt. 1, p. 151.

28. PURSUIT AND RETREAT

1. OR, ser. I, vol. 24, pt. 2, pp. 16, 24, 108, 143; OR, ser. I, vol. 24, pt. 1, p. 151.
2. Grant, *Personal Memoirs*, 1:437; OR, ser. I, vol. 24, pt. 2, p. 256; OR, ser. I, vol. 24, pt. 3, p. 322.
3. Grant, *Personal Memoirs*, 1:437; OR, ser. I, vol. 24, pt. 2, p. 256; OR, ser. I, vol. 24, pt. 3, p. 322.
4. OR, ser. I, vol. 24, pt. 2, pp. 256, 263.
5. Ibid., p. 401; Bell Diary; Affeld Diary.
6. OR, ser. I, vol. 24, pt. 1, pp. 640, 641; OR, ser. I, vol. 24, pt. 2, pp. 59, 60; OR, ser. I, vol. 24, pt. 3, pp. 320, 465.
7. *History of the 46th Regiment Indiana* (1888), 42.
8. OR, ser. I, vol. 24, pt. 1, pp. 151, 616; OR, ser. I, vol. 24, pt. 2, p. 16.
9. OR, ser. I, vol. 24, pt. 1, p. 266.
10. Ibid.

11. Ibid., p. 514; Ballard, *Pemberton,* 103–4.

12. OR, ser. I, vol. 24, pt. 1, p. 266.

13. OR, ser. I, vol. 24, pt. 2, pp. 112, 113, 117, 119.

14. OR, ser. I, vol. 24, pt. 1, p. 266.

29. ROUT IN THE BRIDGEHEAD

1. Raynor Diary; OR, ser. I, vol. 24, pt. 1, p. 266; Greene, "Mississippi," 162, 163.

2. OR, ser. I, vol. 24, pt. 2, p. 136; OR, ser. I, vol. 24, pt. 1, pp. 151, 152, 616.

3. OR, ser. I, vol. 24, pt. 2, pp. 16, 26; Enos Pierson to W. P. Gault, 4 Feb. 1903, VNMP.

4. OR, ser. I, vol. 24, pt. 3, p. 322.

5. OR, ser. I, vol. 24, pt. 2, pp. 136, 137.

6. Ibid.; Sylvanus Cadwallader, *Three Years with Grant, as Recalled by War Correspondent Sylvanus Cadwallader,* ed. Benjamin P. Thomas (New York: Knopf, 1955), 83, 84.

7. OR, ser. I, vol. 24, pt. 2, pp. 23, 119, 137; Crooke, *21st Regiment of Iowa,* 73; Lindsey, *Military Annals,* 526.

8. OR, ser. I, vol. 24, pt. 2, pp. 119, 120, 137.

9. Ibid., pp. 24, 27, 32.

10. Ibid., pp. 27, 33, 132, 139; OR, ser. I, vol. 24, pt. 1, pp. 268, 269; Lockett, "Defense of Vicksburg," 3:488.

11. OR, ser. I, vol. 24, pt. 2, p. 132.

12. OR, ser. I, vol. 24, pt. 1, pp. 640, 641.

13. OR, ser. I, vol. 24, pt. 2, pp. 112, 113, 117, 119.

14. OR, ser. I, vol. 24, pt. 1, pp. 217, 219, 267; OR, ser. I, vol. 24, pt. 3, p. 888.

15. OR, ser. I, vol. 24, pt. 2, p. 256; OR, ser. I, vol. 24, pt. 3, p. 322; Grant, *Personal Memoirs,* 1:437, 1:438.

16. OR, ser. I, vol. 24, pt. 2, pp. 119, 137.

17. Ibid., p. 137.

18. Ibid., pp. 119, 120.

19. Ibid., p. 401.

20. Ibid., p. 73; Lockett, "Defense of Vicksburg," 3:480.

21. OR, ser. I, vol. 24, pt. 1, pp. 268, 269.

30. JOHNSTON AFTER THE BATTLE OF JACKSON

1. OR, ser. I, vol. 24, pt. 3, pp. 883–84.

2. Ibid., p. 881.

3. Ibid., p. 882; Johnston, *Narrative,* 179–80.

4. Johnston, *Narrative,* 180; OR, ser. I, vol. 24, pt. 1, p. 241.

5. Bryner, *Bugle Echoes,* 81–82.

6. OR, ser. I, vol. 24, pt. 2, p. 256; OR, ser. I, vol. 24, pt. 3, p. 322.

7. Bell Diary; Affeld Diary.

8. Johnston, *Narrative*, 186, 187; OR, ser. I, vol. 24, pt. 1, pp. 216–18.

9. OR, ser. I, vol. 24, pt. 3, p. 888.

31. ACROSS THE FINAL BARRIER

1. Johnston, *Narrative*, 185, 186; OR, ser. I, vol. 24, pt. 1, p. 241.

2. Thienel, "Bridges"; OR, ser. I, vol. 24, pt. 1, pp. 153, 181; OR, ser. I, vol. 24, pt. 2, p. 27.

3. Thienel, "Bridges"; OR, ser. I, vol. 24, pt. 2, p. 205.

4. Sherman, *Memoirs*, 1:352.

5. Bell Diary; OR, ser. I, vol. 24, pt. 2, p. 251.

6. OR, ser. I, vol. 24, pt. 2, pp. 256, 253; OR, ser. I, vol. 24, pt. 3, p. 322; Affeld Diary.

7. OR, ser. I, vol. 24, pt. 1, p. 641.

8. Ibid.; OR, ser. I, vol. 24, pt. 2, p. 297; Stockton Diary.

9. OR, ser. I, vol. 24, pt. 1, pp. 153, 187; OR, ser. I, vol. 24, pt. 2, p. 27.

10. OR, ser. I, vol. 24, pt. 3, p. 324; OR, ser. I, vol. 24, pt. 2, pp. 139, 140.

11. OR, ser. I, vol. 24, pt. 2, pp. 343, 350, 401.

12. A. S. Abrams, *A Full and Detailed History of the Siege of Vicksburg* (Atlanta, GA, 1863), 29.

13. OR, ser. I, vol. 24, pt. 3, p. 887; Johnston, *Narrative*, 187, 188.

14. OR, ser. I, vol. 24, pt. 1, p. 271; OR, ser. I, vol. 24, pt. 2, pp. 365, 366.

15. OR, ser. I, vol. 24, pt. 2, pp. 375, 379, 380; ORN, ser. I, vol. 25, p. 6.

16. OR, ser. I, vol. 24, pt. 2, pp. 406, 407; OR, ser. I, vol. 24, pt. 1, p. 271.

17. OR, ser. I, vol. 24, pt. 2, pp. 325, 357, 400.

18. Abrams, *Full and Detailed History*, 29.

19. OR, ser. I, vol. 24, pt. 2, pp. 97, 107, 109, 420.

20. Ibid., p. 353.

21. Ibid., p. 381, 385.

22. Ibid., pp. 375, 379, 380.

23. OR, ser. I, vol. 24, pt. 2, pp. 343, 344, 355; OR, ser. I, vol. 24, pt. 1, p. 264.

32. INVESTMENT OF VICKSBURG

1. OR, ser. I, vol. 24, pt. 2, pp. 256, 263; OR, ser. I, vol. 24, pt. 3, p. 322; Affeld Diary.

2. OR, ser. I, vol. 24, pt. 1, p. 755; OR, ser. I, vol. 24, pt. 2, p. 256; Affeld Diary.

3. OR, ser. I, vol. 24, pt. 1, p. 755.

4. Ibid.

5. OR, ser. I, vol. 24, pt. 2, p. 251.

6. Sherman, *Memoirs*, 1:353.

7. Grant, *Personal Memoirs*, 1:442.

8. Ibid.; Lloyd Lewis, *Sherman, Fighting Prophet* (New York: Harcourt, Brace, 1932), 277.

9. OR, ser. I, vol. 24, pt. 1, p. 641.

10. Ibid.; OR, ser. I, vol. 24, pt. 2, p. 297; Stockton Diary.

11. OR, ser. I, vol. 24, pt. 1, p. 596; OR, ser. I, vol. 24, pt. 2, pp. 17, 33.

12. OR, ser. I, vol. 24, pt. 2, pp. 405, 406; M. Baker to W. T. Rigby, 31 May 1902, VNMP.

13. OR, ser. I, vol. 24, pt. 2, p. 251.

14. Ibid.

15. James T. Hogane, "Reminiscences of the Siege of Vicksburg by Major J. T. Hogane of the Engineer Corps," *Southern Historical Society Papers* 11 (1883): 291.

16. OR, ser. I, vol. 24, pt. 1, p. 273.

17. OR, ser. I, vol. 24, pt. 2, pp. 401, 402, 406.

33. FIRST ASSAULT ON THE STOCKADE REDAN

1. Herman Hattaway, "Jewels of the Mississippi," in The Photographic History of the Civil War, ed. William C. Davis and Bell L. Wiley, 2 vols. (New York: Black Dog and Leventhal, 1994), 2:35, 2:36–37, 2:45, 2:54.

2. OR, ser. I, vol. 24, pt. 2, p. 414; Ephraim McD. Anderson, *Memoirs, Historical and Personal, Including the Campaigns of the First Missouri Confederate Brigade,* ed. Edwin Bearss (Dayton, OH, 1972), 327–28.

3. OR, ser. I, vol. 24, pt. 1, p. 153.

4. OR, ser. I, vol. 24, pt. 2, p. 33; Col. W. J. Landram, "After Action Report, May 25, 1863," in VNMP.

5. OR, ser. I, vol. 24, pt. 2, pp. 17, 18, 230–31.

6. OR, ser. I, vol. 24, pt. 1, pp. 17, 18, 27; Joseph E. Chance, *Second Texas Infantry: From Shiloh to Vicksburg* (Austin, TX, 1985), 104.

7. OR, ser. I, vol. 24, pt. 2, pp. 19, 33; OR, ser. I, vol. 24, pt. 1, p. 154; Landram, "After Action Report."

8. OR, ser. I, vol. 24, pt. 2, pp. 267–68, 271, 276; *The Story of the 55th Regiment Illinois Volunteer Infantry in the Civil War, from Organization to Muster Out, 1861–1865,* committee compilation (Clinton, IL, 1887), 235.

9. OR, ser. I, vol. 24, pt. 2, pp. 263–64.

10. Sgt. W. W. Gardner to Dr. Levi Fuller, 25 May 1863, VNMP; Joseph L. Herr, "Sketch of the 1st Battalion, 13th Infantry," in VNMP.

11. OR, ser. I, vol. 24, pt. 2, p. 264.

12. Ibid., pp. 281, 283, 406; Thomas T. Taylor to W. T. Rigby, 19 Mar. 1903, VNMP; James Kephart to W. W. Gardner, 16 Jan. 1902, VNMP; Joseph A. Saunier, *A History of the 47th Ohio Veteran Volunteer Infantry, 2d Brigade, 2d Division, 15th Army Corps, Army of the Tennessee* (Hillsboro, OH, 1903), 211; Ephraim Anderson, *Memoirs,* 28–29.

13. OR, ser. I, vol. 24, pt. 2, p. 297; Stockton Diary; Wales W. Wood, *A History of the 95th Regiment Illinois Volunteers, from Its Organization in the Fall of 1862, Until Its Final Discharge from the United States Service, in 1865* (Chicago, IL, 1865), 73–74.

14. OR, ser. I, vol. 24, pt. 2, p. 17; OR, ser. I, vol. 24, pt. 1, p. 153; Henry Clay Warmouth, "The Vicksburg Diary of Henry Clay Warmouth, pt. 2 (April 28, 1863–May 26, 1863)," ed. Paul H. Hass, *Journal of Mississippi History* 32 (1970): 72.

15. OR, ser. I, vol. 24, pt. 2, pp. 17, 18, 230–31.

16. Ibid.

17. L. Rassieur to Robert Buchanan, 12 Oct. 1901, VNMP.

18. OR, ser. I, vol. 24, pt. 2, p. 60.

19. Ibid., pp. 18, 27, 229, 231–33; OR, ser. I, vol. 24, pt. 1, pp. 153–54; Marshall, *History of 83rd Ohio*, 85–86; Marcus M. Spiegel, *Your True Marcus: The Civil War Letters of a Jewish Colonel*, ed. Frank L. Byrne and Jean Powers (Kent, OH, 1985), 281.

20. OR, ser. I, vol. 24, pt. 2, p. 406; Winchester Hall, *The Story of the 26th Louisiana Infantry in the Service of the Confederate States*, ed. Edwin C. Bearss (Gaithersburg, MD, 1984), 67–68.

21. Reichelm, "Taking of Vicksburg."

22. OR, ser. I, vol. 24, pt. 2, p. 414; Ephraim Anderson, *Memoirs*, 328–29.

23. OR, ser. I, vol. 24, pt. 2, pp. 9, 33; OR, ser. I, vol. 24, pt. 1, p. 154; Landram, "After Action Report."

34. SECOND ASSAULT

1. Grant, *Personal Memoirs*, 1:444; Greene, "The Mississippi," 177; OR, ser. I, vol. 24, pt. 1, pp. 54, 55.

2. OR, ser. I, vol. 24, pt. 2, pp. 52, 140; OR, ser. I, vol. 24, pt. 1, pp. 726, 731, 768, 780, 784; Bryner, *Bugle Echoes*, 84.

3. OR, ser. I, vol. 24, pt. 1, p. 760; Halsey Diary; OR, ser. I, vol. 24, pt. 2, pp. 262, 285, 407.

4. OR, ser. I, vol. 24, pt. 1, p. 756; OR, ser. I, vol. 24, pt. 2, pp. 257, 264, 269, 282.

5. OR, ser. I, vol. 24, pt. 2, pp. 257, 273; Hugh Ewing, Affidavit, in VNMP; OR, ser. I, vol. 24, pt. 1, pp. 756, 757; Thomas T. Taylor to W. T. Rigby, 19 Mar. 1903, VNMP.

6. OR, ser. I, vol. 24, pt. 2, pp. 273, 415; Bryner, *Bugle Echoes*, 85, 86.

7. George H. Hildt to W. T. Rigby, 8 Feb. 1902, VNMP.

8. Ibid.

9. OR, ser. I, vol. 24, pt. 2, pp. 257, 258, 282.

10. Ibid.

11. Ibid., pp. 258, 264.

12. Ibid., p. 269.

13 OR, ser. I, vol. 24, pt. 1, p. 760.

14. OR, ser. I, vol. 24, pt. 2, pp. 258, 297, 300; Greene, "The Mississippi," 85.

15. OR, ser. I, vol. 24, pt. 2, pp. 258, 415.

16. OR, ser. I, vol. 24, pt. 1, p. 172; Greene, "The Mississippi," 55, 172, 182.

17. David W. Reed, *Campaigns and Battles of the Twelfth Regiment Iowa Veteran Volunteer Infantry* (Evanston, IL, 1903), 123.

18. Bryner, *Bugle Echoes,* 85; OR, ser. I, vol. 24, pt. 1, pp. 757, 760, 768.

19. OR, ser. I, vol. 24, pt. 1, p. 768; Bryner, *Bugle Echoes,* 86.

20. OR, ser. I, vol. 24, pt. 2, pp. 19, 33, 140, 181, 229, 230; OR, ser. I, vol. 24, pt. 1, pp. 597, 598, 617; OR, ser. I, vol. 24, pt. 3, p. 331; Landram, "After Action Report."

21. OR, ser. I, vol. 24, pt. 1, pp. 174, 175.

22. OR, ser. I, vol. 24, pt. 2, p. 140; James B. Black to W. T. Rigby, 15 May 1902, VNMP; Landram, "After Action Report."

23. OR, ser. I, vol. 24, pt. 2, p. 140.

24. Ibid., p. 141; J. D. Pearson to Stephen D. Lee, 17 May 1902, VNMP.

25. OR, ser. I, vol. 24, pt. 2, pp. 141, 357.

26. Ibid.

27. Ibid., p. 141.

28. OR, ser. I, vol. 24, pt. 1, p. 128.

29. Ibid., p. 172; Greene, "The Mississippi," 55, 172; OR, Ser I, vol. 24, pt. 3, p. 172.

30. OR, ser. I, vol. 24, pt. 1, p. 55.

31. Greene, "The Mississippi," 56.

32. OR, ser. I, vol. 24, pt. 1, p. 173.

33. Ibid., pp. 67, 316; J. Q. A. Campbell, 5th Iowa, Diary, in VNMP (hereafter cited as Campbell Diary).

34. OR, ser. I, vol. 24, pt. 1, pp. 67, 316.

35. OR, ser. I, vol. 24, pt. 2, pp. 67, 68, 316; Campbell Diary; Mary Amelia Stone, *Memoir of George Boardman Boomer* (Boston, MA, 1864), 258.

36. J. D. Pearson to Stephen D. Lee, 17 May 1902, VNMP; OR, ser. I, vol. 24, pt. 1, p. 154; OR, ser. I, vol. 24, pt. 2, p. 240.

37. J. D. Pearson to Stephen D. Lee, 17 May 1902, VNMP.

38. OR, ser. I, vol. 24, pt. 2, pp. 20, 27, 28, 232.

39. J. D. Pearson to Stephen D. Lee, 17 May 1902, VNMP.

40. Ibid.; OR, ser. I, vol. 24, pt. 2, p. 141.

41. OR, ser. I, vol. 24, pt. 2, pp. 141, 357.

42. Ibid., pp. 357, 358; E. Root to J. P. Dolliver, 24 Mar. 1903, VNMP; T. N. Waul to W. T. Rigby, 10 Mar. 1903, VNMP.

43. OR, ser. I, vol. 24, pt. 2, pp. 141, 358; Landram, "After Action Report"; E. Root to J. P. Dolliver, 24 Mar. 1903, VNMP.

35. ATTACKS ON THE LOUISIANA POSTS

1. OR, ser. I, vol. 24, pt. 3, p. 846.
2. OR, ser. I, vol. 24, pt. 2, pp. 697, 700; OR, ser. I, vol. 24, pt. 3, pp. 302, 303.
3. Blessington, *Texas Division*, 81, 82; OR, ser. I, vol. 15, pp. 1081–83.
4. OR, ser. I, vol. 24, pt. 2, p. 83.
5. OR, ser. I, vol. 26, pt. 2, p. 12–13, 15; Joseph H. Parks, *General Kirby Smith, C.S.A.* (Baton Rouge: Univ. of Louisiana Press, 1954), 269.
6. Richard Taylor, *Destruction and Reconstruction: Personal Experiences in the Late War* (Nashville, TN, Sanders, 1998), 137–38; Parks, *General Kirby Smith*, 269, 270.
7. Richard Taylor, *Destruction and Reconstruction*, 137–38.
8. OR, ser. I, vol. 25, pt. 2, p. 15.
9. Blessington, *Texas Division*, 91–92, 119 and 148.
10. Ibid.; ORN, ser. I, vol. 25, pp. 147, 148.
11. OR, ser. I, vol. 24, pt. 2, p. 457; Blessington, *Texas Division*, 93, 94, 120.
12. OR, ser. I, vol. 24, pt. 2, p. 458.
13. OR, ser. I, vol. 22, pt. 2, pp. 91–92, 119, 120.
14. OR, ser. I, vol. 24, pt. 2, p. 458.
15. Ibid., p. 467; Blessington, *Texas Division*, 95, 96; Col. Herman Lieb, "After Action Report," in VNMP.
16. OR, ser. I, vol. 24, pt. 2, p. 467.
17. Ibid.; OR, ser. I, vol. 24, pt. 1, p. 102.
18. OR, ser. I, vol. 24, pt. 2, p. 467; ORN, ser. I, vol. 25, p. 163.
19. OR, ser. I, vol. 24, pt. 2, pp. 471, 472.
20. Ibid.; ORN, ser. I, vol. 25, pp. 161, 162; State of Illinois, Office of the Adjutant General, "Report of the Adjutant General of the State of Illinois," vol. 6, pp. 72, 73, 368, 606.
21. OR, ser. I, vol. 24, pt. 2, pp. 471–72.
22. Ibid., pp. 448, 449, 460; OR, ser. I, vol. 24, pt. 3, pp. 405, 406.
23. OR, ser. I, vol. 24, pt. 2, pp. 448, 449, 460.
24. Ibid., p. 461.
25. Ibid.
26. Ibid., pp. 459–61.
27. Ibid., p. 175.
28. Blessington, *Texas Division*, 110–12, 123, 124.
29. Ibid.
30. Ibid., 113, 114; OR, ser. I, vol. 24, pt. 2, p. 466.
31. ORN, ser. I, vol. 25, pp. 213–16; OR, ser. I, vol. 24, pt. 2, p. 450.
32. OR, ser. I, vol. 24, pt. 2, pp. 74, 75.
33. OR, ser. I, vol. 24, pt. 3, p. 997.
34. OR, ser. I, vol. 24, pt. 2, p. 466; Blessington, *Texas Division*, 116–18.

35. OR, ser. I, vol. 24, pt. 2, p. 695.

36. Ibid., pp. 697, 700.

37. Ibid.

38. Ibid., pp. 697, 700; OR, ser. I, vol. 24, pt. 3, pp. 302, 303.

39. OR, ser. I, vol. 24, pt. 3, pp. 375.

40. OR, ser. I, vol. 24, pt. 2, p. 449; ORN, ser. I, vol. 25, p. 163.

41. OR, ser. I, vol. 24, pt. 2, p. 467; Blessington, *Texas Division,* 95, 96; Lieb, "After Action Report."

42. OR, ser. I, vol. 24, pt. 2, p. 467.

43. Ibid.; OR, ser. I, vol. 24, pt. 1, p. 102.

44. OR, ser. I, vol. 24, pt. 2, p. 467; ORN, ser. I, vol. 25, p. 163.

45. OR, ser. I, vol. 24, pt. 2, pp. 471, 472; ORN, ser. I, vol. 25, pp. 161, 162; A. B. Booth to W. T. Rigby, 28 Apr. 1903, VNMP; State of Illinois, Office of the Adjutant General, "Report of the Adjutant General," vol. 6, pp. 72, 73, 368, 606.

46. OR, ser. I, vol. 24, pt. 2, pp. 471–72.

47. Ibid., pp. 448, 449, 460.

48. Ibid., pp. 451–52; ORN, ser. I, vol. 25, p. 175.

49. ORN, ser. I, vol. 25, pp. 213–16; OR, ser. I, vol. 24, pt. 2, p. 150.

50. OR, ser. I, vol. 24, pt. 2, pp. 450, 466, 517.

36. SIEGE: WAR BY SHOVEL

1. Lockett, "Defense of Vicksburg," 3:491.

37. SIEGE OPERATIONS

1. OR, ser. I, vol. 24, pt. 2, p. 174.

2. Ibid., pp. 181–84.

3. Ibid., pp. 181–84; W. H. Whipple, Diary, in VNMP.

4. OR, ser. I, vol. 24, pt. 2, pp. 186–87, 334.

5. Raynor Diary.

6. OR, ser. I, vol. 24, pt. 2, pp. 181–84; T. C. Buck to W. T. Rigby, 21 May 1910, VNMP.

7. OR, ser. I, vol. 24, pt. 2, pp. 186–87, 334.

8. Jack Coggins, *Arms and Equipment of the Civil War* (New York: Doubleday, 1962), pp. 66, 77, 88.

9. OR, ser. I, vol. 24, pt. 2, pp. 173, 365; Lockett, "Defense of Vicksburg," 3:491.

10. OR, ser. I, vol. 24, pt. 2, p. 319.

11. ORN, ser. I, vol. 25, p. 107.

12. OR, ser. I, vol. 24, pt. 2, pp. 318, 339.

13. ORN, ser. I, vol. 25, p. 100.

14. Warren D. Crandall and Isaac D. Newell, *History of the Ram Fleet and the Mississippi Marine Brigade in the War for the Union on the Mississippi and Its Tributaries*, pt. 2 (St. Louis, MO: Buschart, 1907), 307.

15. Ibid., pp. 304, 306, 307.

16. ORN, ser. I, vol. 25, pp. 77–80.

17. OR, ser. I, vol. 24, pt. 2, pp. 202, 232, 367.

18. Ibid., pp. 200–202, 207.

19. OR, ser. I, vol. 24, pt. 2, p. 202; Andrew Hickenlooper, "The Vicksburg Mine," in *Battles and Leaders of the Civil War* (New York: Castle Books, 1956), 3:542.

20. OR, ser. I, vol. 24, pt. 2, pp. 202, 333, 368; Hickenlooper, "Vicksburg Mine," 3:540–41.

21. OR, ser. I, vol. 24, pt. 3, pp. 438, 441; Hickenlooper, "Vicksburg Mine," 3:542.

22. OR, ser. I, vol. 24, pt. 2, pp. 202, 207, 294; OR, ser. I, vol. 24, pt. 3, p. 440; Wilber F. Crummer, *With Grant at Fort Donelson, Shiloh and Vicksburg* (Oak Park, IL, 1915).

23. Hickenlooper, "Vicksburg Mine," 3:542.

24. Ibid.; Crummer, *With Grant*; N. M. Baker, Diary, in VNMP.

25. Hickenlooper, "Vicksburg Mine," 3:542; OR, ser. I, vol. 24, pt. 2, pp. 202, 207, 372, 376; C. E. Bassett to J. A. Edmiston, 12 Mar. 1902, VNMP.

26. OR, ser. I, vol. 24, pt. 1, pp. 294, 312–13.

27. OR, ser. I, vol. 24, pt. 3, p. 441.

28. OR, ser. I, vol. 24, pt. 2, pp. 202, 294, 312–13; Hickenlooper, "Vicksburg Mine," 3:542.

29. OR, ser. I, vol. 24, pt. 2, pp. 202–203; OR, ser. I, vol. 24, pt. 3, p. 456.

30. OR, ser. I, vol. 24, pt. 2, pp. 203, 365; OR, ser. I, vol. 24, pt. 3, p. 456.

31. OR, ser. I, vol. 24, pt. 2, pp. 173, 377; Grant, *Personal Memoirs*, 1:461.

32. OR, ser. I, vol. 24, pt. 2, p. 376.

33. Ibid., pp. 372, 413, 416; A. B. Booth to W. T. Rigby, 28 Apr. 1903, VNMP; J. H. Jones, "The Rank and File at Vicksburg," *Publications of the Mississippi Historical Society* 7 (1903): 27–28.

34. C. E. Bassett to J. A. Edmiston, 12 Mar. 1902, VNMP; Hickenlooper, "Vicksburg Mine," 3:542.

35. OR, ser. I, vol. 24, pt. 2, pp. 372, 416.

36. Ibid., pp. 377, 416.

37. ORN, ser. I, vol. 25, p. 5; OR, ser. I, vol. 24, pt. 3, pp. 326, 327, 328, 329.

38. OR, ser. I, vol. 24, pt. 1, p. 768; Bryner, *Bugle Echoes*, 84.

39. OR, ser. I, vol. 24, pt. 2, pp. 187, 189.

40. Ibid., pp. 187, 188.

41. Grant, *Personal Memoirs*, 1:443.

42. OR, ser. I, vol. 24, pt. 3, pp. 337, 338.

43. Lt. George Hale, Diary, in VNMP (hereafter cited as Hale Diary).

44. ORN, ser. I, vol. 25, pp. 58, 59, 61, 65, 65, 66.

45. OR, ser. I, vol. 24, pt. 1, p. 292; OR, ser. I, vol. 24, pt. 3, pp. 869, 987.

38. FRUSTRATION IN THE MECHANICSBURG CORRIDOR

1. OR, ser. I, vol. 24, pt. 1, pp. 88, 736.

2. Ibid., p. 89; OR, ser. I, vol. 24, pt. 2, p. 441; OR, ser. I, vol. 24, pt. 3, p. 356.

3. OR, ser. I, vol. 24, pt. 2, pp. 285, 302; OR, ser. I, vol. 24, pt. 3, p. 352; Affeld Diary; J. M. Lee, Diary, in VNMP (hereafter cited as J. M. Lee Diary); Oldroyd, *Soldier's Story*, 16.

4. Oldroyd, *Soldier's Story*, 16; J. M. Lee Diary.

5. OR, ser. I, vol. 24, pt. 3, pp. 354, 355.

6. OR, ser. I, vol. 24, pt. 2, pp. 302, 435, 441.

7. Ibid., pp. 209, 219.

8. OR, ser. I, vol. 24, pt. 3, pp. 361, 362.

9. OR, ser. I, vol. 24, pt. 2, pp. 435, 436; Pomutz, *History of the 15th Iowa*, 257; Affeld Diary; J. M. Lee Diary.

10. OR, ser. I, vol. 24, pt. 3, pp. 373, 374; OR, ser. I, vol. 24, pt. 1, p. 359.

11. OR, ser. I, vol. 24, pt. 3, pp. 374, 475; ORN, ser. I, vol. 25, pp. 57, 58.

12. OR, ser. I, vol. 24, pt. 3, p. 379.

13. OR, ser. I, vol. 24, pt. 2, pp. 214, 436–441; OR, ser. I, vol. 24, pt. 3, p. 384.

14. OR, ser. I, vol. 24, pt. 2, p. 439.

15. Affeld Diary.

16. Dana, *Recollections*, 83.

17. OR, ser. I, vol. 24, pt. 3, pp. 409, 410; OR, ser. I, vol. 24, pt. 1, p. 100.

18. OR, ser. I, vol. 24, pt. 1, pp. 95, 96, 98.

19. OR, ser. I, vol. 24, pt. 2, pp. 509–12.

20. Ibid., pp. 295, 296, 303, 533; OR, ser. I, vol. 24, pt. 3, pp. 427, 428; Halsey Diary; H. M. Trimble, Diary, in VNMP.

21. OR, ser. I, vol. 24, pt. 2, pp. 245, 533; OR, ser. I, vol. 24, pt. 3, p. 428.

22. OR, ser. I, vol. 24, pt. 2, pp. 245, 246, 296, 303; OR, ser. I, vol. 24, pt. 3, pp. 430, 431, 442.

23. OR, ser. I, vol. 24, pt. 3, p. 431.

24. OR, ser. I, vol. 24, pt. 2, p. 226; OR, ser. I, vol. 24, pt. 3, pp. 439, 449.

25. OR, ser. I, vol. 24, pt. 2, pp. 247, 248, 309–11.

26. OR, ser. I, vol. 24, pt. 3, p. 450.

27. OR, ser. I, vol. 24, pt. 2, p. 305.

28. Ibid., pp. 302, 435, 441.

29. OR, ser. I, vol. 24, pt. 3, pp. 939, 940.

30. Ibid., pp. 937, 938.

31. Ibid., pp. 939, 940.

32. OR, ser. I, vol. 24, pt. 2, pp. 214, 436–41; Affeld Diary.

33. OR, ser. I, vol. 24, pt. 2, pp. 214, 436–41; OR, ser. I, vol. 24, pt. 3, p. 384.

34. OR, ser. I, vol. 24, pt. 2, pp. 440, 442.

35. OR, ser. I, vol. 24, pt. 3, p. 951.

36. OR, ser. I, vol. 52, pt. 2, pp. 492, 494.

37. OR, ser. I, vol. 24, pt. 3, p. 960.

38. Ibid., pp. 670–73.

39. Ibid., p. 965.

40. Ibid., pp. 960, 961, 964.

41. OR, ser. I, vol. 24, pt. 2, pp. 509–12.

39. OFFENSE AND DEFENSE

1. OR, ser. I, vol. 24, pt. 3, p. 896.

2. Richard B. Irwin, "The Capture of Port Hudson," in *Battles and Leaders of the Civil War* (New York: Castle Books, 1956), 3:593.

3. OR, ser. I, vol. 24, pt. 2, pp. 214–16, 218–23; OR, ser. I, vol. 24, pt. 3, p. 393.

4. OR, ser. I, vol. 24, pt. 3, p. 929.

5. OR, ser. I, vol. 24, pt. 2, pp. 74, 75.

6. OR, ser. I, vol. 24, pt. 1, p. 244; OR, ser. I, vol. 24, pt. 3, p. 969.

7. Greene, "The Mississippi," 192; OR, ser. I, vol. 24, pt. 3, pp. 971, 972.

8. OR, ser. I, vol. 52, pt. 2, p. 502; OR, ser. I, vol. 24, pt. 3, p. 985.

9. OR, ser. I, vol. 24, pt. 2, pp. 227, 228.

10. Ibid., pp. 248, 249; OR, ser. I, vol. 24, pt. 1, p. 113; Crooke, *21st Regiment of Iowa,* 111.

11. OR, ser. I, vol. 24, pt. 3, p. 985; A. D. Kirwan, ed., *Johnny Green of the Orphan Brigade: The Journal of a Confederate Soldier* (Lexington: Univ. Press of Kentucky, 1956), 79, 80.

12. OR, ser. I, vol. 24, pt. 3, p. 986; Samuel G. French, *Two Wars: An Autobiography of Samuel G. French* (Nashville, TN: Confederate Veteran, 1901), 176–82.

13. French, *Two Wars,* 176–82.

14. Johnston, *Narrative,* 203, 204; OR, ser. I, vol. 24, pt. 1, pp. 241, 245.

15. OR, ser. I, vol. 24, pt. 2, pp. 307, 308.

16. OR, ser. I, vol. 24, pt. 1, pp. 57, 58.

17. OR, ser. I, vol. 24, pt. 3, p. 463.

18. Ibid., pp. 462, 463.

19. Ibid., p. 463.

40. FORLORN HOPE

1. OR, ser. I, vol. 24, pt. 1, p. 219.

2. Ibid.; Parks, *General Kirby Smith,* 278; OR, ser. I, vol. 24, pt. 2, p. 43.

3. OR, ser. I, vol. 22, pt. 2, p. 856.

4. Ibid., p. 863.

5. Ibid.; Parks, *General Kirby Smith,* 279.

6. OR, ser. I, vol. 22, pt. 2, pp. 867, 868.

7. Ibid., p. 868.
8. Ibid., p. 879; OR, ser. I, vol. 22, pt. 1, pp. 409, 413.
9. OR, ser. I, vol. 22, pt. 2, p. 899.
10. Ibid., pp. 900, 901.
11. OR, ser. I, vol. 22, pt. 1, pp. 409, 413.
12. OR, ser. I, vol. 22, pt. 2, p. 903.
13. OR, ser. I, vol. 22, pt. 1, pp. 423, 424.
14. Ibid., p. 420.
15. Ibid., p. 429.
16. Ibid., pp. 413, 417, 420, 421.
17. Ibid., p. 410.
18. Ibid., pp. 413, 418, 421.
19. ORN, ser. I, vol. 25, pp. 229, 230.
20. OR, ser. I, vol. 22, pt. 1, pp. 421, 422.
21. Ibid., p. 437.
22. Ibid., pp. 395, 396, 397, 437.
23. Ibid., pp. 433, 435, 436.
24. ORN, ser. I, vol. 25, pp. 229, 230.
25. Ibid.; OR, ser. I, vol. 22, pt. 1, pp. 229, 230.
26. ORN, ser. I, vol. 25, pp. 398, 399, 403.
27. OR, ser. I, vol. 22, pt. 1, p. 411.
28. Ibid., p. 433.
29. OR, ser. I, vol. 22, pt. 2, p. 339.
30. ORN, ser. I, vol. 25, p. 228.
31. OR, ser. I, vol. 22, pt. 2, p. 339.
32. Ibid., p. 335.
33. OR, ser. I, vol. 22, pt. 1, pp. 387, 388.
34. Fletcher Pratt, *War on Western Waters* (New York: Holt, 1956), 182.
35. OR, ser. I, vol. 22, pt. 1, pp. 388, 395, 400.
36. Ibid., p. 388.
37. Ibid., pp. 405-6.
38. ORN, ser. I, vol. 25, pp. 229, 230.
39. OR, ser. I, vol. 22, pt. 1, p. 418.
40. Ibid., p. 425.
41. Ibid.
42. Ibid., p. 411.
43. OR, ser. I, vol. 22, pt. 2, p. 391.
44. OR, ser. I, vol. 22, pt. 1, p. 411.

41. FALL OF THE FORTRESS

1. OR, ser. I, vol. 24, pt. 1, pp. 57, 58.
2. Greene, "The Mississippi," 201.

3. Ibid., 200–201; OR, ser. I, vol. 24, pt. 1, pp. 285–86; OR, ser. I, vol. 24, pt. 2, p. 424.

4. Greene, "The Mississippi," 201; OR, ser. I, vol. 24, pt. 3, p. 286.

5. OR, ser. I, vol. 24, pt. 3, pp. 982–83; ORN, ser. I, vol. 25, pp. 97–99.

6. OR, ser. I, vol. 24, pt. 1, p. 261.

7. OR, ser. I, vol. 24, pt. 2, pp. 347–49.

8. Ibid., pp. 374, 383; OR, ser. I, vol. 24, pt. 1, p. 282.

9. OR, ser. I, vol. 24, pt. 2, pp. 282–83.

10. OR, ser. I, vol. 24, pt. 1, p. 286.

11. Grant, *Personal Memoirs,* 1:465–66; B. J. Williams to W. T. Rigby, 30 June 1905, VNMP; J. H. Jones, "Rank and File," 28.

12. Grant, *Personal Memoirs,* 1:466; OR, ser. I, vol. 24, pt. 3, p. 460.

13. OR, ser. I, vol. 24, pt. 1, pp. 283, 284.

14. Ibid., 544.

15. John C. Pemberton, "The Terms of Surrender," in *Battles and Leaders of the Civil War* (New York: Castle Books, 1956), 3:544.

16. Ibid.

17. Ibid.

18. Ibid.

19. Ibid.

20. OR, ser. I, vol. 24, pt. 1, p. 284; J. H. Jones, "Rank and File," 29.

21. Grant, *Personal Memoirs,* 1:468–69; OR, ser. I, vol. 24, pt. 1, pp. 284–85.

22. Grant, *Personal Memoirs,* 1:468.

23. OR, ser. I, vol. 24, pt. 1, p. 284; OR, ser. I, vol. 24, pt. 3, p. 460; Pemberton, "Terms of Surrender," 3:544; Lockett, "Defense of Vicksburg," 3:492; OR, ser. I, vol. 24, pt. 2, pp. 352, 405.

24. OR, ser. I, vol. 24, pt. 1, p. 285; Lockett, "Defense of Vicksburg," 3:492.

25. OR, ser. I, vol. 24, pt. 3, p. 467.

26. OR, ser. I, vol. 24, pt. 1, pp. 284–85.

27. Frank Moore, ed., *The Civil War in Song and Story* (New York: Collier, 1889), 305–6; Crummer, *With Grant,* 157.

28. Grant, *Personal Memoirs,* 1:472; Hale Diary; Lockett, "Defense of Vicksburg," 3:492.

42. OCCUPATION

1. Richard S. West, *The Second Admiral: A Life of David Dixon Porter, 1813–1891* (New York: Coward-McCann, 1937), 336; Porter, *Incidents and Anecdotes,* 200.

2. Grant, *Personal Memoirs,* 1:474.

3. ORN, ser. I, vol. 25, pp. 103, 258; Richard S. West, Jr., *Mr. Lincoln's Navy* (New York: Longman's, Green, 1957), 223.

4. Richard S. West, Jr., *Lincoln's Navy,* 223.

5. OR, ser. I, vol. 24, pt. 3, p. 483; Kenneth P. Williams, *Lincoln Finds a General* (New York: Macmillan, 1958), 4:420–21.

6. John T. Trowbridge, *The Desolate South, 1865–1866,* ed. Gordon Carroll (New York: Duell, Sloan and Pearce, 1956), 191.

7. Abrams, *Full and Detailed History,* 159.

8. OR, ser. I, vol. 24, pt. 1, p. 62; Abrams, *Full and Detailed History,* 161; OR, ser. I, vol. 24, pt. 2, p. 178.

9. OR, ser. I, vol. 24, pt. 1, p. 292; OR, ser. I, vol. 24, pt. 3, pp. 869, 987.

10. OR, ser. I, vol. 24, pt. 3, p. 478.

11. Ibid.

12. Ibid., pp. 479, 483.

13. Ibid., pp. 484, 487, 502.

14. Ibid., pp. 484, 489; OR, ser. I, vol. 24, pt. 2, p. 325.

15. OR, ser. I, vol. 24, pt. 3, p. 488.

16. Ibid.

17. Ibid., pp. 494–95.

18. Ibid., pp. 485, 493, 494.

19. Ibid., pp. 493–94, 1001, 1002.

43. CLEANING UP LOOSE ENDS

1. Sherman, *Memoirs,* 1:331.

2. Ibid.

3. Ibid.

4. Irwin, "Capture of Port Hudson," 3:597.

5. Ibid.

6. Ibid.

7. Ibid.

8. J. B. Nicolay and J. Hay, *Abraham Lincoln: A History* (New York: Century, 1890), 327; Henry, *Story of the Confederacy,* 265.

Principal Sources

DOCUMENTS

United States. Department of the Interior. National Park Service. Vicksburg
National Military Park, Vicksburg, Mississippi. Files.

AFFIDAVITS:

Ellis, W. C.
Ewing, Hugh.
Gaines, J. W.
Slack, A. L.
Rigby, W. T., ed. "Catalog of Affidavits for the Establishment of the Vicksburg
National Military Park."

DIARIES:

Baker, N. M. Diary.
Bell, Capt. John N. Diary.
Campbell, J. Q. A., 5th Iowa. Diary.
Hale, Lt. George. Diary.
Halsey, W. B. Diary.
Hobbs, Charles A. Diary.
Hunt, Lt. Ira W., Company K, 11th Wisconsin. Diary.
Keene, H. S. Diary.
Lee, J. M. Diary.
Moore, Sgt. Elias, Company A, 114th Regiment, Ohio Volunteer Infantry. Diary.
Raynor, Col. W. H. Diary.
Stockton, Brig. Gen. Joseph. Diary.
Taylor, Capt. James B., Company H, 120th Ohio Infantry Regiment. Diary.
Trimble, H. M. Diary.
Whipple, W. H. Diary.

LETTERS:

Anderson, Frank, to Capt. W. T. Rigby, 10 November 1903.
Baker, M., to W. T. Rigby, 31 May 1902.

Bassett, C. E., to J. A. Edmiston, 12 March 1902.
Black, James B., to W. T. Rigby, 15 May 1902.
Booth, A. B., to W. T. Rigby, 28 April 1903.
Brumbach, Jefferson, to his wife, 20 May 1863.
Buck, T. C., to W. T. Rigby, 21 May 1910.
Capers, W. C., to Starr, 7 April 1863.
Gardner, Sgt. W. W., to Dr. Levi Fuller, 25 May 1863.
Hildt, George H., to W. T. Rigby, 8 February 1902.
Kephart, James, to W. W. Gardner, 16 January 1902.
Norman, H. T., to W. T. Rigby, 5 May 1904.
Payne to W. T. Rigby, 16 December 1910.
Pearson, J. D., to S. D. Lee, 17 May 1902.
Pierson, Enos, to W. P. Gault, 4 February 1903.
Rassieur, L., to Robert Buchanan, 12 October 1901.
Root, E., to J. P. Dolliver, 24 March 1903.
Slack, A. L., to W. T. Rigby, 9 September 1903.
Taylor, Thomas T., to W. T. Rigby, 19 March 1903.
Upton, D. M., to W. T. Rigby, 30 July 1903.
Waul., T. N., to W. T. Rigby, 10 March 1903.
Whitehead, J. T., to VNMP Commission, 7 July 1903.
Williams, B. J., to W. T. Rigby, 30 June 1905.
Yates, J. H., to W. T. Rigby, 22 June 1903.

MAPS:

Obenchain, Francis G. *Part of the Battlefield of Port Gibson, Mississippi, May 1, 1863.*
Topographic Map of the Vicksburg Military Park. 1:10,000. Unpublished.

OTHER DOCUMENTS:

Herr, Joseph L. "Sketch of the 1st Battalion, 13th Infantry."
"Index of Markers and Positions in the Vicksburg National Military Park."
Landram, Col. W. J. "After Action Report, May 25, 1863."
Lieb, Col. Herman. "After Action Report."
Martin, Simeon R. "Facts about Company I, 46th Mississippi Infantry."
"Proposed Battery Inscription—Confederate."

PUBLISHED WORKS

Abrams, A. S. *A Full and Detailed History of the Siege of Vicksburg.* Atlanta, Georgia, 1863.
Adamson, A. P. *Brief History of the Thirtieth Georgia Regiment.* Griffin, Georgia: Mills Printing, 1912.
Anderson, Ephraim McD. *Memoirs, Historical and Personal, Including the Campaigns of the First Missouri Confederate Brigade.* Dayton, Ohio: 1972.
Anonymous. *History of the 35th Regiment, Massachusetts Volunteers, 1862–1865.* Boston, 1884.

————. *History of the 37th Regiment, Ohio Veteran Volunteer Infantry.* Toledo, Ohio, 1890.

————. *History of the 46th Regiment, Indiana Volunteer Infantry, September 1861–September 1865.* Volume 1. Logansport, Indiana, 1888.

————. *The Story of the Fifty-fifth Regiment, Illinois Volunteer Infantry, in the Civil War, from Organization to Muster Out, 1861–1865.* 1887.

Ballard, Michael B. *Pemberton: A Biography.* Jackson: University Press of Mississippi, 1991.

Battles and Leaders of the Civil War. 4 volumes. New York: Castle Books, 1956.

Bearss, Edwin Cole. *The Campaign for Vicksburg.* 3 volumes. Dayton, Ohio: Morningside, 1985–86.

————. "The Vicksburg River Defenses and the Enigma of Whistling Dick." *Journal of Mississippi History* 19 (Jan. 1957): 21–30.

Bearss, Edwin C., and Warren E. Grabau. "The Battle of Raymond"; "Battle of Raymond Had False Reports"; "Rebels Surprise Yanks in Jungle-like Warfare"; "Yanks Begin Victory Move"; "Tide of Conflict Begins to Turn"; "Yanks Win Battle of Raymond." Series in *Jackson (MS) Clarion Ledger,* appearing, respectively, 5 Jan., 12 Jan., 19 Jan., 26 Jan., 2 Feb., and 9 Feb. 1958.

Blessington, Joseph P. *The Campaigns of Walker's Texas Division.* New York: Lang, Little & Co., 1875.

Brown, D. Alexander. *Grierson's Raid.* Urbana: University of Illinois Press, 1954.

Bryner, Byron C. *Bugle Echoes: The Story of the Illinois Forty-seventh.* Springfield, Illinois: Phillips, 1902.

Cadwallader, Sylvanus. *Three Years with Grant, as Recalled by War Correspondent Sylvanus Cadwallader.* Edited by Benjamin P. Thomas. New York: Knopf, 1955.

Capers, W. B. *The Soldier Bishop: Ellison Capers.* New York, 1912.

Chance, Joseph E. *Second Texas Infantry: From Shiloh to Vicksburg.* Austin, Texas: Eakin Press, 1985.

Coggins, Jack. *Arms and Equipment of the Civil War.* New York: Doubleday, 1962.

Crandall, Warren D., and Isaac D. Newell. *History of the Ram Fleet and the Mississippi Marine Brigade in the War for the Union on the Mississippi and Its Tributaries.* Part 2. St. Louis, Missouri: Buschart, 1907.

Crooke, George. *The Twenty-first Regiment of Iowa Volunteer Infantry.* Milwaukee, Wisconsin, 1891.

Crummer, Wilber F. *With Grant at Fort Donelson, Shiloh and Vicksburg.* Oak Park, Illinois, 1915.

Dana, Charles A. *Recollections of the Civil War: With the Leaders at Washington and in the Field in the Sixties.* New York: Appleton, 1898.

Davis, Maj. George B.; Leslie J. Perry; and Joseph W. Kirkley. *Atlas to Accompany the Official Records of the Union and Confederate Armies.* Washington, D.C.: Government Printing Office, 1891–95. Cited as OR Atlas.

Dyer, Frederick H. *A Compendium of the War of the Rebellion.* 3 volumes. New York: Yoseloff, 1959.

Elliott, Isaac H. *History of the Thirty-third Regiment, Illinois Veteran Volunteer Infantry, in the Civil War, 22nd August 1861 to 7th December 1865.* Gibson City, Illinois, 1902.

Evans, Gen. Clement A., ed. *Confederate Military History; a Library of Confederate States History.* 12 vols. Vol. 7. J. Wheeler, "Alabama"; Vol. 11, J. M. Harrell, "Arkansas." New York: Thomas Yoseloff, 1899.

Fiske, Harold N. *Geological Investigation of the Alluvial Valley of the Lower Mississippi River.* Vicksburg, Mississippi: Mississippi River Commission, 1945.

French, Samuel G. *Two Wars: An Autobiography of Samuel G. French.* Nashville, Tennessee: Confederate Veteran, 1901.

Govan, Gilbert E., and Livingood, James W. *The Story of General Joseph E. Johnston, C.S.A.: A Different Valor.* Indianapolis, Indiana: Bobbs-Merrill, 1956.

Grant, Ulysses S. *Personal Memoirs of U. S. Grant.* 2 volumes. New York: Webster, 1885.

Greene, Francis Vinton. "The Mississippi." *Campaigns of the Civil War.* New York: Jack Brussels, n.d.

Hall, Winchester. *The Story of the 26th Louisiana Infantry in the Service of the Confederate States.* Lexington, Kentucky: Lost Cause Press, 1957.

Harper's Weekly, 6 June 1863.

Hart, G. E., ed. *Photographic History of the Civil War.* Volume 3. Secaucus, New York: Blue and Grey Press, 1987.

Hattaway, Herman. "Jewels of the Mississippi." The Photographic History of the Civil War. Edited by William C. Davis and Bell L. Wiley, 2 vols. New York: Black Dog and Leventhal, 1994

Henry, Robert S. *The Story of the Confederacy.* New York: Bobbs-Merrill, 1936.

Hickenlooper, Andrew. "The Vicksburg Mine." In *Battles and Leaders of the Civil War.* Vol. 3. New York: Castle Books, 1956.

Hogane, James T. "Reminiscences of the Siege of Vicksburg by Major J. T. Hogane of the Engineer Corps." *Southern Historical Society Papers* 11: 291.

Irwin, Richard B. "The Capture of Port Hudson." In *Battles and Leaders of the Civil War.* Vol. 3. New York: Castle Books, 1956.

Johnston, Joseph E. *Narrative of Military Operations Directed During the Late War Between the States.* New York: Appleton, 1874.

Jones, J. H. "The Rank and File at Vicksburg." *Publications of the Mississippi Historical Society* 7 (1904): 17–31.

Jones, John B. *Rebel War Clerk's Diary.* New York: Sagamore Press, 1958.

Jordan, Thomas, and J. P. Pryor. *The Campaigns of Lieutenant-General Forrest, and of Forrest's Cavalry.* New Orleans, Louisiana, 1868.

Kirwan, A. D., ed. *Johnny Green of the Orphan Brigade: The Journal of a Confederate Soldier.* Lexington: University Press of Kentucky, 1956.

Lee, Stephen D. "The Campaign of Vicksburg, Mississippi, in 1863." *Publications of the Mississippi Historical Society* 3 (1900): 21–54.

————. "The Siege of Vicksburg." *Publications of the Mississippi Historical Society* 3 (1900): 55–71.

Lewis, Lloyd. *Sherman, Fighting Prophet.* New York: Harcourt, Brace, 1932.

Lindsey, John B. *Military Annals of Tennessee: Confederate.* Nashville, Tennessee, 1886.

Lockett, S. H. "The Defense of Vicksburg." In *Battles and Leaders of the Civil War.* Vol. 3. New York: Castle Books, 1956.

Mahan, A. T. "The Gulf and Inland Waters." In *Campaigns of the Civil War.* New York: Jack Brussel, n.d.

Marshall, Thomas B. *History of the Eighty-third Ohio Volunteer Infantry, the Greyhound Regiment.* Cincinnati, Ohio, 1912.

The Medal of Honor of the United States Army. Washington, D.C.: U.S. Government Printing Office, 1948.

Miers, Earl S. *The Web of Victory: Grant at Vicksburg.* Baton Rouge: Louisiana State University Press, 1955.

Moore, Frank, ed. *The Civil War in Song and Story.* New York: Collier, 1889.

Moore, William T. "The Battle of Baker's Creek—A Thrilling Experience." *Vicksburg (MS) Daily Herald,* 5 Oct. 1902.

Morton, John W. "The Artillery of Nathan Bedford Forrest." In *Wizard of the Saddle.* Nashville, Tennessee: Smith and Lamar, 1909.

Natchez (MS) Daily Courier, 3 July 1863.

Natchez (MS) Daily Courier, 19 May 1863.

Nicolay, John G., and John Hay. *Abraham Lincoln: A History.* 10 volumes. New York: Century, 1890.

Noll, Howard A. *General Kirby Smith.* Sewanee, Tennessee: University of the South, 1907.

Official Records of the Union and Confederate Navies in the War of the Rebellion. 31 volumes. Washington, D.C., 1895–1926. Cited as ORN.

Oldroyd, Osborn H. *A Soldier's Story of the Siege of Vicksburg.* Springfield, Ohio, 1885.

Parks, Joseph H. *General Kirby Smith, C.S.A.* Baton Rouge: University of Louisiana Press, 1954.

Pemberton, John C. "The Terms of Surrender." In *Battles and Leaders of the Civil War.* Vol. 3. New York: Castle Books, 1956.

Pemberton, John C., III. *Pemberton: Defender of Vicksburg.* Chapel Hill, North Carolina: University of North Carolina Press, 1942.

Perry, Oran. "Perry Tells Story of Siege of Vicksburg." *Vicksburg Evening Post,* 6 June 1926. Clipping in files of VNMP.

Pine Bluff (AR) Commercial, 17 Dec. 1904. Clipping in files of VNMP.

Pomutz, George. *History of the 15th Iowa Volunteer Infantry.* Keokuk, IA, 1887.

Porter, David D. *Incidents and Anecdotes of the Civil War.* New York: Appleton, 1885.

———. *The Naval History of the Civil War.* New York: Sherman, 1886.

Pratt, Fletcher. *War on Western Waters.* New York: Holt, 1956.

Prime, Maj. F. E. *Map of the Siege of Vicksburg by the U.S. Forces, 1863.*

Raynor, John H. "Vicksburg Revisited." *Toledo (OH) Daily Blade,* 15 Nov. 1902.

Reed, David W. *Campaigns and Battles of the Twelfth Regiment, Iowa Veteran Volunteer Infantry.* Evanston, Illinois, 1903.

Reichelm, E. Paul. "The Taking of Vicksburg." *Bayonne (NJ) Herald*, 11 Jan. 1902.

Roach, Alva C. *The Prisoner of War and How Treated*. Indianapolis, IN: Railroad City Publ. House, 1865. Reprint, edited by Robert S. Henry, Jackson, Mississippi, 1956.

Roster and Record of Iowa Soldiers in the War of the Rebellion. Volume 3. Des Moines, Iowa, 1908.

Rowland, Dunbar. *The Official and Statistical Record of the State of Mississippi*. Nashville, Tenn., 1908.

Saunier, Joseph A. *A History of the Forty-seventh Ohio Veteran Volunteer Infantry, Second Brigade, Second Division, Fifteenth Army Corps, Army of the Tennessee*. Hillsboro, Ohio, 1903.

Sherman, William T. *Memoirs of General William T. Sherman*. 2 volumes. New York: Appleton, 1875.

Spearing, Darwin. *Roadside Geology of Louisiana*. Missoula, Montana: Mountain Press, 1995.

Spiegel, Marcus M. *Your True Marcus: The Civil War Letters of a Jewish Colonel*. Edited by Frank L. Byrne and Jean Powers Soman. Kent, Ohio, 1985.

State of Illinois. Office of the Adjutant General. "Report of the Adjutant General of the State of Illinois." Vols. 2, 3, 6.

Steele, Matthew Forney. *American Campaigns*. 2 volumes. Washington, D.C.: Adams, 1909.

Stone, Mary Amelia. *Memoir of George Boardman Boomer*. Boston, Massachusetts, 1864.

Swigart, Frank. *Washington (DC) National Tribune*, 23 Dec. 1886.

Taylor, Richard. *Destruction and Reconstruction, Personal Experiences in the Late War*. Edited by Richard B. Harwell. New York: Appleton, 1955.

Thienel, Phillip N. "Bridges in the Vicksburg Campaign." *Military Engineer* 47 (Nov.–Dec. 1955): 456–59.

Thomas, Benjamin P. *Abraham Lincoln*. New York: Knopf, 1952.

Trowbridge, John T. *The Desolate South, 1865–1866, a picture of the battlefields and of the devastated Confederacy*. Edited by Gordon Carroll. New York: Duell, Sloan and Pearce, 1956.

Tunnard, W. H. *A Southern Record of the History of the 3d Regiment, Louisiana Infantry*. Baton Rouge, Louisiana, 1866.

The War of the Rebellion: A Compilation of the Official Records of the Union and Confederate Armies. 73 volumes, 128 parts. Washington, D.C., 1880–1901. Cited as OR.

West, Richard S. *The Second Admiral; A Life of David Dixon Porter, 1813–1891*. New York: Coward-McCann, 1937.

West, Richard S., Jr. *Mr. Lincoln's Navy*. New York: Longman's, Green, 1957.

Williams, Kenneth P. *Lincoln Finds a General*. 5 volumes. New York: Macmillan, 1948–58.

Wilson, Lt. Col. James H. "A Staff Officer's Journal of the Vicksburg Campaign." *Journal of the Military Service Institute* 3 (July–August 1908): 107.

Wood, Wales W. *A History of the Ninety-fifth Regiment, Illinois Volunteers, from Its Organization in the Fall of 1862, Until Its Final Discharge from the United States Service, in 1865.* Chicago, 1865.

Woodworth, Steven E. *Davis and Lee at War.* Lawrence: University Press of Kansas, 1995.

Xenophon. "The Anabasis of Cyrus." In *The Greek Historians.* Edited by Francis R. B. Godolphin. Vol. 2. New York: Random House, 1942.

Index

Maxey, Samuel B., BG, USA, 208, 246

Maxey's BDE (CSA), 244, 245, 335, 470

McArthur, John, BG, USA, 60, 86, 88, 89, 90, 179, 452

McArthur's DIV (USA), 60, 86, 89, 90, 179, 181, 183, 321, 323, 342, 358, 360, 459, 475

McArthur's PROV DIV (USA), 450

McClellan, George, MG, USA, 51

McClernand, John Alexander, MG, USA, 7, 56, 60, 61, 62, 64, 66, 81, 82, 83, 84, 85, 87, 88, 89, 135, 143, 144, 145, 146, 147, 148, 149, 155, 156, 157, 158, 159, 160, 171, 197, 198, 240, 241, 242, 243, 259, 264, 272, 279, 280, 281, 282, 290, 294, 298, 300, 301, 306, 307, 321, 322, 323, 341, 342, 351, 356, 357, 368, 373, 376, 378, 515, 519

McClernand's corps (USA), 56, 64, 135, 142, 144, 145, 149, 179, 199, 243, 249, 259, 260, 263, 264, 273, 285, 348, 351, 367, 416, 441, 442, 515

McCown, James, COL, CSA, 436

McCulloch, Henry E., BG, CSA, 389, 391

McCulloch, Robert, COL, CSA, 103

McCulloch's BDE (CSA), 386, 389, 390, 391, 395

McDowell's Bluff, AL, 35

MCENRR (see Mississippi Central Railroad)

McGinnis, George F., BG, USA, 279, 294, 295

McKay's Ferry (MS), 89, 96, 140, 170, 171

McKay's Ferry road, 96

McNutt Lake, 439

McPherson, James Birdseye, MG, USA, 7, 56, 60, 66, 82, 86, 87, 88, 135, 138, 148, 149, 171, 172, 182, 183, 195, 197, 198, 222, 223, 224, 229, 230, 231, 232, 233, 234, 239, 241, 242, 243, 251, 252, 253, 257, 260, 273, 280, 288, 290, 295, 300, 301, 305, 312, 313, 321, 322, 323,

329, 330, 341, 342, 348, 351, 356, 357, 358, 378, 423, 429, 430, 433, 434, 474, 496, 497, 515, 520

McPherson's corps (USA), 56, 148, 149, 160, 170, 171, 179, 199, 224, 230, 239, 241, 246, 259, 351, 367, 372, 378, 397, 428, 441, 442, 450, 508, 509, 515

McRae, Dandrige, BG, CSA, 480, 481, 485, 486

McRae's BDE (CSA), 482, 483, 484

McRaven house, 428

Meadeville, MS, 121

Mechanicsburg, MS, 338, 403, 441, 447, 448, 450, 451, 452, 453, 454, 455, 456, 457, 458, 460, 461, 462, 463, 464, 465, 466, 467, 470, 517, 518

Mechanicsburg Corridor, 325, 446, 450, 451, 452, 454, 456, 457, 458, 465, 466, 469, 470, 471, 473, 475, 512

Memphis, TN, 5, 7, 8, 15, 29, 34, 35, 52, 58, 68, 69, 72, 80, 94, 99, 100, 102, 108, 109, 110, 111, 118, 180, 182, 183, 206, 245, 384, 394, 404, 441, 455, 456, 477, 480, 486, 487, 491, 508, 514

Memphis, Battle of, 5, 8

Memphis & Charleston Railroad, 5, 6, 8, 33, 35, 99, 102, 108, 110, 206

Memphis to Columbus (telegraph) line, 34

Meridian, MS, 9, 35, 93, 94, 95, 100, 112, 114, 119, 120, 153, 196, 244

Meridianville, MS, 258

Messenger's Creek, 320

Messenger's Ford (Ferry) (MS), 320, 324, 340, 448, 459, 460, 475, 476, 505

Mexico, Gulf of, 4, 5, 30, 74, 250

Mexico, War with, 41, 496

Middle Road, 260, 264, 270, 271, 272, 275, 276, 278, 279, 280, 281, 283, 284, 285, 286, 287, 288, 290, 292, 294, 298, 299, 300, 301, 302, 303, 306, 315, 316, 517, 519

Middle Road Force, 312, 313

Ninety-eight Days was designed and typeset on a Macintosh computer system using PageMaker software. The text is set in New Caledonia and the chapter openings are set in Onyx. This book was designed by Sheila Hart, typeset by Kimberly Scarbrough, and manufactured by Thomson-Shore, Inc. The recycled paper used in this book is designed for an effective life of at least three hundred years.